MICRO FINANCE AND INCLUSIVE GROWTH

MICRO FINANCE
AND
INCLUSIVE GROWTH

B.T. Ramappa

KALPAZ

ISBN: 978-93-5128-128-3
Price : ₹ 1740

First Published, 2015

Published by

Kalpaz Publications
C-30, Satyawati Nagar
Delhi-110052
Ph. : 9212142040
E-mail: kalpaz@hotmail.com

Laser Typesetting: Future Computer, Delhi
Printed at: G. Print Process, Delhi

Cataloging in Publication Data—DK

Courtesy: D.K. Agencies (P) Ltd. <docinfo@dkagencies.com>

Micro finance and inclusive growth / B.T. Ramappa.

pages cm
Contributed articles.
Includes bibliographical references.
ISBN 9789351281283

1. Microfinance—India. 2. Microfinance—India—Karnataka. 3. Financial services industry—India. 4. Financial services industry—India—Karnataka. 5. Women in development—India. 6. Women in development—India—Karnataka. 7. Self-help groups—India. 8. Self-help groups—India—Karnataka. I. Ramappa, B. T. (Bidaragodu Thammaiah Gowda), editor.

DDC 332.0954 23

Contents

Advisor

Conference Director

Prof D.S.Somashekar

Principal,

Tunga Mahavidyalaya

Thirthahalli, Shivamogga,

(Kuvempu University, Karnataka)

Chief Editor

B.T. Ramappa

List of Reviewers

M.V. Srinivasa Gowda

B. Jayarama Bhat

S. Mahendrakumar

B. Prakash Rao

Tunga Vidyavardhaka Sangha

Tunga Mahavidyalaya, Thirthahall-577432

Kuvempu University, Shivamogga district, Karnataka

Message

I am glad to know that the Tunga Mahavidyalaya is bringing out a volume of proceedings of the National Conference on Microfinance and Inclusive Growth in India, held in January, 2015. This volume contains the full text of the papers selected for the presentation. These papers have been contributed by the experts in the field of microfinance covering conceptual, theoretical and empirical research issues. These papers are sure to offer valuable inputs for strengthening the microfinance sector in general, and the livelihood promotions, in particular.

I wish the contents of this volume go a long way in disseminating the knowledge on microfinance and livelihood promotions which would be of great value to the teachers' researchers, MFI and policy makers.

May this volume be a guiding light to new initiatives for the livelihood promotions in India.

Sri Kowlani Dharmaiah,
President & Chief Patrons of the Conference
Tunga Vidyavardhaka Sangha
Tunga Mahavidyalaya
Thirthahalli.

Prologue

Finacial services are necessary for sustainable economic development. These services should be made available not only to the rich, but to the poor masses also. Among these poor, there is a section of people who are so poor that no financial services are reaching them. In reaching this unreached section, microfinance has come into being. It has been successful in extending the financial; services to those who have not been properly served before.

Historically, the micro credit movement in our country was initiated by NABARD from the institutional forum in the year 1992 through Self-Help Group Bank Linkage Programme (SHGBLP). Today, the microfinance sector has a massive institutional infrastructure with a broad spectrum of stakeholders such as RBI, NABARD, SIDBI, the Governments, the NGO sector, the MFI sector, etc. The rise of microfinance industry has made it possible to provide cost-effective financial services to the poor and mobilize enormous financial resources for social investment.

The impact of microfinance, inter alia, on livelihood promotions requires the urgent attention of the researchers, practitioners and policy makers. In this context, the efforts of the faculty & staff of the Tunga Mahavidyalaya in organizing a National Conference deserve our heartfelt appreciations.

In total, more than 60 research papers have been received. This speaks of the appropriateness and contemporariness of the theme selected for deliberations. I am sure that the deliberations of this conference will promote further research in livelihood promotions. Further, I strongly believe that this volume of well-researched papers on microfinance and livelihood promotions would be a torch bearer to the academic and industry.

I wish all the best to my colleagues in Tunga Mahavidyalaya, Thirthahalli.

Prof D.S.Somashekhar
Principal and Conference Director
Tunga Mahavidyalaya
Thirthahalli

Chief Editor's Note

The Microfinance over years registered a high level growth. Its role came to be recognized as a powerful instrument in eradication the pressing social and economic contingencies not only in the Indian conditions but also internationally.

With a goal of reducing the absolute poverty in the world by one-half by the year 2015, the UN Millennium Declaration convened in 2002 was committed to achieve this goal.

The Indian economy is facing severe problems like hunger, malnutrition, gender inequality, illiteracy, ignorance since a long time. To overcome these social and economic problems they traditional banking institutions and they role is really insufficient, particularly in the light of the rural population of the country. The comparatively speaking the rural India is in the high clutches of the poverty, malnutrition, gender inequality, illiteracy, ignorance etc., This expose the rural mass particularly poverty stricken once to the exploitation of the rich and money lenders. It is of a great necessity to liberate the rural poor from the clutches of the exploiting group. It has been considered by several experts and practitioners the Microfinance industry is of a great help. From this angle nowadays the Microfinance sector requires a strengthening tonic from all sides to shoulders its responsibility with all vigor and vitality. For this, Governments, agencies, policy makers, experts in the field have to bear the responsibility.

As academicians have chosen this subject for the conference in the light of our region. The Malnad area is not an exception from the problems noted already. To some extent I feel these problems are more severe poverty stricken masses are exposed for exploitation at all levels. Small agriculturist, landless labourers, petty businessmen, unsupported men and women are being found helpless. Their plight to a square meal a day is a difficult job. From this view

I have thought a strengthening Microfinance industry will go a long way in finding solutions for the needy. When there was a reference from the UGC, I thought this subject a long way in finding solutions for many of our social and economic ills. The supported voice of my colleagues helped me to conduct this programme.

For the conference I have received more than 60 papers, from researchers and experts on the subject. Most of the papers really spoke frankly and authoritatively on the different faces of the subject. These papers with reference to their concentration on different aspects of Microfinance industry were classified under different heads Part 1 Microfinance – Inclusive Growth and Financial Inclusion. Part II Microfinance and Women Empowerment. Part III Microfinance and Self Help Groups. Part IV Microfinance – The Other Contours. Several groups have been formed including all these authors to present and serious deliberations.

I feel the outcome of this will guide to strengthen the Microfinance industry from all angles to frame & execute a suitable policy relating to all the regions to realise the formidable goal eradication poverty.

It is to be noted that the views expressed by the authors are their personal views and the chief editor is not responsible for their statements, arguments and suggestions of any kind.

Chief Editor

Acknowledgements

It is my earnest duty to thank several members and institutions for having supported me in discharging this responsibility of conducting & to bring out a volume containing the papers presented in the conference.

At the outset I thank from the bottom of my heart the University Grants Commission, New Delhi for having extended financial assistance & the Guidance.

I feel that the Management of my institution the Tunga Vidyavardhaka Sangha if not shown a green signal for this purpose, I wouldn't have successful in this endeavour. Hence it is my responsibility & duty to convey my thanks to their present & all the members of the Management

The Conference Director Professor D.S. Somashekhar , Principal, Tunga Mahavidyalaya, Thirthahalli & my colleagues have encouraged me to take up this responsibility & they lend their positive support for this to be successful. They are to be respected & thanked.

A major job was being done by the reviewers of the papers received for the conference & selected for the publication. I thank all these experts & academicians. Our team of reviewers namely Dr. M.V. Srinivasa Gowda, Currently: Adjunct Faculty, National Institute of Advanced Studies, Bengaluru. Dr B.Jayarama Bhat Professor, Department of Studies in Economics Kuvempu University, Shankaraghatta, Dr.Mahendra Kumar, Professor & Chairperson, DOs in Economics and Co-operation, Manasagangotri, University of Mysore, Mysore. Professor Prakash Rao B. H.O.D of Commerce & Management, Coordinator - M.Com Department, Tunga Mahavidyalaya, Thirthahalli. Who invested their time to read, review and recommended the papers for presentation and publication. Their valuable comments on certain papers enabled us to recast them thoroughly.

I render my heart feel thanks to the local organising committee comprising of Chief Patrons Sri Kimmane Rathanakar ,Hon ble minister for Primary & Secondary Education, Government of Karnataka. Sri Kowlani Dharmaiah President, Sri T.R.Arunachala Vice President, Sri Pattamakki Mahabalesh Secretary, Sri U.Don Ramanna shetty Joint Secretary. Dr.K.R.Jagadish Treasurer, Tunga Vidyavardhaka Sangha, Tunga Mahavidyalaya, Thirthahalli. For having assisted me in all respects to make this conference to be successful.

I expressed my thanks to the Conference Director & Principal Professor D.S. Somashekhar, Prof. Prakash Rao B. Conference Joint Organizing Secretary & H.O.D of Commerce & Management, Coordinator - M.Com Department, Dr.M.S.Manjunatha, Conference Joint Organizing Secretary & Assistant Professor Department of Economics, Tunga Mahavidyalaya , Thirthahalli

I thank the donors who have liberally contributed for these purposes.

I am also grateful to Dr D.H.Manjappa Hoseman, Former Vice-Chancellor VSK University, and Bellary for delivering keynote address, and Dr. Yogish S.N. Professor and Chairman, DOS in Economics, Jnana Sahyadri, Kuvempu University, Shankaraghatta, Shivamogga, and Key Speaker in the conference. I have received valuable suggestions from Dr M.G.Basavaraja Professor of Economics and Director Gandhi Bhavan, Manasagangotri, University of Mysore, Mysore, for which we thank wholeheartedly.

I thank all the contributors of the papers for the conference and the publication. These experts & academicians we are deeply obliged to all these contributors who submitted their papers within the stipulated deadlines.

I thankfully acknowledge the wonderful services rendered by student-volunteers, smt. Meenakshi, Superintendent, and Non – teaching staff Tunga Mahavidyalaya, Thirthahalli for this event. Most importantly, I am thankful to my wife smt. Suma and my daughters' Deepthi & Thrupthi.

I owe a special word of thanks to our publisher, Gyan Publishing House, New Delhi for publishing this edited volume. We sincerely hope that this book will be interest to researchers' planners and policy makers and a welcome contribution to the literature on the subject.

Chief Editor

Reviewers

1. Dr. M.V. Srinivasa Gowda (b. 1945), currently Honorary Professor, National Institute of Advanced Studies, Bangalore, India was formerly: SBM Chair Visiting Professor (2008-12), University of Mysore, Mysore, AICTE Member, Court of Jadavpur University, Kolkata(2006-10) and; Professor and University Head, Dept of Agril. Economics, University of Agricultural Sciences, Bangalore (in various capacities from 1972 to 2005). Prof. Gowda has been a post-graduate teacher and researcher for the last over 46 years. Dr. Gowda is currently a guest Faculty for MBA program at a few Universities / Institutes of Management Studies. An alumnus of Bangalore University and the Institute for Studies in Economic Development (ISVE), Naples, Italy, Dr. Gowda has published over 150 papers in Indian and international journals; authored two books, co-authored one book and co-edited six books; apart from producing seven research reports based on field studies and writing a number of popular articles and book reviews in journals and dailies. He has guided the theses of a large number of MSc (Agri. Econ), M.Phil, and Ph.D. students in economics as well as the projects of a very large number of MBA students of Indira Gandhi national Open University in which he is also serving as Academic Counselor for two courses namely Managerial Economics & Macro Business Environment for the past 20 years. A recipient of the ICAR Best Teacher Award and also the Award of Excellence in International Economic Education and Research conferred by Texas A & M University, USA, Dr. Gowda has travelled widely abroad on academic assignments. He has served as a Collaborating Social Scientist in IRRI, Philippines in an IRRI-India collaborative research study and as Visiting Professor of Agricultural Economics for two years in Alemaya University, Ethiopia under the World Bank sponsored Agricultural Research and Training Project.

Dr. Gowda has delivered over 160 lectures at the UGC refresher courses/summer institutes for university/college teachers and served as a member of the boards of post-graduate studies in various universities in India. He is a NABET-accredited socio-economic impact evaluator for government- and corporate-sponsored development projects. He is a member of several professional societies including the Indian Economic Association, Karnataka Economic Association, Indian Society of Agricultural Economics and World Economics Association. Dr. Gowda is President of Karnataka Economic Association for the year 2014-15.

2. **Dr. B. Jayarama Bhat** is Professor of Economics, Department of Studies in Economics, Kuvempu University, Jnanasahyadri, Shankaraghatta. He has been teaching Economics to the Post Graduate Students for the past 27 years. Along with teaching, Prof. Bhat has contributed papers at many of the International (11) and National (22) and State Level (12) conferences held in India and abroad. Prof. Bhat has published about 27 research Papers in National and International Journals of repute. Also, he has visited Singapore, Melbourne, Canberra, Sydney, Paris, London, Thailand and Taiwan. Apart from teaching, he has served as Chairman of the Department, BOS, BOE, Deputy Director, DDE and PMEB of Kuvempu University; as well he served in different capacities at various academic bodies of Kuvempu University and the Universities outside Karnataka. Under the Supervision and Guidance of Prof. Bhat 09 Candidates were awarded with Ph.D., Degree and another 09 Candidates obtained M.Phill. Degree of Kuvempu University. Currently, 07 Candidates are perusing Research Degree under him. He had edited a Volume on Infrastructure Development in India in the year 2008 which received appreciation from the academic circle. He had successfully completed the UGC Major Research Project on Transport and Development in Karnataka in the year 2011.

3 Dr S. Mahendrakumar is presently working as Professor & Chairman , DOS in Economics and Co-operation, University of Mysore, Manasagangotri, Mysore. He obtained his masters and Ph.D from the University of Mysore. He has 26 years of teaching and Research Experience and has published three books. He has published about 30 research paper in International and National journals with high repute. He has guided seven successful candidates for their Ph.D's and eight students are working at present. He has attended many International and National conference, seminars and workshops and Chaired technical sessions. His field of interests are Co-operative Management, Agricultural and Development Economics. He has served as Chairman and member of various academic and non-academic committees.

4 Prof. Prakash Rao B. is presently working as Associate Professor & Coordinator, HOD of Commerce & Management, - M.Com Dept. He obtained his masters and M.Phil. He has 30 years of teaching and research experience and has published five books. He has attended many national conference, seminars and workshops. His field of interests are Commerce & Management. He has served as Chairman and member of various academic and non-academic committees. He has been serving as Yoga Teacher since 1990 in the local Yoga Shikshana Samthi and has attended eight "State Level Yoga Shikshakara Prashikshana Varga (Camp) at various places of the state. Serving as Placement Officer of the Career Guidance Cell of the college since 2008 and helping the students in placements and higher education.

List of Contributors

Akshatha B.G., Lecturer, Department of Studies and Research in Commerce, Jnana Sahyadri, Kuvempu University, Shankarghatta, 9480239979.

Smt. Archana K.U., Lecturer Dept. of Economics Tunga Mahavidyalaya,Thirthahalli.

Archana G.R., Student, Final Year M.A, Post Graduate Studies in Economics, MACW, Mysore.

Dr. M.G. Basava Raj, Professor of Economics and Director Gandhi Bhavan, Manasagangotri, University of Mysore, Mysore-06

Chaithra K., Research Scholar, Sahyadri Arts and Commerce College Shivamogga.

Chandrashekhar Moger, Research Scholar, Dos in Economics, Kuvempu, University, Shankarghatta. Shivamogga.

Chethana. B., Research Scholar, DoS in Economics and Co-operation, Manasagangotri, Mysore,chethanab81@gmail.com 9741676814.

Dr DEVARAJ. P., Principal and Associate Professor , G F G C College, Thirthahalli, Shivamogga District.

Prof Devaraja Nayaka, UGC-CSSEIP, Mysore University ,Ph:9880964840.

Prof. Dhananjaya, HOD, Assistant Professor of Economics, PG-Centre, Sir. M.V. Arts and Commerce College, New Town, Bhadravathi-577 302.

Dharmanna. H.D., Assistant Prof. of Economics, G F G C College, Thirthahalli. Shivamogga District.

Dr. Dinesha P. T., Assistant Professor, Centre for the Study of Social Exclusion and Inclusive Policy, University of Mysore, Mysore.

Divya. B.S., Assistant Professor of Economics, MIG-18, Maruti Temple Road, Gangothri Layout, Mysore - 570 009. bharadwaj.bs@gmail.com 9740701205.

Prof Doddegowda, Assi. Professor of Economics, Maharani's Arts College for Women, Mysore.

ESWAR M.G., Research Scholar, Sahyadri arts and commerce college Shimoga.

Gagan Krishnadas., Research Scholar, Department of Studies in Law, University of Mysore.

Ganaraj K., Lecturer, Department of Economics, SDM College, Ujire, Dakshina Kannada.

Girish G.S., Research Scholar, Department of Economics, Jnana Sahyadri, Kuvempu University, Shankaraghatta.

Dr. Gowda N.K., Chairman and Research Guide, Professor of Economics, DOS in Economics, Shivagangotri, Davanagere University, Davanagere, Karnataka.

Mr. HarshaDhar .G., Ph.D Research Scholar, Dept. of Studies in Economics,Sahyadri Arts College, Kuvempu University, Shivamogga–577 203, Karnataka.

Dr.Huchhe Gowda, Assistant Professor, Department of Studies in Economics, Rani Channamma University, Vidya Sangama, PBNH-4, Belagavi-591156, Karnataka.

Dr. Jagadish.V.V., Assistant Professor of Economics, PG Department in economics, GCWM, Mandy.

Dr. M. Jayaprakash, Faculty Member, Institute of Cooperative Management (ICM), Rajendranagar, Hyderabad, Andhra Pradesh, email: jpmtalkad@yahoo.co.in.

Dr. B.Jayarama Bhat, Professor, Department of Studies in Economics, Kuvempu University, Jnanasahyadri, Shankaraghatta-577 45 ,Karnataka, *bj_bhat1959@yahoo.co.in.*

S. Jyothi Lakhmi, NCIGDR Trust, Mysore.

Ms Kavyashree C.S., Lecturer, Dept.of P.G.Studies in Economics, Sri J.C.B.M.College, Sringeri, Chickmagalur dist.

Dr. N.T. Krishnamurthy, Assi. Professor of Economics, Maharani's Arts College for Women, Mysore.

Dr. KUNDAN BASAVARAJ, Associate Professor, Dept of P. G. Studies Graduate Studies and Research in Commerce, Sahyadri Arts and Commerce College, Shivamogga- 577201.

Dr.D.M. Madari, Associate professor & Research Guide, Department if Economics, Karnataka State Women's University, Bijapur, Karnataka, India.

Madhu G.R., UGC-Senior Research Fellow,Dos in economics and co operation ,University of Mysore, MGM, Mysore,570006 Madhu.rajgowda01@gmail.com.

Mahammad Habeeb, Research Scholar, Dept of Economic,Karnataka University,Dharwad.

Maharani's Arts College, Mysore.

Dr.Mahendra Kumar, Professor and Chairperson, DOs in Economics and Co-operation, Manasagangotri, Mysore.

Dr. Mahesha. M., Associate Professor, DOS in Economics and Cooperation, University of Mysore, Mysore. maheshgundegal@ gamil.com, Mahesh_eco_5800@yahoo.co.in.

Dr. Manjappa D Hosamane, Former Vice-Chancellor VSK University, Bellary. mhosamane@yahoo.com.

Manjushree S., Lecturer , Department of Studies and Research in Commerce, Jnana Sahyadri, Kuvempu University, Shankarghatta, 9480239979.

Dr M.S. Manjunatha, Assistant Professor , Department of Economics, Tunga Mahavidyalya, Thirthahalli, Kuvempu University,Karnataka.

Mr. Nagaraj H.V., Research Scholar, Department of Economics, Jnana Sahyadri, Kuvempu University, Shankaraghat2ta, Shimoga, Karnataka-577451. e-mail: hvnnagaraj@gmail.com.

Dr. D .C Nanjunda, UGC-CSSEIP, Mysore University.

Dr. Narayan D. Arundhekar, Guest Lecturer, Department of Economics, Government First Grade College, Navabhag, Bijapur, Karnataka.

Dr. Padmegowda, A.T. Associate Professor, & HOD of Economics. DVS College of Arts and Science, Shivamogga.

Dr. Padmini S.V., Assistant Professor of Economics, Department of Studies and Research in Economics, Tumkur University Tumkur 572 103.

Dr.R.H.Pavithra, Assistant Pro8fessor, Department of Studies and Research in Economics Karnataka State Open University, Mukthagangothri, Mysore.

Mr. Prasanna Kumar T., Lecturer, Department of BBM, SDM College of Business Management, Mangalore.

Prof.B.Prakash Rao., Associate Prof. & Head, Department of Commerce and Management.

Pushpa Nanaiah., Research Scholar, University of Mysore

Dr. Puttaraja, Associate professor Post graduate Department of Studies in Economics.

Raghavendra C.R., Research Scholar, Dept of Economics, Sahyadri arts and Commerce College, Shivamogga raghavendracr2@ gmail.com.

Raghavendra H., Guest Lecturer, Department of Commerce, Government First Grade College, Holehonnur, Shimoga, Karnataka

Rajeshwari M. Pattar, Research Scholar, Department of Economics, Karnataka State Women's University, Bijapur, Karnataka, India.

Rakshitha. S., Lecturer in Department of Commerce, Tunga Mahavidyalaya, hirthahalli.Rakshtha2405@gmail.com

Dr. M.S. Ramananda, Associate Professor and Chairman, Department of Studies and Research in Economics, Karnataka State Open University

Dr. B.T. Ramappa, Associate Professor and Head, Department of Economics, Tunga Mahavidyalya, Thirthahalli, Kuvempu University,Karnataka,

Dr. T. Ramesh, Faculty Department of Economics, Basudev Somani College, Kuvempunagar, Mysore

Dr. Ravi C.S., Research Scholar,Dept of P. G. Studies and Research in Commerce, Sahyadri Arts and Commerce College, Shivamogga -577201

Rohini R., Assistant professor, G.F.G. College Shiralakoppa, Shivamogga, Kuvempu University

Rupa K. N., Teacher Fellow, DOS in Economics and Co-Operation, Manasa Gangothri, Mysore

Dr. R. Sambashivam, Asso. Prof. and Co-ordinator, P.G Studies and Research in Economics Sahyadri Arts College, Kuvempu University, Shivamogga –*sambasivamraju@gmail.com*

Prof. Sathyanarayana, Principal Department of Economics, Kamala Nehru College for Women,

Dr. Sathyanarayana, Guest Faculty, Department of Studies in Economics, Chamarajanagara Satellite Post Graduation Centre, Chamarajanagara, University of Mysore. Email: sathya956@gmail.com.

Mr. SHANMUGA S., Research scholars Dept of Economics, University of Mysore

Dr. Shashirekha K.R., Associate Professor, P.G Studies and Research in Economics,Sahyadri Arts College, Kuvempu University, Shivamogga–577 203, Karnataka

Mrs. Shilpa M. Wodeyar, Ph.D Research Scholar, Dept. of Studies in Economics, Sahyadri Arts College, Kuvempu University, Shivamogga -577 203

Shivakumar. P. T., Assistant Professor, Department of Commerce, Poorna Prajna College, Udupi, Karnataka,

Dr. Shyamsundar, Associate Professor, Department of Economics, G.F.G. College, Soraba-577429 Shivamogga District, Karnataka, ssundarmgd@rediffmail.com 9448681849

Siddalingareddy, Research Scholar, Department of Economics, Gulbarga University, Gulbarga-585106, +919945616334,E-Mail:siddalingareddy.1985@gmail.com

Dr. Siddaraju V.G., Associate Professor *cum* Deputy Director, Centre for Study of Social Exclusion and Inclusive Policy, University of Mysore, Mysore – 570 006, Karnataka

Dr. N. T. Somashekaraiah, *Assistant Professor, Department of Post Graduate Studies in Economics, Maharani Arts College For Women, Mysore.*

Subramani G. R., Guest Lecturer, Department of Political Science, Government First Grade College, Kalammanagar, Yellapur, Karnataka,

Swetha S., Junior Research Fellow, State Bank of Mysore Chair, Department of Studies in Economics, Manasagangothri, University of Mysore, Mysore. Email: swetha.s55517@gmail.com. Mobile: 9945404638.

Dr. Uma H. R., Professor of Economics, Sir M.V. PG centre, Mandya

Mr. Umashankar B., Hiremath Guest Lecturer, G. F. G. College Yelbuga, Dt: Koppal.

Dr. M.D. Umesha, Faculty, Gandhi Bhavan, University of Mysore, Mysore.

Dr. Vasanthi Reena Williams V., Vikas PG Department of Commerce, Mysore.

Dr. H.C.Veerappa Gowda, Course Co-ordinator, Department of P.G.Studies in Economics, Sri J.C.B.M. College, Sringeri, Chickmagalur dist.

Dr. Venkatesh M., Associate Professor, D.V.S Arts and Science College, Shivamogga.

VIJAY V., Research Scholar, Sahyadri Arts and Commerce College, Shivamogga District.

Vimala B.N. Research Scholar, Department of Commerce, Jnana Sahyadri, Kuvempu University, Shankarghatta, vimalabngowda@gmail.com, 9739269954

Dr. A. R. Viswanath, Professor, DOS in Economics and Cooperation, University of Mysore.

Dr. S.N. Yogish, Professor and Chairman, DOS in Economics, Jnana Sahyadri, Kuvempu University, Shankaraghatta, Shivmogga.

Keynote Address:

Micro Finance: Issues and Challenges for Inclusive Growth in India

Manjappa D. Hosamane

Almost one-fifth of the world's present 1.3 billion population is living in extreme poverty, earning less than one dollar a day. In recent public debates, microfinance has been considered as an important instrument to combat poverty. For decades poverty alleviation has been in the international agenda. The United Nations Millennium Development Goals fixed that by 2015 the number of people living in extreme poverty should be half of what it was in 2000. However, this goal has not been achieved so far. In the meantime, microfinance is an emerging phenomenon that opens access to capital for an individual. Microfinance is deemed as a means to solve the crushing poverty.

The main objective of microfinance is to alleviate poverty by stimulating economic growth through entrepreneurial initiative. As our Prime Minister has announced, poor people should have bank accounts, i.e., inclusive financial scheme is the aim of this drive. Micro-finance should be a part of this drive at present.

Micro-finance can be looked at from three angles. First, poverty is one of the serious socio-economic problems in the country. Through the micro finance scheme, we can achieve reduction in poverty in the country. The second angle is economic growth. Our economy needs inclusive growth. This programme will stimulate economic growth. The third important angle is entrepreneurial talent for industrialization and trade.

Micro finance programme will promote entrepreneur development which is needed at this hour.

There are 1500 micro finance institutions (MFIs) around the world, the smallest loans typically being less than $150 on an average. The micro finance organizations are diverse in nature. Many are non-governmental organizations. Most of them are private or those involving private–public partnership have found that a number of organizations are working for profit (Battluna and Dovado 2010). More than half of the world's population has no access to banking and other financial services, thus the potential market for micro finance is substantial.

It is observed that the capital flow is huge in microfinance. There is a huge international capital inflow, but the cost of funding this segment is a major problem. Now micro savings and micro-insurance are recent additions to the services that micro-finance organizations offer, but they are increasing alongside the traditional loans to individuals and groups.

Micro lending is also evident in several high profiles. For example IPOs of micro financing organisation are in Mexico and India. However, as micro financing is gaining in popularity, observers have recently warned that a potential bubble may be emerging (Gukbale 2009).

We found that capital inflow allowed borrowers to take on more debt than repay which in similar cases is lending them to take out additional loans to repay the each ones. In India, the average individual micro finance debt has gone up five fold, from $27 in 2004 to $135 in 2009 (Gokahle 2009). This leads to conflict with the goals of micro finance. This calls moratoria on loan repayment in some contents. At this point, the industry is ripe for researchers to provide sober and analytically rigorous evaluations of whether micro finance delivers on its promises.

Another problem associated with this scheme is that savings of poor accumulate is vulnerable to depletion by numerous unintended uses. Women in particular find it hard to accumulate savings become their uses for buyers some or their children's education etc. Therefore savings in order to invest becomes notice a psychological struggle of inter-temporal choice but practically a matter of keeping one many safe until an investment opportunity angle.

Traditional financial institutions find serious the par risky and expensive. These institutions have limited information on the credit worthiness and reliability of specific individuals. This leads to agency and transaction cost problems. The issue is how to overcome the asymmetry of information—how to figure art what is a good risk and who is not. This is a need distribution network that reaches the poor which raises costs.

Micro finance is known for popularizing group-based lending. There coexist: is three models of group lending currently joint liability group lending, individual liable group lending and village banking. However, each model is slightly differ in liability criteria, but they are rely on local social networks, the behaviour of small group and dynamic incentives to alleviate the moral hazard and adverse selection problems. The main problem is that micro financing organizations cannot indentify risky borrowers because they have no inflation on that part of behaviours. They set a uniform rate of interest and rely on borrow to self-selected into groups using local information group lenders also mitigate moral hazard because individual in highly because networked communities can observe other choice of project.

Micro-finance has shifted the focus towards women as borrowers in micro-finance high repayment rate as compared to men borrowers. There is a sustainability question. It is found that 346 micro financing organizations, 45 per cent being non-govt organisation (NGOs), 30 per cent are non-bank financial institutions making profit and 10 per cent are banks with changing interest (Cull et al 2009) show that 54 per cent of NGOs and 75 per cent of banks are profitable. Many non-profit organizations take much risk on subsidies from donors to survive. When the mission drifts in view of the industry increasingly commercialization: the question of operational business models and future sustainability.

There are clear differences between NGOs and banks in terms of proportion of women clients; loan some return on equity profitability and instant rates changed. These differences speak to the likelihood of the sustainability of microfinance institutions.

One of the major innovations of micro finance is the relation on group lending practices. There are many advantages and disadvantages in group lending approval. It is based on joint liabilities. Hence, the critically social capital moves from group to individual loans and does not reduce the repayment rate are year after interventions. This may solve most of the problem faced by micro finance organizations in respect of management and risk.

In the present day world scenario, we look microfinance from three angles: capital investment should be from advanced profit; employment generation as a gain corporate sector; social business from social responsibility of corporate sector.

Microfinance institutions also provide wide range of financial services including training to potential borrowers how to run a firm. The non-credit organizations have become more important during the recent years.

Still programme does not included a greater extent extreme poor is not participated. Many countries show the value of loan to be risky. They lack confidence or their micro finance does not reach the poorest of poor (core group) . This has benefited to limits extent. Secondly, one poor is often not accepted in group. Thirdly staff members of micro finance institutions may prefer to exclude core poor since lending to them is extreme risky.

When we look at the research works there is a lack of solid empirical research. After review, the debate on micro finance still doubts whether microfinance substantial contribution of its objectives. Inclusive growth by its very definition implies an equitable allocation of resources with benefits accruing to every section of society, which is a utopian concept. But the allocation of resources must be focused on the indented short and long terms benefits and economic linkages at large and not just equitable mathematically on some regional and population criteria.

As a nation still in the process of developing itself, it would perhaps be very premature to let go of the dream of inclusive growth but with some hard realities thrown in too. Society by its very definition implies coming together of a variety of peoples and sharing of benefits in order to survive and grow. But what we do of the people who are seeped deep in concept of zero sum game, where one has to win at the cost of other across whole gamut of economic activity?

These are two separate issues and one must not be berated and criticized because of deficiency in other. The concept of few people monopolizing and restricting the entry of others is a faulty notion again based on mindset of stagnant economy and static society. In today's increasingly global, dynamic and competitive economy such notions are based on inherent failure to identify the skill/activity linkages present and missing in the real sense. Of course, there is scope for vast improvements and yet the trickledown effect is visible across the country with a few exceptions too. These exceptions are due to various regional, environmental, political and infrastructure deficiencies. Growth in a competitive economy is, and will always be, inclusive because it cannot be otherwise. It is immensely fashionable to criticize and play down innovations in the economy and hence the job market.

Gini coefficient, a measure of income inequality, indicates that income inequality in India has increased at both the overall level and in almost all the states both for urban and rural areas. To tackle this problem, suggests that there are a number of macro and micro level interventions that are poverty reducing and thus conducive to inclusive growth. At macro level, there is little doubt about the usefulness of the augmented Washington Consensus (Rodrik, 2006). At micro level, evidence suggests that improving the following factors will help accelerate poverty reduction: reduction of inequality, not limited to income inequality, access to public infrastructure and services especially health and education, access to markets, accountability and voice, good governance, and the role of civil society organizations, women empowerment. Major cornerstone of inclusive growth is to ensure the benefits and fruits of growth reaches to the bottom of the socio-economic distribution. However, it is never the case.

International organizations' reports recently witness the increasing interest of western banks in new models of finance, particularly Islamic finance and microfinance. This new trend is not only channeled through the frame of corporate social responsibilities programme and policies or limited to ad hoc financial institutions (like microcredit banks or Islamic banks) as it is entering the financial offer of mainstream banks. It is observed that many elements of microfinance could be considered consistent with the broader goals of Islamic banking. Apart from pure economic considerations which are not the aim by addressing new markets and embracing unconventional financial proposals, the global banking sector can contribute to the quest for diversity-oriented policies posed by an increasingly globalised scenario. The consequences this new trend is likely to have on inner banking structures are still unknown and are likely to interest the issue of wealth distribution. Moreover, from a more general point of view, by showing that even different moral ethos deep rooted in different cultural paradigms can be as profitable and available as western capitalistic ones; the banking sector can play a potential role in disseminating awareness on specific cultural and religious issues, resulting in increased integration of Muslim communities and low income investors in the long run and supporting commercial banks the close relation between economy and culture.

Though most of the evidence and literature on the subject appears self-praising, nonetheless there is much more to the concept than one can imagine. The establishment of microfinance institutions (MFIs) world-wide for the provision of collateral free loans to the poor through mechanisms and instruments not known to normal commercial banks has set new milestones in the field of financial services. With 900 million households in the less developed countries left without any access to formal financial services, this might just be the key to address market failures in the financial landscape.

Micro-Finance in India

Since the early national plans, successive governments in independent India have emphasized the link between improving access to finance and reducing poverty, a stance that has had influence globally. The need to improve financial access for India's poor, the overwhelming majority of whom are concentrated in rural areas, motivated the establishment of a vast network of rural cooperative credit banks in the 1950s, followed by a drive to nationalize commercial banks, launched in 1969. This led to thousands of new bank branches in rural areas across the country. The strategy during the 1970s and 1980s gave the lead role to the nationalized (state-owned) commercial banks, which were charged with loosening the grip of traditional informal sector moneylenders through the use of targeted low-priced loans. The 1990s saw the partial deregulation of interest rates, increased competition in the banking sector, and new microfinance approaches, most notably, a nationwide attempt, pioneered by non-governmental organizations (NGOs) and now supported by the state, to create links between commercial banks, NGOs, and informal local groups ('self-help groups', or SHGs). Better known as 'SHG Bank Linkage', this approach has grown dramatically over the past decade, and while its outreach is still modest in terms of the proportion of poor households served, many believe it is destined to become the country's dominant system of mass-outreach banking for the poor. However, informal sector lenders remain a strong presence in rural India, delivering finance to the poor, the vast majority of whom still do not have access to either formal or semi-formal (microfinance) sectors. Scaling-up access to finance for India's rural poor, to meet their diverse financial needs (savings, credit, insurance against unexpected events, etc.) through flexible products at competitive prices, presents a formidable challenge in a country as vast and varied as India. But the opportunities, too, are plentiful, and government has an important role to play in creating space and a flexible architecture for innovations. The review draws on a recent survey conducted jointly by the World Bank and the National Council of Applied Economic Research, India (NCAER) - the *Rural Finance Access Survey, 2003* (RFAS-2003) highlights inadequacies in rural access to *formal* finance and the extortionary terms of *informal* finance, which provide a strong need and ample space for innovative *microfinance* approaches—that combine the safety and reliability of *formal* finance with the convenience and flexibility of *informal* finance—to serve the financial needs of India's rural poor. Some of the key microfinance initiatives in India over the past decade take a closer look at the most dominant among the recent microfinance approaches, SHG Bank Linkage. It evaluates the success with which this approach has been able to reach out to the poor.

Financial depth is attributable in large part to India's vast network of financial institutions, including those focused on rural customers. The 1970s and 1980s saw a rapid expansion of India's financial system into rural areas. Following Indira Gandhi's bank nationalization drive, launched in 1969, commercial banks were required to open rural branches and, between 1973 and 1985, bank branches in rural areas grew at an average of 15.2 per cent each year, about double the growth rate of branches in semi-urban (6.4 per cent), urban (7.8 per cent) and metropolitan (7.5 per cent) areas.

Today, India has over 32,000 rural branches of commercial banks and regional rural banks (RRBs), some 14,000 co-operative bank branches, 98,000 primary agricultural credit societies (PACS), not to speak of the thousands of mutual fund sellers, several non-bank finance companies (NBFCs) and a large post office network with 154,000 outlets that are required to focus on deposit mobilization and money transfers. For a more detailed discussion of the current level and pattern of access to finance in India, see World Bank (2004).

According to the RFAS-2003, some 41 per cent of rural households have a deposit account and 21 per cent of rural households have access to credit from a formal source. Amongst formal institutions, commercial banks are by far the most dominant source of formal finance for rural households.

They have the largest share of household deposits among rural banks, and are also the most important source of credit for those rural households who have access to the formal sector.

While achievements over the past decades should not be underestimated, *poorer* households in rural areas in India still have very little access to formal finance. The RFAS-2003 indicates that rural banks serve primarily the needs of the richer rural borrowers: some 66 per cent of large farmers have a deposit account; 44 per cent have access to credit. Meanwhile, the rural poor face severe difficulties in accessing savings and credit from the formal sector: 70 per cent of marginal/landless farmers do not have a bank account and 87 per cent have no access to credit from a formal source. Resources and the local moneylender dominate. Over 90 per cent of households report financing unusual expenses from cash at home, while the second most important source of financing such expenses was reportedly informal loans from family, friends, or moneylenders. Newer sources, such as the recently introduced Kisan Credit Cards, are still statistically insignificant. Village people are not access to other financial services, such as insurance, also remains limited for the rural poor, although many would like to have access to insurance. Over 82 per cent of households surveyed in RFAS-2003, did not have any insurance, and practically none of the poorest households surveyed had insurance. It should be noted, also, that large regional differences exist in the distribution of financial services, both in terms of the volume of transactions and branch density, with clients in India's economically weaker regions having a disproportionately lower level of financial access; not surprisingly, poor households in the economically weaker regions are particularly starved of financial access. The spread of branches appears to be closely associated with regional shares in population: the eastern and central regions have larger shares in population and therefore, despite their low share in income, occupy the second and third positions in terms of share in branches.

However, the presence of branches alone does not ensure access to finance; as expected, income is a key determinant to financial access. Regional differences in the volume of financial services (volume of credit and deposits) are largely explained by regional income differentials: India's lesser developed and low-income eastern, central and north-eastern regions account for 54 per cent of the population and 40.5 per cent of total branches, but only 20 per cent of outstanding credit and 29 per cent of deposits access to formal credit is particularly a problem for meeting unforeseen expenditures – family.

From the perspective of small, rural borrowers (the users), rural banks are unattractive for the following reasons. First, rural banks do not provide flexible products and services to meet the income and expenditure patterns of small rural borrowers. As noted above, small rural borrowers have irregular/volatile income streams and expenditure needs, and therefore, prefer to borrow frequently, and repay in small installments, but most banks do not offer such products. Also, while small rural borrowers seek savings and lending products, they also seek insurance (life, health, crop), which banks do not generally offer.

Second, the transaction costs of dealing with formal banks are high. In part, high transaction costs stem from distance to the nearest financial institutions. According to the RFAS-2003, the median distance to the nearest financial institution ranges from two kms (post office branches) to five kms (commercial banks, cooperative banks); the median time taken to travel to the nearest commercial bank, cooperative or RRB is 30 minutes (post offices are available at closer proximity). Furthermore, procedures for opening an account or seeking a loan are cumbersome and costly (with high rejection rates) and, as indicated by the RFAS-2003, clients have to pay hefty bribes (ranging from ten per cent–20 per cent of the loan amount) to access loans, so that the ultimate cost to borrowers is very high (despite interest "caps"). On average, some 27 per cent (and 48 per cent in UP) of sample households who borrowed from an RRB report having to pay a bribe to get the loan, a little under 27 per cent of households who borrowed from a commercial bank paid a bribe, and ten per cent of households who borrowed from a credit cooperative paid a bribe. The bribe amounts appear to vary from anywhere between ten per cent of the loan amount (in the case of banks) to 20 per cent (in the case of cooperatives). Moreover, longer processing times for loans, together with bribes, could result in higher effective costs to borrowers and consequent credit rationing. It takes, on an average, 33 weeks for a loan to be approved by a commercial bank.

A third factor that makes formal banks unattractive for rural borrowers is that banks demand collateral, which poor rural borrowers lack. Indeed, the majority of loans extended by appreciation of the interest rate risk involved in such investment allocation decisions, viewing G-Secs as risk-free assets. Income on sale of investments has been rising steadily over the past five years accounting for around 33 per cent of operating profits in FY 2002-03. Simultaneously, the share in total income of interest income on advances has fallen to levels below 40 per cent. As pointed out by RBI, trend and Progress of Banking in India, 2002-03. High transaction costs of dealing with formal banks translate into a low frequency of transactions.

According to the RFAS-2003, more than 60 per cent of households with bank accounts report accessing their accounts at a frequency of less than once a month (62.3 per cent of households with accounts in banks access their accounts less than once a month, while the same percentage amongst households with accounts in RRBs is 70.8). Commercial banks, RRBs and cooperatives are collateralized, with 89 per cent of households who borrowed from RRBs, and 87 per cent of households who borrowed from commercial banks, reporting that they had to provide collateral (RFAS-2003). Land remains by far the most predominant form of collateral. But, this collateral is seldom executed, so it is just another cost, with little benefit in practice. First, MFIs suffer from the lack of a sufficient pool of managerial and technical skills. As microfinance is a specialized activity and given that many MFIs have evolved from NGOs that have otherwise been focusing on grant based activities, staff tend to have a stronger inclination towards social development issues and tend to possess limited skills in finance, accounting and business management. Expertise in internal controls, credit appraisal and risk management, MIS, financial control and management, financial analysis, business planning, systems development, new product design, etc. tends to be lacking.

Partly as a result of their managerial and technical weaknesses, Indian MFIs today find it difficult to mobilize commercial funding. Most MFIs face a serious shortage of equity necessary to leverage debt and increase client outreach at a faster rate. Sa-Dhan, the leading network of MFIs in the country, projects a requirement of equity funds of Rs100 crore ($22 million), that can be absorbed immediately by MFIs. ICICI Bank that has partnership arrangements with 30 MFIs at present, with plans to increase this to around 50.

MFIs in a year's time, also projects the lack of equity for the second rung of MFIs (40-45 out of the 50 they plan to target) as being a constraint/ requirement to scaled up debt financing by them. Also, banks like IDBI Bank indicate that while they are willing and interested in increasing the debt exposure to MFIs, lack of equity capital (and management capacity) amongst MFIs constrains them from doing so. Since 2013, debt financing from banks to MFIs has grown rapidly relative to earlier years – available data from four private sector banks shows that the banks' exposure to MFIs is today in excess of Rs 200 crore ($44 million); this compares to SIDBI's exposure of Rs 120 crore, $26 million) 14. However, this growth has been targeted at a relatively small set of 10-15 better MFIs and commercial banks are still risk averse when it comes to lending to a larger set of MFIs, pointing out that considerable potential to scale up commercial bank lending to MFIs exists. At present, the exposure of commercial banks to lending to MFIs constitutes a miniscule fraction (0.1 per cent) of the balance sheets of these banks.

The cost of funds for Indian MFIs is relatively high, and unlike in Bangladesh and a number of other countries, the Indian MFI sector has not benefited from grants/subsidized funding. Unlike in, say, Bangladesh, where Palli Karma-Sahayak Foundation (PKSF) lends to MFIs at four to six per cent p.a. (less than half the market interest rate), Indian MFIs, right from inception, tend to raise debt (from SIDBI, FWWB or commercial banks) at market rates (between 11-13.5 per cent p.a.). While, in many ways, this is a more sustainable way to grow, in practice, the high cost of funds combined with problems in accessing equity, has meant that achieving profitability and growth has been more difficult for Indian MFIs than their counterparts in countries like Bangladesh.

The absence of an enabling policy, legal and regulatory framework is often cited by MFI representatives as a factor constraining their ability to access funds, and hence, scale-up. MFIs can mobilize deposits only if they convert themselves into an NBFC and receive an 'investment grade' rating from a corporate rating agency. This is difficult for most MFINBFCs; based on past examples, on account of the typically geographically concentrated and non-collateralized portfolios that MFIs have, rating agencies, in almost all cases, have not assigned the required credit rating. The minimum start-up capital requirement for registering as an NBFC (Rs 20 million or $450,000) is typically beyond the reach of most MFI.

From the above analyses there is a need to reform the policies and greater strength to be given to banks and non-governmental organizations and people participation to be consider for microfinance role in inclusive growth.

PART—1
MICROFINANCE—INCLUSIVE GROWTH AND FINANCIAL INCLUSION

1

Determinants of Financial Inclusion in Karnataka—A District Level Analysis

Mahesh M.

Abstract: *Financial inclusion refers to a process that ensures the ease of access, availability and usage of the formal financial system for all members of an economy. Financial inclusion has several advantages. It facilitates efficient allocation of productive resources and thus can potentially reduce the cost of capital. An inclusive financial system can help in reducing the growth of informal sources of credit that are often found to be exploitative. Thus, an all-inclusive financial system enhances efficiency and welfare by providing avenues for secure and safe saving practices and by facilitating a whole range of efficient financial services. With this, backdrop, this paper attempts to measure inter-district variation in access to financial services using Index of Financial Inclusion in Karnataka. Further the study also intends to measure the factors responsible for variation in access to financial services at district level. The results of the study have various policy implications.*

Introduction

The banking industry has shown tremendous growth in volume and complexity during the last few decades. Despite making significant improvements in all the areas relating to financial viability, profitability and competitiveness, there are concerns that banks have not been able to include vast segment of the population and area, especially the underprivileged sections of the society and less developed areas, into the fold of basic banking services. The efforts are being made to study the causes of financial exclusion and designing strategies to ensure financial inclusion of the poor and disadvantaged at international and national levels. The reasons may vary from country to country and state to state and hence the strategy could also vary but all out efforts are being made as financial inclusion can truly lift the financial condition and standards of life of the poor, disadvantaged and less developed areas.

The problem of financial inclusion has a sharp regional dimension. The figures shows that share of bank branches in rural areas had been declined from 58 per cent in 1990 to 36 per cent in 2012. Even today, not more than 40 per cent of the population have access to banks' presence in rural areas, more than half of the 6,00,000-odd villages across the country do not have access to banking. This situation is further intensified by the problem of financial exclusion in the form of outright crash of rural credit-deposit ratio, plunge in the number of small borrowers' accounts of less than Rs 25,000, closure of rural bank branches, increasing concentration of banking business in the top 100 deposit centers of the country etc. All these banking developments show the slow progress of banking and resultant low level of financial outreach in rural and less developed areas. Most of the empirical works pertaining to financial inclusion focussed on measurement of financial inclusion (Mandira Sarma, 2008, Chakravarty, R and Rupayan Pal, 2010) linkages between financial inclusion and development (Leeladhar, 2006, Mandira Sarma and Jasim Pais, 2011) and status financial inclusion (Rangarajan Committee, 2008). But the literature on the determinants of financial inclusion and regional disparities in financial inclusion is scanty both at India and state level including Karnataka. (Kuldeep Singh and Singh Kondan, 2012, Nitin Kumar, 2012). Hence this study made an attempt to analysis the factors determining the financial inclusion in Karnataka by considering district as the unit of study.

Methodology

This study is purely based on cross-sectional data for the year 2011 and collected from various sources, viz, Census Report 2011, CRISIL, Karnataka Economic Survey. To estimate the influence of determining factors multiple regression model has been used. The model has been specified as follows:

$$IFI = a + b_1 Pddp + b_2 Popuden + b_3 Lit + b_4 Urba + b_5 Pov + U$$

Where *IFI* is index of financial inclusion, *Pddp* if per capita district domestic product, *Popu* is population density of the district, Lit is literacy rate, *Urba* is urbanisation and *Pov* represents poverty level of the district, a and b's are the parameters of the model to be estimate. *U* is disturbance term assumed to have all properties of classical regression model.

The dependent variable of the model is *IFI* as a composite measure of financial inclusion taken from Standard and Poor Crisil Incusix. Among the explanatory variables, the population density is the population per square kilometer to capture the district-wise demographics and understand the role of population concentration on the IFI. Income is measured by per capita district domestic product. This variable measures the influence of district economic condition on financial inclusion. The next probable factor affects the financial inclusion is literacy rate and expected to have a positive impact on financial inclusion Finally, level of urbanisation is another important variable included in this study, which is measured as the percentage of population living in urban area.

Results and Discussion

Figure : 1 shows district-wise financial inclusion for the year 2013. It reveals that out of thirty districts only two have above 80 per cent of financial inclusion, i.e., Kodagu top the list with an IFI value of 84.5 followed by Bangalore unban with 81.6. Four districts have an IFI value between 70 to 80 (Udupi, Dharwad, Chickmagalur and D.K) and again four districts have financial inclusion 60 to 70 (Shimoga, Hassan, Mysore and UK) five districts have a financial inclusion between 50 to 60 (Bangalore rural, Gadag, Chithradurga, Gulbarga and Ramnagar). But the majority of the districts, that is, thirteen have financial inclusion between 40 to 50. Two districts Chamaranagar and Yadgiri are lowest level of financial inclusion with IFI values of 39.5 and 36.2 respectively.

Fifure: 1 District-wise Index of Financial Inclusion in Karnataka - 2013

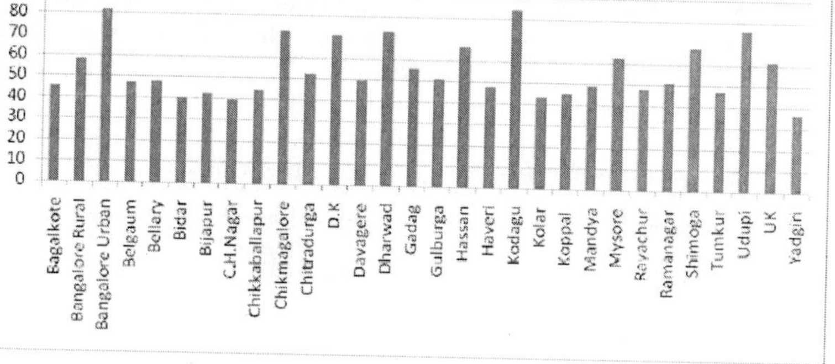

Table 1 shows the classification of the districts as High, Medium and Low financial inclusion districts by considering IFI greater than 55 as High, between 40 and 50 as Medium and less than 40 as low financial inclusiveness. Twelve districts come under the first category, sixteen districts are belonging to medium level and two districts are low level of financial inclusion. This information indicate that there is a wide spread disparity in financial inclusion among the districts of Karnataka. Further the disparity is aggravated if we compare level of financial inclusion across the broad regions, i. e., Hyderabad, Mumbai and southern Karnataka regions. The average IFI score for Hyderabad region is 44.48, for Mumbai region it is 51.88 and southern region has a IFI value of 60.02.

Table: 1 Classification Districts on IFI Value

High	*IFI*	*Medium*	*IFI*	*Low*	*IFI*
Bangalore Rural	58.1	Bagalkote	45.1	C.H.Nagar	39.5
Bangalore Urban	81.6	Belgaum	46.9	Yadgiri	36.2
Chikmagalore	72.9	Bellary	48.1		
D.K	71.1	Bidar	40.2		
Dharwad	73.1	Bijapur	42.7		
Gadag	55.7	Chikkaballapur	44.4		
Hassan	66.7	Chitradurga	52.4		
Kodagu	84.5	Davagere	49.8		
Mysore	62.7	Gulburga	51.1		
Shimoga	67.8	Haveri	47.8		
Udupi	76.4	Kolar	43.6		
UK	61.2	Koppal	45		
		Mandya	49.4		
		Rayachur	48.1		
		Ramanagar	51.1		
		Tumkur	47.2		

There are several factors responsible for financial inclusion and its disparity across the districts in Karnataka, i.e., level of economic status of the district (income), population density, urbananisation and literacy level, and so on. To analyse the influences of these factors the paper used econometric model. The results of the model are reported in Table 2.

Table 2: Results of the Determinants Financial Inclusion in Karnataka

Variable	*Coefficient*	*Std.error*	*t value*	*Pro.value*
Income	.3123	.1123	2.78	0.012
Ln literacy	.7724	.2943	2.62	0.015
Ln branches/thousand				

population	.0743	.0410	1.81	0.082
Lnpopulation density	0289	.0417	0.69	0.494

Number of obs = 30 F(4, 25) = 21.76 Prob > F = 0.0000 Adj R-squared = 0.7412

The results of regression model reveal that the model is a good fit for the data. It explained seventy four per cent of changes in financial inclusion and F value is also statistically significant at one per cent level indicating adequacy of our model. As the study expected the coefficient of income is positive and significant at five per cent level. This implies that the level of financial inclusion is expected to determine by the economic conditions of the districts. The coefficient of value of 0.31 indicate a one per cent increase in district domestic per capita income leads to increase financial inclusion on the average by 0.31 per cent. Hence to increase financial inclusion the government should improve the economic conditions of households.

Per cent level on the financial inclusion in Karnataka. A one per cent increase in literacy rate would expect to increase IFI by an amount of 0.77 per cent. This result reveals the significance of literacy in improving financial inclusion.

The coefficient of branches per thousand population is positive, but marginally significant at ten per cent level. This shows that branch penetration has also some impact on financial inclusion. The influence population density on financial inclusion is positive but not statistically significant.

Conclusion

The objective of this paper is to analyse the factors responsible for the level of financial inclusion in Karnataka. The study made use regression analysis for this purpose. The results of the study reveals that Karnataka's score of 57.7 on a scale of 100 reflects under penetration of banking services in the state. More over there is a wide district-wide disparity with south and coastal regions remaining leaders in financial inclusion. The results of regression model suggest that economic condition, level of literacy and number of branches have a significant influence on financial inclusion. This study strongly argues for a truly inclusive growth and financial inclusion so that inequality in the distribution of banking organisation is lessened. The financially inclusive policy must be the central concern of the policy makers. The long term objective should be the financial inclusion of all persons through the banking system.

REFERENCES

1. Datta, S.K. and M. Chakraborty (2005) "Changing Rural Credit Scenario over a Decade: Experiences of Two West Bengal Villages" www.iima. ac.in/ download.php?downloadid=319
2. Government of Karnataka (2012) *Economic Survey.*
3. Karmakar, K.G. (2007) *Rural Credit and Self-help Groups: Micro-finance Needs and Concepts in India*, Sage Publications.
4. Kumar, A (2005) "Access to financial services in Brazil", The World Bank.
5. Leeladhar, V., (2006) '*Taking Banking Services to the Common Man - Financial Inclusion*', Reserve Bank of India Bulletin.
6. Mohan, R., (2006) '*Economic Growth, Financial Deepening and Financial Inclusion*', Reserve Bank of India Bulletin.
7. Mandira Sarma (2008) "Index of Financial Inclusion" Indian Council for Research on International Economic Relations, Working Paper no. 215.
8. Mandira Sarma and Jesim Pais (2008) " Financial Inclusion and Development: A Cross Country Analysis" Published by Indian Council for Research on International Economic Relations (http://www.icrier.org/pdf/Mandira%20Sarma-Paper.pdf)
9. NABARD (2008) *Report of the Committee on Financial Inclusion*, January 2008.
10. Nitin Kumar (2012) "Financial Inclusion and its determinants: Evidence from state level empirical analysis in India" Indira Gandhi Institute of Development and Research.(http://www.igidr.ac.in/money/Financial%20Inclusion%20and%20Its%20Determinants_Nitin.pdf)
11. Sangwan, S.S. (2008) Financial Inclusion and Self Help Groups, accessed from www.nabard.org/.../Financial%20lnclusion% 20and% 20SHGs.pdf, 10 Feb 2008.
12. Sarma, M (2008) *Index of Financial Inclusion*, Working paper no. 215, Indian Council for Research on International Economic Relations, June 2008.
13. Satya R. Chakravarty and Rupayan Pal (2010) "Measuring Financial Inclusion: An Axiomatic Approach" Indira Gandhi Institute of Development Research, WP-2010- 003.
14. Subba Rao, K. G. K., (2007) '*Financial Inclusion: An Introspection*', Economic Political Weekly, pp. 355-360.
15. Thorat, U., (2007) '*Financial Inclusion-the Indian Experience*', Reserve Bank of India, Bulletin, July, Vol.LXI (7).
16. World Bank (2005) *Indicators of Financial Access: Household Level Surveys*, Financial Sector Vice-Presidency, the World Bank.

2

Micro Finance as a Means to Achieve Inclusive Growth—A Study with special Reference to Stree Shakthi Sanghas

Ramappa B.T., Prakash Rao B., Manjunatha M.S.

Abstract: *Micro finance is intended to play a significant role in poverty alleviation and development. The need, therefore, is to share experience and materials which will help not only in understanding successes and failures but also provide knowledge and guidelines to strengthen and expand micro finance programmes. The ultimate aim is to attain social and economic empowerment. Especially women economic empowerment is so strong by Microfinance through SSSs (SHGs). Successful intervention is therefore, dependent on how each of these stages has been carefully dealt with and also the capabilities of the implementing organisations in achieving the final goal, e.g., if bank credit delivery takes place without consolidation of SHGs; it may have problems of self-sustainability and recovery. A number of schemes under banks, governments offer direct credit to potential individuals without forcing them to join SHGs. Completion and classification of the communication materials in the directory is done based on this development process.*

Micro Finance sector has covered a long journey from micro savings to micro credit and then to micro enterprises and now entered the field of micro insurance, micro remittance, micro pension and micro livelihood. This gradual and evolutionary growth process has given a great boost to the rural poor in India to reach reasonable economic, social and cultural empowerment, leading to better life of participating households. Financial inclusion in the country has been playing a leading role in the micro finance programme for nearly two decades. Now they have joined hands proactively with informal delivery channels to give microfinance sector the necessary momentum. During the current year too, microfinance has registered an impressive expansion at the grass root level. The UN Millennium Declaration, which was convened in 2002, committed the participating country to work together to achieving the Millennium Development Goals (MDGs), the foremost being reducing absolute poverty in the world by one-half by the year 2015. Micro Finance programmes, which serve the poor, are being seen as an important vehicle for realising the MDGs and reducing poverty and vulnerability. Against this background, the paper throws light on the impact of SHGs on savings and incomes of Karnataka, case study of Chavalamane Gramapanchayat Stree Shakhi Sanghas in Koppa Taluk. 2. Outlines the issues and Challenges in microfinance for the development of Rural India. 3. Progress of Stree Shakti Sangha, based on the results, suggestions and recommendations are drawn based on the Primary and Secondary data.

Key words: Microfinance, Stree Shakti Sangha, Women, Banks, etc.

Introduction

India is the fourth largest economy in the world on a purchasing power parity basis and twelfth on a nominal basis. With the GDP at factor cost growing by 7.4 per cent in the year 2009-10, the Indian economy is marching ahead. This rapid expansion is expected to continue as growth in the services and high technology manufacturing sector accelerates. Agriculture, which continues to support around 56 per cent of the population, has grown by a mere 0.2 per cent in the last quarter of 2009-10. In addition, the organised sector employment presently comprises less than 10 per cent of the workforce, leaving the vast majority of the working population with irregular income streams. The Eleventh Five Year Plan (2007-12) envisions inclusive growth as a key objective.

Micro Finance sector has covered a long journey from micro savings to micro credit and then to micro enterprises and now entered the field of micro insurance, micro remittance, micro pension and micro livelihood. This gradual and evolutionary growth process has given a great boost to the rural poor in India to reach reasonable economic, social and cultural empowerment, leading to better life of participating households. Financial instuitions in the country have been playing a leading role in the micro finance programme for nearly two decades. Now they have joined hands proactively with informal delivery channels to give microfinance sector the necessary momentum. During the current year too, microfinance has registered an impressive expansion at the grass root level.

Micro Finance – Sustainable Financial Intermediation Mechanism for Poor

While prevalence of poverty especially among women in developing countries is a major issue, there is also a growing awareness that poor people are ready and willing to emerge out of poverty if given access to basic economic inputs in an enabling environment. This realisation has led to the growing support for micro finance programme that serve the poor people. Micro finance is being increasingly seen as a sustainable financial intermediation mechanism for the development of poor, particularly Women.

Development of SHGs

SHG is brainchild of Prof.Mohammed Yunus of Chittagong University, Bangladesh founded in the year 1975. When Yunus started Grameena Bank, he started giving loans to men, but the repayment rate was poor and Grameena Bank could not grow. He then observed that women were borrowing and repaying much better than men and he allowed women to take the lead. Today, more than 805 of Grameena Banks borrowers are women. In addition, women take the lead in the banks other ventures of telecommunications, handloom and energy production. There has been a major change in the country in the last 20 years. In the years after independence, there was a multiplicity of political and economic interests. Now the economy is being increasingly dominated and controlled by big global and single-vision corporate interests.

The government as well as non government sectors and most recently, the corporate sectors involved themselves in SHG. It is a fact that in few part of the country this has brought tremendous result but in most of the states the real situation is quite disappointing. The SHG model emerged in the 1980s and 1990s.With the tremendous support from the government of India, state governments, NABARD, the banking sector and NGOs, the movement spread like anything. Even such a situation arise that the Indian Government budget presentation has emphasised on SHG bank linkage each year as in many cases it gave the ruling party a political mileage. As per the report of NABARD, by the end of March 2006 there were 3.37 million SHGs in India covering 40.95 million poor households (roughly 200 million people or 20 per cent of total population and 80 per cent of total poor population). As of March 2007, 2.92 million SHGs had received bank loans of Rs 180,410 million. But can we say it has really changed the fate of the poor women.

In Karnataka since inception 2009-10 the total cumulative savings is Rs 611.75 crores, 130000 SHGs have formed, in that 105242 are with bank linkages and Rs 685.375 crores taken as loan from banks. The groups have received Rs 65 crores as revolving fund released by the government. The groups have distributed loan to its members amount is Rs 1739.59 crores, in this 1372.63 crores repaid by the members, its 79 per cent of the loan has repaid it is good sign for development. Mandya, Belagavi and Kalaburgi districts have highest cumulative savings.

Objectives of the Study

This paper throws light on the impact of SSSs on savings and incomes of Karnataka, case study of Chavalamane Gramapanchayat Stree Shakhi Shangas in Koppa Taluk. 2. Outlines the issues and challenges in microfinance for the development of Rural India. 3. Progress of Stree Shakti Sangha, based on the results, suggestions and recommendations are drawn based on the primary and secondary data.

Methodology

The data collected both primary and secondary data. The primary data were collected through questionnaire-cum-interview schedule method. Secondary information is collected from Taluk Development Extension Office Koppa Taluk in Chikkamagaluru district. Koppa taluk has 22 Grama Panchayats under three Hoblis namely, Hariharapura, Kasabha and Megunda in Koppa Taluk. Out of 138 SSSs in Chavalamane Gramapanchayat total eleven Stree Shakhi Shangas in Koppa Taluk, we are selecting four SSSs were randomly selected and then out of four SSSs, all 60 members were selected for the field survey, by using judgment sampling method. The present study covers a period of 12 months from January to December 2013.

The survey carried out for this study is highlighted here: details of division-wise Stree Shakthi Sanghas in Koppa Taluk:

Table 1: Progress under Micro Finance in India – Savings of SHGs with Banks Region-wise/State-wise Agency-wise position as on 31 March 2010 (Rs. lakh)

Sl. No.	*Region/State*	*Commercial Banks*		*Regional Bank*		*Cooperative Bank*		*Total*	
		No. of SHGs	*Saving Amount*	*No. of SHGs*	*Saving Amount*	*No. of SHGs*	*Saving Amount*	*No. of SHGs*	*Saving Amount*
A	**Northern Region**								
1.	Haryana	19167	9465.55	14063	1062.49	3532	234.51	36762	10762.55
2.	Himachal Pradesh	26908	2000.36	6660	849.28	16614	641.26	50182	3490.90
3.	Punjab	37576	3124.24	2825	216.14	4604	304.72	45005	3645.10
4.	Jammu & Kashmir	3511	266.83	437	17034	418	1534.66	4366	1818.83
5.	Rajasthan	96442	7549.18	61355	3360.67	55498	3345.23	213295	14255.08
6.	New Delhi	2191	234.85	Na	Na	Na	Na	2191	234.85
	Total	**185795**	**22641.01**	**85340**	**5505.92**	**80666**	**6060.38**	**351801**	**34207.31**
B.	**North-Eastern Region**								
1.	Assam	77036	3662.24	121298	2637.95	20018	1059.75	298352	7359.74
2.	Meghalaya	7607	193.06	1834	132.51	2346	34.68	11787	360.25
3.	Nagaland	5419	151.37	Na	Na	507	183.00	5926	334.37
4.	Tripura	11244	574.34	15832	2660.60	4273	100.76	31349	3335.7
5.	Arunachal Pradesh	5173	71.51	1038	77.85	207	15.53	6418	164.89
6.	Mizoram	1765	44.23	2643	176.97	689	30.20	5097	251.4
7.	Manipur	4973	118.44	4723	80.00	1135	20.12	10831	218.56
8.	Sikkim	1829	96.74	Na	Na	599	45.24	2428	141.98
	Total	**115046**	**4911.93**	**147368**	**5765.88**	**29774**	**1489.28**	**292188**	**12167.09**
C.	**Eastern Region**								
1.	Bihar	92616	6147.32	48208	2392.25	Na	Na	140824	8539.57
2.	Jharkhand	55252	6159.32	24172	1262.49	Na	Na	79424	7421.81
3.	Orissa	248873	10569.41	185309	18906.09	68990	6998.00	503172	36473.5
4.	West Bengal	304693	15476.46	171226	29358.99	171140	14651.40	547059	59486.85
5.	A&N Islands (UT)	511	18.10	Na	Na	3252	74.77	3763	92.87
	Total	**701945**	**38370.61**	**428915**	**51919.82**	**243382**	**21724.17**	**1374242**	**112014.60**

D.	**Central Region**								
1.	Chattisgarh	42845	2199.47	50762	4626.75	20375	751.84	113982	7578.06
2.	Madhya Pradesh	98015	5745.42	60616	3435.34	19595	970.31	178226	10151.07
3.	Uttarakhand	22060	2295.70	10423	602.41	11514	4272.00	43997	7170.41
4.	Uttar Pradesh	189374	16665.25	237942	9567.55	2444	230.23	429760	26464.03
	Total	**352294**	**26906.84**	**359743**	**18232.35**	**53928**	**6224.38**	**765965**	**51363.57**
E.	**Western Region**								
1.	Goa	4768	3400.37	Na	Na	1977	248.94	6745	3649.31
2.	Gujarat	96674	20313.52	44169	2097.13	27337	9779.50	168180	32190.15
3.	Maharashtra	410864	29428.56	91762	703.82	268069	26695.64	770695	56828.02
	Total	**512306**	**53142.45**	**135931**	**2800.95**	**297383**	**267245.08**	**945620**	**9266748**
F.	**Southern Region**								
1.	Andhra Pradesh	1025638	97455.56	395965	26154.09	26613	19190.33	1448216	125528.98
2.	Karnataka	219056	21224.22	157359	14304.26	158173	27176.84	134588	62705.32
3.	Kerala	306422	322282.68	34190	849.88	53585	4423.76	394197	37556.32
4.	Tamil Nadu	618627	69400.56	75202	4377.38	132881	16595.32	826710	90373.26
5.	Puducherry	15786	1053.38	857	26.96	3080	206.62	19723	1286.96
	Total	**2185529**	**221416.40**	**663573**	**45712.57**	**374332**	**50321.87**	**3223434**	**317450.84**
	Grand Total	**4052915**	**367389.24**	**1820870**	**129937.49**	**1079465**	**122544.16**	**6953250**	**619870.89**

Source: www.http.yahoo.co.in Status of Micro Finance in India 2009-10.

The SSS is a voluntary association of 10-20 members who have common interest and who come from poor background to undertake productive activities. Usually, the members of same community who have poor financial backup join SSSs to undertake productive activities either on individual basis or on group basis to earn income and calculate thrift among the members. The 90 per cent members of SSSs come from Below Poverty Line (BPL) card. Any person who comes up may become the members of the SSSs by making savings regularly. Once or twice of a meeting held collecting Rs 50 each member for every SSS. The money saved the members will be deposited in the banks by opening an account in the name of SSS. Based on the amount of savings made by the members of SSS, the banker finances the SSS without any collateral security. The members themselves are jointly responsible for the payment of loan taken in the name of SSS by undertaking entrepreneurial activities. Economic development of our country can be achieved only through enlistment of the village folk consisting of farmers, women, artisans, etc. Finance being the life blood of every business venture, availability of adequate funds at reasonable terms is a must to ensure speedy economic development of a village and economic empowerment of women. Qualitative research study was done using group discussions with the SHG (SSSs) women in the rural village of all the three division in Koppa taluk. A total focus group discussion was done for nearly one hour duration with ten to twelve members in each focus group. This study reveals both primary and secondary data.

Sampling Details

Table 2: Details of Division – Gramapanchayat Wise Stree Shakthi Shangas in Koppa Taluk (In Rupees)

Name of the Gramapanchayat	*Number of SSSs*	*Number of Members*	*Name of the Gramapanchayat*	*Number of SSSs*	*Number of Members*
1. Hosakoppa	04	81	12. Agalaghandi	03	49
2. Hariharapur	07	119	13. Herur	03	48
3. Bhandigadi	08	130	14. Athikodige	02	36
4. Chavalamane	11	169	15. Kesave	03	47
5. Niluvagilu	02	35	16. Hirekodige	10	179
6. Shanuvalli	04	62	17. Nuggi	04	69
7. Hiregadde	07	121	18. Bhithravalli	06	109
8. Bhuvanakote	01	15	19. Narasipura	08	145
9. Thuluvinakoppa	05	82	20. Marithottlu	12	202
10. Jayapura	07	133	21. Harandur	10	162
11. Guddethotta	02	35	22. Koppa Rural	19	325
Total				138	2353
Category-wise SC 7, ST-2, General 129					

Source: Primary information from Taluk Extension Office, Koppa 03-09-2014.

Table 2 shows the study is based on systematic random sampling technique covering the Gramapanchat-wise in Koppa taluk have 22 Gramapanchayat under 03 Hoblies namely, Hariharapura, Kasabha and Megunda in Koppa Taluk. The details are depicted in Table 2.

Table 3: Sample Details of Division-wise Stree Shakthi Shangas in Koppa Taluk (In Rupees)

Sl. No	*Name of the SSSs*	*No of Members*	*Amount- Savings and deposited to the Bank*	*Internal debt with in the SSSs*	*Rate of Interest (Rs.)*	*External debt– Banks etc*	*External debt– balance*	*Succeeded Rate (per cent)*
1	Eswari Stree Shakthi Sangha, Kerakoppa	15	130600	38050	2 per cent	250000	186828	95
2	Sreenidhi Shakthi Sangha, Halmuthur	15	45600	10000	200	250000	210888	90
3	Sreelakhmi Shakthi Sangha Halmuthur	15	86660	15600	200	200000	Nil	92
4	Vidya Shakthi Sangha, Halmuthur	15	49995	10000	100	150000	12553	98

Source: Primary information, Taluk Development Extension Office, Thirthahalli.

In Koppa taluka the 22 Grama Panchayats have three divisions with a total of 138 SSSs. In each division SSS getting membership is unlimited. But here each SSS has membership ranging from 15 to 20. Total membership of SSSs is 2353. Each group formed executive board. Government giving Rs 5000 through the Taluk Panchayat and Rs 5000 children and Mahila Department of the Koppa taluk office. The distribution of nominal rate of interest among the members is less than five per cent. Collecting per membership fee Rs 50 -100 every month deposited to nearest bank. Bank on the basis of this giving loans to the priority basis each SSS members. They are imposing rate of interest. Repayment of loan who taken the loan their responsibility. Any profit of SSS distribution the members. They are giving the loan priority SC, ST, Minorities etc other their needs. In Chavalamane Gramapanchayat area Halmathur Eshwari Stree Shakthi Sangha total amount deposited in the Karnataka Bank Kammardi is Rs 1,30,600. And taken the loan amount Rs 2,50,000. Srinidhi Stree Shakthi Sangha total amount deposited in the Karnataka Bank Kammardi Rs 45600. Sreelakhmi Stree Shakthi Sangha total amount deposited in the Karnataka Bank Kammardi Rs 86660. Vidhya Stree Shakthi Sangha total amount deposited in Karnataka Bank Kammardi Rs 49,995.

Successfully achieving the welfare of the economy through empowerment of the women possible in all areas of Koppa taluk, banks are giving loans to SSSs with 1:1 deposit-loan ratio. Other details are depicted in Table 3.

Saving Purposes and Interest on Internal Lending

Women and child welfare department and Taluk Panchayat are giving Rs 10,000 to each SSS. This amount Government of Karnataka not imposition any interest. When closing the any SSSs paying to the government of this Rs 10,000.This amount utilises the each SSSs, using the welfare of the SSSs. Majority of the members 78 per cent were not saved the amount before joining to SSSs and few were saving in post office, chit funds in villages. But after becoming the member all the SSSs have started saving the amount. After becoming the member of the group they are to save a minimum amount weekly as decided by the group through consensus. The amount saved by the members varies Rs. 50 to Rs 100 per week; two per cent to five per cent of the members are saving amount more than Rs 500. Thus, the data revealed shows that SSSs has helped them to maximum extent to generate saving thereby getting micro credit, which includes financial inclusion leading to inclusive growth. Lending among the members out of their savings is an important aspect of the group's functioning. Normally, most of the groups start internal lending after three months from the date of formation of groups. The group members develop mutual trust and understanding among themselves before they start their internal lending. The bases for considering eligibility of a member for loan are regularity in their savings, attendance and repayment of earlier loans. The group discusses the loan requests of members and decisions are taken by consensus. SSSs lend money for a variety of purposes, both for consumption needs such as hospital, maternity etc and productive purposes like tailoring, milk dairy, poultry, cloth selling, bangles selling, fish trade, forest resources storage (Honey collecting etc) Ittige (Building Purposes), Paddy Business, Butti Production, Vegetables, and other small business purposes. The normal rate of interest charged by the groups is one per cent to four per cent per month. The interest on internal lending is an important financial resource to SSSs for developing activities.

Repayment of Loans

In any SSS only one member of a group can get loan at one time. The priority of loan is decided by the members themselves (SC, ST, needy). Member's failure to pay loan instalments, interest charges and savings on the day of meeting invites a fine. If any member defaults in repayment of loans in a group, the group brings collective pressure on the defaulter. About 80 per cent of the members have borrowed money from the SSSs and 20 per cent of them have borrowed from the banks in Chavalamane area. Four Sanghas have taken the internal and external loans and repayment regularly (100 per cent) remains members are taken the loan within the SSSs. The amount borrowed from the banks is higher as compared to the SSSs. Overall Koppa taluk, out of the total borrowers from the SSSs, 90 per cent of them have paid the amount regularly and 10 per cent of them are defaulters. In case of banks 80 per cent of them have paid the amount regularly and 20 per cent of them are the defaulters.

Educational Background of Respondents

Out of 60, 33.33 per cent of the women were below primary school and 25 per cent middle school. 20 per cent of the women were in High school and 8.33 per cent in PUC and five per cent of the women were above degree and 8.33 per cent of the women were illiterate.

Table 4: Educational Background of Respondents

Education	*Frequency*	*Percentage (per cent)*
Below Primary 1-4	20	33.33
Middle School 5-7	15	25.00
High School 8-10	12	20.00
PUC 11 and 12	05	8.33
Above Degree	03	5.00
Illiterate	05	8.33
Total	60	100

Source: Primary data.

Occupation

Table 5 depicts that around 50 per cent of the members are involved in house maids and Agriculture and allied activities, 6.67 per cent of the members own agricultural land holdings for her husband.16.8 per cent of the members are self-employed in activities like cow rearing, hen rearing, goat rearing, petty shops, grocery store, tailoring shop etc.

Table 5: Occupation Structure

Occupation	*Frequency*	*Percentage (per cent)*
Self employed	10	16.67
Housemaids, Agricultural and allied workers	30	50
Land holders	04	6.67
Coolies	07	11.67
Tailors and Cloth sellers	05	8.33
Livestock rearing	04	6.67
Total	60	100

Source: Primary data.

Annual Household Income

Table 6 shows that the majority (63.33 per cent) of the members earn per year below Rs 10,000, 16.67 per cent of them earn Rs. 10001 to 15000 per annum and remaining members above Rs 15,000 as depicted in Table 6.

Table 6: Annual Family Incomes

Annual Income	*Frequency*	*Percentage (per cent)*
Below 11000	38	63.33
11001-15000	10	16.67
15001-20000	05	8.33
20001-25000	05	8.33
25001-30000	02	3.33
Total	60	100

Source: Primary data.

Motivating Factors to join SSS

Table 7 reveals that majority 26.67 per cent of the members were influenced by their peer group members, 25 per cent of them joined under the influence of Govt incentives. Self- influenced is the least (five per cent).

Table 7: Motivating Factors to join SSSs

Motivating Factors	*Number*	*Percentage*
Govt incentives	15	25.00
Self	03	5.00
Family members	05	8.33
Friends and Relatives	15	25.00
NGOs–Dharmasthala Sanghas	06	10.00
Peer group members	16	26.67
Total	60	100

Source: Primary data.

Term Saving

Table 8: Term Saving

Amount	*Number*	*Percentage*
Rs 50	35	58.33
Rs 50-Rs 75	11	18.33
Rs 75-Rs 100	14	23.33
Total	60	100

Source: Primary data.

Table 8 shows that highest percentage (58.33 per cent) of the members were save their earnings to SSSs of above, Rs 50 per month, 23.33 per cent of them save the amount ranging between Rs 75-Rs100 and 18.33 per cent of the members were saving the amount in the range between Rs 50 and Rs 75.

Decision Making in SSS Meetings

Table 9 reveals highest percentages (83.33 per cent) of the group were taking the decision on the basis of consensus, 13.33 per cent of group were taking decision by group representatives and 3.33 per cent of the group were taking decision on the basis of voting method.

Table 9: Decision Making in SSS Meetings

Decision	*Number(s)*	*Percentage (per cent)*
By consensus	50	83.33
By voting	02	3.33
By Group representative	08	13.33
Total	60	100

Source: Primary data.

Government Facilities Utilised

Table 10: Subsidies received from the Government are listed below (Rs crores) since its inception-2012-13

Sl.No	*Name of the Gramapanchayat*	*Name of the SSS*	*Suthunidhi (Rs)*	*Subsidies (Rs.)*	*Total (Rs)*
1.	Agalagandi	Sampige SSS	10000	100000	110000
2.	Bhandigadi	Vanitha Raitha Mahila SSS	10000	80000	90000
3.	Athikodige	Gagan SSS	10000	100000	110000
4.	Athikodige	Spurthi SSS	10000	-	10000
5.	Athikodige	Thrupthi SSS	10000		10000
6.	Athikodige	Vinayaka SSS	10000		10000
7.	Athikodige	Divyajothi SSS	10000		10000
8.	Jayapura	Lokaparameswari SSS	10000		10000
9.	Jayapura	Eswari SSS	10000		10000
10.	Athikodige	Divyajothi SSS		83538	83538
11.	Jayapura	Bharathi SSS	5000	115000	120000
12.	Bithralli	Vanadurgasree SSS	5000	115000	120000
13.	Athikodige	Pragathi SSS		115000	115000
14.	Athikodige	Prakruthi SSS		115000	115000
15.	Asagodu	Sadhana SSS	5000	102000	107000

Source: Primary information in Taluk Extension Office Koppa 03-09-2014.

Major Findings:

(1) The majority, i.e., 33.33 per cent of the members have studied upto the middle school. Therefore, from the above analysis we can say that those who are in SSSs movements are able to increase their literacy level.

(2) Around 30 per cent of the members are involved in Housemaids, and Agriculture and allied activities. From the above analysis we can conclude that the women members after joining the SSSs to create self-employment and to offer employment

opportunities to neighbouring family members and then provide employment to people of their area. So, micro finance helps the these village people to increase their mobility, recognition from family, decision making power, participate in village development programmes, meeting etc and to participate in political activities.

(3) All the SSSs are receiving government subsidies and other facilities.

(4) Majority 63.33 per cent of the members are earned per year below Rs 11000 per year. This analysis infers that after joining the SSSs they are able to increase their earning level through doing some self employed activities like selling cloth, bangles, dairy business, petty shops, beedi works, hen rearing etc.

(5) 66.67 per cent of the members joined the SSSs after 2002, i.e., majority of the members were completed more than nine years. The analysis infers that the microfinance programmes were encouraged the rural women to joined the SSSs for easy accessing of credit with lowest interest rate, improving the saving habits of women, improving the accessing health services and to educate the women to participate in the family.

(6) Majority 26.67 per cent of the members were influenced by their peer group members. The analysis infers that the women were encouraged by women, i.e., they were having group discussions. The group discussion helps them to get mutual co-operation with mutual benefits through Microfinance.

(7) Majority of members' position in the group was ordinary members. The above results concluded that even though the Microfinance programmes provides various services to poor and destitute poor women. Women are not ready to accept any position in the group due to high risks.

(8) Term meeting output shows that majority (78 per cent) of the members was conducting the meeting monthly once. The analysis confers that every month twice they were conducting the meeting, the first meeting to discuss the village, group issues and the second meeting to collect saving money and loan amount from the group members.

(9) The highest percentages (58.33 per cent) of the members were save their earnings Rs 50 per month. The result that the rural women earning level were increased. It also says that the Microfinance programmes make the destitute women to save some amount from the total family earnings.

(10) The field study reveals highest percentages (83.33 per cent) of the group were taking the decision on the basis of consensus.

The analysis can be concluded that the Microfinance programmes helps the women to take decision on the basis of consultation and get opinion from every member before taking final decision.

(11) The socio-economic impact from respondents reveals that the Microfinance programme through SHG helps the women to increase all socio-economic impact such as Women were given special respect at home, respect within their community, the SSSs to involve any of the income generating activities/self employment activities. It will help the women to increase the self employment opportunity and to reduce the below poverty line rural women in the study area. All socio-economic impact increased positively except the entrepreneurs skills.

Conclusion

The study brings out a meaningful link between microfinance initiatives and livelihood promotions in rural India. The SSSs for easy accessing of credit with lowest interest rate, improving the saving habits of women, improving the accessing health services and to educate the women to participate in the family and village development activities. This study concludes that modern microfinance sectors needs a maxima list approach in reducing the poverty and economic empowerment of the rural women. Further research attempts can also be initiated to understand the inter-institutional contribution in the promotion of livelihoods in rural areas.

REFERENCES

1. Government of Karnataka, 'SSSs Information,' Koppa Taluk Office, Koppa, Chikkamagaluru District of Karnataka.
2. Dodkey, M.D. (1999), "SHGs and Micro Credit, Sustaining Rural Women", Social Welfare, March, 45(12):19-20.
3. NABARD (2004) Financing Self Help Groups: A Reference Handbook of NABARD, Bangalore, 4-5.
4. Lazar.D 7 Meganathan M.(2011), Socio-economic Empowerment of Schedule Caste Women through Microfinance in Ramanathapuram district edited volume Shollapur and Naveen K Shetty, Microfinance and Sustainable Livelihood Promotions in India, EXCEL Publications New Delhi. 327-337.
5. Pavan K. Bhura: Microfinance in India: A major link to ensure inclusive growth, University of Delhi, India.
6. Elizabeth Rhyne: Microfinance in India, 'Micro-credit is imperilled in India by Defaults" Published November 25, 2010 Re, Action International Washington.

7. Ahmad, M.A. (1999), Women Empowerment: Self-Help Groups, Kurukshetra, Vol. 47 (7).

8. www.microfinancegateway.org

9. Government of Karnataka, (2005), "Economic Survey, 2004-05", *(Bangalore: Planning and statistical department).*

10 Dr. Ramesh T. *"Micro finance – A Drive to Combat Poverty", "The Management Accountant"* Nov. 2008, Vol. 43, No.11, 822-826.

11 Government of Karnataka, Women and Children Development Department, Bengaluru, Report-July 200.

12 Manoj Anand, (1993), "Economic Appraisal Industrial Projects, Schemes for Providing Financial Assistant", Deep and Deep Publications, New Delhi, 242-253.

3

Inclusive Growth and Emerginging Challenges of Micro Finance in India

Ravi C S and Kundan Basavaraj

Abstract: *Microfinance refers to small savings, credit and insurance services extended to socially and economically disadvantaged, segments of society. In the Indian context, the terms like small and marginal farmers, rural artisans and economically weaker sections have been sued extensively to define microfinance customers. The recent task force on microfinance has defined it as provision of thrift, credit and other financial services and products of very small amounts to the poor in rural, semi-urban or urban areas, for enabling them to raise their income levels and improve living standards. Inclusive economic growth has been one of the priority agendas of the Government of India over the past decade. It is widely acknowledged that inclusive economic growth cannot be accomplished without achieving financial inclusion for the nearly two-thirds of India's population who are unbanked. Access to credit by poor and vulnerable sections of the society is the main objective of financial inclusion. Banks play an important role in providing access to credit for the needy people. Financial inclusion can be achieved through an effective credit delivery system. The present study attempts to measure the inclusive growth and emerging challenges of microfinance in India.*

Key Words: Inclusive growth, Microfinance, financial inclusion.

Introduction

Financial inclusion is both a cause and consequence of economic growth. Financial inclusion has become a buzzword in development policy, and has come to be regarded as an important and inevitable milestone in achieving inclusive growth. The process of economic growth, especially when it is on a high growth trajectory, must strive to encompass participation from all sections of society. Lack of access to finance for vulnerable and weaker sections of the society has been recognised as a serious threat to economic progress especially in developing countries. Moreover, persistent deprivation of banking services to a large segment of the population leads to a decline in investment and has the potential to fuel social tensions causing social exclusion. Access to finance, especially by the poor and vulnerable groups is a prerequisite for employment, economic growth, poverty reduction and social cohesion.

The Financial Inclusion Committee defined financial inclusion as the process of ensuring access to financial services and timely and adequate credit where needed by vulnerable groups such as weaker sections and low-income groups at an affordable cost, financial sector reform committee refers to it as the universal access to a wide range of financial services at a reasonable cost. These include not only banking products but also other financial services such as insurance and equity investment products. However, what matters most is not just the access to financial services, but its actual usage. Among the non-users of formal financial services a clear distinction needs to be made between voluntary and involuntary exclusion. The problem of financial inclusion addresses the 'involuntarily excluded' as they are the ones who, despite needing financial services, do not have access to them.one Based on its experience as a rating agency for microfinance institutions, perspective on financial inclusion is that financial inclusion is not just a matter of providing various financial products and services to the excluded population but doing so in a responsible manner.

Financial Inclusion - Indian Scenario

Inclusive economic growth has been one of the priority agendas of the Government of India over the past decade. It is widely acknowledged that inclusive economic growth cannot be accomplished without achieving financial inclusion for the nearly two-thirds of India's population who are unbanked. The committee on financial inclusion was set up to suggest strategies to extend financial services to small and marginal farmers and other vulnerable groups. In the following year, a High Level

Committee on Financial Sector Reforms was set up with the focus on identifying emerging challenges in meeting the financing needs of the Indian economy.

Earlier, the focus of financial inclusion was primarily confined to ensuring a bare minimum access to a savings bank account without frills to all. However, recently in August 2012, RBI has redesigned the NFA with the inclusion of additional common banking facilities. In the first-ever Index of Financial Inclusion conducted to find out the extent of the reach of banking services across the world, India was ranked 50th out of a total of a 100 countries. A comparative perspective on the status of financial inclusion in India and China are presented in Table 1. The data reveal that the level of financial inclusion in India is much lower compared to that in China, except in the case of credit. As per the Findex data, the number of adults having accounts with formal financial institutions in India was little more than 40 per cent for male and about one-third for female, which is much lower than the Sri Lankan case where almost 70 per cent of the people have bank accounts. However, in terms of usage of the accounts for saving and/or borrowing the Indian scenario was abysmally low with only about 10 per cent of the adults with saving or borrowings from a formal institution. This underscores the strong need for widening and deepening of financial services to the unbanked people.

Table 1: Status of financial inclusion in India, 2012

Particulars	*India*	*China*
Account at a formal financial institution:		
All Adults (Percentage 15+)	35.2	63.8
Adults living in a rural area (Percentage 15+)	33.1	58.0
Adults living in an urban area (Percentage 15+)	41.0	82.1
Savings (Percentage 15+)		
Savings any money in the past year	22.4	38.4
Saved at a formal financial institution in the past year	11.6	32.1
Credit (Percentage 15+)		
Loan from a formal financial institution in the past year	7.7	7.3
Loan from family or friends in the past year	19.7	25.0
Loan from an informal private lender in the past year	6.6	1.1
Insurance (Percentage 15+): Personally paid for health insurance	6.8	47.2

Source: The Little Data Book on Financial Inclusion, 2012. The World Bank, p. 74.

Financial Inclusion - RBI Interventions

The conventional view is that financial inclusion cannot be achieved without active support from policy-makers and regulators. The Government of India has made several rounds of efforts at several points over the past few decades to promote inclusive financial growth. Keeping in mind the aim to achieve sustainable and equitable growth, the RBI has taken several initiatives to increase access to banking services, credit markets and financial education. These included the lead bank scheme of the commercial banks and the promotion of self-help groups (SHGs), a programme promoted by NABARD and facilitated by the RBI's acceptance of unregistered groups of low income individuals as an entity for banking purposes. To strengthen the financial inclusion drive, RBI asked banks to cover all villages with a population of more than 2,000 with at least one banking outlet by March, 2012. As much as 74,499 such villages were identified as unbanked, and were allocated to various banks, including regional rural banks (RRBs) for providing banking services by March, 2012. In the Monetary Policy 2012–13, eight RBI has proposed that State Level Banker's Committees (SLBCs) prepare a roadmap for coverage of unbanked villages with a population below 2,000 for providing banking services in a time bound manner.

The current round of initiatives for the promotion of financial inclusion includes:

- Appointment of the Business Correspondent (BC)/Business Facilitator (BF) for outreach to low income families/individuals.
- Introduction of the concept of no-frills accounts and encouraging banks to open such accounts for low income families.
- Encouragement to RRBs/Cooperative banks to sell insurance and other financial products.
- Creation of special funds for financial inclusion.
- Revival of the cooperative credit structure involving PACS, District Central Cooperative Banks (DCCBs) and State Cooperative Banks (SCBs).
- Liberalisation of KYC norms for small accounts and KCC/GCC Guidelines.
- Introduction of technology products and services such as prepaid cards, mobile banking.
- Liberalisation of branch expansion.
- Promotion of financial literacy and strengthen consumer protection.

Initially, the RBI specified that those who could act as BCs were 'not-for-profit' entities who could conduct banking business as agents of the banks at places other than the bank's premises. The activities they could conduct were borrower's identification, collections, preliminary processing and submission of loan applications, creating awareness about savings and opening of account (though KYC compliances were the bank's responsibility), promoting SHGs and JLGs, collection of small value deposits, disbursal of small value loans, follow-up on recovery of principal/interest, sale of micro-insurance, and receipt and delivery of small value remittances. The hesitation of the RBI in mainstreaming agent-banking model was reflected not only in its restriction of the model to not-for-profit entities (though later the engagement of some types for-profits was also permitted), but also by the restrictions imposed on pricing. BCs were to be paid from the bank's margin, and no charges could be imposed on the customer either by the bank or the BC. This limited the viability of the model since the margins of banks are of the order of four per cent, and it is well known that any form of micro banking activity incurs a cost of six to ten per cent of the money value of the transaction. Soon concerned about allowing the links between BCs and bank branches to become too tenuous (leading to a 'lack of supervision'), the RBI limited the distance from the branch within which the BC had to operate. While this was widely seen as a limited step, these provisions led to some experimentation with leading commercial banks establishing pilot programmes with various not-for-profit entities to determine the feasibility of enabling financial inclusion within the strait jacket then imposed by the rules. Essentially, BCs were employed in opening NFA, providing payment services under government welfare programmes and to a lesser extent in mobilising deposits.

Financial Inclusion Plan

The elements of financial inclusion focused in the recent initiatives by RBI include saving-cum-overdraft account, remittance facility, and access to credit through instruments like general credit cards. Performance of providing these services depends on the institutional network coverage of bank branches in the remote areas. The RBI had pursued the financial inclusion agenda more closely and now the banks have prepared plans in each and every State targeting 72,800 villages with the population of more than 2000 that are not covered by mainstream financial institutions.

Financial inclusion plans of banks for three years - achievements

Particulars	*Year ended March 2010*	*Year ended March 2012*	*Progress April 2010 March 2012*
No. of BCs/BC Agents Deployed	33,042	96,828	63,786
Banking Outlets through Branches	21,475	24,701	3,226
Banking Outlets through BCs	32,684	120,355	87,671
Banking Outlets-through other Modes	99	2,478	2.379
Total Banking Outlets	54,258	147,534	93,276
No Frill A/Cs (no. in millions)	49.33	103.21	53.88
Overdraft-No Frill A/Cs (no. in millions)	0.13	1.52	1.39
BC- ICT based A/Cs (no. in millions)	12.54	52.07	39.53

EBT A/Cs-through BCs (no. in millions)	7.48	21.76	14.28
KCC (no. in millions)	17.63	22.34	4.71
GCC (no. in millions)	0.45	1.27	0.82

Source: Reddy, D.R.K. 2012. 'Financial Inclusion: Road Ahead, Bankquest', *the Journal of Indian Institute of Banking and Finance*, 83(2): 40–46.

The number of no-frills savings account with an overdraft facility has increased from 1.3 million in 2010 to 1.52 million in 2012 (Table 4.2). As part of the financial inclusion process, banks have opened 3,226 rural branches in the last two years. To encourage banks to open branches in the rural areas, they are permitted to freely open branches in tier III to tier VI centers, subject to reporting to the RBI. Further, to increase the reach of banking services, the number of business correspondents (BCs) or BC agents deployed by banks jumped nearly three-fold to 96,828 in 2012 from 33,042 in 2010. The number of electronic beneficiary transfer (EBT) accounts opened through BCs rose from 7.48 million 2010 to 21.76 million in 2012. Banks are opening EBT accounts so that social benefits can be transferred electronically to the bank account of the beneficiary. Similarly, the number of KCC issued has increased from 17.63 million in 2010 to 22.34 million in 2012 where as GCC growth was three-fold during this period. The data shows that in the last two years banks done much more compared to the preceding five years when the concept of BC/BF was introduced. The FIP mooted by RBI has been a clear reason for this recent expansion of network of BCs. KYC norms introduced by the RBI are meant for the purpose of customer identification, monitoring of accounts and reporting of suspicious transactions to the appropriate authorities. Among the key elements of the KYC procedure, customer identification was believed to be a major challenge to achieving financial inclusion. Since most excluded people belong to low income households and do not have identity or address documents, it was difficult to insist on these documents as part of the KYC norms. RBI norms clearly prescribe documents both for individual identification and permanent residence proof, and lists the acceptable ID proof documents. But, for first time banking clients, these are more often unusual and strange documents and even if they have one, it is often a challenge to get their names correctly spelled to the satisfaction of the cautious banker. The issue is even more nightmarish when these first timers are women members. For group-based savings units like Self-Help Groups (SHGs) the issue gets even more complex to get a KYC approved. Assessments have shown that 60 per cent of the cases where SHG women desirous of opening accounts have faced challenges in complying with KYC norms.

KYC Norms

Paradoxically, it is more prevalent in resource poor areas, which have also shown slow progress in SHG movement. However, the banks still needed to ensure the integrity of the customer before opening of a bank account for any financial transaction. Considering these issues the latest RBI circular allows flexibility in the requirement of identity and address documents for small deposit accounts. In this context, the introduction of the Aadhar project is expected to address the KYC problem in the near future by providing a Unique Identification Number for each citizen of India. The speed with which UIDs are provided to residents will further facilitate banks' penetration and therefore boost financial inclusion.

Technology and Financial Inclusion

Technology and financial inclusion are the popular coinage in banking parleys in the country. While technological upgradation and mobile banking are catching up so fast, financial inclusion is relatively tardy in progress. Given the reach of the mobile phone connectivity and associated communication technologies in the country, mobile banking has the potential to emerge as a positive strategy in terms of costs, convenience, and speed of reach. Mobile banking is used in many parts of the world with little or no infrastructure, especially remote and rural areas. This aspect of mobile technology is also popular in countries where most of their population is unbanked. In most of these places, banks can only be found in big cities, and customers have to travel long distances to the nearest bank. By 2012, it is estimated that there will be 1.7 billion people with a mobile phone but not a bank account and as many as 364 million unbanked people could be reached by agent-networked banking through mobile phones.

Mobile banking is just one of the reasons India is a place to watch for innovations in financial inclusion. Eko Financial Services Ltd., which had created the software programme five years ago, and which allows migrant workers in cities across India to send money to their families using a mobile phone is now working with two major banks, the State Bank of India and ICICI Bank, to offer financial services to poor and low income customers using local corner stores, pharmacies and airtime resellers as agents. By harnessing the huge potential of domestic remittances as an anchor product, Eko hopes to tap a huge potential market in India, where three quarters of the 1.25 billion people live on less than $2 a day. Eko was the first company dedicated to a mobile phone-based basic savings account and payment service for the unbanked in India.1

Launched in 2007, Eko has developed a mobile-based service usable even on the most basic handsets and continually revised and re-fashioned its approach. At first, Eko experimented with a basic deposit and payment service from one Eko account to another. But by the second half of 2011, Eko had struck on a revised formula that appeared to work as a business—providing a highly efficient and simple payment directly into the account of a bank anywhere in India.

Financial Inclusion - NABARD Initiatives

NABARD focuses its initiatives towards technology up-gradation, capacity building and financial literacy for greater financial inclusion. The 'Financial Inclusion Fund' (FIF) managed by NABARD supports developmental and promotional interventions leading to financial inclusion and 'Financial Inclusion Technology Fund' (FITF) supports investments in meeting the cost of technology adoption aimed at promoting financial inclusion. As on 31 March 2012, the contribution to these Funds stood at Rs 793.2 million (FIF) and Rs 1,304.9 million (FITF), the cumulative sanctions under FIF and FITF were Rs 1,146.2 million and Rs 3,434.8 million respectively, and disbursements were Rs 364.6 million and Rs 1,841.6 million, respectively. In addition to the above, NABARD had initiated the following policy initiatives during 2011–12:

- Sanctioned a project on implementing ICT through Application Service Provider (ASP) Model to RRBs, with a grant support of Rs 1,077 million to 53 RRBs and disbursed Rs 405.2 million during 2011–12.
- Support for CBS to weak RRBs from FITF—It has been decided to support the identified weak RRBs for CBS implementation through ASP Model. Under the scheme of support to 28 identified weak RRBs for CBS installation, proposals were received from 27 RRBs as on 31 March 2012, against which assistance was sanctioned to 26 RRBs for Rs 2,165.2 million with disbursements amounting to Rs.1,395.4 million.
- Establishment of Financial Literacy and Credit Counseling Centre (FLCC) by Lead Banks: Under the scheme, support is being provided from FIF for establishment of FLCCs by Lead Banks in 256 excluded districts and 10 disturbed districts. As on 31 March 2012, Rs 107.1 million has been sanctioned to Lead Banks in 128 districts of 12 States viz., Assam, Bihar, Manipur, Meghalaya, Rajasthan, West Bengal, Uttar Pradesh, Jharkhand, Madhya Pradesh, Maharashtra, Odisha and Gujarat for setting up FLCCs.

- Financial Literacy through Audio Visual medium—Doordarshan: Grant assistance of Rs 32.8 million was provided from FIF to Doordarshan for producing and directing a half-an-hour financial literacy programme in Hindi, to be telecast in six centres.
- NABARD extended support to the extent of Rs 22.5 million from the FIF to Invest India Micro Pension Services to pilot test a micro pension model among SHG members in eight districts of four States, viz., Odisha, Uttar Pradesh, Bihar and Tamil Nadu. The project aims at covering 40,000 rural poor under the old-age pension scheme. So far, Rs 17.4 million has been released covering 16,395 persons.
- Engaging Farmers' Club as BF by RRBs: Financial support is being extended by NABARD for Farmers' Clubs acting as Business Facilitators of RRBs in villages having 2,000+ populations in their command areas. As on 31 March 2012, Rs 20.8 million sanctioned to 22 RRBs in 12 States from FIF. Support was made available from the FIF to RRBs for engaging 'Authorized functionaries of well run SHGs linked to Banks to act as BC/BF', with the purpose of extending financial services in semi-urban and rural areas in their command area. As on 31 March 2012, eight RRBs were sanctioned Rs 4.381 million for training of authorised functionaries of well-run SHGs in six States.

Financial Inclusion-/Issues and Challenges

There have definitely been significant advances in Micro finance operations in recent years and the concept and practice of SHG bank linage model has now developed deep roots in many parts of the country. An attempt is also made in this article to throw a light on some of the pertinent issues and challenges that need the considerable attention of the policy makers.

- **Application of the concept**
  Concerns have been expressed about the application of the concept. Micro savings, micro credit and micro insurance are the main components in microfinance. It is only the micro savings and micro credit aspects have been carrying out by MFIs in India. Micro insurance, micro remittances and micro pension however, are still in experimental stage, till now.
- **Weak microfinance institutions**
  Normally microfinance institutions play a vital role in strengthening the programme of micro finance. Unfortunately,

most of the MFIs which are operating in India suffer from weak governance, defective management structure, absence of adequate internal controls and financial discipline. This also results in lack of financial transparence on their part, making their regulation much more difficult.

- **Absence of proper legal and regulatory mechanism**
  An enabling policy, legal and regulatory framework is prerequisite for the success of microfinance in any country, if this sector were to be scaled up; the government would need to play a positive role in establishing an enabling policy, legal and regulatory framework for microfinance. Unfortunately, this is lagging in India.
- **Geographic Imbalances**
  Another area of concern is that microfinance in India has been very strongly biased towards south and has not provided a balanced access to credit for the poor in other regions. This promotes regional imbalance and aggravates the regional disparities. For instance, 58 per cent of NABARDs clients live in southern India and 78 per cent of loans facilitated by NABARD were disbursed in South India.
- **Product Innovation**
  At present, MFIs tend to be rigid on product features such as loan amount, repayment schedule, and loan tenure, saving instruments, insurance products etc. MFIs need to explore innovative products that suit the requirement of rural poor, particularly women.
- **Transaction Costs**
  Transaction cost is a cause of concern to most of the MFIs because of service delivery at the door steps of the consumers with little or no deployment of technology solutions. This is critical concern in the face of rising competition, public scrutiny and political interference.
- **Manpower shortage**
  Qualified skilled and experienced manpower is grave shortage to this sector. This sector is not able to attract required and capable talent despite offering attractive pay package. This is largely due to the fact that microfinance is still not perceived as a viable business opportunity and professional workplace.
- **Interest rates and service fee**
  Interest rates and service fee charged by MFIs are another issue of great concern and major challenge for this sector in the face of rising competition, public scrutiny and political inference.

- **Finance**
  Long term debt and equity investments can help the MFIs to maintain current growth while maintaining capital adequacy norms. But getting long term debt and equity investment is a major challenge to the MFIs in the given legal and regulatory environment.
- **Unorganised sectoral tendencies**
  Informal sector is still a dominant sector when compared with formal one even in the field of microfinance in India. As a result of this accurate data relating to savings and deposits, credit etc., is not available.

Conclusion

Microfinance scene in India has reached a take off stage. Achievement of inclusive growth can be reached, only when some more efforts of substantial progress can be made in taking microfinance movement to the next orbit of sustainability. This will make this sector vibrant and help to achieve its single-minded mission of providing financial services to the poor and bridge the increasing gap between the demand and supply so as to achieve the ever shining goal of inclusive growth.

REFERENCES

1. Basu, P. 2008. A Financial System for India's Poor. In Microfinance in India ed. K.G. Karmakar, 19-32. New Delhi: Sage Publications.
2. Microfinance: an Emerging Asset Class for Debt and Equity Investors. August 2007.www.MicroCapital.org:
3. Fernandez, A. 2008. Why Sanghamitra is Different? In Microfinance in India, ed. K.G. Karmakar, 219-242. New Delhi: Sage Publications.
4. The Economic Times, 26 February 2007: Andhra experience to have its mark on the bill.
5. Ghate, P. 2007. Indian Microfinance: The Challenges of Rapid Growth. New Delhi: Sage Publications.
6. Action International, Center for Financial Inclusion, Financial Inclusion: What's the Vision?
7. Inclusive Growth – Financial Inclusion an Opportunistic Play' Mr. Koustubh Joshi
8. Stirred, but not shaken Will Vikram Akula's strategy put SKS Microfinance back on track? Business Today June 12,2011.
9. Report of committee on Financial Inclusion by C. Rangarajan (2008).

10. Inclusive growth, K. N. Raj's Essays on economic development, Edited by Ashoka Mody, Orient Longman.
11. Inclusive Growth Development Perspectives in Indian Economy by N.A. Mujumdar.
12. Milford Bateman 2010. Why Doesn't Microfinance Work? : The Destructive Rise of Local Neoliberalism, Zed Books.
13. Pushing Financial Inclusion Issues, Challenges and Way Forward — A Presentation by K.C. Chakraborty Deputy Governor, RBI, July 2009, Mumbai.
14. Karmakar, K.G. 2008. Microfinance in India. New Delhi: Sage Publications.
15. M-Cril and Mix. 2007, India Microfinance Review 2007. Gurgaon/Washington DC: Micro-Credit Ratings International Limited/Microfinance Information Exchange.
16. Nair, T. 2005. The Transforming World of Indian Microfinance. Economic and Political Weekly, 40(17): 1693-1714.

4

Microfinance Services Towards Financial Inclusion and Welfare of the Poor—Evidence from India

Raghavendra C.R., Eswar M.G. and Chaithra K

Abstract: *The objective of 100 per cent financial inclusion cannot be achieved by the Government of India unless it looks for its enforcement in each and every part of the country. The main focus is required in the rural and remote areas. One of the most significant factors which push towards the financial inclusion of the rural and remote population is the microfinance services. In fact, microfinance is the only way through which the financial inclusion can penetrate into the rural and remote areas. This paper mainly focuses upon the achievements of the microfinance services towards financial inclusion. The role of every participant in the microfinance market has been analysed.*

Keywords: Financial Inclusion, Microfinance.

In the Indian context, the microfinance sector has witnessed an unprecedented growth in the last few years, and has firmly established itself as significant potential contributor in the government's agenda of "Financial Inclusion". Financial services for the poor have proved to be a powerful instrument for poverty reduction that enables the poor to build assets, increase incomes, and reduce their vulnerability to economic stress. However, with nearly one billion people still lacking access to basic financial services, especially the very poor, the challenge of providing financial services to them remains, convenient, safe, and secure deposit services are a particularly crucial need. Microfinance sector is both old and new - people have always been borrowing, lending and saving for as long as there has been money (and in kind before). They have done this within their own communities, using their own systems and methods, without any external assistance or resources.

The sector is new in that it has primarily developed as a response to the inability or apathy of commercial banks and the formal financial system to serve the needs of low-income households and micro enterprises. Microfinance plays a significant role overarching goal to reduce poverty in India. Providing access to microfinance can prove to be an effective way of reaching the poor and improving their lives. The availability of adequate and timely microfinance services for low-income households has many effects on the development of a community. It can directly affect community organising and development as a part of the microfinance activities, and it can also indirectly enable and facilitate community development as an externality of credit itself. Microfinance is an enabling, empowering, and bottoms-up tool to poverty alleviation that has provided considerable economic and non-economic externalities to low-income households in developing countries.

Microfinance is being hailed as a sustainable tool to combat poverty, combining a for-profit approach that is self-sustaining, and a poverty alleviation focus that empowers low-income households. Microfinance is increasingly becoming a tool to exercise developmental priorities for governments in developing countries. In order to ensure that the poorest benefit from this growth, and also contribute to it, the expansion and improvement of the microfinance sector should be a national priority. Microfinance programmes have, in the recent past, become one of the more promising ways to use scarce development funds to achieve the objectives of poverty alleviation. Furthermore, certain micro-finance programmes have gained prominence in the development field and beyond. The basic idea of micro-finance is simple: if poor people are provided access to financial services, including credit, they may very well be able to start or expand a micro-enterprise that will allow them to break out of poverty.

Micro Finance – An Overview

Micro finance refers to the provision of financial services to poor or low income clients, including consumers and the self-employed. The term also refers to the practice of sustainably delivering those services. More broadly, it refers to a movement that envisions a world in which as many poor and near poor households as possible have permanent access to an appropriate range of high quality financial services, including not just credit but also savings, insurance and fund transfers. Micro finance can be defined as small loans that help poor people who wish to start or expand their small businesses but are not able to get banks to lend to them. Micro credit is the extension of small loans to entrepreneurs too poor to qualify for traditional bank loans. It is helping millions of poor people, especially poor rural women; with tiny loans so they can start small, create self employment and improve their lives. Microfinance is the supply of loans, savings, and other basic financial services to the poor. People living in poverty, like everyone else, need a diverse range of financial instruments to run their businesses, build assets, stabilise consumption, and shield themselves against risks. Financial services needed by the poor include working capital loans, consumer credit, and savings, pensions, insurance, and money transfer services. Microfinance aims at providing broad range of financial services such as deposits, loans, payment services, money transfers, insurance to poor and low-income households and their micro enterprises.

Financial Inclusion

Financial inclusion is delivery of banking services at an affordable cost to the vast sections of disadvantaged and low income groups. Unrestrained access to public goods and services is the sine qua non of an open and efficient society. As banking services are in the nature of public good, it is essential that availability of banking and payment services to the entire population without discrimination is the prime objective of the public policy. By financial inclusion we mean the provision of affordable financial services, viz., access to payments and remittance facilities, savings, loans and insurance services by the formal financial system to those who tend to be excluded. In the policy framework for development of the formal financial system in India, there is always an emphasis on the need for financial inclusion and covering more and more of the excluded population by the formal financial system.

History of Micro Finance in India

The micro finance activity is the result of NABARD's work in the micro finance sector, which started in 1992 through a pilot project for promoting 500 self help groups (SHGs). As the idea gained acceptance from the banking system and the results were promising, the Reserve Bank of India (RBI) encouraged this positive initiative by issuing instructions to banks in 1996 to cover SHG financing as a mainstream activity under their priority sector–lending portfolio. From 1999 onwards the Government of India (GOI) made linking SHGs with banks a national priority through its periodic policy and budget announcements. Today, the programme is growing at a pace of about 2.5 million households annually. It is the largest and fastest growing microfinance programme in the world in terms of its outreach and sustainability.

Government Measures for Promoting Financial Inclusion

Bringing the larger population within the structured and organised financial system is an important item on the development agenda of the government. With the objective of attracting the financially excluded population into the formalised financial system, given the socio-demographic complexities in India the RBI has introduced a multi-institutional and multi-instrument approach to comprehensively address the issue of financial inclusion. Some of the RBI measures taken in this direction are as follows:

1. *No-Frills Account*: Banks were advised in November 2005 to make available a basic banking 'no-frills' account either with 'nil' or very low minimum balances and charges that would make such accounts accessible to vast sections of population. All the public and the private sector banks as well as the foreign banks, except some, are reported to have introduced the basic banking 'no-frills' account.
2. *General Credit Card (GCC):* With the objective of providing hassle-free credit in rural and semi-urban areas, the banks were advised in December 2005, to consider introduction of a General Credit Card (GCC) to such constituents. The card with the nature of revolving credit was to have a credit limit of up to Rs 25,000, with reasonable interest rate based on the assessment of income and cash flows of the household without insistence on security or purpose or end-use of credit.
3. *Business Facilitator (BF) and Business Correspondent (BC) Models:* In January2006, banks were permitted to utilise the services of NGOs/SHGs micro-finance institutions and other

civil society organisations as intermediaries in providing financial and banking services through the use of business facilitator and business correspondent (BC) models.

4. *Passbook Facility:* Pass books provide ready information to the account holders, of the transactions in their accounts. This document cannot be substituted by bank account statements. Since non-issuance of the pass books to the small customers could indirectly lead to their financial exclusion, the RBI had advised the banks in October 2006 to invariably offer the pass book facility to all its savings bank accountholders without any charge on the customers.
5. *Simplified KYC Procedure:* With a view to facilitate the opening of bank accounts by the common man through a simplified KYC procedure, RBI in 2006-07, announced that the bank could open accounts of low balance /turnover (where the balance does not exceed Rs 50,000 in all the accounts taken together and the total credit in all the accounts taken together is not expected to exceed Rs 2 lakh in a year) only with self-certification of address by the customers and self-photograph.
6. *Credit Counselling and Financial Education:* The banks were also advised by the RBI to make available all printed material used by retail customers in the concerned regional language. RBI itself has launched in 2007, a multilingual website in 13 Indian languages on all matters concerning banking and the common person.

Recommendations of the Committee on Financial Inclusion

Keeping in view the enormity of the task involved, the committee recommended the setting up of a mission mode National Rural Financial Inclusion Plan (NRFIP) with a target of providing access to comprehensive financial services to at least 50 per cent (55.77 million) of the excluded rural households by 2012 and the remaining by 2015. This would require semi-urban and rural branches of commercial banks and RRBs to cover a minimum of 250 cultivator and non-cultivator households per branch per annum. The committee also recommended that the government should constitute a National Mission on Financial Inclusion comprising representatives of all stakeholders for suggesting the overall policy changes required, and in undertaking promotional initiatives.

Major Recommendations for Commercial Banks

Target for providing access to credit to at least 250 excluded rural households per annum in each rural/ semi-urban branch. Targeted branch expansion in identified districts in the next three years, provision of customised savings, credit and insurance products, incentivising human resources for providing inclusive financial services, simplification of procedures for agricultural loans.

Major Recommendations for Regional Rural Banks

- Extending their services to unbanked areas and increasing their credit-deposit ratios. No further merger of RRBs.
- Recapitalisation of RRBs with negative net worth.
- Widening of network and expanding coverage in a time-bound manner.
- Strategic microfinance plan with NABARD support.
- Separate credit plans for excluded regions.
- Pilot testing of B/F, B/C Model.
- Computerisation.
- Strengthening Boards of Management.
- Tax Incentives.
- NABARD to support HR Developments in RRBs.

Major Recommendations to Co-operative Banks

- Early implementation of Vaidyanathan Committee Revival Package.
- Use of Primary Agricultural Credit Societies (PACS) and other primary cooperatives as business correspondents.
- Co-operatives to adopt group approach for financing excluded groups.

Conclusion

The study reveals that despite the measures undertaken by the government and corporations like simplification of procedures, liberalisation of rate of interest, support for capacity building measures, assistance in marketing the products and etc., problems of beneficiaries continued to exist. Like, inadequate credit, poor marketing by the institutions for their products, absence of training and follows up, absence of necessary guidance etc. These problems need immediate redressal by financing institutions. To sum up, there are several challenges that require concerted efforts from banks, the RBI and the Government to ensure convenient and cost-effective delivery of financial services to the public at large. There is a need to cover more people under financial inclusion who deserve and extremely in need of finance. The challenges in particular are, to introduce innovations in identifying such people, re-engineering of financial products as per the requirements, risk assessment, reduce transaction costs, devise new credit delivery channels and use information technology to make financial inclusion a viable model. As a developing country, India faces constraint of resource for rapid socio-economic development. While there may be limitation of financial resources but available human resources are huge and yet to be fully exploited. Thus, it is not only the availability of finance to the targeted class but also about the usage. Therefore there is a need of evolving appropriate strategy for mobilising and training human resources for optimising use of the available financial resources.

REFERENCES

1 Arunachalam, P (2011) (Ed): Microfinance Management, Serials Publications, New Delhi.

2 Das, S K Nanda, B P and Rath, J (2008) (Ed): Microfinance and Rural Development in India, New Century Publications, New Delhi.

3 Feroze, S.M and Chauhan A K (2011): Microfinance in India: A Performance Evaluation, New Century Publications, New Delhi.

4 Government of India (2011): Economic Survey 2010-11, Ministry of Finance, Department of Economic Affairs, Economic Division, Oxford University Press, New Delhi.

5 Prasad, Chandra Shekhar (2008): Economic Survey of India 1947-48 to 2008-09, New Century Publications, New Delhi.

6 Prasad, C S Mathur, Vibha and Chatterjee, Anup (2007): Sixty Years of the Indian Economy 1947 to 2007, Volume 2, New Century Publications.

5

Financial Inclusion of Internal Labour Migrants—Need for Socio-Economic Stability

Madhu G.R., Mahammad Habeeb and H.R. Uma

Abstract: *As discussed in Rio+20, migration has been recognised for its increasing importance and relevance to the social, economic and environmental dimensions of sustainable development. Although the share of international migrants in the world's population has remained at approximately three per cent for more than 20 years, their absolute numbers have increased significantly: in 1990, approximately 156 million people lived outside their country of birth, but today this figure has increased to approximately 215 million. At the same time, today approximately 740 million internal migrants are estimated to have moved away from their places of birth within the borders of their own countries.*

Economic migrants are the world's fastest growing group of migrants. At the micro level, individual migrants can be motivated to leave their homes in pursuit of what are perceived to be better economic and social opportunities elsewhere. On a macro level, migration is stimulated by the globalisation of trade, transport and communications technologies, as well as by demographic dynamics.

Like international migration, movement within the borders of a country is driven by the search for better opportunities. Rural urban and urban urban migration is primarily driven by economic and social causes, with environmental change increasingly influencing movement. In Asia, workers are increasingly moving to cities and manufacturing centers due to wage differentials and labour opportunities. Rural-urban and urban-urban migration is expected to contribute to the significant urbanisation of Africa and Asia in coming decades, with most growth taking place in medium sized cities (those with populations between 500,000 and one million people).

This paper seeks to address this gap by suggesting that targeted financial services are a critical element in enabling social protection of migrant populations. Using a conceptual framework of social protection for migrant workers and detailed case studies of seasonal migrants from the North Karnataka to South Karnataka in India. this paper highlights the following key points:

(i) Seasonal migrants are often affected by erratic incomes and employment, shorter work life and early retirement, cash flow volatilities at source, debt burden and exclusion from formal financial institutions;
(ii) Migrant households adopt various coping mechanisms to manage such risks, but these are not sufficient to reduce vulnerabilities faced by them; and
(iii) Targeted financial services can help in managing the afore-mentioned socio-economic risks. Populations that migrate internally in search of work are an economically active group. Given the magnitude of internal migration in India, the inclusion of this group in the formal financial system is important. The available literature on financial inclusion of migrants provides estimates of the magnitude and composition of remittances and linkages of migrants to bank accounts. India has the second largest domestic remittance market in the world (Tumbe, 2011).

Key words: migration, inclusion, financial, international.

Migration of persons within national borders is far greater in magnitude than migration across international borders and has enormous potential to contribute to economic prosperity, social cohesion and urban diversity. Internal migration is an essential and inevitable component of the economic and social life of the country, given regional imbalances and labour shortages, and safe migration should be promoted to maximize its benefits. However, in the absence of a coherent policy framework and strategy, migration imposes heavy costs on human development through poor labour arrangements and working conditions of migrants, and obstacles in their access to shelter, education, healthcare and food. (UNESCO, 2012).

Migration helps to minimise regional, socioeconomic, and cultural disparities, and is considered to be an integral component of the development process. Migration helps to diffuse development, technology, and innovations from more developed areas or cities to rural or less developed areas. Migration can significantly change the quality of human capital in rural areas, especially when outmigration of highly-skilled people is not compensated by resources, such as remittances becoming available for investment in health and education of children and youth. (FAO, 2009).

Migration has long been an important livelihood strategy for the people of India. Whenever the population rose to such an extent that people could no longer secure a livelihood, they migrated elsewhere. Even today, both poor and better off people pursue migration as a livelihood strategy in India. Choice of destination and levels of benefits and risks, however, vary significantly, according to the economic and social power of the migrant.

The study of migration is important to measure the transitory phases of development in a country and their relation with the population on move especially in the context of internal shifts in population. It is in fact, one of the most important variables for measuring the urbanisation trends as well. In most of the countries, especially of the South East Asia, the urban population is growing at a faster rate than that of rural areas on account of shift of rural people to the urban for seeking opportunities of livelihood because in rural areas the agricultural returns are not sufficient to meet their requirements. (B. K. Roy and Basheer K).

This study has been undertaken in Karnataka state to show the effect of internal migration on financial inclusion. A sample survey has been conducted to show the migration of labourers between north Karnataka to other regions which is mainly due to the economic reasons with the main objective to show how this has helped in the financial inclusion of excluded people.

Research gap

After reviewing the literature of internal labour migration and financial inclusion , studies are done on the different dimensions of internal labour migration and financial inclusion, some of the studies are concentration on internal migration, remittances and poverty: evidence from Ghana and India (Priya Deshingkar et al, 2012) some on The Changing Pattern of Internal Migration in India: Issues and Challenges (Sandhya Rani Mahapatro) Internal Migration, Poverty and Development in Asia (Priya Deshingkar, 2006) Rural out-migration and economic development at origin (Mariapia Mendola, 2006), Financial Inclusion for the Migrant Poor: Experience, Challenges and Data Gaps, Seasonal Migration of Rural Labour in India, (Haberfeld et al 1996), Circular Migration in India (Priya Deshingkar), Karnataka State Government set up a high power committee on redressal of regional imbalances under the chairmanship of Prof. D.M. Nanjundappa (popularly known as Nanjundappa Committee). This report shows that north Karnataka region is more backward in general and Hyderabad Karnataka is the most backward compared to south Karnataka. Interestingly, the Committee has found that some of the taluks in south Karnataka are also backward. Further, the Committee made a number of recommendations for the reduction of regional imbalances in the State. And hardly any study is done internal labour migration from north Karnataka to other parts for social and economic stability though this study concentrates on internal labour migration for financial inclusion.

Objective of the Study: To examine the role of internal labour migration for financial inclusion.

Hypotheses

The study has set the following hypotheses for investigation:

(1) Migration has improved the socio-economic status of migrant agricultural labourers.
(2) Majority of migrants are from socially backward classes and economically depressed classes.

Data Analysis and Interpretation

This study is based on primary data. Primary data is collected from 400 households with scheduled questionnaire in Manvi Taluk of Raichur district of Karnataka. The descriptive statistics of frequencies, weighted averages; cross tabs were used to analyze the data as per the objectives of the study.

Demographic Analysis

Table 1: Gender and Age Group-wise Migrants in Total Households

Age Group	*Children*		*Young*		*Aged*		*Total*
Gender	*Male*	*Female*	*Male*	*Female*	*Male*	*Female*	*All*
No. of Migrants	78	75	323	252	1	1	730
Percentage	10.68	10.27	44.24	34.54	0.13	0.13	100

Source: Field survey.

The above table shows classification of migrants on the basis of gender and age group. The data in the table shows that the young aged labourers constituted more in migration from the study area, within this group number of males is dominant. Whereas number of female is very close to males this shows that females also joining the flow of migration. The other important thing to highlight is the children nearly 20 per cent of children are migrating along with the parents. It was noticed that only two aged people have migrated.

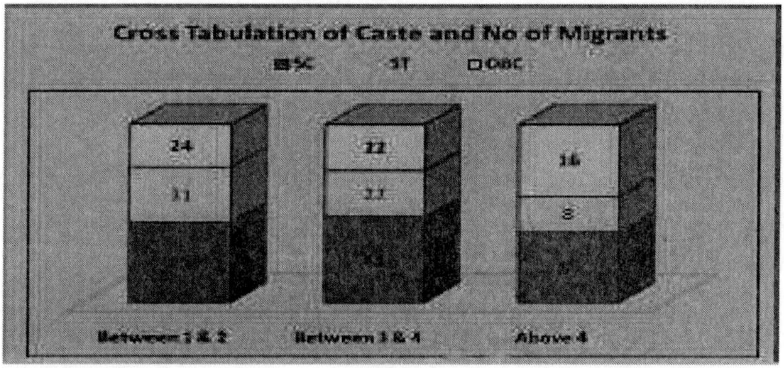

Source: Field Survey.

Fig. 1: Cross Tabulation of Caste and Number of Migrants.

The above chart shows the social identification of migrants. About 45 migrant households belong to Schedule Castes, 31 migrant households belong to Schedule Tribes and 16 migrant households belong to Other Backward Classes are sending labourers between one to two. Whereas 41 Schedule Caste, 22 Schedule Tribes and 22 Other Backward Classes seasonal migrant households sending labourers between three to four. In the same manner 16 Schedule Castes, eight Schedule Tribes and 16 Other Backward Classes households sending the above four seasonal migrant labourers above four. More than four labourers are migrating from 16 households belong to Schedule Caste, eight households belong to Schedule Tribes and 16 households belong to Other Backward Classes.

Socio-Economic Conditions

Table 2: Age-wise and Caste-wise Respondents Details

Age group	*Frequency*	*Percentage*	*Caste*	*Frequency*	*Percentage*
Between 15-30	120	53.3	SC	102	45.3
Between 31-45	85	37.8	ST	61	27.1
Above 45	20	8.9	OBC	62	27.6
Total	225	100.0	Total	225	100.0

Source: Field survey.

Table 2 shows the respondent details regarding age and caste. Most of the respondents fall into the young age group between 15 to 30 years, and they represent 53.3 per cent of the total number of migrants. Whereas the respondent belongs to age between 31 to 45 years represents 37.8 per cent of the total. The age group of above 45 years constitute third highest and represent 8.9 per cent of the total.

Details regarding the caste of the respondents are also shown in the table. The agricultural labourers belongs to Schedule Caste are more likely to migrate in the study area, while labourers belongs to Other Backward Class and Schedule Castes represented second and third highest respectively.

Table 3: Education Level of the Respondents

Education	*Frequency*	*Percentage*
Illiterate	132	58.7
Primary	55	24.4
High School	27	12.0
College	11	4.9
Total	225	100.0

Source: Field survey.

The data in the above table-3 depicted in the pie diagram below. The table as well as diagram shows education levels of the respondents. According to the data most of the respondents are illiterates, who even don't knew to put signature and they represent 58.7 per cent of the total. Whereas 24.4 per cent of the respondents studied only primary level and they constitute the second highest. The percentage of the respondents who got the high school and college level is 12 per cent and 4.9 per cent respectively.

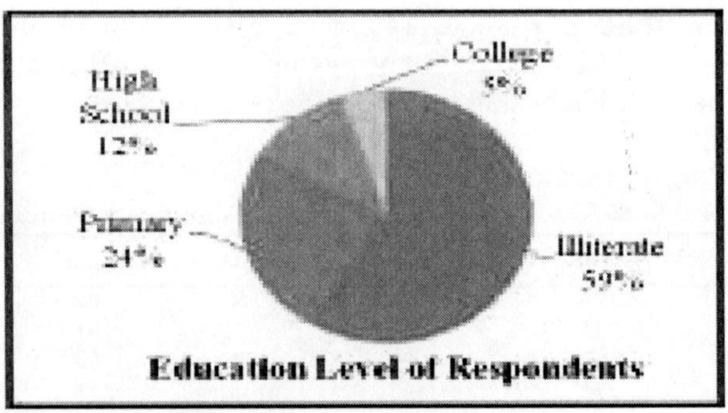

Fig. 2: Education Level of the Respondents.

Table 4: Facilities at Destination

	Housing		*Drinking Water*		*Electricity*	
	Frequency	*Percentage*	*Frequency*	*Percentage*	*Frequency*	*Percentage*
Not good	193	85.8	29	12.9	30	13.3
Good	32	14.2	196	87.1	195	86.7
Total	225	100.0	225	100.0	225	100.0

Source: Field survey.

The table 4 highlights the availability and conditions of the basic living facilities of the respondents at the destination. According to the information given in the table 85.8 per cent of the migrant labourers were living in the tin sheds at destination place which were not in good condition, whereas 14.2 per cent of the people were living in rented houses. They were somewhat in better condition compared to sheds. About 87 per cent of the migrants were living in the sheds near the construction fields and outside the field are getting clean drinking water in the urban migrated place whereas 12.9 per cent of the people were not getting clean drinking water. About 86.7 per cent of respondents in lived sheds and homes having electricity facility, while 13.3 per cent of the migrant labourers were not having even a single bulb in their shed or house.

Table 5: Asset Possession by Respondents

	Land		*House*		*Livestocks*	
	Yes	*No*	*Yes*	*No*	*Yes*	*No*
Frequency	148	77	219	6	64	161
Percentage	65.8	34.2	97.3	2.7	28.4	71.6

Source: Field survey.

The economic status of migrant agricultural labourers before the migration can be analysed on the basis of assets they possess. Here land, house and livestocks have taken into consideration as assets. The above table shows that the 65.8 per cent of the labourers have their own land holdings but this can't be considered as they are economically strong. We will see clearly in the next part of this chapter about what kind of land they have is it irrigated or barren? And what are the holding sizes. So here 34.2 per cent of the people are not having any kind of land. The labourers having house constitute 97.3 per cent whereas 2.7 per cent labourers not having their own house even this too we can't take into consideration as these labourers having their own house because all the labourers in the study area are living in huts not in the constructed homes. The percentage of livestock possess by the migrant agricultural labourers is only 28.4 per cent whereas 71.6 per cent labourers not possess livestocks.

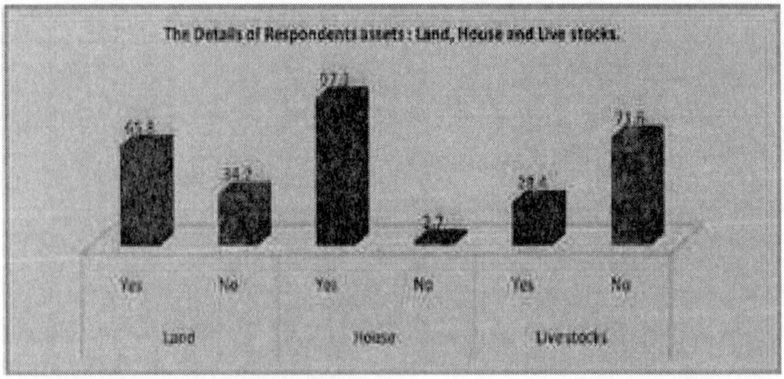

Source: Field Survey.

Fig. 3: Asset Possession by Respondents.

The information relating to the respondents land holdings, housing and livestock assets is given in the above bar chart. Very high percentage of labourers was having land and house but very few labourers were having livestock.

Table 6: Respondent land asset details

	Land	
	Frequency	*Percentage*
Owned	148	65.8
Not Owned	77	34.2
Total	225	100.0

Source: Field survey.

The above table shows that 65.8 per cent of the migrants were having own land whereas 34.2 per cent of the migrants were not having own land. Having own land here cannot be considered as strong economic status because most of them were having less than five acres land, which is mostly barren and rainfed.

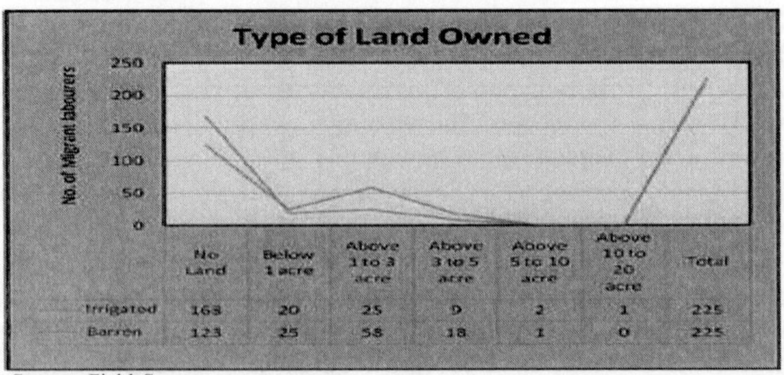

Source: Field Survey.

Fig. 4: Type of land possessed by respondents

The data regarding land assets of the migrant agricultural labourers has depicted in the chart below. The chart shows that the number of households not having the irrigated land out of 225 households is 168, whereas 20 households were having irrigated land below the one acre, 25 households having irrigated land above one to three acres, in the same manner Nine households having the irrigated land above Three to Five acres. Whereas only Two households were having irrigated land above Five to Ten acres and only one household among total is having the irrigated land above 10 to 20 acres.

Borrowing details

Pie chart 5 depicts that the 22 per cent of the migrant labourers did not borrow from any sources, While 17 per cent of the labourers borrowed amounts below Rs 25000. The labourers constituting 33 per cent in the diagram had borrowed between Rs 25001 and 50000, while Nine per cent of the migrant labourers borrowed more than Rs 1 lakh.

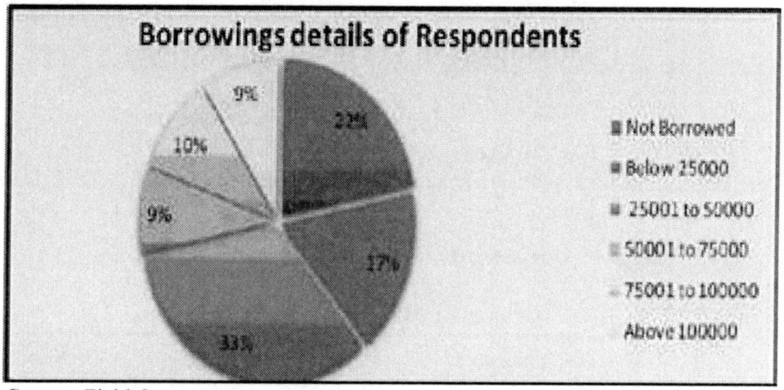

Source: Field Survey

Fig 5: Borrowings.

Table 7: Sources of Borrowing

	Borrowed from institution		Borrowed from Non-institution	
	Frequency	*Percentage*	*Frequency*	*Percentage*
Zero borrowing	48	21.3	48	21.3
Yes	40	17.8	158	70.2
No	137	60.9	19	8.4
Total	225	100.0	225	100.0

Source: Field Survey.

The data in Table 7 have been used to draw the bar chart below. The table and the bar chart show that the borrowing sources of the migrant agricultural labourers of the Manvi Taluk of Raichur district. According to the above table, 48 households have not borrowed from any sources. Out of 100 per cent institutional borrowings only 17.8 per cent of the labourers borrowed from the institutional source. Whereas 60.9 per cent have not borrowed from the institutions and 21.3 per cent labourers were not borrowed from any sources. Out of 100 per cent non-institutional borrowings, 70.2 per cent of the labourers borrowed and only 8.4 per cent have not borrowed from non-institution sources.

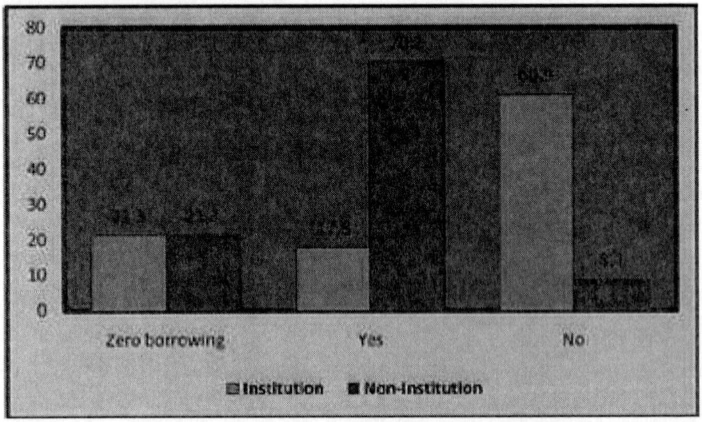

Source: Field survey.

Fig. 6: Borrowings Sources of Respondents.

Table 8: Stream of Migration in Study Area

	Direction of migration		*Time Period*		*Frequency*	
	Within State	*Inter State*	*Within 3 Months*	*3 to 6 Months*	*Every Year*	*Not Every Year*
Frequency	213	12	60	165	175	50
Percentage	94.7	5.3	26.7	73.3	77.8	22.2

Source: Field survey.

Most of the migrant agricultural labourers were migrating within the state boundary. They are more likely to migrate every year and the most important thing is that they were migrating only for seasonally. The above table shows the direction, time period and frequency of migration in the study area. According to the data of table, 94.7 per cent of the people migrating within the state boundary and the 73.3 per cent of the labourers are migrating between three to six months. Whereas 26.7 per cent labourers migrating not more than three months. This stream of migration shows that this is a seasonal and rural outmigration.

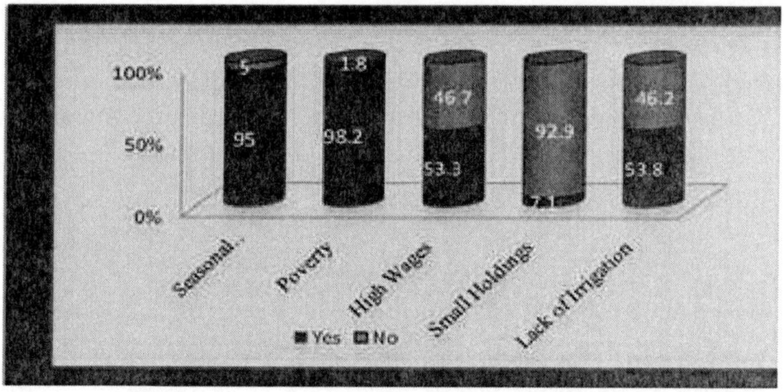

Source: Field survey.

Fig. 7: Reasons for Seasonal Migration.

There are many reasons behind the seasonal migration of agriculture labourers. The above bar chart shows the reasons behind the seasonal migration of agriculture labourers in the study area. The 95 per cent of the labourers are migrating because of seasonal unemploment, 98.2 per cent labourers were revealed that poverty is the reason to migrate, 53.3 per cent labourers said high wages in urban areas is the reason behind their migration where as only 7.1 labourers given small holdings as their reason to migrate and 53.8 per cent labourers were migrating due to lack of irrigation facility.

Table 9: Economic Impact of Seasonal Migration

Impact	*Income*	*Expenditure*	*Savings*	*Debt Position*
Same	0.4	0.0	2.7	11.1
Decreased	0.0	0.0	0.0	73.3
Increased	99.6	100.0	92.0	0.0
Nil	0.0	0.0	5.3	15.6
Total	100.0	100.0	100.0	100.0

The table-9 shows the economic impact of seasonal migration on income, expenditure, savings and debt position of seasonal migrant agricultural labourers. Migration helped to increase the income of 99.6 per cent respondents, and the expenditure of every migrant labour household has increased. Migration also increased the savings of the 92.0 per cent seasonal migrant labourers. Seasonal migration also helped labourers to repayments on debts, so 73.3 per cent migrants said that their volume of debt has decreased.

Conclusion

The migration has been considered as the final livelihood strategy by the migrant agricultural labourers in the study area. Above results shows that migration increases the migrants social and economic status of migrants workers, these changes are very help full to include the excluded group of people to financial inclusion process and achieve the financial inclusion, without economic stability there is no possibility to achieve financial inclusion in the country.

REFERENCES

1. Kaur B, Singh J.M, Garg B.R, Singh Jasdev and Singh S. (2011). "*Causes and Impact of Labour Migration: A Case Study of Punjab Agriculture*" Agriculture Economic Research Review Vol. 24, pp. 459-466.
2. Keshri and Bhagat (2012), "*Temporary and Seasonal Migration: Regional Pattern, Characteristics and Associated Factors*" Economic & Political Weekly, Vol xlvii, no. 4, pp. 81-87.
3. Wani M.H, Shahid Yousuf, Baba S.H. and Wani S.A. (2011). "*Agriculture Labour Migration: Causes and Implications*" Agriculture Economics Research Review Vol.,24.
4. Ahamad M.G, Khondker R.K, Ahmed Z, Tanin F. (2011). "*Seasonal Unemployment and Voluntary Out-Migration from Northern Bangladesh*" Modern Economy, 2, 174-179 http://www.SciRP.org/journal/me
5. Bhattacharya, P. C. (2000). "*An Analysis of Rural-to-Rural Migration in India*". Journal of International Development 12:5, 655–667.
6. [Online]available:http://onlinelibrary.wiley.com/doi/10.1002/1099-1328%28200007%2912: 5%3C655::AID-JID666%3E3.0.CO;2-8/pdf
7. Bryan R. Roberts. (1989). "*Urbanisation, Migration, and Development*" Source: Sociological Forum, Vol. 4, No. 4. http://www.jstor.org/stable/684429.Accessed: 30/04/2013 06:28
8. Census of India, 1981, 1991, 2001, Migration Data. New Delhi: Government of India. http://censusofindia.gov.in
9. Deshingkar P and Akter S (2009), "*Migration and Human Development in India*" MPRA Paper No. 19193. Overseas Development Institute, London. http://mpra.ub.uni-muenchen.de/19193/
10. Deshingkar P. (2008). "*Circular Internal Migration and Development in India*" Overseas Development Institute, London. http://essays.ssrc.org/acrossborders/wp-content/uploads/2009/08/ch8.pdf
11. Deshingkar P. (2010). "*Remote Rural Areas and Chronic Poverty in India*" ODI Working Paper 323 CPRC Working Paper 163 Migration, Overseas Development Institute 111 Westminster Bridge Road London SE1 7JD. http://www.odi.org.uk/sites/odi.org.uk/files/odi-assets/publications-opinion-files/5514.pdf

12. Grau H.R and Aide T.M. (2007), "*Are Rural–Urban Migration and Sustainable Development Compatible in Mountain Systems?*" Mountain Research and Development, 27(2):119-123 2007. http://www.bioone.org/doi/full/10.1659/mrd.0906
13. Haas, H. (2010). "*The Internal Dynamics of Migration Processes: A Theoretical Inquiry*". Journal of Ethnic and Migration Studies 36:10, 1587–1617. http://www.heindehaas.com/Publications/de%20Haas%202010%20JEMS%20the%20internal%20dynamics%20of%20migration%20processes.pdf
14. Haberfeld Y, Menaria R.K, Sahoo, B.B, Vyas R.N. (1999). "*Seasonal migration of rural labor in India*" Population Research and Policy Review 18: 473-489. http://www.ncbi.nlm.nih.gov/pmc/articles/PMC3162249/
15. Hazra A. (2012). "*Rural India Still Floating Towards Cities*" Kurukshetra, Vol. 60 No. 4, pp. 3-5 [Online]available:http://164.100.47.132/fileUpload/writereaddate%5C16-30%20Aprli%202012. pdf
16. Herrmann M. and Svarin D. (2009): "*Environmental pressures and rural-urban migration: The case of UNCTAD*" January 2009. MPRA Paper No. 12879, posted on 20 January 2009, 18:56 UTC, http://mpra.ub.uni-muenchen.de/12879/
17. Hossain, M.Z. (2001). "*Rural-Urban Migration in Bangladesh: A Micro-Level Study*", Paper presented in a Poster Session on Internal Migration at the Brazil IUSSP Conference during August20-24. www.iussp.org/Brazil2001/s20/S28_P02_Hossain,
18. Lee, E. S. (1966). "*A Theory of Migration*", Demography. http://www.students.uni-mainz.de/jkissel/Skripte/Lee.pdf
19. Lusome R. "*Migration in India*" http://community.eldis.org/.59b6a372/Labour%20Migration%20in%20 India.pdf
20. Rajasekhar D., Suchitra J. Y, Madheswaran S. and Karanth G. K. "*At Times When Limbs May Fail: Social Security For Unorganized Workers In Karnataka*" (http://www.isec.ac.in/At%20times%20when%20limbs%20may%20fail%20-%20revised%20draft%2030%20MAY.pdf)
21. Ramesh, Meena H.R. and Singh Y.P. (2012), "*Socio-Economic Status of Small Ruminant Farmers in Different Agro-Climatic Zones of Karnataka, India*" International journal of livestock research; 2(2): 129-136, http://www.scopemed.org/?mno=21763
22. Todaro M.P. (1980). "*Internal Migration in Developing Countries: A Survey*" University of Chicago Press, http://www.nber.org/chapters/c9668.pdf
23. Suryanarayana M.H. (2009) "*Intra-State Economic Disparities: Karnataka and Maharashtra*" Economic and Political Weekly. Vol. XLIV No. 26-27.
24. Vijay K. (2010). "*Nature and Characteristics of Seasonal Labour Migration: A Case Study in Mahabubnagar District of Andhra Pradesh*" Working Paper 433. Centre for Development Studies, Thiruvananthapuram. www.cds.edu/wp-content/uploads/2012/09/wp433.pdf

6

Role of Banks in Achieving Financial Inclusion

Rakshitha. S

Abstract: *In India more than half of the poor are financially excluded from the country's formal banking sector. The poor category or low income people, has very little access to financial services due to this aspect, many of them have to depend on informal source of finance which leads to high cost and also results in uneven spread of formal financial service over the country, so the banking industry in India has expanded' its product i.e.;' expansion of its financial inclusion.*

Financial inclusions are the availability of financial services at an affordable cost to the vast sections of the disadvantaged and low income groups. Financial inclusion provides product link bank accounts, insurance, savings, advisory service, and micro finance etc. RBI vision for 2020 is to open nearly 600 million new customer's account, so they have directed all banks to maintain "no-frills account" or a bank account with zero balance for achieving 100 per cent financial inclusion by creating financial assistance by the government.

An attempt has been made in this paper to provide a brief overview on role of banks in achieving financial inclusion for sustainable growth of Indian Economy.

Key Words: Financial Inclusion, Financial Services, Self-Help-Groups.

1. Introduction

Financial inclusion is one of the positive effects which can facilitate many people to come out of the poverty conditions. It is widely believed that financial inclusion provides access to various services in financial areas. The poverty conditions are majority found in rural areas.

Financial inclusion, with a focus on rural areas, has been one of RBI's main priorities since 2005. The RBI's plan includes provision of banking services to habitations with a population of 2000 and above, as per 2001 census, by March 2012. With this end in mind, in November 2005, the RBI has asked banks to offer a basic banking 'no frills account' with low or zero minimum balance and minimum charges to expand the outreach of such accounts to the low income groups. The business correspondent (BC) model was launched, among other things, in order to extend the reach of banks to remote areas.

The objectives of financial inclusion are to extend the organised financial service. An attempt must be to light the poor so that they come out of poverty. The basic concept of financial inclusion is having a saving or current account with any bank. In reality it includes loans, insurance service and much more. Some of the major efforts made in the last five decades include- nationalisation of banks, co-operative and regional rural banks, lead bank schemes, formation of SHG'S etc. All these initiatives is to reach the large sections of the financial excluded population.

2. Review of Literature

A. Sheshadri A.B. Revealed to ensure financial inclusion can bring in to balanced growth fold the needy and weaker sections. In a country like India with low literacy levels, poverty, unemployment, heavily uneven distribution of income and wealth and opportunities, the government has to aesthetic responsibility to put system in place for reaching the bottom of pyramid.

Srikanth. R (2013) reported that financial inclusion attempt to lift the resource poor from poverty through coordinated action amongst the banks, the government and other related institutions in order to facilitate access to bank accounts and other related services. Indian Institute of Banking and Finance (IIBF) opines financial inclusion is delivery of banking services at an affordable cost (no frills accounts) to the vast sections of disadvantaged and low income group. Unrestrained access to public goods and services is the sine qua of an open and efficient society.

3. Statement of Problem

In India, one-third of the population is financial excluded from access to financial services. There is a need to achieve financial inclusion, access over various financial services to the poor and fills the gap between social classes. Each and every banks must adopt financial inclusion by their own interest but not by force. In Karnataka, only some banks are actively involved in financial inclusion to promote economy. This study helps to know the issues involved in the adoption of financial inclusion plan.

4. Objectives

- To identify various institutions and there role in financial inclusion.
- To study role of banks in achieving financial inclusion with the help of SHGs.

5. Methodologies

The study is analytical and based on the material collected from primary data and secondary data.

The present study was intended to assess the level of financial inclusion among the vulnerable section of society in Kudige, a village in Thirthahalli taluk. To study their awareness about financial inclusion, financial products and financial services offered by banks. For the purpose of this research studies a sample size of 40 women who are members of SHG's of four different groups are selected. Secondary data are collected from reference books, research journals, reports (i.e., RBI, GOI) and relevant internet sources.

6. Financial Inclusions

Financial inclusion is access to financial services and timely and adequate credit to the excluded sections, i.e., weaker sections and low income groups. One segment of the population has access to assortment of banking services encompassing regular banking facilities and portfolio counselling, the other segment of underprivileged and lower income group is totally deprived of even basic financial services.

The banking industry has grown both horizontally and vertically but the branch penetration in rural area has not kept pace with the rising population and the need of accessible financial services. Even after decades of bank nationalisation, whose rational was to shift the focus from class banking to mass banking, we still find usurious money lenders in rural areas continuing to exploit the poor. Financial inclusion of the poor will help in bringing them to the mainstream of growth and would also provide the financial institutions an opportunity to be partners in inclusive growth.

The banking industry has grown both horizontally and vertically but the branch penetration in rural area has not kept pace with the rising population & the need for accessible financial services. Even after decades of bank nationalisation, whose rational was to Repeat the focus from class banking to mass banking, we still find usurious money lenders in rural areas continuing to exploit the poor. Financial inclusion of the poor will help in bringing them to the mainstream of growth & would also provide the financial institutions an opportunity to be partners in inclusive growth.

The committee on financial inclusion under the Chairmanship of Dr. C. Rangarajan has defined financial inclusion "as the process of ensuring access to financial services and timely and adequate credit as needed by vulnerable groups such as weaker sections and low income groups at a affordable cost".

7. Financial Inclusion - Current Status

- Despite various measures for financial inclusion, poverty and exclusion continuous to dominate socio economic and political discourse in India. Even after six decades of post independence era. Through economy has shown impressive growth during post linearisation era of 1991, impact is yet to be percolated to all sections of the society and therefore, India is still home of one-third of world's poor.
- The present banking network of the country (as on 31.03.2014) comprises of a bank branch network of 115082 and an ATM network of 160055. Of these, 43962 branches (38.2 per cent) and 23334 ATMs (14.58 per cent) are in rural areas.

Table: Financial inclusion- Summary progress of all banks including Regional Rural Banks (RRB's) during three years period is as under:

Particulars	*Yr. Ended 2010*	*Yr. Ended 2011*	*Yr. Ended 2012*	*Yr. Ended 2013*
Banking outlets in villages				
(a) Branches	33,378	80,802	37,471	401,837
(b) Villages covered by BC's	34,174	34,811	1,41,136	2,21,341
(c) Other modes	142	595	3,146	6,276
(d) Total	67,674	1,16,208	1,81,753	2,68,456
Urban locations through BS's	447	3,771	5,891	27.143
Basic Saving Bank Deposit a/c –branches				
(a) No in Millions	60.19	73.13	81.20	100.80
(b) Amount in billions	44.33	57.89	109.87	164.89
Basic Saving Bank Deposit a/c –BC's				
(a) No in Millions	13.27	31.63	57.30	81.27
(b) Amount in billions	10.69	18.23	10.54	18.22

OD facility availed in BSBDA's a/c				
(a) No in Millions	0.18	0.61	2.71	3.92
(b) Amount in billions	0.10	0.26	1.08	1.55
(c) KCC's (no. in Millions)	24.31	27.11	30.24	33.79

Source: Table IV. 4, RBI annual reports, 2013.

8. Role of various institutions in achieving Financial Inclusion

8.1 Role of Regional Rural Banks

RRB's have been existence for around three decades in Indian financial scene. In the beginning of six RRB's with 17 branches covering 12 districts in December 1975, the numbers have grown in to 196 RRB's with 14,446 branches in March 2004. A remarkable feature of their performance over the past three decades and the massive expansion of their network in rural areas. Before the existence of RRB's in India, Commercial and Co-operative banks were rendered service to the rural public. These banks were quite inadequate to reach rural population. But RRB's have achieved tremendous growth in terms of reaching rural India. Due to amalgamation the number of RRB's decreased to 86 and number of branches to 15,181 in 2008-09.

8.2 Role of Self help groups

As an innovative credit channel, the SHG was introduced in 1992, to link poor people with bank credit. Under the programme, about 40 million rural families have been linked with banks up to March 2007 (NABARD). The distinguishing feature of their approach as compared to other sponsored credit schemes is learning the management of own money by the poor before availing bank loan. In financing SHG's the requirement of collateral by banks has been replaced by peer group pressure and hence there has been enabled social and economic inclusion of women by waiving the requirement of collateral.

8.3 Role of Commercial Banks towards Financial Inclusion

Bank plays an important role in mobilisation and allocation of resources in any country. Rural people in India are facing problems in the inadequate supply of credit. The major source of credit to rural households, particularly – low income working households, has been the informal sector. Informal sectors advance loans at very high rate of interest. The financial inclusion will not be possible without the contribution of banks. Banks are the key pillar of India's financial system.

9. Results and Analysis

The purpose of financial inclusion is delivery of banking services at an affordable price in a fair and transparent manner to the vulnerable sections of the society.

Socio-economic Status of the Respondents

Table 1: Socio-economic Status

Socio-economic Factors		*No of respondents*	*Percentage*
Age	Below 25 years	5	12.5
	26 - 35 years	10	25
	36-45 years	20	50
	Above 45 years	5	12.5
Education	Illiteracy	12	30
	Primary	18	45
	High School	07	17
	P.U.C.	03	08
	Graduate	-	00
Type of Occupation	Petty Business	05	12.5
	Job	02	05
	Labour	14	35
	Agriculture	19	47.5
Family Monthly Income	Below Rs 500	02	5
	Rs 501-2000	08	20
	Rs 2001-4000	20	50
	Rs 4001-6000	10	25

Source: Field Survey.

Table 1 reveals that 50 per cent of respondents interviewed in selected survey area were in the age group of 36-45 years. It is observed that 45 per cent of the respondents were completed primary level education. Majority of the respondent were working as labour and also dependant on agriculture (35 per cent and 45.1 per cent). It is noted that 25 per cent of the respondents were belonging to family monthly income range of Rs 4001-6000.

Financial Inclusion Status of Respondents

The Financial inclusion status of the selected respondents is self help group with the four women groups.

Membership of SHG's (Women Category)

Table 2: Membership of SHG's

Particulars	*No. of Respondents*	*Percentage*
Yes	40	100
No	0	-
Total	40	100

Source: Field Survey.

Table 2 throws light on the membership in SHG's. Their survey has focused on women category of 40 respondents who were taken for the survey is all members of SHG. Through participating as member they have improved their saving and have taken advantage of their group.

Have a bank account

Table 3: Have a separate bank account

Particulars	*No. of Respondents*	*Percentage*
Yes	36	90
No	04	10
Total	40	100

Source: Field Survey.

Table 3: It is observed out of 100 per cent surveyed respondents 90 per cent are having bank account, whereas 10 per cent of respondents are not having the bank account.

Financial inclusion is gaining its importance as focused on low income group. This survey about bank account helps to know most of the women related to SHG are aware about opening of bank account.

Amount of loan availed by the members of SHG's

Table 4: Loan availed by the members

Loan availed	*No. of Respondents*	*Percentage*
Less than 10,000	06	15
10,000-15,000	10	25
15,000-25,000	15	37.5
25,000-35,000	06	15
35,000 & above	03	7.5
Total	40	100

Source: Field Survey.

Table 4 consists of the members' availed loan through various ways. Majority 37.5 per cent of them are in the categories Rs 15,000-25000, 25 per cent of them take the loan in the category of Rs 10000-15000. Members get an actual idea about loans which prevails in bank along with the interest. Through SHGs, it improves the standard of living of people and also creates financial inclusion.

Amount of Deposits in banks by the members of SHG's (Monthly)

Table 5: Amount of Deposits in Banks

Particulars	*No. of Respondents*	*Percentage*
50 and less than 50	10	25
100 and less than 100	30	75
Total	40	100

Source: Field Survey.

Table 5 consists of the deposits made by the members of SHG's. 75 per cent of members deposits Rs 100 and less, 25 per cent of members deposit Rs 50 and less. Through this they come to know the process of deposit in bank and related to the banking rules.

Receipt of Bank Loan

Table 6: Receipt of bank loan

Particulars	*No. of Respondents*	*Percentage*
Yes	33	82.5
No	07	17.5
Total	40	100

Source: Field Survey.

Table 6: Majority of the members are having bank loan, 17 per cent of the members are not having bank loan. It shows that after joining SHG majority of the members are taking bank loan and utilise their service of bank in generating income through animal husbandry, poultry and other activities. So, this creates active utilisation of financial services of banks.

Awareness about Financial Services offered by banks after opening an account (After joining SHGs)

Table 7: Awareness about Financial Services

Particulars		*No. of Respondents*	*Percentage*
Deposits and Savings	Not familiar	02	05
	Just familiar	38	95
Pass Book and Cheque	Not familiar	06	15
	Just familiar	34	85
Loans and Interest rate	Not familiar	06	15
	Just familiar	34	85
ATM	Not familiar	10	25
	Just familiar	30	75

Source: Field Survey.

Table 7 exhibits that majority (95 per cent) of the respondents are familiar about deposits and saving after opening an account. It is noted that (85 per cent) of the respondents were familiar about pass book, cheque, loan and interest rate. Only 25 per cent of the respondents were not familiar about ATM. Majority in the locality are familiar about various financial services and have access over bank with the linkage of SHG.

10. Suggestions

The following are the suggestions recommended from this study:

- Minority of respondents have not opened bank account due to awareness of banking area. Awareness programms must be organised to influence the vulnerable section of the society and also create awareness related to no-frills accounts.
- Banks should appoint business correspondents to disseminate its service to the unreached area.
- Major respondents are having bank account but are unaware about certain financial service by bank such as ATM (Technology). In this regard account holders must be educated about these services.
- Bank should take special steps in their area of research to reach 100 per cent financial inclusion.
- The government should play all the social security payments through the bank account of the beneficiary. This would enhance the banking habits among villages and thereby pave the way for financial inclusion at gross root level.

11. Conclusion

Financial inclusion is a major criterion to poverty alleviation. RBI's vision for 2020 is to open 600 million new customer's accounts and service them through a variety of channels by leveraging and information technology. In a country like India with low literary levels, poverty, unemployment, heavily uneven distribution of income and wealth and opportunities, the government has the aesthetic responsibility to put the system in place for reaching gross root level and achieve financial inclusion.

REFERENCES

1. Rangarajan Committee Report on Financial inclusion rbi.org.in/scripts.
2. "Financial inclusion": A Road India Need to Travel" K.C. Chakrabarty, Deputy Governor, RBI.
3. State levels Banker Committee "Action plan for comprehensive financial inclusion" (2014).
4. Reserve Bank of India, "Report of the committee on financial inclusion" January 2008.
5. Economic and Political Weekly.

7

Role of Micro Finance for Financial Inclusion of the Tribes: An Empirical Study in Chamarajanagara and Mysore Districts of Karnataka

Puttaraja

Abstract: *The purpose of the present study is to identify and study the causes and consequences of the supply side and demand side factors relating to micro finance and the financial inclusion process with reference to the four major tribes of Mysore and Chamarajanagara districts in Karnataka state. These four sample tribes are at diverse and in different levels of socio-economic transformation. Therefore, the micro finance activity and their response to the programmes of financial inclusion both supply side and demand side is very weak. Among the major tribes of the case study area, on the supply side, there is a total absence of the public sector financial institutions in the tribal areas. The bankers are unwilling to open the branches on account of the absence of demand for banker's financial products and services by the tribes. On the demand side the tribes do not need all the modern banking products and services, since they are at a very low level of subsistence economy. In other words both supply and demand side constraints are responsible for financial exclusion of the tribes in the case study region.*

The tribal economic empowerment goal could be achieved only through transferring adequate real resource to tribes on one hand and providing financial infrastructure facilities to them on the other hand. This is a highly challenging task in India. This could be achieved through adopting Bank correspondence or Bank facilitators model (BC or BF) by Bank-SHGs linkage model of financial inclusion. In the recent past, Government of India has devised and implementing the Bank-SHGs linkage model for promoting financial inclusion among tribal people in India. This is a good beginning and welcome change. But this plan is also not fully successful in the tribal areas. To financial inclusion of the tribes, the rational and suitable measures are urgently needed.

Key words: Inclusive growth, Micro finance, financial inclusion, Self-help group.

Introduction

The tribal population has been most socially and economically excluded in India. Thus, the tribes are also the financially excluded social group who suffer from acute poverty, unemployment and underemployment, hunger and starvation in many South Asian countries including India. The exclusion process in case of tribal people assumes the social, economic and status, and hence they are socially excluded by the main land people. They are economically excluded since the tribes do not produce substantial marketable surplus of private goods. Therefore the tribes have lack of adequate income to buy goods produced by rural and urban communities. Further, more importantly, the difficult geographical conditions like dense forest, hilly and mountainous regions in which tribes live isolates them from mainland habitats financial dimension. This is because; the tribal people are assigned a very low caste status. Thus, partly on account of indifference on the part of the government on one hand and partly on account of lack of demand for infrastructure on the other hand, there is a serious shortage of infrastructure facilities including financial infrastructure. There are supply side and demand side bottlenecks for the development of financial infrastructure in the tribal areas.

In this paper an attempt is made to identify and analyse the role of micro finance and obstacles for the financial inclusion of tribes which hamper their socio-economic empowerment. This is a case study based on primary data collected by using an interview schedule. It deals with the case of four tribes namely, Jenukuruba, Kadukuruba, Soliga and Yarava who live in and closer to the National

Reserve Forest area of Nagarahole, Bandipura, and B.R. Hills spread over in southern part of the Mysore and Chamarajanagara districts in Karnataka state. The tribal population is highly deprived and exploited, thus, it is a very backward segment of Indian society. The tribes of India are subject to a high degree of social exclusion on account of assigning them a low caste status; whereas the Indian tribes also suffer from economic exclusion from the mainstream economy on account of their isolated living and absence of modern educational capability and skills as well as other physical and economic resources. Therefore the tribal people of India suffer from socio-economic exclusion as well as financial exclusion.

II. Conceptual Framework

Micro finance has evolved as an economic development approach, intended to benefit low-income group. Micro finance refers to the provision of financial services to low income clients, including the self employed. Micro finance helps to extend the market, reducing poverty and festering social change through the financial strength.

The majority of tribal people depend on the informal sources of finance for meeting their livelihood and consumption needs (Singh, 2004).The majority of the resources used by them are informal in nature like interest free loans taken from friends/relatives though people were using Micro Finance services, too, but the share of Micro Finance Institutions in total money management transactions was less than 15 per cent (Rutherford, 2003). The major source of finance was found to be the moneylenders, i.e., approximately 80 per cent of the total amount borrowed (Sriram, Parhi, 2006).

Financial inclusion means delivery of banking services and credit at an affordable cost to the vast sections of disadvantaged and low income groups. The various financial services include savings, loans, insurance payments, remittance facilities and financial counselling/ advisory service by the formal financial system. An open and efficient society is always characterised by the unrestrained access to public goods and services. As banking services are in the nature of public goods, financial inclusion should, therefore, be viewed as availability of banking and payment services to the entire population without discrimination of any type. C. Rangarajan Committee Report (2008, pp. 33).

According to the European Foundation the concept of social exclusion refers to "The process which individuals or groups are wholly or partially excluded from full participation in the society in which they live". Various scholars of the sociology and anthropology have shown interest in studying the causes and consequences of social exclusion. On the whole social exclusion is a practice, which is an obstacle to full participation of all the people or group of people in the societal process and thus a welfare depressant. On the whole as C.J. Sonowal has observed social exclusion shows the following features of a 'society at large or individual at least': '(i) inability to participate effectively in economic, social, political and cultural life. (ii) Distance of alienation from the so-called mainstream society. (iii) isolation from major social mechanisms which produce or distribute social resources (C.J. Sonowal; pp.125).

The C. Rangarajan Committee Report (2008) has defined the concept of financial inclusion as "the process of ensuring access to financial services and timely and adequate credit where needed by vulnerable groups such as weaker sections and low income groups at an affordable cost".

The means of financial inclusion implies more and more access to all individuals to institutional credit and financial services for the purpose of productive and social purposes. The Rangarajan Committee (2008: p.1) observed that;

"The essence of financial inclusion is in trying to ensure that a range of appropriate financial service is available to every individual and enabling them to understand and access those services. Apart from the regular form of financial intermediation, it may include a basic no frills banking account for making and receiving payments, as a savings product suited to the pattern of cash flows of poor household, money transfer facilities, small loans and overdrafts the productive personal and other purposes, insurance (life and non-life) etc".

The term 'financial exclusion', the opposite of 'financial inclusion' is defined by the C. Rangarajan Committee (2008 p. 1) as " There is growing divide, with an increased range of personal finance options for a segment of high and middle income population and significant large section of the population who lack access to even the most basic banking services. This is termed 'financial exclusion'. These people, particularly, those living on low incomes, cannot access mainstream financial products such as bank accounts, credit, remittances and payment services, financial advisory services, insurance facilities etc".

The idea of financial inclusion is very powerful and socially important. The achievement of financial inclusion helps to promote personal/individual development/empowerment. This all important aspect is explained by C. Rangarajan Committee Report (2008; pp.34) as under "... the term financial inclusion is perceived in different ways under different contexts. There is a view that only access to credit is treated as financial inclusion whereas the other view that only access to credit is treated as financial inclusion whereas the other view includes all the services extended by the financial institutions. That apart, financial inclusion by banks and other institutions must target, apart from personal/private "investment requirements of individuals and groups, the universal public investment requirement necessary for development of infrastructure, social sector services, public utilities and productive forces/ capacity building efforts, etc. Thus financial inclusion may well be all about money and finance, but with the ultimate objective of directly abolishing the state of social exclusion in the economy".

The study of financial inclusion by the UN (2006) has set the following as its main goals:

(a) Access at a reasonable cost of all households and enterprises to the range of financial services for which they are "bankable", including savings, short and long term credit, leasing and factoring, mortgages, insurance,pensions payments, local money transfers and international remittance.
(b) Sound institutions, guided by appropriate internal management systems, industry performance standards and performance monitoring by the market, as well as by sound prudential regulation where required.
(c) Financial and institutional sustainability as a means of providing access to financial services over time.
(d) Multiple providers of financial services, where feasible, so as to bring cost-effective and a wide variety of alternatives to customers (which could include any number of combinations of sound private, non-profit and public provider).

III. Literature Review

Traditional economic theory deals with interrelationship between finance and economic development. This part of economic theory has evolved the past 150 years. The classical theory of economic growth has examined the significance of an investment function in commencing and increasing the rate of economic growth but, however, it has not dealt with the different sources of finance available in capitalist economy.

Adam Smith (1776) had expressed the view about the significant and crucial contribution of high density of banks in Scotland for invigorating stimulating development of the Scottish economy.

Jude L. Fernando (1997), in his study on empowerment of women by means of micro credit – based income generation programms is a new orthodoxy in the development discourse. In this article he appraises this phenomenon in a broader historical context. It shows how women's interests are being subsumed by and subordinated to the priorities of mainstream development in ways detrimental to the radical aspirations of the NGOs' empowerment project. In addition is a critical evaluation of the current approaches used in studies on micro-credit and empowerment. These studies have mostly focused on the final outcome of micro-enterprise rather than the process through which they are achieved. This study based on field research in Bangladesh, demonstrates that widely documented success of micro –enterprises are a result of the activities of the very institutions that are considered to be oppressive to women. In this process, NGOs contribute to further legitimisation of the same institutions that their micro-enterprises desire to transform.

Mahendra Dev S. (2006) in his study on "Financial Inclusion: Issues and Challenges", examined that financial inclusion is important for improving the living conditions of the poor farmers, rural nonfarm enterprises and other vulnerable groups. Financial exclusion, in terms of lack of access to credit from formal institutions, is high for small and marginal farmers and some social groups. Apart from formal banking institutions, which should look at inclusion both as a business opportunity and social responsibility, the role of Self-Help Groups (SHGs) movement and micro finance institutions is important to improve financial inclusion. This requires new regulatory procedures and de politicisation of the financial system.

Sometimes the attitude of the microfinance provider itself affects the customers perception regarding micro financing services. Particularly, the commercial banks hesitate to provide finance to the poor people as they are considered to be non-bankable, hence, risky too. In a sample study of 10 rural bank branch managers within three district of Madhya Pradesh (Jones et al., 2004), the managers were found to be having the negative attitude towards their role as financial service providers.

Identification of Research Gaps. Some of the important research gaps in the study of financial exclusion/inclusion include the following:

(1) The nature and extent of financial exclusion exist across the sex (female), across different regions, across various occupations (organised and unorganised sector), different regions (progressive and backward regions). Therefore the problem of financial exclusion has to be studied in all these perspectives.

(2) There are few studies on the inclusion and exclusion of the tribes in the development process particularly on the north

eastern tribes. But, on the tribes of Karnataka and particularly in Mysore and Chamarajanagara Districts, the studies on inclusion and exclusion particularly on financial inclusion for tribal development not undertaken.

IV. Results and Discussion

The main objective of this study is to identify and study the causes and consequences of the supply side and demand side factors relating to micro finance and the financial inclusion process with reference to the four major tribes of Mysore and Chamarajanagara districts in Karnataka state.

The present study is based on primary data. The sample size is 100 respondents. Of these, 55 tribal households are selected from Mysore district and 45 households are selected from Chamarajanagara district. The four major tribes namely, Jenukuruba (30), Kadukuruba (20), Soliga (30) and Yarava (30), are selected for the study. Among these four tribes Jenukurba tribe is identified as primitive tribe and the remaining three tribes are viewed as an ancient forest based tribes. Of these tribes, Yarava tribe is found in Mysore district only.

The data are collected by using an interview schedule by the researcher from six Hadies/Podus namely, Attagullypura colony, Melukamenahally, and Mookahally colony of Chamarajanagara district and Shettyhally, Hosahally-A and B hadies and Yashodharapura hadies of the Mysore district. The field study was undertaken during January to March 2014.

The Yashodharadapura where the Soliga tribe lives, is located four Kilometers away from Hunsur town (Taluka headquarter), and Shettyhally, 20 Kms away from Hunsur town and Hosahlly A and B hadi, is located 12 Kms away from H.D. Kote town (Taluka headquarter), where Soliga, Jenukuruba, Kadukuruba and Yarava tribes live, in Mysore district.

The Attagullipura tribal colony, where the Soliga tribe lives, is located 18 Kms away from Chamarajanagara town (District headquarter), Mookahally and Melukamenahally Colony where Soliga, Jenukuruba and Kadukuruba tribes live, is located 12 Kms away from Gundalpet town (Taluka headquarter) in Chamarajanagara district. These tribal settlements are connected by road. There is a public and private transport plying between hadis/podus and towns. Simple average methods and statistical tables are used to analyse the problems.

The geographical proximity influences the people of the interland of a town or city the sample tribes in both the case study districts live at short distance from small towns which have health and educational infrastructure as well as the economic infrastructure like public transport, public road, public telephone, post office, agriculture market, banks, and tiny and small scale industries. Even though, the sample tribes are not highly influenced by the nearby small towns and their economy. This is clear from the data related to employment level and pattern (Table 1.2). The level and variety of banking practices of the tribes (Table 1.5) the mode of saving habits of the sample tribes (Table 1.6). In other words there are no urban influences on the tribal society and economy in our case study region.

Demographic Profile of the Case Study Tribes

In the total tribal population of these two districts, 44,151 and 31,505 are the selected four tribes in Mysore and Chamarajanagara districts respectively which is 16.27 per cent and 29.69 per cent of the total tribes.

Table 1.1: Demographic Profile of the Selected Tribes in Mysore and Chamarajanagara Districts (In Numbers)

Sl. No.	*Number of Hadies*	*Number of Families*	*Total Tribal Population*	*Jenu Kuruba*	*Kadu Kuruba*	*Yarava*	*Soliga*
Mysore District							
1 H.D. Kote	114	4841	23368	16761	2430	1547	2630
2 Hunsur	51	2916	13071	11329	00	93	1649
3 Mysore	01	104	518	0	0	0	518
4 Najangudu	05	247	1235	1195	0	0	40
5 Piriyapatna	30	1201	5959	5783	0	0	176
Mysore Total	**201**	**9309**	**44151**	**35068**	**2430**	**1640**	**5013**
Chamarajanagara District							
1 C.R. Nagara	24	1052	6001	-	-	-	6001
2 Gudlpet	29	1048	4119	1355	750	-	2014
3 Kollegal	80	3176	19506	-	-	-	19506
4 Yalandur	10	462	1879	-	-	-	1879
C.R. Nagara Total	**143**	**5738**	**31,505**	**1355**	**750**	-	**29400**
Grand total	**344**	**15047**	**75656**	**36423**	**3180**	**1640**	**34413**

Source: ITDP Office Report of Mysore and Chamarajanagara Districts 2010.

The Table 1.1 shows that H.D. Kote and Hunsur talukas have highest tribal population in Mysore district than the other talukas. That means in these talukas in 165 (82 per cent) tribal hadies 7757 (83.38 per cent) families are settled which consist of the 36,439 (82.53 per cent) tribal population with good mixture of the four tribes in Mysore district. The Mysore, Nanjanagudu, Piriyapatna talukas have less tribal population and mix of the above said tribes.

Among the selected tribes Jenukurubas (primitive tribe) are the highest in number than the others. In Chamarajanagara district, Soliga is the major tribe. They are living in 143 podus of the 5530 (96.37 per cent) families which consist of 29400 (93 per cent) population and spread over in the four talukas. Kadukuruba and Jenukuruba tribes are very less in numbers and there is no Yarava tribe in the Chamarajanagara district. Comparatively Mysore district has highest in numbers of tribes and good mix of all the four tribes. In both the districts all the selected tribes are unevenly distributed, because of the unequal spread of the forest and different cultural and ethnic nature of the tribes.

Table 1.2: Sources of Employment of the Sample Tribes (In Percentage)

Districts	*Chamarajanagara*				*Mysore*				
Tribes	*JK*	*KK*	*Soliga*	*Average*	*JK*	*KK*	*Soliga*	*Yarava*	*Average*
Sample Size	10	10	25	45	20	10	05	20	55.0
Wage Labour	97	95	97	96.33	98	90	95	85	92.0
Agriculture	50	60	54	54.66	52	65	48	65	57.5
MFP Collection	17	30	45	30.66	40	32	20	20	28.0
Animal Husbandry	15	20	17	17.33	20	30	15	35	25.0
Self Employment	01	00	09	3.33	02	05	15	10	9.25
Govt. Jobs	10	08	06	08.00	12	06	05	05	07.0
Migration	60	65	54	59.66	70	60	50	62	60.5

Source: Compiled from Primary Data.

Of total sample tribal households nearly 85-98 per cent of the Jenukuruba, Kadukuruba, Soliga, and Yarava tribes work as wage labourer in Mysore district. Whereas 95- 97 per cent of Jenukuruba, Kadukuruba and Soliga tribes in Chamarajanagara district work as wage labourer. That means wage labour is major form of labour supply among tribes. Next agriculture tends to be the major source of employment of all the four sample tribes in both the districts (Table 1.2). This is because nearly 35-50 per cent of the total sample tribal households do not own agricultural land. Nearly 50-75 per cent of the total sample tribal households do not have appropriate land records. Thus, 40-60 per cent of the tribal households suffer from unemployment and underemployment problems. It indicates that the tribal rehabilitation programme in Mysore and Chamarajanagara districts is still not complete and it is not tribal friendly (Table 1.4).

The dependency of sample tribes on Minor Forest Produces (MFP) collection and animal husbandry for their livelihood is marginal. The Jenukuruba and Kadukuruba tribes in Mysore district and Soliga as well as Kadukuruba tribes in Chamarajanagara district still relay upon income derived from MFP collection than the other two tribes like Jenukuruba and Yarava in the study area (Table 1.2).

The self employment programme has not made any significant impact on tribes in the case study region. Although the state government as well as NGOs (VGKK and SVYM), offer short duration courses on vocational education and training. The response of the youth of the four sample tribes is highly discouraging (Table 1.2).

The sample tribal population has not taken advantage of job reservation policy of the State, since the level of education and skill formation and training level is very low and qualitatively is very poor. So, they are unable to take advantage of the periodic recent developmental schemes implimented by various State and Central governments (Table 1.2).

All the four sample tribes of the Mysore and Chamarajanagara districts show a high degree of migration characteristics. It was reported that, 50-70 per cent of the different tribal labour migration (Table 1.2) to Coorg and neighbouring districts in Karnataka and Nilgiri and Coimbatore districts of Tamil Nadu State.

Migration of tribal labour from subsistence agriculture to capitalist plantation economy is a recent emerging trend probably since 30 years. The migration of tribal labour from rural to rural area enable more wage income leading to improved and better food security and availability of cheap or low cost labour to the plantation owners. In recent past, they prefer to migrate to the neighbouring coffee plantation, since the employment available help them to overcome income poverty and famine (O.D. Heggade and Puttaraja: 2011).

Table 1.3: Monthly Incomes of the Tribal Families

Districts	*Chamarajanagara*				*Mysore*				
Tribes (Income in Rs)	*JK*	*KK*	*Soliga*	*Average*	*JK*	*KK*	*Soliga*	*Yarava*	*Average*
Below Rs 2500	04	03	05	04	05	02	03	02	03.00
Rs2500-5000	70	65	60	65	75	60	50	58	60.75
Rs5000-7500	15	20	25	20	18	25	30	25	24.50
Rs7500-10,000	10	08	08	08.67	02	10	12	10	08.50
Above Rs 10,000	01	04	02	02.33	00	03	05	05	03.25
Total	**100**	**100**	**100**	**100**	**100**	**100**	**100**	**100**	**100**

Source: Compiled from Primary Data.

Nearly 50 to 70 per cent of the tribal families earn between Rs 2500- Rs 5000 per month through a combination of wage employment, MFP collection, and animal husbandry etc (Table 1.3). That means on an average each tribal family has two to three adult working members.

Thus, each family person earns an average Rs 750 – Rs 1250 per month. However, the income carried by the tribal family is unstable and very low throughout the year. Thus, the incidence of income poverty and human poverty on the sample tribal households in southern Karnataka is very high. This is the major problem responsible for the lack of participation in financial inclusion activities.

A small number, that is 20-24.5 per cent of the total sample households in Chamarajanagara and Mysore districts respectively, earn more than Rs 5000 –Rs 7500 per month. In this category of income earners, more number of Soliga, Yarava, and Kadukuruba tribes is found. In this sense, the Jenukuruba tribe in both the case study districts is economically highly backward and thus, Jenukuruba across to financial inclusion with the modern financial intermediaries is not existent.

Table 1.4: Size of Land Holdings and Source of Income for Agricultural Operation (In Percentage)

Districts	*Chamarajanagara*				*Mysore*				
Tribes	*JK*	*KK*	*Soliga*	*Average*	*JK*	*KK*	*Soliga*	*Yarava*	*Average*
Size of land holding									
< 2 Acre	10	15	32	19.00	11	12	08	12	10.50
2-4 Acre	35	35	20	30.00	30	38	30	35	33.25
Above 4 Acre	05	10	02	05.66	11	15	10	18	13.50
Landless households	50	40	46	45.33	48	35	52	35	42.50
No Land Records	70	75	65	70.00	75	70	50	60	63.75
Institutional Source	05	10	20	11.66	08	10	15	20	13.25
Non Institutional Source	65	72	60	65.66	75	65	55	60	63.75

Source: Compiled from Primary Data.

On an average 40 to 50 per cent of the tribal households own agricultural landholdings between 0.10 to 4 acres (43.75 per cent in Mysore district and 49 per cent in Chamarajanagara district). The total numbers of sample households which own more than four acres of agricultural land are in more number in Mysore district rather than in the Chamarajanagara district (Table1.4). It may also be observed that the land owning tribal households in the case study regions have made inroads into institutional sources of credit and banking services. Whereas, those households which do not own land as well as, those tribal households which do not possess appropriate legal Title Deeds to their land do not have access to institutional source of credit and banking services (Table-1.4).

Table: 1.5: Banking Practices of Tribes (In Percentage)

Districts			*Chamarajanagara*				*Mysore*		
Tribes	*JK*	*KK*	*Soliga*	*Average*	*JK*	*KK*	*Soliga*	*Yarava*	*Average*
Accounts Open	20	25	30	25.00	25	30	35	40	39.5
Transactions	18	15	20	17.66	18	24	25	26	23.25
Know about M.B.I	01	02	05	2.66	01	01	02	02	1.50
Use of M.B.I	00	00	01	0.33	00	00	01	01	0.50
Loans Received	15	20	25	20.00	20	25	30	26	25.25
Loans Repayments	05	06	08	6.33	05	10	15	12	10.50
Response of Bankers	Good	Good	Good		Good	Good	Good	Good	

Source: Compiled from Primary Data, (*Note:* M.B.I- Modern Banking Instruments)

It may be observed from Table 1.5 that, the financial inclusion process of the tribes have begun and it is in its nascent stage in both Chamarajanagara and Mysore districts. About 25 per cent of the sample tribal households in Chamarajanagara districts and on an average 39.5 per cent of the tribal households in Mysore district have bank accounts in public sector banks like Cauvery Kalpataru Grameena Bank, State Bank of Mysore, Vijaya Bank and private sector banks like Karnataka Bank... etc.

Nearly 17.66 per cent and 23.25 per cent on an average of total sample tribal households in Chamarajanagara and Mysore districts have started using various kinds of banking services in conducting financial transaction and about 20 per cent in Chamarajanagara district and 20-25 per cent in Mysore district sample tribal households have availed bank loans. About 6.33 per cent in Chamarajanagara district and 10.5 per cent in Mysore district the tribal borrowers have repaid loans (Table 1.5).

The entire tribal households have expressed their happiness about the banker's response to open bank accounts and avail bank loans. However only a negligible number of tribal households in both the districts have reported that they are aware and using services/ instruments like ATM/credit and debit cards, cheques, MT, overdrafts, DD., etc. The major reason for nearly 97.3 per cent of the sample tribal households in the case study districts are not using banking instruments due to their acute poverty and near obstacles of integration between tribal economy and mainland economy. This suggests that, the need for increasing the avenues for economic interaction between tribes and non-tribes in the study region.

Table 1.6: Mode of Savings of the Tribes (In Percentage)

Districts			*Chamarajanagara*				*Mysore*		
Tribes	*JK*	*KK*	*Soliga*	*Average*	*JK*	*KK*	*Soliga*	*Yarava*	*Average*
Postal Savings	02	04	05	3.66	02	05	10	08	06.25
Micro Saving	01	02	35	12.66	02	02	05	05	03.50

Pigmy Deposits	00	00	00	00.00	00	00	00	00	00.00
Fixed Deposits	00	00	00	00.00	00	00	02	02	01.00
LIC	03	02	05	03.33	02	03	10	03	04.50

Source: Compiled from Primary Data.

Broadly, two trends may be observed about savings behaviour of the four observed tribes of Mysore and Chamarajanagara districts. They are:

(1) A small number of tribal households have undertaken postal and micro savings in this respect, 35 per cent of Soliga households in Chamarajanagara district have undertaken micro savings, because of successive working of the SKS micro finance in Attagullipura colony.

(2) It is discouraging to note that, the tribal households in general have not purchased pigmy deposits or fixed deposits from the nationalised banks (Table 1.6). This empirical data show again that there is a direct link between extreme poverty and financial exclusion.

Districts Chamarajanagara and Mysore

Table 1.7: Performance of Women SHGs (In percentage)

Districts			*Chamarajanagara*				*Mysore*		
Tribes	*JK*	*KK*	*Soliga*	*Average*	*JK*	*KK*	*Soliga*	*Yarava*	*Average*
Membership	52	54	45	50.33	56	57	48	53	53.50
Savings	52	54	45	50.33.	56	57	48	53	53.50
Loans	29	32	38	33.00	40	45	32	46	40.75
Profits Received	52	54	45	50.33	56	57	48	53	53.50
Repayment	10	12	15	12.33	15	20	22	25	20.50
Interest to Continue	40	45	40	41.66	50	40	40	42	43.00

Source: Compiled from Primary Data.

Table 1.7 shows that the women SHGs movement is fairly successful among all the four sample tribes in the case study region, all though, the loan repayment by the women members of the SHGs is low among all the sample tribes of Chamarajanagara and Mysore districts. In terms of other indicators of financial inclusion like membership of the SHGs formation of the tribal women savings and borrowing behaviour, profit received is vary sustained improvements in the employment income generation, integration process between tribal economy and mainland economy will help to further create and develop Bank-SHGs network for the benefit of tribal. About 41.66 per cent in Chamarajanagara district and 43 per cent in Mysore district of the sample households have shown interest to continue to be part of the working of women SHGs. The equal partnership at household level which is an important tribal culture value has supported the attempts to bring tribal women under the SHGs network.

Findings of the study:

1. Comparatively Mysore district has highest in number of tribes and good mix of all the four tribes. In both the districts all the selected tribes are unevenly distributed, because of the unequal spread of the forest and different cultural and ethnic nature of the tribes. All selected sample tribes are suffering from acute poverty and unemployment. So they are excluded from the financial inclusion as well as inclusive growth.
2. Financial inclusion process of the tribes has begun and it is in its nascent stage in both Chamarajanagara and Mysore districts.
3. In both the districts land holding tribes are small and marginal farmers and forty per cent of households are landless. It leads to financial exclusion.
4. Tribal households in general have not purchased pigmy deposits or fixed deposits from the nationalised banks.
5. There is a direct link between extreme poverty and financial exclusion.
6. Majority of tribal peoples are not having the banking practices.
7. Tribal households which do not possess appropriate legal title deeds to their land so they are not eligible have access to institutional source of credit and banking services.
8. Allmost all the tribal households in the study region are wage labourers and they are migration for wage. MFP business also is very low due to the implementation of the forest and wild life protection act and partly implementation of the forest right Act.
9. In the tribal area women SHGs and SHGs bank linkage programme is not success.

Policy Suggestions

1. Rehabilitation and resettlement programme of tribes should properly implementation, including reorientation and resettlement nearby the main land particularly nearby urban and semi-urban areas is required.
2. Proper implementation of the Forest Right Act and distribution of land and title deed of land very urgently needed to access banking facilities and to eliminate the demand side and supply side bottlenecks for the development of financial infrastructure in the tribal areas.

3. Extension of the rural and commercial bank branches to the tribal and hilly regions including mobile banking system.
4. The Local government officials and NGOs should be involved for organising the SHGs among tribal women and encourage to take-up self-employment activities outside the tribal habitats and settlements.
5. Provision of institutional financial facilities to encourage the small and household business in the tribal areas the separate rational and dynamic policies and programmes are timely needed.

V. Conclusion

The foregoing analysis of obstacles for financial inclusion among tribes in southern Karnataka reveals that the continued existence of subsistence tribal economy increased alienation or shifting of tribes from forest to mainland, failures in tribal resettlement and redevelopment programmes, lead to extreme poverty, unemployment and underemployment, shortage of civic amenities and thus poor quality of life of the tribes, all these factors of underdevelopment results in extremely low level of tribal human resource development. Thus, the tribal underdevelopment and threats to their life and livelihoods do not provide opportunities for financial inclusion initiatives among the tribes. Thus, there are, as it is already explained supply side and demand side constraints to bring tribes under financial inclusion process. The State should make efforts to reduce or remove them.

It was also revealed in this study that increased employment opportunities, job securities, encouragement to undertake sustainable agriculture and facilitating labour migration among tribes to help to initiate financial inclusion process in tribal societies and economy. In many of the tribal settlements there are no grampanchayat (Rural Self Governments). Thus, like other mainland villages, the tribal settlement (Popu/hadi) do not receive development grants from the Government of India under its umbrella programme MGNREGP, and other programme under state government except ITDP which are not well-devised and adequately funded. Therefore, based on the present study we conclude that, among four tribes like Kadukuruba, Jenukuruba, Soliga and Yarava, in southern Karnataka, financial inclusion process is just begun and is in its nascent stage.

REFERENCES

1. Alaysius P. Fennandez (1997), Micro Finance Institutions with Difference, Economic and Political Weekly, Vol. 42 (13): pp. 1185-1189.

2. Atkinson Rob, Divoudi Simin (2000), The Concept of Social Exclusion in European Union, Context Development and Possibilities. Journal of Common Market Studies 38(3):427-448.
3. GOI (2008), Report of Committee of Financial Inclusion (New Delhi; Planning Commission, Government of India). Chairman Dr. Rangarajan.
4. Mahendra Dev S. (2006), Financial Inclusion: Issues and Challenges, Economic and Political Weekly, Vol. 31, No. 16, April.
5. O.D. Heggade and Puttaraja (2011), Migration of tribal labour : A Case Study of Rural-Rural Migration in Karnataka. Vol. VII, No. 3, Journal of Rural Development and Social Change, Odyar Publications, Mysore.
6. Schumpeter Joseph (1912), (1992), The Theory of Economic Development, translated by Reveres Opine, with new introduction by E. Elliot, Transaction Publishers, New Brunswick.
7. Smith Adam (1776), (1998), An Enquiry into the Nature and Causes of Wealth of Nations: London; UK.
8. Sonowal C.J. (2008), Indian Tribes and Issue of Social Inclusion and Exclusion, Studies in Tribes and Tribals, 6 (2): pp. 125. Kamal Raj Enterprises, New Delhi.

8

Role of Banks And Other Financial Institutions In Achieving Financial Inclusion

A.R. Viswanath and S. Shanmuga

Abstract: *Financial inclusion is delivery of banking services at an affordable cost to the vast section of the disadvantaged and low income groups. As banking service is considered as a public good, it is essential that availability of banking and payment services to the entire population without discrimination is the prime objective of the public policy. For more than three decades after nationalisation of major commercial banks in 1969, Indian banking has shown tremendous growth in volume and outreach resulting in increase in the total number of branches of schedule commercial banks from 8,321 in the year 1969 to 68,681 as at the end of March 2006 and reduction of the average population per branch office from 64,000 to 16,000 during the same period. Public sector banks were in the forefront of reaching out to sections that were once neglected and designing new, innovative loan products for agriculture and small-scale industries sector is an outstanding example in this regard.*

Financial institutions, both large and small, have an important role to play in financial inclusion. With their organised structure and effective management, larger financial institution could act as mentors for small financial services firm by ensuring a storing financial banking. So present study focusing on role being played by banks and other financial institutions achieving financial inclusion significant and they have started silent revolution heading towards financial inclusion.

Key words: Financial Inclusive, Commercial bank, Cooperative bank, RRB, NBFCs, MFIs, NGO.

Introduction

Financial inclusion or inclusive financing means delivery of financial services at affordable costs to sections of disadvantaged and low-income segments of society, in contrast to financial exclusion where those services are not available or affordable. An estimated 2.5 billion working-age adults globally have no access to the types of formal financial services delivered by regulated financial institutions. For example, in sub-Saharan Africa only 24 per cent of adults have a bank account even through Africa's formal financial sector has grown in recent years. It is argued that as banking services to the entire population without discrimination is the prime objective of financial inclusion public policy.

The term "financial inclusion" has gained importance since the early 2000s, a result about financial exclusion and its direct correlation to poverty. The United Nations defines the goals of financial inclusion as follows.

- Access at a reasonable cost for all households to a full range of financial services, including savings or deposit or services, payment and transfer services, credit and insurance;
- Sound and safe institutions governed by clear regulation and industry performance standards;
- Financial and safe institutional sustainability, to ensure continuity and certainty of investment; and
- Competition to ensure choice and affordability for clients.

Former United Nations Secretary-General Kofi Annan, on 29 December 2003, said: "The stark reality is that most poor people in the world still lack access to sustainable financial services, whether it is savings, credit or insurance. The great challenge before us is to the constraints that exclude people from full participation in the financial sector. Together, we can and must build inclusive financial sector that help people improve their lives".

The Alliance for Financial Inclusion (AFI) is the world's largest and most prominent network of financial inclusion policymakers from developing and emerging economies who work together to increase access to appropriate financial services for the poor.

Financial inclusion in India

The Reserve Bank of India (RBI) set up the Khan Commission in 2004 to look into the mid-term review of the policy (2005-06). In report RBI exhorted the banks with a view to achieving greater financial inclusion to make available a basic "no-frills" banking account. In India, Financial inclusion first featured in 2005, when it was introduced by K.C. Chakraborty, the chairman of Indian bank. Mangalam became the first village in India where all households were provided banking facilities. Norms were relaxed for people intending to open accounts with annual deposits of less than Rs 50,000. General credit cards (GCCs) were issued to the poor and the disadvantaged with a view to help them access easy credit. In January 2006, the Reserve Bank permitted commercial banks to make use of the services of NGOs and SHGs, micro-finance institutions, and other civil society organisations as intermediaries for providing financial and banking services. These intermediaries could be used as business facilitators or business correspondents by commercial banks. The bank asked the commercial banks in different reasons to start a 100 per cent financial inclusion campaign on a pilot basis. As a result of the campaign, states or Union territories like Puducherry, Himachal Pradesh and Kerala announced 100 per cent financial inclusion in all their districts. Reserve Bank of India's vision for 2020 is to open nearly 600 million new customers' accounts and services them through variety of channels by leveraging on IT. However, illiteracy and the low income savings and lack of bank branches in rural areas continue to be a roadblock to financial inclusion in many states and there is inadequate legal and financial structure.

In India, RBI has initiated several measures to achieve greater financial inclusion, such as facilitating no-frills accounts and GCCs for small deposits and credit. Some of these steps are:

- Opening of no-frills accounts
- Relaxation on Know-your-customer (KYC) norms.
- Engaging Business correspondents (BCs)
- Use of technology
- Adoption of Electronic Benefits Transfer (EBT)
- General credit card (GCC)
- Simplified Branch Authorisation
- Opening of branches in unbanked rural centers

Pradhan Manthri's Jan Dhan Yojana

Indian Prime Minister Narendra Modi announced this scheme for comprehensive financial inclusion on his first Independence Day speech on 15th August 2014. The scheme was formally launched on 28 August 2014 with a great to provide 'Universal access to banking facilities' starting with basic Banking Accounts with overdrafts facility of Rs 5000 after six months and Rupay Debit Card with inbuilt accident insurance cover of Rs 1 Lakh and Rupay Kissan Card and in next phase, Micro insurance and pension etc. will also be added. In a run up to the formal launch of this scheme, the Prime Minister personally mailed to CEOs of all banks to gear up for the gigantic task enrolling over 7.5 crore (75 million) households and to open their accounts. He categorically declared that a bank account for each household was a "national priority". On the inauguration day of the scheme, 1.5 Crore (15 Million) bank account were opened.

Financial inclusion is delivery of banking services at an affordable cost to the vast section of the disadvantaged and low income groups. As banking service is a public good. It is essential that availability of banking and payment services to the entire population without discrimination is the prime objective of the public policy. For more than three decades after nationalisation of major commercial banks in 1969, Indian banking has shown tremendous growth in volume and outreach resulting in increase in the total number of branches of schedule commercial banks from 8,321 in the year 1969 to 68,681as at the end of March 2006 and reduction of the average population per branch office from 64,000 to 16,000 during the same period. Public sector banks were in the forefront of reaching out to sections that were once neglected and designing new, innovative loan products for agriculture and small-scale industries sector is an outstanding example in this regard.

The inclusive growth as a strategy of economic development received attention, owing to a rising concern that the benefit of economic growth has not been equitably shared. Inclusive growth as the literal meaning of the time word refers to both the pace and pattern of the economic growth. Financial inclusion broadens the resource base of the financial system by developing a culture of savings among large segment of rural population and plays its own role in the process of economic development. Further, by bringing low income groups within the perimeter of formal banking sector, financial inclusion protects their financial wealth and other resources in exigent circumstances. Financial inclusion also mitigates the exploitation of vulnerable sectors by the usurious money lenders by facilitating easy access to formal credit.

RBI has adopted a bank-led model for achieving financial inclusion and removed all regulatory bottlenecks in achieving greater financial inclusion in the country. Further, for achieving the targeted goals.

RBI has created conducive regulatory environment and provided institutional support for banks in accelerating their financial inclusion efforts. Banks are advised to open Basic Saving Bank Deposit (BSBD) accounts with in common facilities such as no minimum balance, deposit and withdrawal of cash at bank branch and ATMs, receipt/ credit of money through electronic payments channels, facility of providing ATM card.

Progress of Financial Inclusion Drive

Massive expansion of financial sources of credit has taken place after Independence. Now more than 60,000 branches of commercial banks, more than 1,00,000 branches of RRBs and over 2,000 primary urban banks serve the people of the country, apart from several other formal financial institutions. However, this large infrastructure that has penetrated even remote rural areas is still able to serve only a small part of the potential clientele. The problem is particularly severe in rural areas. In this context, it needs to be mentioned that Urban Co-operative Banks (UCBs), Regional Rural Banks (RRBs) and Local Area Banks (LABs) numbering 1606, 64, and 4 respectively are, in fact, small Finance banks operating in this country. These apart, there is a 3-Tier rural Co-operative structure with state Co-operative Central banks (SCCBs) at the apex, District Central Co-operative banks (DCCBs) at the intermediary level and primary Agriculture credit society (PACs) at the grass root level, which number 31, 371 and 92, 432 respectively. These undertake predominantly credit/investment activities.

Progress of financial inclusion since the launch of financial inclusion programme clearly indicates that banks are progressing in areas like opening of banking outlets, deploying BCs, opening of BSBD accounts. The number of commercial banks increased manifold from 68,681 in March 2006 to 1,02,343 in March 2013, spread across the length and breadth of the country. In rural areas, the number of branches increased from 30,572 to 37,953 during March 2006 to March 2013. As compared with rural areas, the number of branches in semi-urban areas increased more rapidly. Total number of banking outlets in villages increased from 67,694 in March 2010 to 2,68,454 in March 2013 (increased around four times during the period of three years). Of total branches, banking outlets through BCs increased from 34,174 to 2,21,341 during the same period (increased around 6.5 times). The financial inclusion was explicitly made as a policy objective and thrust was on providing safe facility of savings deposits through "no frills" accounts. A synoptic view of financial inclusion is as under:

- Number of No. Frill Accounts- 3,30,24,761 at end- March 2009
- Number of rural branches – 31,727 constituting 39.7 per cent of total bank branches (as of June, 31st, 2009)
- Number of ATMs – 44,857 (as on May 31st, 2009)
- Number of POS- 4,70,237 as on May 31st, 2009)
- Number of Cards – 167.09 million (as on May 31st, 2009)
- Number of Kissan Credit Cards- 76 million (*Source:* CMIE publication 2007-08)
- Number of mobile phones – 403 million (as on April 30, 2009) out of which 187 million (46 per cent) do not have a bank account (*Source*: Cellular Operators Association of India)

The number of "no frills" accounts increases from 4,89,497 at end-March 2006 to 3,30,24,761 at end –March 2009. Notably, the public sector banks account for the majority of these "no frills" accounts as at end –March 2009 (Table- 1). Similarly, the number of credit as well as savings accounts per 100 adults has shown increasing trend over a period 2002 to 2007.

Table 1: Progress of No-frills accounts in Indian Banks

Category	*March 31, 2006*	*March 31, 2007*	*March 31, 2008*	*March 31, 2009*
Public Sector Banks	3,32,878	58,65,419	1,39,09,935	2,98,59,178
Private Sector Banks	1,56,388	8,60,997	18,45,869	31,24,101
Foreign Banks	231	5,919	33,115	41,842
Total	**4,89,497**	**67,32,335**	**1,57,88,919**	**3,30,24,761**

Source: Report on Trend and Progress of Banking India – 2007–08.

Conclusion

Financial inclusion is the key to the inclusive growth development is positively related to economic growth. Financial inclusion promotes thrift and develops culture of saving and also enables efficient payment mechanism strengthening the resource base of the financial institution. Banks and Financial institutions play a predominant role in financial inclusion. Financial inclusion, though well recognised as a means for inclusive growth, is constrained by several factors in India. The banks are faced with high operating cost in extending the financial service to remote areas. High maintenance cost of these accounts as well as small ticket size of the transactions is also adding to the problem. Further reaching out of the illiterate people or people who can handle only the regional languages is also difficult without developing a suitable communication mode.

The challenge also lies in offering a single loan product which is not based on or linked to the purpose of the loan, the collateral or assets held or income earned by the household but is purely based on cash flow and credit record of the household. With the arrival of banking technology and realisation that poor are bankable with business prospects, financial inclusion initiatives will strengthen financial deepening further and provide resources to the banks to expand credit delivery. The banking technology initiatives meant for financial inclusion should be collaborative and innovative with an objective to reduce the transaction costs. Thus, financial inclusion along with the governmental programmes will lead to an overall inancial and economic development in our country and as in the case for most developing countries, extending the banking services to everyone in the country will be the key driver towards an inclusive growth.

REFERENCES

1. Reserve Bank of India (2008). Report on currency and Finance 2006-08.
2. Micro- Finance for Self-Help Groups", Kurukshetra.
3. Indian Economy: A performance Review, 1947-48 to 2010-11.
4. www.rbi.org.in
5. www.dandc.eu/en/article
6. www.indianmirror.com/NGO
7. Pratiyogita Darpan-2013.

9

Role of Banks In Achieving Financial Inclusion—An Econometric Analysis

Chethana B and Mahesha M

Abstract: *Financial inclusion has become one of the most critical aspects in the context of inclusive growth and sustainable development in the developing countries like India. Financial inclusion is the delivery of financial services at an affordable cost to the marginalised groups, by providing them with timely and adequate access to the financial products and services and it is also a strategy for eradicating the poverty. It is estimated that globally over 2.5 billion people are excluded from access to financial services, of which one-third is in India. Access to various financial services enables the poor people to participate in the growth of the economy. But India had scored poorly on financial inclusion parameters when compared with the global average, said the Reserve Bank of India in its annual report (2013-14) and another report of the World Bank study in April 2012, which had shown half of the world's population held accounts with formal financial institutions.*

This study revealed that only nine per cent of the population had taken new loans from a bank, credit union or microfinance institution in the past year. In India, only 35 per cent have formal accounts versus an average of 41 per cent in developing economies. India also scored poorly in respect of credit cards, outstanding mortgage, health insurance, origination of new loans and mobile banking. "Financial inclusion remains a substantially unfinished agenda," said the report. Reserve Bank of India vision for 2020 is to open nearly 600 million new customers' accounts. With this backdrop this study is directed towards understanding the importance of Financial Inclusion for Inclusive Growth; it aims at analysing the role of Banks in reaching out to the unbanked and backward areas in achieving financial inclusion and also this study is going to make an analysis of access to financial services by the peoples of India.

Key words: Financial Inclusion, Financial Services, Banks, Inclusive Growth.

Introduction

Financial inclusion is one of the main agenda of many countries in the recent past. Because financial inclusion broadens the resource base of the financial system by developing a culture of savings among large segment of rural population and plays its own role in the process of economic development. Further, by bringing low income groups within the perimeter of formal banking sector. Financial inclusion also mitigates the exploitation of vulnerable sections by the money lenders by facilitating easy access to formal credit. In this regard the role of banks in achieving the financial inclusion is very essential. So, as per the recommendation of Khan Commission-2004, various reformative measures have been taken by banks and Government of India to achieve financial inclusion. The number of financial inclusion strategies has been initiated by the banks to achieve their targets related to inclusion. In developed countries, the formal financial sector comprising mainly the banking system serves most of the population, in developing countries, a large segment of the society, mainly the low-income group, has little access to financial services, either formal or semi-formal. As a result, many people have to necessarily depend either on their own sources or informal sources of finance, which are generally at high cost. Most of the population in developed countries (99 per cent in Denmark, 96 per cent in Germany, 91 per cent in the USA and 96 per cent in France) has bank accounts (Peachy and Roe, 2004). However, formal financial sectors in most developing countries serve relatively a small segment, often no more than 20-30 per cent of the population, the vast majority of who are low income households in rural areas (ADB, 2007).

Importance of financial inclusion arises from the problem of financial exclusion of nearly three billion people from the formal financial services across the world. Financial inclusion may be defined as the process of ensuring access to financial services and timely and adequate credit where needed by vulnerable groups such as weaker sections and low income groups at an affordable cost (The Committee on Financial Inclusion, Chairman: Dr. C. Rangarajan).

Objectives

(1) To study the extent of financial exclusion and inclusion in India.
(2) To examine the determinants of Financial Inclusion.
(3) To study the relationship between Financial Inclusion and Human Development in India.

Hypotheses

(1) There is a significant difference in the number of bank branches across region.
(2) The financial inclusion is significantly influenced by literacy, credit deposit ratio and accessibility to mobile and internet.
(3) There is a positive relationship between financial inclusion and human development.

Methodology

The present study used the secondary data from the RBI reports, Planning Commission Reports, NSSO reports, Census of India, CRISIL's report on Inclusix and ministry of labour and employment, GOI. The data collected for the research were analysed with the help of simple statistical techniques such as AGR, CAGR, percentages and graphs to come to meaningful conclusions. Correlation, multiple regression analysis and ANOVA test have been used to test the hypotheses.

Financial Exclusion in India

In this section the financial exclusion from different perspectives is presented. As per the All India Debt and Investment Survey (NSSO 59th Round) showed 51.4 per cent of farmer households are financially excluded from both formal/ informal sources. Further, only 27 per cent of the total farmer households access to formal sources of credit; one third of this group also borrowed from non-formal sources. Overall, 73 per cent of farmer households have no access to formal sources of credit. Across regions, financial exclusion is more acute in Central, Eastern and North-Eastern regions. All three regions together accounted for 64 per cent of all financially excluded farmer households in the country. Overall indebtedness to formal sources of finance of these three regions accounted for only 19.66 per cent.

One of the RBI Working Paper Study by Sadhan Kumar (2011) worked out an Index on financial inclusion (IFI) based on three variables namely, penetration (number of adults having bank account), availability of banking services (number of bank branches per 1000 population) and usage (measured as outstanding credit and deposit). The results indicate that Kerala, Maharashtra and Karnataka has achieved high financial inclusion (IFI >0.5), while Tamil Nadu, Punjab, A.P., H.P., Sikkim, and Haryana identified as a group of medium financial inclusion (0.3 <IFI<0.5) and the remaining states have very low financial inclusion.

Table 1: Households not availing Banking Services in India (in percentage)

Sl. No.		*Census 2001*	*Census 2011*
1.	Rural	69.9	45.6
2.	Urban	50.5	32.2
3.	Total	64.5	41.3

Source: Department of Financial Services, GoI.

As Table 1 reveals, as per Census 2011, the 41.3 per cent of households were not availing to banking services. Even though the percentage of non-availing to banking services by the people of India is very large, as per the 2011 census it has achieved significant decline compared to 2001 census in both rural and urban areas.

As the standing committee report on finance 2013-14 said the percentage of unbanked population in UK, Sweden, Germany, Canada and Belgium is less than five per cent. But at the same time the percentage of unbanked population in India is more than 40 per cent.

Financial Inclusion in India

The Reserve Bank of India (RBI) set up the Khan Commission in 2004 to look into financial inclusion and the recommendations of the commission were incorporated into the mid-term review of the policy (2005–06). In the report RBI exhorted the banks with a view to achieving greater financial inclusion to make available a basic "no-frills" banking account. In India, financial inclusion first featured in 2005, when it was introduced by K.C. Chakraborty, the Chairman of Indian Bank. Mangalam became the first village in India where all households were provided banking facilities. Norms were relaxed for people intending to open accounts with annual deposits of less than Rs. 50,000. General credit cards (GCCs) were issued to the poor and the disadvantaged with a view to help them access easy credit. In January 2006, the Reserve Bank permitted commercial banks to make use of the services of non-governmental organisations (NGOs/SHGs), micro-finance institutions, and other civil society organisations as intermediaries for providing financial and banking services. These intermediaries could be used as business facilitators or business correspondents by commercial banks. The bank asked the commercial banks in different regions to start a 100 per cent financial inclusion campaign on a pilot basis. As a result of the campaign, states or union territories like Pondicherry, Himachal Pradesh and Kerala announced 100 per cent financial inclusion in all their districts. Reserve Bank of India's vision for 2020 is to open nearly 600 million new customers' accounts and service them through a variety of channels by leveraging on IT. However, illiteracy and the low income savings and lack of bank branches in rural areas continue to be a roadblock to financial inclusion in many states and there is inadequate legal and financial structure.

The Government of India recently announced "Pradhan Mantri Jan Dhan Yojna," a national financial inclusion mission which aims to provide bank accounts to at least 75 million people by January 26, 2015. To achieve this milestone, it's important for both service providers and policy-makers to have readily available information outlining gaps in access and interactive tools that help better understand the context at the district level. In India, RBI has initiated several measures to achieve greater financial inclusion, some of these steps are: Opening of no-frills accounts, relaxation of know-your-customer (KYC) norms, engaging business correspondents (BCs), use of technology, adoption of EBT, GCC and KCC, simplified branch authorisation, opening of branches in unbanked rural centres, direct benefit transfer (DBT), Swabhimaan Campaign, setting up of Ultra Small Branches (USBs), USSD-based mobile banking and banking facilities in unbanked blocks, etc.

Table 2: Comparison of financial inclusion in India with selected countries, 2011

Sl. No.	Country	Number of Bank Branches Per 1000 KM	Number of ATMs	Number of Bank Branches Per 0.1 Million	Number of ATMs	Bank Deposits as per cent to GDP	Bank Credit as per cent to GDP
1.	India	30.43	25.43	10.64	8.9	68.43	51.75
2.	China	1428.98	2975.05	23.81	49.56	433.96	287.89
3.	Brazil	7.93	20.55	46.15	119.63	53.26	40.28
4.	Indonesia	8.23	15.91	8.52	16.47	43.36	34.25
5.	Korea	79.07	...	18.8	...	80.82	90.65
6.	Mauritius	104.93	210.84	21.29	42.78	170.7	77.82

7.	Mexico	6.15	18.94	14.86	45.77	22.65	18.81
8.	Philippines	16.29	35.75	8.07	17.7	41.93	21.39
9.	South Africa	3.08	17.26	10.71	60.01	45.86	74.45
10.	Sri Lanka	41.81	35.72	16.73	14.29	45.72	42.64
11.	Thailand	12.14	83.8	11.29	77.95	78.79	95.37
12.	Malaysia	6.32	33.98	10.49	56.43	130.82	104.23
13.	UK	52.87	260.97	24.87	122.77	406.54	445.86
14.	Switzerland	84.53	166.48	50.97	100.39	151.82	173.26
15.	France	40.22	106.22	41.58	109.8	34.77	42.85

Source: Financial Access Survey, IMF.

From Table 2, it would be observed that in India, financial exclusion measured in terms of bank branch density, ATM density, bank credit to GDP and bank deposits to GDP is quite low as compared with most of developing countries in the world. Further China, Mauritius, Switzerland have achieved very high financial inclusion than India. Because in all these developed countries bank branch density, ATM density, bank branches, ATM branches and the deposit and credit as percentage of GDP are very high compare to India.

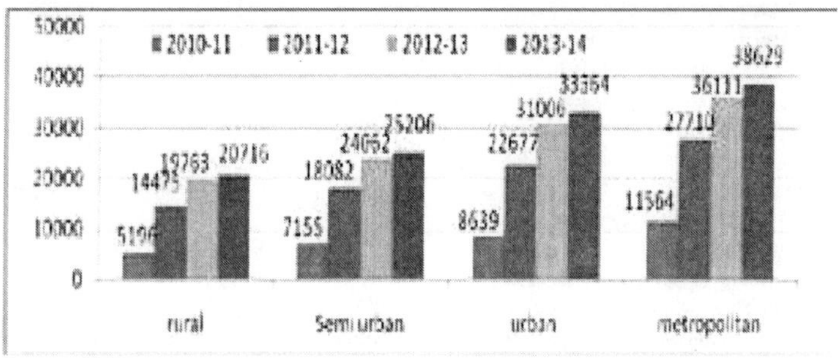

Source: RBI

Fig. 1: ATM network by population group.

The total number of ATMs in rural India witnessed a CAGR of 56 per cent during 2010 to 2013. The number of rural ATMs increased from 5,196 in 2010 to 11,564 in 2013. Even though the CAGR of rural ATMs from 2010 to 2014 is very high than others the percentage of rural ATMs to the total ATMs is less than 18 per cent in the year 2013. Because the banks are feels that the opening of ATMs in rural areas is not much profitable.

Strategies of RBI for Achieving Financial Inclusion

The RBI extends banking facilities in phase-wise manner in all the unbanked villages. During Phase I (2010-13), 74414 unbanked villages with population more than 2000 were identified and allotted to various banks through SLBCs for coverage through various modes, All these unbanked villages have been covered by opening banking outlets comprising 2493 branches, 69589 BCs and 2332 through other modes. In Phase II (2013-16), banking outlets in unbanked villages with population less than 2000, about 490000 unbanked villages have been identified and allotted to banks for coverage in a time bound manner by March 31, 2016. As per the progress reports received from SLBCs, banks had opened banking outlets in 183,993 unbanked villages by March 2014, comprising 7761 branches, 163187 BCs and 13045 through other modes. The financial inclusion plan and performance of RBI can be viewed as in the table 3.

Table 3: Financial Inclusion Plan - Summary Progress of all Banks including RRBs

Particulars	*Year ended Mar-10*	*Year ended Mar-13*	*Year ended Mar-14*	*Progress April 2013 - Mar-14*
1. Banking Outlets in Villages – Branches	33378	40837	46126	5289
2. Banking Outlets in Villages – Branchless Mode	34316	227617	337678	110061
3. Banking Outlets in Villages –Total	67694	268454	383804	115350
4. Urban Locations covered through BCs	447	27143	60730	33587
5. Basic Savings Bank Deposit A/c through branches (No. in millions)	60.2	100.8	126	25.2
6. Basic Savings Bank Deposit A/c through branches (Amt. in billion)	44.3	164.7	273.3	108.6
7. Basic Savings Bank Deposit A/c through BCs (No. in millions)	13.3	81.3	116.9	35.7
8. Basic Savings Bank Deposit A/c through BCs (Amt. in Rs. billion)	10.7	18.2	39	20.7
9. BSBDAs Total (No. in millions)	73.5	182.1	243	60.9
10. BSBDAs Total (Amt. in billion)	55	182.9	312.3	129.3
11. OD facility availed in BSBDAs (No. in millions)	0.2	4	5.9	2
12. OD facility availed in BSBDAs (Amt. in billion)	0.1	1.6	16	14.5
13. KCCs – (No. in millions)	24.3	33.8	39.9	6.2
14. KCCs – (Amt. in billion)	1240.1	2623	3684.5	1061.5
15. GCC- (No. in millions)	1.4	3.6	7.4	3.8
16. GCC - (Amt. in billion)	35.1	76.3	1096.9	1020.6
17. ICT A/Cs-BC- Transaction - (No. in millions) (During the year)	26.5	250.5	328.6	NA
18. ICT A/Cs-BC- Transactions - (Amt. in billion) (During the year)	6.9	233.9	524.4	NA

Source: RBI annual report 2013-14.

The above table tells about the financial inclusion plan of the RBI. As the table shows the number of banking outlets has gone up to 383804. Out of these, 115350 banking outlets were opened during

2013-14. Further during 2013-14, 5289 rural branches were opened. More than 60 million basic savings bank deposit accounts (BSBDAs) were added during the 2013-14 to the total number of BSBDAs (243 million). With the addition of 6.2 million KCCs during 2013-14, there are 39.9 million KCCs as on March 31, 2014 and with the addition of 3.8 million GCCs (non-farm sector) during 2013-14, there are 7.4 million GCCs as on March 31, 2014. Further, 328.6 million transactions were carried out in BC-ICT accounts during the 2013-14 as compared to 250.5 million transactions during 2012-13. Thus the table 3 clearly tells that the progress of banks in financial inclusion.

Table 4: Households availing Banking Services

Areas	*2001* Total no. of households	Number of households availing Banking services	Per cent	*2011* Total no. of households availing Banking services	Number of households	Per cent
Rural	138271559	41639949	30.1	167826730	91369805	54.4
Urban	53692376	26590693	49.5	78865937	53444983	67.8
Total	191963935	68230642	35.5	246692667	144814788	58.7

Source: Census of India and RBI.

As Table 4 reveals, in 2011 the percentage of people access to banking services is very high compared to 2001. The percentage of rural people access to banking services increased to 54.4 per cent in 2011 from 30.1 per cent in 2001. Totally the percentage of people availing to banking services increased from 35.5 per cent in 2001 to 58.7 per cent in 2011.

Table 5: The results of ANOVA test to show the difference in the branches of commercial banks opened in the different population groups

Population group	*Sum of Squares*	*Df*	*Mean Square*	*F*	*Sig.*
Between Groups	1.700E9	3	5.665E8	56.869	.000
Within Groups	2.789E8	28	9961588.344		
Total	1.978E9	31			

Table 5 shows the ANOVA test results, to test the significant difference in the branches of commercial banks opened in the different population groups. Since the probability value is 0.000, the result is statistically significant at one per cent level of significance. It means that there are significant differences in the branches of commercial banks opened in the rural, semi-urban, urban and metropolitans (different population groups) in India. But according to the post hoc test there is no significant difference between the branches of urban and metropolitan groups.

Relationship between Financial Inclusion and Human Development in India

Table 6: Correlations between financial inclusion and human development

		FI	*HD*
FI	Pearson Correlation	1	.791**
	Sig. (2-tailed)		.000
	N	21	21
HD	Pearson Correlation	.791**	1
	Sig. (2-tailed)	.000	
	N	21	21

**Correlation is significant at the 0.01 level (2-tailed).

Table 6 presents the results of correlation between financial inclusion and human development in India. The results are significant at one per cent level. As the results show there is a perfect positive relationship between financial inclusion and human development. It means that as the financial inclusion increases, it leads to increase in the human development of India.

Table 7: Comparison of financial inclusion and human development

States	*HDI*	*Rank*	*CRISIL Inclusix*	*Rank*
Kerala	0.79	1	76.1	1
Himachal Pradesh	0.652	2	58.5	5
Goa	0.617	3	72	2
Punjab	0.605	4	55.7	7
Maharashtra	0.572	5	37.5	12
Tamil Nadu	0.57	6	60.5	4
Haryana	0.552	7	48.4	9
Jammu and Kashmir	0.529	8	33.8	13
Gujarat	0.527	9	38.6	11
Karnataka	0.519	10	57.7	6
West Bengal	0.492	11	28.8	18
Uttaranchal	0.49	12	50.5	8
Andhra Pradesh	0.473	13	61.3	3
Assam	0.444	14	28.2	19
Rajasthan	0.434	15	32.7	15
Uttar Pradesh	0.38	16	33.5	14
Jharkhand	0.376	17	30.1	16
Madhya Pradesh	0.375	18	29.9	17
Bihar	0.367	19	23.5	21
Odisha	0.362	20	40.6	10
Chhattisgarh	0.358	21	27	20

Source: Compiled from HDI 2011 and CRISIL Inclusix report.

Table 7 brings out the relationship between financial inclusion and human development in India for 21 Indian states, which are seem to move in the same direction and closely with each other.

This result shows that states with high level of human development are also the states with relatively high level of financial inclusion and vice versa. The states of Goa, Punjab, Kerala, Himachal Pradesh, Haryana and Tamil Nadu which rank the best in human development are also found to have high financial inclusion. Furthermore, the states of Jharkhand, Madhya Pradesh, Chhattisgarh, Odisha and Bihar which are among the lowest on index of human development perform poorly on financial inclusion as well.

CRISIL's Inclusix – An index to measure India's progress in financial inclusion

CRISIL's Inclusix is India's first comprehensive measure of financial inclusion in the form of an index. It is a relative index that has a scale of 0 to 100, and combines three very critical parameters of basic banking services, branch penetration (BP), deposit penetration (DP), and credit penetration (CP) together into one single metric. For each of these parameters, CRISIL evaluates financial inclusion at the national, regional, state and district level. A CRISIL Inclusix score of 100 indicates the ideal state for each of the three parameters.

Table 8: CRISIL Inclusix Scores showing the Levels of Financial Inclusion

Sl. No.	*CRISIL Inclusix Score*	*Level of Financial Inclusion*	*Number of States/UTs*
1.	>55	High	11
2.	Between 40.1 and 55	Above Average	4
3.	Between 25 and 40	Below Average	17
4.	< 25	Low	3

Source: Report on CRISIL Inclusix, GOI, RBI 2013.

As Table 8 shows, CRISIL Inclusix scores have been divided into four categories that indicate different levels of the financial inclusion in India. Out of 35 states and UTs in India 11 states have high level of financial inclusion, four states are above average, 17 states are below average and only three states have low level of financial inclusion.

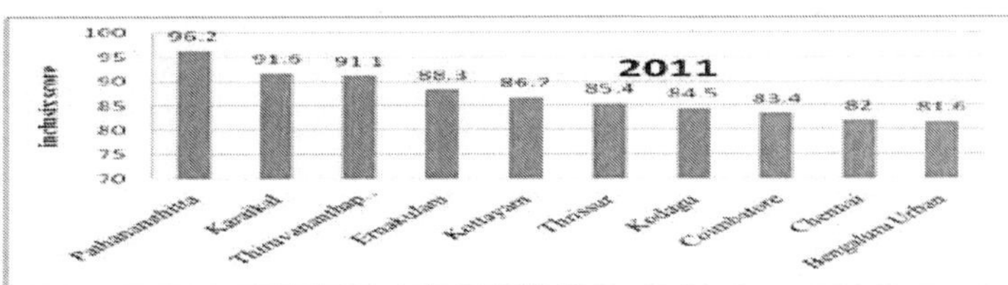

Source: Report on CRISIL Inclusix, GOI, RBI 2013.

Fig. 2: Top 10 districts in terms of CRISIL Inclusix score in India in 2011

Fig. 2 tells us that the top ten districts which have achieved high financial inclusion in India in 2011. Out of these ten districts, five districts belongs to Kerala and out of the remaining five districts, two belongs to Karnataka, two belongs to Tamil Nadu and one belongs to Pondicherry. This clearly indicates that southern region of India has achieved more financial inclusion than other regions. The detailed information related financial inclusion of all the regions of India has explained in the following figure 3.

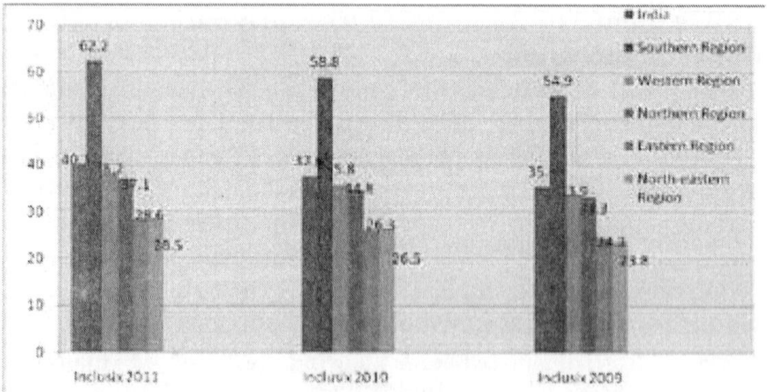

Source: Report on CRISIL Inclusix, GOI, RBI 2013.

Fig. 3: Region wise Index values and trends of INCLUSIX scores.

As Fig. 3 reveals, southern region leads the financial inclusion drive in India. It means that southern states Karnataka, Kerala, Tamil Nadu, Goa, Maharashtra and Andhra Pradesh have contributed more in achieving financial inclusion in India. The Inclusix score of southern region has increased from 54.9 in 2009 to 62.2 in 2011. The western region stands at second followed by northern region, eastern region and north-eastern region in achieving financial inclusion in India. CRISIL score for all India stands at a relatively low level of 40.1 in 2011.

Table 9: Regression results on determinants of Financial Inclusion

Model	*Un-standardised Coefficients B*	*Std. Error*	*Standardised Coefficients Beta*	*t*	*Sig.*	*Adj R square*
1. (Constant)	-16.467	22.075		-.746	.463	
literacy	.399	.281	.201	1.422	.016	.600
CDR	.210	.077	.347	2.716	.012	
mobile	.085	.192	.058	.441	.663	
internet	3.445	.938	.540	3.673	.001	

Dependent Variable: Financial Inclusion

The above table shows the regression results of determinants of financial inclusion. Literacy is positively and significantly associated with financial inclusion implying that higher the literacy, higher will be the financial inclusion. Similarly, Credit Deposit ratio is also positively and significantly associated with financial inclusion, which means that as the CDR increases financial inclusion also increases. Even though the availability of mobiles shows positive relationship with the financial inclusion, the result is not significant. Further, as the results shows increase in the access to internet leads to increase in the financial inclusion significantly. The adj R^2 is 0.600 which means that 60 per cent of the variation in the financial inclusion explained by the literacy, CDR, availability of mobile and access to internet.

Conclusion and Policy Suggestions

The overall conclusion emerging from the analysis of the Role of Banks in achieving financial inclusion is that, financial inclusion playing a very big role in achieving the aim of inclusive growth of the eleventh five year plan.

The analysis of the financial exclusion tells that as per the census 2011, the 41.3 per cent of households not availing banking services and even the studies of RBI and NSSO also expressed their views to reduce the financial exclusion. In this regard the concerned authorities of the government should take care to financially include the excluded people. This study observed that in India, financial inclusion is quite low as compared with most of developing and developed countries in the world. Since the highly capitalised banking systems seem to be less inclusive. This is not surprising that the ATMs opened in urban and metropolitan regions are very high than villages. As this study revealed that even though the number of policies initiated by the RBI, still the percentage of households not availing to the banking services is considerably high. In this regard government should give more importance to increase the access of financial services by the people of India. Further, as the results of ANOVA tells that there are significant differences in the branches opened in different population groups. The total numbers of banks opened in the rural areas are high, but it is not according to the proportion of percentage of the rural population. Because according to the 2011 census still 46 per cent of the rural peoples don't have access to financial services, whereas in urban areas it is only 32 per cent.

The result of correlation tells us that there is a strong positive correlation between financial inclusion and human development.

The states which have highest financial inclusion, they achieve more human development. So to achieve highest human development the policy-makers should have to give more importance to financial inclusion.

CRISIL Inclusix at all India level stood at a relatively low level of 40.1 for 2011. But this is an improvement compare to 37.6 for 2010. Out of the ten states or UTs with highest CRISIL Inclusix score, six are from southern region. Southern region of India leads in terms of financial inclusion in the country with a score of 62.2 for 2011. The western region stood at second followed by other regions. This clearly indicates that southern region of India has achieved more financial inclusion than other regions. This is also supported by the top ten districts of southern region which have highest CRISIL Inclusix score. Further, as the regression results showed the financial inclusion is significantly determined by the literacy, Credit-Deposit ratio and access to internet. So, to achieve highest financial inclusion the policy makers should focus on these indicators.

REFERENCES

1. Archana H. N. (2013), "Financial Inclusion - Role of Institutions", Innovative Journal of Business and Management, pp. 44-48.
2. Godwin Chigozie Okpara (2013), "Developing an Index of Financial Inclusion: An Average Ratio Approach".
3. Gupta, Anurag, Chotia Varun and Muralidhar NV (2014)' "Financial Inclusion and Human Development: A State-Wise Analysis from India", International Journal of Economics, Commerce and Management, Vol. 2, pp. 1-23.
4. Beg, Mahammad Paheem (2014), "The Role of Regional Rural Banks in Financial Inclusion: An Empirical Study in India", Indian Journal of Research, Vol. 3, pp. 129-130.
5. Manoj Kumar (2014), "An Empirical Study of Financial Inclusion in India", International Journal of Informative and Futuristic Research, Vol. 1, pp. 61-72.
6. Nalini, G.S. and Mariappan K (2012), "Role of Banks in Financial Inclusion", Research journal of commerce and behavioral science, Vol. 1, pp. 33-36.
7. Naveen Kumar, H, Manjunath S.J and Arun Kumar G (2012), "Role of Banks in achieving Financial Inclusion", International Journal of Business and Management Research, Vol. 2, pp. 518-521.
8. Radhika Dixit and Munmun Ghosh (2013), "Financial Inclusion for Inclusive Growth of India - A Study of Indian States", International Journal of Business Management and Research (IJBMR), Vol. 3, pp. 147-156.
9. Raihanath M P and Pavithran K B (2014), "Role of Commercial Banks in the Financial Inclusion Programme", Journal of Business Management and Social Sciences Research, Vol. 3, pp. 75-81.

10. Report on CRISIL Inclusix 2013-14, GoI.
11. Reserve Bank of India Annual Report 2013-14.
12. Srikanth R (2013), "A Study on - Financial Inclusion - Role of Indian Banks in Reaching out to the Unbanked and Backward Areas", International Journal of Applied Research and Studies, Vol. 2, pp. 02-20.
13. Tamilarasu A (2014), "Role of Banking Sectors on Financial Inclusion Development in India – an Analysis", International Interdisciplinary Research Journal, Vol. 2, pp. 39-45.

http://www.rbi.org.in

http://planningcommission.nic.in/

http://www.indiastat.com/

http://financialservices.gov.in/

http://www.imf.org/

http://censusindia.gov.in/

10

Role of Banks in Achieving Financial Inclusion

H.C. Veerappa Gowda and C.S. Kavyashree

Abstract: *Financial inclusion is a tool for combating poverty. Access to various financial services enables the poor people to participate in the growth of the economy. Many banks are forced to adopt financial inclusion rather than on their own. Banks have encountered various problems while adopting financial inclusion as financial inclusion relates to the provision of affordable financial services by the formal financial system to those who tend to be excluded. Inclusive economic growth has been one of the priority agendas of the Government of India over the past decade. Banks should encourage people to access banking services by way of no-frills account, financial inclusion campaign and business correspondent. The Government should encourage banks to adopt financial inclusion by means of financial assistance, advertisement and awareness programme etc. The Government of India and the banks functioning in India need to play a major role in imparting financial literacy to include the excluded.*

Introduction

Financial Inclusion growth is possible only through proper mechanism which channelises all resources in all directions towards the customers. It is an innovative concept which provides alternative techniques to promote banking habits among the rural people. The Government of India has set a target of reaching full inclusion by 2015. These objectives are being met through financial instruments, such as micro credit, which have achieved positive results, helping thousands of the world's poor to lift themselves out of poverty. Financial inclusion is the recent concept which helps to achieve sustainable development of the country through making available financial services to the unreached people with the help of financial institutions. The process of financial inclusion consists of ensuring bank accounts to each household and their inclusion in the banking system.

Financial Inclusion - Definition

The Government of India's committee on financial inclusion in India defines financial inclusion as 'the process of ensuring access to financial services and timely and adequate credit where needed by vulnerable groups such as the weaker sections and low income groups at an affordable cost'.

The United Nation defines it as "a financial sector that provides access to credit for all "bankable" people and firms and to savings and payments services for everyone." Inclusive Finance does not require that everyone who is eligible to use each of the services. But they should be able to choose and use them if desired.

Financial inclusion broadens the resource base of the financial system by developing a culture of savings among large segment of rural population and plays its own role in the process of economic development.

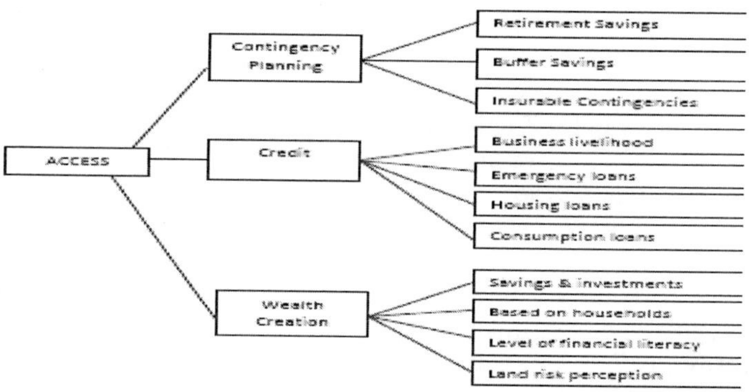

Source: A hundred small steps – Report of the Committee on Financial Sector Reforms (Chairman: Dr Raghuram Rajan).

The essence of financial inclusion is to ensure delivery of financial services which include bank accounts for savings and transactional purposes, low cost credit for productive personal and other purposes; financial advisory services insurance facilities etc.

Financial inclusion initiatives include advice to all banks to open Basic Savings Bank Deposit (BSBD) accounts with minimum common facilities such as no minimum balance, deposit and withdrawal of cash at bank branch and ATMs, receipt/credit of money through electronic payment channels, facility of providing ATM Card, relaxed and simplified KYS norms to facilitate easy opening of bank accounts, especially for small accounts with balances not exceeding Rs 50,000 and aggregate credits in the accounts not exceeding Rs One lakh a year. Further banks are advised not to insist on introduction for opening bank accounts of customers. In addition banks are allowed to use Aadhaar Card as a proof of both identity and address.

In the simplified branch authorisation policy to address the issue of uneven spread of bank branches, domestic SCBs are permitted to freely open branches in Tier 2 and Tier 6 centers with population of less than one lakh under general permission, subject to reporting.

Compulsory Requirement of opening Branches in Un banked villages is another measure where Banks are directed to allocate at least 25 per cent of the total number of branches to be opened during the year in un banked rural centers.

Public and private sector banks had been advised to submit board approved three year financial inclusion plan (FIP) starting from April 2010. These policies aim at keeping self set targets in respect of rural brick and mortar branches opened, BCs employed, coverage of un-banked villages with population above 2000 as well as below 2000, BSBD accounts opened, KCCS, GCCs issued and others. RBI has been monitoring these plans on a monthly basis. Banks have been advised that their FIPs should be disaggregated and percolated down up to the branch level. This would ensure the involvement of all stake holders in the financial inclusion efforts.

In June 2012 revised guidelines on financial literacy centers (FLCs) were issued. It was advised that FLCs and all the rural branches of scheduled, commercial banks should scale up financial literacy efforts through conduct of outdoor financial literacy camps at least once a month. To facilitate financial inclusion through provision to two essentials, i.e., financial literacy and easy "Financial access". Accordingly 718 FICs have been set up as at end of March 2013. A total of 2.2 Million people have been educated through awareness camps/chapels, seminars and lectures during April 2012 and March 2013.

Role of Banking Sector in Financial Inclusion in India

The number of commercial banks in a country provides an opportunity for the people of that country to participate in the formal financial system and to utilise financial services of formal financial system. Larger the number of commercial banks, larger the scope of bringing people in to formal financial system, provided if banks provide suitable financial products and services.

In India financial inclusion first featured in 2005. When it was introduced, that too from a pilot project in UT of Pondicherry by Dr K.C. Chakraborty, the Chairman of Indian Bank, Mangalam village become the first village in India where all households were provided banking facilities.It was found that these intermediates could be used as business facilitators (BF) or business correspondents by Commercial banks. The Reserve Bank of India, therefore, asked the commercial banks in different regions to start a 100 per cent financial inclusion campaign on pilot basis.

As a result of the campaign, States and UTs like Pondicherry, Himachal Pradesh and Kerala have announced 100 per cent financial inclusion in all their districts. Reserve Bank of India's vision for 2020 is to open nearly 600 million new customers' accounts and service them through a variety of channels by leveraging on IT. However, illiteracy and the low income savings and lack of bank branches in rural areas continue to be a road block to financial inclusion in many states. Apart from this there are certain lacunae in the current model that is followed. There is inadequate legal and financial structure. India being a mostly agrarian economy hardly has schemes which lend for agriculture. Along with microfinance we need to focus on micro insurance too.

Suggestions

There is need for coordinated action between the banks, the government and others to facilitate access to bank accounts amongst the financially excluded. Opening of bank accounts should be perceived more as an obligation than a business opportunity by the banks. As people in India are still not aware of banking services, there is a need for financial literacy programmes in rural areas as well as urban slum areas. The business correspondent model should be used more by the banks and should be made available in remotest parts of India. Focus is required to be on customer service, education and protection. There is also a need of financial literacy at the time of account opening, incentives for branch managers delivering on socially responsible schemes, documentation of best practices on such projects etc... and to create a Financial – Inclusion Index (FIT).

Conclusion

There is a long way to go for the financial inclusion to reach to the core poor according to K.C. Chakraborty, RBI Deputy Governor. Even today the fact remains that nearly half of the Indian population doesn't have access to formal financial services and are largely dependent on money lenders. The Indian banking industry today is quite robust and strong to be able to take on the challenges of achieving greater financial inclusion. Banks are the gateways to the most basic forms of financial services extent of financial inclusion by banks.

REFERENCES

1. Suresh Chandra Bihari 2011, Financial Inclusion The key to Emerging India" AIJSH Volume, Issue 1.
2. Mandira Sharma, 2008, "Index of Financial Inclusion, Indian Council" for Research on International Economic Relations working paper.
3. Kelkar V. (2010), Financial Inclusion for Inclusive Growth ASC I Journal of management.
4. Rangarajan C (2008), "Report of the committee of Financial Inclusion".
5. Chakraborty K C (2011) , "Financial Inclusion and Banks: Issues and Perspectives" RBI Bulletin – November 2011 Role of Banks in act.

11

Bank-Led Financial Inclusion—A Case Study in K R Nagara Taluk of Mysore District

Uma H. R. and Rupa K. N.

Abstract: *Financial Inclusion is both challenge and an opportunity to financial system. Financial inclusion is nothing but the inclusion of hitherto excluded poor and deprived section of society into the mainstream economy. Inclusive growth and Participatory development is the policy priority of the Government of India (GOI). GOI and Reserve Bank of India, make coordinated efforts to meet this challenge. RBI adopted bank-led financial inclusion model to attend the issue. The present study is an attempt to assess the changes in banking growth according to different population groups. Branch expansion, deposit mobilisation and credit penetration are the three parameters assess the changes. To check the difference before and after financial inclusion two periods were considered, Period-I (1997 to 2004) and period-II (2005 to 2013). The year 2005 is considered as reference period as the effective financial inclusion mission took off. To test the efficacy of financial inclusion the study attempted to find out the impact of financial inclusion on account holders in K R Nagara taluk of Mysore district. With regard to the impact of social and economic changes of sample account holders after the financial* *inclusion in the study region, the chi-square test revealed that there is a significant change after the financial inclusion. Therefore, considering the positive changes in banking growth and impact on economic and social condition of new account holders, Government of India and RBI may take further efficient steps to reach the unreached effectively.*

Key words: Financial Inclusion, Scheduled Commercial Banks, Branch expansion, Deposit mobilisation, credit penetration.

Introduction

According to the Census of India 2011, the population of India is 1,210 million; with 68.84 per cent of the total still residing in rural areas. India has 6,38,588 inhabited villages. The growth of Indian economy is challenged by poverty, unemployment, income inequality and regional disparity. Financial exclusion is the deprivation of formal banking products and services to needy people. Growth becomes inclusive only when it creates economic opportunities along with ensuring equal access to them. Financial Inclusion is an attempt to include hitherto excluded marginalised people. It is the gateway to achieve inclusive social and economic development.

In India bank-led financial inclusion model was adopted to achieve the target of reaching each and every one of the nation through banking net. 'Bank the unbanked' is the Slogan of financial inclusion. The Eleventh Five Year Plan (2007-12) has specifically underlined the need for "more inclusive growth". The 12th Five Year Plan in India is focusing on "Faster, Sustainable and more Inclusive Growth" for the overall development of the nation. Financial inclusion has current significance and relevance because it leads to social, economic and political inclusion. Financial Inclusion begins with access to financial services in the absence of price and non-price barriers. The access has many dimensions such as basic savings bank account, check in account, micro-credit, savings products, remittances and payment services, insurance, healthcare, mortgage, financial advisory services, entrepreneurial credit, and pension for old age, branchless banking through business correspondents, mobile banking and self help group-Bank linkage, etc. Many studies on bank-led financial inclusion were carried out. But the present study intends to study population-wise growth of banking. The study is for two periods, viz., before and after financial inclusion to assess the impact of financial inclusion. The study attempts to assess the socio-economic impact of financial inclusion on BSBD account holders.

Objectives of the study

(1) To study population-wise growth of financial inclusion at National level.
(2) To assess the socio-economic impact on BSBD account holders' after financial inclusion.

Methodology

The study is based on both primary and secondary data. The secondary data was collected from various reports of Reserve Bank of India (RBI) and publications of Government of India. To test the impact of financial inclusion two periods were considered, i.e., period-I (1997 to 2004) and period-II (2005 to 2013).This is because from year 2005 financial inclusion initiatives were undertaken by both GOI and RBI all with all seriousness. Population-wise growth related to branch expansion, deposit mobilisation and credit penetration are considered to check the efficacy of financial inclusion. The exponential growth model is used to estimate the growth rates for the two periods. Compound growth rates (CGR) for two periods has been calculated to notice the changes.

To assess the changes in economic and social condition after financial inclusion on BSBD account holders, 100 samples were selected at random in K R Nagara taluk of Mysore district in Karnataka. Data was collected from the selected respondents by administering a structured questionnaire to collect the required information. Since the primary data is categorical in nature, Chi-Square test has been employed to draw suitable inference.

The study proposed to test two hypotheses

The first hypothesis is based on secondary data, i.e., There is no difference in growth and impact of financial inclusion on population wise growth of banking.

Second hypothesis is based on primary data, i.e., there is no positive socio-economic impact on BSBD account holders after financial inclusion.

Results and Discussion

Financial inclusion was effectively implemented through various initiatives to include the excluded sections of society into formal financial sector. Branch expansion, deposit mobilisation and credit penetration are the parameters used to check the efficacy of financial inclusion.

Population Group-wise growth of Branches

Under Financial Inclusion, much importance is given to extend banking services to rural people. In the year 1969, there were 1833 bank branches in rural areas, 3342 branches in semi-urban areas, 1584 branches in urban areas and 1503 branches in metropolitan areas. Population Group-wise growth of Branches is depicted in Table-1

Table 1: Population Group-wise Distribution of Branches

Sl No	*Year*	*Rural*	*Semi-Urban*	*Urban*	*Metropolitan*	*Total*
Period-I						
1.	1997	32915	13766	9340	7529	63550
2.	1998	32878	13980	9597	7763	64218
3.	1999	32857	14168	9898	8016	64939
4.	2000	32734	14407	10052	8219	65412
5.	2001	32562	14597	10293	8467	65919
6.	2002	32380	14747	10477	8586	66190
7.	2003	32303	14859	10693	8680	66535
8.	2004	32121	15091	11000	8976	67188
	CGR (per cent)	**-0.40**	**1.30**	**2.20**	**2.40**	**0.80**
Period-II						
1.	2005	32082	15403	11500	9370	68365
2.	2006	30106	15760	12200	11800	69866
3.	2007	30248	16522	13070	12421	72261
4.	2008	30772	17776	14333	13383	76256
5.	2009	31453	19058	15374	14332	80217
6.	2010	32473	20778	16810	15457	85518
7.	2011	33909	23053	17749	16445	91156
8.	2012	36428	25750	18980	17439	98597
9.	2013	39336	28264	19941	18212	105753
	CGR (per cent)	**2.80**	**7.90**	**7.20**	**7.60**	**5.60**

Source: Basic Statistical Returns of Scheduled Commercial Banks in India.

Table 1 depicts the growth of banking sector in period-I and period-II to compare the changes occurred before and after financial inclusion. Compound Growth Rate is calculated for two periods.

In period-I CGR (per cent) for rural areas indicates negative branch expansion and for semi-urban areas it was 1.30 percentages. This is mainly because of closure of rural branches and amalgamation of small bank branches. During the same period growth rate is 2.20 and 2.40 for urban and for metropolitan cities respectively. Branch expansion in urban areas is attributed to liberalised fiscal and monetary policy adopted by the country.

With regard to the growth of banking expansion for the period-II CGR (per cent) for rural areas registered 2.80. Semi-urban areas registered highest growth rate of 7.90. Urban and Metropolitan areas showed CGR per cent 7.20 and 7.60 respectively which is above the average level of 5.60. This information clearly indicates major changes occurred in case of all areas under financial inclusion regime.

In case of rural branch penetration CGR (per cent) has increased from 0.40 to 2.80. Other areas also recorded enormous increase in CGR (per cent) which clearly reflect the positive impact of financial inclusion. Among these population groups semi-urban area recorded highest growth rate because initial attempts of financial inclusion targeted the villages > 2000 population. Now financial inclusion attempts are targeting the villages <2000 population. This will definitely improve rural penetration of banking. But compared to the growth rates of urban and metropolitan areas, branch expansion rate is less in rural areas. As India lies in rural areas, still effective attempts are needed to enhance rural branch penetration.

Commercial banks deposits according to population group

Deposit mobilisation indicates increased access and use of bank accounts which in later stage used productively through lending. Increase in deposit mobilisation leads to increase in capital mobilisation on which all productive activities and economic development relies. Existence of regional disparity is the significant feature of Indian economy. As India is the country of villages, the number of accounts in rural and semi-urban areas is more when compared to urban and metropolitan areas. But regarding amount outstanding huge difference can be **seen as most of rural accounts are small.** The comparative figures of deposit mobilisation according to population group is depicted in Table 2.

Table 2: Deposit of Commercial banks according to population group (Amount in crores)

Sl. No.	*Year*	*Rural*		*Semi-urban*		*Urban*		*Metropolitan*	
		N A	*A O*	*N A*	*A O*	*N A*	*A O*	*N A*	*A O*
Period-I									
1.	1997	116693	737.70	110129	980.45	88645	1125.78	81112	2162
2.	1998	120060	867.06	110705	1156.44	88536	1348.97	80731	2592
3.	1999	122660	1026.97	112376	1360.52	89533	1601.81	81339	2992
4.	2000	125852	1205.39	114109	1619.72	89831	1889.63	83023	3499
5.	2001	131723	1394.31	116400	1861.88	92769	2178.33	87137	4060
6.	2002	133000	1594.23	117394	2149.90	94622	2554.78	94975	4935
7.	2003	136733	1765.02	117537	2417.57	96099	2905.03	95711	5674
8.	2004	138760	1950.82	120651	2682.17	99571	3302.96	98176	7177
	CGR (per cent)	**2.60**	**14.10**	**1.30**	**14.60**	**1.70**	**15.40**	**3.20**	**16.66**
Period-II									
9.	2005	141908	2131.04	125198	2956.85	101376	3748.91	98310	8631
10.	2006	139570	2260.61	121664	3022.13	106172	4308.13	117692	11321

11. 2007	149663	2530.14	132808	3573.95	113422	5325.92	123306	14540
12. 2008	168034	3034.23	148361	4302.80	128021	6576.99	137241	18585
13. 2009	199695	3639.10	169725	5297.58	142272	8229.14	150611	22054
14. 2010	224155	4203.38	189457	6140.47	152323	9449.92	168934	25817
15. 2011	250254	4932.66	212043	7168.31	168037	11105.13	179796	30689
16. 2012	283072	5731.86	239951	8425.45	180626	12725.92	199551	33899
CGR (per cent)	**10.90**	**14.90**	**10.20**	**16.00**	**8.70**	**18.10**	**9.70**	**19.60**

NA - Number of Accounts; AO - Amount outstanding
Source: Handbook of statistics on the Indian economy.

Table 2 indicates growth of deposit mobilisation for two periods related to different population groups. Period-I is the period just before formal financial inclusion steps taken. Period II is the period after the initiatives taken to financial inclusion drive. Regarding deposit accounts in rural areas the growth rate for period-I was just 2.60 and that enhanced to 10.90 in period-II. Significant increase was noticed after initiatives taken for financial inclusion. But related to amount outstanding in deposit accounts marginal increase was noticed from 14.10 to 14.90.This is mainly because under financial inclusion regime poor and marginalized people are included. They have low economic profile and majority of accounts opened were "No Frills" accounts with zero or minimum balance.

In the case of semi-urban areas growth rate related to number of accounts drastically increased from meager1.30 in period-I to 10.20 in period-II. The growth rate is due to effective implementation of financial inclusion measures under which all the villages above 2000 population were covered. The growth rate of amount outstanding in accounts was 14.60 in period-I and it was moderately increased to 16.00 in period-II. Existence of lag between number of accounts and amount outstanding is due to increase in small balance accounts.

The growth rate of deposit accounts for urban centers was just 1.70 in period-I and it steeply increased to 8.70 in period-II. At the same time growth rate related to amount outstanding increased from 15.40 to 18.10. The growth rate of deposit accounts for urban centers was just 3.20 in period-I and it significantly increased to 9.70 in period-II. At the same time growth rate related to amount outstanding increased from 16.66 to 19.60. Simplification of KYC norms, adoption of liberal policy to open accounts, publicity and propaganda, enhanced economic capacity of middle class people, DBT transfers payments are the reasons for opening deposit accounts. Over all statistical data show drastic increase in number of deposit accounts but moderate increase in amount outstanding. To improve this situation, steps are to be taken enhance economic capacity of account holders.

Population Group-wise Credit Penetration

The increase of credit accounts and amount of loan outstanding is another significant indicator of financial inclusion. In credit penetration also, regional disparity can be noticed. Though even today India remains as 'Rural India', it lags behind in getting banking services. The situation moderately improved due to encouraging steps taken for rural penetration of banking services. The growth of credit penetration for two periods is presented in Table 3.

Table 3: Commercial Bank Credit according to Population Group (Amount in Rs. crores)

Sl. No.	*Year*	*Rural*		*Semi-urban*		*Urban*		*Metropolitan*	
		N A	*A O*	*N A*	*A O*	*N A*	*A O*	*N A*	*A O*
1.	1997	27280	403	15839	406	7454	518	5045	1517
2.	1998	26761	481	15083	465	6903	598	4838	1755
3.	1999	24473	539	14458	548	6992	707	6382	2030
4.	2000	25080	594	14865	648	7795	796	6631	2563
5.	2001	22511	689	14047	711	7934	953	7873	3031
6.	2002	25163	877	15037	902	7661	1238	8528	3544
7.	2003	25637	1065	15434	1041	7972	1429	10448	4025
8.	2004	**25556**	1099	16108	1149	8931	1700	15786	4856
	CGR (per cent)	**-0.80**	**15.00**	**0.40**	**15.40**	**2.70**	**17.30**	**15.30**	**16.80**
9.	2005	29357	1605	18226	1428	10177	2123	19391	6369
10.	2006	29054	1994	21475	1748	12919	2764	21988	8633
11.	2007	31029	2357	22099	2128	13254	3501	28060	11484
12.	2008	33546	3231	24021	2560	14194	4306	35230	14073
13.	2009	33823	3096	24973	3111	14750	4986	36690	17284
14.	2010	37074	3852	27047	3679	16242	5936	38285	19985
15.	2011	40018	3924	28772	4520	16896	7795	35038	24517
16.	2012	41749	4422	31292	5283	17740	8549	40099	49779
	CGR (per cent)	**5.50**	**14.20**	**7.00**	**18.70**	**7.01**	**19.80**	**10.00**	**25.60**

NA-Number of Accounts; AO-Amount outstanding
Source: Handbook of statistics on the Indian Economy.

Table 3 depicts the comparative figures of flow of credit to rural, semi-urban, urban and metropolitan centers. The steady increase in number of credit accounts and amount outstanding indicates increased credit penetration which will otherwise improve the consumption capacity and productive activities.

Regarding credit accounts in rural areas, the growth rate for period-I was negative at –0.80 and enhanced to 5.50 in period-II. Drastic changes can be noticed after initiatives taken for financial inclusion. But relating to amount outstanding in credit accounts the growth rate shows marginal decrease from 15.00 to 14.20. The growth rate of credit accounts for period-I in **semi-urban areas** was just 0.40 and it had enhanced to7.00 in period-II. The growth rate of amount outstanding in credit accounts for period-I was 15.40 and it increased to 18.70 in period II. Here also steep rise in credit accounts and moderate increase in amount outstanding can be seen. This is mainly because poor and marginalized people who are included under financial inclusion drive are not in a position to get credit from banking system. Less consumer needs and business requirements, lack of collaterals, low economic condition, and lack of credit worthiness hinder rural masses to get adequate credit. Steps are to be taken to improve credit access to rural masses.

Regarding credit accounts in urban areas, the growth rate of credit accounts was 2.70 in period-I and is enhanced to 7.01 in period-II. The growth rate of amount outstanding in credit accounts in period-I was 17.30 and it increased to 19.80 in period-II. Liberalized policy adopted by India under globalisation led to development of economic activities. This, in turn enhances the credit accounts in urban and metropolitan cities. In metropolitan areas, the growth rate of credit accounts show negative impact as it decreased from 15.30 to 10.00. But growth rate of amount outstanding in credit accounts increased from 16.80 to 25.60. The decreased growth rate of credit accounts under financial inclusion regime may be due to economic recession. But, growth rate of amount outstanding has increased drastically. More demand for consumer loans because of changing lifestyle, increased demand for housing loans because of easy access, increase in business loans to withstand global competition are the reasons for significant increase in amount outstanding in metro areas. All the findings based on the above secondary data disproved the hypothesis that there is no population-wise growth of banking system after financial inclusion.

Impact of Social and Economic condition after financial inclusion

The second objective of the study is to assess the impact of financial inclusion on social and economic condition of BSBD account holders in the study region. The prime objective of financial inclusion is to include poor and backward people into banking net to improve their living standards. Opening the account in bank, push up the confidence level of new account holders. Secured saving facility boosts saving habit of account holders. Overdraft and credit facility help the account holders to avail loan for consumption as well as for small business activities. BSBD accounts also help to get employment and other social security payments directly from government. Changed situation after opening the account bring changes in socio-economic condition of new account holders. Collected data in K R Nagara taluk on changes after introduction of financial inclusion among the sample respondents are presented in Tables 4 and 5.

Table 4: Impact on Economic condition after opening account

	Physical Assets	*Owning of land*	*Live stock*	*Electronic goods*	*Vehicles*
Affirmative	71	65	85	32	82
Non-Affirmative	29	35	15	68	18

Chi-Sq = 81.140**, DF = 4, P-Value = 0.000.

It is very clear that among 100 sample respondents, 71 have informed that their physical assets were increased after financial inclusion; while 29 had no improvements in their physical assets. With regard to owning of land, 65 were affirmative and rests of them were non-affirmative. It is known that the major source of earnings other than farming would be through livestock in the rural areas. The study reports that 85 have opined in favour of financial inclusion. The study also reports that there is increase livestock and 15 were non-affirmative. But regarding the purchase of electronic goods like TV, cell-phone etc. financial inclusion does not bring changes to majority of people as 68 were non-affirmative. This may be due to non-priority of rural people. Regarding the purchase of vehicles, 82 were affirmative. The collected information clearly indicates positive improvement of economic condition of account holders. The chi-square test further revealed that there is a significant impact of the financial inclusion among the respondents.

Table 5: Impact on Social Condition after opening account

	Education Expenditure	*Health Access*	*Confidence Level*	*Skills and Empowerment*	*Risk Management*	*Nutritional Status*
Affirmative	75	85	78	54	79	54
Non-Affirmative	25	15	22	46	21	46

Chi-Sq = 43.700**, DF = 5, P-Value = 0.000.

Improvement in economic condition always has positive impact on social condition of account holders. This has been proved in Table 5. Based on the collected information, the results are presented in Table 5. It is well observed that expenditure on education of their children was conveniently met after financial inclusion in the study area. Access to health has improved, as 85 respondents were affirmative in their response. One of the important reasons for introduction of financial inclusion in the rural and semi-urban areas is to create confidence and increase their skill formation in decision making and empowerment. The study showed an increased confidence level (78 per cent); skill formation and empowerment (54 per cent) among the sample respondents which definitely improve the decision making power of the individuals. 79 per cent were affirmative regarding their risk management capacity. Along with all these, 54 per cent respondents confirmed increase in nutritional status. These empirical findings clearly established the fact that there is a positive change in social conditions of respondents after financial inclusion. The chi-square test has shown highly significant result at one per cent level of significance. The test result has disproved the hypothesis, that there is no impact on social condition of sample respondents in the study area.

Conclusion and Policy Implications

Financial inclusion is a powerful tool for achieving inclusive growth. The potential for growth is enormous if we make use of strength of poor and deprived people in rural areas. But the inability to access necessary financial services like secured savings, loan, remittance, insurance services etc. by the needy people acts as constraint for growth. Financial Inclusion is not an end itself, but rather a gate way, a process. With this view the present study based on secondary data emphatically proved that drastic banking growth had taken place during financial inclusion regime. The present research investigation conducted at the cross-sectional level in K R Nagara taluk of Mysore district has provided clear evidence that there is a positive impact on social and economic condition of BSBD account holders who are covered under financial inclusion. It is clear that financial inclusion is not only a tool to uplift poor but also an opportunity to banks to expand their business transactions. Therefore, considering the positive changes in banking growth and level of living of BSBD account holders, Government of India may take further initiatives to implement ambitious JAN-DHAN YOJANA mission by making use of efficient banking system.

REFERENCES

1. Ananth S, T and Sabri Öncü (2013), Challenges to Financial Inclusion in India: The Case of Andhra Pradesh, Economic and Political Weekly Feb. 16, 2013, Vol. XLVIII, No. 7 pp. 77-83.
2. Anupama Sharma and Sumita Kukreja (2013), an Analytical Study: Relevance of Financial Inclusion for Developing Nations Research Inventory: International

Journal of Engineering and Science, Issue: 2278-4721, Vol. 2, Issue 6 (March 2013), pp. 15-20.

3. Beck, T., Demirgüç-Kunt, A. and Levine, R (2007), "Finance, inequality and the poor", Journal of Economic Growth, 12(1), 27-49.
4. Chittaranjan Mishra (2012), An Analytical Study: Relevance of Financial Inclusion for Developing Nations, The International Journal's Research Journal of Commerce and Behavioral Science, Volume: 01, Number: 08, June, pp. 22 – 27.
5. Chakraborty K.C (2010), Inclusive Growth – Role of Financial Sector, National Finance Conclave 2010 organised by KIIT University Bhubaneswar: KIIT University.
6. Government of India (2014), Annual Report of Ministry of Finance, New Delhi .
7. Government of India (2009), Report of the Committee on Financial Sector Reforms, "A Hundred Small Steps", Planning Commission, Government of India, Sage Publications.
8. Gujarathi, D. B. (2012), Analysis of Various Initiatives on Financial Inclusion, National Monthly Refereed Journal of Research in Commerce & Management, 1(7), 82-95.
9. Karmakar, K.G (2011), Towards Financial Inclusion in India, Sage Publication, New Delhi.
10. Reserve Bank of India (2014), Handbook of Statistics on the Indian Economy Division of Reports and Knowledge Dissemination Department of Economic and Policy Research, Mumbai.

12

Role of Banks in Achieving Financial Inclusion

Rohini R.

Abstract: *The main objectives of the study are to analyse the role of banks in financial inclusion for economic growth and challenges. Sustained growth of the nation depends critically on universal financial services covering all people. Financial inclusion is emerging as the new paradigm of economic growth. Financial inclusion plays a major role in driving a-way the poverty. Further, empirical evidence shows that inclusive financial system significantly raises growth, alleviate poverty and expand economic opportunity. Financial inclusion refers to delivery of banking services to masses including privileged and disadvantaged people at an affordable terms and conditions. It not only enhances overall financial intensity of agriculture but also help in increasing rural non-farm activities which lead to development of rural economy and improve economic condition of people. Financial inclusion is integral to the inclusive growth process and sustainable development of the country. It is a policy of involving a wider section of population deposit mobilisation and credit intermediation.*

The banking industry is making rapid strides with Information Technology driven initiatives and has led to expansion of financial services giving birth to the concept of Financial Inclusion. The Eleventh

Five Year Plan (2007-12) envisaged inclusive growth as a key objective as well as a strategy for economic development. The objective of financial inclusion is to extend financial services to the large hitherto un-served population of the country and achieve broad-based improvement in the living standards of all our people. The three major aspects of financial inclusion are (i) access to financial market (ii) access to credit market and (iii) learning financial matters. Reserve Bank of India and government and other banks play an important role in promoting financial inclusion for economic growth. Government and RBI has taken various steps to increase banking penetration in the country, nationalisation of banks, establishment of RRBs, introduction of SHG and strategy of one person one account for accessing financial market.

Introduction

Financial inclusion is new paradigm of economic growth which plays a major role in driving away the poverty. Lack of access to financial services in most of rural areas due to high informative barriers and low awareness, poor functioning and financial history of financial institutions, near absence of insurance and pension service create the need and scope of financial inclusion. Fruits of development have hardly reached to nearly half of Indian population because no access to loan and insurance and this raises most pertinent issue of financial inclusion. Financial inclusion is integral to the inclusive growth process and sustainable development of the country.

Financial inclusion may be defined as the process of ensuring access to financial services and timely and adequate credit where needed by vulnerable groups such as weaker sections and low income groups at an affordable cost (The Committee on Financial Inclusion, Chairman: C. Rangarajan). Financial Inclusion, broadly defined, refers to universal access to a wide range of financial services at a reasonable cost. These include not only banking products but also other financial services such as insurance and equity products. Financial inclusion broadens the resource base of the financial system by developing a culture of savings among large segment of rural population and plays its own role in the process of economic development. Further, by bringing low income groups within the perimeter of formal banking sector; financial inclusion protects their financial wealth and other resources in exigent circumstances. The objective of financial inclusion is to extend the scope of activities of the organised financial system to include within its ambit people with low incomes. Through graduated credit, the attempt must be to lift the poor from one level to another so that they come out of poverty.

Financial inclusion broadens the resource base of the financial system by developing a culture of savings among large segment of rural population and plays its own role in the process of economic development. Further, by bringing low income groups within the perimeter of formal banking sector; financial inclusion protects their financial wealth and other resources in exigent circumstances. The Government of India and the Reserve Bank of India have been making concerted efforts to promote financial inclusion as one of the important national objectives of the country. Before 1990s several initiatives has been undertaken which included creation of State Bank of India in 1955; nationalisation of commercial banks in 1969 and 1980; initiating the Lead Bank Scheme in 1970; was a big step to expand financial inclusion. Priority sector lending norms, branch licensing norms with focus on rural and semi-urban branches.

National Bank for Agriculture and Rural Development (NABARD) was set up in 1982 mainly to provide refinance to the banks extending credit to agriculture, establishment of regional rural banks in 1975 are also the major steps for same aim which encourage branch expansion in rural area. It also regulate interest rate ceiling for credit in weaker sections. After 1990s there are major important steps taken for financial excluded people as launching SHG-bank linkage programme in1992 by NABARD, which facilitates and provides door step banking. Simplifications of Know your customer (KYC) norms are another milestone. Where NGOs are set up to organise the poor, build their capacities and facilitates the process of empowering them. In 1998 Kissan credit card has been launched and on the suggestion of NABARD in 2005 General credit card has been launched which facility up to Rs 25000. In January 2006 NGOs, SHGs, and Micro Finance Institutions are permitted by RBI. Now MFIs currently cover 8.3 million borrowers. MFIs, self-help groups (SHGs) also meet the financial service requirements of the poorer segments.

Financial tools help entrepreneurs start and expand small businesses which are a source of local job creation, growth and poverty reduction. Financial inclusion has become a national and a government imperative in the last few years. The discussions towards financial inclusion have definitely reached a crescendo this year with increased focus from the government, various policymakers and some genuine progress by the private sector and financial institutions. A well developed, inclusive financial sector is like a good transport system. It is basic infrastructure that everyone in the country - from individuals to governments to business of all sizes - depends upon new technologies such as mobile phones, smart cards, ATMs and business correspondents, coupled with strong banking institutions hold promise of dramatically expanding access by reducing costs for providers and clients alike. Financial inclusion is a win-win proposition. This is further aggravated with a lack of awareness and trust amongst the financially excluded regarding the benefits of the banking system. Hence, reaching out to over 700 million citizens across six lakh villages who don't have access to the formal banking system appears to be a Herculean task.

Technology also plays a major role in financial inclusion in the sense that mobile telephony has reached far flung areas and has facilitated fund transfers even to a village bank through electronic mode / mobile phone. Banks could play a major role in 'inclusive growth through of the excluded' is only a means to financing of MSMEs, especially in rural and semi-urban centres in a big way. Financial literacy is a prerequisite for effective financial inclusion, which will ensure that financial services reach the under banked sections of the society, leading to consumer protection through self-regulation. In recent times, the financial landscape in our country has undergone significant transformation shaped by the forces of globalisation, advances in technology, greater market orientation and financial innovation.

Objectives

(1) To explore the need and significance of financial inclusion.
(2) To analyse the role of banks in financial inclusion.
(3) To examine the initiatives taken by the RBI and Government in financial inclusion.
(4) To study the challenges to the financial inclusion.

Importance of Financial Inclusion

The policy-makers have been focusing on financial inclusion of Indian rural and semi-rural areas primarily for three most important pressing needs:

(1) **Creating a platform for inculcating money saving habit** – The lower income category has been living under the constant shadow of financial duress mainly because of the absence of savings. The absence of savings makes them a vulnerable lot. Presence of banking services and products aims to provide a critical tool to inculcate the habit to save.

(2) **Providing formal credit avenues** – So far the unbanked population has been vulnerably dependent of informal channels of credit like family, friends and moneylenders. Availability of

adequate and transparent credit from formal banking channels shall allow the entrepreneurial spirit of the masses to increase outputs and prosperity in the countryside.

(3) **Plug gaps and leaks in public subsidies and welfare programmes** – A considerable sum of money that is meant for the poorest of poor does not actually reach them. Government is therefore, pushing for direct cash transfers to beneficiaries through their bank accounts rather than subsidising products and making cash payments.

Role of Banks in Financial Inclusion

Banks play a vital role in the economic development of a country like India. Indian economy in general and banking services in particular have made rapid strides in the recent past. Following are the major strides.

(1) **Promotion of Self-Help Groups:** Self-Help Groups in good number appeared in the rural economy due to the promotional efforts made by NABARD. As per the operational guidelines, SHGs are informal groups formed on voluntary basis to attain certain collective goals, both social and economic. In April, 1996, the Reserve Bank of India advised the banks to consider lending to the SHGs as a segment of priority sector advances and integrate it with the mainstream credit operations. There are more than 69.53 lakh savings-linked SHGs and more than 48.51 lakh credit-linked SHGs covering 9.7 crore poor households as on 31st March 2011. This is a good indicator of the sustained efforts made by banks to reach out to the unreached, particularly to the women.

(2) **Opening No-Frills Accounts:** The banking sector has 7.5 crore no-frills accounts, while the total number of savings bank accounts has increased to 55.95 crore, of which 18.46 crore accounts are in the rural sector as on March 2010.

(3) **Evolution of Branchless Banking Model:** An innovation in branchless banking has been adopted by the public sector banks, by appointing business correspondents in selected villages to deal with customers of the bank using smart cards. The business correspondents are the local persons, who are familiar with the local households. Simplicity of operations is the hall mark of branchless banking process. The small electronic gadget identifies the finger prints of the customer and facilitates the transactions like depositing and withdrawing cash. This facility replaces the brick and mortar branch effectively.

(4) **Rural Financial Inclusion:** Some details pertaining to the progress made by the banking sector in enhancing financial inclusion in rural areas are available in the Reserve Bank's Report on Trend and Progress of Banking in India: 2010-11. The progress made so far is not very impressive. Evidently, banks have a long way to go to attain 100 per cent financial inclusion. The 'Task Force on the Aadhaar-enabled Unified Payment Infrastructure headed by Mr. Nandan Nilekani has suggested that ten lakh business correspondents have to be appointed to ensure that social sector schemes' benefits reach the intended beneficiaries in about six lakh villages. This recommendation anticipates that these ten lakh "mini ATMs" could be used to make payments to beneficiaries in 2.25 lakh gram panchayats covering six lakh villages besides serving the urban poor. This is a challenging task indeed.

(5) **Role of Gramin Banks:** The Working Group on Rural Banks, which recommended the establishment of regional rural banks, has formulated the ideological framework of this new credit agency as follows: "One of the most important objectives of the rural banks would be to attempt **effective coverage** of small and marginal farmers, landless labourers, and rural artisans. The performance of these banks will be judged primarily by their success in coverage of such categories of borrowers towards meaningful productive activity and recovery of their advances rather than by the profit they make. The brick and mortar branches of banks are in existence only in 22,684 villages in 622 districts. The number of villages covered through the much talked about business correspondents is not more than 76,801. The number of villages covered through other modes like mobile vans and ATMs is not very significant; it is only 355 as on March 2011.

(6) **An Action Programme for RRBs:** The regional rural banks have to be assigned a strategic role in attaining total financial inclusion, as a part of the overall programmes of a strong base in the rural credit space. They have been running in a handicapped race along with the bigger commercial banks. Their amalgamations in the recent years have expanded their areas of operation and thereby improving their viability considerably. One of the committees appointed by the Reserve Bank of India has identified 256 districts in India out of the 622 districts as financially excluded districts. Districts, where the rural and semi-urban per branch population is more than 19,272 and their corresponding credit gap is more than 95 per cent, are considered

as financially excluded. In Bihar, 37 out of its 38 districts are among the financially excluded districts.

(7) **Empowering MSMEs:** Financing of first time entrepreneurs is a must for financial inclusion enterprises which commenced as small enterprises have grown manifold and both the companies have offices and units well spread out. Both are good examples of inclusive growth. Hence first time entrepreneurs need to be supported and banks have been doing this but still there is a large gap in this area of financial inclusion. Single-widow clearance of credit facilities centralised processing cell with single point appraisal and sanction. Developing cluster-based approach to financing of MSME units will go a long way in promoting inclusive growth.

(8) **Mobile Banking:** It is the current innovation included in the recent initiatives towards achieving greater financial inclusion by banks and the service providers in the banking sector. The guidelines issued by Reserve Bank of India during 2008 for mobile banking transactions have accelerated the process of mobile banking operation in the country. There are several successful experiments in mobile banking. Further, RBI has given banks a clear lead against non-banks, particularly mobile network operators, by allowing only banks to offer mobile banking services. Mobile banking in India has, so far, not reached the poor and illiterate customers. The potential to link banking services to the most widely used gadget by all sections of the society is huge. The number of mobile subscribers in India is more than 860 million or 72 per cent of the population, where as the proportion of the banked population is only around 50 per cent. Thus, from the perspective of facilitating financial inclusion 'mobile banking' offers immense opportunities for the banks.

(9) **Financial Inclusion through Micro Finance Sector:** The Micro Finance Sector over the period has evolved two different delivery models, one focused on Self Help Group (SHG) and its federations based on community participation and other one based on commercially oriented market driven Micro Finance Institutions (MFIs). The former one (SHG channel) is termed as non-profit and non-commercial with perfect integration of the existing financial structure where as the latter one (MFIs) has emerged as a profit oriented entity as a consequence of slow progress of SHG bank linkage model.

(10) **SHG-Bank Linkage Model:** An important regulatory dispensation that facilitated financial inclusion was given in the early 90s, when banks were allowed to open savings accounts

for SHGs, which were neither registered nor regulated. The impressive progress of SHG bank linkage programmes in reaching the poor clients by providing financial services led to greater financial inclusion. At the end of March 2011, 7.54 million groups had been linked with the banking system. Commercial banks had a share of 60 per cent of the amount saved by SHGs and 64 per cent of all the groups with outstanding loans. Further, the federation of SHGs is emerging as intermediary institutional set up between the groups and bank branches and varying degree of success is being observed in several States.

Progress in Financial Inclusion

Banks are increasingly involved in branch expansion in different areas. Due to RBI's concerted efforts since 2005, the number of branches of Scheduled Commercial Banks increased manifold from 68,681 in March 2006 to 1,02,343 in March 2013, spread across length and breadth of the country in rural areas, the number of branches increased from 30,572 to 37,953 during March 2006 to March 2013.

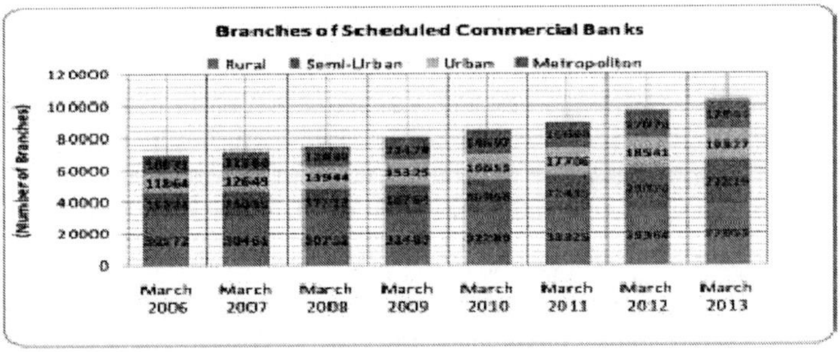

Source: Basic Statistical Returns, RBI and DFS, GoI.

Fig. 1: Branches of Scheduled Commerical Banks.

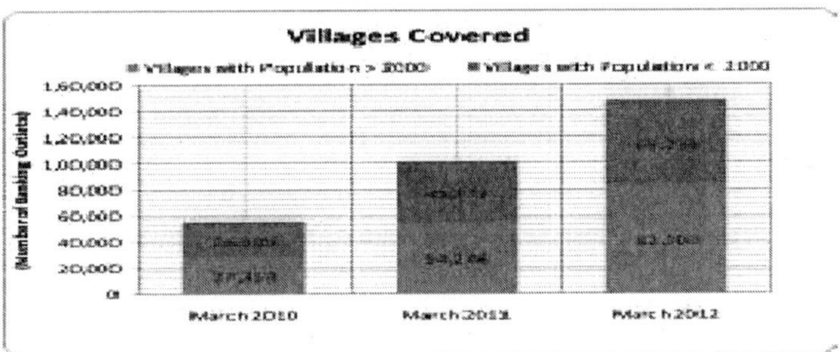

Source: RBI Annual Report, 2011-12.

Fig. 2: Villages Covered.

The number of banking outlets in villages with population more than 2000 as well as less than 2000 increased consistently since March 2010. The total number of banking outlets in villages increased from 67,694 in March 2010 to 2,68,454 in March 2013. Of total branches, banking outlets through BCs increased from 34,174 to 2,21,341 during the same period. The number of BSBD accounts opened increased from 73.45 million.

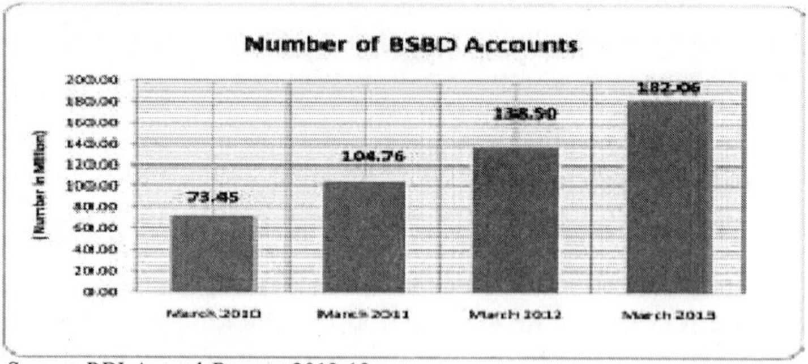

Source: RBI Annual Report, 2012-13.

Fig. 3: Number of BSBD Accounts.

RBI advised banks to provide small overdrafts in BSBD accounts. Accordingly upto March 2013, there were 3.95 million BSBD accounts and OD facility of Rs 1.55 billion (These figures respectively, were 0.18 million and 0.10 billion in March 2010).

Kissan Credit Cards (KCC) Issued

Banks have been advised to issue KCCs to small farmers for meeting their credit requirements. Up to March 2013, the total number of KCCs issued to farmers remained at 33.79 million with a total outstanding credit of Rs 2622.98 billion.

General Credit Cards (GCC) Issued.

Banks have been advised to introduce General Credit Card facility up to Rs. 25,000 at their rural and semi-urban branches. Up to March 2013, banks had provided credit aggregating to Rs 76.34 billion in 3.63 million GCC accounts.

Challenges in the Task of Financial Inclusion

1. The major barriers for financial inclusion, apart from socioeconomic factors such as lack of regular income, poverty, illiteracy, etc.
2. Lack of reach, higher cost of transactions and time taken in providing those services. In a vast country like India viable models for remote areas are difficult to design.

3. Appropriate Business Model to suit urban poor and rural people.
4. Efficient Delivery Mechanism need to be identified. Financial Literacy and financial education need to be taken up on large scale.
5. Lack of ownership by banks in implementation of Financial Inclusion.
6. Lack of co-ordination among different entities Information and Communications Technology (ICT) based BC Model - Yet to stabilise.
7. Infrastructure Problems - Premises, Roads, Power, etc.

Suggestions

(1) Training to Financial Inclusion Agents: The Financial Inclusion agents should be adequately trained on a continuous basis about the products and services provided by banks from time to time.

(2) Women Empowerment: Women empowerment is another *sine qua non* for the success of Financial Inclusion movement.

(3) Banks should prepare comprehensive plans to cover all villages, through a mix of branchless banking and bricks and mortar branch banking.

(4) Speed up enrolment of customers and opening of UID-enabled bank accounts.

(5) Banks must be able to offer the entire suite of financial products and services to poor clients at attractive pricing.

(6) It is important that adequate infrastructure such as digital and physical connectivity, uninterrupted power supply, etc., is available.

(7) All stakeholders will have to work together through sound and purposeful collaborations.

(8) Supply of appropriate and affordable services available to those that need them.

(9) Banks should institute systems of reward and recognition for personnel initiating, ideating, innovating and successfully executing new products and services in the rural areas.

(10) Greater collaboration is also imperative to mitigate the numerous other risks arising out of this new form of banking.

Conclusion

Empirical evidence shows that economic growth follows financial inclusion. Boosting business opportunities will definitely increase the gross domestic product, which will be reflected in our national income growth. Financial inclusion becomes a major prerequisite to poverty alleviation. Even though the measures have been taken by RBI and Government, improper repayment, time consumption, high cost and illiteracy are continuing to be a road block to financial inclusion in many areas. Consequently, many banks are not adopting fully fledged financial inclusion plan. The banks should step up to overwhelm all these problems and to disseminate its service to remote areas. The banks should encourage the people to access banking services by ways of financial inclusion campaign and business correspondent. The government should encourage the banks to adopt financial inclusion by means of financial assistance, advertisement and awareness programme etc. to achieve the aim of 11th plan of Inclusive Growth.

REFERENCES

1. Rangarajan, C. (2008), Report of the committee on Financial Inclusion, GoI, pp. 1.
2. PR Newswire (2000), 6th September.
3. Rao, N, N, D, S, V (2010), "Financial inclusion - Banker's Perspective", 'Bank Quest', Vol. 8, No. 4, Oct-Dec, pp. 20-26.
4. Rao S.K (2010), "Nationalisation of banks – an anchor for financial inclusion", 'Bank Quest', Vol. 8, No. 3, July-September , pp. 17-24
5. Swamy, V and Vijayalakshmi (2010), "Role of financial inclusion for inclusive growth in India- issues and challenges", thttp://skoch.in/fir/role%20%financial (visited on 04/08/11)
6. Badajena, S, N and Gundimeda, H (2010), "Self help group bank linkage model and financial inclusion in India", http://skoch.in/fir/role%20%financial%20% inclusion%20 in(visited on 06/08/11)
7. Nurkse, R(2010), Financial Inclusion "Widening the Bottom of the Pyramid" pp. 6 http://skoch.in/fir/role%20%financial(visited on 04/08/11)
8. Handoo, J(2010), "Financial inclusion in India: Integration of technology, policy and market at the bottom of the pyramid", http://skoch.in/fir/role%20%financial %20%inclusion%20 in(visited on 1/08/11)
9. Chakraborty, K C (2009), A National Initiative for Financial Inclusion at September 18. (visited on 05/06/11)
10. JJFLCC Trust (2010), 'All about financial literacy and financial inclusion' first edition, Jnana Jyothi Financial Literacy and Credit Counseling Trust, Manipal.
11. Kibua, T.N. (2007), "Poverty reduction through enhanced access to financial services: case studies of Botswana, Kenya and Namibia" IPAR Occasional Paper

Series, occasional paper No. 010/2007, seapren.org/publications/ PovertyReduction 2008 (visited on 4/08/11)

12. Agarwal, A (2008), "The need for financial inclusion with an Indian perspective" 'Economic Research' March-3, www.oecd.org/dataoecd/16/55/40339652. (visited on 01/08/11)

13

Role of Indian Banking Sector in Financial Inclusion

Umashankar B. Hiremath

Abstract: *Access to finance by the poor and vulnerable groups is a prerequisite for poverty reduction and social cohesion. This has become an integral part of our efforts to promote inclusive growth. In fact, providing access to finance is a form of empowerment of the vulnerable groups. Financial Inclusion denotes delivery of financial services at an affordable cost to the vast sections of the disadvantaged and low-income groups. The various financial services include credit, savings, insurance and payments and remittance facilities.*

The objective of financial inclusion is to extend the scope of activities of the organised financial system to include within its ambit people with low incomes. Through graduated credit, the attempt must be to lift the poor from one level to another so that they come out of poverty. Financial inclusion is the availability of banking services at an affordable cost to disadvantaged and low-income groups. In India the basic concept of financial inclusion is having a saving or current account with any bank. In reality it includes loans, insurance services and much more.

The first-ever Index of Financial Inclusion to find out the extent of reach of banking services among 100 countries, India has been ranked 50. Only 34 per cent of Indian individuals have access to or receive banking services. In order to increase this number the Reserve Bank of India had the Government of India take innovative steps. One of the reasons for opening new branches of Regional Rural Banks was to make sure that the banking service is accessible to the poor. With the directive from RBI, our banks are now offering, No-Frill, Accounts to low income groups. These accounts either have a low minimum or nil balance with some restriction in transactions. The individual bank has the authority to decide whether the account should have zero or minimum balance.

Access to safe, easy and affordable credit and other financial services by the poor and vulnerable groups in disadvantaged areas and lagging sectors is recognised as a pre-condition for accelerating growth and reducing income disparities and poverty. Access to a well-functioning financial system, by creating equal opportunities, enables economically and socially excluded people to integrate better into the economy and actively contribute to development and protects themselves against economic shocks. Despite the broad international consensus regarding the importance of access to finance as a crucial poverty alleviation tool, it is estimated that globally over two billion people are currently excluded from access to financial services.

Key Words: Financial Inclusion, Banking Sector, SCB's, RRB's, RBI, Development.

Introduction

Financial inclusion is a tool for combating poverty. It is estimated that globally over two billion people are excluded from access to financial services, of which one-third is in India. Access to various financial services enables the poor people to participate in the growth of the economy. Many banks are forced to adopt financial inclusion rather than their own interest. The banks have encountered various problems while adopting financial inclusion viz. improper repayment, need for additional workforce, more time consumption, heavy work load, high cost etc. The main objectives of this study were to know the measures taken by the banks for financial inclusion, to examine the difficulties involved in the adoption of financial inclusion and also to enhance the extent of financial inclusion. The data required for the study was collected from both primary and secondary sources. The total numbers of samples were 50. The study was conducted among the banks in Tiruchendur area of Tamil Nadu. Reserve Bank of India's vision for 2020 is to open nearly 600 million new customers' accounts. The banks should encourage the people to access banking services by ways of 'no-frills' account, financial inclusion campaign and business correspondent. The government should encourage the banks to adopt financial inclusion by means of financial assistance, advertisement and awareness programme etc.

In order to expand the credit and financial services to the wider sections of the population, a wide network of financial institutions has been established over the years in India. The organised financial system comprising Commercial Banks, Regional Rural Banks (RRBs), Urban Co-operative Banks (UCBs), Primary Agricultural Credit Societies (PACS) and post offices caters to the needs of financial services of the people. The initiatives taken by the Reserve Bank and the Government of India towards promoting financial inclusion since the late 1960s have considerably improved the access to the formal financial institutions. Banking sector plays considerable role in bringing financially excluded people in to formal financial sector as policies of the government and Reserve Bank towards financial inclusion are implemented through banking sector.

This article makes an attempt to assess the role of banking sector in financial inclusion process in India. Role of banks in financial inclusion process in India is examined on the basis of data available from the institutional sources such as Reserve Bank of India (RBI), National Bank for Agriculture and Rural Development (NABARD), Scheduled Commercial Banks (SCBS), RRBs, UCBs and PACS from different viewpoints namely, branch penetration, ATM penetration, population per branch, distribution of banking branches, credits, including micro finance, of SCBs and Co-operative banks, deposits of SCBs and Co-operative banks, credit-income ratio, deposit-income ratio and cash-deposit ratio in India.

Over the past 20 years, the Indian financial system has made significant progress in terms of resource mobilisation, geographical and functional reach and financial viability. The banking sector comprised 86 scheduled commercial banks with a consolidated asset base of Rs 73 Lakh crore. In addition, there were 82 Regional Rural Banks (RRBs) consolidated from the 196 that originally existed before the amalgamation process started in 2006.

In 1996, the RBI mandated the establishment of Local Area Banks – essentially RRBs under private ownership – but only six were ever licensed and just four are functioning today. In addition, there were 12,375 Non Bank Finance Companies in India in May 2012, out of which just 271 were permitted to accept/hold public deposits. There is also a network of cooperative banks, with 31 state cooperative banks (SCBs) and 371 district central cooperative banks (DCCBs). The main aim of the rural cooperative banks is to provide crop and other working capital loans, primarily for short-term purposes to farmers and rural artisans. The cooperative banks do this either directly or by financing those of the 93,400 primary agricultural cooperatives functioning in their operational areas. In urban areas, the financial services of the banks and NBFCs are supplemented by the operations of over 1,645 urban cooperative banks.

Financial exclusion is often the symptom as well as the cause of poverty. Financial exclusion has been predominant in rural areas primarily due to poor infrastructure. As a result, necessarily many people have to depend either on their own sources or informal sources of finance, which are generally at high cost. Most of the population in developed countries (99 per cent in Denmark, 96 per cent in Germany, 91 per cent in USA and 96 per cent in France) has bank accounts. However, formal financial sectors in most developing countries serve relatively a small segment, often no more than 20-30 per cent of the population, the vast majority of who are low income households in rural areas (ADB, 2007).

Financial inclusion is intended to connect people with banks for consequential benefits, ensuring that the financial system plays its due role in promoting inclusive growth which is one of the biggest challenges facing the emerging economies. Access to a well-functioning financial system enables economically and socially excluded people to integrate better into the economy and actively contribute to development and protects themselves against economic shocks.

Scope of the Study

There are various types of banks which operate in our country to meet the financial requirements of different categories of people. On the basis of function, the banks can be classified into five categories, viz. central bank, commercial bank, development bank, co-operative bank and specialised bank.

Objectives

The main objectives of this study were: (1) to study the measures taken by the banks for financial inclusion, (2) to examine the difficulties involved in the adoption of financial inclusion, and (3) to suggest steps to enhance the extent of financial inclusion.

Methodology

The data required for the study was collected from both primary and secondary sources. The primary data was collected from the banks using structured questionnaire. The secondary data was collected from the published journals, books and various websites. The samples were selected by administering convenience sampling technique. The total numbers of samples were 50. The various statistical tools used to analyse the primary data were percentage analysis, mean score analysis and correlation. The present study had undertaken a period from December 2010 to March 2011.

Financial Inclusion Plan of Banks

We have encouraged banks to adopt a structured and planned approach to financial inclusion with commitment at the highest levels, through preparation of Board approved Financial Inclusion Plans (FIPs). The first phase of FIPs was implemented over the period 2010-2013. The Reserve Bank has used the FIPs to gauge the performance of banks under their FI initiatives. In this direction we have put in place a structured and comprehensive monitoring mechanism for evaluating banks' performance vis-à-vis their targets. To ensure support of the Top Management of the Bank to the FI process and to ensure accountability of the senior functionaries of the bank, one on one annual review meetings, chaired by the Deputy Governor, are held with CMDs/CEOs of banks. A snapshot of the progress made by banks under the three Year Financial Inclusion Plan (April 10 - March 13) for key parameters during the three year period indicates that banking outlets increased to nearly 2,68,000 banking as on March 13 as against 67,694 banking outlets in villages in March 2010. 7400 rural branches have been opened during this period of three years. Nearly 109 million Basic Savings Bank Deposit Accounts (BSBDAs) have been added taking the total no. of BSBDA to 182 million. Share of ICT-based accounts have increased substantially - Percentage of ICT accounts to total BSBDAs has increased from 25 per cent in March 10 to 45 per cent in March 13. About 4904 lakh transactions have been carried out in ICT-based accounts through BCs during the three year period.

After completion of the first plan period, we realised that there is an Access Usage conundrum a large banking network has been created along with the opening of large number of bank accounts. However, we have realised that simply creating the banking infrastructure and opening banking accounts will not fulfil our objectives of achieving total Financial Inclusion. To take the process, forward banks have been advised to draw up fresh Three Year Financial Inclusion Plans for the period 2013-16 ensure involvement of all the stake holders in the FI efforts and to ensure uniformity in the reporting structure under the Financial Inclusion Plan, banks have are to ensure that the FIPs prepared by them are disaggregated and percolated down upto the branch level. The focus under the new plan is to ensure that the large banking network created is utilised for extending other products viz. credit products, which will help make the business more viable for banks. This would also ensure that a large number of accounts are opened and equally large volume of transactions takes place and people reap the benefits of getting linked to the formal financial institutions.

Financial Inclusion Plans - Progress at a Glance

Sl. No.	*Particulars*	*Year ended March 10*	*Year ended March 11*	*Year ended March 12*	*Year ended March 13*	*Progress 10-March 13 April*
1.	Banking Outlets in Villages – Branches	33378	34811	37471	40837	7459
2.	Banking Outlets in Villages – BCs	34174	80802	141136	221341	187167
3.	Banking Outlets in Villages – Other Modes	142	595	3146	6276	6134
4.	Banking Outlets in Villages – TOTAL	67694	116208	181753	268454	200760
5.	Urban Locations covered through BCs	447	3771	5891	27143	26696
6.	Basic Savings Bank Deposit A/c through branches (No. in millions)	60.19	73.13	81.20	100.80	40.61
7.	Basic Savings Bank Deposit A/c through branches (Amt. in billions)	44.33	57.89	109.87	164.69	120.36
8.	Basic Savings Bank Deposit A/c through BCs (No. in millions)	13.27	31.63	57.30	81.27	68.00
9.	Basic Savings Bank Deposit A/c through BCs (Amt. in billions)	10.69	18.23	10.54	18.22	7.53
10.	BSBDA Total (in millions)	73.45	104.76	138.50	182.06	108.61
11.	BSBDA Total Amt. (in billions)	55.02	76.12	120.41	182.92	127.90
12.	OD facility availed in Basic Savings Bank Deposit A/c (No. in millions)	0.18	0.61	2.71	3.95	3.77
13.	OD facility availed in Basic Savings Bank Deposit A/c (Amt. in billions)	0.10	0.26	1.08	1.55	1.45
14.	KCCs - (No. in millions)	24.31	27.11	30.24	33.79	9.48
15.	KCCs - (Amt in billions)	1240.07	1600.05	2068.39	2622.98	1382.91
16.	GCCs - (No. in millions)	1.39	1.70	2.11	3.63	2.24
17.	GCCs - (Amt in billions)	35.11	35.07	41.84	76.34	41.23
18.	ICT A/Cs-BC- Transactions – No. in millions	26.52	84.16	155.87	250.46	490.49
19.	ICT A/Cs-BC- Transactions –Amt in billions	6.92	58.00	97.09	233.88	388.97

Assistance provided by Shri Ajay Kumar Misra, GM, Smt. Sushma Vij, DGM, and Smt. Mruga M Paranjape, Manager is gratefully acknowledged.

Results

The findings which arrived from the analysis on Banks Role in Financial Inclusion are presented below:

- Profile of the Respondents;
- Target for Financial inclusion;
- Getting refinance for financial inclusion;
- Inducement for financial inclusion;
- Conducting financial inclusion campaign;
- Focused people for financial inclusion;
- Benefits obtained from financial inclusion;
- Reason for financial exclusion;
- Perception towards financial inclusion;
- Expected assistance from the government.

Measures Taken For Financial Inclusion

Services	*Yes*	*No*
No frills account	31(62 per cent)	19(38 per cent)
Core banking	41(84 per cent)	8(16 per cent)
E-banking	25(50 per cent)	25(50 per cent)
Mobile banking	25(50 per cent)	25(50 per cent)
Issue of Kissan credit card	15(30 per cent)	35(70 per cent)
Biometric ATM	-	50(100 per cent)
Bancassurance	31(62 per cent)	19(38 per cent)
Microfinance	30(60 per cent)	20(40 per cent)
Trading of shares	31(62 per cent)	19(38 per cent)
Ties up with NGOs	17(34 per cent)	33(66 per cent)
Advertisement for financial inclusion	20(40 per cent)	30(60 per cent)
Business correspondent model (Smart card system)	16(32 per cent)	34(68 per cent)
Financial Literacy and Counseling Centre (FLCC)	10(20 per cent)	40(80 per cent)

Table 2 depicts that 62 per cent of the banks have offered no-frills accounts, bancassurance, trading of shares and the remaining 38 per cent of the banks have not offered such services. 84 per cent of the banks are offering core banking service and the remaining 16 per cent of the banks are not offering core banking service. 50 per cent of the banks have offered e-banking, mobile banking service and the remaining 50 per cent of the banks have not offered such services. 70 per cent of the banks have not issued Kissan credit card and the remaining 30 per cent of the banks have issued Kissan credit card to the farmers. No bank has offered Biometric ATM facility to the customers. 60 per cent of the banks have offered microfinance and the remaining 40 per cent of the banks have not offered microfinance to the vulnerable people. 66 per cent of the banks have not tied up with NGOs and the remaining 34 per cent of the banks have been tied up with NGOs to disseminate their service. 60 per cent of the banks have not given advertisement for financial inclusion and the left over 40 per cent of the banks have given advertisement for financial inclusion. 68 per cent of the banks have not preferred business correspondent and the rest 32 per cent of the banks have preferred business correspondent. 80 per cent of the banks have not established financial literacy and counselling centre and the remaining 20 per cent of the banks have established financial literacy and counselling centre to educate the customers.

Suggestions

The following are the suggestions recommended from this study to various beneficiaries like Banks and the Government.

To the Banks: The banks should offer all forms in the regional language of the customers. The banks must create awareness among the people concerning the significance of banking services by advertisement and financial inclusion campaign. ATMs are one of the most cost effective ways of reaching the rural poor. Thus, new biometric ATMs have to be established to assist the customers who are unable to memorize PIN. The banks should constitute Grievance Redressal Machinery to redress the customer's discontent promptly. And also it should offer no-frills account in order to turn unbankable into bankable.

To the Government: The government should include financial literacy in the curriculum of schools and colleges. The government should also raise the Financial Inclusion Fund and a Financial Inclusion Technology Fund to reach banking services to the unbanked areas. The government should pay all the social security payments through the bank account of the beneficiary.

Conclusion

Financial inclusion becomes a major prerequisite to poverty alleviation. Reserve Bank of India's vision for 2020 is to open nearly 600 million new customers' accounts and service them through a variety of channels by leveraging on information technology. However, the improper repayment need for additional workforce, time consumption, high cost and illiteracy are continuing to be a road block to financial inclusion in many areas. Consequently, many banks are not adopting fully fledged financial inclusion plan. The banks should step up to overwhelm all these problems and to disseminate its service to remote areas. The banks should encourage the people to access banking services by ways of no-frills account, financial inclusion campaign and business correspondent. The government should encourage the banks to adopt financial inclusion by means of financial assistance, advertisement and awareness programme etc. to achieve the aim of 12th plan of Inclusive Growth.

Inclusive economic growth has been one of the priority agendas of the Government of India (GOI) over the past decade. It is widely acknowledged that inclusive economic growth cannot be accomplished without achieving financial inclusion for the nearly two-thirds of India's population who are unbanked. FI is the road that India needs to travel toward becoming a global player. Financial access will attract global market players to our country and that will result in increasing employment and business opportunities. Inclusive growth will act as a source of empowerment and allow people to participate more effectively in the economic and social process. It is evident from the data given above and the RBI annual report that even though various measures have been taken and more flow of credit to various sector of the economy, still majority of the population in rural areas have not come under the concept of financial inclusion. The Government of India and Banks functioning in India have to play a major role in imparting financial literacy to include the excluded.

REFERENCES

1. Narendra, M (2011), "Financial Inclusion Gains Urgency", the Hindu Survey of Indian Industry.
2. Raj Kapila, and Uma Kapila, (Eds.) (2008), "Inclusive Growth: The Role of Banks in Emerging Economies", Economic Developments in India, Academic Foundation.
3. Sendhilvelan, M., and Karthikeyan, K., (2006), "No Frills Account: A Basic Drive for Financial Inclusion", Southern Economist, Vol. 45.
4. Subhash Narayan, (2011), "Fund to Boost Financial Inclusion in the Works".
5. Nageswara Rao (2010), Financial Inclusion - Banker's Perspective. The Journal of Indian Institute of Banking & Finance, October –December.
6. Suresh Chandra Bihari (2010), Financial Literacy - The Key to Financial Deepening, The Journal of Indian Institute of Banking & Finance, October–December.
7. The international journal RJCBS: Volume: 01, Number: 04, Feb-2012.
8. Chakraborty, K.C. (2011), "Financial Inclusion and Banks: Issues and Perspectives" Address delivered at the FICCI – UNDP Seminar on "Financial Inclusion: Partnership between Banks, MFIs and Communities" at New Delhi on October 14, 2011.

14

An Empirical Analysis of Micro Finance And Inclusive Growth in India

Shashirekha K. R. and Harshadhar G.

Abstract: *Microfinance has implicit a huge importance throughout the national and international position in sight of its efficacy in credit dispensation, loan repayment, looking for sustainability and reduction of poverty. The experience world over has proved that hassle free and repetitive amount of credit is the basic need of the poor which has become the hallmark of microfinance. In the Indian perspective, the microfinance sector has witnessed a unique growth in the last few years and has firmly established itself as significant potential contributor in the government's agenda of "Financial Inclusion". Microfinance aims at providing broad range of financial services such as deposits, loans, payment services, money transfers, insurance to poor and low-income households and their micro enterprises to arrive the target of an inclusive growth. India has the potential of becoming a leading economy and has the unique opportunity to make that growth inclusive, provided there is willingness on the part of all sections of society to put in hard and disciplined work, together with serious, sustained and purposeful planning. Microfinance is being hailed as a sustainable tool to battle poverty, combining a for-profit approach that is self-sustaining and a poverty alleviation focus that* *empowers low-income households. Microfinance helps to achieve inclusive growth in the path of sustainable development.*

Keywords: Microfinance, Inclusive growth, Enterprises, Eco–social, Comprehensive.

Introduction

Microfinance plays an appreciative role with the help of government and NGO to reduce the poverty level in India. Providing access to the microfinance can prove to be an effective way of reaching the poor and improving their lives. Microfinance is creature sleeted as a sustainable tool to struggle against the poverty, combining for profit approach that is self-sustaining and a poverty alleviation focus that empowers low-income households. Microfinance is increasingly becoming a tool to exercise developmental priorities for governments in developing countries like India. In order to ensure that the poorest benefit from growth and also contribute to it, the expansion and improvement of the microfinance sector should be a national priority.

The primary scheme of microfinance is simple: If poor people are provided access to financial services, including credit, they may very well be able to start / expand a microenterprise that will allow them to break out of poverty. Hence, LEDGE WOOD says, Microfinance is a source that provisions of financial services like saving credit insurances and payment services to low income clients including the self employed. Regarding that, microfinance is a designed financed service for the micro enterprises helping them by running and expending business. There are two models of microfinance which are established in India: ***(a)*** Direct Financing Model / Micro Finance Institution Model. Here the bank lends money to an NGO. The NGO promotes and imparts training to the Self Help Groups and also gives credit to them.

SHG-Bank Linkage Model: Here SHGs act as a bridge between bankers and the grass root clients. Banks transfer funds to microfinance bodies that are responsible for disbursal and collection. The intermediation cost could be around six per cent of the loan value. The risk completely lies with the banks. The advances to the SHGs would be reflected in the portfolios of the banks. Banks do not mind taking the risk as servicing the grass-root level customers who are illiterate would otherwise involve a lot of transaction cost. A majority of these grass-root level customers have no means to produce ration card, identity card and even filling up request forms, which are the bare necessities to obtain loans in the normal course of bank lending operations. NABARD oversees the linking programme of banks to SHGs and offers refinance for it whereas SIDBI, through the SIDBI base for micro-credit (SFMC) lends to Microfinance Institutions. The Self-Help and Group-Bank Linkage Programme implemented by commercial banks, Regional Rural Banks and Co-operative banks has emerged as a major micro finance programme in India.

An Overview of Micro Finance

Microfinance refers to the provision of financial services to the poor, low income clients, including consumers and the self employed. More broadly, it conveys to a movement that envisions a world in which as many poor and near poor households as possible have permanent access to an appropriate range of high quality financial services, with not just credit but also savings, insurance and fund transfers. Microfinance can be defined as small loans that help poor who wish to start / expand their small businesses but are not able to get banks to lend to them. Microcredit is the extension of small loans to entrepreneurs too poor to qualify for traditional bank loans. It is helping millions of poor people, especially poor rural women; with tiny loans so they can start small, create self employment and improve their lives.

The Microfinance supplies the loans, savings, and other basic financial services to the poor people who suffering in poverty, like they need a diverse range of financial instruments to run their businesses, build assets, stabilise consumption and shield themselves against risks. Financial services needed by the poor include working capital loans, consumer credit, savings, pensions, and insurance and money transfer services. Microfinance aims at providing broad range of financial services such as deposits, credits, payment services, money transfers, insurance to poor and low-income households and their microenterprises. Accordingly all these things microfinance has their own professional role, those are:

- Credit to Rural Poor
- Poverty Alleviation
- Improve the Conduction of Women Empowerment
- Struggling for Economic Growth
- Mobilisation of Savings
- Development of Life Skills
- Improving in Mutual Help and Cooperation
- Looking for Social Welfare
- Accomplish the Sustainable Development

History of Micro Finance in India

Microfinance in India started in 1974 at Gujarat with SEWA (Self Employed Women's Association) Sahakari Bank. Latter on Microfinance arrives is the result of NABARD's work in the micro finance sector, which started in 1992 through a pilot project for promoting 500 self help groups (SHGs). As the idea gained acceptance from the banking system and the results were promising, the Reserve Bank of India (RBI) encouraged this positive initiative by issuing instructions to banks in 1996 to cover SHG financing as a mainstream activity under their priority sector–lending collection.

From 1999 onwards the Government of India made linking SHGs with banks a national priority through its periodic policy and budget announcements. Today, the programme is growing at a speed of about 2.5 million households annually. It is the largest and fastest growing microfinance programme in the world in terms of its outreach and sustainability.

Comprehensive Growth of Microfinance in India

During the 1960s and 1970s the key issue in agriculture and rural development was agricultural production. Apart from improved seeds and seedlings, fertiliser, pesticides, tools and machines agricultural credit was an input for improved agricultural production. The target groups were farmers and the issue was how to disburse agricultural credit to farmers. The funds were provided by the governments and donors. The main disbursement channels were agricultural development banks and projects. Agricultural credit was a service, not a business. The strategy had much to show: the green revolution, driven by technology, financed on credit, with subsidized interest rates. The produce was purchased by government at guaranteed prices. So green revolution succeeded thereby ignoring the business of the financial services. But when farmers didn't repay their loans, the banks didn't cover their costs and the governments ran out of money to finance the subsidies, the banking business finally failed and so did the service. Meanwhile, with the rapidly growing population, increasing numbers of rural people could not live on agriculture alone.

To survive they had to engage in numerous activities such as on-farm, off-farm and non-farm activities. Rural households and rural economies got increasingly diversified. Access to finance was the limiting factor. Agricultural credit had been exclusive. It excluded all those who didn't own and cultivate the land. In addition to this, labourers, small and micro-entrepreneurs, traders, women and large numbers of small-holders were too poor to pay the bribes and also too uneducated to do the paperwork. The unsatisfied demand prepared the ground for a revolution on the supply side and microfinance took its birth. Perhaps this might have been called the 'Blue Revolution', the blue being the bankers' colour. The new emerging issue was to link microfinance to rural entrepreneurs through inclusive financial systems development.

Due to the overall failure of capital transfer and government-directed credit during the 1960s and 1970s, the emphasis on development policy shifted from targeting bigger farmers and SMEs to inclusive finance, including micro-entrepreneurs, women and the poorer segments of the population; from the development banks and subsequently from credit Non-Governmental Organisations to rural financial system development with a conducive policy framework and the building of self-reliant, sustainable institutions; in rural areas from agricultural credit to rural financial services for a diversified economy; and from development banking to microfinance.

Microfinance through SHGs has become a ladder for the poor to bring them up not only economically but also morally, socially and culturally. Initially, SHGs and microfinance, as the instrument for social and economic empowerment, were established by the non-governmental organisations. In the period of 21st century, NGOs have been transformed them selved from non-profit to profit making business models. Especially, the success formula of microfinance not for profit model has been learned from the concepts of PRODEM of Bolivia and Grameen Bank of Bangladesh. It has been proved that committed for the social development, NGOs can develop the society through providing finance accessibility to the poor based on self-help model. Many NGOs in India came forward to promote microfinance. At present more than 1000 NGOs are implementing micro-finance projects in India.

Objectives of the Study

The major and specific objectives of the present study shall be:

- To study the overviews and history of microfinance in India.
- To examine the comprehensive growth of microfinance in India.
- To evaluate the problems and challenges in front of an inclusive growth in India.

Hypotheses

The following tentative hypotheses will be framed to meet the objective of the study.

- Microfinance devotes their presence to concentrate for inclusive growth and eco–social welfare.
- Microfinance's economic and commercial activaties are always correlates with the inclusive growth and sustainable development of the nation.

Methodology

The methodology is very essential to construct the research work. Both qualitative and quantitative methods were used for the study. The article has required secondary data. Secondary data has been gathered from published sources such as various journals, periodicals, articles, books, literatures, reports and projects on the subject. For the purpose of gathering the latest updated information on the topic E–sources has also consulted.

Requirements of Inclusive Growth in India

Inclusive growth is necessary for sustainable development and equitable distribution of wealth and prosperity. Achieving inclusive growth is the biggest challenge in a country like India. As democratic country, India bringing 600 million people living in rural into the mainstream is the biggest concern. The challenge is to take the levels of growth to all section of the society and to all parts of the country. The best way to achieve inclusive growth is through the developing life skills. Mr. Jeffrey, Chairman and CEO of Manpower Planning, USA, said that, a multifaceted approach towards education and skills development is necessary to achieve grow. He said the challenge of skills shortage can be addressed through public-private partnership. Since independence, significant improvement in India's economic and social development made the nation to grow strongly in the 21st century. The following factors encouraged our India to concentrate more on inclusive growth.

- India is the 7th largest country by area and 2nd by population. Approximately, it is the 12th largest economy at market exchange rate. Yet, India is far away from the development of the neighbourhood nation, which means China.
- The exclusion in terms of low agriculture growth, low quality employment growth, low human development, rural-urban divides, gender and social inequalities, and regional disparities etc. are the problems for the nation.
- Reduction of poverty and other disparities and rising of economic growth are the key objectives of the nation through inclusive growth.

- Studies estimated that the cost of corruption in India amounts to over 10 per cent of GDP. Corruption is one of the ills that prevent inclusive growth.
- Although child labour has been banned by the law in India and there are stringent provisions to deter this inhuman practice. Still, many children in some limited area are unaware of education as their lives are spoiled to labour work.
- Literacy levels have to rise to provide the skilled workforce required for higher growth.
- Achievement of nine per cent of GDP growth for country as a whole is one of the boosting factor which gives the importance to the Inclusive Growth in India.
- Inclusiveness benchmarked against achievement of monitorable targets related to (i) Income and Poverty, (ii) education, (iii) health, (iv) women and children, (v) infrastructure, (vi) environment.
- Even at international level also, there is a concern about inequalities and exclusion and now they are also taking about inclusive approach for development.

Problems relating to Inclusive Growth Strategies in India

For a developing nation like India, there is a need of inclusive growth be vital to achieve the overall progress of the country. Though it is positive for macro-economic stability, 2008-09 effected a relative growth slowdown, mostly from the spillover effects of the weakening of the global economic momentum and volatile financial markets. The following problems are the major concerns for developing countries like India to achieve the inclusive growth. They are:

(a) Poverty;
(b) Unemployment and
(c) Agricultural Risks.

Traditionally, India is considered as the agricultural-based country. As the majority of Indians are engaged in agriculture for employment, the recent developments in the other sectors decreased this major sector's growth. Some of the problems in Indian agriculture are:

- Long term factors like steeper decline in per capita land availability, shrinking of farm size.
- Slow reduction in share of employment.
- Low labour productivity in agriculture and the gap between agriculture and non-agriculture is widening.
- Decline in yield growth due to land, water and power problems, vulnerability to world commodity prices, farmer's suicides.

- Disparities in growth across regions and crops, which means growth rate declined more in rain fed areas.

Thus these problems became the hurdles in the key area for the economic development of the nation, that is to say agriculture.

Problems in Social Development

Social development is also one of the key concerns in inclusive growth. The social development became the hot criteria in the recent past in India. Social development is also facing some difficulties, which is making the path critical to inclusive growth in the country. Some of the problems in social sector are:

- Significant regional, social and gender disparities.
- Low level and slow growth in public concerns particularly in employment opportunities and emergencies.
- Deprived quality delivery systems.
- Achievement of 119th rank among 170 countries on Human Development Index.
- Social indicators are lower for scheduled castes and scheduled tribes.
- Malnutrition among children is one major problem.
- Social advancements in India are still at substandard growth due to the strong influence of culture disparities.

Regional Disparities

These are all the main visible problems which are affecting for the India as a big task to achieve the inclusive growth.

Challenges before Inclusive Growth Strategies in India

The key components of the inclusive growth strategy included a sharp increase in investment in rural areas, rural infrastructure and agriculture spurt in credit for farmers; increase in rural employment through a unique social safety net and sharp increase in public spending on education and health care. The government also should exit for a variety of legislative interventions to empower the disadvantaged. Some of the challenges and opportunities before inclusive growth strategies in India are:

- **Poverty alleviation** is one of the big challenges for India. Eradication of poverty in India is generally only considered to be a long-term goal. Poverty alleviation is expected to make better progress in the next 50 years than in the past, as a trickle-down effect of the growing middle class. Increasing stress on quality education, reservation of seats in government jobs and the increasing empowerment of women and the economically weaker sections of society, are also expected to contribute to the alleviation of poverty.

- For **agricultural growth**, the private players can participate in to bridge the gap including providing microfinance. Contract farming, setting up storage facilities for agro-produce, and producing them from farmers. The private sector could also develop heritage sites and tourist spots and encourage the promotion of traditional arts and crafts in joint ventures with rural enterprises. The Government of India should also increase its present moratorium on interest payments, lowering of farm credit rates for increase in agricultural growth.
- Government schemes should target eradication of both **social deficiency** and **unemployment** attempt to solve the problems by providing financial assistance for setting up businesses, skill honing, setting up public sector enterprises, reservations in governments, etc. The decreased role of the public sector after liberalisation has further underlined the need for focusing on better education and has also put political pressure on further reforms.
- **Child labour** is a difficult task that is basically rooted in poverty. The Indian government is implementing the world's largest child labour elimination programme, with primary education targeted for around 250 million. Numerous non-governmental and voluntary organisations are also involved. Special investigation cells have been set up in states to enforce existing laws banning employment of children under 14 in hazardous industries. The allocation of the Government of India for the eradication of child labour was $10 million in 1995-96 and $16 million in 1996-97. The allocation for 2007 is $21 million. Failure to implement the law and poor rehabilitation policies need urgent attention which is a big challenge for India to achieve inclusive growth.
- Social development is possible through achieving **Women Empowerment** and eradicating the **regional disparities**. Though the government is giving the women empowerment by benevolent special reservations and awareness programme. The women's progress in India is still not matched the prospect for inclusive growth. Presently, the women are committing with the top posts in India like President, Lok Sabha Speaker and Railway Minister etc.
- To bring in inclusive growth, it is necessary to enhance the capabilities of women by providing proper valuable education,

so that they will get an opportunity to occupy employment and be self sustainable.

The Government of India has stepped up for inclusive growth by launching many initiatives with features that are innovative, flexible and reform oriented such as:

(a) Rural Infrastructure (Bharat Nirman)
(b) Employment (Mahatma Gandhi National Rural Employment Guarantee Scheme)
(c) Regional Development (Backward District Development Programme)
(d) Education (Sarva Shiksha Abhiyan)
(e) Rural Health (National Rural Health Mission)
(f) Urban Infrastructure (National Urban Renewal Mission)

Findings

The major optimal issues and findings are as follows:

- Microfinance unswervingly contributes to improve the credits and national income.
- Microfinance is a best example for money circulation and commercial business.
- Inflation, deflation and depreciation are impacts for microfinance activities.
- Share markets and liquid moneys are correlated with microfinance.
- In sustainably developed nations microfinance are practicing in healthy position.

Suggestions

On the origin of our above study, the following suggestions are optional to attain of inclusive growth through the valuable assist of microfinance. Also these are all vital perception of microfinance for effective and sustainable expansion of the nation.

- Avoid black money and black marketing system to improve the conduction of microfinance.
- Educate and train the employs, subordinates and members of the microfinance.
- Coordinate the microfinance groups to concentrate the well being for inclusive growth and sustainable development.
- Motivate the microfinance group members to serve for the socialistic economic.

- Aware the microfinance organisation as skilled advanced and well civilised to improve our national economic condition.

Conclusion

Microfinance involves in assortment of services that is saving, credit, finance, money transfers, from the over initiative. It is clear that microfinance has an important role to recompense in favour of inclusive growth. Moreover microfinance is undoubtedly the most visible innovation in anti-poverty policy in the last half century as what we have sighted. The major benefit of microfinance projects and schemes is that it allows low income families to save their money. Microfinance helps the poor people to get access / save funds over a period of time with low interest rates. Also the poor could solve their own issues by working together as a community and it creates trust and social capital in their communities. It also leads to stability and growth in their households. So consequently all these things microfinance motivates the inclusive growth in respective manner for the nation.

REFERENCES

1. Morduch Jonathan, "The Microfinance Promise", Journal of Economic Literature Vol. XXXVII, (December 1999).
2. Campion, Anita and Sahra Halpern, "Automating Microfinance", Occasional Paper No. 5, Microfinance Network, Washington, DC, (2001).
3. Ravikumar and B. Ratna, "A Primer on Micro Finance – The Paradox of Plenty in Poverty", The Chartered Accountant, (May 2006).
4. Santosh Ranganath N and Prakash Babu B, "Inclusive Growth in India: The Role of Financial Sector, Inclusive Economic Growth in India: Issues, Challenges and Implications", ValarPirai Publication Pvt. Ltd., Chennai, (2011); pp. 872–875.
5. Jeet Singh and Preeti Yadav, "Micro Finance as A Tool for Financial Inclusion & Reduction of Poverty" Journal of Business Management & Social Sciences Research (JBM&SSR) ISSN No. 2319-5614 Volume 1, No. 1, (October 2012); PP. 02–13.
6. Manmohan Mall and P K Mishra, "Micro Credit for Sustainable Development: Role of NGOs", International Journal of Management and Social Sciences Research (IJMSSR) ISSN: 2319-4421 Volume 2, International Research Journal Consortium, (April 2013); pp. 05–09.
7. N. Santosh Ranganath and Prof. G. Tulasi Rao, "Inclusive Growth and Sustainability: Role of Banking Sector in India", International Journal of Research in Advent Technology, Volume 1, Issue – 5, (December 2013); pp. 04–12.

8. Gurushree College of Commerce of Social Work, "Emerging Trends in Microfinance and Sustainable Social Development", Proceeding of National Conference on Role of Microfinance in Sustainable Social Development, (15th March 2014); pp. 233–237.
9. http://www.ijrat.org
10. http://www.irjcjournals.org
11. http://www.mfinindia.org

PART—II
MICROFINANCE AND WOMEN EMPOWERMENT

15

Microfinance And Women's Empowerment—Issues and Challenges

Pavithra R.H. and Ramananda M.S.

Abstract: *Women Entrepreneurs plays an important role in boosting the Indian economy system. The development of the business sector may be an indicator of a predictable legal structure and a prosperous economy. Entrepreneurship development for women is an important factor in economic development of India. Women entrepreneurs in India are handicapped in the matter of organizing and running business on account of their generally low levels of skills and for want of support system. The transition from homemaker to sophisticated business woman is not that easy. But the trend is changing. Women across India are showing an interest to be economically independent. Women are coming forth to the business arena with ideas to start small and medium enterprises. They are willing to be inspired by role models the experience of other women in the business arena.*

Microfinance is emerging as a powerful instrument for poverty alleviation, employment generation and empowerment of womenfolk. In India Microfinance for women is mainly empowering than the individual lending. Many successful women forums and organisations are trying to bring rural women together for development of women folk like Working Women's Forum (WWF), Self-Employed Women's Association (SEWA), Shri Mahila Griha Udyog, Mhaswad, Maharashtra etc.

Keywords: Microfinance, Empowerment, Women Entrepreneurs.

Introduction

Women play a decisive role in the process of moving their families out of poverty. Around 30 per cent to the rural Indian households are estimated as headed by women. Even when there is a male earner, woman's earning forms a significant part of the income of the poor household. Yet they remain as most vulnerable, marginalised and excluded from the mainstream of the society. In spite, her contribution not being measured she continues to do her best in contributing herself to the nation through the family. "Perhaps one would call her the unsung heroine of our country who without any glare of publicity contributes her best to the progress of country" (Amarjit Kaur, 1989). Even though half of India's population consists of women, they are subjected to all kinds of domination. It is only after the international year of women (1975) government paid focused attention to integrate them into national planning and progress by striving to have a closer look at their problems and potentialities. The early planning was oriented towards the welfare, from 70's there was a shift from welfare to development. In 1980's government of India laid stress on family welfare and social uplift. During the 1990's more importance was given to political empowerment and now it is economic empowerment.

Women Entrepreneurs plays an important role in boosting the Indian economy system. The development of the business sector may be an indicator of a predictable legal structure and a prosperous economy. Microfinance is an efficient tool to fight against poverty, but also as a means of promoting the empowerment of the most marginalised sections of the population, especially women. Entrepreneurship is a form of human resource and entrepreneurial behaviour depends on a number of factors like skill, knowledge of the enterprise, risk taking ability, achievement motivation, exposure to mass media, trainings received, and moreover, with innovativeness of the entrepreneur. Entrepreneurial behaviour can be attributed as the change in knowledge, skills and attitude of entrepreneurs in the enterprise they have taken up. Women have been starting businesses at a higher rate than men for the last 20 years and tend to create home-based micro (less than five employees) and small businesses. Women will create over half of the 9.72 million new small business jobs expected to be created by 2018 and more and more are doing this from home offices across the country. It's a surprising statistic, especially considering that women-owned businesses only created 16 per cent of total U.S. jobs that existed in 2010.

There is evidence of significant potential for micro-finance to enable women to challenge and change gender inequalities at all levels if there is a strategic gender focus. There have also been many important recent innovations in products and services to enable women to better benefit. Nevertheless benefits cannot be assumed and even financially sustainable micro-finance if it is gender blind, it may seriously disempower women and increase inequality. These are: (i) official definition of microfinance, (ii) ensuring the microfinance services, (iii) approach to subsidy, (iv) banking policies, (v) management information system and (vi) legislation processes.

Today's women are taking more and more professional and technical degrees to cope up with market need and are flourishing as designers, interior decorators, exporters, publishers, garment manufacturers and still exploring new avenues of economic participation. It is perhaps for these reasons that Government Bodies, NGO's, Social Scientists, Researchers and International Agencies have started showing interest in the issues related to entrepreneurship among women in India. Women Entrepreneurs may be defined as the women or group of women who initiate, organise and co-operate a business enterprise. Government of India has defined women entrepreneurs as an enterprise owned and controlled by a woman having a minimum financial interest of 51 per cent of the capital and giving.

Empowerment of Women

In India, females head only ten per cent of the total households and the ownership of land and other properties are mainly in the name of the male members of the family. Hence, women have hardly any ownership of resources and autonomy to take decision.

However, the participation of women in income generating activities of the family has been increasing over time. Female work participation not only increases their family income but also brings economic independence among women in the household. This helps them to participate more effectively in intra-household decision-making and have better access to information. Moreover, where women are economically active, female children are perceived as potential wage earners and they receive a higher share of household resources than where women are economically unproductive. But female work participation alone cannot ensure true economic empowerment as the ownership of resources may still lie in the hands of the male members. Thus, female work participation rate is a necessary condition but is not a sufficient condition for economic empowerment of women. Economic empowerment of women is possible only when women have full autonomy to spend their income and also control resource.

Entrepreneurship development among women can be considered a possible approach to economic empowerment of women. A woman as an entrepreneur is economically more powerful than as a mere worker because ownership not only confers control over assets (and liabilities) but also gives her the freedom to take decisions. This will also uplift her social status significantly. Through entrepreneurship development a woman will not only generate income for herself but also will generate employment for other women in the locality. This will act as an employment in the women sector.

Women Entrepreneurs

In India, very few women entrepreneurs are in the big enterprises. They are mainly concentrated in the Small Scale Industries (SSIs). In the SSI sector the participation of women can be classified into three types.

- Women as the owners of enterprises.
- Women as managers of enterprises, and
- Women as employees.

With regard to ownership an SSI managed by one or more women entrepreneurs in propriety concerns or in which she/they individually or jointly have a share capital of not less than 51 per cent as partners/ shareholders/Directors of Private Limited Company/Member of Cooperative Society is called a women enterprise. The share of the units managed by women in terms of employment was 7.14. The employment generated per Rs one lakh investment is the units managed by women was 2.49.

Women in India are still less likely to start a new business than men, although the gap seems to be declining. The share of female entrepreneurs (10 per cent) is still significantly low when compared to their work participation rate (25.7 per cent. Hence, it is very important to know the impediment to growth of women entrepreneurship.

Women Entrepreneurship: Indian scenario

Traditionaly it was believed that women are physically and mentally weak and, hence, they are not fit for hard, hazardous and risky tasks. But with the increasing empowerment of women in the world, now no job, profession or enterprise is such which women cannot undertake. Contrary to it, it can be observed that in oriental societies the women are born- risk seekers. They grow up with the feeling of management of risk and adjustment/adaptation with the changing environment they have to take care of kids, the house and related and activities. It has also been observed that women are most passionate and reliable agents of development if they are supported by capital and opportunities. This is the assumption by which micro finance has started with the extension of small loans to groups of women; too poor to qualify for bank loans. Micro-credit programmes have brought the vibrancy of the market economy to the poorest villages and the people of the World" says World Bank President, James D.Walfensohn while Prof. M. Yunus, founder of Grameen Bank, remarked, "Micro-credit helps to create self-employment and put the poor, particularly women in the drivers' seat." Thereby Self-help-groups are seen as viable vehicle of empowering women through micro credit and facilities offered through this forum.

SHG movement was sown in Indian soil way back in the 1970's as a small effort by the foreseeing people and organisations. The projection was that the development of marginalised and less privileged 'could be achieved through their own support and involvement. Hence they are called SHGs. SHG is a voluntary association of persons with common interests. Such groups are organised for mutual help and benefit.

They come together for the purpose of solving their common problems through self help and mutual trust. These groups inculcate the habit of thrift among the members. They also mobilise the small saving from the members of group. These groups advance loans to the needy members. ·Today they are considered as effective instruments of rural development. These groups help in creating a self-dependency and self-sufficiency among the members. It has been realised that an effective way to tackle poverty and to enable community to improve the quality of it through social mobilisation of disadvantaged people. The concept of SHG is based on the idea of community participation, as sustainable community development requires the active participation of the entire community. The NABARD has recognised the importance of SGH's and has initiated the SGH-bank linkage programme, which has emerged as the largest microfinance programme in the world.

Micro Finance

Microfinance can be considered as a pro-poor credit access method as against the formal financial institutions, who pose several practical difficulties to the poor to access credit, very specially women. The microcredit summit 2007 defines micro credit as the extension of small loans to very poor people for self-employment projects that generate income and allow them to take care of their families. This has proved as an effective and popular measure in the on-going struggle against poverty, enabling the poor who do not access to lending institution at affordable cost to start any economic activity. Therefore the prime objective is to alleviate poverty through extended access to finance.

The defining criteria used include:

1. *Size*: they are very small in size micro loans.
2. *Target user*: micro entrepreneurs and low income house-holds
3. *Utilisation*: the use of fund is mainly for income generating activities and enterprise development and community use (productive purpose).
4. *Terms and conditions*: are flexible easy to understand and suited for local conditions of the community.

Hence micro finance is financial service of small quantity provided by the financial institutions to the poor. These financial services may include thrift savings, credit and insurance etc., i.e., any financial service provided to meet the financial needs with the rider that (i) the transaction value is very small and (ii) customers are 'poor'; micro credit as a tool of poverty alleviation and empowerment has gained credence in development dialogue the world over. Provision of credit requires initiatives from the government as well as non-government organisations in making available smaller amounts of credit to the Poor clients without any collateral security on loans and with shorter repayment periods and amounts. The Poor need credit for small productive assets, working capital, housing and money to meet illness and emergencies. The demand for credit here is not only large but also heterogeneous as well.

Micro Credit in India

In India the major objective of nationalisation of banks was to improve the flow of credit to the poor households. Priority sector lending was one of the most important goals. In spite having large network of banks they were not able to connect to the poor and large number of poor remained outside the purview of banking system and continued to be exploited by the money lenders. The meagre impact of various programmes for the uplift of the poor is because subsidised credit is not effectively reaching the poor. The results indicated that the poor need small and frequent doses of credit for consumption and emergency purposes. In response to this, the NABARD sponsored a research programme through an NGO namely, MYRAQA. Encouraged by the results of the group-based approach for lending to the poor, the NABARD in1992 launched a pilot project linking SHGs with Banks. This could be considered as a landmark development in the history of micro-finance for the poor in the country. Micro credit in India is largely linked with Self-help groups. It has made remarkable advancement in India is considered as the largest micro finance programme in terms of outreach in the world. This rapid growth process has a boost to the rural poor particularly women to reach reasonable economic, social and political empowerment leading to a better life. It has given poor in India specially women, an opportunity to become agents of change. Table 1 depicts the cumulative progress of SHG's and the bank loans over the years. We observe a rapid growth in the formation of SHG's as well as in the bank loans every year. As on 31st March 2010, there were more than 77 lakh saving-linked SHG's and more than 42 lakh credit-linked SHG's covering about 8.6 crore poor households under the programme.

Table 1: SHGs and Bank Loan (Rs. in crores)

Year	*No. of SHG's Linked*		*Bank Loan*	
	During the year	*Cumulative*	*During the year*	*Cumulative*
1992-93	255	255	0.29	0.29
1993-94	365	620	0.36	0.65
1994-95	1502	2122	1079	2044
1995-96	2635	4757	3.62	6.06
1996-97	3841	8598	5.78	11084
1997-98	5719	14317	11.92	23.76
1998-99	18678	32995	33.31	57.07
1999-00	81780	114775	135.91	192.98
2000-01	149050	263825	287.89	480.87
2001-02	197653	461478	545.47	1026.34
2002-03	255882	717360	1022.33	2048.67
2003-04	361731	1079091	1855.53	3904.2
2004-05	539365	1618456	2994.26	6898.46
2005-06	620109	2238565	4499	13397.46
2006-07	1105749	3344314	6570	199967.46
2007-08	1227770	4572084	8849.26	208816.72
2008-09	1609586	6181670	-	-
2009-2010	1586822	7768492	-	-

Source: NABARD, Status of Microfinance in India, 2008-09.

Objectives and Research Methodology

The study is based on secondary data which is collected from the published reports of RBI, CMIE, Economic Surveys, newspapers, journals, websites, etc. The study was planned with the following objectives:

(i) To provide a national networking forum for women in business that will support them in starting and growing their businesses.

(ii) To identify problems unique to women in setting up and running their enterprises.
(iii) To suggest certain remedial measures to solve the problems of Women Entrepreneurship in Indian Economy.
(iv) To study the policies, programmes, institutional networks and the involvement of support agencies in promoting women's entrepreneurship.

Women Entrepreneurship in India

Women have gradually been changing with the sensitivity to their role and economic status in the society. Women are increasingly being conscious of their existence, their rights, and work situation. However, the position of women work participation as well as both is low in India in comparison to selected countries of the world. Women work participation in India is 31.6 per cent where as in USA it is 45 per cent, UK 43 per cent, Canada 42 per cent, France 32 per cent, Indonesia 40 per cent, Sri lanka and Brazil both 35% Table 1 refers women entrepreneurship position in the selected states of India is 30 per cent on an average, but in Bihar it is only 15.04 per cent. Further, in India, men generally take the lead in the entrepreneurial world. With the change of time as well as cultural norms, and increase in literacy, women are increasingly ready to enter the field of entrepreneurship.

(i) Women entrepreneur is a person who accepts challenging role to meet her personal need and become economically independent. There are economic, social, religious, cultural and other factors existing in the society which responsible for the emergency of the entrepreneurs.
(ii) "Women entrepreneur refers equally to someone who has started a one women business to someone who is a principal in family business or partnership or to someone who is shareholder in a public company which she runs".

Table 1: State-wise Distribution of Women Enterprises in 2011

States	*No. of Units Registered*	*No. of Women Entrepreneurs*	*Percentage*
Tamil Nadu	9618	2930	30.36
Uttar Pradesh	7980	3180	39.84
Kerala	5487	2135	38.91
Punjab	4791	1618	33.77
Maharashtra	4339	1394	32.12
Gujarat	3872	1538	39.72
Karnataka	3822	1026	26.84
Madhya Pradesh	2967	842	28.38
Bihar	7344	1123	15.04
Other States & UTs	14576	4185	28.71
Total	64,796	19,971	32.82

Source: CMIE Report – 2011.

Challenges faced by Women Entrepreneurs

While empowering women entrepreneurs faced the following problems. Women Entrepreneurs encounter two sets of problems, i.e., general problems entrepreneurs and problems specific to women entrepreneurs. These are discussed follows.

(a) Male-dominated Society

The greatest deterrent to women entrepreneurs is that they are women. The Constitution of India speaks about the equality between both the sexes, i.e., men and women. But in practice, women are looked upon *as "abala"*, i.e. weak, in all respects. In the male-dominated Indian society, women are not treated equal to men. This serves as a barrier against women's entry into business.

(b) Problem of Finances Arrangement

The women entrepreneurs are suffering from, inadequate financial resources and working capital. The women entrepreneurs lack access to external funds due to their inability to provide tangible security. Very few women have the tangible property in hand. Women entrepreneurs suffer from shortage of finance on two counts: (i) women do not generally have property on their own names to use that as collateral security for obtaining loans from banks and other financial institutions. Thus their access to external sources is very limited. (ii) banks also consider women less credit-worthy and discourage women borrowers on the belief that they cannot repay the amount of loans taken by them.

(c) Scarcity of raw materials required for productive capacities

Most of the women enterprises are plagued by the scarcity of raw materials and necessary inputs. Knowledge of alternative source of raw materials availability and high negotiation skills are the basic requirement to run a business. Getting the raw materials from different source with discount prices is the factor that determines the profit margin. Lack of knowledge of availability of the raw materials and low-level negotiation and bargaining skills are the factors, which affect women entrepreneur's business adventures.

(d) Market-oriented Risks

A number of women have to face the challenges of market because of stiff competition. Many business women find it difficult to capture the market and compete with their product. They are not fully aware of the changing market conditions.

(e) Stiff competition with men and established self-sufficient entrepreneurs

Women entrepreneurs do not have a proper organisational set-up to pump in a lot of money for canvassing and advertisements. Thus, they have to face a stiff competition with the men entrepreneurs who easily involve in the promotion and development area and carry out easy marketing of their products with both the organised sector and their male counterparts. Such a competition ultimately results in the liquidation of women entrepreneurs.

(f) Lesser-risk and uncertainty-bearing Tendency

Women in India lead a protected life. They are neither even less educated and economically nether stable nor self-dependent. All these factors reduce their ability to bear risks and uncertainties involved in a business unit, which is the most important criterion for survival in every business activity.

Women in India have done very well for themselves and the country. Indra Nooyi –Chairman and Chief Executive Officer of PepsiCo, is the most well-known face amongst Indian businesswomen, HP Managing Director Neelam Dhawan, ICICI Bank Limited Managing Director and CEO Chanda Kochhar and IBM India CMO Virginia Sharma are just a few examples that exemplify the strength of Indian women.

While there are women who have become successful businesswomen and role models for the Indian Industry, there are others including Ekta Kapoor who changed the face of Indian television, Neeta Lulla who is an Indian fashion stylist and made a mark for herself in the fashion industry and Shahnaz Husain, one of the most prominent Indian female entrepreneurs known for her herbal cosmetics and beauty products.

Table 2: Top 10 Women Entrepreneurs and Leaders of India for the year 2012

Sl. No.	*Name*	*Company*
1.	Chanda Kochhar	ICICI Bank
2.	Kiran M Shaw	Biocon
3.	Shobhana Bhartia	HT Media
4.	Shikha Sharma	Axis Bank
5.	Naina Lal Kidwai	HSBC India
6.	Kalpana Morparia	JP Morgan India
7.	Neelam Dhawan	Hewlett-Packard India
8.	Mallika Srinivasan	TAFE
9.	Preetha Reddy	Apollo Hospitals
10.	Roppa Kudva	CRISIL

Source: Women web 2012.

Conclusion

Women entrepreneurship must be moulded properly with entrepreneurial traits and skills to meet the changes in trends, challenges global markets and also be competent enough to sustain and strive for excellence in the entrepreneurial arena. Micro finance is playing a vital role in the success of SHGs; particularly the entry of rural women in micro enterprises will be encouraged and aggravated. Women are facing great challenges at the family, community and state levels, ranging from poverty, illiteracy, and irreligious patriarchy to socio-political exclusion. The government should embark on a comprehensive programme for local women, focusing on enhancing their capacity building and increasing their productivity. The rural women are having basic indigenous knowledge, skill, potential and resources to establish and manage enterprise. Now, what is the need is knowledge regarding accessibility to loans, various funding agencies procedure regarding certification, awareness on government welfare programmes, motivation, technical skill and support from family, government and other organisation. Some microfinance practitioners, community social workers, donor agencies and academic, alternative models of microfinance are needed in the near future to reduce poverty and increase women's empowerment. Capacity building involves more than simply stimulus assistance through microfinance.

REFERENCES

1. S. P. Gupta (2009), "Statistical methods", Thirty eight revised Editions, Sultan Chand & Sons, New Delhi.
2. C.R Kothari (2007), Research Methodology Methods and Techniques, Second Edition, and New Age International Publishers, New Delhi.
3. Manjula Bolthajjira Chengappa, "Micro-Finance and Women Empowerment: Role of Nongovernment Organizations" http://www.istr.org/Abstracts2010/pdf/ISTR2010_0212.pdf.
4. Rajendran N (2003), "Problems and prospects of women Entrepreneurs" SEDME.
5. Sharma, Sheetal (2006) "Educated Women, powered, women" Yojana, Vol. 50, No. 12.
6. www.ghallabhansali.com
7. www.icfaijournals.com

16

Empowerment Of Women Through Micro Finance—A Means of Achieving Gender-Related Human Development

Somashekaraiah N. T., and Mahendra Kumar

Abstract: *Micro finance is emerging as a powerful instrument for poverty alleviation in the new economy. In India, Microfinance scene is dominated by Self Help Group – Bank Linkage Programme as a cost effective mechanism for providing financial services to the unreached poor which has been successful not only in meeting financial needs of the rural poor women but also strengthen collective self help capacities of the poor, leading to their empowerment. Economic empowerment results in women's ability to influence or make decision, increased self confidence, better status and role in household etc. Micro finance is necessary to overcome exploitation, create confidence for economic self reliance of the rural poor, particularly among rural women who are mostly invisible in the social structure.*

National development could be achieved only by achieving the human development. Human development means improvement in the quality of life of people. Quality of life is determined by a number of factors like income, employment, education, good health including nutritious food etc. No human development could be achieved in rural India on sustainable basis until and unless its women fold are developed and empowered socially and economically. In this paper, an empowered woman is considered to be one who has made her life better by having access to and utilisation of resources provided by microfinance programme. She also exerts and participates in the household decision-making. She shows self-confidence and also participates in the democratic institutions in the rural area. She has general awareness of the existing social, economic and political environment. Hence, this paper puts forward how micro finance has received extensive recognition as a strategy for economic empowerment of women. This paper also seeks to assess the human development through empowerment of women.

Keywords: Microfinance, women's empowerment, human development.

Introduction

Microfinance is the provision of financial services to low-income clients, including consumers and the self-employed, who traditionally lack access to banking and related services. Microcredit, or microfinance, is banking the unbankables, bringing credit, savings and other essential financial services within the reach of millions of people who are too poor to be served – by regular banks, in most cases because they are unable to offer sufficient collateral. In general, ***"banks are for people with money, not for people without"*** is based on the premise that the poor have skills which remain unutilised or underutilized. Microcredit fits best to those with entrepreneurial capability and possibility. Ultimately, the goal of microfinance is to give low income people an opportunity to become self-sufficient by providing a means of saving money, borrowing money and insurance.

The main aim of microfinance is to empower women. Women make up a large proportion of microfinance beneficiaries. Traditionally, women (especially those in underdeveloped countries) have been unable to readily participate in economic activity. Microfinance provides women with the financial backing they need to start business ventures and actively participate in the economy. It gives them confidence, improves their status and makes them more active in decision-making, thus encouraging gender equality.

The most of the microcredit institutions and agencies all over the world focuses on women in developing countries. Observations and experience shows that women are a small credit risk, repaying their loans and tend more often to benefit the whole family. In another aspect it's also viewed as a method giving the women more status in a socioeconomic way and changing the current conservative relationship between gender and class when women are able to provide income to the household.

National development could be achieved only by achieving the human development. Human development means over all development of people to improve their quality of life. Quality of life is determined by number of factors like income, employment, education, good health including nutritious food etc. No human development could be achieved in rural India on sustainable basis until and unless its women fold are developed and empowered socially and economically. Women's development is directly related to human development. The effective management and development of interest, skills and other potentialities are of paramount importance. Women's development could be achieved by empowerment which enabled them to be the agents of social change. Organisational behaviour is the key to women's empowerment. Women's organisations in groups provide them a platform to discuss helplessness in their own society. In this process the women will not only identify their problems but also become aware of their innate capabilities in order to raise their status in the family and in the society.

Since the 1990's women have been identified as key agents of sustainable development and women's equality and empowerment are seen as central to a more holistic approach towards establishing new patterns and processes of development that are sustainable. The World Bank has suggested that empowerment of women should be a key aspect of all social development programmes (World Bank, 2001). Empowerment is a process of awareness and capacity building leading to greater participation, to greater decision-making power and control and to transformative action. Women's empowerment is defined as "women's ability to make strategic life choices where that ability had been previously denied them" (Kabeer 1999). Empowerment is midway in the change processes that benefit women at individual, household, community and broader levels. At the most basic level, innovations can benefit women simply by improving their well-being in terms of health, nutrition, income, life span, etc. Beyond vital improvements in well-being, changes can result in women's empowerment, where women gain agency and resources to make decisions, build confidence and act in their own interests. Deeper and truly transformative changes reshape societal norms, attitudes and institutional practices. Greater gender equality in markets, political institutions, family systems and social roles provide an ongoing foundation for sustaining women's well-being and empowerment.

Hence, this paper puts forward how micro finance has received extensive recognition as a strategy for economic empowerment of women. This paper also seeks to assess the human development through empowerment of women.

Review of Literature

Malhotra and Mather 1997; Kishor 1995 and 2000b; Hashemi et al, 1996; Beegle et al, 1998; Batliwala 1994; Bisnath and Elson 1999; Kabeer 2001; Narasimhan, 1999; Sen and Grown 1987, Naila Kabeer (2003), UNDP Annual Report (2006) as their work seems most relevant for rural women empowerment in India and these literature have been reviewed.

Objectives

- To analyse the Women's Empowerment through Microfinance.
- To assess the impact of Women's Empowerment on Human Development.

Methodology

In this paper an attempt is made to present the Empowerment of Women through Micro Finance – A Boon for Human Development. The paper is based on only the secondary sources of data. The secondary data were collected from books, journals, published and unpublished theses, reports of the bureau of economics and statistics, Government of India publications on women's empowerment, economic survey- India, etc.

Empowerment of Women through Microfinance

Empowerment is a process of awareness and capacity building leading to greater participation, to greater decision-making power and control and to transformative action. Women's empowerment is defined as "women's ability to make strategic life choices where that ability had been previously denied them" (Kabeer 1999). Empowerment is midway in the change processes that benefit women at individual, household, community and broader levels. At the most basic level, innovations can benefit women simply by improving their well-being in terms of health, nutrition, income, life span, etc. Beyond vital improvements in well-being, changes can result in women's empowerment, where women gain agency and resources to make decisions, build confidence and act in their own interests. Deeper and truly transformative changes reshape societal norms, attitudes and institutional practices. Greater gender equality in markets, political institutions, family systems and social roles provide an ongoing foundation for sustaining women's well-being and empowerment.

Strategies

To adopt a Sector-specific three-Fold Strategy for Empowering Women based on the prescriptions of the National Policy for Empowerment of Women. They include:

- **Social Empowerment:** To create an enabling environment through various affirmative developmental policies and programmes for the development of women besides providing them easy and equal access to all the basic minimum services so as to enable them to realise their full potentials.
- **Economic Empowerment:** To ensure provision of training, employment and income-generation activities with both forward and backward linkages with the ultimate objective of making all potential women economically independent and self-reliant, and
- **Gender Justice:** To eliminate all forms of gender discrimination and thus, allow women to enjoy not only the de-jure but also the de-facto rights and fundamental freedom on par with men in all spheres like political, economic, social, civil, cultural etc.

A majority of microfinance programmes target women with the explicit goal of empowering them. There are varying underlying motivations for pursuing women empowerment. Some argue that women are amongst the poorest and the most vulnerable of the underprivileged and thus helping them should be a priority. Whereas, other believe that investing in women's capabilities empowers them to make choices which is a valuable goal in itself but it also contributes to greater economic growth and development. It has been well-documented that an increase in women's resources results in the well-being of the family, especially children (Mayoux, 1997: Kabeer, 2001: Hulme and Mosley, 1997). A more feminist point of view stresses that an increased access to financial services represent an opening/opportunity for greater empowerment. Such organisations explicitly perceive microfinance as a tool in the fight for the women's rights and independence.

MFIs are autonomous financial institutions, which help members to keep their savings safe in the form of grant loans to people in exigencies without any troublesome procedure. It is argued that, through microfinance, poverty can be reduced as well as the resultant increased access and control over financial resources by women can itself become an empowering instrument. In microfinance sector, many private sector banks came forward three to four years back to provide credit to poor through SHGs and MFIs.

Today, the concept of Self Help Groups (SHGs) we catching up as the most viable means to empower women, especially at the grass root level. Women have shown extraordinary dynamism in organising themselves in group activities for income generation, better bargaining power and improvement in the quality of life. Membership in a group provides women a legitimate forum beyond the private domestic sphere, and inputs to which they previously lacked access. It permits a gradual building of her capacity to interact effectively and redistribute economic opportunity. It is against this backdrop that the SHGs have emerged as an alternative banking structure to cater to the needs of women.

SHG is a voluntary association of persons with common interests, formed democratically without any political affiliations. They are small and homogenous groups of 15-30 members. The uniqueness of these groups lies in the fact that to a large extent they are self supporting, self governing organisations free from bureaucratization and politicisation. The process empowers the poor and enables them to control direction of own development by identifying their felt needs. The SHG is a viable alternative to achieve the objectives of rural development and specially women empowerment. Through the SHG the micro credit is disbursed to rural women for the purpose of making them enterprising women and encouraging them to enter entrepreneurial activities.

Credit needs of rural women can be fulfilled totally through the SHG. The group members save a regular amount of Rs 20 to Rs 100 every month. The group rotates the money to the needy members for various purposes at a specified interest rate. As the repayment is cent per cent and the recycling is fast, the savings amount increases rapidly owing to the accumulation of income from interest. The savings habit helps the members to escape clutches of money lenders.

It paves the way for the empowerment of women and builds confidence in them to stand on their own feet. After the group stabilises over a period of six months or more in the management of its own funds, it conducts regular meetings, maintains savings and gives loans to members on interest. The SHGs are linked with the banks for external credit under the projects of rural development. The banks provide assistance for various entrepreneurial activities such as setting up small shops, vegetable shops, tailoring units, charcoal making units, dairies, etc.

The borrowers repay the bank loans properly. The SHGs repay more than 90 per cent loans of the banks on time. Besides focusing on entrepreneurial development and empowering women, SHGs concentrate on algound development of the beneficiaries and their village as a whole. The groups undertake the responsibility of delivering non-credit services such as literacy, health and environmental issues. The concept of SHG moulds women as responsible citizens of the country achieving social and economic status. There are many successful women forums and organisations that are trying to bring the rural women together for developmental works. The examples are- Working Women's Forum (WWF), SEWA, Shri Mahila Griha Udyog Lijat Papad or Lijat and Mann Deshi Mahila Shahakara Bank Ltd., Mhaswad, Maharashtra.

The strengthening of Self-help Groups is necessary for community-based organisations and for the empowerment of women. Special attention needs to be given to increasing employment opportunities and productive resources of women through special financial intermediaries, building women's competitiveness and increasing economic exchanges among women entrepreneurs.

The role and impact of microfinance programme on the various domains of women empowerment has been measured as discussed below:

Economic Empowerment

Microfinance through SHGs has linked rural poor women with formal credit delivery system, provided micro-loans and has encouraged them to start micro enterprises. This programme has helped in increasing self-employment as well as income of the participants and helped them to become economically more empowered than non-participants.

Access to Employment

Traditionally, it was used to be thought that women are capable of performing domestic chores only. But, employed women, wage or self-employed, discard this social belief. Employment provides them an opportunity to come out of the four walls of their house. Employment leads to possession over income, knowledge, awareness and self-confidence. Employment gives exposure to the outside world. Therefore, women's access to employment is an important indicator of empowerment. As per literature, the microfinance programme has helped the participants in increasing employment, particularly self-employment. With the help of micro-loans the programme participants have become self-employed in small business such as stitching and embroidery, rearing milk animals, rope and garland making, soap, surf, jam, chalk and candle making and have started petty shops.

Contribution to Household Income

The addition in household income improves the status of a woman within her family. This increases her recognition, self-esteem, power and control over the family. The contribution to the household income helps women to become economically independent and financial decisionmaker in the household expenditure. Microfinance programme has helped the women participants to increase their contribution to the household income.

Access to and Control over Family Resources

Access to and control over household resources has been considered as the possession of house, land, gold and jewellery, etc. If a woman owns the house/land, she gets more respect and feels more control over the family. The possession of gold and jewellery leads to economic security. Microfinance programme increases the economic prospectus of the participants, which helps them to have access to and control over the household economic resources.

Role in Household Financial Decision-making

Women involved in the household financial decision-making are definitely more empowered because generally male members of the family dominate in financial decision-making. The microfinance beneficiaries were asked about their independence and contribution in making financial decisions like budget allocation, when get a loan, amount and source of loan, buying and selling of household durables etc.

Savings in Bank Account

If a woman having a savings bank account, deposits money regularly in the account in her individual capacity, she is considered to have more foresightedness and economically aware as compared to those who do not take this initiative. Here, the amount of deposit, which is necessary for SHG to get microfinance benefit, is not given any significance. However, the saving in addition to this compulsory monthly saving has been considered for empowerment. Microfinance programme has developed the banking habits of self-help group members who contribute to the group savings fund through fixed installments at regular intervals. This develops the habit of thrift and banking.

Socio-cultural and Familial Empowerment

Microfinance programme pursued through SHGs is a collective effort of group participants. The members co-operate one another, deal with other members of the society and meet the members of other groups in their joint group meetings. In this way, they develop a social behaviour. Women are given an opportunity to come out of the four walls of their houses and meet other members of the society, which leads to their socio-cultural and familial empowerment.

Political Empowerment

Self-confident and conscious women are capable of taking part in the election process and village polity. It has been observed that microfinance programme has empowered the women participants socio-economically as well as politically. They feel themselves to be in the mainstream of the village affairs, hence, play a significant role in the village polity. The impact is measured by comparing the level of political awareness among the programme participants and non-participants as well as the interest taken by them to participate in the village political affairs.

Education, Skill and Training Empowerment

Besides the socio-economic and political empowerment of the programme participants, microfinance programme also develops the overall personality of its participants. The group activities lead to the development of basic skills like writing their name, reading numbers, doing basic arithmetic, filling bank forms and understanding pass-book entries etc. SHGs influence the level of comfort and confidence of its members by developing these basic skills in them. All this generates knowledge, self-confidence and self-esteem which are the indicators of their empowerment.

Microfinance programme may be an important programme but not a panacea to end all the problems that poor face. Hence, the programme beneficiaries must efficiently use the financial support to start small businesses that will help in uplifting standard of life and empowerment of women.

Impact of Women's Empowerment on Human Development

Human development is a process of widening people's choices as well as raising the level of well-being achieved. The most critical ones are to lead a long and healthy life, to be educated and to enjoy a decent standard of living. Additional choices include political freedom; other guaranteed human rights and various ingredients of self respect. According to Mahbub-ul-Haq, there are four essential components in the human development paradigm; equity, sustainability, productivity and empowerment. An empowered woman is vital role in human development. The impact of women empowerment on human development can be analysed on the basis of following factors.

Poverty alleviation

Poverty opportunity for participation of women in skilled activities has direct impact on poverty alleviation. Members of the women's cooperative, active in other income generating activities are found to gain from their affiliation with the micro-enterprise. Their marketing skills have opened a new source of income, in addition to the remuneration obtained from the assembly work. In general, women are not remunerated for their household work and hence they do not play any significant role in the financial decision-making. It has been found that engaging in the micro enterprise has created the opportunity for women to earn for themselves and thereby increased their stay in financial matters in the family. With rise in family income, overall expenditure patterns and priorities are expected to change. More emphasis can now be given to issues of better quality of life for the family. For example, scope for investment in children's education is now increased who would otherwise be required to contribute to the family income.

Employment

Employment provides economic power, and any power affects gender relations. Employed women develop a greater degree of self-confidence, become conscious of right and develop a sense of protest, opposition and contest. Provision of financial services and easy access is important for the development of poor women. Numbers of SHGs members are being trained for undertaking various productive activities like making agarbathi, candle, papad, pickles etc. Hence, after the women's empowerment in rural area, there is many small micro enterprises were started. SMEs are usually the prime drivers of jobs. Small enterprises are an important source of employment in many rural areas, often a sizable share of the labour force. As small firms are more labour intensive, it is suggested that they should be encouraged as a way of generating employment.

Income

Among the indicators of human development, income is also considered one of the important factors to determine the human development. The tiny loans are enough for hardworking micro women entrepreneurs to start or expand small businesses such as weaving baskets, raising chickens, or buying wholesale products to sell in a market. Income from these businesses provides better food, housing, healthcare and education for entire families, and most important, additional income provides hope for a better future.

Education

Education besides providing reading, writing and counting skills enables women to possess degrees, which in turn, qualify them for different kinds of white collar jobs. Even in business and social life educated people, especially women, enjoy greater status. In UNDP'S human development index education has been considered as a first indicator for human development. Mahatma Gandhi emphasised basic education to all so that people can live a happy life in villages itself. Moreover, he advised government to educate women who are the main pillars of society. On the basis of this statement, empowered women are capable to provide quality education facilities to her family members.

Health

Health is also one of the important indicators of the human development. Health is a positive condition in which a person is free from all diseases. It is the most essential component of human life. Healthy citizens are economically useful, progressive, and productive and thus, are an asset to the nation. Better the quality of citizens, better the quality of life. When women are empowered, they are able to provide good health facilities to their family and also contribute healthy people to the nation.

Household Goods

After women empowerment, many rural women started using electric appliances, radios, fans, mixer, refrigerator etc. This increase in the use of household goods can also be attributed to the improved economic conditions of the rural women after their empowerment.

Banking Habit

The empowerment of women has influenced the banking habits of the rural people. After the empowerment, women are accustomed to banking habit by becoming members in SHGs and Co-operative Banks. The banking habit is relatively common among the women, perhaps because of their better savings capacity, particularly after the introduction of SHGs. The number of debtors too, increased after the introduction of this facility, mainly because loans were obtained for household productive activity purposes. The introduction of SHGs also developed contacts between women and money lending institutions.

Market Contacts

The interdependence of economic activities accentuates market contacts between rural and urban societies. Rural women buy household inputs and sell their output in urban markets. The introduction Self Help Groups and Women's Co-operative Societies increased these market contacts.

Social Impact

Ownership and operation of the small business has given women the empowerment they would never had otherwise. Division of labour has now become participatory. The women are participating equally with men in negotiations on business deals for their cooperative. Women are now managing and keeping accounts of the business operations and engaging male employees as necessary. Their level of knowledge and awareness has increased because of higher access to mass media. Some of them are using computers for keeping accounts for the micro enterprise, word processing, day-to-day management activities and training others. Overall, the status of women in rural area will increased considerable from their involvement in the business activities.

Extension Activities

After the empowerment the social development of the women has undergone radical change in the rural area. There has also been change in the involvement of the women in political and economic institutions. The women have acquired a social status by becoming members of the Panchayat Boards and member in Welfare Associations. Their involvement in politics is also noteworthy. Many have become party secretaries: joint secretaries: ward members and active members. A remarkable improvement in these social and political organisations enables one to infer that the socio-economic conditions have changed after the empowerment.

Conclusion

In conclusion, it may be said again that no human development could be achieved in rural India on sustainable basis until and unless its women fold are developed and empowered socially and economically. It is well understood today that without economic and social liberalisation of women is possible and also without the provision of equal economic and social opportunities to women no emancipation of women truly occurs. Further, it is only when the rural women is allowed to participate as an equal partner in the most vital process of development of the nation, the human development will take place in a real sense. Microfinance brought psychological and social empowerment than economic empowerment. Impact of micro finance is appreciable in bringing confidence, courage, skill development and empowerment. Therefore, **Empowerment of Women through Micro Finance** is one of the means for human development.

REFERENCES

1. Batliwala, Srilatha, 1994, "The meaning of Women's Empowerment: New Concepts from Action." pp. 127-138 in *Population Policies Reconsidered: Health, Empowerment and Rights.* G. Sen, A. Germain, and L.C. Chen, eds. Cambridge, MA: Harvard University Press.
2. Bisnath, Savitri and Diane Elson, 1999, *Women's Empowerment Revisited.* Background Paper, Progress of the World's Women. UNIFEM.
3. Gurumoorthy T.R. (2000), "Self Help Groups-Empower Rural Women". Kurukshetra, Vol. 48, No. 5.
4. Jayanti C, "Empowering Women". Yojana, June 2001.
5. Someshekhar, Ne. Thi Adunika Bharathada Arthashastra, Chaitra Book House, Bangalore, 2011.
6. Devadas, Rajmmal P, "Empowerment of Women through SHGs", 1999.
7. NARABAD, Annual Report 2006-07.
8. *The Hindu,* March 18, 2006.

17

Role Of Micro Finance in Women's Empowerment

D.M. Madari and Rajeshwari M. Pattar

Abstract: *Microfinance is a type of banking service that is provided to unemployed or low-income individuals or groups who would otherwise have no other means of gaining financial services. Micro finance through Self Help Group (SHG) has been recognised internationally as the modern tool to combat poverty and for rural development. Micro finance and SHGs are effective in reducing poverty, empowering women and creating awareness which finally results in sustainable development of the nation. The main aim of microfinance is to empower women. In this paper the role played by Microfinance in women's empowerment are considered into three dimensions namely psychological, social and economical. The objectives of the study are: (i) to assess the performance of SHG's in Koppal region, (ii) to analyse the freedom women members get in decision making in SHG's, (iii) to document the problems women members face in SHG's, (iv) to analyze the empowerment of the women psychologically, economically, sociologically and politically and; (v) to offer suggestions for further empowerment of women in SHG's.*

The study was undertaken in the rural areas of Koppal region. Both primary and secondary data's were used. Primary data were collected from a field survey in the study region. Secondary data were collected from NGOs' reports and other documents. The researchers have used percentage method, simple correlation coefficient, paired t-test and cross tabulation for analysis purpose. Analysis showed that there is a gradual improvement in empowerment of rural women. From the interaction among the respondents it is noticed that some members are expecting the NGO to come up with more training sessions in income generating activities. They need an effective way to develop their skills and talents by participating in various training programmes. There is a definite improvement in the psychological well being and social empowerment among rural women as a result of participating in micro finance through SHGs.

Keywords: Microfinance, women's empowerment, Non-Governmental Organisation, Self Help groups.

Introduction

Microfinance is the provision of financial services to low-income clients, including consumers and the self-employed, who traditionally lack access to banking and related services. Microcredit, or microfinance, is banking the unbankables, bringing credit, savings and other essential financial services within the reach of millions of people who are too poor to be served by regular banks, in most cases because they are unable to offer sufficient collateral.

In general, "banks are for people with money, not for people without." (Gert van Maanen, Microcredit: Sound Business or Development Instrument, Oikocredit, 2004) is based on the premise that the poor have skills which remain unutilis ed or underutilized. Goal of microfinance is to give low income people an opportunity to become self-sufficient by providing a means of saving money, borrowing money and insurance. The main aim of microfinance is to empower women. Women make up a large proportion of microfinance beneficiaries.

Traditionally, women (especially those in underdeveloped countries) have been unable to readily participate in economic activity. Microfinance provides women with the financial backing they need to start business ventures and actively participate in the economy. It gives them confidence, improves their status and makes them more active in decision-making, thus encouraging gender equality. According to CGAP, long-standing MFIs even report a decline in violence towards women since the inception of microfinance. The most of the microcredit institutions and agencies all over the world focuses on women in developing countries. Observations and experience shows that women are a small credit risk, repaying their loans and tend more often to benefit the whole family. In another aspect it is also viewed as a method giving the women more status in a socioeconomic way and changing the current conservative relationship between gender and class when women are able to provide income to the household.

There are many reasons why women have become the primary target of microfinance services. A recent World Bank report confirms that societies that discriminate on the basis of gender pay the cost of greater poverty, slower economic growth, weaker governance, and a lower living standard for all people. At a macro level, it is because 70 per cent of the world's poor are women. Women have a higher unemployment rate than men in virtually every country and make up the majority of the informal sector of most economies. They constitute the bulk of those who need microfinance services. Giving women access to microcredit loans therefore generates a multiplier effect that increases the impact of a microfinance institution's activities, benefiting multiple generations. NABARD (2005) explains that the Self Help Group is a group with "an average size of about 15 people from a homogenous class. They come together for addressing their common problems. They are encouraged to make voluntary thrift on a regular basis. They use this pooled resource to make small interest bearing loans to their members. The process helps them imbibe the essentials of financial intermediation including prioritisation of needs, setting terms and conditions and accounts keeping. This gradually builds financial discipline in all of them. They also learn to handle resources of a size that is much beyond the individual capacities of any of them. The SHG members begin to appreciate that resources are limited and have a cost. Once the groups show this mature financial behaviour, banks are encouraged to make loans to the SHG in certain multiples of the accumulated savings of the SHG. The bank loans are given without any collateral and at market interest rates. The groups continue to decide the terms of loans to their own members. Since the groups' own accumulated savings are part and parcel of the aggregate loans made by the groups to their members, peer pressure ensures timely repayments." In this paper the role played by microfinance in women's empowerment are considered into three dimensions namely, psychological, social and economic.

Review of Literature

What is meant by empowerment? When does the well-being of a person improve?

Sen (1993) explains that the freedom to lead different types of life is reflected in the person's capability set. The capability of a person depends on a variety of factors, including personal characteristics and social arrangements. Malhotra (2002) constructed a list of the most commonly used dimensions of women's empowerment, drawing from the frameworks developed by various authors in different fields of social sciences. Allowing for overlap, these frameworks suggest that women's empowerment needs to occur along multiple dimensions including: economic, socio-cultural, familial/ interpersonal, legal, political, and psychological. The World Bank defines empowerment as "the process of increasing the capacity of individuals or groups to make choices and to transform those choices into desired actions and outcomes.

According to Krishna (2003) empowerment means increasing the capacity of individuals or groups to make effective development and life choices and to transform these choices into desired actions and outcomes. It is by nature a process and/or outcome.

Microfinance and Women Empowerment

A majority of microfinance programmes target women with the explicit goal of empowering them. There are varying underlying motivations for pursuing women empowerment. Some argue that women are amongst the poorest and the most vulnerable of the underprivileged and thus helping them should be a priority. Whereas, other believe that investing in women's capabilities empowers them to make choices which is a valuable goal in itself but it also contributes to greater economic growth and development.

It has been well-documented that an increase in women's resources results in the well-being of the family, especially children (Mayoux, 1997; Kabeer, 2001; Hulme and Mosley, 1997). A more feminist point of view stresses that an increased access to financial services represent an opening/opportunity for greater empowerment. Such organisations explicitly perceive microfinance as a tool in the fight for the women's rights and independence. Finally, keeping up with the objective of financial viability, an increasing number of microfinance institutions prefer women members as they believe that they are better and more reliable borrower.

Statement of the Problem

In olden days women were restricted to take part in any social activities and not given roles in decision-making in her family. The situation was even more worsening in rural and remote areas. Now the situation has been changed. She is given freedom to do what she wishes. In today's scenario more women are engaged in income generating activities. This is because of NGO and other financial institution came forward to provide microfinance to poor women. They believe that a woman is the small credit risk and often benefits the whole family. The main aim of microfinance is to empower women. This induced the researcher to focus more on the empowerment of rural women who participates in the microfinance.

Objectives of the Study

(a) To review the performance of SHGs in Koppal rural region.
(b) To study the problems women members face in SHG.
(c) To analyse the freedom women members get in SHG.
(d) To discuss the empowerment of the women psychologically, economically and sociologically.
(e) To offer suggestions for the betterment of women's empowerment in SHG.

Research Methodology Sources of Data

The study was undertaken in rural areas of Koppal region. Both primary and secondary data were used. Primary data were collected from a field survey in the study region. Secondary data were collected from NGOs' reports and other documents. One NGO is selected and three Self-Help Groups promoted by that NGO in rural areas of Koppal are taken for study. Areas covered under the study were: Gangavati, Kustigi and Yalaburga.

Sampling Method

Cluster sampling and area sampling was followed. Since the members are large in number they are divided by groups and randomly selected for data collection. Sample Size: 181 samples have been collected for the research from all the three rural areas of Koppal region. Statistical tools used: Simple correlation coefficient, paired t-test, cross tabulation and percentage analysis has been used to analyse and interpret the data. Method of Data Collection: A structured interview schedule was prepared by the researcher and used for collecting data from the rural SHG women members who are engaged in Micro enterprises through microfinance.

Limitations of the Study

(a) The study was confined with the rural areas of Koppal. Hence the results may not be applicable to urban area SHG members.
(b) The data were collected only from those who were engaged in income generating activities.

Findings

Educational qualifications of respondents

About 36.5 per cent of the women are illiterate and the next majority of the women have done up to secondary education.

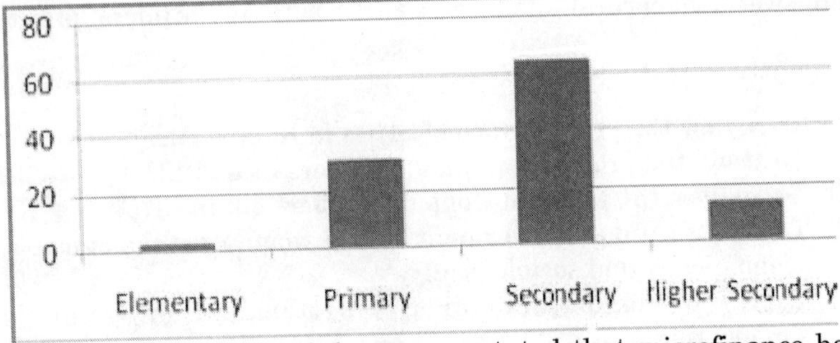

About 92 per cent of the women stated that microfinance has reduced their poverty level to a greater extent.

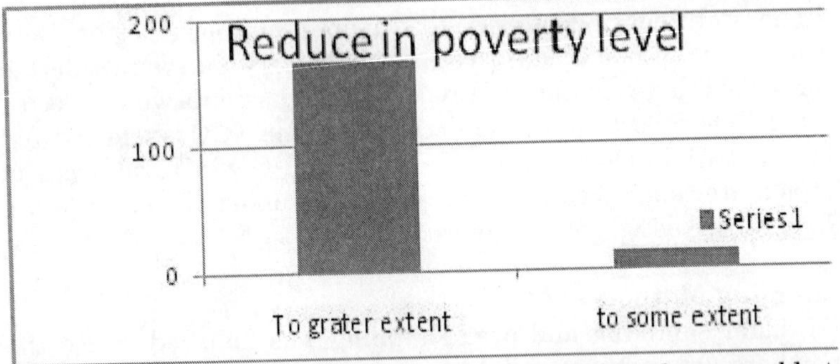

About 130 respondents out of 181 reported that they are able to maintain their family to some extent followed by the 44 respondents who accepted to greater extent they are able to maintain their family after joining in SHG.

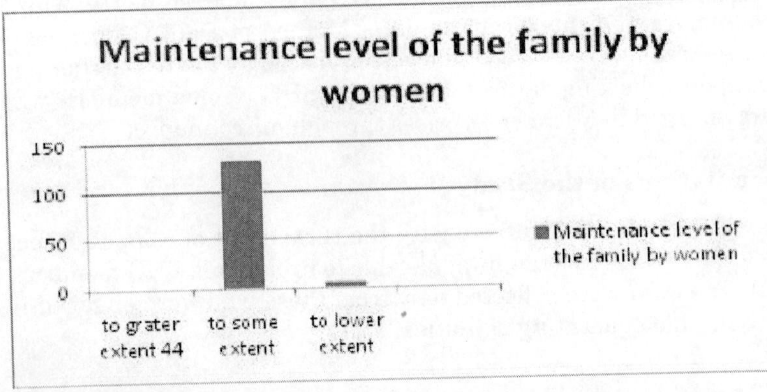

All the respondents agreed that micro finance brought courage and self-confidence and improved their skills and self-worthiness. Microfinance improved the literacy level of rural women and their improved awareness on children education.

Majority of the respondents expressed that their awareness about environment improved after actively taking part in micro finance programmes. Maximum number of respondents accepted that microfinance has brought about economic development directly and indirectly happiness and peace in the family.

Women are economically and socially empowered after joining SHG and getting micro finance as 92 per cent of the respondents reported that poverty level was reduced by participating in the micro finance programme.

As far as the self help group is concerned they don't face any type of problems or compulsions from leaders or from other members in the group. Women are given full freedom to express their opinions.

It is also noticed that most of the women are not aware of the trainings organised by the NGO. The NGO shall actively take part in various trainings sessions provided to all women members wherein they can gain more knowledge about the various income generating activities.

Conclusion

The rural area Self Help Groups are performing well. The study concludes that microfinance brought psychological and social empowerment than economic empowerment. Impact of micro finance is appreciable in bringing confidence, courage, skill development and empowerment. The SHG members feel free to move with their groups and leaders. It leads them to participate on various social welfare activities with good cooperation. While interacting with the respondents, it is noticed that some members are expecting the NGO to come up with more training sessions in income generating activities. All they need is a way to develop their skills and talents by participating in various training programmes.

REFERENCES

1. Gupta S. P. (2009), "Statistical methods", Thirty eight revised Editions, Sultan Chand & Sons, New Delhi.
2. Kothari C.R (2007), Research Methodology Methods and Techniques, Second Edition, New Age International Publishers, New Delhi.

3. Manjula Bolthajjira Chengappa, "Micro-Finance and Women Empowerment: Role of Nongovernment Organizations".
4. Rajendran K. and Raya R.P. (2010), Impact of Micro Finance - An empirical Study on the Attitude of SHG Leaders in Vellore District (Tamil Nadu, India).

18

Micro Finance And Women Empowerment in India—Issues And Challenges

Sathyanarayana

Abstract: *Micro finance Sector has grown rapidly over the past few decades. One of the significant initiatives by the NABARD was the SGH-Bank Linkage Programme initiated in 1992. Micro Finance is playing a crucial role in the field of rural development in general and women empowerment in particular. Micro credit has been hailed as the method of creating additional employment and reducing poverty with economic freedom. The strategy is redistribute, entrepreneurial and empowering. Especially rural women empowerment through pro-active role is getting momentum due to shift in policies from bureaucratic 'top centric' to ground up interactive schemes has changed the socio-economic environment in rural areas.*

Introduction

Micro Finance covers a wide range of services like credit, savings, insurance, remittances and also non-financial services like training, counselling, etc.

In this paper an attempt has been made to discuss Micro Finance and Women Empowerment including the issues and challenges by taking into account SHGs. This paper throws light on women empowerment through SHGs. Micro Finance Sector has grown rapidly over the past few decades Noble Laureate Mohammed Yunus is credited with laying the foundation of the modern Micro Finance

Institutions with establishment of Grameena Bank, Bangladesh in 1976. Today it had evolved into a vibrant industry exhibiting a variety of business models. Micro Finance Institutions in India exists as NGOs, Commercial Banks, Regional Rural Banks, Co-operative Societies and other large lenders have played an important role in providing refinance facility to MFIs. Banks have also leveraged the Self Help Group channel to provide direct credit to group borrowers.

"Micro Finance is the provision of financial services to low income clients or solidarity lending groups including consumers and the self-employed who traditionally lack access to banking and related services". Micro finance is not just about giving micro credit to the poor rather it is an economic development tool whose objective is to assist poor to work their way out of poverty. It covers a wide range of services like credit, savings, insurance, remittances and also non-financial services like training, counseling, etc. In general Micro Finance sector is having a healthy growth rate there have been a number of concerns related to the sector, like grey areas in regulation, transparent pricing, low financial literacy, etc. In addition to these concerns there are a few emerging concerns like cluster formation, insufficient funds, multiple lending and over-indebtedness which are arising because of the increasing competition among the MFIs.

On a national level there has been spate of actions taken to strengthen the regulation of Micro Finance Sector including enactment of Micro Finance Regulation Bill by the Govt. of Andhra Pradesh, implementation of sector – specific regulation by RBI and recently release of Draft Micro Finance Institutions Bill 2011 for comments. The challenge is related to supervision, ground realities, and operational efficiency of MFIs. Women Empowerment through micro finance is possible. Especially rural women empowerment is linked with SHGs and NGOs mechanism. The strategy is redistributive, entrepreneurial and empowering. Especially rural women empowerment through pro-active role is getting momentum due to shift in policies from bureaucratic 'top centric' to ground up interactive schemes has changed the socio-economic environment in rural areas. According to Mehamood Yonus, Micro Credit Pioneer, "If you can run a bank, lend money and get it back cover all your costs and made a profit and people get out of poverty, what else you name?" "A nation would not march forward if the women are left behind". Women play a vital role in the social and economic transformation of a country. The empowerment of rural women is crucial for the development of Rural Bharat.

Majority of Micro Finance programmes focus women with a view to empower them. They are varying underlying motivations for pursuing women empowerment. A more feminist point of view stresses that an increased access to financial services represent an opportunity for greater empowerment. Such organisations explicitly perceive Micro Finance as a tool in the fight for the womens right and independence. Keeping up with the objection of financial viability on increasing number of micro finance institutions prefer women members as they believe that they are better and more reliable borrowers. Self-help groups intermediated by micro credit have been shown to have positive efforts on women, with some of these impacts being ripple effects. They have played valuable roles in reducing the vulnerability of the poor, through asset creation, income, consumption smoothing, provisions of emergency assistance and empowering and emboldening women by giving them control over assets and increased self-esteem and knowledge, Several recent assessment studies also generally reported positive impacts. Malhotra constructed a list of dimensions of womens' empowerment. They are linked with economic, socio-cultural, inter-personal, legal, political and psychological. It has been well documented that an increase in women's resources results in the well being of the family, especially children.

Swain (2007) has opined that women are in the process of empowering themselves and NGOs that provide support in financial services and specialised training, have a greater ability to make a positive impact on women empowerment. Swain and Wallentin (2009) have inferred that SHG members are empowered by participating in micro finance program in the sense that they have a greater propensity to resist existing gender norms and culture that restrict their ability to develop and make choices. Batliwala identified three approaches to womens' empowerment (a) The integrated development approach which focused on womens' survival and livelihood needs, (b) The Economic development approach which aimed to strengthen womens' economic position and the consciousness approach which organized women into collectiveness that address the source of oppression.

According to Sen, "Women are less likely to secure favourable outcomes for themselves in household decision making processes. They feel that their long terms security lies in subordinating their well-being to that of make authority figures." Women in India miss many opportunities, especially due to their limited access to crucial inputs like credit. Women have become victims of deprivation, discrimination and atrocities. The SHGs would provide a permanent forum for articulating their needs and contributing their perspective to rural development. Women empowerment is basically concerned with equality, participation in influencing decisions and access to opportunity. The SHGs are called as thrift and credit groups. The SHGs provide group approach to the micro credit programme. Along with implementing the micro credit programmes, SHGs take up many other important issues like healthcare, sanitation, family planning, literacy, management of common resources etc. The SHG itself with the help of NGO makes assessment of individual credit needs of its members and submits to the bank for sanction of collective loan in its name. The NGO helps the SHG in processing raw materials and also marketing of the produce. The entire loan amount disbursed to the SHG is re-financed by NABARD to the financing banks. So, there is a shift in emphasis from the rapid disbursement of subsidised loans to target population towards the building of local sustainable institutions. So women empowerment is possible through SHGs.

Although the SHG-Bank linkage model is well managed in India by NABARD, currently there is no proper regulatory body for the supervision of MFIs. The presence of institutions with a variety of legal forms makes it difficult for the regulation of all such institutions by a single regulatory body in the current Indian legal structure. Though NBFCs which cover the major part of the outstanding loan portfolio by the Micro-Finance channel are regulated by RBI, other MFIs like societies, trusts, Co-operative Societies, etc. fall outside the purview of RBI's regulation. The micro finance institutions Bill 2011 is a major step in the Micro Finance sector. The proposed bill clarifies all doubts pertaining to regulation of the MFIs by appointing RBI as the sole regulator for all MFIs.

It is necessary to create awareness of Micro Finance among women, because there is financial illiteracy. They are also unable to generate own funds. Majority of the Micro Finance loans are disbursed on group lending concept and a past record of the group plays an important role in getting new loans either through SHG-Bank linkage or through MFIs. The two major problems with the group concept are drop-outs and migration. Another problem is cluster formation is restricting MFIs from reaching to rural areas where there is the actual need for Micro Finance. People in urban, semi-urban areas are already having access to Micro Finance through SHG-Bank linkage. But in rural areas people do not have access to banks. It is limited in rural sector. MFIs are not willing to go to remove locations. So, there is low penetration of micro finance in rural area and remote areas. Another problem is multiple lending and over-indebtedness. Multiple lending is eating away the opportunity of new borrowers. MFIs are getting affected because borrowers are failing to make payments and hence their recovery rates are falling. On the other hand over-indebtedness is making the borrower go to depression. So, at present Micro Finance sector should include new clients and new locations.

SHG-Bank linkage programme has brought out the traditional skills, organisational skills and collective power of women, especially from economically disadvantaged background to the forefront. SHG Women members have ventured into hitherto unemployed areas and proved that they can deliver when trusted and entrusted. NABARD brought out the booklet 'SHGs "Paving Pathways to possibilities", highlighting the organisational skills of women SHG members for taking up assignments and contracts offered by State government departments. The booklet documented 50 case studies spanning across 13 States. Apart from traditional activities like running canteens, stitching uniform for school students etc., the SHGs are also managing rural call centres, re-cycling of plastic waste, procurement of food grains, etc.

The SHG-Bank linkage programme has completed over two decades. In this journey of twenty years over 73 lakh SHGs predominantly women have gained access to financial services from the formal banking system. This has helped feminise the credit portfolio of banks to a marginal extent and made substantial impact on the lives and livelihoods of SHG families.

The Union Ministry of Rural Development launched the National Rural Livelihood Mission by restructuring Swarnajayanthi Gram Swarozgar Yojana and replacing the same with effect from 1st April, 2013. The interest subvention scheme under NRLM for eligible women SHGs in identified 150 districts is being implemented by NABARD for RRBs and co-operative banks. Under this scheme the women SHGs in 150 districts shall be eligible for interest subvention and avail the credit upto Rs 3.0 Lakh at 7 per cent per annum. Further the SHGs will be provided with an additional 3 per cent subvention on prompt repayment of loan.

From this study, following inferences have been drawn with regard to micro finance and women empowerment.

- An enabling regulatory environment protects interest of stake holders as well as promotes growth.
- Field supervision helps to monitor the performance of ground staff of various MFIs and their recovery practices.
- It is necessary to encourage rural penetration and to check up multiple lending.

- MFIs should provide complete range of products including credit, savings, remittance, finance advice and also non-financial services like training and supply.
- MFIs are employing different patterns of charging interest rates. So a common practice for charging interest should be followed.
- Operation costs should be reduced through new technologies.
- As funds are inadequate MFIs can raise their funds through alternative sources.
- Rural female education is necessary to tackle women empowerment.
- Self employment opportunities will increase among women through Micro Finance.
- Through the role of women in borrowing and lending of funds management corruption will decrease to a great extent.

On the basis of the findings of the study, the following suggestions are made to empower women through Micro Finance and SHGs.

- Effective training programmes should be conducted by the NGOs to the rural women who are involving in Self Help Groups.
- SHGs are required to maintain books that give details regarding its accounts, number of meetings held, decision taken in the meetings, amount of savings and credit availed and repayment.
- Awareness programmes are the need of the hour with regard to group formation, its operations and activities.
- Evaluation of prospective members should be undertaken by examining the background of each of the members of the group.
- SHG should try to maintain financial health, financial discipline and quality oriented activities and operations.
- NGOs should guide about participatory planning, holistic approach, resource mobilisation, self-management, self-help and mutual help.

Conclusion

In this way Micro Finance helps to a great extent to empower women through SHGs. The efficiency of SHGs rests on the role of NGOs. NGOs should not only facilitate the availability of credit from the financial institutions to SHGs but also assist them in understanding and implementing the basic requisites laid down by NABARD. NGOs could also aid SHGs in identifying suitable products that they can manufacture and sell. Further they should impart the necessary skills and training to the members of SHGs and provide for effective marketing outlets for the products manufactured by SHGs. On the other hand, State Governments and Panchayats should actively promote the formation of women SHGs. If State government could put SHGs prominently on its agenda, times ahead can be promising.

REFERENCES

1. Nair, Tara S (2012), "Financing of Indian Micro Finance: Evidence and Implications" Economic and Political Weekly, 33-40, June 23.
2. N C A E R (2008), Impact and Sustainability of SHG-Bank Linkage Programme, New Delhi, India.
3. Cheston and Lisa Kuhn (2002), Empowering Women through Micro Finance.
4. Ghate, Prabhu (2008), Micro Finance in India – A state of the sector report, New Delhi, Sage Publication.
5. Naik, Kabeer, (2005), Is micro finance a magic bullet for women empowerment?
6. Rajgopal S (2006), Micro Finance: Case Studies ICFAI University Press Hyderabad.
7. Reddy Y V (2006), Micro Finance, RBI's Approach, August 2006.
8. Abdul Raheem A (2005), Micro Finance and Self Help Groups to alleviate poverty. Facts for you. Vol. 25 No.11 August pp. 33-36.
9. Annual Report NABARD 2013-14.

19

Selp Help Group for Women Empowerment

T. Ramesh

***Abstract**: Today's world is caught in a great economic crisis. Liberalisation has brought several multinational companies into developing countries. Due to this the local enterprises are unable to compete with the products that are better in quality as well as lower in prices. In this economic environment, the women self- help groups (SHGs) are building themselves up as a power to be reckoned with. Many political parts and women's organisations have failed to recognise the potential of this power. While the multinational companies have more money power, these groups have within them the extensive market potential of their own families and companies. When organised effectively, this could prove to be a true challenge to counter the influx and influence of multinational companies in India.*

Concept of SHG

Self-Help Group (SHG) is a small voluntary association of poor people, preferably from the same socioeconomic background. They come together for the purpose of solving their common problems through self-help and mutual help. The SHG promotes small savings among its members. The savings and kept with a bank. This common fund is in the name of the SHG. Usually, the number of members in one SHG does not exceed twenty.

The concept of SHG is based on the following principles:

- Self-help supplemented with mutual help can be a powerful vehicle for the poor in their socioeconomic development;
- Participative financial services management is more responsive and efficient;
- Poor need not only credit support, but also savings and other services;
- Poor can save and are bankable and SHGs as clients, result in wider outreach, lower transaction cost and much lower risk costs for the banks;
- Creation of a common fund by contributing small savings on a regular basis;
- Flexible democratic system of working;
- Loaning is done mainly on trust with a bare documentation a amounts loaned are small, frequent and for short duration;
- Defaults are rare mainly due to group pressure; and periodic meetings non-traditional savings.

Micro Finance programmes are currently being promoted as a key strategy for simultaneously addressing both poverty alleviation and women's empowerment. Before 1990s, credit schemes for women were almost negligible. There were certain misconception about the poor people that they need loan a subsidised rates of interest on soft terms, they lack skills capacity to save, credit worthiness and therefore are no bankable. Nevertheless, the experiences of several and SHG; reveal that rural poor are actually efficient managers of credit and finance. Availability of timely and adequate credit is essential for them in their enterprises rather than subsidies. Earlier government efforts through various poverty alleviation schemes for self employment by providing credit and subsidy received little success. Since most of them were target based involving various government agencies and banks.

Meaning of Empowerment

Empowerment is not essentially political alone; it is a process having personal, economic, social and political dimensions with personal empowerment being the core of the empowerment process. In fact political empowerment will not succeed in the absence of economic empowerment. The Scheme of Micro-financing through SHGs create empowerment promoting conditions for women to move from positions of marginalisation within household decision-making process and exclusion within community, to one of greater centrality, inclusion of voice. The social processes of micro financing programmes strengthens women's self esteem and self worth, instil a greater sense of awareness of social and political issues leading to increased mobility and reduced traditional seclusion of women.

Most importantly micro-finance programmes enable women to contribute to the household economy, increasing their intra-household bargaining power. Thus, micro financing through self-help groups has transferred the real economic power in the hands of women and has considerably reduced their dependence on men. But the lack of education often comes in the way and many a times they had to seek help from their husbands or any other educated man/woman for day-to-day work. The political as well as economic empowerment will not succeed in the absence of women education in skills and vocations they .require the most. The governments in developing countries therefore must take effective steps to enrol the members of SHGs in the schemes of open schooling or any other distance mode to impart education. Although it is also true that economic empowerment alone does not always lead to reversal in gender relationship.

Strategy of Women Empowerment

In view of low literacy rate of women and the gigantic task of educating rural women a suitable strategy will have to be planned. The major task is to identify the areas where these groups in fact, are fairing problems because at this stage only the problem solving adult learning technique will attract these rural poor to improve their working and income.

The success of any strategy of women empowerment depends upon the following factors:

- Level of education, hard work
- Social custom
- Family planning, small family
- Health, medical services, cleanliness
- Environment, tree growing, kitchen gardening.

Various case studies show that there is a positive correlation between credit availability and empowerment of women.

Major Findings

The SHGs voluntarily formed by women save whatever amount they can save every month and mutually agree to contribute to a common fund to be lent to the members for meeting their productive and emergent credit needs. These groups are linked to the banks once their activities are stabilised. Besides focusing on entrepreneurial development of the beneficiaries, the SHGs undertake the responsibility of delivering non-credit services such as literacy, health and environmental issues.

Each Self-Help Group consists of 10-20 members. The members of SHGs met three to four times a week. There is a president, a secretary and a treasurer in each SHG. All the groups maintain the records such as membership register, minute's book, cash book, savings ledger and the loan ledger. They prepare action plans after a detailed discussion of their proposed activities. Every member of the group gets an opportunity to put fetch her views. Thus, the SHGs have achieved success in bringing women to the mainstream of decision making. The study has found a remarkable change in the personality of women after joining the SHGs.

Constraints

- Lack of support from male members (of the families) as well as banks
- Large magnitude of the target group of poor people
- Difficulty in creating awareness among people
- Limited resources with the NGOs
- Large requirements of training and sensitization of issues
- Limited number of experienced intervention agencies

Overall Impressions

- Adoption of non-traditional activities
- Improvement in the income levels of SHGs members
- Nearly 100 per cent recovery of loans
- Generation of small savings in the rural sector among women
- Use of local knowledge and resources in productive activities
- Reduction in transaction cost for both banks as well as SHGs
- Maintenance of minimum records in the form of registers
- Maintenance of proper accounts by the SFIGs
- Regular meetings of the SHGs members to tackle problems among themselves
- Healthy relation and coordination between SHGs, NGOs and bank
- Support services to NGOs by banks for networking with other smaller NGOs

Conclusion

The SHGs have made a lasting impact on the lives of the women particularly in the rural areas. Their quality of life has improved a lot. There is an increase in their income, savings and consumption expenditure. This shows an improvement in their standard of living. The women have gained self-confidence. They got an opportunity to improve their hidden talents after joining the SHGs. They can speak freely in front of large groups of people. They got recognition in the family and society SHGs have also given women a greater role in household decision making.

Besides, the SHGs have created better understanding between the members of the different religious groups as the members of SHGs belong to different religions. This is a welcome change to have understanding and tolerance towards the members of other religions particularly in a country like India where there is a diversity of religions and castes.

REFERENCES

1. Gariyai, C. K and Vettivel, S. K., "Women's Own the Self-help", Commonwealth Publishers, New Delhi, 2004.
2. Karmakar, K. G., "Rural Credit and Self-help groups: "Micro Finance Needs and Concepts in India". Sage Publication, New Delhi 1999.
3. Birendra Kumar Jha (2009), "Empowerment of Rural Women in India" Kanishka Publishers, New Delhi.
4. APMAS (2005), A Study on Self-help group (SHG) - Bank Linkage in Andhra Pradesh, Andhra Pradesh Mahila Abhivrudhi Society, Hyderabad.
5. Arunachalam, Ramesh, S. (2011), The Journey of Indian Microfinance: Lessons for the Future, Aapti publications, Chennai.
6. K. G Karmakar, "Rural credit and Self help group – Microfinance needs and concepts in India", New Delhi, Sage Publication India Pvt. Ltd., 2003.
7. Dasgupta, R., "An informal journey through Self Help Group" Indian Journal of Agriculture Economic, Vol. 56, No. 3, July-September, 2001.
8. Rao, V. M., 'Women self help group profiles from Andhra Pradesh, Kurushetra, Vol. 50, No. 6, Apr. 2001.
9. Chandrasekhar, H.M and Lokesh M.U. (2009). Role of SHGs in socio-economic change of vulnerable poor, International NGO Journal.

20

Role of Micro Finance in Women Empowerment

Swetha S., and Sathyanarayana

Abstract: *Women's empowerment is one of the prerequisites of human development in a country. Introduction of micro finance institutions and SHGs with bank-linked credit schemes has of late been enabling women to engage themselves in various economic and social activities without any restrictions. Against this background, the present paper tries to highlight on the role and status of micro finance in women's empowerment and to examine the performance of SHG-bank linking programme (SBLP) in empowering women. It is found that both the micro-finance institutions and SBLP have positive influence on women's empowerment in India.*

Key words: Micro Finance, SHGs, Women Empowerment, JEL Classification: G21, E5.

Introduction

The UN Millennium Declaration (2002) committed the participating countries to work together in achieving the Millennium Development Goals (MDGs), the foremost being reducing absolute poverty in the world by one-half by the year 2015. The steps initiated by the Government of India since independence, have not reduced poverty and income inequality completely. Micro finance programmes, which serve the poor, are being seen as an important vehicle for realising the MDGs and reducing poverty and vulnerability. The problems of hunger, malnutrition, gender inequality, illiteracy continue to exist. One of the factors considered the cause of this is the non-availability of micro level financing for the needy poor. They are forced to turn to the traditional moneylenders by paying exorbitant interest rates. The conditions of the poor women are even worse. The Government of India has been making efforts to develop rural areas through various banking networks to help the poor especially women. Micro finance plays a vital role in promoting economic activities, health, infrastructure and education for rural people.

For sustenance/better growth of the world, the deprived sections should be drawn into the mainstream of growth. A number of progressive measures are initiated in the Indian banking sector to reach the vulnerable sections of the society. Yet, the economically disadvantaged people are outside the range of the formal banking system. The size and frequencies of transactions of these people are cost prohibitive. In addition, the general apathy that the poor are not bankable and they are not trustworthy did come in the way of taking the financial services to these people. In this context, micro finance has come as an innovative movement; it is a quite promising and cost-effective tool in reaching the poor and fighting against the poverty.

Defining Micro Finance

Micro Finance is a broad term that includes deposits, loans, payments services and insurances to poor. The concept of micro finance and micro credit are used interchangeably. Today micro finance is very much in the agenda of public policy and it has been increasingly used as a vehicle for reaching the otherwise unreachable poor in the country. The need, therefore, is to share experience and materials, which will help in not only understanding successes and failures but also provide knowledge and guidelines to strengthen and expand micro finance programmes. The ultimate aim is to attain social and economic empowerment.

micro finance sector has covered a long journey from micro savings to micro credit and then to micro enterprises and now entered the field of micro insurance, micro remittance, micro pension and micro livelihood. This gradual and evolutionary growth process has given a great boost to the rural poor in India to reach reasonable economic, social and cultural empowerment, leading to better life of participating households.

Micro Finance and Women Empowerment

Women have been the most underprivileged and discriminated strata of the society not only in India but the world over. In spite of all Government and Non-Governments' efforts, they have been highly ignorant clients of the financial sector. In the recent times, microfinance has been emerging as a powerful instrument for empowering women particularly, the rural women. Apart from the informal sector of finance the formal and semi-formal sectors like commercial banks, NGOs etc, are taking much interest in providing microfinance to women considering it to be a profitable commercial activity. Women are also participating in the microfinance movement by availing the microfinance services being provided by the various financial channels. Women economic empowerment is so strong by Micro Finance through SHGs.

The main aim of microfinance is to empower women. Women make up a large proportion of microfinance beneficiaries. Traditionally, women (especially those in underdeveloped countries) have been unable to readily participate in economic activity. Microfinance provides women with the financial backing they need to start business ventures and actively participate in the economy. It gives them confidence, improves their status and makes them more active in decision making, thus encouraging gender equality. Majority of microfinance programmes focus women with a view to empower them. There are varying underlying motivations for pursuing women empowerment. Some argue that women are amongst the poorest and the most vulnerable of the underprivileged and thus helping them should be a priority.

Literature Review and Research Gap

The fast-paced growth of microfinance industry has invited widespread recognition, from national as well as international policy makers and donors/agencies. It has been well-documented that an increase in women's resources results in the well-being of the family, especially children (Mayoux, 1997; Kabeer, 2001; Hulme and Mosley, 1997). A more feminist point of view stresses that an increased access to financial services represent an opening/opportunity for greater empowerment. Such organisations explicitly perceive microfinance as a tool in the fight for the women's rights and independence. Swain, R. B. (2007) concluded that NGOs support in financial services and specialised training, have a greater ability to make a positive impact on women empowerment. Swaina, R . B. and Wallentin, F. W. (2009) noted that SHGs members are empowered by participating in microfinance program in the sense that they have a greater propensity to resist existing gender norms and culture that restrict their ability to develop and make choices. Self-help groups intermediated by microcredit have been shown to have positive effects on women (Zaman, 2001, Simanowitz and Walker, 2002).

There are few systematic studies done on the status and role of microfinance in women's empowerment. Moreover, there are also few studies done on the role of SHG-bank linking programme regarding empowering women. The present study attempts to fill this gap.

Objectives and Methodology

- To highlight on the status and role of microfinance in women's empowerment.
- To examine the performance of SHGs-banking linking programme in empowering women.

The present study is purely based on secondary sources of data. It is collected from NABARD report on status of micro finance and respective official websites. The simple descriptive statistical techniques have been used for data analysis.

Micro Finance and Women Empowerment

Dr Mohammed Yunus is credited with pioneering microfinance in the 1970s, for giving small loans to the women of Jobra village in Bangladesh. He went on to found the Grameena Bank in 1983. The World Bank says that MFIs serve around 160 million people in developing countries. Between 1950 and 1970, the Indian Government focused on reaching out to the unbanked with subsidised agricultural credit and small loans. It also launched many initiatives including the Lead Bank Scheme, Priority Sector Advances, JRY (Jawaharlal Rozgar Yojana) and PMRY (Prime Minister's Rural Employment Scheme) to benefit and in the 1990s transformed themselves into unbanked and underdeveloped regions; however, these did not penetrate as deeply as intended. In order to address this issue, the government proposed the introduction of MFIs, to be regulated and supervised by the RBI, which would lend to the poor at subsidised interest rates. This paved the way for the entry of MFIs in the 1980s. In the late 1990s, institutions such as SIDBI and NABARD entered the arena to assist the ailing microfinance business.

The Eleventh Five Year Plan (2007-12) envisioned inclusive growth as a key objective. It is a powerful instrument for reducing poverty and income disparities among the people in the country. Financial inclusion is necessary to enable the weaker sections of the society to participate in the formal financial system as they are otherwise disadvantaged sections and low income groups. Further, the 12th Five Year Plan has also adopted "faster, sustainable, and more inclusive growth as the key development paradigm". For last two decades in India the microfinance services have expanded considerably in alleviating the country's poverty.

In India, two broad approaches prevail in case of micro financing viz. self help group–bank linkage (SHGB) and micro finance institutions (MFIs). NABARD has been supporting the SHG-Bank linkage programme since 1992. In the context of growing demand for micro finance by self help groups, RBI made linkage of self help groups with banks as a priority sector activity in 1996. The Government of India has been supporting the programme by making special budgetary provision for promotion of self help groups since 1999.

Micro finance through Self-Help Group (SHG) has been recognised internationally as the modern tool to combat poverty and for rural development. Micro finance and SHGs are effective in reducing poverty, empowering women and creating awareness which finally results in sustainable development of the nation. Self-help groups intermediated by microcredit have been shown to have positive effects on women, with some of these impacts being ripple effects. They have played valuable roles in reducing the vulnerability of the poor, through asset creation, income and consumption smoothing, provision of emergency assistance, and empowering and emboldening women by giving them control over assets and increased self-esteem and knowledge (Zaman, 2001). Several recent assessment studies have also generally reported positive impacts (Simanowitz and Walker, 2002).

Table 1: Client outreach—SBLP and MFI models (in crores)

Year	Number of Clients (crore)			Loan Outstanding (Crore)			Share of MFI in
	SBLP	*MFI*	*Total*	*SBLP*	*MFI*	*Total*	*Incremental Micro Lending per cent*
2006-07	3.8	1	4.8	12,366	3,456	15,822	—
2007-08	4.7	1.4	6.1	16,999	5,954	22,953	35
2008-09	5.4	2.3	7.7	22,679	11,734	34,413	50
2009-10	6	2.7	8.7	28,038	18,343	46,381	55
2010-11	6.3	3.2	9.4	31,221	21,556	52,777	50
2011-12	6.1	2.7	8.8	36,340	20,913	57,253	-14
2012-13	6.5	2.8	9.3	39,375	22,300	61,675	31

Source: NABARD. Status of Microfinance in India 2012–13.

There are 6.5 and 2.8 crore active clients of SBLP and MFIs respectively (Table 1). Both client outreach and outstanding loans of MFIs have not increased since 2010–11. The number of active clients has remained around nine crore over the last four years, if one ignores the possible overlapping between the SBLP and MFI models. The loan outstanding was stagnant around 21,000 crore, and increased marginally by about 1,300 crore between 2011–12 and 2012–13. In 2007–08, SBLP accounted for about two-thirds of the incremental loan amount disbursed within the microfinance system. During the subsequent three years, the period of hyper growth of MFIs, this share came down by about 15 percentage points. In 2011–12, all the incremental lending within the system was due to SBLP. The share of MFIs improved substantially to 31 per cent in 2012–13 (table 1).

Table 2: Estimate of Micro Finance Credit Clients (in millions)

	2008	*2009*	*2010*	*2011*
Commercial banks (including RRBs) small loan accounts	41	39.2	45.2	43.3
PACs borrowers (small vulnerable)	28.5	28.7	30	31.0
SHG members	47.1	54	59.6	62.5
MFI clients	14.1	22.6	26.7	31.8
Total	130.7	144.5	161.5	168.6

Source: Microfinance India- State of the Sector Report (2013).

Table 2 shows the total number of microfinance sector clients stood at 168.6 million as at the end of March 2011. Of this, 43.3 million were customers of commercial banks. This number had declined from the previous year's level of 45.2 million. Overall, like in the previous year, the SHGs and MFIs put together had reached about eight million clients more than the commercial banks.

SHG-Bank Linking Programme and Women Empowerment

Self-Help Groups (SHGs) movement has triggered off a silent revolution in the rural credit delivery system in India. It is a small voluntary association to form a group. SHGs have proved as an effective medium for delivering credit to rural poor for their socioeconomic empowerment especially women. Self Help Group (SHG) in India has come a long way, since its inception in 1992. The spread of SHGs in India has been phenomenal. It has made dramatic progress from 500 groups in 1992 (Titus, 2002) to some 16, 18,456 groups that have taken loans from banks. About 24.25 million poor households have gained access to formal banking system through SHG-bank linkage programme and 90 per cent of these groups are only women groups (NABARD 2005). The NABARD (2006) homepage declares that more than 400 women join the SHG movement every hour and an NGO joins the Micro Finance Programme every day.

The formation of SHGs have benefited its members in numerous ways; not only have the assets, incomes and employment opportunities for the women but also enhance the equality of status of women as participants, decision-makers and beneficiaries in the democratic, economic, social and cultural spheres of life (Ritu Jain 2003). The basic principles of the SHGs are group approach, mutual trust, organisation of small and manageable groups, group cohesiveness, spirit of thrift, demand based lending, collateral free, women-friendly loan, peer group pressure in repayment, skill training capacity building and empowerment (Lalitha and Nagaraj, 2002). The growth of self help groups in India is shown in the Table 3 given below.

Table 3: Number of SHGs in India

Year	*Number of SHGs*	*Growth Rate*
2005-06	2238565	
2006-07	2924973	30.66
2007-08	5009794	71.28
2008-09	6121147	22.18
2009-10	6959250	13.69
2010-11	7547269	8.45
2011-12	7960349	5.47

Source: NABARD, *Status of Microfinance in India 2012–13.*

Table 3 shows the number of SHGs in increased from 2238565 (2005-06) to 7960349 (2011-12) but it has registered declining growth rate.

SHG – Bank Linkage Programme

The Self - Help Group Bank Linkage Programme (SHBL) which started as a pilot programme in 1992 has developed at a very fast rate with time. SHG - Bank Linkage Programme was started on the basis of the recommendation of SK Kalia Committee. While the SHG - bank linkage Programme has experienced exponential growth over the past decade, there remain large regional disparities in the growth of the SHG movement with limited progress in certain regions. Though the SHG- Bank Linkage Programme contributed to improve economic conditions, social change was not as apparent, and there are concerns of sustainability and further development of self reliance of the institutions. The SHG-Bank Linkage Programme has the following objectives:

- To develop mutual faith and confidence between the rural poor and bankers
- To combine sensitivity, flexibility and responses of the informal credit system with the strength of administration capabilities, technical strength and the financial resources of the formal financial institutions.

- To expand credit flow/ financial services to the rural poor with less transaction costs.
- To alleviate poverty and empower the women.

Table 4: Growth trends in SHGs Bank Linking Programme

Particulars	*2009*	*2010*	*2011*	*2012*	*2013*
No. of SHGs with outstanding bank loans	42,24,338	48,51,356	47,86,763	43,54,442	44,51,434
Loans disbursed to SHGs (billion)	122.54	144.53	145.48	165.35	205.85
Total bank loan outstanding to SHGs (billion)	226.79	280.38	312.21	363.41	393.75
No. of SHGs with savings accounts with banks (million)	6.12	6.95	7.46	7.96	7.32
Total saving of SHGs with banks (billion)	55.46	61.99	70.16	65.51	82.17

Source: Microfinance India- State of the Sector Report (2013).

The progress of SBLP since 2009 is given in Table 4. All the particulars relating to growth trends of SHGs bank linking programmes like number of SHGs with outstanding, loans disbursed to SHGs, total bank loan outstanding to SHGs, number of SHGs with saving accounts with banks and total saving of SHGs with banks are increasing in nature. This shows that SHGs bank linking programmes are playing very important role in providing the finance to economic activities especially women economic activities.

Though there are different models for purveying microfinance, the Self-Help Group Bank Linkage Programme has emerged as the major programme in the country. It is being implemented by commercial banks, regional rural banks (RRBs), and cooperative banks. In 2009-10, 15.87 lakh new SHGs were credit-linked with banks, and bank loan of Rs 14,453 crore was disbursed to these SHGs. While there was a continuous increase in the amount of credit outstanding per SHG, there was a fluctuating trend in the amount of saving per SHG in the recent years (Table 5).

Table 5: New SHGs Financed by Banks during the year

Year	*No.(Lakh)*	*Amount(Rs.Crore)*	*Growth percentage*
2007-08	12.28	8,849.26	-
2008-09	16.09	12,256.51	38.50
2009-10	15.87	14,453.30	17.90
2010-11	11.96	14,547.73	0.65

Source: NABARD, Status of Microfinance in India 2011–12.

Several factors and strategies have been provided by the SHGs that have made a positive contribution to the empowerment of women. These are full support and timely advice for balancing family and business responsibilities, leadership, experience in decision-making and discussions on social issues. As a result, the numbers of SHGs have been increasing day by day. The details of total number of women SHGs saving linked, credit linked and loans outstanding for the last four years are given in the Tables 6, 7 and 8.

Table 6: SHGs Saving Linked with Bank and Women Empowerment-2008-2012

Year	*Total SHGs (lakh)*	*Women SHGs (lakh)*	*per cent Total women SHGs to total SHGs*	*Women SHGs Amount (crore)*	*Amount (crore)*	*per cent of women SHGs Amount to total SHGs*
2008-09	50.1	22.38	44.67	3785.39	3108.65	82.12
2009-10	61.21	48.64	79.46	5545.62	4434.3	79.96
2010-11	69.53	53.10	76.37	6198.71	4498.66	72.57
2011-12	74.62	60.98	81.7	7016.30	5298.65	75.5

Source: NABARD, Status of Microfinance in India 2011–12.

Table 6 shows the SHGs saving linked with bank during 2007-1012. It can be found that the number of women SHGs saving linked with bank is increasing in nature. It was 22.38 per cent in 2008-09 and followed by 48.64 per cent (2009-10), 53.10 per cent (2010-11) and 60.98 per cent (20111-12). But the percentage of women SHGs amount to total SHGs is declining in nature. It was 82.12 per cent in 2008-09 and followed by 79.96 per cent (2009-10), 72.57 per cent (2010-11) and 75.5 per cent (2011-12).

Table 7: Loan Disbursed of SHGs and Women Empowerment- 2008-2012

Year	*Total SHGs (lakh)*	*Women SHGs (lakh)*	*per cent Total women SHGs to total SHGs*	*Women SHGs Amount (crore)*	*Amount (crore)*	*per cent of women SHGs Amount to total SHGs*
2008-09	50.1	22.38	44.67	3785.39	3108.65	82.12
2009-10	16.09	13.74	85.39	122253.51	10527.38	85.91
2010-11	15.87	12.94	81.54	14453.30	12429.37	85.99
2011-12	11.96	10.17	85	14547.73	12622.33	86

Source: NABARD, Status of Microfinance in India 2011–12.

Table 7 shows the loan disbursed of women SHGs during 2007-12. It found that the total loan disbursed of women SHGs during 2008-12 has been decreasing in nature. It was 22.38 per cent in (2008-09) and followed by 13.74 per cent (2009-10), 12.94 per cent (2010-11) and 10.17 per cent (2011-12). On the other the percentage of women SHGs amount to total SHGs are also increasing in nature. It was

82.12 per cent in 2008-09 and followed by 85.91 per cent (2009-10), 85.99 per cent (2010-11) and 86 per cent (2011-12).

Table 8: Loan outstanding by SHGs and Women Empowerment-2008-2012

Year	*Total SHGs (lakh)*	*Women SHGs (lakh)*	*Per cent women SHGs to total SHGs*	*Total Amount (crore)*	*Women SHGs Amount (crore)*	*per cent of women SHGs Amount to total SHGs*
2008-09	36.26	29.17	80.45	16999.91	13335.61	78.45
2009-10	42.24	32.77	77.58	22769.84	18583.54	81.93
2010-11	48.51	38.91	80.33	28038.38	23030.36	82.14
2011-12	47.87	39.84	83.2	31221.17	26123.75	83.7

Source: NABARD, Status of Microfinance in India 2011–12.

Table 8 shows the loan outstanding of women SHGS during 2008-2012. Both the percentage of women SHGs in number and amount are increasing in nature over a period of time. Further the percentage of loans outstanding of exclusive women SHGs to loans outstanding of total SHGs which was 78.45 per cent in 2008-09 and it is increased to 83.7 per cent in 2011-12. It shows that women SHGs are playing very important role in women empowerment.

Tables 6, 7 and 8 reveal the progress of women SHGs during the year 2008 - 09, 2009 – 10, 2010 –11 and 2011-12. Saving-linked, loan disbursed and loan outstanding amount of women SHGs as a percentage of amounts of total SHGs has been increased during 2008-12. It was also found that employment generation with the help of SHGs is more in below poverty line families than APL (above poverty line) families as a member of SHGs. There is an increase in the expenditure of beneficiaries from last year to the current year. That means it shows a positive impact of SHGs on employment generation. The problems of unemployment as well as poverty in the economy can be solved in this way if SHGs continuously provide help to these people. As majority of beneficiaries of all SHGs accepted expansion of employment after getting loans. Thus, SHGs leads to the way through which the problem of unemployment can be solved and poverty can be removed in the Indian economy.

Conclusion and Policy Recommendations

It is clearly found that microfinance and SBLP are positively influence on women's empowerment through the provisions of loans, saving, employment, and income and so on. So, empowering the poor and vulnerable women of the society through microfinance is the great task to the government. In this direction the objective of our country is to enroll at least 50 per cent of all rural women in as members of SHGs over the next few years and link these SHGs to banks.

Self Help Groups, which play a pivotal role in microfinance, are overwhelmed by problems, such as poor accounting and management. So this should be immediately taken into consideration. MFIs do not have adequate access to financial capital unlike the rest of the financial sector, and as a result are burdened by high debt equity ratios and equity shortfall. So, there is need to support from state government, NGO concentration and public awareness regarding the introduction of MFIs and SHGs. The current policies of micro finance and SHGs are outdated and they need to reset.

Existing MFIs should also start looking at other initiatives, such as larger loans for different segments, technology advancement and professional processes, participation by private sector banks, better monitoring and control by the authorities to ensure that the funds reach the needy, awareness building through media, and federations such as Micro Finance Development Equity Fund (MFDEF) recently set up by NABARD, are expected to play a vital role in meeting the equity needs of MFIs. More such agencies are required to support the government in making microfinance a success.

REFERENCES

1. Jayanthi K J (2011), Microfinance: Implementations and Policy Challenges. Thought paper, Infosys, Finacle.
2. NABARD (2010), Status of Micro Finance in India 2009-10.
3. NABARD (2012-13), *Status of Microfinance in India* 2012–13.
4. Nair T and Tankha A (2013), Microfinance India – State-of-the-Sector Report 2013. Sage Publications India Pvt. Ltd, New Delhi.
5. Narang, U (2012), Impact of Self-Help Groups Bank Linkage Programme in India. *International Journal of Trade and Commerce-IIARTC, 1 (2).*
6. Narang, U (2012), Self Help Group: An Effective Approach to Women Empowerment in India. International Journal of Social Science and Inter-disciplinary Research, 1(8).
7. Sarumathi, S and Mohan, K. (2011), Role of Micro Finance in Women's Empowerment - An Empirical study in Pondicherry region rural SHG's, Journal of Management and Science, 1 (1).
8. Swaina, R B and Wallentin, F Y (2009), Does microfinance empower women Evidence from self-help groups in India. *International Review of Applied Economics,* 23(5), pp. 541–556.

21

Women Empowerment Through Micro–Entrepreneurship

Girish G.S., Nagaraj H.V., Gowda N.K and Yogish S.N.

Abstract: *In recent years micro-finance has become a much favoured intervention for poverty alleviation in the developing countries. Microfinance programmes are currently being promoted as a key strategy for, simultaneously addressing both poverty alleviation and women's empowerment. Providing access to microfinance is considered pre-condition for poverty alleviation and also women empowerment. Providing for women with effective financial services helps them to deal with vulnerability and can be there by help to reduce poverty. Financial services to low income entrepreneurs maybe the single most effective way to reduce poverty and achieve broad-based economic growth. Against this background this paper focuses on the role of microfinance in empowering women in particular. Furthermore, empowerment involves both the individual change and collective action. For an empowerment approach the development to be successfully implemented, changes are needed in the abilities of individuals and groups to identify and meet their own need in the households, communities, organisations, institutions and society. Empowerment enables woman to control their own lives and to set their own to organise, to help each other and to make demand on the state and on society itself for change. With the collective empowerment of women, of course, would bring* *with it the individual empowerment of women. While studying empowerment it is also essential to locate individuals within the historical, social and political contacts of their social group to correctly interpret the impact of development outcomes. In this regard, present paper reviews the women empowerment through micro entrepreneurship by the means of micro-finance, along with key strategies in overcoming the inherent limitations in empowering women.*

Key Words: Micro-finance, Micro-Entrepreneurship, Women-Empowerment, SHGs, Poverty Alleviation.

Introduction

Women entrepreneurship plays a critical role in the economic development of societies in its smallest manifestation, it enhances livelihoods with the family while on larger and deeper levels, and national wealth accrues. However for long, women entrepreneurs have low business performance compared to their male counterparts. And this has been attributed to factors which normally affect entrepreneurial performance such as lack of credit, saving, education, or training, and social capital. Women entrepreneurs play a significant role in local economies and women developing countries are undertaking a good number of small-scale enterprises. In a developing country like India where economic status of women is very painful especially in rural pockets and opportunities of earning are very less, entrepreneurship in small enterprise is an option for women either individually or through SHGs. The growth rate of women's participation in economic activities is much lower than the expected rate. If we look at the developed countries we see that women are actively participative in the business and trade activities, including agriculture, without any social or other restrictions. But in India, there are still many social and cultural restrictions on women. Hence, women participation in entrepreneurial activities is less than the requirement of the fast growth of India.

Microfinance serves as a means to empower the poor, and provides a valuable tool to assist the economic development process. While the main objective of the microfinance is to enable the poor to acquire productive assets, in practice the size of the loan being very small and the repayment period being very short, microfinance activity in India does not lead to the creation of sustainable micro enterprises. The nature of the target group and the absence of security for the loan generally tend to create an atmosphere of utmost caution, which is reflected in the size, and the duration of the loan. Further, microfinance is by its very nature a group activity and therefore may not promote individuals excelling to set up thriving micro-enterprises. The answer to this seems to be that the initial phase of microfinance activity should lead to a second phase of financing where individuals with proven record are picked up for commercial scale financing operations.

Micro Finance and Micro Enterprise

Microfinance means providing small loans very poor families to help them engage in productive activities or grow their tiny business. Microfinance originally established to impel the moneylender out of business and to bridge the capital gap apparently unfilled by the rural co-operatives and commercial banks. Microfinance is a logical approach to development because it functions at the grass root level, can be sustainable, is capable of involving large segments of the population and builds both human and productive capacity. Microfinance is the provision of a broad range of financial services to low-income micro enterprise and households. Robinson (2001 defines microfinance as) "small-scale finance services-primarily credit and savings-provided to people who farm, fish or herd" and adds that it "refers to all types of financing services provided to low-income households and enterprise". It is observed that the micro-finance activities are mainly offered by formal financial institutions with the help of SHGs. As a result, micro-finance programme is growing in those areas where there is incredible growth of formal financial institutions.

Micro enterprise is a term used often in development programmes such as poverty alleviation and self–employment in particular. The micro and small sector has been a major component of industrial growth of the developing countries where these can be regarded as an absolute force of innovation and development. There was no definition of micro enterprise earlier. In accordance with the provision of Micro, Small and Medium Enterprise Development (MSMED) Act, 2006 the Micro Enterprises are further classified in two classes.

- **Manufacture Enterprises:** The micro manufacturing enterprise is defined in terms of investment in plant and machinery. The investment should not exceed twenty-five lakh rupees.
- **Service Enterprises:** The enterprises engaged in providing or rendering of services and are defined in terms of investment in equipment. The limit of investment in plant and machinery /

equipment for micro service enterprises should not exceed ten lakh rupees.

Objectives of the Study

The basic objectives of this study are:

(a) To discuss the significance of Women Development programmes in general.

(b) To trace out the status of women in their ordinary business of life.

(c) To analyse the levels of Attitude, Skill and Knowledge gained by women entrepreneurs through microfinance (SHGs).

(d) To analyse the impact of empowerment of women entrepreneurs.

(e) To suggest some remedial measures to improve upon the efficiency and effectiveness of micro-finance in developing women entrepreneurship.

Statement of the Problem

In olden days, women were restricted to take part in any social activities and not given roles in decision making in her family. The situation was even more worsening in rural and remote areas. Now the situation has been changed. She is given freedom to do what she wishes. In today's scenario more women are engaged in income generating activities. This is because of NGO and other financial institution came forward to provide microfinance to poor women. They believe that a woman is the small credit risk and often benefits the whole family. The main aim of microfinance is to empower women. This induced the researcher to focus more on the empowerment of rural women who participates in the microfinance.

Woman Entrepreneur and Her Qualities

She is a woman of commitment, independently employed, she has a close relationship with her father and after obtaining an undergraduate and subsequently a graduate degree in some area of liberal arts, marries, has children and starts her first significant entrepreneurial venture in the service area in her late 30s or early 40s. Her biggest problems at start-up later in the venture reflect a lack of business training and generally in the financial area.

Leadership Qualities

Some of the outstanding qualities of women entrepreneurs are;

Accept challenges	Ambitious
Drive	Enthusiastic

Hard work
Industrious
Skillful
Adventurous
Educated
Keenness to learn and imbibe new ideas
Intelligent
Studious
Patience
Motivator
Potential Optimism
Conscious
Determination to excel
Experienced
Perseverance

In spite of the remarkable importance of women's participation, their jobs have been considered as an "extra income" to family survival or simply to improve its living conditions. Moreover, micro-enterprises owned by women have been considered as a way to meet primary needs instead of a profitable source of income. Women have had to lead fight against an adverse environment, which traditionally had been minimising and exploiting their capacities. As a consequence of this reality, in some cases, women are just satisfied with the non-financial benefits, such as the psychological satisfaction of social contact.

Benefits of a Women Entrepreneur

First-born child of middle class parents
Father and /or mother in independent business
College-educated
Married
Early 30s for the first significant venture
Previous experience in new venture
Desires independence
Motivated by desire for independence and job satisfaction
Small and young business
Self-confident
Moderate risk-taker
High tolerance for ambiguity
High energy level
Biggest problems in start-up
Lack of business training
Personnel management
Biggest problems in current operations;

- Lack of experience in financial planning
- Weak collateral position
- Cash flow management
- Taxation

With education and training, the women have gained confidence to do all work, which was the prerogative of man and do it excellently, rather better than men. Over the years, the educational women have become ambitious, acquired experience and basic skills of competency and self-assurance.

Women's Micro-Enterprises; Main Characteristics

Considering the entrepreneurial environment, women's activities are very interesting as they offer a great source of knowledge and innovation. For example, there is no single type of female micro-entrepreneur; they differ in social background, educational level, experience and age. One important element, and perhaps the only characteristic that men will never have, is the possibility to transfer "motherhood skills" to job. These include fostering of other people's development through guiding, monitoring and sharing information. Women are experienced in balancing claims, in the organising and pacing, and in handling difficulties.

Businesswomen in developing countries share the following general characteristics:

- They are concentrated in market sectors that have low barriers to entry and low levels of outside communication (transfer to other markets) they focus on trade, services and light manufacturing activities.
- Their business is smaller than others, employing less than five employees.
- The owners have relatively little previous working experience.
- They use traditional technologies.
- Most employees are family related.
- They are often home based.
- Business growth strategies are affected by household responsibilities.
- Owners tend to have lower levels of education and literacy.
- Women start their enterprises with less professional work experience and knowledge of their sector than their male counterparts.

Women's Participation in Micro Finance Activities

Although men, as well as women, face difficulties in establishing an additional enterprise, women have barriers to overcome. Among them are negative socio-cultural attitudes, legal barriers, and practical external barriers, lack of education and personal difficulties.

In spite of this, for women and especially for poor women, micro-enterprise ownership has emerged as a strategy for economical survival. One of the most essential factors contributing to success in micro-entrepreneurship is access to capital and financial services. For various reasons, women have had less access to these services than men.

In general, women need access to small loans (especially for working capital), innovative forms of collateral, frequent repayment schedules more appropriate to the cash flows of their enterprises, simpler application procedures and improved access to savings accounts. Surveys have shown that many elements contribute to make it more difficult for women in small business to make a profit.

SHGs' Women Entrepreneurship Development

A Self Help Group is defined as a "self governed, peer controlled informal group of people with similar socio-economic background and having a desire to collectively perform common purpose."

The SHG is considered as a viable organisation of the rural poor particularly women for delivering micro credit in order to undertake entrepreneurial activities. Some of the SHGs managed by the rural poor women successfully demonstrated how to mobilise and manage thrift activities, appraise credit needs enforce financial disciplines, maintain credit linkages with banks and effectively undertake income generating activities. In the last decade, SHGs have gained increased attention among women entrepreneurs. They have become increasing important programme of the development process in the women in all of these main areas of work such as attitude, skill and knowledge. On the other hand, there is a current view that SHGs constitute a viable alternative to government as channels of development assistance, particularly in developing countries.

Microfinance is a critical tool in addressing the issues of financial exclusion is the inability of individuals, households or groups to access necessary financial services in an appropriate form. In India, microfinance scene is dominated by Self Help Groups (SHGs) - Banks linkage Programme, aimed at providing a cost effective mechanism for providing financial services to the 'unreached poor'.

In the last decade, SHGs have gained increased attention among women entrepreneurs. They have become increasing important programme of the development process in the women in all of these main areas of work such as attitude, skill and knowledge. On the other hand, there is a current view that SHGs constitute a viable alternative to government as channels of development assistance, particularly in developing countries.

Impact of Micro-Finance on Women

Microfinance in India is woman centric. Reports and evaluation studies indicate that these activities have led to creation of awareness among rural women, promotion of savings habit, better utilisation of money to generate income, and general improvement in the respect for women in the rural society.

At the same time, fear is expressed that in the social milieu where the women can come under the family/male pressure, she might be forced to misdirect the loan. In other words, the women may be used as a front by the society. Such apprehension is quite realistic because of the still widely prevalent illiteracy among women. Therefore microfinance, as is envisaged, will succeed and will be sustainable in areas where female literacy is high and programme is accompanied by good amount of training and awareness building.

Progress of Micro-finance Programme

Year	*SHGs Financed by Banks during the Year*			*Bank Loan Outstanding*		
	No. (lakh)	*Amount (Rs.Crore)*	*Growth (per cent)*	*No. (lakh)*	*Amount (Crore)*	*Growth (per cent)*
2007-08	12.28	8849.26	-	36.26	16999.90	-
2008-09	16.09	12256.51	38.50	42.24	22679.85	33.41
2009-10	15.87	14453.30	17.90	48.52	28038.28	23.62
2010-11	11.96	14547.73	0.65	47.87	31221.17	11.35
2111-12	11.48	16534.77	13.66	43.54	36340.00	16.40

Source: NABARD.
Note; *Includes new well as repeat loans to SHGs.

Under the SHG-Bank Linkage Programme, as on 31 March, 2012, 79.60 lakh SHG-held savings bank accounts with total savings of Rs 6,551 crore were in operation. By November 2012 another 2.14 lakh SHGs had come under the ambit of the programme, taking the cumulative number of savings-linked groups to 81.74. As on March 2012, 43.54 lakh SHGs had outstanding bank loans of Rs 36,340 crore. During 2012-13 (up to November 2012) 3.67 lakh SHGs were financed with an amount Rs 6,664.15 crore.

This provides ample evidence to the fact that micro finance through SHGs laid the seeds for social and economic empowerment of women. 'Banking the Unbankable' through micro finance is a valuable contribution to development planning as it presents an alternative way to development. Micro finance has ushered in a new life of liveliness, joy and jubilations for them. It has aided in making the passage from darkness to light for thousands of women struggling to breathe in the quagmire of poverty.

Reasons for Women Opting for Entrepreneurship:

Self determination, expectation for recognition, self esteem and career goal are the key drivers for taking up entrepreneurship by women. Sometimes, women chose such career path for discovering their inner potential, caliber in order to achieve self satisfaction. It can also provide a mean to make best use of their leisure hours. However, dismal economic conditions of the women arising out of unemployment in the family and divorce can compel women into entrepreneurial activities.

Obstacles for Women Entrepreneurship

The entrepreneurial process is same for men and women. Successful men and women entrepreneurs undergo similar motivations and thus achieve success in largely same way under similar challenges. They are also found to have access to fund from the same sources.

The same condition both men and women can be successful entrepreneurs. However, in practice most of the upcoming women entrepreneurs face problems that are of different dimensions and magnitudes than that faced by their male counterparts. These problems, generally, prevent these women entrepreneurs from realising their potential as entrepreneurs. The major hurdles that the women face during starting and running a company generally come from financing and balancing of life. The balancing of life is caused due to lack of family support for the women. The other hindering external factors include gender discrimination, inaccessibility to information, training opportunities, infrastructure etc. Some internal factors like risk aversion by women, lack of confidence, lack of vision of strategic leader etc. can also create obstacles for the women entrepreneurship development.

Problems of Women Entrepreneurship in India

Definitely, there are a number of problems regarding women entrepreneurship in India, researchers having identified issues relating to social aspects, economic life, skill problems, problems of family support, courage etc.

1. Absence of Definite Agenda of Life
2. Absence of Balance between Family and Career Obligations
3. Poor Degree of Financial Freedom
4. No Direct Ownership of the Property
5. Paradox of Entrepreneurial Skill and Finance
6. No Awareness about Capacities

7. Low Ability to Bear Risk
8. Problems of Work with Male Workers
9. Negligence by Financial Institutions
10. Lack of Self-Confidence
11. Lack of Professional Education
12. Mobility Constraints
13. Lack of Interaction with Successful Entrepreneurs

Measures to Remove the Obstacles

The elimination of obstacles for women entrepreneurship requires a major change in traditional attitudes and mindsets of people in society rather than being limited to only creation of opportunities for women. Hence, it is imperative to design programmes that will address to attitudinal changes, training, supportive services.

A. The basic requirement in development of women entrepreneurship is to make aware the women regarding her existence, her unique identity and her contribution towards the economic growth and development of country.

B. The basic instinct of entrepreneurship should be tried to be reaped into the minds of the women from their childhood. This could be achieved by carefully designing the curriculum that will impart the basic knowledge along with its practical implication regarding management (financial, legal etc.) of an enterprise.

C. Adopting a structured skill training package can pave the way for development of women entrepreneurship. Such programmes can train, motivate and assist the upcoming women entrepreneurship in achieving their ultimate goals. Various schemes like the World Bank sponsored programmes can be undertaken for such purposes. The course design should focus on imparting input on profitability, marketability and practical management lessons. Besides, there should be consideration in helping the women entrepreneurs in balancing their family life and work life.

D. As a special concern, computer illiterate women can be trained on Information Technology to take the advantage of new technology and automation. The established and successful women entrepreneurs can act as advisors for the upcoming women entrepreneurs.

E. The initiatives taken from these well established entrepreneurs for having interaction with such upcoming women entrepreneurs can be proved to be beneficial in terms of boosting their morale and confidence. It may result in more active involvement of women entrepreneurs in their enterprises.

F. Infrastructure set up plays a vital role for any enterprise. Government can set some priorities for women entrepreneurs for allocation of industrial plots, sheds and other amenities. However, precautionary measures should be undertaken to avoid the misuse of such facility by the men in the name of the women.

Even in today's era of modernisation the women entrepreneurs depend on males of their family for marketing activities. This is simply because they lack the skill and confidence for undertaking such activities. Women development corporations should come forward to help the women entrepreneurs in arranging frequent exhibitions and setting up marketing outlets to provide space for the display of products or advertisement about services made by women.

Measures to Increase and Support Women's Participation in Microfinance Activities

Governments should explore ways of developing innovative credit programmes using intermediary channels or institutions closer to the target groups such as co-operatives, women's group associations and other grassroots organisations. Savings and credit programmes should be designed in a way not to exclude women from participating. Additionally, there is a need to examine the impact of structural adjustment policies on men and women at the family level as well as within various sub-sectors of the labour market and within the small enterprise sector itself.

In general terms, in order to facilitate the participation of women in micro and small enterprise, donors should:

- Encourage micro-enterprise programmes to develop specific strategies for recruiting women as clients from within their existing target groups.
- Encourage micro-enterprise programs to expand their target groups to include the sizes and types of enterprise activities in which women engage and/or experiment with, business and technical assistance according to the needs of these types of enterprises.
- Consider expanding support to a broader range of organisations, especially those organisations active in rural areas that aim at poverty eradication. Support for these organisations should include technical assistance and training in programme

planning, management and in developing teams of female staff to assist clients in business planning and management.

- Increase the availability of working capital;
- Experiment with lending programmes that do not require conventional forms of collateral;
- Replicate and expand existing successful methodologies for delivering small working–capital loans;
- Introduce savings mobilisation components in the context of credit or other enterprise assistance programmes;
- Promote credit policies that are open to both small-scale enterprise activities and enterprises operating in trade, commerce and other small enterprise sectors where women have higher participation rates.

Technical assistance for micro-enterprise development should focus more on basic training in product marketing and design concepts and on transmitting skills to increase and diversify production. Governments can also directly increase the market for micro-enterprise products by improving rural and urban infrastructures.

Findings and Suggestions

- Donor agencies should promote studies to support local women's groups in educational and promotional campaigns and launch special studies on specific policy problems related to the micro-enterprise sector and gender issues in microfinance activities.
- Short-term assistance programs might aim at increasing the productivity of women's labour by providing credit, technology, and skill training.
- Long-term objectives could emphasise eliminating institutional constraints which limit women's access to productive resources, creating social, technological and economic mechanisms to reduce conflicts between women's productive and reproductive roles, as well as defining strategies to address traditional and legal barriers that hamper or preclude the active participation of women in the productive sectors of the economy.
- The key issue for successful microfinance programme focused on women should consider them in a broader context, as a family nucleus, that is vital for societal improvement and progress. Following this idea, microfinance programmes should provide women with specific adapted products through appropriate methodologies, which can offer competitiveness to their business but also well-being to them and their families.

Conclusion

Traditionally women have been marginalised. A high percentage of women are among the poorest of the poor. Microfinance activities can give them a means to climb out of poverty. Microfinance could be a solution to help them to extend their horizon and offer them social recognition and empowerment.

On the other hand, thanks to women's capabilities to combine productive and reproductive roles in microfinance activities and society has enabled them to produce a greater impact as they will increase at the same time the quality of life of the women micro entrepreneur and also of her family. The question is not whether we should focus on women or men. Both female and male play vital role in creating income and jobs. Their capacity for innovation stimulates general economic growth. Microfinance programmes should be accessible to both of them (male and female entrepreneurs) and offer adequate policies regarding to market interchange, access to financial services, and training and technical assistance.

Microfinance through SHGs laid the seeds for social and economic empowerment of women. 'Banking the Unbankable' through micro finance is valuable contribution to development planning as it presents an alternative way to development. Micro finance has ushered in a new life of liveliness, joy and jubilations for them. It has aided in making the passage from darkness to light for thousands of women struggling to breathe in the quagmire of poverty.

REFERENCES

1. Sarumathi S. and K.Mohan, *Role of Micro Finance in Women's Emperment* (An Empirical study in Pondicherry region rural SHG's), Journal of Management and Science Vol. 1, No. 1 (Sep'2011) ISSN: 2249-1260.
2. Ruth Marjor 4 Adhiambo Ocholah Simeo Okelo Cainan Ojwang Fredrick Aila Patrick B. Ojera, *Literature Review on the Relationship between Microfinance Provision and Women Enterprise Performance*, Greener Journal Social Sciences, GJSS ISSN: 2276-7800, Impact Factor 2012, (UJRI): 0.7863 ICV 2012: 5.99.
3. Dr. Jyotish Prakash Basu, Reader and Head, Department of Economics, Raja Peary Mohan College, Uttarpara, Hooghly, *Microfinance and Women Empowerment an Empirical Study with special reference to West Bengal.*
4. Isidore Ekpe Norsiah Binti Mat Razli Che Razak, *The Effect of Microfinance Factors on Women Entrepreneurs' Performance in Nigeria: A Conceptual Framework*, International Journal of Business and Social Science, Vol. 1 No. 2; November 2010.
5. Moin Qazi, *Microfinance and Women's Empowerment*, Himalaya Publishing House, Mumbai, 2007.

6. Dr Vasant Desai, Director, Visvesvararaya Institute of Socio-economic Research (VISER), Mumbai, *Small- Scale Industries and Entrepreneurship,* Himalaya Publishing House, 2008.
7. Chanchal Charan, *Micro-Finance in India; Rural Development and Poverty Alleviation*, Southern Economist, Nov. 15, 2013.
8. Sivakkolundu C. and Lognanthan, *Micro Finance and Self Help Groups*, Southern Economist, Nov. 15, 2013.
9. Chakraborty K.C., *Financial Inclusion in India; Journey so far and way forward,* Southern Economist, Nov. 15, 2013.
10. Angel Anila A., *Impact of EDP Curriculum on the SHG Women Entrepreneurship Development,* Southern Economist, July 1, 2013.

22

Women Empowerment Through Microfinance—Its Impact on Different Self Help Groups

Narayan D., Arundhekar Subramani G. R. and Raghavendra H.

Abstract: *Microfinance is a type of banking service that is provided to unemployed or low-income individuals or groups who would otherwise have no other means of gaining financial services. Microfinance through Self -Help Group (SHG) has been recognised internationally as the modern tool to combat poverty and for rural development. Microfinance and SHGs are effective in reducing poverty empowering women and creating awareness which finally results in sustainable development of the nation. The main aim of Microfinance is to empower women. In this paper the role played by Microfinance in women's empowerment are considered into two dimensions namely social and economical. The objectives of the study are (i) To understand the impact on income before and after joining different SHGs in Bijapur District, Karnataka (ii) To analyse the freedom and problems a women members get in SHG's (iii) To analyse the relationship between literacy level and awareness of education after joining SHGs (iv) To analyze the relationship between the empowerment of the women economically and socially after joining SHGs.*

This study was undertaken in rural areas of Bijapur District, Karnataka both primary and secondary data are used. Primary data are enumerated from a field survey in the study region Secondary data are collected from NGOs reports, magazines, journals etc. The statistical tools used are Sign Test, Correlation Test and Percentage. Analysis showed that there is a gradual impact on the income among rural women's. From the interaction among the respondents it is noticed that some members are expecting more training sessions in income generating activities. All they need is to interact and attend many training programmes. There is definite improvement in empowerment among rural women as a result of participating in micro finance after joining different SHGs programme.

Keywords: SHGs, Microfinance, Women's Empowerment, Sign Test, Correlation Test.

1. Introduction

Microfinance is the provision of financial services to low-income clients, including consumers and the self employed, who traditionally lack access to banking and related services. Microcredit, or Microfinance, is banking the on bankable, bringing credit, savings and other essential financial services within the reach of millions of people who are too poor to be served by regular banks, in most cases because they are unable to offer sufficient collateral. In general, banks are for people with money, not for people without. (Gert van Maanen, Microcredit: Sound Business or Development Instrument, Oikocredit, 2004) is based on the premise that the poor have skills which remain unutilised or underutilised. Microcredit fits best to those with entrepreneurial capability and possibility ultimately; the goal of microfinance is to give low income people an opportunity to become self-sufficient by providing a means of saving money, borrowing money and insurance.

The main aim of microfinance is to empower women. Women make up a large proportion of microfinance beneficiaries. Traditionally, women (especially those in underdeveloped countries) have been unable to readily participate in economic activity. Microfinance provides women with the financial baeking they need to start business ventures and actively participate in the economy. It gives them confidence, improves their status and makes them more active in decision-making, thus encouraging gender equality. According to CGAP, long-standing MFIs even report a decline in violence towards women since the inception of microfinance.

The most of the microcredit institutions and agencies all over the world focuses on women in developing countries. Observations and experience shows that women are a small credit risk, repaying their loans and tend more often to benefit the whole family. In another aspect it´s also viewed as a method giving the women more status in a socioeconomic way and changing the current conservative relationship between gender and class when women are able to provide income to the household. There are many reasons why women have become the primary target of microfinance services.

A recent World Bank report confirms that societies that discriminate on the basis of gender pay the cost of greater poverty, slower economic growth, weaker governance, and a lower living standard for all people. At a macro level, it is because 70 per cent of the world's poor are women. Women have a higher unemployment rate than men in virtually every country and make up the majority of the informal sector of most economies. They constitute the bulk of those who need microfinance services. Giving women access to microcredit loans therefore generates a multiplier effect that increases the impact of a microfinance institution's activity, benefiting multiple generations.

NABARD (2005) explains that the Self Help Group is a group with "an average size of about 15 people from a homogeneous class. They come together in addressing their common problems. They are encouraged to make voluntary thrift on a regular basis. They use this pooled resources to make small interest bearing loans to their members. The process helps them imbibe the essentials of financial intermediation including prioritisation of needs setting terms and conditions and accounts keeping. This gradually builds financial discipline in all of them. They also learn to handle resources of a size that is much beyond the individual capacities of any of them. The SHG members begin to appreciate that resources are limited and have a cost. Once the graphs show this mature financial behavior, banks are encouraged to make loans to the SHG in certain multiples of the accumulated savings of the SHG. The bank loans are given without any collateral and at market interest rates. The groups continue to decide the terms of loans to their own members. Since the groups' own accumulated savings are part and parcel of the aggregate loans made by the groups to their members, peer pressure ensures timely repayments." In this paper the role played by microfinance in women's empowerment are considered in three dimensions namely, psychological social and economical.

2. Statement of the problem

In olden days women were restricted to take part in any social activities and not given roles in decision making in her family. The situation was even more worsening in rural and remote areas. Now the situation has been changed she is given the freedom to do what she wishes. In today's scenario more women are engaged in income generating activities. This is because of NGO and other financial institution like Self-help groups came forward to provide microfinance to poor women. They believe that a woman is the small credit risk and often benefits the whole family. The main aim of Microfinance is to empower women. This induced the researcher to focus more on the empowerment of rural women who participates in the microfinance.

3. Objectives of the study

1. To understand the impact on income before and after joining different SHGs Groups in Bijapur District, Karnataka.
2. To analyse the freedom and problems a women members get in SHGs.
3. To analyse the relationship between literacy level and awareness of education after joining SHGs.
4. To analyse the relationship between the empowerment of the women economically and socially after joining SHGs.

4. Hypotheses

- **H0- Null Hypothesis:** There is a significant difference between income before and after joining different SHGs Groups.
- **H1- Alternative Hypothesis**: There is no significant difference between income before and after joining different SHGs Groups .

5. Research Methodology

The study was undertaken in a few taluks of Bijapur district by using random sampling method. Both primary and secondary data were used for the study. Primary data were enumerated from a direct interview and questionnaire in the study region. Secondary data were collected from NGOs reports and other documents. Since the number was rather large, random sampling was followed. Altogether 100 samples were chosen for research from five taluks of Bijapur district. A structured questionnaire was used for collecting primary data from the women members of rural SHGs who were engaged in micro enterprises through Microfinance. Sign Test, coefficient of correlation and percentages were used for the analysis and interpretation of data. The analysis and interpretation of data have been done by using Excel and SPSS 16 software.

Table 1: Area covered under different SHGs

Taluks	*Name of the SHGs*
Bijapur	Sri Bhavani Stree Shakthi Sangha
	Sri Yallamma Mahila Swasahaya Sangha
Basavan Bagewadi	Renuka Devi Swasahaya Sangha
	Durga Parmeshwari Swasahaya Sangha
Muddebihal	Saraswathi Mahila Swasahaya Sangha
	Sri Laxmi Stree Shakthi Sangha
Sindgi	Ganga Mahila Swasahaya Sangha
	Jai Bhavani Swasahaya Sangha
Indi	Sri Kalikamba Mahila Swasahaya Sangha
	Durga Mata Swasahaya Sangha

Source: Primary data and random method used.

6. Limitations of the Study

The study was confined to five taluks of Bijapur District. The data were collected only from those who were engaged in income generating activities.

7. Results and Discussion

7.1. Age of Women from different SHGs

Out of the 100 respondents 58 per cent of the respondents are under the age group of less than 30 who are in different SHGs. 24 per cent are under the age group of 30-45, 18 per cent are under the age group of 45 and above, this indicates that most of the women are young.

Table 2: Frequency Distribution of Age of Women

Age Group	*No. of Respondents*	*Percentage*
Below 30	58	58
30 to 45	24	24
Above 45	18	18

Source: Primary Data.

7.2. Literacy of Women

Out of the 100 respondents 55 per cent of the respondents are illiterate who are in different SHG's. 25 per cent have studied up to Secondary, 11 per cent have studied up to Primary and only few per cent of people have studied Higher and UG level. This shows that even now the most of the women are still uneducated.

Table 3: Qualification

Qualification	*No. of Respondents*	*Percentage*
Elementary	4	4
Primary	11	11
Secondary	25	25
Higher Secondary	2	2
UG	3	3
Illiterate	55	55

Source: Primary Data.

7.3 Microfinance helps to reduce Poverty Level

Out of the 100 respondents 93 per cent of the respondents say that microfinance helps to reduce the poverty level and only seven per cent won't believe that it reduce the poverty level.

Table 4: Microfinance helps to reduce the Poverty Level

Responses	*No. of Respondents*	*Percentage*
Yes	93	93
No	7	7
Total	100	100

Source: Primary Data.

7.4. Women's Empowerment

Out of the 100 respondents 91 per cent of the respondents say that, they can express their opinions freely both in group and in the family also i.e., they don't have any problem with the group and leader.

Table 5: Women's Empowered Socially

Responses	*No. of Respondents*	*Percentage*
Yes	91	91
No	9	9
Total	100	100

Source: Primary Data.

7.5. Women's Freedom to move independently

Out of the 100 respondents 88 per cent of the respondents say that, they can move to any place without the help of their family members to bank, government places which indicates social mobility.

Table 6: Women's Freedom to move independently

Responses	*No. of Respondents*	*Percentage*
Yes	88	88
No	12	12
Total	100	100

Source: Primary Data.

7.6 Purpose of Getting Microfinance

Out of the 100 respondents 58 per cent of the respondents say that, they want to start the new business through microfinance. This shows that women's are getting confident towards microfinance to start a business.

Table 7: Purpose of getting Microfinance

Purposes	*No. of Respondents*	*Percentage*
Household	14	14
To Start a Business	58	58
To Promote an Existing Business	6	6
Children Education	9	9
Agriculture	13	13
Total	100	100

Source: Primary Data.

7.7. Correlation Test

7.7.1. Correlation between Improvement in literacy level and Awareness on Education

The correlation between the improvement in literacy level and Awareness on Education is 0.941 which is highly significant positive correlation indicating that improvement in the respondent's literacy level leads to awareness in a child's education after joining SHGs.

Table 8: Correlation between Improvement in literacy level and Awareness on Education

		Improvement in Literacy Level	*Awareness in Education*
Improvement in literacy level	Pearson Correlation	1	.941**
	Sig. (2-tailed)		.000
	N	100	100
Awareness in education	Pearson Correlation	.941**	1
	Sig. (2-tailed)	.000	
	N	100	100

**Correlation is significant at the 0.01 level (2-tailed).
Source: Primary and Computed Data using SPSS 16.

7.7.2. Correlation between joining SHGs and Empowerment of Women Socially and Economically

The correlation between after joining SHGs and empowerment of women socially and economically is 0.720 which is high positive correlation indicating that joining of SHGs made the women's more empower socially and economically.

Table 9: Correlation between joining SHGs and Empowerment of women socially and economically

		After Joining SHG's	*Empowerment of Women Socially and Economically*
After Joining SHG's	Pearson Correlation	1	.720**
	Sig. (2-tailed)		.000
	N	100	100
Empowerment of women socially and economically	Pearson Correlation	.720**	1
	Sig. (2-tailed)	.000	
	N	100	100

** Correlation is significant at the 0.01 level (2-tailed).
Source: Primary and Computed Data using SPSS 16.

7.8. Average Income before and after joining SHGs

Table 10: Sign Test

Name of SHGs	*Average Income Before joining SHG's(Annually)*	*Average Income After joining SHG's(Annually)*	*SIGN*	
			Positive	*Negative*
Sri Bhavani Stree Shakthi Sangha	55000	80000	+	
Sri Yallamma Mahila Swasahaya Sangha	68000	65000		-
Renuka Devi Swasahaya Sangha	58000	100000	+	
Durga Parameshwari Swasahaya Sangha	75000	120000	+	
Saraswathi Mahila Swasahaya Sangha	100100	100099	0	0
Sri Laxmi Stree Shakthi Sangha	85000	98000	+	
Ganga Mahila Swasahaya Sangha	56000	92000	+	
Jai Bhavani Swasahaya Sangha	49000	48000		-
Sri Kalikamba Mahila Swasahaya Sangha	69000	73000	+	
Durga Mata Swasahaya Sangha	89000	12200	+	
Total	7	2		

Source: Primary Data.

Sign Test

Frequencies		*N*
Average Income After joining SHG's (Annually) - Average Income Before joining SHG's (Annually)	Negative Differences	2
	Positive Differences	7
	Ties	1
	Total	10

8. Findings

1. Most of the respondents are of the age of below 30 years. This shows that women of young age are interested in joining SHGs.

2. The qualification of women is less educated. This shows that even now the most of the women are still uneducated
3. As far as the self help group is concerned they don't face any type of problems or compulsions from leaders or from other members in the group. Women are given full freedom to express their opinions.
4. Respondents believe that microfinance helped to remove the poverty level and lead a normal life.
5. Respondents believe that improvement in literacy level helps to increase in awareness of children's education.
6. Respondents believe that after joining SHGs it has helped for empowerment of women socially and economically.
7. Respondents say that there is a significant impact on income before and after joining different SHGs.

Conclusion

The rural area Self-Help Groups are performing well. The study concludes that microfinance through different SHGs brought social empowerment and economic empowerment. Impact of microfinance is appreciable in reducing poverty line. The SHG members feel free to move with their groups and leaders. It leads them to participate in various social welfare activities with good cooperation. There is lot of impact on income after joining SHGs and finally it is noticed that all they need is a way to develop their skills and talents by participating in various training programmes.

REFERENCES

1. Agarwal S, "Technology Model for Women Empowerment", Kurukshetra (2007): May, pp.18-28.
2. C.R Kothari, "Research Methodology methods and techniques", 2nd Edition (2007). New Age International (P) Ltd. Publishers, New Delhi.
3. http://papers.ssrn.com/sol3/papers.cfm?abstract_id=722614, accessed on 4th April 2013.
4. http://www.deccanherald.com/content/275414/F , accessed on 4th April 2013.
5. http://www.kolar.nic.in/Taluk_Info.html, accessed on 1st April 2013.
6. J.K Sharma, "Business Statistics", 2nd Edition (2007), Dorling Kindersley (p) Ltd. publishers, New Delhi.
7. Nagayya, "Microfinance for self help groups", Kurukshetra (2000): August, pp. 15-28.

8. Reserve Bank of India, Report of the Internal Group to examine issues relating to rural credit and Microfinance, (2005).
9. Sharma K.C, "Microfinance Through self help groups", Indian Journal of Agricultural Economics, 56 (3), (2001): pp. 76-86.

23

Microfinance and Women's Empowerment: A Contemporary Issues and Challenges

Raghavendra C R and Venkatesh M

Abstract: *According to 2001 Census, women constitute about 48 per cent of the total population of the country. Their participation at grass root level is increasingly recognised for empowerment and developmental perspectives. Microfinance, the current buzzword in the developmental sector, delves with the problems of community development. "Microfinance" is defined as financial services for poor and low-income clients offered by different types of service providers. In practice, the term is often used more narrowly to refer to loans and other services from providers that identify themselves as "microfinance institutions" (MFIs). The history of micro financing can be traced back as long to the middle of the 1800s when the theorist Lysander Spooner was writing over the benefits from small credits to entrepreneurs and farmers as a way getting the people out of poverty. The modern use of the expression "micro financing" has roots in the 1970s when organisations, such as Grameen Bank of Bangladesh with the microfinance pioneer Muhammad Yunus, were starting and shaping the modern industry of micro financing.*

Most of the research studies and annual reports found that credit programme allows women to take a greater role in household decision making, greater access to financial and economic resources, more bargaining power and greater of mobility. Activities are carried out by various forms of institutions and individuals such as microfinance institutions (MFIs), Non Governmental Organisations (NGOs), Government Institutions, Self Help Groups (SHG) and commercial Banks. MFIs offer a variety of financial products including credit, savings, insurance, business development services. The study known about major aspects like source of awareness about microfinance, saving patterns, loan and Income Generating Activities (IGA) etc, some other aspects viz., promoting womens' access to public services, and employment opportunities, stronger partnerships between private banking sector and MFIs, inclusion of women empowerment indicators used to achieve this noble idea with full potential. This paper also made an effort to suggest the ways to increase women empowerment as to enhance the literacy rate, organised and planned way for intervention in schemes, group cohesion.

Keywords: Microfinance, Women Empowerment.

Introduction

According to 2001 Census, women constitute about 48 per cent of the total population of the country. Their participation at grass root level is increasingly recognised for empowerment and developmental perspectives. Rajasthan has historically been a patriarchal and feudal society where gender discrimination has been a concern. This has drastically affected women's health, financial status, literacy level and political involvement. The paradigms for social development have been rapidly changing with greater attention to gender issues both at the global and national levels. Since 1970s the attempts to redefine development in terms of women and her productive role are increasingly in consideration. During the 1980s various perspectives labeled, "mainstreaming women" which called for bringing women towards development efforts. The empowerment approach, which evolved in the 1990s, has interpreted it in terms of participation in policymaking and planning process. For womens' participation and empowerment, the organisation of women into self-help groups (SHGs) and provision of microfinance through them is to be viewed in this background.

In 2001, the "National Policy for Empowerment of Women" was adopted in India, with the ultimate objective of ensuring women their equitable place in the society by empowering them as 'catalyst' of societal change and development. Since womens' empowerment became key to socio-economic development, bringing women into the mainstream of national development has been a major concern of government. The ministry of rural development has special gears for women in its programmes. Funds are earmarked as "Women's component" to ensure flow of adequate resources for facilitation. Ministry of Rural Development is implementing various schemes like Indira Awas Yojana (IAY), Restructured Rural Sanitation Programme, Accelerated Rural Water Supply Programme (ARWSP) Swarnajayanti Grameen Swarozgar Yojona (SGSY), by National Social Assistance Programme (NSAP), the (erstwhile) Integrated Rural Development Programme (IRDP), the (erstwhile) Development of Women and Children in Rural Areas (DWCRA) and the Jawahar Rozgar Yojana (JRY) are the schemes having women's component.

Many MFIs in India, viz., Asmitha – Provides rural poor women access to financial resources in the form of collateral free small loans for income generation and livelihood promotion. Bandhan MF – In this microfinance activities are carried on by Bandhan Financial Services Pvt. Ltd. (BFSPL), incorporated under the Companies Act, 1956 and also registered as a Non Banking Financial Company (NBFC) with the Reserve Bank of India (RBI). Grameen Foundation – Works in six key areas: Connecting microfinance institutions with capital markets, strengthening organisations by building people practices, harnessing the power of technology, helping track people's movement out of poverty, sharing knowledge widely for broader impact and Social Business. Cash poor India –is to identify and motivate poor women in the rural areas and to deliver financial services to them in an honest, timely and efficient manner. Saadhana – is a non-profit organisation established in the year 2001 to reach out to the urban and rural poor women with the specific mandate to catalyze the 'Endeavour of the Poor for Self-Sufficiency'.

Need of Micro Finance in India

Finance is spine code for development of any country and as India depending on agriculture base production dependence on ruler segment of economy is the most. Banking sector provide its services to the larger segment of India but still to reach to the lower segment for their upliftment is still missing and so need such system which is essentially for development of poor class. "To help poor people out of poverty" aim of the MFS. Basically ruler segment is interested in reasonable credit available to them and so they selected "Local Lndlord" who gives them credit without any documentation and easy when needed. Initially they feel it's so easy to have cash without any hurdles but when the landlords makes collection it is really so difficult for them to repay. An analysis of 28 studies of informal money lending rates in 14 countries in Asia,

Latin America and Africa concluded that 76 per cent of moneylender rates exceed 10 per cent per month, including 22 per cent that exceeded 100 per cent per month. Moneylenders usually charge higher rates to poorer borrowers than to less poor ones.

MFIs in India

After 9/11 tragic event world gravity forces need the strong economy for sustainable development and in this India and China got attention. To improve GDP is become essential for Indian economy for survival purpose and in this case the best answer would be the MFIs which serve the purpose with the best intention. "SEWA" in Gujarat, SHARE and BASIX in Southern India have convinced to the public at mass that with such institution real services reaches to the Indian economy for upliftment and for betterment. NABARD's SHG-Bank linkage programme also provides the "largest microfinance network in the world". The Indian microfinance NGOs – SHARE, BASIX, SEWA, MYRADA and PRADAN proves and grab attention in to the Indian scenario for its own development and also economic growth also. In the investment bases MFIs reaches to the 52 million borrowers including MFIs solidarity lending methodology 99.3 per cent women client and among over all scenario 51 per cent users are female. In India through banking sector MFIs reaches to the ruler segment and did the milestone work for ruler sector. As per 2001 RBI report in India 14000 branches in 375 districts of India. On an average about three villages have one bank branch; this is the best coverage system over all worlds. RRBs provides Nationalised commercial banks and credit co operatives, together, the RRBs, the nationalised commercial banks and the credit co-operatives comprising of PACS and P/SLDS Primary Agricultural Credit Societies (PACS) and Primary/State Land Development Banks (P/SLDS) have one branch for every 4,000 rural residents.

Women's Empowerment and Microfinance

Empowerment implies expansion of assets and capabilities of people to influence control and hold accountable institution that affects their lives. Empowerment is a multi-dimensional social process that helps people to gain control over their own lives, communities and in their society, by acting on issues that they define as important. Microfinance, the current buzzword in the developmental sector delves with the problems of community development. "Microfinance" is defined as financial services for poor and low-income clients offered by different types of service providers. In practice, the term is often used more narrowly to refer to loans and other services from providers that identify themselves as "microfinance institutions" (MFIs).

The history of micro financing can be traced back as long as to the middle of the 1800s when the theorist Lysander Spooner was writing over the benefits from small credits to entrepreneurs and farmers as a way getting the people out of poverty. The modern use of the expression "micro financing" has roots in the 1970s when organisations, such as Grameen Bank of Bangladesh with the microfinance pioneer Muhammad Yunus, were starting and shaping the modern industry of micro financing. Microfinance commonly works through group systems like the Grameen Bank of Bangladesh, solidarity groups of Latin America, and self-help groups of India. Self-help groups, the most common microfinance institutions in India, are small voluntary associations of poor people from the same socioeconomic background who come together for the purpose of solving their common problems through self-help and mutual help.

MFIs offer a variety of financial products including credit, savings, insurance, business development services. Microfinance clients are poor and low-income people that do not have access to other formal financial institutions. They are often self-employed, household-based entrepreneurs with their diverse micro enterprises viz., small retail shops, street vending, artisanal manufacture, and the like. In rural areas, micro entrepreneurs often have small income-generating activities such as food processing and trade. Hard data on the poverty status of clients is limited, but tends to suggest that most microfinance clients fall near the poverty line, both above and below. Households in the poorest 10 per cent of the population, including the destitute, are not traditional microcredit clients because they lack stable cash flows to repay loans. Women often comprise the majority of clients. By helping women meet their practical needs and increase their efficacy in their traditional roles, microfinance may in fact help women to gain respect and achieve more in their socially defined roles, which in turn may lead to increased esteem and self-confidence. MFIs are autonomous financial institutions, which help members to keep their savings safe in the form of grant loans to people in exigencies without any troublesome procedure. It is argued that, through microfinance, poverty can be reduced as well as the resultant increased access and control over financial resources by women can itself become an empowering instrument.

Focus on Poor Women

Above data reflect that in India higher scale gender inequality. With MFI it would attempted to reduce such in equality and resolve problem of society. To develop any society it is essential to empower women. Women face problem of inequality not in the field of society but face gender specific problem to education, health, employment and in home also. MF deals with women below the poverty line. For that target group should be identify. Their feature for selection, criteria for selection, type of help – all points should be kept in mind. MFI basically interested in social mobility, poverty eradication and give upward economic push. Much evidence proves that in Indian women have to face low social status and lack of key resources. Still they are better customers and able to manage resources in better way they are not able to obtain such benefits. To empower women and upward status of women national development authority focuses on it. Special attention given to women in different programme like: Swarnajayanti Gram Swarozgar Yojona (SGSY), the Indira Awas Yojona (IAJ), National Social Assistance programme (NSAP), Restructured Rural Sanitation Programme, Accelerated Rural Water Supply programme (ARWSP) the (erstwhile) Integrated Rural Development Programme (IRDP), the (erstwhile) Development of Women and Children in Rural Areas (DWCRA) and the Jawahar Rozgar Yojana (JRY).

Women Entrepreneurship in India

Women have gradually been changing with the sensitivity to their role and economic status in the society. Women are increasingly being conscious of their existence, their rights, and work situation. However, the position of women work participation as well as both is low in India in comparison to selected countries of the world. Women work participation in India is 31.6 per cent whereas in USA it is 45, per cent UK 43 per cent, Canada 42 per cent, France 32 per cent, Indonesia 40 per cent, Sri lanka and Brazil both 35 per cent. The following table showing that women entrepreneurship position in the selected states of India is 30 per cent on an average, but in Bihar it is only 15.04 per cent, further in India, men generally takes the lead in the entrepreneurship world. With the change of time as well as cultural norms, and increase in literacy, women are increasingly ready to enter the field of entrepreneurship.

States	*No. of Units Registered*	*No. of Women Entrepreneurs*	*Percentage*
Tamil Nadu	9,618	2,930	30.36
Uttar Pradesh	7,980	3,180	39.84
Kerala	5,487	2,135	38.91
Punjab	4,791	1,618	33.77
Maharashtra	4,339	1,394	32.12
Gujarat	3,872	1,538	39.72
Karnataka	3,822	1,026	26.84
Madhya Pradesh	2,967	842	28.38
Bihar	7,344	1123	15.04
Other States and UTS	14,576	4185	28.71
Total	64,796	19,971	32.82

Source: CMIE Report – 2011.

Challenges Faced by Women Entrepreneurs

While empowering women entrepreneurs faced the following problems. Women entrepreneurs encounter two sets of problems that are general problems entrepreneurs and problems specific to women entrepreneurs. These are listed as follows.

- Male dominated Society
- Problem of Finances arrangement
- Scarcity of raw materials required for productive capacities
- Market oriented risk
- Mobility Constraints
- Overlapping of Responsibility of Business and Family
- Lack of Education and Technology
- Lack of self confidence and optimistic attitude amongst women
- Motivational Factors

Major uplift to women entrepreneurs

- Enroll women organisations for government schemes and incentives
- Get collective representation of women business on major forums, economic policy making, banking and funding etc.
- Providing marketing platforms for products produced by women business, give women businesses global representation
- Leadership training and advanced skill development programmes of the highest standards to compete globally
- Provide opportunities for women to get them a level playing field

Government adopt steps to draw more women into entrepreneurship.

Increase the ability of women to participate in the labour force by ensuring the availability of affordable child care and equal treatment in the workplace. More generally, improving the position of women in society and promoting entrepreneurship generally will have benefits in terms of women's entrepreneurship.

- Incorporate a women's entrepreneurial dimension in the formulation of all SME related policies. This can be done by ensuring that the impact on women's entrepreneurship is taken into account at the policy stage.
- Improve the factual and analytical underpinnings of our understanding of the role of women entrepreneurs in the economy by strengthening the statistical basis for carrying out gender related cross country comparative analysis and longitudinal studies of the impact of important developments and policies.

All the government bodies should induct women entrepreneurs on their boards, to generate gender sensitivity and create policies which are conducive for the growth of women entrepreneurship.

Future prospects of development of women entrepreneurs

The following efforts can be taken into account for effective development of women entrepreneurs.

- Easy availability of credit and at preferential interest rate for women entrepreneurs remains long standing demand.
- Better educational facilities and schemes should be extended to womenfolk from government part.
- Government should felicitate various schemes and plans for the encouragement of women's entrepreneur.
- Women's entrepreneur should more competitive and efficient in the local and international market. There should be a strong monitoring of these policies at different levels of execution.
- Counseling through the aid of committed NGOs, Psychologists, managerial experts and technical personnel should be provided.
- Government making provisions of marketing and sales assistance and making provisions of micro credit system and enterprise credit system to the women entrepreneurs.
- The banks should simplify the procedural formalities in extending loans for women entrepreneurs. The managerial staff in the banks should assist women applicants in understanding the formalities in simple manner.

Conclusion

Women entrepreneurship must be molded properly with entrepreneurial traits and skills to meet the changes in trends, challenges global markets and also be competent enough to sustain and strive for excellence in the entrepreneurial arena. Micro finance is playing a vital role in the success of SHGs particularly the entry of rural women in micro enterprise will be encouraged and aggravated. Women's are facing great challenges at the family, community and state levels, ranging from poverty, illiteracy, and irreligious patriarchy to sociopolitical exclusion. The government should embark on a comprehensive programme for local women. Focusing on enhancing their capacity building and increasing their productivity. The rural women are having basic indigenous knowledge, skill, potential and resources to establish and manage enterprise. Now what is the need is knowledge regarding accessibility to loans, various funding agencies procedure regarding certification, awareness on government welfare programmes, motivation, technical skill and support from family, government and other organisation. Some microfinance practitioners, community social workers, donor agencies and academic, alternative models of microfinance are needed in the near future to reduce poverty and increase women's empowerment. Capacity building involves more than simply stimulus assistance through microfinance.

REFERENCES

1. Basu, P. 2008, A Financial System for India's Poor. In Microfinance in India ed. K.G. Karmakar, 19-32. New Delhi: Sage Publications.
2. Microfinance: an Emerging Asset Class for Debt and Equity Investors, August 2007, www.MicroCapital.org
3. Fernandez, A. 2008, Why Sanghamitra is Different? In Microfinance in India, Ed. K.G. Karmakar, 219-242. New Delhi: Sage Publications.
4. The Economic Times, 26 February 2007, Andhra experience to have its mark on the bill.
5. Ghate, P. 2007, Indian Microfinance: The Challenges of Rapid Growth. New Delhi: Sage Publications.
6. Action International, Center for Financial Inclusion, Financial Inclusion: What's the Vision?
7. Koustubh Joshi Inclusive Growth – Financial Inclusion an Opportunistic Play.
8. Stirred, but not shaken! Will Vikram Akula's strategy put SKS Microfinance back on Track? Business Today, June 12, 2011.
9. RBI (2008), Report of committee on Financial Inclusion by C. Rangarajan.

10. Inclusive growth, K. N. Raj's Essays on Economic Development, Edited by Ashoka Mody, Orient Longman.
11. Inclusive Growth Development Perspectives in Indian Economy by N. A. Mujumdar.
12. Milford Bateman 2010, Why Doesn't Microfinance Work? : The Destructive Rise of Local Neoliberalism, Zed Books.
13. Pushing Financial Inclusion Issues, Challenges and Way Forward A Presentation by K.C. Chakraborty Deputy Governor, RBI July 2009, Mumbai.
14. Karmakar, K.G. 2008, Microfinance in India. New Delhi: Sage Publications.

24

Emerging Issues on Empowerment Of Women and Inclusive Growth in India

Padmini S.V.

Abstract: *Women empowerment nowadays is gaining increasing importance. To provide equal opportunities to women education and employment and to bring economic status to women central and state governments implemented many programmes. As a result of this, status of women in India has been subject to many great changes over the past few millennia. In modern India, women have held high offices including that of the President, Prime Minister, Speaker of the Lok Sabha and Leader of the Opposition. Economic empowerment is also the empowering of previously disadvantaged sections of the population.*

The major objectives of the study are to examine education, economic development workforce participation of women and, economic benefits of women empowerment, to examine MDG's Goal to promote gender equality and to empower women, to analyze the role of women in government. As a result of successful implementation of women empowerment programmes the status of women in India has been subject to many great changes over the past few millennia.

It is evident from the analysis of the study that enhancement of the number of women compared to their male counterparts, increase in the literacy rate of women, key positions held by women, participation of women in the mainstream of economic development which shows that empowerment of women happened which is expected to achieve faster rate of growth with gender equity.

Introduction

Women empowerment nowadays is gaining increasing importance. To provide equal opportunities to women education and employment and to bring economic status to women central and state governments implemented many programmes. As a result of this, status of women in India has been subject to many great changes over the past few millennia. In modern India, women have held high offices including that of the President, Prime Minister, Speaker of the Lok Sabha and Leader of the Opposition. Economic empowerment is also the empowering of previously disadvantaged sections of the population.

"Empowerment is not giving people power; people already have plenty of power, in the wealth of their knowledge and motivation, to do their jobs magnificently. We define empowerment as letting this power out." It encourages people to gain the skills and knowledge that will allow them to overcome obstacles in life or work environment and ultimately, help them develop within themselves or in the society.

To empower a female "...sounds as though we are dismissing or ignoring males, but the truth is, both genders desperately need to be equally empowered." Empowerment occurs through improvement of economic, financial and social conditions, standards, events, and a global perspective of life. Organisations can use to open the knowledge, experience, and motivation power that people already have. The three keys that managers must use to empower their employees are:

1. Share information with everyone
2. Create autonomy through boundaries
3. Replace the old hierarchy with self-managed teams (Ken Blanchard, John P. Carlos, and Alan Randolph: *Empowerment Takes More Than a Minute)*

In order to guarantee a successful work environment, managers need to exercise the "right kind of authority" (p. 6). Hence it can be summarised that "empowerment is simply the effective use of a manager's authority", and subsequently, it is a productive way to maximise all-around work efficiency and skills (Stewart, in her book *Empowering People: Empowerment Takes More Than a Minute).*

Methodology

The major objectives of the study are to examine education, economic development, work force participation of women and economic benefits of women empowerment, to examine MDG's to promote gender equality and to empower women, to analyse the role of women in government. The study conducted with the help of secondary data obtained through journals, reports, periodicals, newspapers, magazines and internet. The study is analytical in nature.

In India nowadays women participate fully in areas such as education, research activities, development activities, sports, politics, media, art and culture, service sectors, science and technology etc. The Constitution of India guarantees to all Indian Women Equality (Article 14), no Discrimination by the State (Article 15(1)), Equality of Opportunity (Article 16), and equal pay for equal work (Article 39(d)). Apart from this, it allows special provisions to be made by the State in favour of women and children (Article 15 Moreover (3)), renounces practices derogatory to the dignity of women (Article 51(A) (e)), and also allows for provisions to be made by the State for securing just and humane conditions of work and for maternity relief (Article 42).

During 1990s, grants from foreign donor agencies enabled the formation of new women-oriented Non Government Organisations. In India,Self-help groups and NGOs such as Self Employed Women's Association (SEWA) have played a major role in the advancement of women's rights. Some women have emerged as leaders of local movements; for example, Medha Patkar of the Narmada Bachao Andolan.

The Government of India declared 2001 as the Year of Women's Empowerment (*Swashakti*). The National Policy for the Empowerment of Women was introduced in 2001. On March 9, 2010 the Women's Reservation Bill was passed, as a result of which 33 per cent of seats in India's Parliament and state legislative bodies are reserved for women.

MDG's to Promote Gender Equality and Empowerment of Women:

Eliminate gender disparity in primary and secondary education and at all levels by 2015

- Ratios of girls to boys in primary, secondary and tertiary education

- Share of women in wage employment in the non-agricultural sector.
- Proportion of seats held by women in national parliament.
- For girls in some regions, education remains elusively.
- Poverty is a major barrier to education, especially among older girls.
- In every developing region except the CIS, men outnumber women in paid employment.
- Women are largely relegated to more vulnerable forms of employment.
- Women are over-represented in informal employment, with its lack of benefits and security.
- Top-level jobs still go to men — to an overwhelming degree
- Women are slowly rising to political power, but mainly when boosted by quotas and other special measures.

All the above problems should be resolved to improve the status of women socially and economically.

Government programmes to achieve empowerment of women

Government has implemented various programmes all over the country for the social and economic empowerment of women.

To provide education to women two important programmes: 'Sarva Shiksha Abhiyan' and 'Mahila Samakhya, have been implemented. To achieve economic empowerment and welfare of women, the following programmes have been implemented. Swayam Sidha, Swa-Shakti Project, Support for Training and Employment Programme of Women (STEP), Swavalamban, Shishuvihara/ Babycare Centres for employed and suffered women, Hostels for working women, Swadhar, Rashtriya Mahila Kosh, which will be helpful for the enhancement of confidence among women which in turn will be helpful for the upliftment of socially and economically oppressed women.

Conclusion

It is evident from the above analysis that enhancement of the number of women compared to their male counterparts, increase in the literacy rate of women, key positions held by women, participation of women in the mainstream of economic development which shows that empowerment of women happened which is expected to achieve faster rate of growth with gender equity.

Suggestions

1. Literacy rate among female should be strengthened, then only it is possible to achieve cent per cent literacy rate in Indian economy.
2. Health conditions of women should be improved so that we can expect increase in the life expectancy at birth.
3. More number of women should have higher education, technical education, and they should engage in research, then only we can expect very good contribution from women towards government as well as private sector.
4. Central government and State governments should provide adequate support to women in agricultural sector, industrial sector and tertiary sector then only it is possible to expect good performance of these sectors.

REFERENCES

1. United Nations Development Programme, Human Development Report 2013, p.156.
2. The Global Gender Gap Report 2012, World Economic Forum, pp. 10-11.
3. Mishra, R. C. (2006), Towards Gender Equality: Authors press, ISBN 81-7273-306-2.
4. Pruthi, Raj Kumar, Rameshwari Devi and Romila Pruthi (2001), Status and Position of Women: In Ancient Medieval and Modern India, Vedam Books, ISBN 81-7594-078-6.
5. Jyotsna Kamat (2006), Status of women in Medieval Karnataka, Retrieved 24, Dec. 2006.
6. Singh, S. and Hoge, G. (2010), Debating Outcomes for 'Working' Women – Illustration from India, The Journal of Poverty, 14 (2), 197-215.
7. Carol S. Conrod (June 1998), Chronic Hunger and the Status of Women in India, Retrieved 24 December 2006.
8. The Sexual Harassment of Women at Workplace (Prevention, Prohibition and Redressal) Act, 2013.
9. Beaman, Lori, Raghabendra Chattopadhyay, Esther Duflo, Rohini Pande, and Petia Topalova, 2009, Powerful Women: Does Exposure Reduce Bias? The Quarterly Journal of Economics 124(4):1497-1540. http://www.povertyactionlab.org/evaluation/perceptions-female-leaders-India.

25

Microfinance a Boon to Women Empowerment—With Special Reference to Bhadravathi Taluk

Vimala B N

Abstract: *The present paper provides a platform to understanding the role of Microfinance in women Empowerment in Bhadravathi Taluk, Shivamogga district. Microfinance programs are treated as key strategy in addressing development issues across nations since the last three decades. This study attempts to explore on the much debated question of the role of Microfinance as a financial intermediary for enhancing women empowerment a primary survey has been carried out to capture the realistic experiences and observation from beneficiaries of members in the self help groups this research has been taken adopted a mix of empirical and theoretical approach with the objective to identify a comprehensive range of implementation and impact issues of Microfinance. It has universally been accepted that the Micro financing is a well successful instrument for eradication of poverty. Most of the government in developing countries is encouraging micro financing for alleviation of poverty and empowerment of women In their countries. The scope of this plan is confined only to Bhadravathi Taluk only. The study was conducted to know the performance of "MICRO FINANCE A BOON TO WOMEN*

EMPOWERMENT" in the development of rural areas. The study was intended to know the developmental activities undertaken in rural areas.

This Paper seeks to examine to impact of Microfinance with respect to poverty alleviation and socioeconomic empowerment of rural women. An effort is also made suggest the ways to increase women empowerment.

Key Terms: Poverty Alleviation, Women Empowerment, Self Help Groups, Microfinance, Decision-making.

Introduction

Women have been described as the embodiment of shakti. But in real life she is treated as Abala. Women in traditional societies are still continued to the four walls of home. Children, household affairs and family rituals very few get the opportunity to come out of four walls and economic activities. Women, over a long period of time, have been considering themselves as powerless. One can say that men have had this kind of attitude towards women and women accepted it and developed a sense of weakness. In many countries, more than one-quarter of women were, over the millennia, physically abused, and a very large number of them were subjected to emotional and psychological abuse. There have also been increasing number of cases of ill-treatment, bride burning and violence against women due to dowry-related and other causes.

The absence of proper recognition of women's positive contribution and participation is due to the contention that their activities are economically unproductive, supplementary, optionally intermittent and dispensable. Throughout the world, the rural women have been underrepresented in the development processes and are discriminated and exploited.

Finance is the lubricant, which oils the wheels of development. Microfinance, finances in small amount to poor especially women in rural areas and support them to start their own enterprise in their own villages. The finance is provided with very reasonable rate of interest and flexible repayment facilities. There is huge potential for microfinance to emerge as a successful model to address the problems of unemployment, women backwardness and poverty in India. Through microfinance emphasises on poor without categorising the gender and taking an impartial stand on providing financial resources, fortunately most of the beneficiaries are women entrepreneurs. This may create an environment for women can give a platform for women empowerment.

In the Microfinance system, self help groups are the basic unit. The sustainability of the system largely depends upon the stability and performance of the self help groups. Self help groups is a homogeneous group of micro entrepreneurs with affinity among themselves, voluntarily formed to save whatever amount they can conveniently save out of their earnings and mutually agree to contribute to a common fund of the group from which small loans are given to the members for meeting their productive and emergent credit needs at such rate of interest, period of loan and other terms as the group may decide. These self help group consists of 10 to 20 rural women from the same village, mostly for poor women, come together to contribute weekly or monthly.

Concept of Microfinance

Microfinance refers to the entire range of financial and non financial services including skill upgradation and entrepreneurship development rendered to rural poor for enabling them to overcome poverty. Finance is basic to any economic activity; the basic Philosophy of rural finance is the dispensation of loans at a concessional rate through administrative control targeting the rural people.

Microfinance, finances in small amount to poor especially women in rural areas and support them to start their own enterprise in their own villages the finance is provided with very reasonable rate of interest and flexible repayment facilities, the concept of micro finance has become a major credit disbursement mechanism in many parts of the world. It now refers to loans savings, Insurance, transfer services and other financial products targeted low income clients it covers the following activities:

- *Micro credit:* It is a small amount of money lent to a client by a bank or other institutions.
- *Micro savings:* These are deposit services that allow one to save small amounts of money for future use.
- *Micro Insurance:* It is system by which business and other organisations make a payment to share risks.
- *Remittances:* These are transfers of funds from people in one place to people in another.

Concept of Women Empowerment

The concept of women's empowerment is the outcome of several important critiques and debates generated by the women's movement throughout the world. Dictionary meaning of "empower" is "to authorize". Global conference on women empowerment held in 1988 defined women empowerment as "the surest way of making women, partners in development". In a broader sense, women empowerment means making the women self-reliant, giving her the liberty to make choice in her life and providing her with information and knowledge to take decisions.

Microfinance its Impact on Women Empowerment

Microfinance programmes are important institutional devices for empowering women in order alleviate poverty. Micro financing programme introduced and explained in several part of India have the potential to minimise the problems of women and enable them to empower in all aspects of life. Women have empowered them in the following aspect:

- Empowerment in family
- Empowerment in the community
- Economic empowerment

Profile of SHGs Groups

Kasthuri Sangha

This self help group was started on 28th June 2008 under the presence of the Bhavani madam and Dayanand sir. These two members gave name to the group as "Kasthuri" and the total number of members were 12.

Group members names

1. Vasima banu
2. Bhuvaneshwari
3. Salma
4. Nelamma
5. Nagamma
6. Gulabamma
7. Lakshmamma
8. Nageeba anjum
9. Hemavathi
10. Bannijana
11. Rashmi
12. Marsath banu

In the year 2009 on November 5th Vasima Banu, Nageeba Anjum and Bhuvaneshwari left the group. In that place Jainaaba and Sujatha were entered.

Meetings

The meetings were held once in a week that is on Saturday 5 pm at Mahila samaja. The weekly savings amounts to Rs 10 per week. Up to now 273 weeks were conducted and the total savings amount is Rs 29,910.

Pragathi Nidhi

For every business finance is very important. It acts as a back bone for business. For starting or developing a business, finance is important. In this pragathi nidhi loan will be given to women's with less interest.

For the first time pragathi nidhi is used by eight members. They are,

1 Bhuvaneshwari, Rs 5000 for purchasing household products.
2 Salma, Rs 5000 for doing painting work.
3 Neelamma, Rs 10000 for doing bangles business.
4 Nagamma, Rs 10000 for development of hotel business.
5 Gulabamma, Rs 10000 for development of hotel business.
6 Lakshamma, Rs 10000 for development of shop.
7 Marsath banu, Rs 10000 for development of provision store.
8 Hemavathi, Rs 10000 for doing bangles business.

Review of Literature

An attempt is made here to review few literatures relating to microfinance, women empowerment. The major findings of the surveyed literature are presented below.

R. Subramanian (January, 2007)[1] He made a study on Microfinance, A promoting instrument for SHGs

He says that Indian banking scenario is very dynamic, and fast changing in its dimension and is understanding the complex environment in the right perspective. The self help group-bank linkage programme aimed at connecting self help groups of poor people with banks and in the process created the largest microfinance net work in the world. And he discussed mostly about self help groups.

P. Sreelakshmi and Niranjan Shetty (January, 2008)[2] Empowerment Through Microfinance

They says that poverty has been degrading human lives for centuries. Reduction of poverty will be one of the greatest achievements of any economy. Empowerment of the poor is automatically achieved with financial stability.

Vasudha Vasakarla (April, 2008)[3] Microfinance, Modern Initiative to Promote Social Welfare.

She says that about one-fourth of the population worldwide, particularly in African countries and in India, is living in below poverty line and facing troubles because of the brokers and middlemen who charge higher interest. Due to the globalisation of economy, the rich are getting richer while the poor are becoming still poorer.

Objectives of Study

1. To study the performance of selected self help groups in Bhadravathi Taluk.
2. To study the theoretical background of the microfinance and women empowerment.
3. To study the management of microfinance by women's in selected self help groups.
4. To know the role of microfinance in women empowerment.
5. To study the economic status of women's before and after join the self help group.
6. To offer suitable suggestions based on the findings of the study.

Scope of the Study

The scope of the mainly confined to management of microfinance by selected women self help groups in Bhadravathi taluk, Bommanakatte village.

Methodology

For the purpose of this study 50 sample sizes selected on the basis of groups for the purpose of the study data collected into two ways that is primary and secondary data. The primary data collected by selected self help groups directly and issuing the questionnaire and collect the data structured. And secondary data is collected through articles, magazines, library books and website.

Analysis And Interpretation of Data

Table 1: Showing Socio Economic Profile

Group	*No. of Respondents*	*Percentage (per cent)*
Age (Years)		
15 to 20 years	0	0
21 to 30 years	13	26
31 to 40 years	16	32
41 and above	21	42
Total	50	100

(Contd.)

Contd.

Educational Level		
Illiterate	25	50
Up to SSLC	20	40
Up to PUC	2	4
Degree and above	3	6
Total	50	100
Monthly Income		
Below Rs 4000	31	62
Rs 4000 to Rs 6000	12	24
Rs 6000 to Rs 8000	5	10
Rs 8000 to Rs 10000	2	4
Total	50	100

(*Source:* Survey data)

From the above table it shows that out of 50 respondents 26 per cent of the respondents belonged to the age group of 21 to 30 years, 32 per cent of the respondents belonged to the age group of 31 to 40 years, and 42 per cent of the respondents belongs to the age group of 41 and above years and there is no respondent between the age group of 15 to 20 years.

From the above table it shows that the academic qualification of the 50 respondents. 50 per cent of the respondents are illiterate, 40 per cent of respondents are up to SSLC, four per cent of respondents are up to PUC, six per cent of respondents are Degree and above.

From the table it shows that monthly income of the respondents. 62 per cent of respondents monthly income is below Rs 4000, 24 per cent of respondents monthly income is between Rs 4000 to Rs 6000, 10 per cent of respondents monthly income is between Rs 6000 to Rs 8000 and four per cent of is between Rs 8000 to Rs 10000.

Statistical Tools and Techniques

In order to extract meaningful information from the data collected data analysis was carried out the collected data were edited. Coded and tabulated for the purpose or analysing them are following statistical tools and test were used as Chi- square test.

HYPOTHESIS TEST - 1

H_{01}: There is no significant relationship between the role of Microfinance in the Women Empowerment.

Particulars	*Beneficiaries*	*Non Beneficiaries*	*Total*
Getting Microfinance assistance	30	10	40
Not Getting Microfinance assistance	4	6	10
Total	34	16	50

Source: Survey Data (April 2011)

The table value X^2 for 1 degree of freedom at five per cent level of significance is 3.841The calculated value ofX^2 is 4.502. The calculated value of X^2 is much Higher than the table value and hence we reject the new hypothesis and strongly agreed that there is a relationship between role of Microfinance in the women empowerment basis of alternative Hypothesis.

Major Findings of the Study

Based on the detailed study, found some of the finding they are as follows:

- Lack of Education : From the study we can find that majority of the respondents are illiterate
- Low Level of Income : The studies have found that many SHG members are from house wives and daily agriculture labourers.
- No security: The SHGs work on mutual trust and confidence of the members because there is no security and safety for their deposits.
- Economic independency strengthens and boost up women empowerment level.
- Asset positions women have impact on their empowerment level.
- Availing Microfinance loans, does not automatically empower the women, proper utilisation loan in productive purpose fetch the ways out of poverty.
- There is definite improvement in psychological well being and social empowerment among rural women of participating in Microfinance through SHG programme.

Suggestions

- Giving Education: The SHG members and other authorities have to come front in educating them like Micro Finance Institutions (MFIs) during at the time of sanctioning the loans and also compulsory education for women's by lending through evening learning centers at villages.
- Income Generating Activities: Income generating activity should be conducted in every village areas in order to earn income for day to day expenses.
- Co-ordination: Old group's members can be motivated to take up promotional and conflict resolution responsibilities in the new SHGs. They can visit problematic groups to explain and resolve various issues for smooth functioning of the new SHGs.
- Easy availability of credit and at preferential rate for women entrepreneurs remains longstanding demand.

- Government should felicitate various schemes and plans for encouragement of women entrepreneurs.

Conclusion

Poverty has ever remained a burning problem for India. It has become a hurdle to the development of the national economy. It has adverse effects on social, economic and political life of the country. Economic distortions, social evils and political instability and demoralisation are the main outcomes of poverty. It has degraded individual as well national status.

In a nut shell, it can be pointed out that Microfinance has contributed considerably for the empowerment of women. They are highly empowered in their family. However, their empowerment in the community, government authorities and economic aspect is only medium.

REFERENCES

1. Christabell, P.J. (2009), Women Empowerment through capacity building, The Role of Microfinance". Ashok kumal mittal concept publishing company. New Delhi, First Edition pp. 23 - 41,65 -206. New Delhi, First Edition. pp. 1-132.
2. Dr Laxmi. (2012), women Empowerment through Self Help Groups. Prateeksha publications. Jaipur (India), First Edition. pp. 1-60.
3. Bhaktapada Sinha Roy. (2007), Rural Banking and Poverty Alleviation, Abhijeet Publications. Delhi 110094, First Edition. pp. 1-20.
4. Ajay Tankha, (2012), Banking on SHG Twenty years on Sage Publications India Pvt. Ltd. New Delhi, First Edition. pp. 9-66.
5. M R Biju, (2006), Women's Empowerment. Amittal Publications. New Delhi, First Edition. pp 129-136, 215-230.

PART—III
MICROFINANCE AND SELP HELP GROUPS

26

Self Help Groups And Micro Finance In India—Some Reflections

Dr. Shyamsundar

Abstract: *Micro finance is emerging as the powerful instrument for poverty alleviation, ensuring equality, inclusive growth and women empowerment. Micro finance promotes rural development through micro enterprises. Because formal credit institutions (capital market) and informal lending system either failed miserably to deliver the goods or have not been conducive to the growth of micro enterprises. Hence a dire need to promote alternative credit delivery system. The Indian micro finance scene is dominated by Self Help Groups (SHGs) and their linkage to banks. In India, the credit delivery through thrift and credit groups emerged as an alternative to the existing system of credit disbursement by the banks. It is fervently hoped that micro finance leads to poverty reduction in rural India and enables the rural masses to raise their income levels and thereby increases their living standard. Under the circumstances, an attempt, based on secondary data gathered from different sources, is made here, to focus on the different dimension of micro finance and SHG-Bank linkage programme.*

Key words: Self Help Groups, Poverty Alleviation, Empowerment. NABARD, MFIs.

Introduction

Any economic policy should focus on empowering people particularly poorer of the poor so as to enable them lead a life without poverty and hunger. Otherwise, poverty leads to a downward cycle of malnutrition, Illiteracy and poor health pushing into further poverty and hunger. India is no exception (This is more true in India than in other places). The inability to get the basic needs-food, clothing and shelter as a consequence of low income, lack of productive assets partial use of human resource owing to insufficient access to education and health and no access to break out poverty due to weak economic and social status are the important aspects of poverty[1] The eradication of poverty is one of the Millennium Development Goals which aims to halve the proportion of people living in extreme poverty by 2015.

The malady of poverty in India certainly warrants the need for innovative measure to ensure a strategic approach to empower the poor people not only to eke out their livelihood but also to improve their social status. Otherwise, it creates crisis shading the economy of a nation and engulf hiatus between the haves and have nots. In short, the need of the hour is to fight out and eradicate poverty so as to ensure decent and comfortable living for the people. Micro finance, the development buzzword of the 90s is believed to cure the ills of poverty.

Micro finance is a buzzword in the financial sector of every nation after the United Nations launched the *International Year of Micro Finance 2005*.It got further impetus when *Mohammd Yunus,* the Founder of Grammeen Bank and a pioneer of micro credit for women was awarded Nobel Prize for peace in 2006. With this, concepts such as self-reliance, self-sufficiency and self- help gained momentum.

The development paradigm in India has witnessed a shift in its focus from growth, increase in GDP and Per Capita Income to non economic factors like social justice, poverty alleviation, redistribution of income, equality and women empowerment, rural development and sustainable development. Micro finance through Self Help Groups (SHGs) is an innovative approach for the financial inclusion of the rural poor. Credit has been an element in linking factor and commodity markets. Credit helps the rural poor in the acquisition of income generating assets and create self employment opportunities thereby alleviating rural poverty SHGs provide an innovative system of financial intermediation to provide micro financial assistance to the rural poor. Access to and control over land, technologies, labour, raw materials and markets.(ILO) Micro finance scene in India is dominated by SHG Bank linkage programme aimed at a cost effective mechanism for providing financial services to the rural poor.

Providing financial services to the poor and underprivileged section of the society has been given top priority on the agenda of many anti poverty programme initiated by the Government of India ever since independence. This involves formal financial institutions. In spite of the best efforts of these financial institutions, in reaching the deprived sections of the society living in rural areas, still, a large chunk rural under privileged poor failed to get their due share from the institutional finance.

Even by early 1990s, the share of informal financial institutions (informal sector) was quite high at 39.6 per cent of the total credit as per the data provided by the RBI. It was in this backdrop, the need for alternative financial innovation that should penetrate into rural hinterland and provide formal financial services without any hurdles was strongly felt. It was in such an environment micro finance emerged as a strong and suitable innovation that bridges the existing gaps in the present financial system[7].

Objectives

- To present, in brief, the origin of Micro Finance and Bank linkage.
- To narrate the role of banks, NGOs and NABARD in micro finance.
- To highlight the contributions of banks in the SHG-Bank Linkage Programme.
- To focus the Micro Finance Institution (MFI)-Bank Linkage programme.
- To offer some pragmatic suggestions for the effective functioning of micro finance institutions.

Methodology

The present paper depends on the secondary data gathered from different sources-both published and unpublished for its analysis. The data gathered are presented in a tabular form and are analysed by using percentage

Origin and History of Micro Finance and Bank Linkages

The country of Bangladesh is the best example of nourishing the idea of Micro Finance where Muhammed Yunus, the proponent, deserves all the credit as regards mooting the idea of Grameena Bank. The project was started in 1976 and later this was recognised as a formal bank by the Government of Bangladesh. It got the status of Schedule Bank (SB) in 1986 and began lending to landless poor particularly women to promote them for self employment.

The Bangladesh Rural Advancement Committee (BRAC), the Association for Social Advancement (ASA) and PROSHIKA are the other micro finance giants operating for over two decades. The BRAC is the largest Non-Governmental Organisation (NGO) addressed the issues of poverty alleviation and empowerment of poor especially women in the rural areas of the country. It has spread its functions in the fields of literacy, legal education and human rights, health, nutrition and other supportive services. It is well understood that the micro finance is the powerful instrument to alleviate vicious poverty circle and to empower the women. With this intention in the country, the SHGs and credit management groups are started and the journey of SHG is started to the liberalised and globalised economy.

In India, banks are considered to be the predominant agency for delivery of micro credit. In 1970s, Ilaben Bhat, Founder Member of Self Employed Women's Association (SEWA), Ahmadabad had developed a concept of Women and Micro Finance. The Annapurna Mahila Mandal in Maharashtra and Working Women's Forum in Tamil Nadu and many NABARD sponsored groups has followed the path of SEWA. Since 1987, Mysore Resettlement and Development Agency (MYRADA) has promoted Credit Management Groups (CMGs) which are similar to SHGs with an aim to bestow social empowerment of women.

In 1991-92, the NABARD started promoting SHGs in a large scale and it was the real take-off point for the SHG movement in India. With an addition to this, in 1993, the Reserve Bank of India (RBI) allowed SHGs to open saving accounts in banks and avail the banking services which was the major boost to the movement. Now, nearly, 560 banks including Nationalised Banks (NBs), Scheduled Banks (SBs), Regional Rural Banks (RRBs) and the Government institutions like District Rural Development Agency (DRDA), local elected bodies and more than 3024 NGOs are collectively and actively involved in the promotion of SHGs towards booming economy.

The Concept of Micro Finance

In the most simplistic way, micro finance can be termed as "banking for the poor". Suggested by the name, most transactions under 'micro finance' involve small amount of money. But the connotation of the term has a much wider meaning[8].

Micro finance has been defined by the task force on micro finance as provision of thrift, credit and other financial services and products of various small amount to the poor in rural, semi urban or urban areas for enabling them to raise their income lives and improve living standards[9].

According to the Norwegian Committee (2006) micro finance can help people to break out poverty which in turn is seen as important prerequisites to establish long lasting peace.

Micro finance institutions embrace refinance institutions, NGOs and SHGs which provide micro credit to the poor, encourage thrift habits in order to enable them to raise income levels and thereby increasing their living standard.

Role of Banks in Micro Credit

There is another potentially hopeful development. The involvement of traditional commercial banks in micro credit is growing rapidly around the world. In several developing countries large state banks and private banks have started to provide micro credit services[10]. In India, NABARD recently initiated a programme to involve private banks in micro finance. According to recent studies, the growth of micro credit in India is led by a number of commercial banks such as ICICI, HSBC and ABNAMRO, together with private venture capitalists (Lakshman 2006, Iyer 2006).

Role of NGOs in Micro Credit Sector

The first phase of micro credit was for income generating activities to small farmers like credit for cattle, setting up grocery shops etc. Today with strong community based structure, it is possible to give credit to groups to form such social infrastructure projects, which are not income generating. The NGOs across the country have asked the states and other institutions engaged with SHGs to make available the data related to achievement in poverty alleviation, employment and literacy. Such data should be disaggregated by caste and class categories to enable a realistic assessment. The groups were of the opinion that there was no data on the number of SHGs in the country, their deposits and the loans disbursed to them or even the impact these have had in empowering women.

Micro Finance –Role of the NABARD

Indian public policy for finance right from1950s till date reflects the patterns observed worldwide. Increasing access to credit for the poor has always remained at the core of Indian planning to fight against poverty. The rationale behind expanding outreach of financial services particularly credit was that the welfare cost of exclusion of the rural poor from the banking services was very high. Late 1960s had been euphemistically referred to associal banking' phase. It witnessed the nationalisation of existing private commercial banks, massive expansion of branch net work in rural areas, mandatory directed credit to priority sectors, subsidised rates of interest and creation of a new set of rural banks at the district level and Apex Banks at the national level. These measures resulted in an impressive gains in rural outreach and volume of credit.[11] However, these gains were not without costs. Government interventions through directed credit, State owned Rural Financial Institutions (RFIs) and subsidised interest rates increased the tolerance for loan default, loan waivers, and tax appraisal and monitoring of loans. This was the situation at the beginning of 1990.

The emergence of micro credit in India has to be seen in this backdrop for a better appraisal of the current paradigm. Successful micro finance interventions across the world and in parts of India by NGOs provided further impetus. In this backdrop, NABARD's search for alternative models of reaching the rural poor brought the existence of informal groups of poor to the fore. It was realised that the poor tended to come together in a variety of informal ways for pooling their savings and dispensing small and unsecured loans at varying costs to group members on the basis of need. The concept of self help was discovered by social development NGOs in 1980s. Realising the only constraining factor in unleashing the potential of these groups was meagreness of their financial resources, NABARD designed the concept of linking these groups with banks to overcome the financial constraint. The programme has come a long way since 1992 passing through stages of pilot (1992-1995), mainstreaming (1995-1998) and expansion phase (1998 onwards) and emerged as the world's biggest micro finance progrmme in terms of outreach, covering 1.6 million groups as on March 2005. It occupies a preeminent position in the sector accounting for nearly 80 per cent market share in India. NABARD is also providing grants on a selective basis to NGOs, primarily for promoting and nurturing SHGs. NABARD has provided financial and other types of support for training of bank staff, NGOs and government agencies engaged in the field of micro finance.

Two broad approaches characterise the micro finance sector in IndiaSelf Help Groups(SHGs)-bank linkage(SBL) and micro finance institutions (MFIs)[12]. The former dates from the NABARD initiated pilot of 500 SHGs in 1992.NABARD had a key role to play in initiating and nurturing India's unique SBL programme. It has largely been responsible for the RNI including Linkage Banking as a main stream activity of banks under "priority sector" lending in 1996. Beginning as pilot in 1992 with 500 SHGs by March 2006 over 22 lakh SHGs had been provided with bank loans. The banks are well on the way to achieving the target set down by NABARD to finance a third of India's rural population through SHGs by 2007 Micro credit and SHGs are only one of the inputs enabling conditions that is required for empowerment and poverty alleviation.

Concept of Self Help Groups (SHGs)

Self Help Groups (SHGs) form the basic constituent unit of the microfinance movement in India. A SHG is a group of a few individuals – usually poor and often women – who pool their savings into a fund from which they can borrow as and when necessary. Such a group is linked with a bank–a rural, co-operative or commercial bank–where they maintain a group account. Over time the bank begins to lend to the group as a unit, without collateral, relying on self-monitoring and peer pressure within the group for repayment of these loans. A SHG consists of five to twenty individuals, usually all from different families. Often a group like this is given a name. Each such group has a leader and a deputy leader, elected by the group members. The members decide among themselves the amount of deposit they have to make individually to the group account. The starting monthly individual deposit level is usually low – Rs 10 or Rs 20 (about 20-40 US cents). For a group of size 10, this translates to Rs 100 to 200 (about $2 to $ 4) of group savings per month. On the basis of the resolutions adopted and signed by all members of the group, the manager of a local rural or commercial bank opens a savings bank account. The savings are collected by a certain date (often the 10th of every month) from individual members and deposited in the bank account.

Role of SHGs

The SHGs play a vital role in the upliftment of the rural poor by providing loans at a reasonable rate of interest. This helps the rural poor to improve employment and economic support. SHGs in most of the villages have been successful in breaking the stranglehold of money lenders. SHGs bank linkage progrmme has been advantageous not only to the members of SHGs but also to the banks. The advantages to the banks are the lower transaction cost by providing loan to the groups for internal lending. There are no recovery problems for banks in loans given to SHGs i.e., near zero nonperforming assets. The SHGs will help economic independence of the rural people and economic development of our country.The SHGs produces the products according to the local demands. By pursuing productive activities the group enhances its income, repays the loan amount to the banks, and spend it on basic health, education etc. so as to drive out of the poverty trap.

SHGs Model

The banks can make use of different models developed by the NABARD for providing micro credit through SHGs. Banks can also design several innovating products best suited to the borrowers' in the specific locations to meet different kinds of credit needs Microfinance services in India are provided mainly by two different models viz., SHG-bank linkage model and MFI-bank model. Out of these two models, SHG-bank linkage model has emerged as the more dominant model due to its adoption by formal financial institutions namely, Commercial Banks, Regional Rural Banks and Cooperative Banks. The MFI-bank model is also gaining importance due to its massive supports by various private sector and foreign funding agencies.

(i) SHG-Bank Linkages (SBL-Model)

The SBL approach involves the formation of SHGs (mainly of women) These women regularly save money that is placed in a local (generally public sector) bank account. According to many studies, the creation of a safe avenue for saving on which interest is earned is an attractive feature of SHGs. The SHG has a set of bye-laws devised and agreed by the members themselves, which include rules of monthly saving, lending procedures, periodicity and timings of meetings, penalties for default etc. Accounts and records are maintained meticulously. The SHG itself functions like a bank. After a certain period (six months to a year) of disciplined functioning, it becomes entitled to a loan from the bank where it has account. A number of studies document the positive impact of SHGs on indicator such as average value of assets per household, average net income per household, employment and borrowing for income generation activities. It is argued that SHGs help inculcate banking.

The problem with the SBL model is that it is largely a government 'pushed' model and has, therefore suffered from all the infirmities any bureaucratic programme, run in a mindless target driven sort of way. All members of government officials including Anganawadi and forest guards, have been asked to form SHGs. Hence the impressive figures of the fast growth of SBL model hide a lot of poor quality work. This has destroyed the credibility of SBL model in the eyes of key stakeholders including potential women members and also bankers.

The real power of SBL model lies in the enormous economies of scale that are created by the power of SHGs federations (each of 150-200 members), for example in bulk purchase of inputs and marketing of output. Besides providing larger loans for housing and health facilities, a variety of insurance services are also made available. Yet there is some critique of SHGs charging high rate of interest to their members. But it is counter argued that SHGs (unlike

MFIs) are members run mini banks. What they charge is also what they earn. The money remains with them. Of course, there is a need for interest rate caps in micro finance but it is useful to members that the money earned on interest by an SHG accrues to itself.

(ii) MFI Model

The newly emerging MFI model is a different ball game altogether. Here the sponsor is a profit oriented venture capitalist, who sees the rural credit market as fresh business opportunities. The MFI apparently brings great professionalism, innovations and technology to its enterprise. It also ventures to provide loans that banks do not. But MFIs form no groups that are engaged in governance functions of SHGs even when they operate through NGOs. MFIs are primarily concerned with lending and recovering (mostly every week) what they lend to cohorts of people at times at very high rates of interests.

The recent suicide episodes in Andhra Pradesh are a grim reminder of the possible extreme consequences of MFIs lending. Since profits are overwhelming considerations for an MFI, there is enormous pressure to lend at all costs and concomitantly, to recover. A high rate of interest is inevitable because of high transaction costs and a relatively low scale of operations. Another dubious practice of many MFIs is that they charge borrowers interest on the entire remaining period as well even if they were to return the loan early. This could become a killing penalty with long remaining periods. There is also lack of transparency especially in 'start up' MFIs about such practice. In addition, borrowers' illiteracy leads to explosive situation which in a vulnerable situation was bound to explode. Finally the really poor do tend to be implicitly or deliberately excluded as they are unable to bear the pressure of recovery.

A major demand of MFIs is that they should be allowed to raise interest rates in an unfettered manner. The enactment of anti usury laws is said to have led to a reduction in supply of credit and rise in interest rates. There was a massive expansion in the supply of credit to the poor in the social banking era. And this was at lower rate of interest. It is only in the reform era that the supply of institutional credit has contracted and the usurious money lender has made a comeback.

SHG-Bank Linkage Programme

An analysis of the SHG-Bank Linkage Programme across the geographical spread of the country and across the financing agencies is being presented here. The analysis covers the broader components of the programme, namely inclusive growth, savings, loans and the recovery performance. Table -1 is worth observing.

Table-1: Overall Progress under SHG-Bank Linkage for last three years.
(Amount in Rs Crores Numbers in lakhs)

Particulars		*2009-10*		*2010-11*		*2011-12*	
		No. of SHGs	*Amount*	*No. of SHGs*	*Amount*	*No. of SHGs*	*Amount*
SHG Savings with Banks as on 31st March	Total SHGs	69.53 (13.6 per cent)	6198.71 (11.8 per cent)	74.62 (7.3 per cent)	7016.30 (13.2 per cent)	79.60 (6.7 per cent)	6551.41 (-6.7 per cent)
	Of which SGSY Groups	16.94 (12.5 per cent)	1292.62 (-17.3 per cent)	20.23 (19.4 per cent)	1817.12 (40.6 per cent)	21.23 (5.0 per cent)	1395.25 (-23.2 per cent)
	per cent of SGSY Groups to Total	24.4	20.9	27.1	25.9	26.7	21.3
	All Women SHGs	53.10 (9.18 per cent)	72.6	60.98 (14.8 per cent)	5298.65 (17.8 per cent)	62.99 (3.3 per cent)	5104.33 (-3.7 per cent)
	per cent of Women Groups	76.4	72.6	81.7	75.5	79.1	77.9
Loans Disbursed to SHGs during the year	Total SHGs	15.87 (-1.0 per cent)	14453.3 (17.9 per cent)	11.96 (-24.6 per cent)	14547.73 (0.01)	11.48 (-4 per cent)	16534.77 (13.70 per cent)
	Of which SGSY Groups	2.67 (1.0 per cent)	2198 (9.1 per cent)	2.41 (-9.9 per cent)	2480.37 (12.8 per cent)	2.10 (-12.9 per cent)	2643.56 (6.6 per cent)
	per cent of SGSY Groups to Total	16.9	15.2	20.1	17.0	18.3	16.0
	All women SHGs	12.94 (5.8 per cent)	12429.37 (18.1 per cent)	10.17 (-21.4 per cent)	12622.33 (1.6 per cent)	9.23 (-9.2 per cent)	14132.02 (12.0 per cent)
	-per cent of Women Groups	81.6	86	85	86.8	80.4	85.5

(Contd.)

Contd. Table

Particulars		*2009-10*		*2010-11*		*2011-12*	
		No. of SHGs	*Amount*	*No. of SHGs*	*Amount*	*No. of SHGs*	*Amount*
Loans outstanding against SHGs as on 31 st March	Total SHGs	48.51 (14.8 per cent)	28038.28 (23.6 per cent)	47.87 (-1.3 per cent)	31221.17 (11.4 per cent)	43.54 (-9.0 per cent)	36340.00 (19.4 per cent)
	Of which SGSY Groups	12.45 (27.5 per cent)	6251.08 (6.6 per cent)	12.86 (3.4 per cent)	7829.39 (25.2 per cent)	12.16 (-5.4 per cent)	8054.83 (2.9 per cent)
	per cent of SGSY Groups to Total	25.7	22.3	26.9	25.1	27.9	22.2
	No of All women SHGs linked	38.98 (18.9 per cent)	23030 (23.9 per cent)	39.84 (2.2 per cent)	26123.75 (13.4 per cent)	36.49 (-8.4 per cent)	30465.28 (16.6 per cent)
	per cent of Women SHGs	8.3	82.1	83.2	83.7	83.8	83.8

Source: NABARD-Status of Micro Finance, 011-12, p. 5,

The data presented in Table-1 indicate the growth of SHGs – saving as well as credit linked for the last three years, separately for all Groups, Groups formed under SGSY and exclusive Women Groups. Under the SHG-Bank linkage programme, over 103 million rural households have now access to regular savings through 7.96 million SHGs linked to banks. About 27per cent of these SHGs are savings linked through the SGSY programme – the rural poverty alleviation programme of the Government of India where predominantly households below the poverty line are admitted as members.

There has been a decline in the amount of savings balance with banks to the extent of 6.7 per cent as compared to the previous year although the number of SHGs saving linked has shown a growth of 6.7 per cent during the year. This decline is almost entirely attributable to the groups formed under SGSY where the decline was to the extent of 23.2 per cent. The number of SHGs, the bank loans and other details are furnished in the ensuing Table-2

Table-2: SHG-Bank Linkage

Year	*No of SHGs*	*Bank Loan (Rs.Crores)*	*No. of Families Assisted (In lakhs)*	*Average Loan per SHG (Rs)*	*Average Loan per Families*
2000-01	1,49,050	28,789	25.33	19,315	1,136
2001-02	197,653	54,554	33.60	27,601	1,624
2002-03	2,55,882	1,02,231	37.54	26.985	1,799
2003-04	3,61,731	1,85,550	45.86	36,180	2,412
2004-05	5,18,173	2,96,180	77.74	42,971	2,864
2005-06	4,82,598	3,09,613	72.38	64,155	4,277
2006-07	11,05,749	6,57,039	154.80	59,420	3,961
2007-08	12,27,770	8,84,926	171.88	72,076	5,148
2008-09	16,09,586	12,25,351	225.64	76,108	5,436
2009-10	15,87,000	14,45,330	222.18	91,073	6,505
2010-11	11,96,000	14,54,773	167.44	1,21,636	8,688
2011-12	17,60,346	16,63,477	191.53	94,497	9,685
Percentage change over 2000	**1081**	**5678**	**656**	**389**	**753**

Note. The percentage change is computed
Source: NABARD-Micro Finance Status in India 2011-12.

The data presented in the Table 2 reveals that the number of SHGs registered an increase of 1081 per cent in 2011-12 over 2000-01 Similarly the bank loan witnessed an increase of 5678 per cent during the same period. It is obvious that over a period of time the average loan per family did increase from Rs 19,315 lakhs in 2000-01 to Rs 121639 lakhs up to 2010-11 but during 2011-12 it showed a decline. It is easy to comprehend that the average loan per families also registered an increase with a percentage change of 753.

MFI-Bank Linkage Programme

MFIs act as an important conduit for extending financial services to the micro finance sector in the country by raising resources from Banks and other institutions. MFIs could be (i) NGO MFIs – registered under the Societies Registration Act, 1860 or the Indian Trusts Act, 1880 (ii) Cooperative MFIs – registered under the State Cooperative Societies Act or Mutually Aided Cooperative Societies Act or Multi State Cooperative Societies Act, (iii) NBFC MFIs incorporated under Section 25 of Companies Act, 1956 (These NBFCs are working "not for profit"), and (iv) NBFC MFIs incorporated under the Companies Act, 1956 and registered with RBI. In addition to their internal resources, these MFIs seek and obtain bulk loans from Banks/ other Financial Institutions for providing micro credit. Though most of these MFIs entered the micro finance sector only after the SHG-Bank linkage programme was well entrenched, the turnover of these institutions grew at a much larger scale than the former. They were more aggressive and innovative in reaching out to the rural poor than the formal banking system. Of late, however, the functioning of these institutions (mostly "for profit" NBFCs) were being subjected to closer public scrutiny on account of alleged unethical business practices and questionable recovery practices. Table 3 reflects the progres under MFI- Bank linkage.

Table 3: Progress under MFI-Bank Linkage Programme (Amount in Rs crores)

Particulars	*2008-09*		*2009-10*		*2010-11*		*2011-12*	
	No. of MFI	*Amount*	*No. of MFI*	*Amount*	*No. of MFI*	*Amount*	*No. of MFI*	*Amount*
Loans disbursed by banks to MFIs	581 (12.2 per cent)	3732.33 (89.4 per cent)	779 (34 per cent)	10728.50 (187.4 per cent)	471 (-39.5 per cent)	8448 (-21.3 per cent)	465 (-1.3 per cent)	5205.29 (-38.39 per cent)
Loans outstanding against MFIs as on 31 March	1915 (72.7 per cent)	5009.09 (82.2 per cent)	1659 (-13.4 per cent)	13955.75 (178.6 per cent)	2315 (39.5 per cent)	13730.62 (-2.0 per cent)	1960 (-15.3 per cent)	11450.35 (-16.6 per cent)
Fresh loans as per cent of Loan Outstanding		74.5		76.9		61.5		45.5

Source: NABARD- Micro Finance Status in India 2011-12, p. 14.

It follows from the data presented in Table-3 that Commercial Banks (and financial institutions like SIDBI) are losing their confidence in lending to MFIs is evident from the fact that the fresh lending to MFIs by banks during 2011-12 declined by over 38 per cent as compared to the last year. There has also been a marginal decline in the number of MFIs availing fresh loans from Banks in spite of the fact that the loan outstanding against MFIs has come down by almost 17 per cent during the year. If the trend continues, this sector is likely to face serious resource crunch and could affect its outreach plans in the near future.

The agency wise details of loans extended to MFIs are shown in Table-4.

Table 4: Loans to MFIs by banks/ Financial Institutions

Financing Agency	*Period*	*Loans Disbursed to MFIs during the year*		*Loans outstanding against as on 31st March*	
		No. of MFIs	*Amount (Crores of Rs)*	*No. of MFIs*	*Amount (Crores of Rs)*
All Commercial Banks	2008-09	522	3718.93	1762	4977.89
	2009-10	645	8038.61	1407	10095.32
	2010-11	460	7601.02	2153	10646.84
	2011-12	336	4950.98	1684	9810.98
Regional Rural Banks	2008-09	59	13.40	153	31.20
	2009-10	46	24.14	103	52.22
	2010-11	9	4.16	23	42.01
	2011-12	113	13.28	128	37.51
Cooperative Banks	2008-09	NA	NA	NA	NA
	2009-10	0	0	3	.0.01
	2010-11	NA	NA	NA	NA
	2011-12	4	1.61	19	4.75
SIDBI	2008-09	NA	NA	NA	NA
	2009-10	88	2665.79	146	3808.20
	2010-11	2	843.78	139	3041.77
	2011-12	12	239.42	129	1597.11
Total by all agencies	2008-09	581	3732.33	1915	5009.09
	2009-10	779	10728.50	1659	13955.75
	2010-11	471	8448.96	2315	13730.62
	2011-12	405	5205.29	1960	11450.35

Source : NABARD –Status of Micro Finance in India 2011-12, p. 15.

The figures given in Table-4 reflect that both the loans disbursed to MFIs and loans outstanding by all commercial banks increased in 2011-12. The RRBs share in loans disbursed to MFIs has declined during the same period though the loans outstanding against has increased. In short, the loans disbursed and outstanding against by all agencies are found increasing. Commendable indeed!

Some Suggestions: Based on the above analysis, the following suggestions are put forth here.

- Micro finance should be given only to income generating activities.
- The bankers should lend to SHGs as a normal banking activity.
- Lending to SHGs at subsidised interest rate is to be treated as a temporary measure.

- There is a dire need to bring SHGs to the manifold regulatory framework.
- Regulations pertaining to the entry of private banks to rural areas are to be relaxed.
- Banks should minimise the documentation process while granting loans to SHGs.

Conclusion

Based on the above analysis, it can be concluded that micro finance has really emerged as a powerful tool for poverty alleviation The effects of micro finance services hardly go unnoticed. Micro finance helps to raise the income of the vulnerable group, promotes higher level of consumption, helps in asset accumulation and enables future investment and thereby contributes to eradicate poverty and empower the deprived group. However, more meticulous and expeditious efforts are required to accelerate the tempo of the movement. Then only the benefits of the development of the country can trickle down to the unreached poor in a rapid fashion.

Notes

1. See Ramesh Babu et al. 'Micro Finance: An Approach for Poverty Alleviation' in Southern Economist, Vol. 49 (10) p. 23
2. See Venkatesh Murthy S.S and Dinish G.M. 'Self help Groups and Empowerment of Women' in Southern Economist, Vol. 49(08) p. 35.
3. Chavan V.M. and Mukund M.M. 'Micro Finance and Financial Inclusion of Poor through Self Help Group Bank Linkage' Southern Economist Vol. 49(14) p. 8.
4. *Ibid* p. 8.
5. *Ibid* p. 8.
6. See Dinesh. B. Raghuwanshi, Micro Fincance : Present Scenario and Emerging Challenges' Southern Economist Vol. 49 (1) p. 15.
7. *Ibid*. p. 15.
8. See Khandelwal Anil. K. (2007) 'Micro Finance Development Strategy for India' Economic and Political Weekly, 31 March p.1127).
9. *Ibid* p. 1127.
10. It is interesting to note that (i) In Pakistan a number of private commercial banks have moved into microfinance. Similarly in Malaysia, Nepal and Thailand, there are programmes stimulating commercial banks to become involved in micro credit

11. It is appropriate to mention here that between 1961 and 2001 the average population per bank branch fell ten fold from 140 thousand to 14000 and the share of institutional agencies in rural credit increased from 7.3 per cent to 66 per cent between 1991 and 2002.
12. It is needless to write here that SBL is the larger model and is unique to India where as MFIS is internationally more established and is the one that appears to be the increasingly favoured route.
13. It is appropriate to mention here that NABARD's work with its partner NGOs (MYRADA, Pradan and Dhan) also led to the government according national priority' to the programme in the Union Budget of 1999.
14. A study of four SHGs federations (including India's oldest one) shows that federations make SHGs financially viable for reducing transaction and promotional costs as also default rates; provide them economies of scale, create value added services and build local capital.

REFERENCES

1 NABARD- Micro Finance Status in India, 2009-10, 2010-11 and-2011-12.

2 Rais Ahmed, (2009), Micro Finance and Women Empowerment, Mittal Publications, New Delhi.

3 Somanath,V.S., (2009), Mircro Finance –Redefining the Future, Excel Books, New Delhi.

27

Financial Inclusion through SHGs—Micro Finance in India

Huchhe Gowda

"You can tell condition of a nation by looking at the status of its women". "Freedom depends on economic conditions even more than political. If a woman is not economically free and self – earning she has to depend on her husband or someone else and dependents are never free" - *Jawaharlal Nehru.*

Abstract: *India falls under low income class according to World Bank. It is second most populated country in the world and around 71 per cent of its population lives in rural areas and 54 per cent of the people depend on agriculture. As a result there is chronic underemployment with a per capita income of hardly $3262. This is not enough to provide food to more than one individual. The obvious result is abject poverty, low rate of education, low sex ratio, and exploitation. The major factor which accounts for high incidence of rural poverty is the low asset base. According to Reserve Bank of India, about 51 per cent of people possess only 10 per cent of the total assets of India. This has resulted in low production capacity both in agriculture (which contributes around 13 per cent of GDP) and in the Manufacturing sector. Rural people have very low access to institutionalised credit (from commercial bank). There are substantial disparities within the country as the gulf between the rich and poor is widening. The Indian government's poverty reduction strategy focuses on infrastructure, social development (especially education* *and health), and rural livelihoods. The improvement in rural livelihoods through inclusive growth is the prime objective of the MFIs. This study thus looks at how the organisational structure of MFIs contributes to inclusive growth. The study is based largely on secondary data, supplemented with some primary data.*

Key Words: Population, Agriculture, Poverty, Education and Development.

Introduction

Financial Inclusion and Microfinance have provided a platform for the underprivileged people in India especially the rural poor to improve their standard of living and attain a level of social, cultural and economic empowerment. Microfinance broadly encompasses providing a range of financial services such as micro credit, deposit, money transfers, micro insurance and micro pension to the deprived and low-income households for a better livelihood. It enables them to engage in micro enterprises and other economic activities. Economic freedom is the edifice on which micro-finance rests. If poor and needy people are provided access to financial assistance and financial services it would enable them to come out the chasm of poverty. It is an enabler for leveraging their initiatives which are lying dormant in them, thereby accelerating the process of building incomes, assets and economic security. Eventually it empowers the underprivileged and brings them into mainstream financial system and development process.

Rationale for the study

Even after six decades of independence, 850 million people in India are living on less than Rs100 per day. Poverty alleviation is a major challenge faced by the government. Since 1991, the government has intensified its efforts for inclusive growth with its outreach programs. Banks and financial institutions are engaged in massive financial inclusion programs. The present study examines the growth and spread of microfinance in India as a poverty alleviation initiative.

Objectives of the study

- To analyse the growth of microfinance sector developed in India and see potential for the microfinance institutions, NGOs, SHGs in the market.
- To analyse the structure and pattern of microfinance programme in rural Indian by the MFIs, NBFCs.
- To study the importance and role of microfinance in poverty alleviation and profitable agriculture activities.

Methodology

This is a descriptive research paper based on secondary data which were gathered from various published sources, viz., books, journals, newspapers, websites, research studies, etc.

Review of Literature

Several research studies are made by both Indian and foreign researchers on microfinance. According to the study by Economic Development Association, Gurgaon, Haryana (2006), microfinance has helped to uplift the poor and empower the women who have no access to credit. Ghate et al, (2007) concluded that microfinance routed through SHGs has emerged as a visible credit channel to the poor as their access to conventional credit channels is constrained by the requirements of collateral, and high transaction cost. Kaptan and Lata Swaminathan (?) examined microfinance through women cooperative banks. They concluded that since women constitute about 50 per cent of the population, their involvement in economic activity will fasten the pace of economic development in the nation. Mahajan and Nagasri (1999), observes that high transaction cost, low scale of operation, high clients turnover, high frequency of transactions, etc. are inhibiting factors for microfinance from the formal channels. Mahajan (2005) says that the role of government, formal financial institutions, Non Government Organisation (NGOs), and people participation play important role in success of microfinance as a medium of poverty alleviation.

Indian Environment

Demand side attributes

India's development over the last 60 plus post-independence years has however not resulted in the income disparity being reduced. The vast majority of the Indian population is still rural and relies on agriculture as the prime means of survival. However, the lack of political stability coupled with the bureaucracy has not helped in bridging the income divide. To alleviate the poverty stricken and propel the economic growth pace forward the government is hard pressed to ensure that the poor receive microfinance. This will prevent mass unemployment/famine and will also result in the betterment of agricultural products and will over all help India to move successfully from a protectionist economy to one that is quite close to a market economy.

The poor and the low-income households also need a broad range of finance such as deposits, loans, payment services, money transfers and insurance. Microfinance satisfies these large demands from the diverse poor such as farmers, women and micro-entrepreneurs.

Supply side attributes

All the major international organisations like the U.N., World Bank, IFC, etc have initiated and are executing microfinance projects in India. The government primarily due to the financial constraint has looked at external agencies for partnership for microfinance projects. In addition in India there are several community-based sources and chit funds which are involved in micro credit but on a very small scale and it often regionalised.

Micro finance

Micro-finance economically disadvantaged segments of society, for enabling them to raise their income levels largest in term of population after China. India's GDP ranks among the top 15 economies of the world. However, around 300 million people or about 80 million households are living below the poverty line, i.e. less than $2 per day according to the World Bank and the poorest are which earns $1 per day. It is further estimated that of these households, only about 20 per cent have access to credit from the formal sector. Out of these 80 million house hold, 80 per cent takes credit from the informal sources i.e., local Zamindars, Chit Funds etc. With about 80 million households below MFIs include non-governmental organisations (NGOs), credit unions, non-bank financial intermediaries, and even a few commercial banks.

Microfinance is to provide financial services like small loans, credit, deposit service and insurance to very poor people for self-employment projects that generate incomes, supporting economically themselves and their family. Some of the defining criteria used include: Size: Loans are micro or very small for targeted users between as little as $5 ~500 Market: Micro entrepreneurs and low-income households Use of funds: For income generation and enterprise development, but also community use like health and education, etc Terms and conditions: Flexible and easy to understand and suited to the local conditions of the community.

Its impact is overwhelming in a number of ways. First, microfinance has provided financial services to people who are largely excluded from the formal financial industry mostly due to the lack of collateral. It helps people to escape from vicious poverty trap. Secondly, microfinance is an innovative program that breaks common industry wisdoms and it is also relevant to many other industries that are looking for the development of new market.

Thirdly, microfinance provides poor people with education and experience in financial service, market economy and entrepreneurial culture.

Findings of the Study

Spread of SHGs: Savings-linked SHGs

The SHG movement has spread to all parts of India with varying degrees of speed and density. Table 1 gives region-wise and agency-wise, savings linked SHGs. At the end of March 2010, there were 69.53 lakh SHGs with savings accounts in banks with balances to the tune of Rs 6,198.71 crore. Bulk of these savings were with the commercial banks aggregating Rs 3,673.89 crore followed by RRBs with Rs1,299.37 crore and cooperative banks with Rs1,225.44 crore. Commercial banks share of savings of SHGs were close to 60 per cent with the rest almost equally shared by the RRBs and cooperative banks.

In terms of spatial dispersal of SHGs across the country, southern region constitute more than 46 per cent in number of SHGs savings accounts and 51 per cent in terms of amount. Eastern region is a distant second with 20 per cent and 18 per cent respectively in terms of number and amount of savings linked SHGs. Northern and North-Eastern regions are lagging far behind.

Table 1: Agency-wise and Region-wise SHGs' Savings with Banks as on 31 March 2010

Region	*Commercial Banks*		*RRBs*		*Cooperative Banks*		*Total*	
	No. of SHGs	*Saving Amt in Lacs*	*No. of SHGs*	*Saving Amt in Lacs*	*No. of SHGs*	*Saving Amt in Lacs*	*No. of SHGs*	*Saving Amt in Lacs*
Northern	185795	22641	85340	5505.9	80666	6060.4	351801	34207.3
	(2.67)	(3.65)	(1.23)	(0.89)	(1.16)	(0.98)	(5.06)	(5.52)
North-Eastern	115046	4911	147368	5765.9	29774	1489.3	292188	12167.1
	(1.65)	(0.79)	(2.12)	(0.93)	(0.43)	(0.24)	(4.20)	(1.96)
Eastern	701945	38370	428915	51919.8	243382	21724.2	1374242	112014.6
	(10.10)	(6.19)	(6.17)	(8.38)	(3.50)	(3.50)	(19.76)	(18.07)
Central	352294	26906	359743	18232.4	53928	6224.4	765965	51363.6
	(5.07)	(4.34)	(5.17)	(2.94)	(0.78)	(1.00)	(11.02)	(8.29)
Western	512306	53142	135931	2800.9	297383	36724.1	945620	92667.5
	(7.37)	(8.57)	(1.95)	(0.45)	(4.28)	(5.92)	(13.60)	(14.95)
Southern	2185529	221416	663573	45712.6	374332	50321.9	3223434	317450.9
	(31.43)	(35.72)	(9.54)	(7.37)	(5.38)	(8.12)	(46.36)	(51.21)
Total	**4052915**	**367389**	**1820870**	**129937.5**	**1079465**	**122544.6**	**6953250**	**619870.9**
	(58.29)	**(59.27)**	**(26.19)**	**(20.96)**	**(15.52)**	**(19.77)**	**(100.00)**	**(100.00)**

Source: Status of Micro Finance in India 2009-2010, NABARD.
N.B.: Figures in brackets indicate percentages to the total.

One-third of the commercial banks SHG savings come from southern region. RRBs and cooperative banks are relatively more active than commercial banks in eastern region while commercial banks lead in southern and western regions. Cooperative banks are next to commercial banks in western region; in all other regions they are lagging behind both the agencies. RRBs and cooperative banks together have a greater share in North-Eastern region in both number of SHGs and their savings. RRBs have less than five per cent share in Northern, North-Eastern and western regions in both number of SHGs and savings amount. Only in eastern and southern regions, RRBs have share ranging between five per cent and ten per cent. Cooperative banks have more than 4 per cent share only in western and southern regions; in all other regions it is less than four per cent.

Credit Linked SHGs

As at the end of March 2010, there were 48.51 lakh SHGs credit linked with outstanding bank loans of Rs. 28,038.28 crore. Commercial banks again had the major share with an amount of Rs. 20,164.71 crore amongst 32.37 lac SHGs. Their share was 71.9 per cent in loan outstanding and 66.7 per cent in number of credit linked SHGs. The RRBs were second with 21.9 per cent and 22.8 per cent in loan outstanding and number of SHGs respectively.

Table 2 shows the SHG credit linkages, region-wise and agency-wise. Southern region again leads with a share of more than 53 per cent in number of SHGs and more than 67 per cent in loans outstanding at the end of March 2010. Northern and North-Eastern regions share are abysmally low-less than four per cent. All the three agencies viz., commercial banks, RRBs and cooperative banks are active in southern region. Commercial banks are leading in all regions with sizable margins in both number of SHGs credit linked and amount outstanding. In terms of loans outstanding they have more than 50 per cent share in all regions. RRBs are second in all regions except western region where cooperative banks are second. It is significant to note that RRBs and cooperative banks are lagging behind commercial banks in credit linkages. Share of commercial banks in all India base is close to 40 per cent in southern region in terms of number of SHGs credit linked and more than 50 per cent in terms of amount outstanding. On the other hand, share of all three agencies are less than five per cent in Northern and North-Eastern regions. RRBs have double digit (more than ten per cent) share only in southern region. Cooperative banks share is less than four per cent in all regions.

Table 2: Agency-wise and Region-wise Bank Loans Outstanding against SHGs as on 31st March 2010

Region	*Commercial Banks*		*RRBs*		*Cooperative Banks*		*Total*	
	No. of SHGs	*Loan o/s (Rs in lacs)*	*No. of SHGs*	*Loan o/s (Rs in lacs)*	*No. of SHGs*	*Loan o/s (Rs in lacs)*	*No. of SHGs*	*Loan o/s (Rs in lacs)*
Northern	65759	49748.24	41415	17852.18	45317	13912.91	152491	81513
	(1.36)	(1.77)	(0.85)	(0.64)	(0.93)	(0.50)	(3.14)	(2.91)
North-Eastern	69571	38826.10	50297	22853.97	13917	5667.72	133785	67347
	(1.43)	(1.38)	(1.04)	(0.82)	(0.29)	(0.20)	(2.76)	(2.40)
Eastern	561579	236556.29	313118	108645.63	152873	24288.96	1027570	369490
	(11.58)	(8.44)	(6.45)	(3.87)	(3.15)	(0.87)	(21.18)	(13.18)
Central	317021	157725.85	153582	77276.47	27319	11237.28	497922	246239
	(6.53)	(5.63)	(3.17)	(2.76)	(0.56)	(0.40)	(10.26)	(8.78)
Western	331693	104591.78	38064	13365.98	87719	18990.72	457476	136948
	(6.84)	(3.73)	(0.78)	(0.48)	(1.81)	(0.68)	(9.43)	(4.88)
Southern	1891640	1429022.95	507504	374464.01	182968	98801.03	2582112	1902287
	(38.99)	(50.97)	(10.46)	(13.36)	(3.77)	(3.52)	(53.22)	(67.85)
Total	**3237263**	**2016471.21**	**1103980**	**614458.24**	**510113**	**172898.62**	**4851356**	**2803828**
	(66.73)	**(71.92)**	**(22.76)**	**(21.91)**	**(10.51)**	**(6.17)**	**(100.00)**	**(100.00)**

Source: Status of Micro Finance in India 2009-2010, NABARD. Figures within brackets indicate percentage to total.

Reasons for Regional Disparities

Spread of microfinance is uneven in the country. While it has grown phenomenally in southern states, other regions are lagging behind. Eastern region is a distant second. Other regions have to do some catching up. The success of microfinance in southern region is because apart from banks, NGOs and Micro Finance Institutions (MFIs) are also active. In other regions especially in northern and North-eastern, the microfinance is predominantly through banking channels; there are lesser number of NGOs and MFIs are few and far between. Success of SHGs also depends on law and order situation. This explains why southern states are more successful than the rest of the country. Insurgency problems in north and north-eastern states, naxalite menace in central and parts of western region are affecting SHG movement in these areas.

Southern states have better literacy rates and awareness; this is helping spread of SHG movement faster. NGOs are in larger numbers in southern states and also more active. MFIs too are active in southern states. These are contributing to acceleration in SHGs in South India. MFIs registered in various legal forms are supplementing the efforts of the formal banking network in providing credit support to the economically excluded for inclusive growth.

The initiative of 1992 to make the traditional and formal banks to extend financial services to deprived sections through informal Self Help Groups (SHGs), has now blossomed into a "monolith" micro Finance initiative. It has been recognised as a decentralised, cost-effective and fastest growing micro finance initiative in the world, enabling over 103 million poor households' access to a variety of sustainable financial services from the banking system by becoming members of nearly eight million SHGs. The linkage with banks has provided the members of the groups the facility of not only pooling their thrift /savings and access to credit from the banking system, but also created a platform through which they could launch a number of livelihood initiatives and also facilitate the empowerment process.

While the first decade of the programme was meant to demonstrate the potential of SHGs to organise themselves and be instrumental in managing their own savings and extending emergent micro credit needs, the second decade laid emphasis on establishing the replicability of the model across the regions, with focus on resource poor regions of the country. This decade also witnessed greater confidence among the financing banks to "own" up the programme as a potential business model thereby extending its outreach to the current level. The development planners including the Government of India and the State Governments also recognised the real potential of the SHG movement in development of the poor and it was made an essential ingredient of all poverty alleviation programmes of the Government.

Even the private sector started realising the untapped potential of SHGs for deep penetration to the emerging rural markets. The turbulence witnessed in the micro finance sector in the recent past due to the mushrooming growth of Micro Finance Institutions (MFIs) and their questionable ways in which they went ahead in extending their outreach and credit intensification, could not make any significant dent in the popularity of the SHG-Bank Linkage Programme.

The small beginning of linking only 500 SHGs to banks in 1992, had grown to over 0.5 million SHGs by March 2002 and further to eight million SHGs by March 2012. From almost 100 per cent of the SHGs linked to Banks at the pilot stage from southern states, the share of southern States in the total number of SHGs linked shrank to 46 per cent by March 2012, while the share of eastern States (especially, West Bengal, Odisha, Bihar) shot up to over 20 per cent.

The third decade of the programme promises to be one of maturing the linkage programme with livelihoods support, lot more innovations in the product range offered through SHGs and path breaking reforms in leveraging technology to improve efficiency, while extending its outreach to more geographical regions, especially the most resource poor regions of the country. It is widely believed that the SHGs of the poor will be the vehicles leading the march of India's emergence as a super economic power in the next decade. A number of countries, especially the developing countries and international agencies are turning to India to learn from its experiments with micro finance and to explore possibilities of replication of the model in other parts of the globe.

Policy Imperatives

Disparity in the spread and success of microfinance across India is all too evident. While southern states are way ahead, other regions are lagging far behind in SHG movement. The success in Southern region is not merely due to micro lending agencies but due to host of other factors like the literacy rate, better economic infrastructure, active NGOs and MFIs. Rural women are more actively involved in SHGs. Therefore one can reasonably surmise that microfinance alone cannot help in upliftment of poor. Spread of education and development of economic infrastructure are vital.

MFIs can play a major role in facilitating financial inclusion, as they are distinctively placed in reaching out to the rural and urban poor. Many of them operate in a limited geographical area, have a better understanding of the issues specific to the rural poor, and enjoy greater acceptability amongst the rural people. They are flexible in operations providing a level of comfort to the rural people. There is however a need to regulate and streamline the MFIs especially the small and start-up MFIs. There is also need for bringing greater transparency in the activities of the MFIs. The government with the Micro Finance Institutions (Development and Regulation) Bill proposes to bring the MFIs under the purview of the RBI. This would need to be done with a sense of urgency.

While the reach and coverage of MFIs is small as of now, they have the potential to reach the far corners of the rural India. They have the look and feel of the local population and can therefore empathise with them better. It will be possible for them to structure their products and services to suit the local needs. They have to however overcome the inhibiting factors viz., professionalism and governance issues. A facilitative environment and enabling regulatory regime would contribute to their success. Their foray in microfinance to become successful should be coterminous to all the developmental programs across sectors.

To push microfinance in northern and north-eastern states, the government has to initiate a two pronged strategy of spread of education and infrastructure development. People in Border States live under constant threat to their life due to poor governance.

The insurgency problems in Border States and law and order in central India would need to be tackled alongside the outreach programme. There is need for more NGOs and MFIs in North India. Educational institutions and Panchayats should actively promote NGOs. Banks and NABARD should finance more MFIs in northern states. The UID Project should also help in speeding up the microfinance movement across the country.

While banks are leading in microfinance, RRBs and cooperative banks with their focus on neglected sectors of society should play more active role. But they are constrained due to lack of professionalism in pushing the inclusive agenda. They are also plagued by political interference and lack of corporate governance. These issues would need to be addressed at once. Closer monitoring and guidance by the RBI and NABARD would help.

Suggestions

India has shown promising growth after 1991 in which the policy reforms occurred. In order to continue the development it is highly critical to alleviate poverty and ensure that the poor get access to capital and finance. The bureaucracy and political instability will test the government's initiatives to roll out new Microfinance projects. An establishment of a solid governing institution for MF coupled with assistance in terms of monetary and knowledge from international organisations will lead to better and bigger projects. Based on the analysis some of the key recommendations are as follows:

- Professional management – Import the best practices from around the world.
- Educate and increase the awareness about the benefits
- Setting up of independent MFI's in collaboration with Grameen banks, etc.
- Reach out to more people through the projects. Different initiatives need to be implemented. It is clearly not a one size fits all strategy.

Conclusion

The main objective of microfinance is to provide an umbrella of micro services to the poor so as to enhance their creditworthiness and make them bank worthy to financial institutions. SHG movement inculcates financial discipline and timely repayment among small borrowers so that they can seek long-term financial assistance and banking services from the formal sector eventually. Microfinance in India has brought number of people above the poverty line. But the coverage is uneven with large number of people in rural hinterland still remaining out of the ambit of the outreach programmes. There is an imperative need for coordinated action among the various agencies such as the government, financial institutions, NGOs and like-minded people. Economic, developmental and infrastructure issues should engage the attention of the government and other stakeholders. Involvement of women especially the rural women in SHG movement will go a long way in achieving "purna swaraj" in inclusive growth agenda.

REFERENCES

1. Das K, (2009), Microfinance in India: Prospects and Challenges, *Professional Banker*, December 2009, pp. 39-42.
2. EDA Rural systems, Gurgaon, and APMAS (Andhra Pradesh Mahila Abhivruddhi Society), Hyderabad, (2006), "Self Help Groups in India: A Study of Lights and shades", a report prepared for the Catholic Relief Services (CRS), Cooperative Assistance for Relief Everywhere (CARE), USAID, GTZ/NABARD, and Microfinance India, New Delhi.
3. Ghate P, et al. (2007), *Microfinance in India: A State of the Sector Report 2007*, CARE, Ford Foundation, and Microfinance India, Delhi, in association with Access Development Services, and Sage Publications India, Delhi.
4. Dr Kaptan S, Swaminathan Lata, "Microfinance through women coop banks to achieve millennium development goals in developing nations", published in NABARD web site; http://www.nabard.org/databank/IARD%20Web/csidfiles/Microfinance%20through%20women%20co-op%20banks.pdf (accessed 27/08/2014).
5. Huchhe Gowda (2013) (ed) "*Empowerment of Women During 21st Century in India*" *Himalaya Publishing House, Mumbai ISBN No. 978-93-5142-250-1.*
6. Mahajan V, (2005), "From Micro Credit to Livelihood Finance", *Economic and Political Weekly*, Vol. 40, No. 41, pp. 4416-4419.
7. Mahajan V and Nagasri G, (1999), "Building Sustainable Microfinance Institutions (MFIs) in India", BASIX, Hyderabad.
8. Rajasekar D (2004), "Microfinance, Poverty Alleviation, and Empowerment of Women: A Study of two NGOs from Andhra Pradesh and Karnataka", A Monograph.
9. Subrahmanyam N, (2009-10), "Micro-Finance and SHG-Bank Linkage: Regional Analysis and Perspectives", *Prajnan*, Vol. XXXVIII, No. 3, pp. 183-202.
10. Tiwari P and Fahad S M, "Concept Paper: Microfinance Institutions in India", Retrieved from: http://theatreforum.in/static/upload/docs/MICROFINANCE.pdf (accessed 27/08/2014).

11. NABARD, (2010), "Status of Micro Finance in India 2009-2010", Retrieved from: http://nabard.org/pdf/Status%20of%20Micro%20Finance%202009-10%20Eng.pdf (accessed 27/08/2014).
12. NABARD Annual Report 2009-10, published by NABARD.

28

Financial Inclusion of Dalit Women Through SHG—Bank Linkage Programme

H.R. Uma and Pushpa Nanaiah

Abstract: *India is home to the largest population of poor in the world. Microfinance in India has emerged as a powerful tool for financial inclusion. The 'SHG – Bank Linkage' programme plays a predominant role in the financial inclusion of excluded poor. The programme is coming up well and being implemented widely across the country. But there is a need to strengthen the SHG-Bank Linkage Programme to fully mainstream it with the commercial banking system. The programme is scaling up at a rapid pace in South India, while the progress in other regions is slow. The variations in performance across the regions, both in terms of reach and quality needs immediate attention.*

Key words: Financial Literacy, Financial Inclusion, Microfinance.

Introduction

Micro Finance is emerging as a powerful instrument for poverty alleviation in the new economy.The term micro finance is of recent origin and is commonly used in addressing issues related to poverty alleviation, financial support to micro entrepreneurs, gender development etc. There is however, no statutory definition of micro finance. The taskforce and supportive policy and regulatory frame work for micro finance has defined micro finance as "provision of thrift, credit and other financial services and products of very small amounts to the poor in rural, semi urban or urban areas for enabling them to raise their income levels and improve living standards".

The definition for microfinance is best given by Robinson, Marguerite. According to her Microfinance refers to small-scale financial services for both credits and deposits — that are provided to people who operate small or micro enterprises where goods are produced, recycled, repaired, or traded; provide services; work for wages or commissions; gain income from renting out small amounts of land, vehicles, draft animals, or machinery and tools; and to other individuals and local groups in developing countries, in both rural and urban areas, delivery of financial services at an affordable cost to vast sections of disadvantaged and low income groups. 'It includes Savings, Credit, Insurance, Remittance facilities etc.

Delivery of financial services at an affordable cost to vast sections of disadvantaged and low income groups is known as Financial Inclusion. Only 31 per cent of the Indian population has access to Banking services. The rest 69 per cent are still deprived of bare minimum banking services for which they are totally dependent on informal banking sources like private money lenders.

FI is needed because of High transactions costs of borrowers, High transactions costs of savers, High transactions costs of banks, High risk cost, and inappropriate products. In India Marginal Farmers, Landless Farmers, Oral Lessees, Self Employed, Urban slum developers, Migrants, Minorities, Senior citizens and all socially excluded groups including Women are the excluded lot.

Measures to promote Financial Inclusion

Certain intermediaries can be used for promoting financial inclusion. They are,:

1. Linkage of Self Help Groups with bank.
2. Linkage of Microfinance Institutions with banks.
3. Business facilitators and correspondence model.

This paper studies linkage of SHGs with banks for the promotion of financial inclusion of rural Dalit women. For the sake of survey Hunsur taluk is considered.

Linkage of SHGs (self-help groups) with Bank:

Status of SHGs in India

A review of the genesis and development of SHGs in India reveals that the existing formal financial Institutions have failed to provide fiancé to landless, marginalised, and disadvantaged groups. The origin of SHGs could be traced to mutual aid in Indian village community. Co-operatives are formal bodies, where as SHGs are informal. SHGs encourage savings and promote income generating activities through small loans. The experiences available in the country and elsewhere suggest that SHGs are sustainable, have replicability, stimulate savings, and in the process help borrowers to come out of vicious Circle of poverty.

As regards micro finance in India, it is a new concept, perhaps influenced by the success of Grameena Bank of Bangladesh. Along with Government of India, NABARD and Rashtriya Mahila Kosh have been promoting SHGs through non government organisations (NGOs) and banks. Self-Help Group is a small economically homogeneous and affinity group of rural poor, voluntarily formed to save and mutually agreed to contribute to a common fund to be lend to its members as per groups decision. The great merit of SHGs has been their ability to inculcate among members sound habits of their savings and banking. SHGs or micro credit groups have been recognised as useful tools to help poor access financial resources not available to them previously and help them breakthrough the strong hold of exploitative money lenders.

India can boast of having the fastest growing and the most cost effective micro finance concept in the world. Poor families have been able to get banking services from the banking system through a network of over 1.5 rural banking outlets and over 16 lakh SHGs in the country. Till 31st March 2005, 16-18 lakh groups have been linked with formal banking system including 5,39,385 fresh groups linked during 2004-05. The SHGs bank linkage programme has benefited 242.5 lakh families, covering 1212.50 lakh poor people. During 2004-05, bank loan of Rs 2,994 crore were provided to 10 SHGs taking the cumulative figure upto 31st March 2005 to Rs 6,898 crore with refinance support and Rs 3092 crore from NABARD.

Indian Initiatives

The first effort was taken by NABARD in 1986-87 when it supported and funded an action research project on "Saving and credit management of SHGs" of Mysore Resettlement and development Agency. (MYRADA). Then NABARD launched a pilot project to provide micro credit by linking SHGs with bank in 1991-92. During the project period, some NGOs like Association of Sarva Seva Farms (ASSEFA), peoples Rural Education Movement (PREM) etc have done excellent work in promotion of SHGs and mobilisation of thrift and disbursal of credit. In 1999, RBI had set up a micro credit cell to make it easier to micro credit provides to pursue institutional development process. Although these developments are commendable, a lot more needs to be done. There are still three to four million households in rural areas and about one to five million poor in urban areas who do not have access to financial services from formal or semi-formal sources.

Significance of Establishing Linkages of SHGs with Banks

The linking of the SHGs with banks aims at using the intermediation of the SHGs between the banks and the rural poor for cutting down the transaction costs for both banks and their rural clients. Of late especially since late eighties it is being realised in India that SHGs can establish relationship between the formal financial institutions and the poor for providing credit and other banking facilities. The SHG approach involves formation of informal groups for pooling their savings through regular periodical meetings and then on lending among the members at some self decides rate of interest ranging from 1 to 3 per cent per month. Women led SHG's in many parts of the country have achieved success in bringing the women to the mainstream of decision making. SHG is also a viable organised setup to disburse micro credit to the rural women and encouraging them to enter into entrepreneurial activities.

Micro finance provides credit access to poor with no collateral obligations. It encourages savings and promotes income generating activities. Loans are provided at the market driven rates of interest and peer pressure is used in repayment. Micro finance is carried out through self help groups where poor come together in the range of 10 – 20 by weekly, fort nightly and monthly meetings through their savings and loading. It is hoped that through such interventions uncovered groups are covered with credit and in the process get empowered.

In 1987, NABARD made an attempt to search for alternative mechanism to improve the access of the poor for financial services in a cost effective and sustainable manner. This search led to the development of a delivery mechanism which encompasses financial relationship between informal organisations of the poor like the SHGs and formal organisations like Banks. Later on with the needed back up policy support from the Reserve Bank and the Central Government, the SHG – Bank linkage programme was launched by NABARD as a pilot project in February 1992. Currently about one lakh SHGs have been linked through various banks under the aegis of NABARD for which it has refinanced Rs 150 crores to the banks. Within this overall objective NABARD and Rashtriya Mahila Kosh have their own special objectives.

SHG – Bank linkage programme

With a view to facilitate smother and meaningful banking with the poor, a pilot project for purveying micro credit by linking SHGs with banks was launched by NABARD in 1991-92. RBI had advised commercial banks to actively participate in this linkage program. The scheme has since been extended to RRBs and co-operative banks.

A target of one lakh SHGs was set for 2000-01 for linkage by banks. The number of SHGs linked to banks aggregated to 1.50 lakh by the end of 2000-01. This translates into an estimated 1.9 million very poor families brought within the fold of formal banking services. More than 88 per cent of the groups linked with banks are exclusive women groups while cumulative disbursement of bank loans to these SHGs stood at Rs193 crores as on March 31, 2000. Commercial banks, RRBs and co-operative banks all now associated with the SHG bank linkage programme.

Since 1970s developing country like India have increasingly focused on micro credit to facilitate the access of poor households to financial services like credit, savings, insurance etc., micro credit, which includes micro savings, is gradually emerging as one of the most effective strategies to alleviate poverty. It can effectively generate employment and sustain the income of the households by giving them opportunities of work. Although micro credit Institutions is effective weapons in the war against rural poverty they alone cannot neutralise non physical symptoms of poverty which deprive the poor of a full social existence. Efforts are needed to promote and strengthen micro finance institutions to optimise their war against poverty.

Role played by Banks in credit lent to SHGs in Karnataka

The number of SHGs linked with banks increased from 22,742 in 2003 to 1, 37,000 by March 2007. During the same period, the amount of credit disbursed through SHGs increased from Rs 21.8 crores to 144 crores. SHG clusters and SHG federations have also been established in the state.

The banking system also has been directed to play its role in this process. In rural credit disbursement, concerted efforts are made to promote the non-farm activities in rural areas. Self-employment ventures in trading the farm and non farm products and production of consumer goods, food articles, garments are some of the programmes commonly promoted by banks, through the SHGs.

These are reasons to believe that given the necessary support and guidance, some of the SHGs have been successful in influencing the employment environment of their members. It may be intangible in some cases, explosive in some others. There is a need for documenting their achievements, for drawing inferences from their experiences.

SHG-Bank linkage – Agency-wise cumulative participation in Karnataka upto March 2006

Sl.No.	*Name of the Agency*	*No. of SHG'S*	*Bank Loan (In Millions)Rs.*
1.	Commercial Banks	38, 605	1, 006.79
2.	Regional Rural Banks	37, 087	1, 094.73
3.	Co-operative Banks	28, 174	734. 66
Total	103, 866	2836. 18	

Source: NABARD Report.

The above table clearly shows that all the financial institutions have provided maximum bank loan to SHGs. Commercial Banks have provided Rs 1006.79 million and they have formulated 38,605 SHG in Karnataka up to 2006. Regional Rural Banks have also played a significant role in providing bank loans to SHGs and even Co-operative Banks also participated in promoting SHGs in Karnataka. Savings made by members are pooled and loaned to be another. SHG members determine the terms and conditions.

SHG members consider their ability to raise loans from banks and their ability to negotiate with banks directly as a major indicator of increased levels of confidence and self esteem. This provides some insights into SHG member's ability to access finance from mainstream institutions. Many members say that they have learnt to sign after joining the group. Although this might seem like a minor achievement to most of us, to SHG members, it seems to be a way of gaining, acceptance in the mainstream and a source of pride. Many members spoke of how they were previously ashamed to conduct bank transactions, as they used thumb impressions in place of signatures. Only after learning to sign they were comfortable about going to a bank. It was after joining the SHG that they had gained the confidence of conducting bank transactions on their own and approaching bank officials for loans.

In the survey area when asked about reasons for joining SHG, members cited as many as nine reasons, to avail credit, developing saving habit, to meet unexpected demand for cash, peer pressure, motivated by NGO officials, Solidarity, exchange of ideas, experiences, attend adult education classes, and empowerment. Among all the reasons mentioned, to avail credit, to meet unexpected demand for cash, and develop saving habit are the prime factors to join the SHGs. However there are minor variations across various categories of women. Regular meetings, compulsory attendance and savings are the features of these SHGs. The meetings are conducted at the group leader's house either weekly or fortnightly depending on the convenience of the members. There is a penalty for late attendance and absentees.

SHG-Bank Linkage in Hunsur Taluk

Finance being the life blood of every commercial venture, availability of adequate funds at reasonable terms is a must to ensure speedy economic development of a village and empowerment of women. There are a good number of financial institutions that support women to start any new enterprises in Hunsur taluk. They have stressed on the need to include those who are financially excluded. It was very clear that lot of stress was made to improve the financial status of Dalit women by providing financial facility to them. Some of the banks which are working in the area under the guidance of RBI are: Karnataka Bank, Canara Bank, State Bank of Mysore, Mysore and Chamarajanagar District Co-Operative Bank, Vijaya Bank, Cauvery Kalpataru Grameena Bank.

These banks played a key role in advancing loans to the women groups in improving their economic status. About six Banks in Hunsur are advancing loans to more than 239.53 lakh people. This indicates the growing economic awareness about rural credit among the groups. This facility enabled the rural women to achieve self sufficiency in economic field. The objective of these Banks is to develop sustainability in the field of economic development by encouraging group activities to generate self employment products. These banks are providing the loan for agricultural purpose, rearing the cows, sheep and goats, and financial assistance for agarbathi manufacturing, sambar powder preparation and papad making, etc. Thrift and credit system of SHGs is a great revolution in this taluk in bringing socio economic transformation among the uneducated rural women. Internet and computer facilities are already provided to these banks for the quick processing of loans to priority groups.

When asked about reasons for joining SHG, members cited many reasons, Among all the reasons mentioned, to avail credit, to meet unexpected demand for cash, and develop saving habit are the prime factors to join the SHGs. However there are minor variations across various categories of women. Regular meetings, compulsory attendance and savings are the features of this SHGs Depending on the economic status of the group; women saved Rs 75 to Rs 150 / month. Generally, after five to six months of operation, savings are used for internal lending. The amount of loan and number of loaners are decided by the members depending on the savings, need, and urgency. Loans are sanctioned at a rate of interest. Women said that they suddenly realised that they have not only access to but control over an amount which they had never dream in their lives that they would ever see. They opened bank account in the name of group to ensure safety of money saved and to access more mainstream credit. These groups are also linked with banks to undertake income-generating activities through which women could achieve economic independence and self-confidence to some extent. Thus women belonging to lowest strata of the society are getting habituated to savings and managing SHGs efficiently. AIDS, dowry, nutrition, legal literacy, sanitation, already involves some of these groups multiple roles of women etc.

The status of women is intimately connected with their economic position, which in turn depends on opportunities for women for participation in economic activities. Though women work more than a man, most of her work in not recognised in monetary terms, particularly in rural areas. This is one of the reasons along with low level of education which is making her more vulnerable to all sorts of exploitations. Women ability to save and access to credit would give them an economic role not only with in the household but, also, outside the house as well. Investment in economic activities of women would improve employment opportunities for women.

The socio-economic survey of SHGs in this area helped rural women to earn an additional monthly income ranging from Rs 500 to Rs 2500 depending on the income generation activity learnt the art of improving their socio-economic status by participating in Government.

Educational status of beneficiaries

Education	Members
10th	2
9th	5
8th	7
7th	3
6th	6
5th	0
4th	5
3rd	2

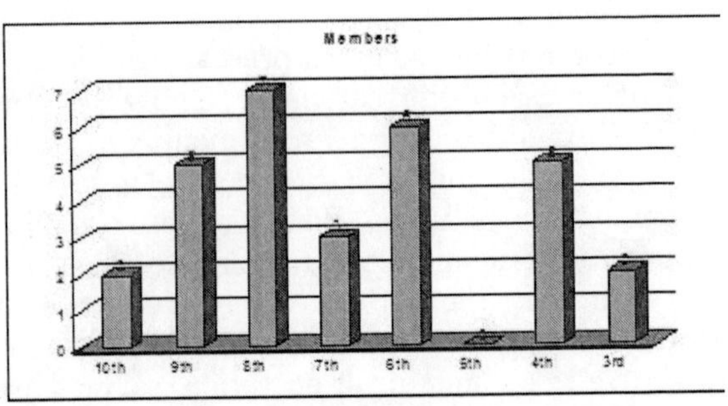

FINANCIAL DETAILS OF SHGS

[illegible]	[illegible]	[illegible]	[illegible]	[illegible]	[illegible]	[illegible]	[illegible]	[illegible]	[illegible]	[illegible]	[illegible]

Conclusion

It has been proved in the study that there is a link between education and the number of beneficiaries who have taken the help of SHGs. In the study area most of the beneficiaries are having primary and secondary education. As per the data most of the beneficiaries are able to understand the significance of SHGs in improving their financial status.

To achieve 100 per cent financial inclusion, financial literacy among the women should be high. Micro finance is emerging as a powerful instrument for poverty alleviation in the current economy. In the case study area micro finance scene is dominated by SHG – bank linkage programme as a cost effective mechanism for providing financial services to the unreached Dalit poor which has been successful not only in meeting financial needs of the rural Dalit women but also strengthen collective self – help capacities of the poor, leading to their empowerment. Rapid progress in SHG formation has now turned into an empowerment movement among women across the study area. If Dalit woman is financially literate it is very easy for her financial inclusion through government programmes.

REFERENCES

1. NABARD (1989), Studies on self help groups of rural poor, NABARD, Mumbai. NABARD (1994), Banking with the poor; Financing self – help groups, NABARD, Hyderabad.
2. NABARD (1985) Study of credit management groups, NABARD, Mumbai. NABARD (1996), Linking self – help groups with banks, NABARD, Pune.

3. NABARD (1998), Banking with the poor – financing self – help group NABARD Hyderabad.
4. Shakti Samachar, October-December 2001, published by women and child development department, government of Orissa, Bhubaneswar.
5. Kumar, Ashok and Harish, Women power; status of women in India, GIAN Publishing House, New Delhi 1991.
6. Annual Report, Ministry of Rural Development; 2001-02 to 2004-05.
7. NABARD's Annual reports (1996-97 to 2004-05).
8. NABARD's statistical reports (1996-97 to 2004-05).
9. The Economic Times – 2005 RBI Bulletins (1999-2000 and 2003-04).
10. Central Statistical Organisation (2003), Statistical Abstract India, CSO New Delhi.
11. NABARD; progress of SHG Bank linkage in India; various years Mumbai.
12. Husheni, S; RS Schuler and I Riley (1996), Rural credit programmes and women's Empowerment in Bangladesh world development, Vol. 24(4), 635-53.
13. Kabeer (2001) "Conflicts over credit, Re-evaluation the Empowerment potential of loans to women in Rural Bangladesh world development", Vol. 29, No. 1.

29

Micro Finance for Women Empowerment—A Study of Self-Help Groups in Thirthahalli Taluk

H.D. Dharmanna

Abstract: *Micro Finance programmes in inclusive growth have been receiving a considerable attention to world over for their potentiality to generate Income, Employment and Alleviation of Poverty. The experience shows that micro finance through Self-Help Groups (SHGs) has a high degree of outreach to women. In India NABARD and some NGOs are sponsored Self-Help Groups Bank linkage programme caused to fast growing of micro finance programmes. The research paper has focused on finding out whether micro finance has really contributed to the socio-economic empowerment of the SHG members; whether micro financing through the SHGs encourages and supports entrepreneurial activities and; the extent to which the SHGs could mobilise the saving habit among Thirthahalli taluk's women,. Out of 525 SHGs in Thirthahalli taluk, 53 groups (10 per cent) were selected randomly for study. All members from each group (900) were selected randomly. After joining the groups, the monthly average income and savings of the respondents had shown increase by 629.63 per cent and 69.62 per cent respectively. The confidence level of the respondents had increased to a great extent.*

They had reported active participation in socio-economic activities. Overall personality index had shown growth of 37 per cent. It was inferred that micro financing through women Self-Help Groups had brought a positive change in the life of the member respondents. The study concluded that poor, discriminated and unprivileged women if join the groups can come out of poverty.

Keywords: Micro Finance, Self Help Group, Empowerment, Entrepreneurship, Income Generation, Capacity Building.

Introduction

In recent years, Micro Finance has become an important intervention as a tool for rural development and poverty alleviation. In India many micro finance institutions including NGOs, NBFIs and Government agencies had intensively intervened innovation of group based (SHG) Garmin (Rural) joint liability groups, Mutually Aided Cooperative Societies etc., which replaced the physical collateral with moral and social collateral for micro-loans had improved the life standard and style of the rural poor and women in particular.

Microfinance is the provision of financial services to low-income clients, including consumers and the self-employed, who traditionally lack access to banking and related services. Microcredit, or microfinance is banking for the non-bankable, bringing credit, savings and other essential financial services within the reach of millions of people who are too poor to be served by regular banks, in most cases because they are unable to offer sufficient collateral. In general, banks are for people with money, not for people without money. It is based on the promise that the poor have skills which remain unutilised; microcredit fits best to those with entrepreneurial capability and possibility. Ultimately, the goal of microfinance is to give low income people an opportunity to become self sufficient by providing a means of saving money, borrowing money and insurance Micro Finance is being practiced as a tool to attract poverty in the world over. The term microfinance could be defined as 'provision of thrift, credit and other financial services and products of very small amounts to the poor in rural, semi-urban or urban areas, for enabling them to raise their income level and improve living standards'. Micro finance institutions are those which provide thrift, credit and other financial services and products of very small amounts mainly to the rural poor, semi-urban or urban areas for enabling them to raise their income level and improve their living standard. The potentiality of Micro Finance Institutions (MFIs) as promising institutions to meet the consumption and micro-enterprise demands of the poor has been realised.

Credit Needs of the Poor

It is estimated that in India there exist approximately 7.5 crore poor households, out of which six crore are in rural and 1.5 crore are in urban area. One estimate assumes that the total annual requirement of credit for the rural poor families would be at least Rs 15000 crore on the basis of a maximum need of assuming Rs 2000 per family. Another estimate for requirement of credit (excluding housing) is Rs 50000 crore assuming average credit usage are Rs 6000 per rural household and Rs 9000 for poor in urban household. The Credit for empowerment is about meeting daily consumption need of the poorest. It entails trying to build capacities of a large number of individuals, usually collectives, to increase credit absorption and undertake sustainable livelihoods. The Self-Help Group (SHG) is conceive as a sustainable people's Institution, which provides the poor with the space and support to necessary for them to take effective steps towards receiving greater control of their lives in society. The focus is on mobilising the poor to pool their own funds, building their capacities, and empowering them to leverage external credit. In other word credit for empowerment is about organising people, particularly around credit and building capacities to manage money.

Growth of Microfinance

This approach was institutionalised in 1976 by Muhammad Yunus, an American Bangladeshi economist who had observed that a significant percentage of the world's population has been barred from acquiring the capital necessary to get out of poverty. The Gramin approach is unique because the small loans are guaranteed by members of the borrower's community, pressure within the group to encourage borrowers to pay back the loans in a timely manner Gramin clients are among the poorest of the poor, many of whom had never possessed any money and relied on a barter economy to meet their daily needs. Using microloans, borrowers are able to purchase livestock or start their own business by 1996 Gramin had extended to more than three million borrowers and was the largest bank in Bangladesh with more than 1000 branches.

The growth of microfinance is visible in many aspects. There are more than 2000 NGOs involved in the NABARD, SHG-Bank linkage programme. Out of these, approximately 800 NGOs are involved in some form of financial intermediation. Further, there are 350 new generation co-operatives providing thrift and credit services. The growth of community institutions has taken place with the role to take social and financial intermediation. A numbers of community banks have came into existence at village and block levels call 'federation of Self-help groups'.

The inadequacies of the formal financial system to cater the needs of the poor and the realisation of the fact that the key to success lies in the evolution and participation of community based organisations at the grassroots level led to the emergence of a new generation of Micro Financial Institutions. One kind of MFI is an NGO engaged in promoting Self Help Groups and their Federations at a cluster level and linking SHGs with Banks under the scheme. Examples are MYRADA in Karnataka, which has promoted Sanghamitra, a company of its village saving and credit Sanghas; PRADAN which has established a large number of SHGs and federated them under Damodar in Bihar, Sakhi Samiti in Rajasthan.

Another kind of NGO-MFI directly lending to the poor borrowers, who are either organised into SHGs or into Gramin Bank type of groups after borrowing bulk funds from SIDBI, RMK and FWWB. Examples in this category are Rashtriya Gramin Vikas Nidhi (RGVN) which runs credit and savings programme in Assam and Orissa on the lines of Gramin Bank in Bangladesh. Also we have SHARE in AP, ASA in Tamil Nadu under this category.

Meaning of Microfinance

As per the Encyclopaedia Britannica, microcredit or microfinance also called Micro banking or a means of extending credit usually in the form of small loans with no collateral to non-traditional borrowers such as the poor in rural or underdeveloped areas.

Micro finance refers to a variety of financial services that target the low income clients, particularly women. Since the clients of microfinance institutions (MFIs) have lower incomes and often have limited access to other financial services, microfinance products tend to be for smaller monetary amounts than traditional financial services. These services include loans, savings, insurance and remittances. Micro loans are given for a variety of purposes frequently for micro enterprise development. The diversity of products and services offered reflects the fact that the financial needs of individuals, households and enterprises can change significantly over the time, especially for those who live in poverty. Because of these varied needs and the industry's focus on the poor, microfinance institutions often use non-traditional methodologies, such as group lending or other form of collateral not employed by the formal financial sector.

Micro finance is a type of banking service that is provided to unemployed or low-income individuals or groups who would otherwise have no other means of gaining financial services. Ultimately the goal of microfinance is to give an opportunity to low income people can become self sufficient by providing a means of savings money, borrowing money and insurance. Like conventional banking operations, microfinance institutions must charge their lenders interest on loans. While these interest rates are generally lower than those offered by normal banks, some opponents of this concept condemn microfinance operations for making profits of the poor. Micro finance refers to a variety of financial services that target low-income clients, particularly women. These services include loans, savings, insurance and remittances. Because of these varied needs, and because of the industry's focus on the poor, microfinance institutions often use non-traditional methodologies, such as group lending or other forms of collateral not employed by the formal financial sector.

Review of Literature

Access to financial services has got significance in the context of empowering the poor households and achieving millennium development goals. A few research studies have attempted to investigate the impact of Micro finance or Self-Help Groups on women empowerment.

Sen (1993) explains the words like empowerment; well-being of a person is that the freedom to lead different types of life is reflected in the person's capability set. The capability of a person depends on a variety of factors, including personal characteristics and social arrangements.

The World Bank defines empowerment as "The process of increasing the capacity of individuals or groups to make choices and to transform those choices into desired actions and outcomes.

Suguna (2006) conducted a study on empowerment of rural women through Self-Help Groups-An-in-depth study of Self-help groups in Chittoor district of Andhra Pradesh. A total sample of 300 beneficiaries had been selected for the study. The objectives of the study are to analyse the role of SHGs in the social, economic and political empowerment of women, to assess the extent of awareness regarding the governmental programme nature of participation of women in SHGs, and to examine and evaluate the specific problems of the beneficiaries with regard to saving, revolving fund productivity marketing.

Pangannavar (2010) reviews the incidence of poverty and efforts made through rural development programmes to overcome the problem of poverty since the incidence of poverty is more acute in rural India. Government has been making efforts to alleviate poverty through various programmes.

Venkatappa and Sivaiah (2011) report that rural development implies both the economic betterment of people and greater social transformation in order to provide the rural people with better prospects for economic development.

Chitra Ramachandran (2008) conducted a study on 202 SHG leaders of Madurai district in Tamil Nadu with a view to understanding the impact of micro enterprises on the quality of life of the women which was measured in terms of their living standards. She observed that most of the women in micro enterprises wanted to reduce poverty and to share their family responsibilities. The survey demonstrated that quality of life of the rural women had substantially increased the objective of the establishment of the micro enterprises successfully.

Dhillion (2010) Observed that the banks perceive poor rural women as higher risky group with limited liability to pay back their loans. The loans demanded by poor people are small in size and not sufficient to cover the transaction cost. Collateral requirements are difficult for women as the property is generally registered in the names of the male members of the family.

Usha (2010) studied 200 women SHGs from Srikakulam and Godavari districts of Andhra Pradesh. Recovery of loans was found very encouraging. Forty six members got elected to various posts of Panchayat committees and ZPs. Around 90 per cent of the members was aware about family planning.

Sarumathi and Moha (2011) made a study on "Role of Micro finance in women's empowerment, an Empirical study in Pondicherry region rural SHGs. In their article they found that the microfinance is a type of banking service that is provided to unemployed or low income individual groups who would otherwise have no other means of gaining financial services. Microfinance through Self-help Group has been recognised internationally as the modern tool to combat poverty and for rural development. Micro finance and SHGs are effective in reducing poverty, empowering women and creating awareness which finally results in sustainable development of the nation. The main aim of microfinance is to empower women.

Statement of the Problem

In olden days women were restricted to take part in any social activities and not given any roles in decision making in their family.

The situation was even more worsening in rural and remote areas. Now the situation has been changed. She is given freedom to do what she wishes. Today's scenario is more women's are engaged in income generating activities. This is because of NGO and other financial institution came forward to provide microfinance to poor women. They believe that a woman is the small credit and often benefits the whole family. The main aim of microfinance is to empower women. This induced the researcher to focus more on the empowerment of rural women who participate in the microfinance especially the Self Help Groups in Thirthahalli taluk. The movement for financial inclusion has been one of the real hopes for inclusive growth management of Microfinance and its programmes are currently being promoted through the Self-Help Groups. In India over the years various poverty alleviation programs have been initiated by government as well as voluntary organisations, despite these efforts not much difference is seen in the magnitude of poverty. Micro credit has now emerged as a financial strategy to reach the urban and rural poor and is emerging as a movement as the global level over the past two decades member in the SHGs their families below poverty line the landless and access to formal credit institutions. The need of the hour is women should be brought into the main stream of the credit system through Self Help Groups.

Meaning of Self Help Group

Self-Help Groups are both by definition and in practice is a group of individual members who by free association come together for a common collective purpose. In practice SHG comprises individual members known to each other coming from the same village, community and even marketing neighbourhood. That is they are homogeneous and have certain pre group social binding factors. In the context of micro-finance, SHGs are formed around the theme of savings and credit.

Self-Help groups don't start with credit, they start as savers group, with regular, weekly, or for fortnightly saving targets. Each member of the group has to save small amount money per month. The savings are deposited in a meeting on an appointed time every week or schedule and the collected saving are lent to members. With the decision of group one who gets the loan being taken by the group. In many groups savings are entered in individual members' passbooks. Some groups pay interest on saving, others pay dividends, but most groups have retained their earnings as part of their capital. An account is opened to maintain a bank deposit in any surplus savings. After some six months the bank where the savings were deposited examines the performance of the group and issues loans to the group. The SHG in turn increases its capacity to manage high amount of finance, develop entrepreneurial and communication skills and logical ability cooperative sense and finally income and employment generating confidence.

The main objective of the SHG is to inculcate the habit of thrift, saving and banking culture to gain economic prosperity through credit. The most important component of SHG is the mobilisation and organisation of women towards the basic strength of solidarity informality and collective action. Self-Help Group methodology is a novel approach in development of economy. These groups can create a unique, alternative, need-based credit delivery mechanism by pooling their insufficient resources for catering to their consumption and occupational requirement.

Characteristics of a Good Self Help Group

- Well functioning SHG should have the following structural features.
- An ideal SHG comprises 15-20 members.
- All the members should belong to the same socio-economic strata of society specifically poor.
- Group should have strong bond of affinity.
- Rotational leadership should be encouraged for distribution of power and to provide leadership pportunities to all the members.
- Members should attend meetings, save and participate in all activities voluntarily.
- To provide gainful employment and to involve the poor in productive activities.
- An SHG should be socially viable institution.
- The procedure of decision making in SHG should be democratic in nature.
- It should be non-partisan in nature.
- The group is frame rules and regulations, which are required for its effective functioning to involve women in decision making and to promote leadership qualities among them.

Objectives of the Study

The important objectives of this paper are: to study the importance and role of the self help groups and micro finance in poverty alleviation; to analyse the growth and performance of microfinance and self help groups in Thirthahalli taluk; to study the role of MFIs and SHGs in women entrepreneurship and women empowerment in Thirthahalli taluk and; to offer suggestions for further empowerment of women through microfinance.

Women's Empowerment

Awareness, participation and mobility primarily constitute the information base and provide the necessary prerequisites for empowerment to take place. While the three factors are interlinked it is generally assumed that awareness in inclusive of participation. Although the process of empowerment varies from culture to cultures, several types of changes are considered to be relevant in vide range of cultures. Some of these changes include: enhancing self-esteem and self-confidence in women, enabling women to gain equal access to control and over resources, faster decision making and action through collective process, and providing information, knowledge and skill for economic independence, transforming the institutions such as family education, religion, media, etc., and structure such as legal, political economic and social etc., to develop them in an ability to think critically.

Methodology

This is a descriptive research paper based on the Primary and Secondary data. Primary Data have gathered through field investigation and by administering questionnaires to women entrepreneurs. Data regarding SHGs collected through direct interview and simple randomly selected members of the SHGs. Secondary data's are obtained from articles which are published in the sources like books, journals, reports of the training institute, magazines and periodicals, etc. Relevant information has also been collected from the different websites.

A brief Profile of Thirthahalli Taluk and SHGs

Thirthahalli taluk is one of the 7 taluks of Shivamogga district. The taluk is situated in the south- western ghat region and belongs to the core Malnad area. The taluk has one ULB and 35 Gram Panchayats covering 247 villages out of which 245 villages are having inhabitants and two villages are un-inhabited. The taluk has an area of 1254 Sq kms. The population of the taluk as per the 2001 census was 1,43,207 out of which 70,734 were males and 72,473 were females. But as per 2011 census the population of the taluk has decreased to 1,41,453, with 69,593 males and 7 males 1860 females. The population of the taluk decreased by 1.22 per cent between the two recent censuses. The decrease in population is due to migration of the rural youths to the cities in search of education and better livelihood. The total number of households in the taluk is 31,102, out of which 27,784 are rural and the remaining 3,318 are the urban households. The sex ratio of the taluk is 1025 females for every 1000 males. The sex ratio of the taluk is more than that of the district. The density of population in the taluk is 114, which is the lowest as compared to the district average. The population in the age group of 0-6 years is 16,292. The literacy rate in the taluk is 78 per cent, the male literacy being 85 per cent and female literacy being 71 per cent.

Shivamogga district has 4329 Self-Help Groups with a total membership of 54,831. Out of this, 13,421 women belong to the SCs and 3,840 women belong to the STs while the remaining 37,570 women members belong to the other categories. Shikaripura taluk has the highest number of the SHGs in the district. Thirthahalli taluk has 525 registered Self-Help Groups with 8,671 total women members. Among these, 632 members belong to SCs, and 363 to STs, and 7,676 to the other categories. Out of the 525 Self-Help Groups more than 450 Groups had availed financial assistance from different banks for productive purposes. To study the performance of SHGs in the taluk towards the women empowerment the researcher selected 53 Self-Help Groups by simple random sampling method out of the 525 groups in taluk, amounting to ten per cent of the total.

Data Analysis and Discussion

Young and Dynamic members of the Self-Help Group in Thirthahalli taluk were found instrumental in leading their groups in right direction. The study found that majority of the respondents, i.e., 63.78 per cent were in the age group of 36-50 years. Adult women members were found guiding the young members properly. As regards to marital status of the respondents, it was found that 88.55 per cent of the respondents were married and 1.56 per cent of respondents are unmarried. It is noteworthy that the remaining respondents, i.e., 0.77 per cent and 8.66 per cent are being Divorcees and Widows respectively, were well supported by the groups. Out of which 900 respective group members, 90.22 per cent of members were from general category, where as only 9.77 per cent of the group members belonged to the Reserve category. No discrimination was observed in working of the groups on the basis of caste or religion. Women Self-Help groups are instrumental in evolving social engineering and integration. With regard to the literacy level, the study disclosed that majority of the respondents (90.22 per cent) were literate. However, only 8.44 per cent of the members had completed their ten plus and graduation level of education in the taluk.

Table1: Socio-economic Profile of Thirthahalli Taluk (n=900)

Age Group	*< 21years*	*21-35 yrs*	*36-50 yrs*	*51-65 yrs*	*Total no.*
	16	240	574	70	900
Marital Status	Unmarried	Married	Divorce	Widow	-
	19	797	07	77	900
Social Category	General	Reserve	-	-	-
	812	88	-	-	900
Literacy level	Illiterate	Primary	Secondary	PUC & Graduation	-
	89	414	321	76	900
Occupation	Agriculture	Agriculture labour	Small Business	Service	-
	331	443	69	57	900
Housing	Pukka	Kuccha	-	-	-
	629	271	-	-	900
Monthly	Rs 1000	Rs 1500	Rs 2000	Rs 2500	-
income	252	206	212	230	900
Monthly	Rs 50	Rs 100	Rs 150	250	-
Savings	419	374	20	87	900

Source: Field Survey - September 2014.

As far as the occupational pattern is concerned, majority of the respondents (49.22 per cent) were Agricultural labourers and 36.77 per cent of respondents were marginal farmers. It was noticed that the earnings of these respondents were uncertain and irregular. Of 900 women respondents, just 6.44 per cent were engaged in Services like Anganavadi Savakis and Arogya Sevakis in villages. And another interesting thing among the members of Self-Help Groups in Thirthahalli taluk is 7.67 per cent of respondents were engaged in small business development and earnings in the taluk. The dwelling houses of the respondents in rural areas of Thirthahalli taluk are simply constructed with having mud or bricks with a cement plastering or mud finishing wall. The roofing of these houses in Malnad regions are covered with Mangalore tiles. The flooring of the houses is made with cement or glass finished tiles and some houses may be constructed with cement slab are as Pukka houses and remaining houses like mud wall tiled roofing houses are to be considered as Kuccha houses. With this 69.88 per cent of the respondents houses were pukka houses and around 30.12 per cent of the house of the respondents are Kuccha houses as in observation. This can clearly show in the above Table 1.

Entrepreneurship

Women entrepreneurship development is an essential part of human resource development women entrepreneurs have started showing more interest because it provides them an opportunity to be one's own boss the challenges they want to face and chance of making money. Entrepreneurship is the purposeful activity undertaken by individual or a group of individuals to earn profit by producing, processing or distributing goods and services. The various NGOs had organised entrepreneurship development programmes and skill development programmes in association with other training agencies in order to train and guide the group members. The groups meetings were found instrumental in encouraging the members to start income generating activities.

As study reveals that the SHG members in taluk have involved themselves in various economic activities by taking the assistance of the group or the bank. A total of 132 business activities were undertaken in the taluk, of which tailoring had the major share with 46 units. It represents the share of 16.55 per cent of total investment made by the SHGs in the taluk. The investment in tailoring is less expensive, but low income generating activity compared to other activities. The total investment made in different activities was Rs 35,86,000 with a share of Rs 27166.66 per activity. The income generation is Rs 3458 per activity. The activity wise investment and income generation as well as creation of jobs in each activity are shown in Table 2.

Table 2: Activity-wise Investment, Income and Jobs created by SHGs in Thirthahalli taluk-2013-14

Business Activity In Rs.	*Number*	*Invest* ment created	*Income* In Rs.	No.of Jobs enterprise	*Investment* per	*Income* enterprise	*No Jobs* per enterprise
Dairy	30	19500	21500	30	6500	716.66	1
Chicken centre	04	170000	23000	08	85000	5750	2
Goat rearing	02	40000	20000	04	20000	10000	2
Vegetable shop	33	11,8000	16250	25	3575.75	8125	0.75
Bangle shop	06	160000	8000	06	80000	4000	01
Saree centre	03	125000	13000	03	41666.66	6500	01
Papad	28	60000	50000	40	2142.85	1785.71	1.42
Pickles	23	95000	45000	35	4130.43	1956.52	1.52
Grocery shop	15	214000	43000	18	14266.66	2866.66	1.2
Tea stall	08	65000	20000	10	8125	10000	1.25
Tailoring	46	388000	24600	47	8434.78	534.78	1.021
Poultry	07	1175000	61000	12	167857	8714	1.71
Transportation	04	130000	26000	08	33500	6500	02
Brick making	01	50000	30000	04	50000	30000	4
Grain selling	09	33000	6600	10	3666.66	733.33	1.11
Floor mill	06	315000	25000	09	52500	416.66	1.5
Canteen	03	120000	2000	06	40000	666.66	02
Fish Sales	01	2000	1500	02	2000	1500	2
Agarbathi making	05	13000	7000	10	2600	1400	2

(Contd.)

Contd.

Business Activity In Rs.	*Number*	*Invest* ment created	*Income* In Rs.	*No.of* Jobs enterprise	*Investment* per	*Income* enterprise	*No Jobs* per enterprise
Beedi rolling	43	88000	10000	43	20465	232.55	1
Weaving	07	30000	3000	10	4285.71	428.57	1.42
Total	**284**	**3586000**	**456450**	**340**	**649717.15**	**102827.43**	**32.901**

Source: Field survey, September-2014.

Financial Resource Mobilisation

Financial resources of the groups under study consisted monthly savings (thrifts) by the members, on an average, the investment and income per activity Rs 649717.15 and Rs 102827.13 respectively as shown in the above Table-2. Around 90 percent of the group members were found having investment in the form of income generating assets such as machines and shops of their own. However, most of the activities started by the respondents were traditional and labour intensive. The study also disclosed that the respondents had to use their own funds as well as funds borrowed from their respective groups to invest in business activities. At times, they were assisted by the groups with internal money lending for meeting domestic needs, borrowings from banks, interest on loans etc. One of the basic activities of the self help group is savings collection from the members in order to create its own fund. When enquired about monthly savings, the respondents reported that before joining the groups, saving activity was irregular and the amount of savings varied from Rs 50 to Rs150 per month. After joining the groups, saving a particular amount became mandatory and the amount ranged between Rs100 to 250 and more per month. As a result of certainty in income, the members were found comfortable to collect savings with their respective groups.

Table 3: Average monthly Savings, income and loan Assistance

Sl.no.	*Particulars*	*Pre-joining In Rupees*	*Post-joining In Rupees*
1.	Aggregate monthly savings of the respondents	81,000	6,44,994
2.	Average monthly saving per member	90	716.66
3.	Aggregate monthly income of the respondents	90,0000	59,99,994
4.	Average monthly income per member	1000	6666.66
5.	Aggregate loan assistance by the SHGs to the members	----	1,62,00,000
6.	Average loan assistance obtained per member	----	18,661
7.	Internal lending per member	----	5000-10000

Source: Field survey- September 2014.

On an average monthly saving amount before joining the group was 90 rupees per respondent which rose to 716.66 rupees per respondent after joining the group, registering the growth by 69.62 per cent (Table-3). In the pre joining period, the average monthly income of the respondent was 1000 Rupees which increased to Rs 6666.66 per respondent in post joining period registering a significant growth by Rs 629.63 per cent. The women members agreed that after joining groups, their risk bearing capacity had increased to a great extent.

As regards loan assistance to the members, it varied between Rs 5000-25000. On an average loan assistance during study period was Rs 18,661 per member. Internal money lending was in practice in all groups. The assistance was available for needy group members to meet emergency needs. Majority of the respondents (85.71 per cent) had availed the loan amount for three times. It was interesting to note that 81 per cent respondents had used borrowed funds for productive purpose or for income generating activities, whereas 19 per cent had used funds for unproductive purposes such as marriages, housing repairs, repayment of old debt etc. More than 91 per cent of the respondent reported paying their dues on due date, however nine per cent of the respondents had delayed the repayment of loan amount. Reasons stated by the respondents were high interest rate, inadequate income, emergencies and disablement.

Impact of SHGs on overall personality of the Respondents

Impact of the Self-Help Group was evaluated on the basis of a five point continuum and the scoring pattern was 5,4,3,2 and one for very low, low, moderate, high, very high respectively. The aspects covered for assessing the impact were regarding their self confidence, self esteem, decision making ability and capacity building. The approach applied was before and after joining SHGs. The impact index was computed by using the formula; impact index= Actual Score/Maximum scores*100

Table 4: Impact of SHG activities on personality of the respondents in Thirthahalli taluk for the year 2013-14

Impact Factor	*Pre-joining*			*Post-joining*			*Incremental*
	Actual scores	*Max. scores*	*Index A/M*	*Actual scores*	*Max. scores*	*Index A/M*	*growth index*
A. Self Confidence:	**285**	**900**	**31.66**	**558**	**900**	**62.00**	**30.34**
I speak confidently with family members	94	300	31.33	222	300	74	42.67
I speak confidently with outsiders	96	300	32.00	119	300	39.66	7.66
I speak confidently in public	95	300	31.66	217	300	72.33	40.67

(Contd.)

Contd. Table

B. Self esteem:	**286**	**900**	**31.77**	**619**	**900**	**68.77**	**37.00**
I feel respected	102	300	34.00	231	300	77.00	43.00
I feel self relied	98	300	32.66	207	300	69.00	36.34
I feel self secured	86	300	28.66	181	300	60.33	31.67
C. Decision making:	**252**	**900**	**28.00**	**611**	**900**	**67.88**	**39.88**
I take decisions in family matters	88	300	29.33	214	300	71.33	42.00
I take buying/selling decisions	86	300	28.66	197	300	65.66	37.00
I take decisions in financial matters	78	300	26.00	200	300	66.66	40.66
D. capacity building:	**230**	**900**	**25.55**	**605**	**900**	**67.22**	**41.67**
I Started own venture	80	300	26.66	214	300	71.33	44.67
I have risk taking attitude	71	300	23.66	182	300	60.66	37.06
I can overcome problems	79	300	26.33	209	300	69.66	43.33

Source: Compiled on the basis of Responses collected-September 2014.

Various indices i.e., self-confidence index, self esteem index, decisiveness index and capacity building index given in Table-4 indicate that overall personality of the group members had increased significantly. It was noteworthy that after joining the groups, more than 68 per cent of the respondents felt respected by family members and others and 60.33 per cent of the respondents had expressed feeling more secured because of financial and social support extended by the groups.

Women Empowerment through SHGs in Thirthahalli Taluk

As far as decision making is concerned, after joining the groups more than 69 per cent of the respondents had reported their major role in family decisions. More than 71 per cent of the respondents had started their own economic activities after joining the groups, which indicated their risk taking attitude and problem solving capacity. After joining the groups, more than 50 per cent of the respondents had reported active participation in attending social meetings, participating anti dowry campaign, anti alcoholism campaign and organising group marriages. This can be clearly understood through Table 5.

Nirmal Gram Programme which is related to village cleanliness and hygiene attracted more than 41 per cent of the respondents. However, the fact should be disclosed here that yet there were nearly 50 per cent members as non participants in various social activities. So, in order to empower the women members in its true sense, there is need for active participation of all members in social activities.

Table: 5 Women empowerment through SHG in Thirthahalli Taluk 2013-14

Sl.No.	*Empowerment dimensions*	*Number of Respondents*	
	Social empowerment:	Pre-joining	Post-joining
1.	Attending social meetings/gatherings	180 (20 per cent)	453 (50.33 per cent)
2.	Participating anti-dowry campaign	45 (5 per cent)	198 (22 per cent)
3.	Participating anti-alcoholism campaign	63 (7 per cent)	238 (26.44 per cent)
4.	Participating Nirmal Gram programme	70 (7.7 per cent)	370 (41.11 per cent)
5 .	organising group marriages	65 (7.22 per cent)	265 (29.44 per cent)
	Political Empowerment:		
1.	Attending political meetings	86 (9.55 per cent)	359 (39.88 per cent)
2.	Election campaigning	58 (6.44 per cent)	275 (30.55 per cent)
3.	Contesting in election	20 (2.22 per cent)	125 (13.88 per cent)
4.	Elected members of ZP,BC,VC	10 (1.11 per cent)	38 (4.22 per cent)
	Economic empowerment		
1.	Average monthly income per member (Rs)	1000	6666.66
2.	Average monthly saving per member (Rs)	90	716.66

Sources: Compiled from Questionnaire-September 2014.

Political empowerment

The disclosure of the study was that women members were somewhat hesitative for joining political activities before joining the groups. As a result of awareness created by the groups more than 39 per cent of the respondents started attending in political meetings, 30.55 per cent of the respondents joined election campaigns. It was noticeable that 13.88 per cent of the respondents had contested in the elections and 4.22 per cent of the members in a group got elected to the various positions on Zilla Panchayat, Taluk Panchayat and Gram Panchayats.

Economic empowerment

It was disclosed that average monthly income was Rs 1000 per member before joining the group which increased to Rs 6666.66 per member after joining the groups registering an increased by 629.63 percent. After joining the groups, the average monthly savings increased to Rs 626.66 per member from Rs90 per member earlier, posting an increased by 69 per cent.The groups were instrumental in developing entrepreneurial skills and encouraging them to start own activities. All 900 members had started own economic activities. The study disclosed that majority of the respondents i.e. more than 90 per cent were in the age group of 21 to 50 years. Young and dynamic women were found ready to take business risk and lead the groups. About 88.55 per cent of the respondents were married. So, it helped the groups to foster social integration and equality; the group consists of the members from all strata of the society. As a part of group activities, 9.88 per cent of the respondents being illiterate were taught writing their names and sign. Educated members were found aware, active and having interest in group activities. Most of the respondent's i.e., 49.22 per cent were agricultural labourers and 36.77 percent of the respondents were being marginal farmers. Before joining the groups, more than 60 per cent of the respondents had daily earning less than Rs 90. But after joining the groups, there was significant growth in the average monthly income of the respondents by Rs 6666.66. Majority of the groups had availed loan amount for three times. It was interesting to note that 81 per cent of the respondents had used borrowed funds for productive purpose, i.e., for income generating activities whereas 19 per cent had used funds for non productive purposes such as marriages, housing repairs, repayment of old debts etc. The respondents reported positive changes of participation in social life, interaction with outsiders i.e. bank officers, Government officers etc respect and honour given by the family members, taking decisions and participating in political activities. The dependency of the members on money lenders had reduced to a great extent. Being the member of SHG was a matter of pride and status.

Conclusion

The study inferred that group association and access to financial services certainly brings positive changes among group members leading to their socio-economic empowerment. However, there is need of employing long term policy measures to empower women in its true sense. Some key issues such as training, awareness and viability of the group activities need to be addressed in order to strengthen women empowerment process through micro financing. The study concluded that poor, discriminated and underprivileged women if join the groups, can come out of poverty. So, a conducive environment is needs to be created in the country to give a boost to women self-help groups.

In the rural area Self-help Groups are performing well. The study concludes that microfinance brought psychological and social empowerment than economic empowerment. Impact of micro finance through SHGs is appreciable in bringing confidence, courage, skill development and empowerment. The SHG members feel free to move with their groups and leaders. It leads them to participate on various social welfare activities with good cooperation. While interacting with the respondents, it is noticed that some members are expecting the NGO to come up with more training sessions in income generating activities. All they need is a way to develop their skills and talents by participating in various training programmes.

India still is the home to the largest population of the poor in the world and about 37 per cent of population is below poverty line. The levels of poverty are high and because of this problem Self-help Groups movement occupies a significant agenda in the poverty reduction and empowerment of women for poor people.

Micro-finance programme are important institutional devices for providing small credit to the rural people in order to alleviate poverty and SHG bank linkage, have the potential to minimise the problems of inadequate access of banking services to the poor. Many studies highlighted that SHGs have inculcated saving habits in poor. Many studies reveal that increased availability of micro-credit to the poor through SHG bank linkage program will help rural people to take up larger productive activities, empower the poor women and decrease the dependence on money lenders. But, in spite of the impressive figures of micro finance in India as have exposed in tables. It is still too small to create a massive impact in poverty alleviation. However, Indian experience in the case of Micro finance and SHG is shown that this strategy is suitable strategy for developing and underdeveloped countries against poverty.

REFERENCES

1. Women Development Report-2011-12.
2. Singh B.N., 2009, Micro finance for rural women's Empowerment: a perspective, an article published in a conference issue, Deep and Deep Publication, New Delhi, p. 464.
3. The World Bank report 2010.
4. Nanda Y.S., Significance of Establishing Linkages with Self help Groups and banks, NABARD website.
5. Raghavendra T.S (2001), Indian journal of Agricultural Economics 56(3), 466-467.
6. Ramanathan A (2008), Micro finance and Poverty Eradication 123-131.
7. Thimmaiah N. (2013), Journal of Media and Social Development 1(1), 104-105.
8. Bainkumar, Women Empowerment and Sustainable Development, Regal Publication.
9. R.Ventakta Ravi and V Narayana Reddy, 'Empowerment of People' Kanishka Publishers.
10. Karnataka at glance 2011-12 data published by Directorate of Economics and Statistics, Bangalore.
11. Shivamogga district at a glance 2011-12 data published by Shivamogga District officer of Economics and Statistics department, Shivamogga.
12. Data Pertaining to Self-Help Groups in Thirthahalli taluk available from the Dept of Women and Children in the Taluk Office.

30

Micro Finance in India—A Micro Level Study

B.T. Ramappa and M.G. Basava Raja

Abstract: 'Microfinance' is a mechanism of financial support for small businesses, providing small loans to businesses that have limited access to traditional sources of financing. Thus, in order to reach these poor people microfinance acts as the most efficient and effective tool. The ultimate aim is to attain social and *economic empowerment. Especially Women Economic Empowerment is so strong by Micro Finance through SHGs. Micro Finance sector has covered a long journey from micro savings to micro credit and then to micro enterprises and now entered the field of micro insurance, micro remittance, micro pension and micro livelihood. This gradual and evolutionary growth process has given a great boost to the rural poor in India to reach reasonable economic, social and cultural empowerment, leading to better life of participating households. Financial intuition in the country has been playing a leading role in the micro finance programme for nearly two decades. Now they have joined hands proactively with informal delivery channels to give microfinance sector the necessary momentum. During the current year too, microfinance has registered an impressive expansion at the grass root level. Against this background, the paper throws light on the impact of SHGs on savings and Incomes of Karnataka, case study of SHGs Koppa Taluk. (2) Outlines the Issues and Challenges in microfinance for* *the development of Karnataka. (3) Progress Report under SHG Bank Linkage in Karnataka, based on the results, suggestions and recommendations are drawn based on the Primary and Secondary data.*

Key words: Microfinance, SHGs, Women Economic Empowerment, Bank Linkage, micro credit.

Introduction

The Millennium Development Goals were adopted by the world leaders in the year 2000 set to be achieved by the year 2015. These goals provide an agenda for the entire international community to come together towards a common conclusion of human development for everyone, everywhere. If these goals are achieved, world poverty will be cut by half, tens of millions of lives will be saved, and billions more people will have the opportunity to benefit from the global economy. India like many other countries has committed to achieve the MDGs and the researcher has analysed India's present status and future prospects in attainment of the goal to reduce extreme poverty by half by 2015.The biggest challenge faced by India today, is the problem of poverty and its eradication. India has the world's largest number of poor people living in a single country. Presently India has a population of 121 crore people and it grows annually with more than one per cent (Micro finance India, 2010; CIA Fact book, 2010). Of its population, nearly more proportion of population is still lives below $ one a-day (below income poverty line). 'Microfinance' is a mechanism of financial support for small businesses, providing small loans to businesses that have limited access to traditional sources of financing. Thus, in order to reach strong by Micro Finance through SHGs.these poor people microfinance acts as the most efficient and effective tool. The ultimate aim is to attain social and economic empowerment. Especially Women Economic Empowerment is so.

Methodology

Qualitative research study was done using group discussions with the SHG in the rural village of Koppa taluk of Karnataka. A total ten focus group discussions were done for nearly one hour duration with five members in each focus group. This study reveals both primary and secondary data.

Table 1: Progress of SHGs in Karnataka (March 2012) (Rs in crores)

Sl.No.	District	Total No. of SHGs	Saving Accumulated	No. of Groups Loan taken from the Bank	Total loan taken from bank	Revolving fund released from Bank	Loan amount distributed by SHG	Total repayment to SHGs	Total repayment to bank
1.	Bengaluru(U)	3161	43.39	3096	58.20	1.50	121.93	156.81	71.65
2.	Bengaluru(R)	3365	33.49	3075	31.44	1.57	105.39	85.17	49.24
3.	Bagalkote	4010	35.96	3895	26.46	1.92	49.08	39.72	21.93
4.	Belaguam	14134	73.40	12550	131.56	6.70	100.50	87.25	61.78
5.	Bellary	5220	41.92	4751	46.84	2.44	69.24	43.98	36.91
6.	Bidar	2939	26.92	2611	25.84	1.37	56.91	48.60	26.47
7.	Bijapur	3888	22.06	3002	15.88	1.80	37.39	37.19	26.13
8.	Chamarajanagar	3928	30.26	4022	73.26	1.85	122.34	101.30	85.75
9.	Chikkamagalur	3283	27.46	3028	21.65	1.46	100.87	88.82	36.90
10.	Chikkaballapur	4989	34.46	4448	61.85	2.27	102.45	86.97	80.11
11.	Chitradurga	5075	43.81	4876	40.68	3.26	109.23	87.27	46.93
12.	Davanagere	4822	39.15	4422	58.49	2.22	79.53	53.58	38.01
13.	Dakshina Kannada	3663	34.14	3649	76.18	1.82	139.87	118.75	89.81
14.	Dharwad	3029	17.67	2488	14.96	1.35	21.24	17.98	9.03
15.	Gadag	3476	16.45	2839	17.15	1.52	34.27	25.68	18.68
16.	Gulbarga	6349	59.73	4656	36.86	1.31	138.49	96.93	46.91
17.	Hassan	6471	56.16	6861	26.92	3.02	252.40	202.60	84.66

(Contd.)

(Contd. Table)

18.	Haveri	4659	32.58	4249	37.17	2.13	123.72	83.50	40.28
19.	Kodagu	1082	15.70	938	9.80	0.46	50.27	48.56	25.93
20.	Kolar	4213	27.07	2764	23.90	1.96	74.12	68.84	34.79
21.	Koppal	2868	18.22	1840	17.40	1.32	28.01	19.13	15.28
22.	Mandya	6638	73.02	6215	53.56	3.11	263.51	227.66	110.57
23.	Mysore	6602	48.78	5779	80.12	3.08	129.09	115.90	58.53
24.	Raichur	5045	32.51	4831	25.41	2.38	51.04	28.48	17.95
25.	Ramanagar	4635	44.78	4100	61.78	2.20	179.76	145.12	175.47
26.	Shivamogga	4329	30.75	3819	47.58	1.94	128.43	122.60	62.70
27.	Tumkur	10234	72.82	9574	107.60	7.19	233.44	189.66	166.13
28.	Udupi	2846	26.82	2670	42.61	1.34	116.25	117.90	75.89
29.	Uttar Kannada	2259	14.86	1769	11.71	0.89	79.32	72.87	14.50
30.	Yadagiri	2771	5.36	2085	1.30	2.94	3.98	3.78	3.51
	Total	**139983**	**1079.70**	**124902**	**1284.16**	**68.32**	**3102.07**	**2622.60**	**1632.43**

Source: State Level Bankers 'Committee Karnataka, Agenda Notes of 121st Meeting 29th May 2012, Syndicate Bank, Bengaluru p.81

Development of SHG-Bank Linkage in Karnataka

The government as well as non-government sectors and most recently, the corporate sectors involved themselves in SHG. It's fact that in few part of the country this has brought tremendous result but in most of the states the real situation is quite disappointing. The SHG model emerged in the 1980s and 1990s.With the tremendous support from the government of India, state governments, NABARD, the banking sector and NGOs, the movement spread like anything. Even such a situation arise that the Indian Government budget presentation has emphasised on SHG bank linkage each year as in many cases it gave the ruling party a political mileage. As per the report of NABARD, at the end of March 2006 there were 3.37 million SHGs in India covering 40.95 million poor households (roughly 200 million people or 20 per cent of total population and 80 per cent of total poor population). As of March 2007, 2.92 million SHGs had received bank loans of Rs 180, 410 million. But can we say it has really changed the fate of the poor women.

Table 1 reveals that all groups have started savings; the total cumulative savings is Rs 1079.70 crores, 139983 SHGs have formed, in that124902 are with bank linkages and Rs 1284.16 crores taken as loan from banks. The groups have received Rs 68.32 crores as revolving fund released by the Government. The groups have distributed loan to its members amount is Rs 3102.07 crores, in this 2622.60 crores repaid by the members, total repayment amount to bank Rs 1632.43 crores. Its 79 per cent of the loan has repaid it is good sign for development. Mandya, Belguam and Gulbarga, these districts have highest cumulative savings.

Findings

Table 2: Details of Operations of Grama Panchayat-Wise Self Help Groups in Koppa Taluk in 2012-13 (Rs in Crores)

Sl.No.	*Name of the G.P.*	*Name of the Grama*	*Name of the SHG*	*Purpose*	*Govt. Subsidies*
1.	Agalagandi	Horasige	Krishna	Collecting forest products	115000
2.	Agalagandi	Ethinatti	Sreenidhi	Dinishi shop	100000
3.	Bhandigadi	Saralathota	Lokaparameswari	Diary	115000
4.	Harandur	Kuvempunagar	Surabhi	Tailoring, Cloth selling	70000
5.	Harandur	Kuvempunagar	Mariya	Condiments, Happala	115000
6.	Thuluvinakoppa	Lokanathapura	Bharath	Ittige	115000
7.	Niluvagilu	Kalanaikanakatte	Bhandya	Fisheries	80000
8.	Niluvagilu	Niluvagilu	Eshwar	Paddy selling	115000
9.	Chavalamane	Kammardi	Sree Durgaparameswari	Ittige	100000
Total					**925000**

Source: Primary Data and Taluk Panchayat Koppa.

In the field study, we personally studied the phenomenon and obtained the first-hand information on SHGs. In seven Grama Panchayats, we selected nine SHGs receiving government subsidies of Rs 9,25,000 crore as shown in Table 2.

Table 3: Details of Grama Panchayat-wise SHGs Operations in Koppa Taluk - Own Construction Building 2012-13 (Rs in Crore)

Sl.No.	*Name of the G.P.*	*Name of the Grama*	*Purpose*	*Total Amount*
1.	Athikodige	Siddanagudda	Building-SHG	230000
2.	Harandur	Chikkanagundi	Building-SHG	230000
3.	Niluvagilu	Yadathanal	Building-SHG	352000
4.	Bhandigadi	Hosur	Building-SHG	352000

Source: Primary Data and Taluk Panchayat Koppa

The survey carried out for this purpose highlights here:

1. Predominant Economic Activities:
   Predominant economic activities carried out in the district are Agricultural and Allied activities like diary, sheep, poultry, wood crafts, and small businesses etc.
2. Major Food, Commercial and Plantation/Horticulture Crops.
   Major Food, Commercial and Plantation/Horticulture Crops grown in the taluk are Paddy, Ragi, Maize, Pulses, Oilseeds, Tobacco, Sugarcane, Coconut, Mango, Banana, Areca nut and Coffee etc.
3. Educational Background

Table 4: Educational Background

Education	*Frequency*	*Percentage (per cent)*
Below Primary 1-4	10	20
Middle School 5-7	25	50
High School 8-10	10	20
PUC 11 & 12	03	6
Above Degree	02	4
Total	**50**	**100**

Out of 50, 20 per cent of the SHGs were below Primary school and 50 per cent middle school. 20 per cent SHGs were in High school and six per cent in PUC and four per cent SHGs were above degree.

4. Occupation Structure

5. **Table 5: Occupation Structure**

Occupation	*Frequency*	*Percentage (per cent)*
Self employed	15	30
House maids and Agriculture and allied activities	05	10
Land holders	20	40

Coolies	05	10
Tailoring and Cloth sellers	04	8
Live stock	01	2
Total	**50**	**100**

Source: Primary Data.

Table 5 result depicts that around ten percent of the members are involved in House maids and Agriculture and allied activities, 40 per cent of the members own agricultural land holdings for her husband. 30 per cent of the members are self employed in activities like Collecting forest products cow rearing, diary, grocery store, condiments, happala, Ittige, tailoring shop fisheries and paddy selling etc.

6. Annual Family Income

   Table 6 shows that the majorities 50 per cent of the members are earn per year below Rs 10000 per year, 30 per cent of them earn Rs 10001 to 15000 per annum and the remaining members depicted in Table 6.

Table 6: Annual Family Incomes

Annual Income	*Frequency*	*Percentage (per cent)*
Below 11000	25	50
11001-15000	15	30
15001-20000	03	6
20001-25000	02	4
25001-30000	05	10
Total	**50**	**100**

Source: Primary Data.

7. Term Savings

   Table 7 shows that highest percentage (62 per cent) of the members were saving their earnings in the SHG upto Rs 50 per month, and 58 per cent of the members were saving the amount in the range Rs 50 - Rs 100.

Table 7: Term Saving

Amount	*Number(s)*	*Percentage (per cent)*
Rs 50	31	62
Rs 50-Rs 100	29	58
Total	**50**	**100**

Source: Primary Data.

8. Husband's Occupation and Income

   Tenper cent of the Husband's Occupation is in to Agricultural Land Holder and their income yearly less than one lakh, 50 per cent Agricultural small holding s less than one hector and their income is not more than yearly net income Rs 12000. Remaining members working business, Coolies, Helping to build houses, Agricultural labourers and other works and their income is less than Rs 7000.

9. Dependents and Joint family Culture
   90 per cent of the families they are serving their old age persons and disabled persons
10. Habits of Husband

    1. 80 per cent of the Husband's are increasing welfare of the family.
    2. Ten per cent Drunkards are beating to their wives
    3. Ten per cent of the people are idle, going to different places and return to the home.
    4. 100 per cent women are ready to serve their husbands lifelong by making them to sit in houses if they are hard work.

11. Nutritious food
    They spend on growing village vegetables than corns and good quality of rice (Ration rice or own growing paddy.
    Majority (78 per cent) of the members were conducting the meeting once a month, followed by 16 per cent who held the meeting every fortnightly and the remaining six per cent were conducting the meeting weekly.

Major Findings

1 The majority i.e., 28 per cent of the members are in the middle school. Therefore, from the above analysis we can say that those who are in SHGs movements are able to increase their literacy level.

2 Around 28 per cent of the members are involved in House maids and Agriculture and allied activities. From the above analysis we can conclude that the women members after joining the SHGs to create self-employment and to offer employment opportunities to neighbouring family members and then provide employment to people of their area. So, micro finance helps the these village people to increase their mobility, recognition from family, decision making power, participate in village development programmes, meeting etc and to participate in political activities.

3 Majority 62 per cent of the members are earned per year below Rs 10000 per year. This analysis infers that after joining the SHGs they are able to increase their earning level through doing some self employed activities like selling cloth, bangles, dairy business, petty shops, beedi works hen rearing etc.

4 Majority of the members were influenced by their peer group members. The analysis infers that the women were encouraged

by women i.e., they were having group discussions. The group discussion helps them to get mutual co-operation with mutual benefits through Microfinance.

5 Term meeting output shows that majority of the members was conducting the meeting monthly once. The analysis confers that every month twice they were conducting the meeting, the first meeting to discuss the village, group issues and the second meeting to collect saving money and loan amount from the group members.

6 The highest per cent (62 per cent) of the members save their earnings at the rate of Rs 50 per month. The result that the rural women earning level were increased. It also says that the Microfinance programmes make the destitute women to save some amount from the total family earnings.

7 The field study reveals highest percentages (90 per cent) of the group were taking the decision on the basis of consensus. The analysis can be concluded that the Microfinance programmes helps the women to take decision on the basis of consultation and get opinion from every member before taking final decision.

8 The socio-economic impact from respondents reveals that the Microfinance programme through SHG helps the women to increase all socio-economic impact such as Women were given special respect at home, Respect within their community, the SHGs to involve any of the income generating activities/self employment activities. It will help the women to increase the self employment opportunity and to reduce the below poverty line rural women in the study area. All socio-economic impact increased positively except the entrepreneurs skills.

Suitable Policy Measures

It is highly necessary to over-come the problems and difficulties of SHGs. These institutions are possible to be strengthened by framing suitable policy measures.

Firstly, there must be supervisory more of an advisory and guiding staff be provided to monitor the activities. Secondly, insurance coverage is provided to all members of the Sanghas and also on live-stock purchased out of the loan amount. Lastly the office bearers and members' in charge of management are to be given suitable training to run the Sanghas effectively and efficiently.

Conclusion

Microfinance has proved to be an effective tool for inclusive growth. SHGs if encouraged play a dominant role in creating economic stability and economic freedom to the rural poor, particularly for women flock. They provide primary training ground for rural women from weaker sections for future leadership. In total, these Sanghas when organised to function effectively and efficiently serve as tools in mitigating rural poverty. In India women are not empowered much than compare with any other people even though the government was introduced many central and states schemes but now both government schemes was given more important for inclusive growth for improving the socio-economic condition, creation of employment opportunities and development of various skills like communication, self confidence, etc.

REFERENCES

1. Syndicate Bank (2012), State Level Bankers 'Committee Karnataka, Agenda Notes of 121st Meeting 29th May 2012, Bengaluru p. 81
2. Government of Karnataka, Women and Children Development Department, Taluk Office and BDO, Koppa.
3. Ramesh T. "Micro finance – A Drive to Combat Poverty", "The Management Accountant" Nov. 2008, Vol. 43, No.11, 822-826.
4. Lindal Mayoux (September 2005), Women's Empowerment through Sustainable Microfinance: Rethinking Best Practice.
5. Shollapur and Naveen K Shetty (2011) 'Microfinance and Sustainable Livelihood Promotions in India, edited volume Socio-economic Empowerment of Schedule Caste Women through Microfinance in Ramanathapuram District, EXCEL Publications, New Delhi.
6. Ahmad, M.A. (1999), Women Empowerment: Self-Help Groups, Kurukshetra, Vol. 47 (7).
7. www.microfinancegateway.org.
8. Government of Karnataka, (2005), "Economic Survey, 2004-05", *(Bangalore: Planning and statistical department)*
9. http:/ /www.microfinacefocus.com/

31

Women Entrepreneurship Development and Self Help Groups: Empirical Evidence from Dakshina Kannada and Udupi Districts of Karnataka

Shivakumar P.T. and Ganaraj K.

Abstract: *Women represent half of the world's population as well as production and considered a significant part in the economy. Traditionally, women are believed to be a 'guarantor' of the household in times of economic crisis. However, despite their importance in the economy, women are disadvantaged, financially excluded and virtually marginalised vis-à-vis men in the society. Several studies conducted at national and international levels reveal that one of the good ways to empower women is to encourage them to develop the skills of entrepreneurship which may lead to financial inclusion and bring them to the mainstream of the society. Here, again we find that the present world of entrepreneurs is dominated by men. In this context micro-finance through self help groups can work as a powerful tool to empower women by inculcating the entrepreneurial skill among women. Against this background the study is designed with the following objectives (1) To find out the importance of SHG's in women* *entrepreneurship; (2) To critically examine the problems faced by women entrepreneur; (3) To suggest suitable policy prescriptions.*

The study was conducted in Dakshina Kannada and Udupi districts of Karnataka State during 2011-2012. A sample of 240 female entrepreneurs of SHGs of three different promotes, i.e. NGO, Co-operative and Government were interviewed for collection of primary data. The major findings of the study are, Firstly, SHG's have made women economically independent and become effective approach of financial inclusion. Secondly, government and Cooperative promoted SHG members have not invested much micro credit on agriculture and related Income Generating Activities (IGA's) due to lack of land and support from their respective promoters. Thirdly, because of small sized group and better marketing strategy performance of NGO promoted groups are good compared to other groups. Fourthly, inadequate finance, lack of better marketing facilities, conflict among group members, lack of follow up and training by promoters are the major problems faced by the entrepreneurs.

Key Words: Self Help Groups, Entrepreneurship, Empowerment, Microfinance, Inclusion.

The Context

Women represent half of the world's population as well as production and considered a significant part in the economy. Traditionally, women are believed to be a 'guarantor' of the household in times of economic crisis. The data indicate that in the global level about 54 per cent of working women are in the labour force. About 20 per cent of households worldwide are female-headed and this figure overtime is increasing. In 2009-2010, in India, women were 26.1 per cent of all rural workers, and 13.8 per cent of all urban workers. It is said that unpaid work of these women comes to around $ 11 trillion per annum, which is equal to half of the world's GDP. But, these income statistics are not entering national accounts and thus they are considered to be 'invisible workers' (Rao 2001:1). Despite their importance in the economy, women are disadvantaged, financially excluded and virtually marginalized vis-à-vis men in the society. In this context several studies conducted at national and international level revealed that one of the good ways to empower women is to encourage them to develop the skills of entrepreneurship which may lead to financial inclusion and bring them to the mainstream of the society. Here again we find that the present world of entrepreneurs is dominated by men. Due to various reasons and hurdles we can see only a very few successful entrepreneurs in the world as well as in India. Governments of various levels have made several efforts to uplift women through several innovative women entrepreneurship programmes. As a complementary to the efforts of the government, micro-finance through self help groups working as a powerful tool to fight poverty became the effective approach of empowering women by inculcating entrepreneurial habits among them. However, it also faces many problems and has not succeeded up to a satisfactory level due to many confronting issues and inhibitions.

Objectives and Methodology

Keeping the above facts in view, this paper has been prepared with the following objectives; 1. To find out the importance of SHG's in women entrepreneurship; 2.To critically examine the problems faced by women entrepreneur; 3. To suggest suitable policy prescriptions. The study is based on both primary and secondary sources of data. The secondary information was gathered from publications of government departments, journals, books, and newspapers. The primary sources of data were collected by canvassing the structured interview schedule for the 240 sample households of in Dakshina Kannada and Udupi districts of Karnataka State. The sample members of SHGs of three different promotes, i.e., NGO, Co-operative and Government were interviewed for collection of primary sources of data. From each promoter, the members of SHGs belonging to the Scheduled Caste (SCs), the Scheduled Tribes (STs) and Others (Other castes includes Other Backward Castes also) were considered as the target group members. From each promoter 80 SHG members consisting 40 members from each district 20 members from two taluks (totally 8 taluks), 10 SHG members from each village (totally 16 taluks) were selected for the interview. The total size of the sample SHG members was estimated at 240 from the four chosen taluks of the two districts. The data were analysed by using the simple percentage, average and indices, wherever appropriate.

Role of SHG's in Women Entrepreneurship

Entrepreneurship refers to the act of setting up a new business or reviving an existing business so as to take advantages from new opportunities. The Government of India has defined women enterprise as an enterprise owned and controlled by women having a minimum financial interest of 51 per cent of the capital and giving at least 51 per cent of the employment generated in the enterprise to women. In general women entrepreneurs may be defined as the women or a group of women who initiate, organise and operate a business enterprise. According to the Third All India Census of Small

Scale Industries conducted in 2001-02 and subsequent estimates made, only 10.11 per cent of the Micro and Small Enterprises in India are owned by women while 9.46 per cent of the MSEs are managed by women. In 2006-07 their estimated number was 12.99 lakh women managed enterprises and 12.15 lakh women managed enterprise. There are several factors responsible for increasing level of female entrepreneurship in India, namely,nature of entrepreneurship, motivation, empowerment, social conditions, economic conditions, literacy and education etc. Entrepreneurship is being seen as the key driver of not just economic development but also social advancement. Expanding the entrepreneurial talent and managerial pool in developing and emerging economies among women is one of the most important means to reducing inequality and promoting financial inclusion. It gives immense scope for women and human development through innovations and best practices of management. Entrepreneurial development provides tools like decision-making and planning to fight disparity and inequity. Studies also show that promotion of women entrepreneurship leads to economic stability of women, family and the community. In spite of the growing rate of work participation of women, the share of female entrepreneurs is still significantly low when compared to their work participation rate.

Access to production credit of SHG's enables women to undertake income-generating activities (IGAs) through which poverty can be reduced. Studies like Carr *et al* (1996), Harper (1998), Dadhich (2001), Sudarshan Synghal (2002), Venkatarao (2009), Reddy Narasimhalu (2009), Vimala (2009) and Tankha *et al* (2005) (2004), Purohit (2003), Isabelle (2006) and Jayasheela and Palanna (2005) showed that participation of women in women organisations like SHGs has changed their lives economically, socially and politically and inculcated entrepreneurial abilities among them. They argue that there is a positive correlation between women empowerment and SHG microfinance. Schreiner et al argues that Micro enterprise development programs make loans to poor people to help them to start or to strengthen their business (Schreiner, Mark and Woller, Garry, 2003). It is believed that the micro-finance programmes will help the rural poor in accessing markets. It also helps in addressing the problems of the women in undertaking IGAs such as inadequate access to skills, raw materials and marketing. The federations of micro-finance groups help the poor especially women not only in negotiating with the market and other suppliers of the critical inputs but also in accessing them at reduced costs. The rural poor also learn how to select viable and feasible IGAs, and acquire skills on business operations.

Results and Discussion

Before describing the socio-economic background of the sample respondents, it is better to look at the distributional pattern of sample households by different socio-economic indicators in the study areas. The data (Table 1) indicate that the sample households selected for the present study are even distributed across different promoters, namely NGO, Co-operative and Government. The distribution of sample households is not even across social groups in the case of NGO and Co-operative, whereas in the case of government, it is by and large, even. Out of the selected sample households, majority of them covered by NGO are belonged to minority such as Christian, Muslim and Jain and a larger proportion covered by Co-operative are belonged to SCs and STs as compared to that of others.

Table 1: Distribution of Sample Households by Social Groups and Promoters

Promoters *Social groups*	*NGO*	*Co-operative*	*Government*	*Total*
SCs	(15) 24.19	(28) 45.16	(19) 30.65	(62) 100
STs	(19) 23.91	(19) 41.30	(16) 34.78	(46) 100
Others	(54) 40.91	(35) 26.52	(43) 32.58	(132) 100
All	**(80) 33.33**	**(82) 34.17**	**(78) 32.50**	**(240) 100**

Note: Figures in the parentheses indicate the actual numbers.
Source: Primary Survey.

Educational Background

Lack of literacy is a major constraint to empower women through SHGs. The savings account, loan account, Income Generating Activities, repayment of loan etc., in SHGs was supposed to be self-managed by the members. However, lack of basic literacy deprived many members to understand this kind of information of SHGs. Lack of literacy is also a major obstacle for promotion of IGAs. It is evident from the discussion held with the less literate members that, they cannot understand entirely the training programme given by the promoters for IGAs and hardly absorb the skills required to market the manufactured goods. The empirical evidence from the field observation support that view that, relatively better literate women have undertaken more IGAs and have got success.

Table 2 presents the data on educational background of SHG members across promoters. The data reveals that most of the respondents are illiterates and some of them have studied upto primary and middle school i.e., upto seventh standard. However, the responds educated PUC and above is much less. The data clearly indicate that educational background of SHG members was awfully unsatisfactory.

Table 2: Educational Background of the Respondents

Educational Level	*Number*	*Per cent*
Illiterate	83	34.58
Primary school	63	26.25
Middle school	48	20.00
High school	34	14.17
PUC and Above	12	5.00
All	**240**	**100**

Source: Field Survey.

Educational status starting from primary level to PUC indicate that the proportion of members tended to decline, in most cases, as the level of educational attainments tends to rise. This follows that as we move along higher spectrum of educational attainments, the proportion of members was found to be far less. The proportion of members with lower educational attainments was higher and lower at the higher level of educational attainments. Such observation was quite pronounced in the case of members formed by Government and Co-operative as compared to NGOs. It is very difficult to handle many things with a huge number of members with illiteracy and literacy at lower levels. The huge illiteracy was found to be one of the biggest constraints in the process of women's empowerment and undertake various entrepreneurial or income generating activities. Due to the lack of education and that too qualitative education, women are not aware of business, technology and market knowledge. Also, lack of education causes low achievement motivation among women. Thus, lack of education creates problems for women in the setting up and running of business enterprises.

Reason for Starting Micro Enterprise

Data reveals that out of total sample 40.0 have started entrepreneurial activity because of emergency and 22.50 per cent started to supplement family income. This indicate two things; one, the main motive for majority was to earn some money for supplementing their husbands' income; two, the women did not have confidence in their income earning potential or in the growth potential of the group enterprise, though in case of some, these perceptions may have changed later. Besides this, 7.50 per cent started to work as an entrepreneur because of unavailability of proper work. However it is interesting that 40 per cent of the respondents started this work to meet emergency needs of the family.

Table 3: Reason for Starting Micro Enterprise

Reason	*Number*	*Frequency*
To Meet Emergency	96	40.00
Supplement Family Income	54	22.50
No Other Work	18	7.50
Easy Availability of Loan	44	18.33
Encouragement by Friends and Family	28	11.67
All	**240**	**100**

Source: Field Survey.

Training Programmes

Training programs and workshops for every type of entrepreneur is available through the social and welfare associations, based on duration, skill and the purpose of the training program. Such programme are really useful to new, rural and young entrepreneurs who want to set up a small and medium scale unit on their own. Table 4 depicts that, out of the total sample 38.33 per cent of the respondents, have did not attend any training, 22.83 per cent have expressed that they are not interested in attending the training offered for SHGs. The table also shows that, 35.87 per cent of the respondents have said that they have no opportunity for attending the training. 15.22 per cent of them have stated that they have no time to attend the training. 26.09 per cent have mentioned other reasons.

Table 4: Training Programmes Attended

Training	*Number*	*Frequency*
Attended	148	61.67
Not attended	92	38.33
All	**240**	**100**
Reasons for not attending		
Not Interested	21	22.83
No Opportunity	33	35.87
No Time	14	15.22
Other Reasons	24	26.09
All	**92**	**100**

Source: Field Survey.

Type of Activity

SHG generates employment opportunities in the rural India by providing many self employment programmes and reduces the level of disguised unemployment which is found in India agricultural sector. The Table 5 shows the distribution of respondents according to their type of income generating activity or entrepreneurial activity of the data reveals that 28.33 per cent members are involved in Agarbathi/ Incense Sticks which is the major and easily performed work in the study area. It requires less skill and education though it yields less income, however because of its easy nature most of the respondents are engaged in this work. 12.91 per cent are engaged in tailoring and bag making and it is a good entrepreneurial activity because it requires little education and gives more income compared to other activities. And 21.67 per cent are engaged in producing food items like bakery items, pickles, pappads etc. 11.67 per cent are engaged in preparing soaps, phenol and other detergents. 17.50 per cent of members are engaged in other business like cement brick making, Areca nut plate making etc. Income is the yard stick to measure the economic condition of the society.

Table 5: Distribution of Respondents According to their Type of Activity

Activity	*Number*	*Frequency*
Agarbathi/Incense Sticks	68	28.33
Food Items	52	21.67
Tailoring/Bag	31	12.92
Agriculture and Allied	19	7.92
Soap/ Phenol	28	11.67
Others	42	17.50
All	**240**	**100**

Source: Field Survey.

Problems faced by the SHG Women Entrepreneurs

Women entrepreneurs face a series of problems right from the beginning till the enterprise functions. Being a woman itself poses various problems to a woman Entrepreneur. The problems of Indian women pertain to her responsibility towards family, society and lion work. Women in India are faced with many problems to get ahead their life in business. Following are some of the major problems faced by the SHG women entrepreneur in the present study.

Financial Problems

One of the main problems faced by the SHG members is problem of credit or finance. In general women do not have property on their names to use them as collateral for obtaining funds from external sources. Thus, their access to the external sources of funds is limited. Besides this the banks also consider women less credit-worthy and discourage women borrowers on the belief that they can at any time leave their business. Given such situation, women entrepreneurs are bound to rely on their own savings, if any and loans from friends and relatives who are expectedly meager and negligible. Thus, women enterprises fail due to the shortage of finance. The Table 6 shows that out of sample 13.33 per cent members have admitted that they are not facing any financial problems. However 48.50 per cent of the respondents opine that microcredit is too small to expand or facilitate for IGAs and manage unexpected shocks in a business. Members opine that, microcredit could supplement the existing small business but may not support much to start a new one. In the case of all the promoters, at a time Rs 45,000 to 50,000 fixed as an upper limit for IGAs. Any further sanction of loan is met only after the repayment of at least half of the earlier credit. Around 16 per cent of the respondents opine that high rate of interest of the SHG's is a problem for them. Apart from this there are also problems like underutilisation of capital, Negative attitude of banks and tight repayment schedule hinders the entrepreneurs.

Table 6: Financial Problem

Problems	*Number*	*Frequency*
No Problem	32	13.33
Lack of Credit	114	48.50
Underutilisation of capital	18	7.50
Higher rate of interest	38	15.83
Negative Attitude of Bank	23	9.58
Tight Repayment Schedule	15	6.25
All	**240**	**100**

Source: Field Survey.

Problem related to Production

Besides the problem of finance, women entrepreneurs also face the problem of production. Data reveals that 19.58 per cent of respondents face the problem of high cost of production. High production cost of some business operations adversely affects the development of women entrepreneurs. The installation of new machineries during expansion of the productive capacity and like similar factors dissuades the women entrepreneurs from venturing into new areas. 15.83 per cent of the women enterprises face the problem of scarcity of raw material and necessary inputs. Added to this are the high prices of raw material, on the one hand, and getting raw material at the minimum of discount, on the other, also hampering their development. However most of the respondents that is 30.83 per cent of the respondents opine that lack of infrastructure like availability of electrically, power are the main problems of production. Finally, 23.75 per cent of the respondents opine that old and outdated technology also became the problem for the women entrepreneurs.

Table 7: Production Problem

Problems	*Number*	*Frequency*
High Cost of Production	47	19.58
Infrastructure Problem	74	30.83
Problem of Raw Material	38	15.83
High Transportation Cost	24	10.00
Obsolete Technology	57	23.75
All	**240**	**100**

Source: Field Survey.

Problem of Marketing

The limited market for their products or services is one of the biggest constraints that the most of the members and promoter faced while putting the micro credit into small scale investment in the countryside. Poor roads, water supply, inadequate access of electrification found to be added fuel to a greater obstacle for optimum utilisation of micro credit for income generation. It has affected for the marketing of both agricultural produce and finished goods. The villages located in Dakshina Kannada have limited infrastructure. The problem is more pronounced in case of relatively more poor, SCs and STs. A majority of them are living in remote areas and far away from the main roads and having improper electric connection which made them hard to market their agricultural produce.

Women entrepreneurs do not have organisational set-up to pump in a lot of money for canvassing and advertisement. Thus, they have to face stiff counterparts. Such a competition ultimately, results in the liquidation of women enterprises. Besides this, lack of information and experience makes it very difficult for her to select technology, market and location, and also to tackle problems related to labour and finance. The government realising the need and importance of women entrepreneurs' participation in the contribution to the economy has offered some assistance, thereby trying to created a favouable climate for woman entrepreneurs to play a significant role in the rapid development of India. Table 8 reveals that 11.67 per cent of the respondents are facing the problem of competition and 13.75 per cent are facing the problem of poor quality of production. Respondents also face the problem of lack of information's i.e., 14.17 percent. However, major problem is faced by the respondents are the problem of Lack of advertisement i.e., 35 percent. In addition to above problems, inadequate infrastructural facilities, shortage of power, high cost of production, social attitude and other socio-economic constraints also hold the women back from entering into business.

Table 8: Marketing Problem

Problems	*Number*	*Frequency*
Competition	28	11.67
Poor Quality	33	13.75
Lack of Advertisement	84	35.00
Dependence on Suppliers	18	7.50
Lack of Information	34	14.17
Distance of Market	43	17.92
All	**240**	**100**

Source: Field Survey.

Conclusion

Indian society needs to bring about an attitudinal change in regard to the role of women as entrepreneurs. This will lead to the development of an appropriate environment in which women will come forth and give vent to their entrepreneurial talents. Ultimately women entrepreneurship must be recognised for what it is. Nationally, it has great importance for future economic prosperity. Based on the findings of the study, the following policy measures can be suggested for better functioning of income generating activities of SHG members and their sustainability to ensure women's empowerment and bring them on mainstream development:

- Government promoted group are availing much internal loans which is much less amount compared to external loans. They face the problem of lack of active support or guarantee agencies like NGOs. Hence, for such groups government should support through some policy measures. Loan amount should be increased to the extent that they can take up an income generating activity.
- The members of SCs/ STs and low-income group households have not invested much micro credit on agriculture and related IGA's. The main problem of them is the lack of land. Even though these communities have some amount of land they are not suitable for cultivation. It is in mostly hilly regions and even irrigation facility is not good. Thus for time being training should be given them to concentrate on much IGA's other than agriculture related like tailoring, soap, phenol making, Agarbathi (incense sticks) making since it does not need any land.
- Module training centers nearer to the women will attract more women to entrepreneurship. Women entrepreneurs also should be encouraged to start and develop their enterprises into medium and large size; and emerge as professional and competent entrepreneurs ready to compete at par with others.

- Women's family and personal obligations are sometimes a great barrier for succeeding in business career. Only few women are able to manage both home and business efficiently, devoting enough time to perform all their responsibilities in priority.
- Groups formed by NGOs have motivated more members to undertake IGAs through micro credit. Hence, it is suggested that co-operatives and governments have to train their SHG members to undertake more and more IGAs. Special attention should be given to SC, ST and low income groups. Promotes have to motivate their and respective members to change their occupation in favour of better paid self employment.
- Simple procedure and right encouragement from the financial agencies may enable women to form more and more SHGs in their locality. The financial institutions including various government departments should give wider publicity on the availability of credit facilities and others benefits that can be offered to the SHGs.
- The main problem faced by the SHG members in adopting income generating activity is due to the lack of better marketing facilities. Even though the groups formed by NGOs has some ray of hope since their promoting agency created a Marketing agency called *'Siri'* to some extent they too face the problem of marketing for some goods. Hence, there is a need of aggressive policy by the state governments on the provision of marketing facilities. A place to market the products must be established in the gram panchayat area or village. So that the respondents can have access to market to sell their products and thereby grow in their business.
- Stiff competition in the market and lack of mobility of women make the dependence of women entrepreneurs on middleman indispensable. Many business women find it difficult to capture the market and make their products popular. They are not fully aware of the changing market conditions and hence can effectively utilise the services of media and internet. Hence, care should be taken towards this direction.
- Women must be educated and trained constantly to acquire the skills and knowledge in all the functional areas of business management. This can facilitate women to excel in decision making process and develop a good business network.
- Various institutions in the financial sector extend their maximum support in the form of incentives, loans, schemes etc. Even then every woman entrepreneur may not be aware of all the assistance provided by the institutions. So the sincere

efforts taken towards women entrepreneurs may not reach the entrepreneurs in rural and backward areas.

- Women are hesitant to find out the access to cater their needs in the financial and marketing areas. In spite of the mushrooming growth of associations, institutions, and the schemes from the government side, women are not enterprising and dynamic to optimise the resources in the form of reserves, assets mankind or business volunteers.

A reduction in women's vulnerability can sometimes also translate into empowerment if greater financial security allows the women to become more assertive in household and community affairs. By providing access to finance for income-generating activities, micro finance institutions can significantly, reduce women's vulnerability to poverty. By putting financial resources in the hands of women, micro finance institutions help level the playing field and promote gender equality. To conclude, an integrated approach is necessary for making the movement of women entrepreneurship a success. For this purpose, both the Government and non-Governmental agencies have to play a vital role. In order to achieve the desired goal, there should be re-orientation of educational system for women, curriculum change, career guidance; reservations, scholarships, and timely assistance are required. The joint efforts of both men and women entrepreneurs can change developing India into a developed country.

REFERENCES

1. Dadhich C.L (2001): 'Micro-finance –A Panacea for Poverty Alleviation: A Case Study of Oriental Grameen Project in India', *Indian Journal of Agricultural Economics*, Vol. 56, No. 3, pp. 419-421.
2. Harper, Malcolm (1998): *'Profit for the Poor: Cases of Microfinance'*, Oxford and IBH Publishing Company Private Limited, New Delhi.
3. Isabelle Guerin, (2006): 'Women and Money: Lesson from Senegal', *Journal Development and Change,* Vol. 37, No. 3.
4. Jayasheela and Palanna V K (2005): 'Role of Self-Help Groups in Enhancing Sericulture Productivity: A case study in Karnataka'. *SEDME*, Vol. 32, No. 1.
5. Purohit, Sheela (2003): 'Microcredit and Women's Empowerment", *Swa Shakti Bulletin,* April, pp. 15-20.
6. Rao V. M. (2001): *'Empowering Rural Women through Dairy Co-operative'*, Anmol Publications, New Delhi.
7. Reddy, Reddeppa A and K Narasimhalu (2009): 'SHG in India: A Tool for Urban Poverty', *Southern Economist*, Vol. 48, No. pp. 39-40.

8. Schreiner, Mark and Woller, Gary (2003). *Microenterprise development programs in the United States and in the Developing World.* World Development.
9. Schreiner, Mark and Woller, Gary (2003): Microenterprise development programs in the United States and in the Developing World. *World Development*, Vol. 31 No. 9.
10. Sudarshan, Synghal (2002): 'Taking Micro-credit to Women', *Financing Agriculture*, Vol. 34, No. 2.
11. Tankha, Ajay Rewa Shankar Misra and Prabhat Labh (2005): 'Case for Microfinance in India', *Mainstream,* Vol. XLIII, No. 16, pp. 3-6.
12. Venkatarao P (2009): 'Role of SHGs in the Empowerment of Women' *SEDME*, Vol. 35, No.1, pp. 29-45.
13. Vimala P (2009): 'Kudumbashree: A Model for Women Empowerment', *Southern Economist*, Vol. 48, No. 14, pp. 37-38.

32

Self Help Groups as a Link for Inclusive Growth—An Impact Study in N.R. Pura Taluk of Chickmagalur District

Archana K.U.

Abstract: *India's performance in recent years has been among the best in the World. Growth may be higher in the last new two decades but inclusive growth has been missing. The income distribution has been unequal and only some sections of the population are benefited more from higher growth and prosperity. Exclusion continued in terms of low agriculture growth with increasing visibility in farmer's suicides low quality of employment growth, inadequate development of women and children, concentration of poverty and low human development, increase in rural urban divides and regional disparities. Among the poor, women are considered the most disadvantaged due to their limited access to economic opportunities and basic social services and the excessive burden of household chores on them. Self-help Group (SHG) approach is the key element in social mobilisation. The microfinance project intervention in terms of formation and stabilisation of SHGs for extending credit support and promotion of thrift to promote visible economic activities is significant. Against this background the paper throws light on the impact of SHGs on savings and incomes of the rural poor in N.R.*

Pura Taluk of Chikkamagalur district in Karnataka.

Introduction

India's performance in recent years has been among the best in the world. The reforms initiated since the early 1990s have unshackled the economy. The long-term trend rate of growth has steadily increased from it an average of 3.5 per cent a year between the 1950s and 1970s, to above a per cent in 2006 and 2007. The powers of India's IT and IT-enabled services, biotechnology, pharmaceuticals and various manufacturing segments is being recognised the world over. Its macro-fundamentals are sound and foreign exchange reserves are comfortable at around $ 250 billion (Arunachalam-2010). Growth may be higher in the last two decades but inclusive growth or equitable development has been missing.

The exclusion problems have not been seriously addressed by the government programmes and strategies. Exclusion continued in terms of low agriculture growth with increasing visibility in farmer's suicides, low quality employment growth inadequate development of women and children, concentration of poverty and low human development both geographically and in terms of social categories, increase in rural urban divides and regional disparities. The economic independence of the lower sections is the key driver towards eradicating this inequality and establishing an inclusive growth model.

India's development agenda will need to be expanded to include not only the eradication of extreme poverty but an inclusive growth strategy to address the legitimate concerns of this large segment of the population. Although the banking sector has made significant developments in many areas of their performance, there still exist large portions of the population which are yet to be brought under the umbrella of banking services. Financial inclusion efforts are essential to bring those portions of the population into the mainstream.

This would enable banks to expand their market share but expand the overall market, in the process of tapping the Bottom of pyramid (Borchra, 2009). Self-help groups and micro finance are very closely linked, in that the former is used as a medium to generate and distribute financial capability so as to help deprived people to move up the income ladder. In fact self-help groups are one of the models of microfinance that is very popular in India. An SHG has 10 to 20 people from a homogenous class. They come together for addressing their common problems. They are encouraged to make voluntary thrift on a regular basis pooled resources to make small interest bearing loans to their members. The process helps them imbibe the essentials of financial intermediation including prioritisation of needs. Setting terms and condition and accounts keeping gradually build financial discipline in all of them. They also learn to handle resources of a size that is much beyond individual capacities of any of them. The SHG members begin to appreciate that resources are limited and have a cost. Once the groups show this mature financial behaviour banks are encouraged to make loans to the SHG in certain multiples of the accumulated savings of the SHG. The bank loans are given without any collateral and at market interest rates. The groups continue to decide the terms of loans to the members. Since the groups own accumulated savings are part and parcel of the aggregate loans made by the groups to their members, peer pressure ensures timely repayment (NABARD-2005). In cases where groups have been given a reasonable operating shape by promotional agencies like non-government organisations, and an SHGs thus formed is stabilised, it is possible to introduce external funds. Ultimately the single most important quality of the self-help groups that help to sustain it as well as its activities and help its members to obtain capabilities is its voluntary nature.

Methodology

The primary data related to the study are collected with a semi-structured interview schedule. Besides this, Focus Group Discussion was help to know the people's perception regarding the SHGs functioning. The secondary information is collected from District statistical office, Chikkamagalur and Taluk office, N.R.Pura. The study is based on systematic random sampling technique. Covering the villages namely Kadinabailu, Mutthinakoppa, Nagalapura, Magundi, Seethuru. Ten SHGs from each village (10x5 = 50 SHGs) and two members from each SHGs (2x50 = 100 members) have been selected on systematic random sample basis. The total sample size of the study is 100.

Table 1: Sampling Details

Sl. No.	*Village*	*Number of SHGs*	*Number of Members*
1.	Kadinabylu	10	20
2.	Mutthinakoppa	10	20
3.	Nagalapura	10	20
4.	Magundi	10	20
5.	Seethuru	10	20
	Total	**50**	**100**

Source: Field study.

N.R.Pura is a Taluk in Chikkamagalur district, in the Indian state of Karnataka. With an area of N.R. Pura is located at 13.62^0 North 75.52^{0}E[(1)]. It has an average elevation of 643 metres (2109 feet). The larger portion of the taluk consists of the hill area which contains some of the wildest mountain scenery in Southern India. The chief natural wealth of N.R. Pura is its, forests, which contains inexhaustible supplies of the finest timber, and rubber. As per 2001 census, N.R. Pura had a population of 65,639 living in 14,793 houses. Spread across total 354 villages and 15 Panchayats males are 32,559 and females are 33,080. N.R. Pura has an average literacy rate of 77 per cent higher than the national average of 59.5 per cent male literacy is 82 per cent and female literacy in 73 per cent. In N.R. Pura 12 per cent of the population is less than six years of age.

Social-economic Profile

In the study area 62 per cent of the respondents are belonging to OBC, remaining members are from SC/ST communities 86 per cent of the respondents are from Hindu religion and 14 per cent of them from Muslim and other religion. 70 per cent of them are belongs to nuclear family. The SHGs composition is dominated by middle age group of 26 to 45 followed by below 25 age groups (chart-1). 60 per cent of the respondents are married and 16 per cent of them are widowed. This shows that the SHGs are providing safety net to married as well as widow women to overcome their family financial problems by empowering them for Graph-1.

Graph-1: Social-economic Profile

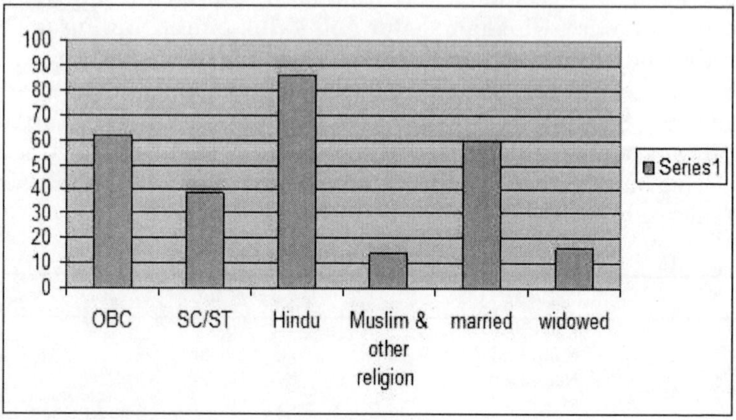

Education

Education is a prime determinant of quality of life in the poverty alleviation efforts. The education status of SHGs members in the study area indicates that 32 per cent of them are illiterate and majority of them are from Kadinabylu, and Mutthinakoppa. About 10 per cent of the members are studied more than graduation. The literacy level is more among the villages near to taluk place N.R. Pura compared to far-off rural areas. However the education status is diverse among the groups (draw chart).

Occupational Structure

Occupational structure determines the earning capacity of the household members. About 21 per cent of the members are housewives, about 32 per cent of the members work as daily wage earners and self-employed (14 per cent). Predominately the daily workers work in the agricultural related activities, as the area is predominated by Areca nut and paddy cultivation. Most of the self employed have petty shops. However, occupational structure does not reveal the real intensity of work behaviour, as this is highly correlated to day-to-day affairs. (Chart)

Graph 2: Occupational Structure

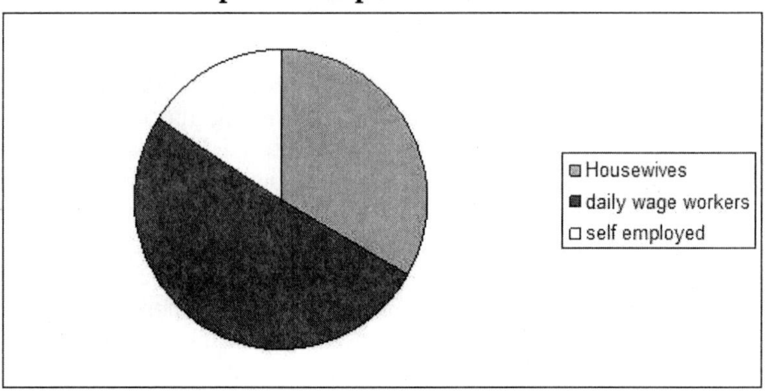

Income Level of Households

The level of income is a major determinant factor for participation in the microfinance. Generally low-income needy people will participate to overcome their short-term financial problems by saving small portion of their income. About 46 per cent of the respondents had income below Rs 11,000 but after becoming member only 30 per cent of them are in this category. In the other income categories like 11,001 to > 1,00,000 there was improvement in the member's performance. The comparison of the income before and after the SHGs membership increase in other category shows the positive impact made by financial inclusion through the self-help groups leading to inclusive growth (Graph-3).

Graph-3: Income Level of Households

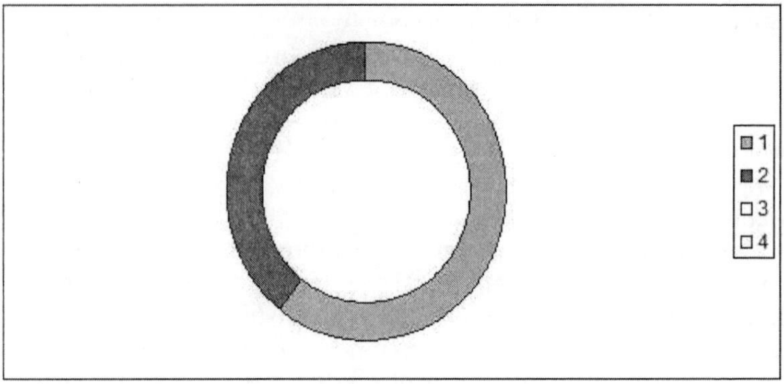

Source: Field study.

Impact of SHGs on Economic Condition:-

SHGs generate the saving among the poor and provide them micro credit which is required for their day-to-day life, and which helps them to improve their economic conditions.

Inception and Size of Groups

The inception of SHGs has a vital bearing on saving and credit creation. Older the SHGs higher are the saving and higher is the credit generation. Whereas the size of the SHGs has a positive relation with the saving, higher the members larger are the saving and vice-versa. Majority of the SHGs started in 2007 (43 percent), and 22 per cent of them are started in 2006. 16 per cent in 2005, 14 per cent in 2008 and only 6 per cent in 2009. The size of groups indicates that 64 per cent of them have 10-15 members and 36 per cent have 16-20 members. The average size of SHGs in study area is 14 members. There is close relation between size of SHGs and its inception. (Chart)

Motivation and Consistency of SHG's

Getting attached to the SHGs needs motivation, while joining the SHGs. The permanent membership also plays a vital role in sustainability of SHGs. Majority of the members are motivated by friends. Who includes neighbors; self-motivation is only 12 per cent, whereas family members and NGO workers (24 per cent) respectively had a role in motivation. The consistency of members in the group shows that, majority (48 per cent) of the SHGs the membership has increased; this indicates that the SHGs have created a positive response towards the microfinance.

Meetings

Meetings are held regularly; attendance is maintained and averages over 80 per cent. Sanctions for default on repayment and for deviant behaviour are imposed. The books (Admission Book, Attendance Register, Minutes Book, Members saving ledger', Members pass book, Receipt voucher, payment voucher, cash book, general ledger, loan ledger, stock book etc.) are maintained either by a literate member of the group or by the NGO staff. Gender issues concerning women in private and public life are raised and discussed. They begin to interact with other groups, government agencies and private institutions.

The meetings were held monthly, fortnightly and weekly. In case of 52 per cent it is held weekly, 32 per cent fortnightly and 16 per cent monthly. In most cases (48 per cent) all members attended the meeting whereas 34 per cent attended a few meetings because of family problems.

Group members' calls for meeting in most of the cases: Sometime NGO workers also call for meeting. About 54 per cent of the decisions in the group are taken by the consensus; 12 per cent by group representative. In certain critical issues decisions (26 per cent) are also made by voting.

Members' Awareness about the working of SHGs

When a member joins the group, it is responsibility of each of them to get acquainted with working of SHG, which indicates high level of participation by the members. The awareness level about objective of the group is very high of 55 per cent, followed by saving of the group 63 per cent. Cash in hand and the name of the bank having the account of the group is 50 per cent respectively.

Savings

Regular savings and lending operations gather strengths for the operation and the sustainability of SHG's. Women themselves also often value the opportunity to be seen to be making a greater contribution to house-hold well being giving them greater confidence and sense of self-worth. They act as the forum for the members to provide space and support to each other. The group decides on the rate of savings, timing and reasons for the loans, the schedule of payments and repayments, and on the interest rates, it assesses whether member is able to use the loan effectively and repay according to the schedule decided on. Majority of the members (58 per cent) were not saved the amount before joining to SHGs and few were saving in post-office pygmy and chit funds in villages. But after becoming the member all the SHGs members have started saving more or less amount.

As the main objective of the SHGs is micro saving and macro credit to the people from the group. After becoming the member of the group they are expected to save a minimum amount weekly as decided by the group through consensus. The amount saved by the members varies Rs 10 to Rs 100 per week; Most of the members (28 per cent) of them are saving Rs 120 per month followed by Rs 80 and Rs 40 respectively. Only two per cent of the members are saving amount more than Rs. 400. Thus, the analysis shows that SHGs has helped them to maximum extent to generate saving there by getting micro credit which includes financial inclusion leading to inclusive growth. (Chart)

Purposes of Saving

SHGs enhance the equality of status for women as participants, decision-makers and beneficiaries in the democratic, economic, social and cultural spheres of life. The SHGs provide savings mechanism which suits the needs of the members. It also provides a cost-effective delivery mechanism for small credit to its members. The major purpose indicated by the members are support family income in case of urgency (44 per cent), education of the children (24 per cent), health problem (22 per cent), and marriage of the children (10 per cent). (Chart)

Sources of Loan and its Utilisation

Sanction of loans to SHGs by banks is based on the quantum of savings mobilised by the SHGs, but not for any specific purpose unlike in case of other schematic landing. The members borrow from SHGs and also from bank depending upon the need. The borrowings from SHGs are made on the basis of three member witness giving the surety of repayment on behalf of member. The member has to repay the loan within stipulated time period with interest laid down by the group from the bank the members can avail the individual loan on the recommendation of the group or group get loan sanctioned by bank under various schemes to the group which can be distributed among the members.

The sources of loan are two types SHGs and bank. Four per cent from SHGs and 35 per cent from B the Banks have not taken any loans respectively. For smaller amount the members are depended on SHGs for instance 72 per cent of the member's have borrowed less than Rs 10,000 from SHGs: Whereas 47 per cent of them have borrowed more than Rs 10,000 from banks. This supports that the

SHG's are able to generate micro credit required by the rural people for their day today activities. The borrowings from the SHGs are used for family expenses, illness, education, celebrations of the festivals etc.; whereas the borrowings from banks are usually used for some specific purposes like marriage, land development, petty business etc. Thus the SHGs are able to provide micro credit to the rural people and bringing them out of indebtedness of the moneylenders.

Repayment of Loan

Only one member of a group gets a loan at one time. The preference in getting loans is decided by the member themselves. The member availing loans have 10 pay interest 2 per cent per month. Out of the total borrowers from the SHGs, 65 per cent have repaid the amount regularly and 35 per cent of them are defaulters. In comparison to this, in case of banks 48 per cent of them have repaid the amount regularly and 52 per cent of them are defaulters. This shows that recovery of the loan by the SHGs is better than by the bank.

Comparison of Status

From the analysis we can conclude that, SHGs membership has helped the members to improve upon the socio-economic status, recognition in community. This is the clear indication of empowerment of women through SHGs. Thus, SHGs has created a positive impact on rural poor women and helped them in getting recognition in community. This proves that "Self-help Groups have made a positive impact on financial inclusion of the members, linking to inclusive growth".

Recommendations

Before providing credit, professional skill and training should be given, if the borrowers are unskilled or semi-skilled. A consultation services should be provided to the borrowers to select the appropriate profitable enterprises. Sufficient amount of loan should be given to start up the selected enterprises at a lower interest rate. A strong monitoring and follow-up support and services should be given in executing the enterprises especially in the first few months. Micro-credit should be given in kind not in cash. So that borrowers will be benefited by getting goods and services is fare prices. Monitor the enterprises taken by the borrowers at least once of a week and prepare a progress report. Provide suggestions regarding further improvement.

India has the potential of becoming a leading economy and has the unique opportunity to make that growth inclusive. Provided there is willingness on the part of all sections of society to put in hard and disciplined work, together with serious, sustained and purposeful planning.

REFERENCES

1. Boochra, Anchal (2009), 'A Pathway for Microfinance in India', http:// www.indianmba. com/ occasional papers (op 201.htm)
2. Dodkeq, M.D. (1999), "SHGs and micro credit, sustaining Rural women", Social Welfare, March. 45 (12): 19-20.
3. Mujumdar N.A. (2007), "Inclusive Growth: Development perspectives in Indian Economy, Academic foundation, New Delhi.
4. NABARD (2005) - 'Progress of SHG-Bank linkage in India'. 2004-2005 Micro credit Innovations Department, NABARD Mumbai.
5. Editorials (2007), 'Focus on inclusive growth' The Hindu, Tuesday. Jul 07, www.hindu.com /2009/07/07/stories/2009070759720800.htm.
6. Parambi, Raphael (2003), – 'Microfinance: Towards inclusive growth; Microfinance News. http://infcny.org 1 content/microfinance-towards-inclusive growth.

PART IV: MICROFINANCE—THE OTHER CONTOURS

33

Cooperatives as Community Based Organisations for Elimination of Rural Poverty in Andhra Pradesh

M. Jayaprakash

Abstract: *The Society for Elimination of Rural Poverty (SERP), through the grass root level functioning of Village Organisations - Self Help Groups (SHGs), Mandal Samakhyas (Block Level Cooperatives) and Zilla Samakhyas (District Level Cooperatives) known as Community Based Organisation Structure, has worked on a comprehensive multi-dimensional poverty alleviation strategy by focusing equally on the Human Development Value Chain and livelihoods value chain by working with the poorest of poor through the Community Based Organisations involving cooperatives registered under Mutually Aided Cooperative Societies Act of Andhra Pradesh. This write-up attempts to analyse the components of the said multi-dimensional strategy of SERP for poverty alleviation in rural areas of Andhra Pradesh.*

Introduction

The Society for Elimination of Rural Poverty (SERP) was established by the Government of Andhra Pradesh (GOAP) as a sensitive support structure to facilitate poverty reduction through social mobilisation and improvement of livelihoods of rural poor in Andhra Pradesh. SERP is implementing Indira Kranthi Patham (IKP) in all the 1098 rural Mandals of 22 rural districts in A.P.

Work with Poorest of Poor

SERP designed special processes and initiatives to work with the poorest of poor, including SC/ST, coastal fisher-folk, disabled, elderly and other vulnerable and marginalised, so that they overcome their peculiar constraints and attain secure and sustainable livelihoods and good quality of life.

Based on the vision and objectives, SERP has undertaken programme to enable the poor to come out of poverty through a systems approach. The non-negotiable principle of SERP is to facilitate the CBOs consists SHGs, village organisations, Mandal Samakhyas (Block Cooperatives), Zilla Samakhyas (District Cooperatives) to provide end-to-end solutions for the poor in all dimensions of poverty. SERP works on a comprehensive multi-dimensional poverty alleviation strategy by focusing equally on both the Human Development Value Chain and the Livelihoods Value Chain. The approach is through the empowerment process of poor through the networks of SHGs and their federations (Cooperatives at the Mandals and Zilla level) by leveraging the power of the collectives to access their rights and entitlements. The livelihoods strategy of SERP aims to capitalise on all the livelihood assets available in the local communities so that sustainable, relevant and effective poverty reduction is possible. Physical, Natural, Social, Financial and Human capital must be nurtured and built upon in order to achieve the rapid results that one would expect of a mature poverty eradication strategy.

SERP Vision

"Every poor family in rural Andhra Pradesh comes out of poverty; is stabilised against hocks that threaten their advancement; improves its livelihoods options; and enjoys a decent quality of life". Society for Elimination of Rural Poverty (SERP) unleashes the creative energy of each household in rural Andhra Pradesh (AP) to the benefit of the households and of the society.

This means that every family

- Earns decent incomes: A Minimum of Rs100,000 per annum, from three to four sources of livelihoods (agriculture, allied, non-farm, jobs in urban areas, etc),
- Plan their household expenditure and economise on their household running costs,
- Protected from risks to - life, health, assets and enterprises,
- Is free from hunger,
- Enjoys secure shelter,
- Access to quality education,

- Enjoys good health, through interventions that prevent ill health, promote good health and secure quality health services when they require it, and
- Leads life with dignity and women enjoy equality within family and outside.

This vision is within the reach of the poor and their institutions, provided the effort so far is continued and pursued vigorously to make the foundation stronger.

SERP Objectives

SERP aims at inclusive growth of the rural poor, including the poorest of the poor, and enhancing opportunities for them to participate in the market for products, services and jobs existing and emerging, while strengthening their institutions at the group, village, mandal and district level and, eventually, at state level towards their full potential with self-reliance. Its objectives are stronger institutions of the poor – SHG:

- Mobilising all poor on a saturation basis into existing or new SHGs and their federal institutions, mostly in co-operative form.
- Nurturing these institutions to become self-governed, self-managed and self-reliant, leveraging technology where relevant.
- Convergence of CBOs with other institutions of poor so as to make them more transparent and ensuring that institutions run programme and deliver services.
- Visible empowerment of women socially and financially.

Organisation Structure of SERP

The day-to-day management of the Society for Elimination of Rural Poverty (SERP) organisation is carried out by the CEO and his/her team of officers. The functions, programme and their relationship are illustrated below. The top decision making activities are carried out in the State Project Management Unit headed by the CEO and State project directors and other functional specialists as indicated. At the district level there is a District Project Management Unit to headed by a Project Director, (District Rural Development Agency) assisted by functional specialists. PD, DRDA implements all the programme of IKP at the district level under the overall guidance and support of the district collector.

Fig. 1: State Project Management Units (SPMU)

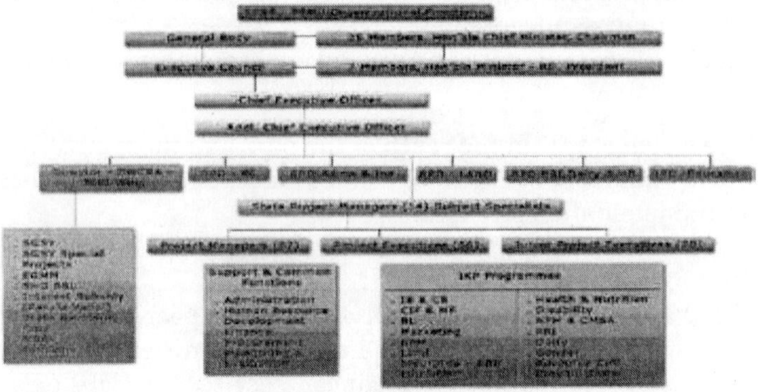

Fig. 2: District Project Monitoring Units (DPMU)

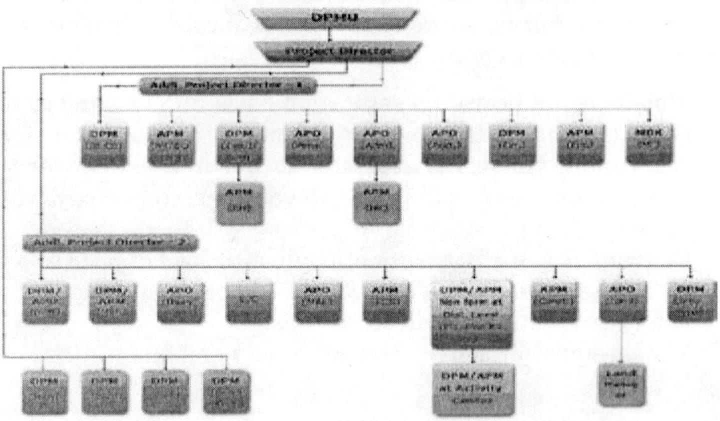

Fig. 3: Tribal Project Management Unit (TPMU)

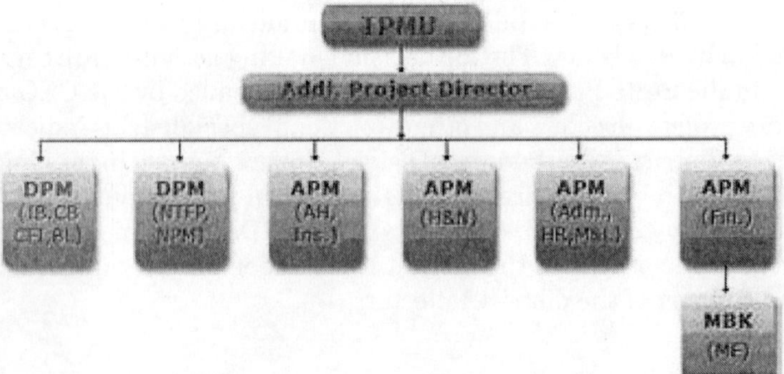

Fig. 4: CBO's Organogram

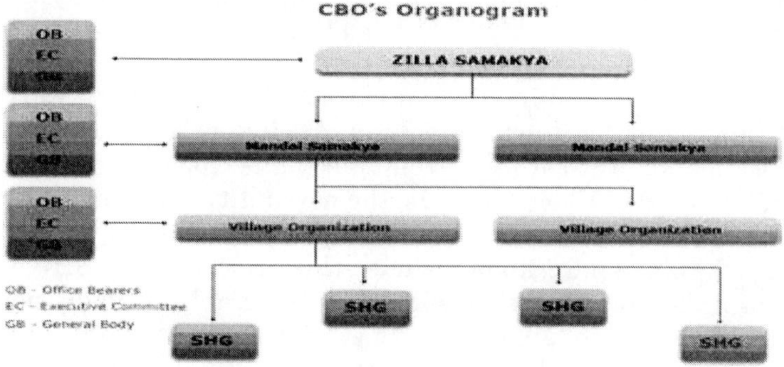

As could be seen from the above diagram, the fundamental unit of development for SERP is the rural household. All interventions through the Human Development Value Chain as well as the Livelihoods Value Chain strive to achieve essentially two outcomes- sustainable per capita household income of minimum Rs 1,00,000 per annum from various sources, and improved Human Development Indicator (HDI). The means through which these are achieved is by organising all rural households into Community Based Organisations (CBOs) and giving them inputs on Institution Building, Capacity Building, adequate credit and hand holding support to make the livelihoods sustainable.

SERP has relentlessly worked on a unique structure of community-based organisation by organising 1.14 crore rural women into 10.27 lakh SHGs, 38646 Village Organisations, 1098 Mandal Samakhyas (Block level Cooperatives) and 22 Zilla Samakhyas (District level Cooperatives). SHG membership in Andhra Pradesh is the largest in the country with around 30 per cent of total SHG members in the country. SERP has established a unique institutional structure for the Community Based Organisations in the World. The structure of CBOs in A.P. has facilitated cumulative loans of Rs 34,889.41 crore by commercial banks to SHG members, Collective Marketing to the tune of Rs 3925 crore resulting in a benefit of Rs 75 to Rs 100 per quintal to the farmers, pesticide free cultivation in 23 lakh acres in 2010-11 alone resulting in a saving of Rs 3000 to Rs 15,000 per acre to the farmers, etc. This unique model has been adopted by Ajeevika (National Rural Livelihoods Mission) at the National level in India.

SHG - Bank Linkage

To reduce the financial vulnerabilities of the poor, several initiatives have been taken up by the Bank Linkage unit of SERP that ensure that commercial banks finance and lend support to the activities undertaken by SHGs. Years of effort in this regard has resulted in Andhra Pradesh leading the SHG Bank Linkage programme by accounting for almost 50 per cent of all bank loans given to SHGs in India. Earlier the poor were not credit worthy as they could not muster any kind of collaterals for loans from these banks. But through group discipline, repayment culture and accumulated corpus funds, the possibility of money lending to the groups has been established thus resulting in the SHG-Bank Linkage programme. Under this project, every SHG has been linked to a bank for servicing this credit needs as per a Micro Credit Plan (MCP). Having started in the year 2000, Bank Linkage has gradually moved to become the flagship programme of SERP.

The progress made by the Bank Linkage unit of SERP has been gradual yet assured. From a meagre 88.63 crore in 1999-2000, the bank linkages have grown to more than 8000 crore at the beginning of 2012.

District-wise Bank Linkage Data

Sl.No.	*District*	*Target for the FY 2011-12*		*Achievement for the FY 2011-12*	
		PHY	*FIN (Rs. In Crores)*	*PHY*	*FIN (Rs. In Crores)*
1.	Adilabad	11,033	206.71	10,598	198.95
2.	Anantapur	16,488	415.50	18,886	485.42
3.	Chittoor	22,916	633.36	20,990	680.01
4.	East Godavari	17,154	433.48	22,833	574.06
5.	Guntur	17,939	416.86	18,169	390.06
6.	Kadapa	10,975	327.31	12,277	318.60
7.	Karimnagar	13,567	340.76	14,011	351.80
8.	Khammam	14,462	352.77	18,683	364.49
9.	Krishna	15,890	512.38	21,127	557.96
10.	Kurnool	13,808	293.26	15,029	322.40
11.	Mahabubnagar	17,638	398.78	13,463	258.41
12.	Medak	11,973	329.18	15,177	340.56
13.	Nalgonda	17,835	332.91	20,397	342.82
14.	Nellore	13,234	286.74	12,434	280.57
15.	Nizamabad	10,439	236.18	10,987	251.64
16.	Prakasam	21,252	441.70	18,633	416.79
17.	Ranga Reddy	14,162	322.88	12,302	284.89
18.	Srikakulam	16,796	370.36	16,163	326.60
19.	Visakhapatnam	15,848	323.16	12,652	291.84
20.	Vizianagaram	16,218	339.52	13,025	255.49
21.	Warangal	17,926	300.22	16,786	321.87
22.	West Godavari	15,101	472.55	19,169	465.17
	TOTAL	**3,42,654**	**8,086.65**	**3,53,791**	**8,080.41**

Source: SERP, Annual Report 2012.

Other innovations brought about by the Bank Linkage unit include Bima Mitras and Community-based Recovery Mechanism. The concept of Bank Mitra had been taken up to increase the communication between the various stakeholders. Bima Mitras are usually educated women who are trained in the various nuances of the programme and act as the interface between the SHGs and banks. The progress is monitored by various committees at the village, mandal and district level through more than 4300 community resource persons. These CRPs are generally selected from the best practitioners in the community who have managed to wriggle themselves out of poverty. All in all, the Bank linkage programme has been largely responsible for the transformation of lives of the poor by ensuring direct benefit and guaranteed access to cheap and safe credit in the time of distress.

Community Investment Fund

CIF is provided by the IKP to enable the poor including disadvantaged communities to access credit facility services seamlessly to improve and diversify their livelihoods. CIF supports the poor in prioritising livelihood needs through investments in sub-projects, proposed and implemented by the Community Based Organisations (CBOs). The cumulative CIF up to November 2011 is Rs 1092.02 Crores and the total numbers of beneficiaries is 28,53,850.

Community M.arketing

Community Marketing Strategy of the project is to enable the small and marginal farmers and NTFP collectors to obtain the best price for their agricultural commodities and forest produce. The marketing interventions through IKP VOs is being promoted mainly to eliminate unfair trade practices, to increase the bargaining power of small and marginal farmers in rural areas and also to generate employment/income to the VOs. The VOs have successfully implemented village level collective marketing of Paddy, Maize, Neem, Red gram, Cashew, and NTFP besides Agricultural Inputs. The marketing interventions of IKP have registered a significant increase in this financial year with pick up in paddy procurement activity.

Table – An Overview of Marketing Interventions

Item	*2006-07*	*2007-08*	*2008-09*	*2009-10*	*2010-11*	*2011-12*
No. of MMS Involved	533	1036	845	835	839	675
No. of VOs involved	783	2071	1662	1443	1341	1607
No. of Families	101790	301172	216792	279306	130120	326872
No. of Commodities	81	79	65	67	65	14
Volume (lakh)	18.25	47.3	59.3	65.6	40.78	188.18
Turnover (Rs. Crores)	126.38	320.15	492.16	611.24	418.87	1956.94

Source: www.scrap.gov.in.

Employment Generation and Marketing Mission (EGMM)

EGMM was set up to address the needs of the next generation of the large network of SHGs created and nurtured by IKP. It aims at to create employment/employability for the rural/tribal underprivileged youth. It works in a public-private partnership mode to identify, train and place youth in entry level corporate jobs in hospitality, retail, sales, tourism, banking, rural BPOs, manufacturing, textiles and construction sectors. Total number of jobs created up to November 2011 is 3,06,183. EGMM has been focusing strongly on retention of trained candidates, as the migration sometimes necessitated by the employment offers, was traumatic for many youth. To counter this, a counselling facility, zero balance bank accounts and a hostel directory have been set in place so that youth who start new jobs are able to transition to their roles smoothly.

Non-Farm Employment

Apart from sector jobs, nurturing non-farm employment is another objective at SERP. Around 30,000 enterprises exist currently and provide employment to over a lakh and half persons and generate considerable wealth in the villages. The entrepreneurs have developed market linkage with local and district level retail and whole-sellers to sell their products. They have also developed links with raw material suppliers for their products. The units have been able to sell products in the local and district level markets as of now. However, their penetration of larger markets is limited. This is due to problems like poor infrastructure, outdated tools and machinery, difficulty in credit access as they are not legally registered, marketing at higher level markets like metros or large cities, better packaging and branding, thereby limiting their growth and potential to excel.

In view of this, an initiative linking rural entrepreneurs to design, packaging, business and marketing skills is underway through EGMM apart from skill upgradation for better product development, quality and better management of their units. Activities under this initiative are still under way, but it is expected that this will create the following outcomes in the medium term.

- 60000 SHG Enterprises supported by SNLP
- 200000 HHs helped out of poverty
- Average income increase per family per annum is Rs 30,000

Dairy

In the agriculture dominated rural part of our country, Dairy acts not just as a valuable alternate source of livelihood for the rural dwellers, but also as a cushion in cases of bad crop. The story of Dairy unit of SERP started off as a pilot project in Nizamabad and Mahabubnagar districts in 2006-07 which helped milk producers to get better price for their milk by ensuring transparency and accuracy in milk procurement operations. The primary goal was to provide marketing support and guaranteed support price to the poor. Gradually, the establishment of milk procurement centres and Bulk Milk Cooling units at mandal levels through SHGs led to profitable dairying process. Focus slowly shifted to the development and strengthening of backward linkages for enhancement of Milk productivity levels through APBN Fodder development as lack of availability of seed material was of major concern.

Achieving a 2/3rd increase in milk production and productivity is the essential goal of the initiative. As much as 65 per cent of the Bank linkage amount has been put into dairying business in the villages of Andhra Pradesh by SERP. The 187 Bulk Milk Cooling Units (BMCUs) have played a major role in ensuring that the poor get remunerative prices for milk. It has been envisaged to conduct group rearing of milch animals under Pala Pragathi Kendralu (PPK). Under this scheme, each eligible group shall be encouraged to take up community dairy farming with eight milch animals housed under a single shelter. For sustenance of these centres, mini feed mixing plants, breeding services, mineral mixture plants were provided as part of the backward linkage and support services. As many as 117 PPKs have been established in the calendar year of 2012.

The dairy activity is a major livelihood opportunity for the rural poor in the state. This intervention helped the Milk Producers to get better price for milk and promoted transparency in milk procurement in 20 districts.

No. of BMCU Mandals	No. of Milk Producers	Milk Collected/Day (Litres) Peak Season	Lean Season	SHG Managed BMCUs Milk Procured	Milk Supplied
193	1,45,000	2.71 Lakh	1.79 Lakh	16,966 Lakh	77,122 MTs

Source: Human Development Value Chain.

Under Social and Human Development (Addressing Millennium Goals), Social action for gender equity, recognising the people with disabilities, among the poorest of the poor, Health and Nutrition intervention, quality education through community participation as intergenerational poverty alleviation strategy are covered.

Gender Initiative

The gender strategy envisages that the poor women are able to access and have control over assets, incomes and all services available at village and individual level. Gender programme helps preventing discrimination against girl child, tackling domestic violence, helps women to increase their understanding of intra family equity issues, decision making levels, free mobility and necessity of building a safe environment. Under this component, 552 Mandal Level Social Action Committees with membership of 5480 women are formed. Community Managed Family Counselling Centres run by SHG women are 490. Women are actively mobilised into V.O. Social Action Committees (VOSACs) in the villages to work on social agenda and gender discrimination cases. At the village level, 13,058 Village Organisation Social Action Committees are formed with a membership of 1,12,739. Number of cases dealt with by these committees and family counselling centres together are 32,710 and number of cases resolved are 23,425 as of November 2011. IKP is playing an important role to prevent infanticide by organising women into Social Action Committees. The Gender Unit is working in 374 mandals of 14 districts.

The activities of Gender unit kicked off with the establishment of Social Action Committees (SACs) at the village and mandal level in more than 200 mandals in the districts of Krishna, Guntur, West Godavari and Prakasam. To address gender issues, a social agenda had been developed and the training was provided to the SHG leaders on women laws, counselling techniques, negotiation and conflict resolution skills. Gender CRPs were selected and trained on universalisation of social agenda. The SAC members have played an active role in tackling various issues brought up by victims through rigorous counselling and workshops.

Disability Initiative

Recognising that people with Disabilities are among the poorest and most vulnerable of the poor, IKP has adopted a participatory development approach to support them by building their capacities to improve life skills and self esteem. IKP has extended the support to enhance their livelihoods by creating linkages to government benefits and entitlements. Provision of assessment, treatment and rehabilitation services were made through community managed interventions through 88 neighbourhood centres. Intensive activities are carried out in 816 mandals. 377891 Persons with Disabilities (PWDs) are organised into more than 41000 exclusive SHGs, 262 Mandal Vikalangula Samakhyas (MVS Cooperatives), and three Zilla Samakhyas in the State. PWDs are given an assistance of more than 200 crores through CIF, Bank Loans and Revolving Fund for enhancing their Livelihood. Further, 7984 Surgical Corrections were carried out and 43697 PWDs were issued assistive devices at no cost to them in the programme mandals. Through *Software for Assessment of Disability for Access Rehabilitation and Empowerment (SADAREM),* the Persons with Disabilities shall be assessed a fresh recording per centage of disability and all the existing Disability Certificates shall be replaced by re-accessing the persons with disabilities by concerned District Medical Boards. So far 9.53 lakh PWDs are assessed against the target of 11.55 lakh. Under Jansree Bima Yojana (JBY) 41,343 were covered and three lakh PWDs were proposed to be covered under JBY for 2011-12. 6094 Srama Shakti Sanghams are formed, exclusively for PWDs under MGNREGS. With regard to job placements for PWDs, Centre for Person with Disability Livelihoods (CPDL), provided 902 placements in the Public Sector as against 1493 trained.

Health and Nutrition

The major goal of the Health and Nutrition strategy under the APRPRP operates in a convergent mode with the line departments by looking at gaps in the existing public health and nutrition services that are provided by the line departments. It is being implemented in 293 pilot mandals covering 4382 Village organisations of the state. The extensive health and nutrition strategies being adopted across 293 mandals include fixed schedule for regular capacity building of stake holders at mandal and district levels, institutionalisation of the fixed Nutrition and Health Days (NH days) in convergence with line departments and regular health savings by 2.83 lakh members in 47752 SHGs to an amount of Rs 5.25 crores as safety nets for health emergencies. The intensive health and nutrition strategies focus on Health CRP strategy. 600 best practitioners from the pilot mandals are working as health CRPs. Since January 2007, this is being implemented in 4201 Nutrition cum day care centres and the impact has been tremendous. The prenatal and neonatal outcomes among the members that attended the Nutrition cum day care centres showed 94 per cent safe deliveries, No low birth weight baby being born. No maternal, infant and neonatal deaths happened in the 9400 deliveries that occurred among the members enrolled at these centres.

The Community Managed Nutrition-Cum Day Care Centres (NDCCs) have made a visible difference in the lives of rural women of Andhra Pradesh. Although it is too early to measure overall reductions in malnutrition levels, early indicators show that the NDCCs display promising potential to improve the nutritional status of pregnant and lactating women and their children in the long term. A number of innovative aspects account for the pilot programme's success. These NDCCs are owned and managed by the communities they serve making them accountable and responsive towards the needs of beneficiaries.They have been built on the strong social infrastructure of Andhra Pradesh's women's Self Help Groups (SHG), their village organisations, and federations that has been established cross the state over the past 16 years. With local women functioning as leaders, mentors, and trainers, the programme has been able to gain wide acceptance within communities and scale up across the state with ease.

Community-managed Educational Services (CMES)

Under the Community Managed Education Services (CMES), the programme has 1031 Early Childhood Education (ECE) centres that are functioning in 65 mandals in 16 districts with enrolment of 16000 children. It is proposed to start 2000 more ECE centres in mandals where NDCC centres are functioning. The targeted enrolment by the end of this financial year is 45000 children in 3031 centres. Quality Improvement Programme is in progress across 40 mandals in 10 districts. In this intervention, 40 Mandal Mahila Samakhya education subcommittees and 1200 VO subcommittees have been formed with support from Education Resource Persons at Mandal and district Level. These sub committees have been trained to monitor the quality of education in government schools. In this regard, convergence meetings have been held at district levels to solicit support from all the line departments. In the scheme of corporate education for weaker sections, admission for 19376 students so far has been facilitated in private/corporate junior colleges for two year intermediate course integrated with focused coaching for IITJEE/

AIEEE/EAMCET. The success of the scheme in the past two years has generated a substantial demand for good quality education at intermediate level among the marginalised and economically vulnerable social categories. Under a scheme to access higher education by the children of rural poor, 19376 children were enrolled in Corporate Junior Colleges with no cost to the students.

Social Security: Pension Scheme: The Government of Andhra Pradesh have introduced pension scheme for the SHG women to provide income security in their old age and social security to all women SHG members to enable them to lead secure life with dignity in old age. This scheme is visualized for SHG women over and above the age group of 18 years, in rural and urban areas to provide social security in their old age. This scheme envisages contribution of Re. one per day by the SHG woman and Government co-contribution of Re. one per day into her pension account.

Death of the earning members in a family was found to be one of the major reasons behind the poor falling into the clutches of poverty, especially in case of the death of the sole bread winner. Keeping in view, the vulnerabilities of poor and the need for an initiative that ensures financial security, the Social Security unit of SERP has been working towards providing a shield to the poor through its Insurance and pension schemes. Dr. Y.S.R Abhaya Hastham is a contributory pension scheme with the primary objective of providing income security and dignity to the SHG women who are 60 years and above. Aam Aadmi Bima Yojana (AABY) is a Group Insurance scheme that caters to earning members of rural landless families with agricultural labour as the primary livelihood. With a contribution of Rs 100 per annum each from Central and State Government, the members are provided life and disability cover.

The pension scheme has been conceived for all SHG women above the age of 18 years in rural as well as urban areas to avail a monthly pension ranging from 500 to 2200 when they attain an age of 60 years. Insurance is also covered under this scheme. As of today, around 48.70 lakh women have been registered under Abhaya Hastham. As many as five lakh members have already started receiving pension amounts. Insurance cover is provided by AABY and Jansree Bima Yojana under which 49 lakh landless agricultural labour and 39 lakh spouses of the SHG women are covered respectively. Also, SERP has enrolled 0.6 lakh SHG women and their family members under National Pension Scheme "SWAVALAMBAN" scheme, under credit linked loan insurance. A MoU has been entered by SERP with Life Insurance Corporation to provide life insurance cover to the SHG members. The risk cover is provided to the extent of the loan amounts availed from banks on a pilot basis in the districts of Medak, East Godavari and Chittoor districts. The Government of Andhra Pradesh has also been actively involved in distributing social security pensions to old age persons, widows and disabled persons.

Major Activities of Institution Building

Ever since its existence, it has been the belief of everyone at SERP that the primary reason for the rural parts of our country to languish in poverty is the existence of institutionalised obstacles for effective growth and development. Building organisations of the poor was envisaged to be an essential requirement for poverty alleviation as it reduced the excessive dependence on state for initiative and made the poor stakeholders in the development process. This paved the way for the establishment of women groups on the principles of self-help resulting in Andhra Pradesh being at the forefront of SHG centric development. Through internal lending and mutual assistance, the SHG movement that started in 1995 has transformed the lives of millions of rural poor in the state.

These member-owned and member-managed financial institutions empowered the poor to assert the right to resources intended for them and lead a life of dignity and self-respect. Special focus was given to the poorest of the Poor among the SC/ST communities who were particularly vulnerable. Gradually, SERP has ventured into new avenues of empowering poor through transferring funds to Mandal Samakhyas, preparation of Micro Credit plans for utilisation of finances, ensuring effective communication by having direct interactions with communities through Video conferences and sending all circulars and instructions both to DPMU and MSs directly in the local language. With the help of Community Resource Persons (CRPs), the implementation has been taken up on a larger scale since 2006 covering all 1098 mandals in the 22 rural districts.

Presently, as many as 10,59,101 Self Help Groups have been formed and organised into 8,821 village organisations which are in turn categorised under various Mandal Samakhyas (MSs). With more than 1.15 crore SHG members, the total savings stand at 4054.44 crores. This concept of executing developmental programmes by making use of Community based organisations (CBOs) has been pivotal for SERP to leverage resources from various development agencies and non-profit organisations. Other activities of the IB unit include Social Mobilisation, Capacity building, Bookkeeping and auditing, preparation of micro credit plans. Regular training programmes and innovations have been taken up to keep the SHG members motivated to innovate and take up responsibility. Over the years, this robust structure has been able to assist the poor and enable them to have a major say in the planning as well as execution of various growth interventions.

Conclusion

Some of the other key results of SERP are:

- 3,06,211 Persons with Disabilities (PWDs) in 32,182 exclusive SHGs for PWDs.
- 4500 acres of fertile land with assured sources of water purchased and handed over to the rural poor.
- 3,15,676 jobs provided to rural youth.
- 48.92 lakh women enrolled in Abhaya Hastham and another lakh rural poor household enrolled in JBY through the largest social security programmes in the country.
- 4201 Nutrition and Day Care Centers established.
- 1186 Early Child Education Centers established with 2171 students.
- 19376 Children enrolled in Corporate Colleges with no cost to them.
- 32710 cases pertaining to women resolved.

The decadal experience at SERP has shown the success in terms of Universal Approach. The challenge to SERP is now to design focused interventions for the poorest of poor (PoP) households in rural A.P. Given this, SERP has clearly articulated the need for a new vision and a fresh approach to finish the unfinished business of the elimination of poverty elimination in the POP households. SERP's comprehensive new approach is aimed at achieving minimum income levels of Rs 1,00,000 per annum per family for all the 30 Lakh PoP households identified in the State in addition to improved human development indicators.

REFERENCES

1. Government of Andhra Pradesh, Department of Rural Development, Annual Report (2009).
2. APMAS (2007): "Emerging SHG Federations and Challenge", by CS. Reddy, N. Tirupathaiah, S. Ramalakshmi, APMAS, Hyderabad, India.
3. APMAS (2011), Self Help Movement, Annual Report.

4. D. Rajasekhar (2004): "Social and Economic Change Monographs", Micro- Finance Poverty Alleviation and Empowerment of Women: A study of Two NGOs from Andhra Pradesh and Karnataka, Institute for Social and Economic Change, Bangalore, India.
5. Ghate Prabhu (2007), Indian Microfinance – The Challenges of Rapid Growth, Sage Publication, New Delhi.
6. NABARD (2010). Banking with the poor; Financing Self Help Groups, NABARD, Hyderabad.
7. Narasimha Rao, C. (2009). *Rural Development in India: A Multi Disciplinary Analysis.* New Delhi: Serials Publications.Rajan Vithal (2010), Killing the FMI Golden Goose, Economic and Political Weekly, December 4, Vol. XLV, No. 49. SERP (2011), Annual Report **SEWA** (1996). "Self Employed Women's Association (SEWA)", Ahmedabad: SEWA.http://www.scrap.gov.in

34

Self Help Groups and Social Inclusion of Women: A Few Stylized Facts

Siddaraju V.G

Abstract: *Social exclusion, discrimination and identity formation have become central focus of discourses in India today. Social exclusion and discrimination refer to the process and outcome of keeping a social group outside the power centres and resources. Poverty and unemployment are the two major problems of under developed countries, to which India is no exception. Self Help Groups (SHGs) can be defined as supportive educational and usually change oriented mutual aid group that addresses life problems or conditions commonly shared by all members. Empowerment is a multi-dimensional process, which should enable women or group of women to realize their full identity and power in all spheres of life. Many studies show that the functional SHG respondents had expressed personal empowerment in terms of authority in planning, decision making, implementation and evaluation of the SHG's programmes.*

With this background, the present study aims to identify the motivational factors of the women's for formation of SHGs and to analyse the decision making power of women in SHGs. The study was conducted in Shimoga district of Karnataka during 2010-11.

SHGs play an important role in empowering women in India. A considerable proportion of members had acquired the vital personal skills including affixing their signature and dealing with cash. Almost all members had these basic skills which were essential for them when dealing with the SHGs. But the important skills of reading and calculating continued to remain un-upgraded since no specific activities were taken up by the SHGs in this regard. Partial improvement in making need-based communication, acquiring information, acquiring higher skills in financial dealings, asserting themselves in children's education decisions was seen among majority of the members.

Keywords: Social exclusion, SHGs, Motivating factor, Decision making and Empowerment

Introduction

Social exclusion, discrimination and identity formation have become central focus of discourses in India today. Social exclusion and discrimination refer to the process and outcome of keeping a social group outside the power centres and resources. Identity formation on the one hand refers to the process and the effect of articulating this social isolation and on the other hand reformulating ones social characteristics and consequently self-determination. As long as those individuals and social groups who are subject to exclusion remain silent then there is no conflict. However, the moment they articulate their exclusion and demand their constitutional and human rights then those who had subjected them to exclusion unleash a reign of terror on them. Exclusion, discrimination and identity formation are both individual and collective processes. Moreover, exclusion, discrimination and identity take place in an interactional process. Further, exclusion and discrimination take different form in different societies. Moreover, they adapt and change themselves according to the changing social reality. Hence, to state that in the modern, liberal society and polity, exclusion and discrimination are reduced or eliminated seem to be not in tune with the reality. In the same vein to deny, the scope of identity formation of even the most discriminated social group also seems to be unrealistic. Social exclusion defines boundaries between groups, locates the different social groups in a hierarchy, regulates, and guides their interaction. Since social exclusion is intimately and inherently related to systems of domination and oppression, it is often highly resistant to change and transformation. Thus, social exclusion becomes a focal point for social conflict.

In the Indian context, the following are the excluded persons:

- **Social Groups:** Dalits/ untouchables/ lower castes, Tribals/ Adivasis/Indigenous peoples, religious and linguistic minorities, the most backward castes, especially women and children among these social groups.
- **Sectoral Groups:** agricultural labourers, marginalised farmers, child labourers, domestic workers, informal workers/ unorganised sector workers, contract workers, plantation workers, fisher communities, manual scavengers, rural and forest based communities, vernacular speaking social groups, people with disability etc.

Poverty and unemployment are the two major problems of under developed countries, to which India is no exception. In India, at the end of the tenth five year plan, 26 per cent of the population was living below the poverty line and in the rural area, the percentages slightly higher (27.10 per cent). The overall employment rate is estimated to be at 7.32 per cent, while the female employment rate is around 8.5 per cent. But, the rate of growth of women unemployment in the rural area is estimated to be around 9.8 per cent. This is because of the low growth rate of new and productive employment opportunities. The union government has implemented various schemes to reduce poverty and promote gainful employment opportunities. But the most attractive scheme with less effort is the "Self Help Groups". It is atoll to remove poverty and improve rural development (Sabyasachi Das, 2003).

Self Help Groups (SHGs) can be defined as supportive educational and usually change oriented mutual aid group that addresses life problems or conditions commonly shared by all members. The purpose may be personal or for societal change or for both. In view of this, the success of the SHG's is crucial in channelising their efforts constructively through motivated and inspired individuals in the fields. In India, self help groups have been in operation for a long time in many fields. Most of the SHG's have come up due to the dynamic leadership of certain individuals with in a group or through the catalytic role played by some in developing in such groups. In rural areas, to encourage decentralised problem analysis and collective action, the formation of SHG is a positive initiative.

Empowerment is a multi-dimensional process, which should enable women or group of women to realise their full identity and power in all spheres of life (Surekharao and Rajananananna, 1999). It consists of greater access to knowledge and resources, greater autonomy in decision making to enable them to have greater ability to plan their lives, or to have greater control over the circumstances that influence their lives and free from shocks imposed on them by custom, belief and practice. Generally development with justice is expected to generate the forces that lead to empowerment of various sections of population in a country and to raise their status especially in case of women. In the present century the terms women empowerment, women welfare, gender justice have come to light in the social, economic and political development perspective of both developed and developing nations. Traditionally women in all most every society have remained a second grade citizen. Hence, neither they are allowed to get themselves educated nor they were given legal rights in the property, government and in administration.

Tripathy (2004) in the study conducted at different parts of the country revealed that the success of the economic activities taken up by the self-employed persons in SHGs largely influenced other poor people. The poor people were motivated by the decision making process, broader financial base of the SHGs in their village. They were impressed by the assets created by the group members and realized that group approach through SHGs was the only means to achieve desired goals. Sherin (1999) found that 82.69 per cent of the functional SHG respondents had expressed personal empowerment in terms of authority in planning, decision making, implementation and evaluation of the SHGs programmes while only 55.17 per cent of the non-functional SHGs respondents claimed that they had been similarly empowered. With this background, the present study is set for the following objectives.

Objectives

(a) To identify the motivational factors of the women's to formation of Self Help Groups.
(b) To analyse the decision making power taken by women in Self Help Groups.

Methodology

The study was conducted during 2010-11 in Shimoga district of Karnataka. Shimoga district has been front running districts in the SHG program in Karnataka. The districts provide an ideal region to undertake the study in view of the diverse culture, climate encompassing the *Maidan* region consisting of Shikaripura, Soraba, Shimoga and Bhadravathi blocks and *Malnad* region consisting of Thirthahalli, Sagara and Hosanagara blocks endowed with majestic Sahyadri hill range and thick forest cover. Out of 30 districts in

Karnataka, Shimoga, district was purposively selected, because of the effective and efficient functioning of the groups formed in this district. Shimoga district consists of only 7 taluks. Among the seven taluks, maximum women SHG's are concentrated on 2 taluks, namely Shimoga and Bhadravathi Taluk. Of these, Shimoga and Bhadravathi taluks were purposively selected for the study as they rank first and second in the number of women SHG's presence. The list of the villages having women SHG's was obtained from the Krishi Vigyan Kendra (KVK). Shimoga Taluk has women Self Help Groups in 58 villages and Bhadravathi Taluk has women SHG's in 92 villages. From each Taluk, five villages were selected based on the highest number of women Self Help Groups presence. From each of selected Self Help Groups, women representatives were selected as a sample for data collection. Thus, a total of 120 women were selected randomly from Self Help Groups spread throughout two taluks. The data collected from the respondents were scored, tabulated and analysed using suitable methods.

Results and Discussion

The results of data analysis are presented under the following major heads in accordance with the objectives of the study.

Socio-Economic Characteristics of SHG Members

Table 1 shows the characteristics of SHGs Members in the study area.

Table 1: Socio-economic Characteristics of SHG Members

Age *Sl. No.*	*Categories*	*Frequency*	*Percentage*
1	Young (up to 35 years)	86	71.67
2	Middle (36 to 50 years)	30	25.00
3	Old (51 years and above)	4	3.33
	Total	**120**	**100**
Education			
	Illiterate	14	11.67
	Functionally illiterate	25	20.83
	Primary school	5	4.16
	Middle school	14	11.67
	High school	48	40.00
	College	14	11.67
	Total	**120**	**100**
Marital Status			
	Married	104	86.67
	Unmarried	13	10.83
	Widow	3	2.5
	Total	120	100.00
Family Type			
	Nuclear family	79	65.83

	Joint family	41	34.17
	Total	**120**	**100.00**
Family Size			
	Small size (1-3)	7	5.82
	Medium size (4-6)	76	63.33
	Large size (above 7)	37	30.85
	Total	**120**	**100.00**
Occupation			
	Agriculture	74	61.67
	Non-agriculture	26	21.67
	Agriculture +non-agriculture	20	16.66
	Total	**120**	**100.00**

Source: Survey Data.

Table 1 shows that age and socio-economic activities are inter-related. The young and middle age group people can actively participate in the socio-economic activities, which is true in the activities of SHGs in the study area. It is observed from the Table-1 the majority of the respondents (71.67 per cent) were young aged, while 25 per cent of them aged were middle and remaining belonged to old age category (3.33 per cent). Educational background of the sample household is very important to describe as the bulk of their access to market, employment, credit, institutions, etc., is mainly dependent on the level of educational attainment by the members of the sample households. It is an essential element of human resource development as it improves the knowledge and develops required skill base among the individuals. It is observed that 40 per cent of the respondents had studied up to high school, followed by 11.67 per cent each of them were having middle school level and college level education, while 4.16 per cent of them were having just primary school level education, respectively, while 20.83 per cent and 11.67 per cent of them were functionally literate and illiterate, respectively. It was noticed that 86.67 per cent of the respondents were married, while 10.83 per cent of them were unmarried and remaining 2.5 per cent were widows. Majority of the SHG members (65.83 per cent) belonged to nuclear family and the rest (34.17 per cent) belonged to joint family category. It could be noted that 63.33 per cent of the respondents belonged to medium size family, followed by 30.85 per cent of them belonged to large size family and remaining 7.72 per cent were found to have small family size. Majority of respondents (61.67) were dependent on agriculture for their livelihood and it is considered major occupation in the sample area, while 21.67 per cent were involved in non-agricultural activities.

Table 2: Motivational Factors in the Formation of SHG's

Sl.No.	*Source*	*Proportion (per cent)*
1.	NGOs	90
2.	Other SHG members	80
3.	Bank	35
4.	Own volition	30
5.	Family members	20
6.	Neighbours	15
7.	Other Organisations	5
8.	Individual Volunteers	5
9.	Members obtaining family approval before joining SHGs	90

Source: Survey Data.

Table 2 shows the sources of motivation for the sample SHG members, for associating themselves with SHGs. Totally eight distinct sources were iterated by the respondents among which NGOs topped the list with 90 per cent of the respondents quoting it as their source of motivation followed by motivation by members of other SHGs in the locality which were quoted as the reason by 80 per cent of the sample members. Similarly bank officials were quoted as motivators by 40 per cent of the respondents. Thirty per cent of the members quoted they had joined the SHGs through their own will. Members of own family were the source of inspiration in case 20 per cent of the members. Fifteen per cent of the respondents had joined after being influenced by neighbours followed by five per cent by other organisations such as cooperative societies, mahila mandals and five per cent of the respondents being influenced to join by individual volunteers who were mostly social workers. Ninety per cent of the respondents stated they had obtained prior permission of their families before associating themselves with the SHGs.

Decision-making Behaviour

Table 3 throws light on the decision-making behaviour of the SHG members while availing credit from their SHGs. Among 55 per cent of the members borrowing from the SHG was a personal decision while in the case of 50 per cent members it was a joint decision of the member and her family. Among another 15 per cent of the members the family directed the member avail SHG loan and also decided its utilisation. Loan utilisation was left to the member's discretion in 40 per cent of the cases while both the member and the family decided the utilisation in 50 per cent of the cases.

Table 3: Decision-making behaviour of SHG members *vis-a-vis* SHG credit

Sl.No.	*Particulars*	*Proportion of SHGs members reporting (per cent)*
1.	Decision to avail loan taken as own decision by the SHG member	55.00
2.	Decision to avail loan taken as joint decision by the SHG member and her family members	50.00
3.	Decision to avail loan imposed by the SHG member's family members	15.00
4.	Utilisation of loan left to the discretion of the SHG member	40.00
5.	Utilisation of loan decided jointly by the SHG member and her family members	50.00

Source: Survey Data.

Table 4: Decisions implemented by the SHG members in their family after being influenced by their association with the SHG (percentage of members)

Sl.No.	*Activity*	*Before SHG Association*	*After SHG Association*	*Implemented as own decision*	*Implemented as personal and family decision**
	Education				
1.	Personally continuing education				
	Adult literacy programmes	—	5.00	—	100
	From primary to secondary	—	—	—	—
	From Secondary to intermediate	—	2.5	—	100
	From Intermediate to graduation/professional	—	—	—	—
2.	Details of education initiated among family members (percentage)				
	-To kindergarten	—	25.00	20.00	80.00
	-From kindergarten to primary	—	15.00	40.00	65.00
	-From secondary to intermediate	—	2.5	100	—
3.	Family education status (Percentage of beneficiaries reporting)				
	-Primary education	66.66 (2.29)	79.16 (2.44)	—	100.00
	-Secondary education	41.66 (0.78)	70.83 (1.14)	—	100.00
	-Intermediate education	23.33 (0.26)	33.33 (0.58)	—	100.00
	Total members per family	3.46	4.16	—	—
4.	Adopting/Implementing				

family planning	33.33	41.66	29.16	70.83
5. Maintaining nutrition in family's food	5.00	20.00	00	100.00
6. Maintaining general cleanliness in the premises	66.66	10.00	00	100.00
7. Encouraging general cleanliness in the vicinity of the premises	50.00	30.00	00	100.00
8. Discouraging the use of tobacco/alcohol in the family	33.33	50.00	100.00	00

Source: Survey Data.
*Figures in brackets indicate sample family averages.

Table 4 indicates the percentage of members who had implemented household decisions after being influenced by their association with SHGS. About five per cent of the members and 2.5 per cent of the members had decided to continue their education through adult literacy programme and from secondary to intermediate education respectively. Education had been initiated among the family members at the kindergarten level among 25 per cent respondents, from kindergarten to primary level by 15 per cent and from secondary to intermediate level among 2.5 per cent of the respondents. More members stated that they had ensured the initiation of education within their family after joining SHGs. At the primary education level the proportion of SHG members whose family members had enrolled for primary education rose from 66.66 per cent before association to 79.16 per cent after SHG association. Similarly the increases at the secondary level were from 41.66 per cent to 70.83 per cent and at the intermediate level it was from 23.33 per cent to 33.33 per cent.

The adoption of family planning was reported to be practiced even before their association with the SHG by 33.33 per cent of the respondents while 41.66 per cent of the respondents reported that they started family planning after SHG association. Similarly 5.00 per cent of the members said they had practiced nutrient management before joining SHG and 20.00 per cent reported that initiated nutrient management after joining SHG. About 66.66 per cent of the SHG members reported that they maintained general cleanliness in their houses even before their association while 10.00 per cent of the members stated that they had started giving extra attention to cleanliness within the house. As regards to the cleanliness in the vicinity of their houses, 50.00 per cent of the members said they maintained such cleanliness even before their association with the SHG while 30.00 per cent of the members said they had initiated cleanliness after joining the SHGs. While 33.33 per cent of the members stated that they had been discouraging the use of tobacco and alcohol even before their association with the SHGs, about 33.33 per cent of the respondents stated that they started fresh campaigns against the usage habits after they were associated with the SHGs. Except in the case of initiating education at the kindergarten, primary levels and in the case of adoption of family planning, most of the decisions were implemented by members jointly with their respective families.

Table 5: Social and personal skills gained by the members from their association with the SHG

Sl.No.	Aspect	More than before	Partially more	No Change	Can't say
1.	More confidence and improvement in dealing with people	35.00	45.00	15.00	5.00
2.	Able to contact people when confronted with problems or when in need of information	10.00	75.00	15.00	0
3.	Able to commute freely without hesitation, self consciousness	20.00	30.00	50.00	0
4.	Able to communicate freely (socially) with people without hesitation, self consciousness	0	15.00	75.00	10.00
5.	Able to conduct dealings at the bank freely without hesitation, self consciousness	80.00	20.00	0	0
6.	Able to pay bills at offices, visit post offices etc without hesitation, self consciousness	40.00	10.00	50.00	0
7.	Confident of conducting business at Gram Panchayats, and other govt offices without hesitation, self consciousness	40.00	10.00	50.00	0
8.	Learnt to affix personal signature	40.00	0	60.00	0
9.	Learnt to read	0	0	100	0
10.	Learnt to write	0	0	100	0
11.	Learnt to calculate	0	25.00	75.00	0
12.	Able to collect information on new topics such as:				
	-nutritious food	15.00	80.00	5.00	0
	-domestic cleanliness	10.00	80.00	10.00	0
	-personal hygiene	15.00	80.00	5.00	0
13.	Able to influence/ take personal decision				
	-in personal finance	25.00	40.00	30.00	0
	-routine household matters	0	0	75.00	25.00
	-in cash dealings	40.00	5.00	55.00	0
	-in the sale/purchase of property (land, buildings)	0	20.00	65.00	15.00
	-purchase of personal clothes, jewellery	20.00	80.00	0	0
	-family planning	0	0	75.00	25.00
	-children's education	0	30.00	45.00	25.00
14.	Status of self-esteem within the family	5.00	15.00	75.00	5.00

Source: Survey Data.

Table 5 displays the social and personal skills as reportedly gained by the members from their association with the SHG. A note-worthy per cent of members expressed a definite positive personal improvement in their ability/confidence to deal with people, ability to conduct dealings at the bank, at post offices, gram panchayats, and other government offices. The proportion of such members ranged from 35 per cent to 80 per cent. Learning to affix personal signature, ability to take personal decisions in personal finance, ability to conduct cash dealings were reported by 40 per cent, 25 per cent and 40 per cent of the respondents. Nearly 80 per cent of the respondents reported partial changes in matters their ability to collect information on new matters of household importance. No change was observed or required especially in matters such as commuting freely, communicating freely, dealing in post offices or gram Panchayats, affixing personal signature, ability to do basic calculation, deciding in routine household matters, transaction of property, family planning, children's education or in their perception of treatment by their respective families.

Conclusion

The overall study shows that the availing, utilisation and repayment of loans showed an asymmetry which was progressively biased against the individual women members. The proportion of members who were able to take loans based on their own decision. Thus there was a restriction as well as encroachment on the members' prerogative *vis-a-vis* her family, in the availing and utilising SHG loans. It may be recalled from the table on factors motivating the members to join SHGs, that even though 30 per cent of the members purportedly joined the SHGs on their volition, another 20 per cent members joined on the behest of their family members. Most noteworthy in this regard was that nearly 90 per cent of the members, (perhaps excluding those members who were single parent families, widows, deserted women) had to obtain prior permission to join SHGs. Thus it was evident women members had to operate within the directions of their respective families even when it came to the availing of loans. In the cases of independent utilisation the members were able to take their own decisions and were single-adult families comprising of widows, aged spinsters, and separated women. Members with age seniority in their respective homes also came under this category. Not much assertion of decision-making process of the members within their families was seen even after their association with the SHGs except for a few cases of continuation of education among children in the family, adoption of family planning and in discouraging the use of tobacco and alcohol in the families. Otherwise much of the decisions made within the families were joint decisions in which the positive note was that the women members too took part.

Most of the members had acquired social skills that they had been exposed to during the course of interaction with their respective SHGs such as conducting dealings at banks, post offices etc. A considerable proportion of members had acquired the vital personal skills of affixing their signature and dealing with cash. Almost all members had these basic skills which were essential for them when dealing with the SHGs. But the important skills of reading and calculating continued to remain un-upgraded since no specific activities were taken up by the SHGs in this regard. A lesser proportion of members professed confidence to conduct dealings in local self-administration and government offices as well - situations which they perceived to be similar to that of dealing with banks and organisation of events within the SHG. Partial improvement in making need-based communication, acquiring information, acquiring higher skills in financial dealings, asserting themselves in children's education decisions was seen among majority of the members. These could at least be partly attributed to their observation, participation in the routine as well as extra-curricular activities of the SHGs. The impact of seminars, public functions participated by the SHG had their impact in aspects of maintaining cleanliness, improving nutritional value of the food etc.

Women should be willing to take additional effort for building a mindset which is suitable for their overall empowerment. It is a gradual and consistent process which requires the support of many who cure related to them in one way or other. In a developing country like India, women empowerment is indispensable for restructure and reorientation of the society as a whole. Women empowerment means inculcating a sense of condition among the women, and making them realise that they have the ability to earn their living and a right to exercise their choices, a sense of self-worth along with the power to control their own lives, both within and outside the home. Self Help Groups play an important role in empowering the women in India.

REFERENCES

1. Das, Sabyasachi (2003), 'Self Help Groups and Micro Credit Synergic Integration", *Kurushetra* Vol. 51, No. 10, pp. 25-28.

2. Sherin, K. J. (1999), Dynamics of Self Help Group Formation - A Case Study in Thrissur District. *M. Sc. (Agri.) Thesis,* Kerala Agricultural University, Thrissur.
3. Surekharao, K. and Rajananananna, J. (1999), "Empowerment of rural women through DWCRA programme", National Conference on Empowerment of Women for National Development, Dhole, pp. 101-107.
4. Tripathy, K.K (2004), Self-help Groups, A catalyst of Rural Development, *Kurukshetra,* 34(3.): 40-43.

35

Empowering Women During Five Year Plans in India

Krishnamurthy N.T., Doddegowda and Archana G.R.

Abstract: *After independence, Indian women experience a major change in their status, her role was changed with the changing socio-economic and political environment. Now Indian women make their marks in the field of business, science and technology, education, politics, media and corporate world. At the same time the changing situation creates new problems like atrocities against women, sexual harassment, dowry deaths and gender based discrimination etc. The Government of India has taken many steps for providing equal status for women against men. In view of this the government declared the year 2001 as the 'year of women's empowerment'. In 2001 the national policy for empowerment of women and an action plan has also been adopted. The strategies of women empowerment includes: social empowerment, economic empowerment and gender justice. There is no doubt about the fact that development of women has always been the central focus of planning since independence. Empowerment is a major step in this direction but it has to be seen in a relational context. An attempt is made in this paper is to discuss the empowering women in India's five year plans.*

Key words: Empowerment, Women Development, National Commission.

Introduction

The ability of women to control their own fertility is absolutely fundamental to women's empowerment and equality. When a woman can plan her family, she can plan the rest of her life. When she is healthy, she can be more productive. And when her reproductive rights-including the right to decide the number, timing and spacing of her children, and to make decisions regarding reproduction free of discrimination, coercion and violence- are promoted and protected, she has freedom to participate more fully and equally in society. Where women's status is low, family size tends to be large, which makes it more difficult for families to thrive. Population and development and reproductive health programmes are more effective when they address the educational opportunities, status and empowerment of women. When women are empowered, whole families benefit, and these benefits often have ripple effects to future generations.

Women empowerment refers to the process of strengthening the hands of women who have been suffering from various disabilities, inequalities and gender discrimination. Women others and it is the process of providing equal right, responsibilities and opportunities to women. Empowerment is the process of providing power to women to become free from the control. There is no doubt about the fact that development of women has always been the central focus of planning since independence. Empowerment is a major step in this direction but it has to be seen in a relational context. In recent years there have been explicit moves to increase women's political participation. The Women's reservation policy bill is however a very sad story as it is repeatedly being scuttled in parliament. But after a long battle, the resolution has been passed in parliament on ninth March 2010. A clear vision is needed to remove the obstacles to the path of women's emancipation both from the government and women themselves. Efforts should be directed towards entire development of each and every section of Indian women by giving them their due share.

The Government of India had ushered the new millennium by declaring the year 2001 as 'Women's Empowerment Year' to focus on the theme 'women are equal partners like men'. The most common explanation of 'women's empowerment' is the ability to exercise full control over one's actions. The last decades have witnessed some basic changes in the status and role of women in our society. There has been a shift in policy approaches from the concept of 'welfare' in the seventies to 'development' in the eighties and now to 'empowerment' in the nineties. An overview of how the Five Year Plans looked at women in India in the context of development gives us a clear picture of changes in vision, strategies of welfare in involving programmes.

Objectives

The main aim of this paper is to analyses the empowering women during plan periods. It also aims at studying the national commission for women.

Methodology

The paper is based on only the secondary sources of data. The secondary data were collected from books, journals, published and unpublished thesis, Five Year Plan Document, reports of the bureau of economics and statistics, Government of Karnataka publications on women empowerment, etc.

Women in Development Planning

The importance of the role of women in development had been recognised by the Government of India right from the very first five year plan (1951-56). However, women in these earlier plans were treated as subjects of 'welfare' and clubbed together under the category of disadvantaged groups such as destitute, disabled, aged, etc. The Second to Fifth Plans (1956-79) continued to reflect the very same welfare approach, besides giving priority to women's education, and launching measures to improve maternal and child health services, supplementary feeding for children and expectant and nursing mothers. The Central Social Welfare Board (CSWB), set up in 1953, served as an Apex Body at the national level to promote voluntary action at various levels, especially at the grassroots, to take up these welfare-related activities for women and children.

Women as Partners in Development

In the beginning of seventies, the development was not proceeding as planned and the fact was realised that women did not actively participate in the process. It was underlined that women must be urgently equipped with the capabilities required for them to take up these new responsibilities. These revelations and recommendations gave birth to the concept of women as "partners" in development and took the importance of their education to a new threshold. However, it was after the early seventies, that there was a gradual shift in the approach from welfare to development, which started recognising women as important participants of the developmental process.

In 1971, in response to request from the United Nations, the Government of India appointed a Committee on the Status of Women in India (CSWI) to examine all questions relating to the rights and status of women in the context of changing social and economic conditions in the country. The Committee's comprehensive report named "Towards Equality" saw a significant change in the government's policies for women. Women were now no longer viewed as targets of welfare policies but as critical groups for development. This was reflected in the Sixth Five Year Plan (1980-85) where strategies for women's employment and economic independence, education, healthcare and family planning and the creation of a supportive legal and institutional environment were conceived. It was for the first time the Planning Commission included a separate chapter on 'Women and Development' in the Sixth Five Year Plan.

In the Seventh Plan (1985-90), the developmental programmes continued with the major objectives of raising the economic and social status of women and bringing them into the mainstream of national development. In the year 1985, the Department of Women and Child Development was set up as a part of the Ministry of Human Resource Development. This department plans and implements certain innovative programmes for women and children. The major policy initiatives undertaken by the department in the recent past include the establishment of the National Commission for Women (NCW), Rashtriya Mahila Kosh (RMK), adoption of National Nutrition Policy (NNP), setting up of National Creche Fund (NCF), launching of Indira Mahila Yojana (IMY), Balika Samriddhi Yojana (BSY) and Rural Women's Development and Empowerment Project (RWDEP).

The Eighth Plan (1992-97), with human development as its major focus, played a very important role in the development of women. The Eighth Plan promised to ensure the benefits of development from different sectors and did not by-pass women, the Eight plan implemented special programmes to complement the general development programmes and to monitor the flow of benefits to women from other development sectors which enabled women to function as equal partners and participants in development process.

Life Cycle Approach

In the Ninth Plan (1997-2002), the Planning Commission, with a view to converge the benefits in the social and economic development sectors for women had requested all the Secretaries of the various

Ministries and Departments of the Government of India to draw up a Women's Component Plan to identify allocation in all the sectors at the Centre by aggregating them in an integrated manner. The Ninth Plan adopted the Life Cycle approach in the empowerment of women which categorises women in to five district sub-groups (population as projected for 2001). They include:

- Girl children in the age group 0-14 years who account for 171.50 million (34.6 per cent), deserve special attention because of the gender bias and discrimination they suffer from at such a tender age.
- Adolescent girls in the age-group 15-19 years who account for 52.24 million (10.5 per cent) are very sensitive from the viewpoint of planning because of the preparatory state for their future productive and reproductive roles in the society and family, respectively.
- Women in the reproductive age-group 15-44 years numbering 233.72 million (47.1 per cent) need special care and attention because of their reproductive needs.
- Women in the economically active age group 15-59 years, who account for 289.40 million (58.4 per cent) have different kind of demands like education/training, employment, income generation and participation in the developmental process, decision making etc.
- The elderly women in the age-group 60+ years numbering 34.87 million (Seven per cent) have limited needs mainly relating to health, financial and emotional support.

Commitments of Ninth Plan

The main objective is to empowering Women as the Agents of Social Change and Development.

Strategies

- To create an enabling environment for women to exercise their rights, both within and outside home as equal partners along with men through early finalisation and adoption of "National Policy for Empowerment of Women.
- To expedite action to legislate reservation of not less than 1/3rd seats for women in the parliament and in the State Legislative Assemblies and thus ensure adequate representation of women in decision making.
- To adopt and integrated approach towards empowering women through effective convergence of existing services, resources,

infrastructure and manpower in both women specific and women related sectors.

- To adopt a special strategy of "Women's Component Plan" to ensure that not les than 30 per cent of funds/benefits flow to women from other developmental sectors.
- To organise women into Self Help Groups and thus mark the beginning of a major process of empowering women. The Self-Help Groups developed and to provide a permanent forum for articulating their perspectives to development.
- To increase access to credit through setting up of a Development Bank for Women Entrepreneurs in small and tiny sectors.

Commitments of the Tenth Plan

This plan approach is to continue with the major strategy of Empowering Women as Agents of Social Change and Development.

Strategies

To adopt a Sector-specific Three-Fold Strategy for Empowering Women based on the prescriptions of the National Policy for Empowerment of Women. They include:

- **Social Empowerment:** To create an enabling environment through various affirmative developmental policies and programmes for the development of women besides providing them easy and equal access to all the basic minimum services so as to enable them to realise their full potentials.
- **Economic Empowerment:** To ensure provision of training, employment and income-generation activities with both forward and backward linkages with the ultimate objective of making all potential women economically independent and self-reliant, and
- **Gender Justice:** To eliminate all forms of gender discrimination and thus, allow women to enjoy not only the de-jure but also the de-facto rights and fundamental freedom on par with men in all spheres like political, economic, social, civil, cultural etc.

Eleventh Plan and Women Empowerment

The main task of the XI FYP is to ensure that women are at the centre stage of all the activities–economic, social and political. The crucial areas concerning themselves, to a large extent, suggest the thrust areas that are required to be kept in view in the Eleventh Plan, while priority will continue to be laid on health, nutrition, education, income generating activities, relief and rehabilitation for women in distress. Micro credit will be continued to remain the backbone of SHG finances and therefore will need to be strengthened and streamlined in the Eleventh Plan. There have been many instances of exploitative rates of interest charged by the unscrupulous agencies which has led to economic distress in many parts of the country. Therefore it is imperative that the Ministry of Finance formulates a regulatory mechanism for micro credit lending to make the system more transparent and beneficial.

National Commission for Women

The National Commission for Women was set up in 1992 to protect and safeguard the rights of women. The activities of the Commission include receiving complaints or suo moto enquiring in cases of deprivation of rights of women, providing counseling, conducting Parivarik Lok Adalats and legal awareness programmes and organising public hearings. The National Commission for Women being the nodal agency for protection of the rights of women needs to be strengthened. The NCW Act needs to be suitable amended to give the Commission more power. The requirement of funds for the XI Plan for the activities of the Commission is estimated as Rs 35 crore.

The Ministry of Women and Child Development, as the nodal agency for all matters pertaining to welfare, development and empowerment of women, has evolved schemes and programmes for their benefit. These schemes are spread across a broader spectrum such as women's need for shelter, security, safety, legal aid, justice, information, material health, food, nutrition etc as well as their need for economic sustenance through skill development, education and access to credit and marketing. The schemes of the Ministry like Swashakti, Swayamsidha, STEP and Swawlamban enable economic empowerment. Working Women Hostels and Creches provide support services. Swadhar and Short Stay Homes provide protection and rehabilitation to women in difficult circumstances. The Ministry also supports autonomous bodies like National Commission, Central Social Welfare Board and Rashtriya Mahila Kosh which work for the welfare and development of women. These schemes were run in the Tenth Plan. It was proposed to continue some in the Eleventh Plan and also to take up new schemes.

Recently, the Sexual Harassment of Women at Workplace (prevention, prohibition and redressal) Act 2013 enacted on 9th December 2013 covers all women against sexual harassment at the workplace in both the public and private sectors. Similarly, in order to prevent violence against women, comprehensive amendments were introduced in the Indian penal code through the Criminal Law (Amendment) Act 2013 that makes provisions more stringent. A high-level committee on the status of women was also set up on 24th May 2013 to prepare a report on the current socio-economic, political, health, and legal status of women in India and recommend measures for empowerment of women. The committee is mandated to present its report within two years.

Conclusion

We may conclude that, women in modern India comparatively in a more respectable position. The constitution of India provides equal rights and opportunities to women. The development in the field of science and technology, universalisation of education, socio-political movement, modernisation, globalisation and similar development changed the approach of people towards Women to a certain extent. The celebration of International Women's Year in 1975 and the activities of UNESCO also created awareness of the problems of women. There development boasted the morale and self–confidence of women as a result Indian women now feel that they too have their own individuality, personality, self respect, talent, capacity and efficiency. The changing socio-economic conditions provide both opportunities and challenges for women. It is true that, during five year plans, Government of India have taken a number of policies and progammes to empowerment of women but empowerment by itself may not place women on an equal status with men. The greatest need is to change of social attitudes towards women.

REFERENCES

1. Reports of Five Year Plans.
2. Census of India, 2011 and www.google.com.
3. Annual Report, NABARD, 2006-07.
4. Lalitha N. "Rural Women Empowerment and Development Banking" Kaniska Publishers, New Delhi.
5. Economic Survey 2013-14.
6. Adhunika Bharathada Arthikathe- Dr. Ne.Thi. Somashekar, Chaithra Publication, Bangalore.

36

Micro Finance as a Powerful Tool for Rural Agriculture Development in India

V. Vijay and P. Devaraj

Abstract: *Microfinance stands as one of the most promising and cost effective tools which fight against global poverty. Need of Micro Finance is more essential in India especially, in every rural economy. The responsibility of meeting the credit needs in the rural areas of India was entrusted primarily with the cooperative sector and later to the commercial banks. Micro finance interventions are well organised world over as effective tool for poverty alleviations and improving socio-economic status of rural farmers. The need for micro finance arises especially in rural India because rural people require finance for poverty alleviation, procurement of farm inputs.*

Micro finance is a programme to support the rural farmers to pay its debt and maintain socio-economic status in the villages. As we know that India is agriculture based economy and most of rural farmers suffer from poverty and lack of finance. Micro finance may be a tool to empower the farmers and rural people to make agriculture profitable. Our research work includes various data relating to micro finance institutions and their lending model. This research paper attempts to bring out the effectiveness of micro finance in rural development. The study focuses on various factors contributing to rural development in India. It shows how the micro finance

Institutions can help the people of rural India, especially how micro finance institutions help to promote rural development by accelerating farm and non-farm activities in rural areas. An attempt is made to study the impact of financial inclusion and micro finance on income generation and livelihood of the farmers in villages.

Key words: Micro finance, poverty alleviations, credit delivery, rural / agriculture development.

Introduction

Today the world is reeling under the sub-prime crisis and the impact of so-called innovative finance derivative products. What has this got to do with small farmers in India? First, we are having farmer's suicides, the main cause of which is high debt. And since these farmers don't have protection under any 'limited liability' laws, nor are their bonuses protected, they stand to lose their land, and pass on their liability to their helpless children. Micro finance programme has been introduced in many countries since it has been considered as an important Tool to combat poverty, especially powerful weapon to fight against farmer's problems in villages. Micro finance is a type of banking service that is provided to unemployed or low-income individuals or poor farmers who would otherwise have no other means of gaining financial services. Ultimately, the goal of microfinance is to give low income people an opportunity to become self-sufficient by providing a means of saving money, borrowing money and insurance. Micro finance is not just about giving Micro credit to the needy farmers rather it is an economic development tool to assist poor farmers to work their way out of poverty. It also covers a wide range of services like credit savings, insurance, remittance and also non financial services like training, consulting etc.

Need for Microfinance

- The need for microfinance arises because the rural India requires sources of finance for poverty alleviation, procurement of agricultural and farms input.
- Micro finance is a programme to support the poor rural farmers to pay their debt and maintain social and economic status in the villages.
- As we know that India is agriculture based economy so microfinance may be a tools to empower the farmers and rural peoples to make agriculture profitable.

- Micro finance also need so it help and act as most powerful instrument to raise productivity and activities of farmers in every rural area.
- So the researchers are interested to find out the scopes of microfinance in rural India. This research paper is highlighting a picture rural India as a profitable segment for microfinance institutions.

Objective of the Study

The prime objective of this study is to show real effects of Microfinance on rural development especially how it makes impact on poor farmers and how change their socio-economic life. It concentrates on studying effect of Microfinance on rural people in general and poor farmers in particular.

Methodology and Limitations of the Study

Our study is based on the secondary data collection and therefore the accuracy and the reliability of the data is based on the same. Data taken from NABARD issues related to micro finance institutions, from many of micro finances institutions and from journals, newspapers etc. Further this study limits only effectiveness of MFIs in rural areas. This study explains growth of MFIs how it helps to accelerate farm activities and how it act as important tool for rural agriculture development.

International scenario

Microfinance as a part of financial sector is expected to be influenced directly or indirectly by the positive or negative changes that take place in the global economy or the regional financial market. Ranking of the top ten countries in micro finance revealed that Peru continued to top the list with the highest score followed by Bolivia and Pakistan. India which was in the list of the top ten countries during the year 2010 could not retain their position in 2011 and hence got hence got dropped from the list. On the other hand, countries such as Uganda, Mexico and Panama have gained entry into the list of the top ten countries. Mexico and Panama, have occupied the tenth position. Now India has been pushed to the 27th rank with a score of 43.1 in the overall microfinance business environment. It occupied the 22nd rank in regulatory framework and practices, the 20th place in supporting institutional framework and 40th rank in terms of stability. The government of India strongly promoted the Self Help Group model through the National Livelihood Mission (NLM) by offering cheap funding and also restricted market based lending.

Table 1: Ranking of top 10 countries in micro finance in 2011-2012

Rank	*Country*	*Score in 2011-12*	*Change from 2010*
1.	Peru	67.8	-6.5
2.	Bolivia	64.7	-4.9
3.	Pakistan	62.8	-2
4.	Kenya	60.3	5.3
5.	El Salvador	58.8	-2.5
6.	Philippines	58.5	-13.3
7.	Colombia	56.0	-0.8
8.	Ecuador	55.1	-0.8
9.	Uganda	53.7	New entrant
10.	Mexico and Panama	53.6	New entrant
27.	India	43.1	Not in list of top 10 countries

Sources: Global Microscope on the Micro Finance Business Environment, 2009-12.

National Scenario

In India development of different micro finance institutions since from long time period ago. We have different MFIs working with different branches and with different lending model. In Karnataka some working of MFIs likes Shri Ksehetra Dharmasthala Rural Development Projects (SKDRDP), BSS Micro finance Pvt Ltd (BMPL), Grameen Financial Services Pvt Ltd (GFSPL), Ujjivan Financial Services Pvt Ltd (UFSPL), RORES Micro Entrepreneur Development Trust (RMEDT) Etc. some other working of MFIs like SKS Micro Finance Ltd (SKSMFL), Spandana Sphoorty Financial Ltd (SPFL), Share Micro Finlimited (SML), Future Financial Services Ltd (FFSL) ETC. In India various MFIs works with different places in our country with different legal status and different loan lending model.

The growth of microfinance is visible in many aspects. There are more than 2000 NGOs involved in the NABARD SHG-Bank linkage programme. Out of these, approximately 800 NGOs are involved in some form of financial intermediation. Further, there are 350 new generation co-operatives providing thrift and credit services. According to our estimate, the present total outstanding, including Sa-Dhan members and bank linkages is approximately Rs 700 crores (Rs 150 crores of Sa-Dhan members and another Rs 550 crores from the Banking system). The total client base is estimated at six to eight million as opposed to the Government of India (GOI) intention to reach 25 million clients. The growth of community institutions has taken place with the role to take social and financial intermediation. A numbers of community banks have come into existence at village and block levels call 'Federation of Self Help Groups'. The inadequacies of the formal financial system to cater to the needs of the poor and the realisation of the fact that the key to success lies in the evolution and participation of community-based organisations at the grassroots level led to the emergence of new generation of MFIs.

One kind of MFI is an NGO engaged in promoting Self Help Groups (SHGs) and their federations at a cluster level and linking SHGs with Banks under the Scheme. Examples are MYRADA in Karnataka, which has promoted Sanghmitra, a company of its village saving and credit Sanghas, PRADAN which has established a large number of SHGs and federated them under Damodar in Bihar, Sakhi Samiti in Rajasthan. Another kind is NGO-MFI directly lending to the poor borrowers, who are either organised into SHGs or into Grameen Bank type of groups after borrowing bulk funds from SIDBI, RMK and FWWB. Examples in this category are Rashtriya Gramin Vikas Nidhi (RGVN) which runs credit and savings programme in Assam and Orissa on the lines of Grameen Bank, Bangladesh. Also we have SHARE in AP, ASA in Tamil Nadu under this category. There are MFIs which are specifically organized as cooperatives, such as over 500 Mutually Aided Cooperative Thrift and Credit Societies (MACTS) in AP, promoted among others by Cooperative Development Foundation (CDF) and the SEWA Bank in Gujarat which also runs federations of SHGs in nine districts. Then we have MFIs, which are organised as Non-Banking Finance Companies (NBFC) such as BASIX, CFTS Mirzapur, and SHARE Micro Fin Ltd and Sarvodaya Nanofinance Ltd.

Table 2 shows working of some MFIs in rural areas for promoting rural and farm activities in India which appeared on the basis of loan amount outstanding in India. It also shows its lending model and its total loan borrowers. Ratios are computed as the MFIs acquired loan portfolio only upto September 2008-2009.

Table 2: Microfinance institutions in India (On the basis of loan amount outstanding)

Name of MFIs	*Headquartered in*	*Legal status*	*Lending model*	*Number of Branches*	*Loans o/s (Rs Mln)*	*Borrowers (No)*
1. SKS Micro finance Ltd (SKSMPL)	Secunderabad, Andhra Pradesh	Pvt Ltd. Company (NBFC)	JLG	1,413	18,227	25,90,950
2. Shree Mcrofin Ltd (SML)	Hyderabad, Andhra Pradesh	Public Ltd. Company (NBFC)	JLG	666	8,568	1,231,556
3. Shri Kshetra Dharmasthala Rural Development Project (SKDRDP)	Dharmasthala, Karnataka	Trust	SHG	22	4,060	612,482

4. Bandhan	Kolkata, West Bengal	Society	JLG	385	3,389	851,713
5. Grameen Financial Services Pvt Ltd (GFSPL)	Bangalore, Karnataka	Pvt. Ltd. Company (NBFC)	JLG	62	1,287	153,453
6. S.M.I.L.E Microfinance Limited	Chennai, Tamil Nadu	Public Ltd. Company	JLG	87	757,7	141,879
7. Gram Utthan	Kendrapara, Orissa	Society	Jlg	20	439	64,100
8. Centre for Rural Reconst-ruction through Social ACTION	Rajahmundry Andhra Pradesh	Society	JLG	15	200	32,491
9. Village Financial Services Pvt Ltd (VFSPL)	Kolkata, West Bengal	Pvt. Ltd Company (NBFC)	JLG	13	209	55,371
10. Gandhi Smaraka Grama Sava Kendram	Alappuzha, Kerala	Society	SHG	15	162	24,201

Source: NABARD Publications related to micro finance.

In India micro finance operates two channels:

1. SHG-Bank Linkage Programme (SBLP)
2. Micro finance Institutions (MFIs)

SHG-Bank Linkage Programme

This is the bank led microfinance channel which was initiated by NABARD in 1992. Under the SHG model the members, usually women in villages are encouraged to form groups of around 10-15. The members contribute their savings in the group periodically and from these savings small loans provided to members. In the latter period these SHGs are provided with the bank loans generally for income generation purposes. the group's members meet periodically when the new saving come in, recovery of past loans are made free from the members and also new loans are disturbed. The SHGs are self sustaining and once the groups become stable it starts working on its own with some support from NGOs.

Micro finance institutions

Those institutions which have microfinance as their main operation are known as micro finance institutions. A number of organisations with varied size and legal forms offer micro finance services. These institutions lend through the concept of Joint Liability Group (JLG). A JLG is an informal group comprising of five/ten individuals members who come together for the purposes of availing bank loans either individually or through the group mechanism against a mutual guarantee.

Table 2: Shows structure and organisation of MFIs in India

Sl.No.	*Type of MFI*	*Number*	*Legal Registration*
		Not-for-Profit MFI	
1.	NGOs	400-500	Society Registration Axt, 1860 Indian Trust Act,1882
2.	Non-profit companies	20	Section -25 of Indian Companies Act, 1956
		Mutual Benefit MFIs	
3.	Mutual Benefit MFIs-Mutually Aided cooperatives societies (MACS)	200-500	Mutually Aided Co-operatives societies, Act enacted BY State Government
	For Profit MFIs		
4.	Non Banking Financial Companies (NBFCs)	45	Indian Companies Act, 1956 Reserve Bank of Indian Act, 1934

Source: NABARD Publications related to micro finance.

Need for Microfinance in India

According to the latest research done by the World Bank, India is home to almost one-third of the world's poor. Though many central government and state government poverty alleviation programme are currently active in India, Micro finance plays a major contributor to financial inclusion. In the past few decades it has helped out remarkably in eradicating poverty. Many of reports shows that people who have taken micro finance have been able to increase their income and hence the standard of living.

About half of the Indian population still doesn't have a savings bank account and they are deprived of all banking services. Poor also need financial services to fulfil their needs like consumption, building of assets and protection against risk. Micro finance institutions serve as a supplement to banks and in some sense a better one too. These institutions not only offer micro credit but they also provide other financial services like savings, insurance, remittance and non financial services like individual counselling, training and support to start own business and the most importantly in a convenient way. The borrower receives all these services at their door steps and in most cases with repayment schedules of borrower's convenience. Some MFIs were created with a mission to serve poor farmers, but most have focused on urban and peri-urban clients and rural areas with high population densities. Increasingly, however, many have begun to penetrate further into rural areas and serve farm clients. Underserved markets, overconcentration and saturation in urban areas, and a drive to realize economics of scale have contributed to this trend.

There are clear linkages between food production at small scale as a problem and micro finance as a solution to that problem. Food production is a multi dimensional problem and micro finance encompasses a multi dimensional response. Further micro finance can play an instrumental role in moving small holder farming from subsistence to commercial farming. Micro finance is considered as a development tool to alleviate poverty in Asian, African and South American countries. Micro finance gives quick and tangible results to the poor people especially women. Micro finance is required by the poor people to invest in income generating activities which will break their vicious cycle of poverty. It has been accepted that micro finance plays a vital role in reducing poverty since it paves way for employment and empowerment which leads to economic development. Poverty can be eradicated only by employment opportunities and the employment seeker and worker should become a job provider. This is possible through micro finance coupled with micro enterprises. But still micro finance plays a modest role in India. At all India level, less than five per cent of rural poor households have access to micro finance as compared to 65 per cent in Bangladesh.

Effectiveness of Micro finance on Rural Agriculture Development

Poverty alleviation in rural areas has been one of the important programmes of the Indian government has considerably enhanced allocation for the provision of agricultural inputs like tools, machines and other equipments which promote capacity building and well being of the rural farmers. The development of micro finance as the most effective tools for financial inclusion was started year ago which promote activities and socio economic life of poor farmers in village areas. The biggest challenge for our country is generate enough employment and income opportunity for the rural and urban poor, but in a sustainable manner. That can be easily done through development of micro finance institutions which empowers rural farmers in village sector.

Empowerment of the rural farmers with micro finance institution is a powerful instrument to change the conditions of farmers socially and economically in every rural area. The number of micro finance institutions enables economic, social, political and psychological empowerment of rural farmers. It provides many economic benefits to the farmers by providing income generating activities through many loans lending schemes and providing other services. It improves status of the farmers which has been proved very fruitful to reduce the poverty of the rural farmers. Getting of economic support or loans through various micro finance institutions helps the rural farmers not only economically but also socially, further this strengthens the whole village sector areas in general. Micro enterprises can play an important role in improving the quality of life of the poor farmers through creating income generation activities. Micro enterprises contribute significantly to economic growth, social stability especially in rural agriculture areas.

We find effects of micro finance on individual low income households and on poor farm group in maximum village sectors have been studied through microeconomic impact studies. There aspects are generally highlighted. Firstly, there is an increased capacity to deal with risk through the withdrawal of savings or obtaining credit in the case of an emergency. This may mean that productive assets (machinery, inventory, land, livestock) need not be sold during the emergency thus that the flow of income need not interrupted. Secondly, there is an improved management of consumption requirements over the year, to maintain adequate levels of food intake. This is major importance, as labour is often the main resource of low income households. Thirdly, opportunities to invest in productive enterprises increase. These increased capabilities of rural households to produce, consume and invest may be reflected only partly in the actual credit and savings relationships with the micro finance institutions, because reliable access to microfinance forms a potential that can be tapped if and when required.

Extrapolate the effects of microfinance on individual households to rural areas in total gives some idea of the overall consequences. The increased individual capacity to deal with shocks reduces the effects of a co-variant shock for the rural population as a whole, at least when substantial proportion of the population is within the financial frontier. Further, increased saving in financial assets means a shift away from storing wealth in assets with zero or low productivity. The financial savings become available for investment in agriculture, in agriculture related trade, and processing, and in a host of other enterprises with expected benefits for technological. In a later stage, when remunerative investment opportunities in rural areas become limited and volume of savings overtakes the volume of credit, excess capital can be channelled via microfinance institutions and the national banking system to urban areas where large scale industries and services offer extensive investment opportunities. In this way, rural savers will benefits from those investment and children of the savers might find the urban jobs they are looking for. So process of increased saving in financial assets followed by intermediation by the banking system and investment by borrowers has been increased extensively at the national level.

Findings of the Study

The study proved that there is improved credit availability through development of micro finance Institutions to the farmers, who so far remained out of the institutional credit delivery and also shows that development of micro finance institutions helps to promote agriculture and allied activities such as rearing sheep, goat and milch animals. Growth of micro finance institutions also help to promote nonfarm activities in rural areas. Micro finance has contributed for the increased income as well as increased the expenditure. It has significantly contributed to the improvements in the economic growth of the respondents by increasing income and changing expenditure and consumption pattern.

Policy Suggestions

Our study on micro finance institutions shows the promotion in rural activities and farm activities in various agriculture sector of our economy. But strengthening micro finance institutions is necessary in many unreachable places where people far away from institutional credit delivery. Meeting, orientation programme, workshops and seminars may be organised where the members will get a chance to exchange their views and able to develop their group strength by infractions. Secondly, active intervention by district administration, professional bodies and voluntary organisation is pre conditions for the successful connectional of empowerment of farm activities through the micro finance in terms of credit delivery, skill training, assets building, enhancing decision making skills related to monetary issues and other issues of famers in rural economy. People should come forward to create awareness about Microfinance institutions and its participations for rural agriculture development.

Conclusion

In conclusion, I will like to say that it has been an interesting endeavour conduct survey on the microfinance institutions. If the plans for microfinance are executed then India will definitely have new dimension to it. It will increase India's standard and make it one of the powerful nations of the world economically. Finance is the lubricant, which oils the wheels of development. Indian economic development relay mainly on development of agriculture. All economies rely upon the intermediary function of finance to transfer resources from savers to investors. In market economies, this function is performed by commercial banks, financial institutions and capital markets. The potential for growing micro finance institutions in India is very high. Major cross-section can have benefit if this sector will grow in its fastest pace. Financial institutions will need to educate villagers on the ease of procedures for availing loans and at reasonable rates of interest. Micros financing through SHG help the poor save more get easy credit which promote their income generate activities. Hence microfinance should provide both savings and loan facilities. Bringing financial services to rural clients is the biggest challenge in the quest for broad-based financial inclusion. Often the main barrier to financial inclusion in rural areas is the great distances that rural residents must travel to reach a bank branch. In many developing countries there are fewer bank branches per rural resident than per urban resident. But development of microfinance institutions helps to extends credit and savings to the poor. Development of MFIs help to accelerates rural economy by promoting the rural farm works, so in developing economy like India micro finance institutions treated as a powerful tool for removing poverty and develop farm work in rural agriculture sector.

REFERENCES

1. Karmakar, K. G, "Rural Credit and Self Help Groups: Mir Finance needs and concepts in India". Sage Publication, New Delhi, India.
2. Anish Chowdhury, "Micro Finance as a Poverty Reduction Tool - A critical Assessment" (Desa Working Paper No. 89).
3. Basu, P. and P. Srivastava (2005), "Exploring Possibilities: Microfinance and Rural Credit".
4. Gupta, M.S. 2008. "Micro Finance through Self Help Groups: An emerging Horizon for Rural Development", Indian Journal of Commerce.
5. Ghate, P. (2006): "Microfinance in India: A State of the Sector Report, 2006", CARE & Ford Foundation, New Delhi.
6. Barry (1996), "Role of Micro Finance Institution in Rural Development," International Journal of Information Technology and Knowledge Management, pp. 435-41.

7. NABARD (2012), "Status of Micro Finance In 2011-2012" http://www.nabard.org
8. Government of India Economic Survey 2009, New Delhi, 2010.

37

Micro Finance in India—The Legal Hurdles

Gagan Krishnadas

Abstract: *Micro Finance can be defined as financial packages which extend small loans to very poor people for self-employment projects that generate income, allowing them to care for themselves and their families. Micro Finance is helpful for small traders and helps the economy in a big way due to the presence of large number of traders who borrow small amounts.*

This paper studies the historical development of micro finance in India; Micro Finance institutional structure; the problems faced by the mainstream micro finance institutions. The study is based on data from the secondary sources. Two case studies have been discussed in order to know the way in which micro finance works in India. In conclusion, the paper suggests certain reforms in the micro finance sector and recommends the government to pass the long pending Micro Finance Bill to enforce these reforms.

"My vision for the future? Two things: to make credit a human right so that each individual human being will have the opportunity to take loans and implement his or her ideas so that self-exploration becomes possible. And second: that it will lead to a world where nobody has to suffer from poverty - a world completely free from poverty."

- Muhammad Yunus[1]

Introduction

Micro Finance can be defined as financial packages which extend small loans to very poor people for self-employment projects that generate income, allowing them to care for themselves and their families.[2]

The institutions providing Micro Credit facilities are either registered as:

1. Society under Societies Registration Act 1860,
2. Trust under Indian Trusts Act 1920,
3. Company under Indian Companies Act, 1956.

The ministry of corporate affairs is primarily concerned with administration of the Companies Act, 1956 and carrying out the functions of the Central Government relating to administration of Societies Registration Act, 1980.[3] Hence, the knowledge of micro credit will be of academic interest to the company secretaries' professionals.

History of Microfinance in India

In India, institutional credit agencies (banks) made an entry in rural areas initially to provide an alternative to the rural money lenders who provided credit support, but not without exploiting the rural poor. There are three main factors that count to the success of *Microfinance* as a Policy in India:

1. The first of these pivotal events was Indira Gandhi's bank nationalisation drive launched in 1969 which required commercial banks to open rural branches resulting in an increase in rural bank branches in India between 1973 and 1985.[4]
2. The second national policy that has had a significant impact on the evolution of India's banking and financial system is the Integrated Rural Development Programme (IRDP) introduced in 1978 and designed to be 'a direct instrument for attacking India's rural poverty.' This programme is interesting to this study because it was a large programme whose main thrust was to alleviate poverty through the provision of loans and it was considered a failure.
3. The last major event which impacted the financial and banking system in India was the liberalisation of India's financial system in the 1990s characterised by a series of structural adjustments and financial policy reforms initiated by the Reserve Bank of India (RBI).

Micro-Finance Institutional Structure in India

The different organisations in this field can be classified as "Mainstream" and "Alternative" Micro Finance Institutions (MFI).[5]

Mainstream Micro Finance Institutions

NABARD, Small Industries Development Bank of India (SIDBI), Housing Development Finance Corporation (HDFC), Commercial Banks, Regional Rural Banks (RRBs), the credit co-operative societies etc are some of the mainstream financial institutions involved in extending micro finance.

Alternative Micro Finance Institutions

These are the institutions, which have come up to fill the gap between the demand and supply for microfinance. MFIs were recently defined by the Task Force as "those which provide thrift, credit and other financial services and products of very small amounts, mainly to the poor, in rural, semi-urban or urban areas for enabling them to raise their income level and improve living standards."

The MFIs can broadly be classified as:

1. NGOs, which are mainly engaged in promoting self-help groups (SHGs) and their federations at a cluster level, and linking SHGs with banks, under the NABARD scheme.

2. NGOs directly lending to borrowers, who are either organised into SHGs or into Grameen Bank style groups and centres. These NGOs borrow bulk funds from RMK, SIDBI, FWWB and various donors.

3. MFIs which are specifically organised as cooperatives, such as SEWA Bank (Self Employed Women's Association, Gujarat), Amarnath Cooperative Bank (Karnataka), Mann Deshi Mahila Sahakari Bank (Maharashtra).

4. MFIs, which are organised as non-banking finance companies, such as BASIX, CFTS, Mirzapur and SHARE Microfin Ltd.

Problems associated with Mainstream MFIs

Following are the factors which hinder the reach of MFI:

1. Borrower Unfriendly Products and Procedures
   With a majority of the customers being illiterate, and a majority of them needing consumption loans and a majority of them

requiring high documentation and collateral security, the products are not reaching the rural poor.

2. Inflexibility and Delay
   The rigid systems and procedures result in lot of time delay for the borrowers and de-motivate them to take further loans.

3. High Transaction Costs, both Legitimate and Illegal
   Although the interest rate offered to the borrowers is regulated, the transaction costs in terms of the number of trips to be made, the documents to be furnished etc. plus the illegal charges to be paid result in increasing the cost of borrowing.

To enable the reach of micro finance services to the needy, the problems associated with the legal, regulatory, organisational systems and the attitudes should be addressed.

Success Stories in Micro Finance

1. **SEWA Bank:** In 1972 the Self Employed Women's Association (SEWA) was registered as a trade union in Gujarat (India), with the main objective of "strengthening its members' bargaining power to improve income, employment and access to social security." In 1973, to address their lack of access to financial services, the members of SEWA decided to found "a bank of their own". Four thousand women contributed share capital to establish the Mahila SEWA Co-operative Bank. Since then it has been providing banking services to poor, illiterate, self-employed women and has become a viable financial venture with today around 30,000 active clients.[6]
2. **The Mann Deshi Mahila Sahakari Bank:** of Mhaswad village is unique in the fact that it is the country's first rural cooperative bank of its kind – for and by women. The absence of a formal education has not deterred these women from managing a system of microcredit that is suited to their needs when the big nationalised banks have failed to see any value in serving them. In the process, they have changed the quality of life in their villages by empowering themselves economically, educationally and politically. Now, even the big nationalised banks want them as clients.[7]

Micro Finance Bill 2007

There has been an attempt to promote and regulate the micro financial sector. In this regard, The Micro Financial Bill 2007 was introduced in 2007, but could not be passed due to the dissolution of Parliament.[8] Highlights of the Bill were:

The Micro Financial Sector (Development and Regulation) Bill, 2007 seeks to promote the sector and regulate micro financial organisations (MFO).

- National Bank for Agriculture and Rural Development (NABARD) shall regulate the micro financial sector.
- Every MFO that accepts deposits has to create a reserve fund by transferring a minimum of 15 per cent of its net profit realised out of its thrift and micro finance services every year.
- The central government may establish a Micro Finance Development Council to advise NABARD on formulation of policies related to the micro financial sector.

Key Issues and Analysis

- NABARD is designated as the regulator of the micro financial sector. However, its dual role as a key participant in the sector and the regulator could lead to conflict of interest.
- The Bill defines 'micro financial services' to include insurance and pension services without specifying to whom such services are to be provided. This implies that every insurance and pension company would be regulated by NABARD.
- Attempt to either use micro finance institutions as substitutes for formal banking or even as agents of the formal banking sector were opposed by All India Democratic Women's Association and Samata, Bharat Gyan Vigyan Samiti. These organisations demanded that there should be representatives from the National Commission for Women, Rashtriya Mahila Kosh and the Ministry of Women and Child Development and Panchayat Raj.[9]

Micro Finance Bill 2013

The Micro Finance Bill 2007 lapsed due to the lack of consensus. It lapsed again in 2010, 2012 and 2013 due to the same reason. The Bill is about to come up for discussion again in the upcoming Parliament session. The sources in the Finance Ministry have confirmed that the bill won't cap interest rates on micro lending and will leave self-help groups and small community service firms out of its regulatory ambit. However, the regulatory body will advise the micro-finance institutions to keep rates low and will closely monitor them.[10]

Conclusion

Micro Finance is not charity. This is business: business with a social objective, which is to help people get out of poverty. The

Government should make programmes which will educate and create awareness among the poor about micro finance. It is the responsibility of each stake holder of the micro finance machinery to work with utmost honesty which will eventually help us to realise the ideal of *Sarvodaya* propagated by Mahatma Gandhi.[11]

REFERENCES

1. Field, E., and Pande, R. (2008) Repayment Frequency and Default in Microfinance: Evidence from India. *Journal of the European Economic Association*, *6*(2/3), 501–509.
2. Ghate, P. (2000) Linking Formal Finance with Micro and Informal Finance. *The Bangladesh Development Studies*, *26*(2/3), 201–215.
3. Joshi, D. P. (2004) Organisation of Micro-Finance. *Economic and Political Weekly*, *39*(14/15), 1475–1476.
4. Kalpana, K. (2006) Microcredit Wins Nobel: A Stocktaking. *Economic and Political Weekly*, *41*(50), 5110–5113.
5. Mayoux, L. (1998) Women's Empowerment and Micro-Finance Programmes: Strategies for Increasing Impact. *Development in Practice*, *8*(2), 235–241.
6. Nair, T. S. (2000) Rural Financial Intermediation and Commercial Banks: Review of Recent Trends. *Economic and Political Weekly*, *35*(5), 299–306.

38

Institutional Financial Support to Rural Women Entrepreneurship Development

Akshatha B.G. and Manjushree S.

'Woman is the full circle, within her is the power to create, nurture and transform.'

Abstract: *This paper concentrates on the institutional support to the development of rural women entrepreneurship. For a country whose population of women alone is more than the total population of many other countries, India fares low where their treatment is concerned. The emergence of women entrepreneurs and their contribution to the national economy is quite visible in India. The number of women entrepreneurs has grown over a period of time, especially in the 1990s. Women entrepreneurs need to be lauded for their increased utilisation of modern technology, increased investments, finding a niche in the export market, creating a sizable employment for others and setting the trend for other women entrepreneurs in the organised sector. While women entrepreneurs have demonstrated their potential, the fact remains that they are capable of contributing much more than what they already are. Women entrepreneurs create new jobs for themselves and others and also by being different. The number of sexual abuse and domestic violence cases against women clearly shows that women in India do not enjoy even basic human rights. Given such a scenario, it becomes clear* *that women charities have an important role to play. The growth and development of women entrepreneurs have accelerated because entrepreneurial development is not possible without active participation of women. So a suitable environment has been created for growth of women entrepreneurs. Because of the importance of women entrepreneurs, a number of institutions have emerged for growth of women entrepreneurs.*

Key words: Entrepreneurship, Institutions, Rural development, Women Charities, Women Entrepreneurship etc.

Introduction

Entrepreneurship so defined, pertains to any new organisation of productive factors and not exclusively to innovations that are on the technological or organisational cutting edge, it pertains to entrepreneurial activities both within and outside the organisation. Entrepreneurship need not involve anything new from a global or even national perspective, but rather the adoption of new forms of business organisations, new technologies and new enterprises producing goods not previously available at a location. This is why entrepreneurship is considered to be a prime mover in development and why nations, regions and communities that actively promote entrepreneurship development, demonstrate much higher growth rates and consequently higher levels of development than nations, regions and communities whose institutions, politics and culture hinder entrepreneurship.

Women in India consistently lag behind the men in terms of access to education, healthcare, jobs etc. Apart from the economic and social inequality, women in India are victims of heinous crimes such as, dowry deaths, rape, molestation and immoral trafficking. As per the latest statistics:

- The female child sex ratio (0-6 years) is 914 per 1000 males
- Rural female literacy rate only 58 per cent while rural male 78 per cent
- A woman employment in urban areas is only 13.9 per cent while in rural areas is 29.9 per cent. With the rise in poverty, many women are forced to work in very low end and low paid jobs.
- Employment of women in organised sector is less than eight per cent.
- Women especially in the child bearing age often deficient in nutrition due to poverty. As a result the number of maternal deaths in India is one of the highest in the world and 87 per cent of all pregnant women in India are anaemic.

Rural women's access to financial services is a key factor of successful rural development strategies for inclusive growth. Designing appropriate financial products for women to be able to save, borrow and insure is essential to strengthen women's role as producers and widen the economic opportunities available to them. For this purpose it is essential to understand how context-specific legal rights, social norms, family responsibilities and women's access to and control over other resources shape their need for capital and their ability to obtain it. It is important that development strategies that aim to boost rural women's productive capacity must enhance women's direct access to financial services, i.e., not mediated through their husbands. A second benefit of improving women's direct access to and control over resources is that this leads to higher investments in human capital and have a stronger impact on children's health, nutrition and education with important long-term implications for families and societies.

Concept of Women Entrepreneurship

Women Entrepreneurship Development an essential pre-condition to the development of the nation as a whole. Entrepreneurship amongst women has been a recent concern. The development of women entrepreneurship is very low in India, especially in the rural areas. Women have become aware of their existence, their rights and their work situation. The educated women do not want to limit their lives in the four walls of the house. They demand equal respect from their partners. However, Indian women of middle class as well as in rural area shave to go a long way to alter their role and to achieve equal rights and position because traditions are deep rooted in Indian society. The progress is more visible among upper class families in urban cities.

Institutional Support to Women Entrepreneurship – An overview

There are number of problems regarding women entrepreneurship in India. Some of them are absence of definite agenda of life, absence of balance between family and career obligations, poor degree of financial freedom, no direct ownership of the property, lack of entrepreneurial skill and finance, no awareness about capacities, low ability to bear risk, problems of work with male workers, lack of self confidence, lack of professional education, mobility constraints and lack of interaction with successful entrepreneurs. To overcome these problems, followings are some of associations or institutions which have played pivotal role for growth and development of women entrepreneurs:

1. Federation of Indian Women Entrepreneurs (FIWE)

Federation of Indian Women Entrepreneurs (FIWE), which is a National-level organisation, founded in 1993, is today, one of India's Premier Institution for Women thoroughly devoted towards Entrepreneurship Development, having a large membership base of 15,000 individual members /professionals and more than 28 Member Associations spread throughout the country. The objective of the organisation is to foster the Economic Empowerment of Women, particularly the SME segment, by helping them to become successful entrepreneurs and become a part of the mainstream industry. FIWE endeavours to provide: Networking platform for women, Technical know-how, Industry research and expertise, Skill development and training and brings the businesswomen on a Common Forum; and ensures that their opinions, ideas and visions are collectively and effectively taken up with policy-makers and various other agencies respectively for the development of Enterprise in Women.

When FIWE was established at Hyderabad (India) by converting the Women's Wing of the erstwhile National Alliance of Young Entrepreneurs (NAYE) into an Autonomous National Level Women Entrepreneurs Organisation. The main objective of FIWE is development of women entrepreneurship in the country. It have a large membership base of 15000 individual members/professionals and 28 member associations spread across the country and also affiliated with International Federation of Women Entrepreneurs (IFWE), which has a membership base of 21 countries and more countries are being added soon.

FIWE provides business counselling to aspirant women start-ups. It also provides hand holding and networking opportunities to start-ups and also to women interested in growing their business further.

2. Centre for Women Entrepreneurship and Gender Studies

Women Entrepreneur Trainer - Motivators (ETMs) Programme –Programme for promoting women entrepreneurship.

For Entrepreneur Trainer-Motivators involved in promoting women to take up entrepreneurship as a career option. The strength of an ETM lies in providing all the necessary motivation, training and assistance to potential and existing entrepreneurs. However, if one looks at the complexities at the behavioural and resource levels in the case of women, the significance of an ETM's role becomes further concretized. Considering this, gender sensitisation becomes an indispensable component of such a programme to bring about an attitudinal change and noticeable improvement.

This programme has been designed in view of the aforesaid need, for trainers and resource persons to help them disseminate the required inputs in such a way that the integration of women into the mainstream of socio-economic life is facilitated. The aim is to develop a cadre of hard core professionals who will work for the promotion of economic activities among women. The major objectives of the programme are to:

- train the participants to identify and analyse constraints and barriers to women entrepreneurship development and devise appropriate strategies
- train them to initiate, plan and implement entrepreneurship development activities for creation of small enterprises
- inculcate in them strategic skills to sensitise the environment for extending timely support required for establishment of small business ventures
- groom them for effective counselling of women entrepreneurs
- share the Indian experience in small enterprise creation by women and its sustainability

The participants are equipped with new tools and techniques to lead women to new enterprise creation and growth of existing small enterprises. The course curriculum focuses on subjects such as; entrepreneur, enterprise and entrepreneurship, women and entrepreneurship, analysis of competencies and assessment of women entrepreneurs, business opportunity identification and plan preparation, small business management information technology, effective business counselling and designing and managing support services for women entrepreneurs, etc.

3. State Bank of Mysore

(a) Small and Medium Enterprises (SMEs)

Stree Shakthi Package for Women Entrepreneurs – Women Entrepreneurs comprise those small scale units managed by one or more women entrepreneurs who have stake not less than 51 per cent of the equity. The important features of the package are: the Entrepreneurs who have undergone EDP conducted by State Level Agencies or programmes co-sponsored by Bank are eligible for financial assistance. Branch Manager and the field staffs will provide necessary inputs and assistance to those women who do not plan to set full pledged industrial ventures but would like to do something at home.

Table 1: Assistance of SBM in the field of Women Entrepreneurship (Concession Margin)

Particulars	*Category Limit Slab in Rs.*	*Margin Concession*
Retail Traders	Over Rs 5000 up to Rs 25000	NIL
	Over Rs 25000 up to Rs 1.00 lakh	5 per cent
Business Enterprises	Up to Rs 25000	NIL
	Over Rs 25000 up to Rs 1.00 lakh	5 per cent
Professional and Self employed women	Up to Rs 25000	NIL
	Over Rs 25000	5 per cent
SSI	Up to Rs 25000	NIL
	Above Rs 25000	5 per cent

Source: http://www.statebankofmysore.co.in/advances/micro-and-small-enterprises-mses/stree-shakthi-package-for-women-entrepreneurs.html

Interest Concessions

- No interest concession in respect of SSI units enjoying credit limits over Rs 25000 but up to Rs 2 lakh
- Above Rs 2 lakh and up to Rs 50 lakh, interest rate lower by 0.50 per cent than the applicable rate
- For Small Business enterprises under the scheme, interest rate lower by 0.50 per cent than the applicable rate
- For advances to professionals and self employed persons interest rate lower by 0.50 per cent than the applicable rate
- No interest concession to advances granted to private retail traders

(b) Annapurna - Scheme for Financing Women for Establishing Food Catering Unit

Table 2: Profile of the Annapurna Scheme

Particulars	*Requirements*
Eligibility	Women (both individual and Partnership firms)
Purpose	For establishing food Catering Unit for selling tiffin/ food/lunch packs etc.
Extent of Finance	Maximum loan of Rs.50000
Purpose of Loan	Term Loan component can be used for purchase of utensils and cutlery, gas connection, Refrigerator, Mixer cum Grinder, Hot case, Utensil stand, Tiffin boxes, Working table, Water filter etc
Repayment	Up to 36 monthly instilments including one month moratorium period.
Margin	10 per cent
Rate of Interest	As per prevailing rates
Security	Hypothecation of assets created out of Bank Loan
Guarantee	One guarantor (with sufficient means) acceptable to the Bank

Source: http://www.statebankofmysore.co.in/advances/micro-and-small-enterprises-mses/stree-shakthi-package- *Source:* for-women-entrepreneurs.html

4. Central Bank

Cent Kalyani – Scheme for Loan to Women Entrepreneurs

This scheme is specially introduced to offer financial assistance to Women Entrepreneurs for economic pursuits in Industry, Agriculture and Allied Activities, Business or Profession. The bank with network of branches spread throughout the country welcomes women entrepreneurs to avail financial assistance for pursuing vacations to their choice.

Credit facilities are available for Women Entrepreneurs for the following:

(a) **Small Business:** For Entrepreneurs who intend to provide service (not a professional service) such as setting up to small lunch/canteen, mobile restaurant, circulating library etc.

(b) **Professional and Self Employed:** Entrepreneurs who are specially qualified / skilled and experienced like Doctors, Chartered Accountants and Engineers or trained in Art or Craft etc.

(c) **Retail Trade:** For entrepreneurs who intend to engage in retail trading of various commodities.

(d) **Village and Cottage/Tiny Industries:** For entrepreneurs who are engaged in manufacturing, processing, preservation and services such as Handloom, Weaving Handicraft, Food-processing, Garment making etc. in village and small towns with a population not exceeding 50,000 utilising locally available resources/skills.

(e) **MSME:** Micro, Small and Medium Enterprises- To start a unit engages in manufacture, processing or preservation of goods.

(f) **Agriculture and allied Activities:** For women entrepreneurs who are engaged/intend to engage in agriculture and allied activities, such as raising of crops, floriculture, fisheries, bee-keeping, nursery, sericulture etc. and also trading in agriculture inputs.

(g) **Government Sponsored Programme:** Apart from the above schemes, women entrepreneurs are also financed under the various Government Sponsored Programmes where Capital subsidies are available.

5. Tamilnad Mercantile Bank Ltd.

Mahalir Loan – exclusive loan for women entrepreneurs

This scheme is exclusively tailored for women in business to give them that extra edge and succeed. This loan scheme is suitable for all the general business that need funding for the working capital and other business related funding necessities. This scheme is attractive and offers loan up to Rs. 10 lakhs with interest on diminishing balance.

Table 3: Profile of the Mahalir Loan

Particulars	*Details*
Purpose	Working Capital requirements / term loan to purchase fixed assets such as plant and machinery etc..
Eligibility	Women Entrepreneurs consisting of all units managed by one or more women entrepreneurs in proprietary concern or in which she / they individually or jointly have a share of not less than 51 per cent as partners / share holders / directors of private limited company / members of co-operative society.
Form of Advance	WCTL / WCDL / Term Loan / Demand Loan / Working Capital Limits such as OD, CC etc.
Loan Quantum	The requirement of the borrower is assessed on case to case basis. The total credit exposure under this loan scheme is restricted up to Rs 10 lakhs.
Repayment	• Working Capital Limit - one year. • Term Loan / Demand Loan: The repayment period shall be fixed on the basis of income generation of the borrower upto the maximum of seven years.
Security	• Primary: Hypothecation of Stock / Book Debts / Equipments / Machineries and Fitting and Furniture etc. • Collateral: Collateral Security should be obtained to fully cover the advance.
Guarantee	The guarantee should be obtained from husband / father of (borrower) the proprietor / partner. Third Party guarantee need not be insisted.
Insurance	Comprehensive insurance has to be made on all the assets hypothecated to the bank. Machineries and Collateral Security like Building should also be insured.
Rate of Interest	• BR+4.75 per cent (15.50 per cent p.a.) for Loans up to Rs. 2 Lakhs. • BR + 5.75 per cent (16.50 per cent p.a.) for Loans above Rs. 2 Lakhs and up to Rs. 10 Lakhs. Current Base Rate for Lending (BR) is 10.75 per cent p.a.
Margin	• Loans up to Rs. 25,000.00 - Nil • Loans Above Rs. 25,000.00 - 20 per cent
Penal Interest	Any irregularity or default in repayment will attract penal interest of 2.00 per cent p.a. over and above rate of interest on the balance outstanding.
Processing Charges	• Term Loan: one per cent of Limit sanctioned without any maximum cap. • Working Capital [Fund and Non-Fund Based]: 0.50 per cent of the loan amount without maximum cap.

6. **SIDBI** - SIDBI stands for Small Industries Development Bank of India. It is a national level institution which extends facilities for growth of small scale industries. This organisation has

introduced two special schemes for small scale industries by women. These are:

- Mahila Udyam Nidhi
- Mahila Vikash Nidhi

These two special schemes for women entrepreneurs provide equity and developmental assistance to women entrepreneurs. These organisations provide financial assistance to women to start entrepreneurial work in the field of spinning, weaving, knitting, embroidery and block printing. Besides the above schemes, SIDBI has lunched the following schemes to provide assistance to women entrepreneurs:

- Micro Credit Scheme
- Women Entrepreneurial Development Programme
- Marketing Development Fund for Women.

7. **SIDO** - SIDO stands for Small Industries Development Organisation. The primary objective of this organisation is to conduct various programmes including entrepreneurship development programme for women. This organisation has introduced various development programmes in the areas of TV repairing, leather goods, screen printing and preparation of circuit boards.
8. **CWEI** - Stands for Consortium of Women Entrepreneurs of India. In the context of the opening up of the economy and the need for upgradation of technology, the Consortium of Women Entrepreneurs of India started in the year 2001 provides a common platform to help women entrepreneurs find innovative techniques of production, marketing, and finance. CWEI consists of NGOs, voluntary organisations, self-help groups, institutions, and individual enterprises, both from rural and urban areas, which collectively support and benefit from the activities taken up by the consortium. CWEI takes up integrated activity linked with product development and manpower training. It also acts as an intermediary between Indian entrepreneurs and overseas agencies for marketing and exports.
9. **WIT** - WIT denotes Women India Trust. The promoter called Kamila Tyabji has taken initiative for establishment of this trust in 1968. The sole objective of this trust is to help women entrepreneurs. With the establishment of Kamila Trust in U.K., it has facilitated its members to market their product in London. It has also extended export support to the countries like Australia, Europe and Germany.

10. **SEWA** - SEWA stands for Self Employed Women Association. It is a trade union of women which was registered under Trade Union Act, in 1972. The primary objective of this organisation is to empower women entrepreneurs in rural sector. Most of members of this organisation are originated from unorganised sector. At present SEWA has shifted its operations from rural areas or level to global level and receive substantial grant from international organisations like Ford Foundation and UNICEF.
11. **SHGs** - SHGs denotes Self Help Groups. It is regarded as an association consisting of small group of self employed women entrepreneurs. The women entrepreneurs may be either from rural or urban areas. The primary objective of SHG is to take care as welfare of its associated members. It provides financial assistance as welfare of its members through financial institutions and non-government organisations.
12. **FIWE** - FIWE stands for Federation of India Women Entrepreneurs. It came into existence in the year 1993 on the outcome of resolution in 7th International conference of women entrepreneurs. It has helped women entrepreneurs in diversified activities through interaction with various women organisations and associations.
13. **NABARD** - NABARD stands for National Bank for Agriculture and Rural Development. It is an autonomous organisation. The primary objective of this autonomous organisation is to provide liberal credit facilities to women entrepreneurs. The followings are some of essential characteristics of NABARD on liberal credit to women entrepreneurs.

    1. It launched the project in 12992 to provide finance to SHG.
    2. It provides facilities on resources and training in NGO Formation.
    3. It arranges training to bank official on formation of SHG.
    4. It provides refinance to bank against lending to SHG.

Conclusion

Women in India have come a long way from being just 'homemakers'. The world now sees them with a different eye and a new respect. Women entrepreneurship in India has come a long way from women working only part time. Successful women entrepreneurs in India have made their presence felt in every field be it the world of politics, music, fashion, movies and entertainment or business. In the recent era, the Indian women entrepreneurs are eager to do the business. Women have been taking interest in income generating activities through entrepreneurship. Because of the establishment of lot many institutions and centers for supporting women entrepreneurship, women identified their needs, demands and their selves. So they expect the equal status and respect from the society. Government of India took many initiatives to develop and improve the position of women and thereby promoting their entrepreneurial skills and capabilities like adequate training programmes on management skills, encourage women participation in decision-making and vocational training extended to women community that enables them to understand production processes and production management. Financial institutions provide more working capital assistance both for small scale venture and large scale venture. Financial help from the government as well as from their families to support the business affect their satisfaction level but it does not hold good in the case of their orientation because satisfaction is more reflected in the financial gains of the business, which can occur only when they have initial access to it, whether through financial institutions or through their families.

REFERENCES

1. Afrin, S., Islam, N., and Ahmed, S. U. (2008) *A multivariate model of micro credit and rural women entrepreneurship development in Bangladesh.* International Journal of Business and Management, 3(8), pp.169–185.
2. Bellu, R. R. (1993) *Task role motivation and attribution style as predictors of entrepreneurial performance: Female sample findings.* Entrepreneurship and Regional Development, 5, pp. 331–344. .
3. Birley, S., Moss, C., and Saunders, P. (1987) *Do women entrepreneurs require different training?* American Journal of Small Business, 12(1), pp.27–35.
4. Brush, G. C., Bruin, A. D., and Welter, F. (2009) *A gender-aware framework for women's entrepreneurship.* International Journal of Gender and Entrepreneurship, 1(1), pp. 8–24.
5. Buttner, E. H., and Rosen, B. (1988) *Bank loan officers' perception of the characteristics of men, women and successful entrepreneurs.* Journal of Business Venturing, 3, pp. 249–258.
6. Byrd, W.A. (1987) *Entrepreneurship, capital and ownership.* Washington, D.C. The World Bank. Mimeo.
7. Charumati, B. (1997) *Women entrepreneur's challenges and prospects.* Indian Journal of Commerce, 1(9), pp. 286–294.
8. Ganesan, R., Kaur, D., and Maheswari, R. C. (2002) *Women entrepreneurs: Problems and prospect.* Journal of Entrepreneurship, 11(1), pp.75–93.

9. Greene, P. (1993) *The role of ethnic sponsorship of female business activities in economic development.* Journal of Business Management, 12(2), pp. 43–54.
10. Habib, W. M., Roni, N. N., and Haque, T. (2005) *Factors affecting women entrepreneurship in India: A multivariate analysis.* Journal of Business Studies, 16(1), pp. 249–258.
11. Hisrich, R.D. and C. Brush (1984) *The Women Entrepreneurs: Management Skills and Business Problems.* Journal of Small Business Management, 22, pp. 30-37.
12. Hisrich, R. D., and Brush, C. G. (1985) *Women and minority entrepreneurs: A comparative analysis.* In J. A. Hornaday, E. B. Shils, J. A. Timmons and K. H. Vesper (Eds.), Frontiers of Entrepreneurial Research, Boston, MA: Babson College. pp. 566–87.
13. Humbert, A., and Drew, E. (1998) *Gender, entrepreneurship and motivational factors in an Irish context.* International Journal of Gender and Entrepreneurship, 2(2), pp.1–30.
14. Inman, K. (2000) *Women's resources in business start-ups. A study of black and white women.* International Journal of Entrepreneurial Behaviour and Research, 30(1), pp. 58–65.
15. Mohanty, A. (2004) *Women in management of micro-enterprises: Problems and prospects.* Journal of Social Science, 8(3), pp.245–251.
16. Mukherjee, S. (2006) *What motivates women entrepreneurs: Factors influencing their motivation.* ICFAI Journal of Entrepreneurship, 3(4), pp. 7–20.
17. Nigam, S., and Sharma, S. K. (1997) *Problems and prospects of women entrepreneurs in Agra.* Indian Journal of Commerce, 2(1), pp.243–248.
18. Parasuraman, S., Purohit, Y. S., Godshalk, V. M., and Beutell, N. J. (1996) *Work and family variables, entrepreneurial career success, and psychological well-being.* Journal of Vocational Behavior, 48, pp. 275–300.
19. Stathopoulou, S., Demetrios, P., and Dimitris, S. (2004) *The female poverty trap.* International Journal of Entrepreneurial Behaviour and Research, 10(6), pp.404–425.
20. Stoner, C. R., Hartman, R. I., and Arora, R. (1990) *Work-home role conflict in female owners of small business: An exploratory study.* Journal of Small Business Management, 28(1), pp. 30–38.
21. Twaalfhoven, B.W.M. and N. V. Indivers (1993) *The Role of Dynamic Entrepreneurs in Dynamic Entrepreneurship in Eastern Europe,* D.F. Abell and T. Koellermeier (eds), Delwel Publisher, The Hague, 1993, pp. 7-13.
22. Tyson, L., T. Petrin and H. Rogers (1994) *Promoting Entrepreneurship in Central and Eastern Europe, Small Business Economics 6,* pp. 1-20.

http://www.statebankofmysore.co.in/advances/micro-and-small-enterprises-mses/stree-shakthi-package-for-women-entrepreneurs.html

http://www.fiwe.org/

http://www.tmb.in/business_mahalir_loan/exclusive_loan_for_women_entrepreneurs.html

https://www.serudsindia.org/donate-money-for-zari-work-trainings-for-rural-women.php

http://youthveerangnayen.org/

http://www.ediindia.org/InterCore5.asp

http://www.giveindia.org/c-58-women.aspx?gclid=COvRvPbGx7kCFQTLpAod3HAABQ

http://www.unido.org/fileadmin/user_media/Publications/Pub_free/A_path_out_of_poverty.pdf

http://www.microfinancegateway.org/p/site/m/template.rc/1.1.4805/

http://www.fao.org/docrep/w6882e/w6882e02.htm

http://www.theijes.com/papers/v2-i3/I023052055.pdf

39

Role of Micro Finance in Empowerment of Fisherwomen in Coastal Karnataka—A Study

Chandrasekhar Moger

Abstract: *The poor, especially the coastal fisher community, has found it extremely difficult to locate alternate sources of income and employment opportunities, in the wake of their inadequate financial credibility. But the recent economic perspectives on development have pointed towards the importance of micro finance in the empowerment of the fisherwomen. One method of access to micro finance by the coastal fisher community, fisher women in particular, is the Self Help Group-Bank linkage programme, where banks provide finance to the groups for undertaking economic activities. Thus the programme provides access to associations of fisher women, who, otherwise un-united, would have found themselves not eligible for bank finance. It is expected that the access of such institutional credit would bring in social, personal and financial empowerment of fisher women. The present paper is an evaluation of the findings of the study undertaken to reveal the role of micro finance in coastal fisher women empowerment.*

The study utilised both primary and secondary data. Primary data relating to the socioeconomic background and various other aspects relating to empowerment of the fisherwomen were collected through pre-designed questionnaire from 100 fisherwomen representing 20 SHGs from the selected five coastal villages in Uttara Kannada District of Karnataka state. A separate interview schedule was designed, pilot tested and used for data collection. The schedule was used to collect specific information from each member of the fisherwomen SHGs.

The study found that Women status increased after joining of the SHGs 90 per cent in the study area. It is noticed that all the respondents agreed that micro finance brought Respect from Layman or Society and self confidence and improved their skill. Majority of the respondents expressed that their awareness about environment improved after taking part in micro finance programmes actively. Maximum number of respondents accepted that microfinance has brought economic development directly and indirectly happiness and peace in the family. The present study evidences the existence of strong linkages of the SHGs with banks for empowerment of fisherwomen. The very reason of members, as opined by them, in joining the group is the improved chances of accessibility to loans. Thus, there exists strong positive relation between the reasons for joining the group, and the existence of bank linkages. The strong bank linkage that exists, can visibly enhance the opportunity of members to access loans, undertake economic activities, and develop skills. But, the SHG-driven micro-finance may suffer from serious limitations, reducing its positive impact on empowerment. The lack of transparency in the SHG activities, and inaccessibility to official records may further hinder the effectiveness of the movement. To conclude, the economic activities of SHGs are quite successful. In this way, SHGs in two villages of Uttara Kannada District were very successful to develop Fisher women empowerment in coastal belt activities.

Keywords: Self Help Groups, Microfinance, Women Empowerment, Income Generating.

Introduction

Without personal assets, paid or self employment, the world's poor has found it exceptionally gruelling to generate sustainable income opportunities. Where commercial financial lending demands collaterals to acquire credit, their unenviable and impoverished circumstances render the impoverished so incompetent to access external financial support mechanisms.

Micro finance has increasingly begun to be seen as a contributor to the reduction of poverty in developing countries, by creating opportunities for the poor to engage in economic and productive activities[1] [UNESCO 1997]. The concept of micro-finance involves the accessibility to collateral-free loans from financial institutions by small groups or associations of poor individuals. The membership fee collected by the group is deposited in banks as savings, which in turn imparts eligibility to these groups to access institutional financial assistance.

Microfinance is the provision of financial services to low-income clients, including consumers and the self- employed, who traditionally lack access to banking and related services. Microcredit, or microfinance, is banking the un bankable, bringing credit, savings and other essential financial services within the reach of millions of people who are too poor to be served by regular banks, in most cases because they are unable to offer sufficient collateral. In general, banks are for people with money, not for people without. It is based on the premise that the poor have skills which remain unutilised or underutilized. Microcredit fits best to those with entrepreneurial capability and possibility. Ultimately, the goal of microfinance is to give low income people an opportunity to become self-sufficient by providing a means of saving money, borrowing money and insurance. The main aim of microfinance is to empower women. Women make up a large proportion of microfinance beneficiaries. Traditionally, women (especially those in underdeveloped countries) have been unable to readily participate in economic activity. Microfinance provides women with the financial backing they need to start business ventures and actively participate in the economy. It gives them confidence, improves their status and makes them more active in decision-making, thus encouraging gender equality. According to CGAP, long-standing MFIs even report a decline in violence towards women since the inception of microfinance[2]. The most of the microcredit institutions and agencies all over the world focuses on women in developing countries. Observations and experience shows that women are a small credit risk, repaying their loans and tend more often to benefit the whole family. In another aspect it is also viewed as a method giving the women more status in a socioeconomic way and changing the current conservative relationship between gender and class when women are able to provide income to the household. There are many reasons why women have become the primary target of microfinance services.

A recent World Bank report confirms that societies that discriminate on the basis of gender pay the cost of greater poverty, slower economic growth, weaker governance, and a lower living standard for all people[3]. At a macro level, it is because 70 per cent of the world's poor are women. Women have a higher unemployment rate than men in virtually every country and make up the majority of the informal sector of most economies. They constitute the bulk of those who need microfinance services. Giving women access to microcredit loans therefore generates a multiplier effect that increases the impact of a microfinance institution's activities, benefiting multiple generations. NABARD (2005) explains that the Self Help Group is a group with "an average size of about 15 people from a homogenous class. They come together for addressing their common problems. They are encouraged to make voluntary thrift on a regular basis. They use this pooled resource to make small interest bearing loans to their members. The process helps them imbibe the essentials of financial intermediation including prioritisation of needs, setting terms and conditions and accounts keeping. This gradually builds financial discipline in all of them. They also learn to handle resources of a size that is much beyond the individual capacities of any of them. The SHG members begin to appreciate that resources are limited and have a cost. Once the groups show this mature financial behaviour, banks are encouraged to make loans to the SHG in certain multiples of the accumulated savings of the SHG. The bank loans are given without any collateral and at market interest rates. The groups continue to decide the terms of loans to their own members. Since the groups' own accumulated savings economic are part and parcel of the aggregate loans made by the groups to their members, peer pressure ensures timely repayments".[4]

Women in India constitute about 50 per cent of the total population and comprise one-third of the labour force. It is, therefore, important that when considering the economic development of this segment of the population, due attention is given to their socio-economic empowerment. In India, of the total population of 5.4 million active fishers [Marine and inland fisheries], 3.8 million are fishermen and 1.6 million are fisherwomen.[5] These fisherwomen are engaged in several fisheries vocations. The major activities in which women's contribution can be noticed throughout the country are fish processing and marketing. However, their participation and contribution are increasing in the areas of aquaculture, development and education. The involvement of women in these activities generates supplemental income to support their families. Even though women are as efficient as men, earnings are not always the same. The wages for men and women are often different with men being paid at least 30 per cent more than that received by women. Microcredit for self help groups is fast emerging as a promising tool of promoting income generating enterprises for reaching the 'unreached' for credit delivery in rural areas, particularly the women who are often considered to have very low net worth for availing any credit facilities from the formal financial institutions, the banks. Microcredit is also considered as the vehicle for achieving empowerment of the women, in all spheres viz., social, cultural, political and economic. It is a way of self-sustenance without looking for financial help or subsidy from 'elsewhere'. In this paper the role played by Microfinance in fisher women's empowerment are considered into three dimensions namely, personnel, social and economic.

The efforts of the SHGs have played a positive role in helping the fisher folk in their socio-economic development, emancipation and empowerment. Their technical knowledge has improved, and their inter-personal and financial management skills have been sharpened. The entrepreneurship helped them to express their individuality and also increased self-confidence among members. As Muhammad Yunus, founder of Grameen Bank of Bangladesh succinctly points out, "women have plans for themselves, for their children, for their home, and the meals. They have a vision. A man wants to enjoy himself"[6]. The present study focuses on an attempt has been made to provide insights on the fishing sector, fishing community, and focused micro-credit for fisherwomen.

Review of Literature

Jayaraman (2000 and 2002) reported on the role and performance of fisherwomen SHGs in India. He found the fisherwomen SHGs performing well in availing microcredit, utilising it and repaying it in time. The microcredit programme implemented through SHGs contributed to the socio-economic welfare and empowerment of the fisherwomen. It also contributed to the eradication of usury and illicit liquor[7]. Nagayya (2000) stated that there has been a massive expansion in the formal credit delivery network in the last three decades and there is an acceptable gap in financing the genuine poor, especially in remote rural area.[8]

Deepti Agarwal (2001) reported that the status of women is low and their socio-economic conditions are much more depressed than that of men.[9] Jeyesh Talati and Venkatakrishnan (2001) explained women's empowerment in Jhabua district, Madhya Pradesh[10]. The women 'leaders' elected by the group members were responsible for the maintenance of group records and management of group. These women's groups laid the foundation for the empowerment of women. Radhakrishna Rao (2002) says, Kerala's remarkable achievements in education and health have been greatly facilitated by its social and physical terrain. Socially speaking, community-based social reform movements competed with each other for social advancement[11].

Shetty (2002) reported on the impact of Rural Self Help groups and other forms of micro-financing[12]. FAO (2003) reported on the best practices and success stories in microcredit programmes for women in coastal fishing communities in India.[13]

Sabyasachi Das (2003) reported on the functioning of Self-Help Groups and microcredit. He reported that, NGOs gave some training to the SHGs for awareness building, entrepreneurship and skill training and some help in arranging inputs, and marketing, introduced saving and internal lending, helped in the maintenance of accounts and linked them with the banks for credit requirements.[14]

Meenambigai (2004) stated that self-help groups play a major role in transforming rural economy. Microcredit helps the rural poor to improve their standard of living and fulfills their credit needs. Microcredit encourages savings, promotes income generating activities and benefits women.[15]

Sheik Mohammed (2004) reported that Self-Help Groups worked for the success of women entrepreneurs[16]. Senthil Vadivoo and Sekar (2004) stated that the self help groups is a movement for women empowerment; it covered women collectively struggling against direct and indirect barriers to their self development and their social, political and economic participation. Women's empowerment can be viewed as a continuous process of several inter-related and mutually reinforcing components. Empowerment is a process of awareness and capacity building, leading to greater participation, greater decision-making power and control the transformative action to overcome the constraints in this process.[17]

Tripathy (2004) explained economic empowerment through income generating activities through self help groups and also explained its importance in education, mid-day meals scheme, health, agriculture and allied activities, community action and sustainable development and rural sanitation.[18]

Thus, the SHGs have been found to be an effective tool of micro-credit delivery for women empowerment and rural development. There are several success stories of how SHGs have benefited the poverty-ridden people in the rural areas in emerging empowered and how lending to SHGs have made loss-making branches of banks to turn around. Although SHGs have come to stay there are some germane issues that need to be sorted out.

Statement of the Problem

Micro finance or provision of financing services to low income households has come to be accepted as the most efficacious intervention to alleviate poverty among the policy circles in the developing countries. Till recently fisherwomen under the Indian rural set up were not able to actively participate in income generating activity due to historical and social cultural reasons. Their socio-economic conditions, decision taking ability and confidence level were very low. Low level of skills, lack of access to training facilities and credit, literacy, ignorance coupled with their invisible contribution to family economy, restricted mobility as a result of gender bias and lack of linkage facilities are some of the contributory factors for the backwardness of the fisherwomen in the coastal areas. The approach towards uplifting the poor fisher women economically should be Self Help. In fact, even the individual effort is too inadequate to improve their economic status. At this juncture, organising the poor fisher women in a group is the need of the hour. Thus, the SHG is considered as the movement of self development. The SHG is the institutional informal setup through which the micro credit is routed by the formal and semi-formal micro finance institutions to assist the poor fisherwomen. The NGOs on the other hand directly lend micro credit to the members of the SHGs out of their own corpus.

Micro credit for fisherwomen self help groups is fast emerging as a promising tool of promoting income generating enterprises for reaching the unreached for credit delivery in coastal area of Uttara Kannada district. It is also considered as the vehicle for achieving empowerment of the women in all spheres viz., social, political, personal and economic. Micro finance through SHGs has empowered the SHGs in many aspects of life. The review of literature reveals that no study has been conducted on the empowerment of women in the coastal areas of Uttara Kannada district of Karnataka state. Therefore, it was thought conducive to conduct study in different coastal villages of Uttara Kannada district to assess the impact of microfinance on empowerment of fisherwomen SHG members.

The above in context, the present study titled 'Role of Micro Finance on Empowerment of Fisherwomen in Coastal Karnataka.

Objectives of the study

1. To study the Socio-Economic status of the members of Fisherwomen SHGs in the study area.
2. To compare the impact of SHGs on the Socio-Economic conditions of fisherwomen before and after the formation of SHGs.
3. To assess the role of SHGs towards in Fisherwomen empowerment.

4. To suggest suitable measures for effective improvement of functioning of fisherwomen SHGs.

Hypothesis

1. Empowerment can serve as a powerful instrument for women to achieve upward social and economic mobility and power and status in society.
2. Micro credit is a potential tool for socio-economic empowerment of the fisherwomen in coastal area.
3. SHGs positively impact on the confidence level of fisherwomen in the study area.

Limitations of the study

The inferences drawn for the study were based on the data collected from the specific beneficiaries in the study area selected for the study. Hence, though general observations were drawn, the outcome pertains only to the study area and the perceptions of the beneficiaries and the investigators.

Methodology of Study

Exploratory Research Design is used for the study. The study was conducted in the district of Uttara Kannada of Karnataka State. Uttara Kannada is the most backward district in fisheries in Karnataka. It has a coastline of 160 kilometers. The district has Five coastal taluks. Bhatkal taluk, with 12 villages, formed the locale of the study. Bhatkal taluk has vast coastal area and a population of 17364. Two villages, namely, Heble and Mavinkurve were selected to form the sample. The villages are very distinctive on account of its location in the coastal belt. Thus, the study was narrowed down to the various women-Self Help Groups formed and functioning within the coastal locale. Personal visits were conducted to a number of such SHGs, with a view to further narrow down the number of SHGs to be subjected to study. Giving due consideration to important facts like category [on basis of formation of SHG], conduct of commercial activities [groups conducting and not conducting activities], representativeness of different religious community of the locale population etc, 20 Self Help Groups were finally selected, on stratified sampling basis, as final sample groups. The study predominantly depends on Primary Data. Attempt was made to elicit response from at least Five members of each of the selected 20 SHGs. Primary data were collected by employing a structured questionnaire.

Findings of the Study

The following form the major findings of the study:

1. Social and Economic Profile of the Respondents:

Out of the total, 76.0 per cent of the respondents were married, while ten per cent were single and six per cent were widowed. As regards the education of the respondents, 20 per cent had education up to +2, while ten per cent were graduates. The rest included 37 per cent who had studied till the fifth standard. Occupational status of the respondents revealed that 35 per cent were self-employed, 32 per cent were housewives, eight per cent were salaried and 25 per cent were daily labourers. As regards the monthly income, 36 per cent of the respondents belonged to the income category of Rs 2,000 - Rs 3,000, while 30 per cent belonged to below Rs 1,000 and 22 per cent to Rs 1,000 - Rs 2,000 category.

2. Motivations for joining SHG

The study identified that the major motivators for the respondents in joining SHGs were their friends [27 per cent], neighbours [24 per cent], personal interest [20 per cent], NGO officials [15 per cent], and other SHG members [14 per cent].

Table 1: Motivators for joining SHG

Motivators	*No.*	*Per cent*
Friends	27	27
Neighbours	24	24
Personal Interest	15	15
NGO Officials	23	14
Other SHG Members	21	
TOTAL	**100**	**100**

Source: Primary Data.

It was revealed that easy access to loans [58 per cent], development of skill sets [53 per cent], participation in economic activity [53 per cent], and inculcation of savings habit [50 per cent], and opportunity of social interaction [47 per cent] and participation in social activity [25 per cent] were among the major motivational factors behind the joining of the SHGs.

Reasons	*Frequency*	*Per cent*
Easy Access to Loans	58	58
Development of Skill Sets	53	53
Participation in Economic Activity	53	53
Inculcation of Savings Habit	50	50
Opportunity of Social Interaction	47	47
Participation in Social Activity	25	25
TOTAL		

Source: Primary Data.

3. Important Roles of SHGs

The below Table shows that after joining of the SHGs income level of the individual women in income level have been increased over all percentage of (26 per cent) and the lowest percentage of (nine per cent) shows low level income of women when compare to before joining SHGs after poverty level decried. Awareness in children and improved literacy level of women are gradually increased.

Table: Important Roles of SHGs

Sl. No.	*Roles of SHGs*	*Frequency*	*Percentage*
1.	Improvement in literacy	21	21
2.	Awareness in children	12	12
3.	Reduce in poverty level	17	17
4.	Improvement in standard of living	15	15
5.	Income of respondents before joining SHG's	9	9
6.	Income of respondents after joining SHG's	26	26
	Total	**100**	**100**

Source: Primary Data.

5. Nature of Operations and Group Characteristics of SHGs

The opinion of the respondent SHG members regarding the nature of operations of their group revealed that feelings of trust among the group members [66 per cent] and group interaction between members [52 per cent] existed at high levels. Nearly 63 per cent of respondents were highly satisfied about the operations of SHGs. Leadership qualities and accountability existed at medium levels for 67 per cent and 47 per cent respectively. As regards transparency of operations, nearly 82 per cent agreed with medium to low levels of existence of transparency. Group cohesion was medium according to 63 per cent

Table: Opinion on Group Characteristics of SHG

Group Characteristics	*Level of Characteristics*					
	High		*Medium*		*Low*	
	No.	*Per cent*	*No.*	*Per cent*	*No.*	*Per cent*
Trust Between Members	66	66	19	19	15	15
Interaction	52	52	44	44	4	4
Satisfaction	63	63	13	13	24	24
Leadership	29	29	67	67	4	4
Cohesion	29	29	63	63	9	9
Accountability	35	35	47	47	19	19
Transparency	19	19	53	53	29	29

Source: Primary Data.

6. Role of Decision Making in Family

The below Table shows that most of the 94 respondents (94 per cent) agreed they play a vital role in decision-making in their houses.

Table: Role of Decision Making in Family

Sl. No.	*Options*	*Frequency*	*Percentage*
1.	Yes	94	94
2.	No	6	6
	Total	**100**	**100**

Source: Primary Data.

7. Personal Empowerment after joining SHG

Personal empowerment achieved by the respondents after joining the SHGs was identified as being composed of improvements in confidence [62 per cent], decision-making capability [68 per cent], and mutual respect [47 per cent] at high levels, and independence [60 per cent], mobility [38 per cent], self-respect [56 per cent], and family acceptance [37 per cent] at medium levels. For 31 per cent, family acceptance, for 28 per cent, mobility and for 18 per cent, self-respect improved only by low levels.

Table: Personal Empowerment of SHG Members

Personal Empowerment	*Extent of Empowerment*					
	High		*Medium*		*Low*	
	No.	*Per cent*	*No.*	*Per cent*	*No.*	*Per cent*
Confidence	62	62	38	38	00	00
Independence	22	22	60	60	18	18
Decision making	68	68	32	32	00	00
Mobility	34	34	38	38	28	28
Self respect	26	26	56	56	18	18
Mutual respect	47	47	34	34	18	18
Family Acceptance	3	31	37	37	31	31

Source: Primary Data.

8. Social Empowerment after joining SHG

Social empowerment as achieved by the respondents after joining the SHGs were identified to be composed of improvements in participation in social programmes [61 per cent high improvement level and 39 per cent medium improvement level], organisational skill [66 per cent high and 28 per cent medium], interactive skills [48 per cent high and 52 per cent medium], group cohesiveness [43 per cent high and 57 per cent medium], awareness on social problems [47 per cent high and 43 per cent medium], membership in other organisations [47 per cent high and 29 per cent medium], acceptance by society [37 per cent high and 43 per cent medium], public speaking skills [29 per cent high and 48 per cent medium] and awareness on rights [43 per cent low and 37 per cent medium].

Table Social Empowerment after joining SHG

Social Empowerment	Extent of Empowerment					
	High		Medium		Low	
	No.	Per cent	No.	Per cent	No.	Per cent
Confidence	62	62	38	38	00	00
Organisational kill	66	66	28	28	6	6
Group Cohesiveness	43	43	57	57	00	00
Interactive Skill	48	48	32	32	00	00
Public Speaking	29	29	48	48	23	23
Awareness on Rights	20	20	37	37	43	43
Awareness on Social Problems	47	47	43	43	9	9
Acceptance in Society	37	37	43	43	30	30
Participation in social Programmes	61	61	39	39	00	00
Membership in other Organisations	47	47	29	29	23	23

Source: Primary Data.

9. Financial Empowerment after joining SHG

Financial empowerment achieved by the respondents after joining the SHGs were identified to be composed of improvements in income [85 per cent high improvement and 11 per cent medium improvement], financial security [56 per cent high and 23 per cent medium], financial management capability [49 per cent high and 33 per cent medium], living conditions [46 per cent medium and 39 per cent high], savings [76 per cent medium and 24 per cent high], and expenditure [61 per cent medium and 23 per cent high].

Table: Financial Empowerment of SHG Members

Financial Empowerment	Extent of Empowerment					
	High		Medium		Low	
	No.	Per cent	No.	Per cent	No.	Per cent
Confidence	62	62	38	38	00	00
Income	85	85	11	11	04	04
Savings	24	24	76	76	00	00
Financial Management	49	49	33	33	18	18
Living Conditions	39	39	46	46	15	15
Expenditure	23	23	61	61	15	15
Financial Security	56	56	23	23	21	21

Source: Primary Data.

10. Micro-Finance through SHGs

The study also identified that nearly 58 per cent of the respondents depended on their income for sources of finance, while 52 per cent depended on moneylenders for external financing sources. It was also found out that 74 per cent of the respondents depended on SHG loans provided through the bank linkage programme as a source of finance. Among the 74 per cent of the total respondents who had availed of the loan facility of the SHG- bank linkage programme, 82 per cent utilised a part of the loan amount for their children's education, while 56 per cent utilised it for agricultural purposes and 43 per cent utilised it for marriage purposes of family members. Use of the micro finance for income generating purposes such as animal husbandry or poultry and small business ventures were limited to 11 per cent and 45 per cent, respectively. Another 34 per cent of the respondents employed a part of the money for repayment of other existing loans.

Findings

Self Help Groups of Fisherwomen can form the heart of community development activities. The pooling of minuscule and individual financial savings of the members through group activities can act as a strong back-bone for women empowerment. Supplemented by the linkages of the self help groups with banks, thereby enabling micro-credit facilities, the financial power of these Fisherwomen gets substantially increased.

The study reveals that Women status increased after joining of the SHGs 90 per cent. It is noticed that all the respondents agreed that micro finance brought Respect from Layman or Society and self confidence and improved their skill. Majority of the respondents expressed that their awareness about environment improved after taking part in micro finance programmes actively. Maximum number of respondents accepted that microfinance has brought economic development directly and indirectly happiness and peace in the family

The present study evidences the existence of strong linkages of the SHGs with banks for empowerment of fisherwomen. The very reason of members, as opined by them, in joining the group is the improved chances of accessibility to loans. Also the opportunity to undertake economic activities through group efforts, and the concomitant learning of entrepreneurial and technical skill sets act as motivators for group membership. Thus, there exists strong positive relation between the reasons for joining the group, and the existence of bank linkages. The strong bank linkage that exists, can visibly enhance the opportunity of members to access loans, undertake economic activities, and develop skills.

On the realistic aspect, it is also found that the members still depend enormously on indigenous money lenders, forcing high interest payments. The high incidence of bank linkage and accessibility to finance through SHGs is still not relieving the rural population from the clutches of money lenders and exorbitant interest rates. It points to the important fact of insufficiency of funding through the bank linkage programmes. Thus, the SHG-driven micro-finance may suffer from serious limitations, reducing its positive impact on empowerment. The lack of transparency in the SHG activities, and inaccessibility to official records may further hinder the effectiveness of the movement.

Probably, the most disappointing fact relating to financial access is the limited employment of SHG credit facilities for economic and other income generating activities. Use of finance for entrepreneurial activities is deplorably low. The vagaries of indebtedness can only increase by using SHG credit facilities for refinancing pre-existing loans or for financing marriages.

It is also noticed that most of the women are not aware of the trainings organised by the NGO. The NGO shall actively take part in various trainings sessions provided to all women members wherein they can gain more knowledge about the various income generating activities. There is a definite improvement in psychological well-being and social empowerment among fisher women as a result of participating in micro finance through SHG programme.

Conclusion

Thus, what emerges from the present study is in rural area, Self Help Groups are performing very well. The study concludes that microfinance brought psychological and social empowerment than economic empowerment. Impact of micro finance is appreciable in bringing confidence, Better Access to Healthcare, skill development and empowerment. The SHG members feel free to move with their groups and leaders. It leads them to participate on various social welfare activities with good cooperation. Insufficiency of finance, lack of transparency in activities, and poor use of finance for productive, income-generating activities act as a limiting factor in achieving the intended empowerment. While interacting with the respondents, it is noticed that some members are expecting the NGO to come up with more training sessions in income generating activities. All they need is a way to develop their skills and talents by participating in various training programmes.

REFERENCE

1. UNESCO 1997 Position Paper No. CAB-97/WS/2, Microcredit Summit, February 2-4, Washington.
2. CGAP, (1997), Introducing Savings in Micro-credit Institutions : When and How?, Consultative Group to the Poorest Focus Note 8, World Bank, Washington DC, USA.

3. World Bank Report.
4. National Bank for Agriculture and Rural Development (1999), "Task Force Report on Supportive Policy and Regulatory Framework for Micro Finance", Mumbai, India, < rbidocs.rbi.org.in/rdocs/Bulletin/DOCs/10307.doc>
5. Jayaraman, R. 2005 Performance analysis of fisherwomen Self Help Groups, Final Report submitted to National Bank for Agricultural and Rural Development, Department of Fisheries Resources and Economics, Fisheries College and Research Institute, Tamil Nadu Veterinary and Animal Sciences University, Thoothukkudi, 63 pp.
6. Muhamnad Yunus[2008], http://www.soc.titech.ac.jp/icm/wind.html
7. Jayaraman, R., (2000), Role of Self Help Groups in Fisherwomen Development in India, Paper Presented at the (Fourth International Conference of the Coastal Zone, Canada Association held during 17-21 September 2000, Saint John, NB, Canada).
8. Nagayya, D., (2000), Microcredit for Self Help Groups, Kurukshetra, 48(11): 10-15.
9. Deepti Agarwal, (2001), Empowerment of Rural Woman in India, Social Welfare, 48(4):3-4.
10. Jayesh Talati and Venkatakrishnan V., (2001), Women's Empowerment in Jhabua District, M.P., Social Welfare, 47(11):15-18.
11. Radhakrishna Rao, (2002), Sustainable Technology for Rural Development, Kurukshetra, 50(5):41-42.
12. Shetty, S.L., (2002), Working and Impact of Rural Self-Help Groups and Other Forms of Micro Financing, Indian Journal of Agricultural Economics, 57(1):31-32.
13. FAO, (2003), Fisheries Report, National Workshop on Best Practices in Micro-Finance Programmes for Women Coastal Fishing Communities in India, Panaji, Goa, India, No.724, 1-4 July, 2003.
14. Sabyasachi Das, (2003), Self Help Groups and Microcredit Synergic Integration, Kurukshetra, 51(10): 25-30.
15. Meenambigai, J., (2004), Self Help Groups in Rural Economy, Kissan World, 31(4):17-18.
16. Sheik Mohamed, (2004), Self-Help Group for the Success of Women Entrepreneurs, Kisan World, 52(8):41-43.
17. Senthil Vadivoo, K. and V. Sekar, (2004), Self Help Groups: A Movement for Women Services : How the Poor in India Could be Better Served, Kissan World, 31(7):13-14.
18. Tripathy, K.K., (2004), Self-Help Groups—A Catalyst of Rural Development, Kurukshetra, 52(8): 40-43.

40

Economic Development Through Micro-Insurance and Thrift Management—A Case of Underprivileged Sections of Society

Vasanthi Reena Williams and S. Jyothi Lakhmi

Social inclusion has become the buzz word and various organisations are putting effort either individually, through their Corporate Social Responsibility activities or by joining hands with the government to ensure inclusion of the weaker sections of society and bringing them into mainstream. This study which is based on secondary research, tries to study the significance of Micro-Insurance and how it could help in supporting the underprivileged by covering risk and ensuring economic stability amongst them. The industry is still in its infancy and there is need to popularise the concept through extensive awareness programmes aiming at the target groups. The study identifies that micro-insurance can categorically help the poor and underprivileged people in society thereby assisting the economic development of the country as a whole. The focus of the study is to highlight the observations made with regard to Thrift Management and Micro Insurance among the underprivileged who are the target group in this study.

Key words: Micro-Insurance, Thrift Management, Self-help groups, Non-governmental organisations, Insurance Regulatory and Development Authority (IRDA).

Introduction

According to the definition provided by Wikipedia[1], '*Micro insurance is the protection of low-income people (those living on between approximately $1 and $4 per day) against specific perils in exchange for regular premium payment proportionate to the likelihood and cost of the risks involved*'. This definition gives the same connotation as the meaning for the term 'Insurance'. However, the concept here is the focus on the marginalised and underprivileged sections of society, basically the low income groups; with an intention of bringing them into the mainstream. The target people for micro insurance are those who have hitherto been ignored by mainstream commercial and social insurance schemes and those who have not been able to access appropriate insurance products to cover risk. The unorganised sector clearly fit the bill in terms of being underprivileged, coming under the tab –'weaker sections' in society, as they have lower job security and having lesser chances of growth and protection, both in terms of individual and economic development.

According to the Central Board for Workers Education[2] (CBWE), Ministry of Labour and Employment, Government of India, the unorganised sectors covers most of the rural labour and a substantial part of urban labour. The unorganised sector adds more than 60 per cent to the national income while the contribution of the organised sector is almost half of that depending on the industry. Similarly, a study on social security benefits for unorganised workers in Karnataka, commissioned by the German Federal Ministry for Economic Cooperation and Development[3] (BMZ), executed by the Department of Labour, Government of Karnataka between 2008 and 2013 has identified that in India, the unorganised workers make up over 90 per cent of the workforce. The study focused on select districts of Karnataka State. Through the study, 220,000 households were surveyed with over 240,000 individuals being identified as beneficiaries of various social security programmes. The study has also initiated a management and information system, developed and put into operation for effective monitoring and decision making.

The term Unorganised Sector, when used in the Indian context is defined by National Commission for Enterprises in the Unorganised Sector, in their report on Conditions of Work and Promotion of Livelihoods in the Unorganised Sector as 'Consisting *of all unincorporated private enterprises owned by individuals of households engaged in the sale or production of goods and services operated on a proprietary or partnership basis and with less than ten total worker's.* The Wikipedia identifies the characteristic features of this sector through ease of entry, smaller scale of operation, local ownership, uncertain legal status, being labour-intensive and operating using lower technology based methods, lower entry barriers for employees, a higher proportion of migrants with a lower rate of compensation, etc. The sector can, therefore, be defined as that workforce having constraints involving illiteracy and ignorance, casual nature of employment and scattered nature of establishments. The sector consists of basically private enterprises having less than ten total workers an operating on a proprietary or partnership basis- as defined by the National Commission on Enterprises in the Unorganized/ Informal Sector (2004). This can be identified on the basis of the nature of the work that the group or individuals are engaged in and on the number of employees in undertakings. Categories of unorganised labour include, contract labour including construction workers, casual labourers, labour employed in small scale industry, handloom/power-loom workers, beedi workers, employees in shops and commercial establishments, sweepers and scavengers, workers in tanneries, and other unprotected labour.

Micro-insurance is insurance with low premiums and low caps/ coverage. It deals with small financial transactions that each insurance policy generates. This includes health insurance contract, contracts covering belongings such as place of residence like hut, livestock, tools, instruments and any other personal accident contract either for an individual or a group. Further the term life micro insurance product describes any term insurance contract with or without return of premium, any endowment insurance contract or health insurance contract with or without an accident benefit rider.

Micro-insurance is synonymous and connected to community-based financing arrangements, which includes community health funds, mutual health organisations, rural health insurance, revolving drugs funds, etc. It has been observed that most community financing schemes have evolved in the context of severe economic constraints, political instability and lack of good governance. Like Microfinance, Micro Insurance involves the active involvement of a group or community in revenue collection, pooling, resource allocation and most importantly service provision. Therefore we can deduce that micro insurance includes: (a) Transactions that are cost effective (b) Clients are from economically weaker sections of society and (c) Risk coverage specifically for the underprivileged.

The Government of India has taken initiatives through the Insurance Regulatory and Development Authority[4] (IRDA) under the IRDA Micro-Insurance Regulations, 2005, by issuing a revised set of proposals on micro insurance products. The authority has created a special category of insurance policies called micro-insurance policies to promote insurance coverage among economically vulnerable sections of society.

A micro-insurance policy could be either a general policy or life insurance policy with a sum assured of Rs 50,000 or less. All micro variable life insurance products have a lock-in period of five years from the date of inception of the policy. However partial withdrawals may be permitted, for certain policies and under certain conditions. Micro-insurance business is usually done through intermediaries like non-government organisations, self-help groups or through Micro-finance institutions. Presently, India is considered to be having the most dynamic micro insurance sector in the world. Since Micro-insurance is a low-price, high-volume business, its success and market sustainability is dependent on keeping the transaction costs down. Studies[5] on the subject suggest that progress in micro insurance can be made successful particularly when public and private sector work together, which means Public –Private Partnership, to generate demand and also for creation of innovative products.

The concept of Insurance by itself is supply driven and therefore to determine demand for insurance products is quiet a tough task by itself. Micro-insurance on the other hand is a low-price, high-volume business and such business can be successful only when the insurance providers can work hand-in-hand with non-governmental organisations (NGO's) and Self-Help Groups. The Self-help groups could assist in a better way as they are part of the target groups and secondly they would know how to address and seek approval from their counterparts. With India's population of around 70 per cent coming from rural areas, the concept of Micro insurance would seem to have a positive impact but would definitely require the creation of awareness amongst the rural masses.

In India, it is often assumed that a micro insurance policy is simply a low-premium insurance policy. However, there are a number of related factors[6] regarding clients for micro insurance as observed. They include the following characteristics:

- Live in remote rural areas, requiring a different distribution channel to urban insurance products.
- Are often illiterate and unfamiliar with the concept of insurance, requiring new approaches to both marketing and contracting.

- Tend to face more risks than wealthier people do because they cannot afford the same defenses. Therefore, for example, on an average they are more prone to illness because they do not eat as well, work under hazardous conditions and do not have regular medical check-ups.
- Have little experience of dealing with formal financial institutions, with the exception of the National Bank of Agriculture and Rural Development (NABARD) Linkage Banking programme with cooperative banks and nationalised banks for securing agricultural loans.
- For a low-income policy holder, submitting a claims form may require an expensive trip lasting a day to the nearest insurance office (thereby losing a day of work and wages), obtaining a form and paying a typist to type up the claim, sending in the claim followed by a long trip back home. Aside from the real costs of doing this, the low income policy holder may be uncomfortable with the process; clerks and other officials are often not courteous with such low-income clients and can make them feel ill at ease.
- Designing micro insurance policies requires intensive work and is not simply a question of reducing the price of existing insurance policies.

A set of regulations published in 2002 by the IRDA, entitled the '**Obligations of Insurers to Rural Social Sectors**'. This is essentially a quota system. It compels insurers to sell a percentage of their insurance policies to de facto low-income clients. It was imposed directly on those new insurers that entered Indian insurance after the market was liberalised. The old public insurance monopolies had no specified quotas, but had to ensure that the amount of business done with the specified sectors would "*not be less than what had been recorded by them for the accounting year*."

With the exception of the social-sector target, the regulations[7] do not specify the income levels of clients directly. They specify that clients must come from rural areas. With poverty in India largely located in rural areas, the effect of such a stipulation is to ensure that poor clients are sold micro insurance policies.

The unorganised sector is identified as being labour-intensive, operating using lower technology based methods, inadequate access to government schemes and government aid, and a higher proportion of migrants with a lower rate of compensation. Another distinctive feature being that those under the Unorganised Sector have a lower job security and poorer chance of growth and protection both in terms of individual and economic development. A preliminary study was conducted for identifying the reason for residents in slum areas not opting for higher education. The study brought out certain facts with regard to their social and cultural outlook; factors relating to lack of confidence, diffidence and insecurity were in many ways not encouraging these residents from opting for higher education though the government has been providing scholarships for such groups. During the course of the preliminary study it was identified that majority of the respondents were labourers from the unorganised sector and lived basically a hand-to-mouth existence. They were not aware of the various schemes and provisions that the government has been providing.

Educating the focus group on their rights and also creating in them the concept of Thrift Management and Micro Insurance would help in instilling confidence and ensuring economic development of the class.

Objectives of the Study

1. To examine the scope of Micro Insurance and Thrift Management initiatives as a catalyst in economic development of those in the unorganised sector.
2. To identify the factors influencing success and failure of Micro Insurance initiatives and interventions in the sector.
3. To examine the initiatives already being undertaken by corporate in the area of Micro Insurance.

Results and Discussion

Designing micro insurance policies requires intensive work and is not simply a question of reducing the price of existing insurance policies. It requires among other things different marketing, and different distribution and servicing channels. In addition, public reimbursement of claims could be arranged at village meetings as it would bring awareness and remove the doubts regarding reimbursement of claims among the illiterate clients. This is also an activity that could demonstrate the advantage of having insurance with a real example. Because of the quota system the largest and best-known intermediaries (NGOs/MFIs) already have existing relationships with commercial insurers that they often wish to keep. The implication of this is that insurers will need to think more creatively about their products and relationships with the intermediaries if they hope to convince them to change companies. It also implies that insurers should start exploring distribution models other than partner-agent. It is also important to demonstrate to the clients how claims are accepted or rejected.

Initiatives by TATA AIG[8]

Tata-AIG for example, has a team of 14 people working solely on micro insurance. Tata-AIG has had success building trust with the potential micro insurance market by emphasising its Tata links. Tata is a trusted company or at least deemed unlikely to misappropriate premiums by low-income clients. Others insurers with trusted local partners could make use of their connection to these partners for the same purpose.

Initiatives by ICICI Prudential[9]

ICICI Prudential has an extensive coverage in 22 states in-coordination with 274 partners aimed to reach remote rural areas in a sustainable manner. They have presently insured more than one million rural lives. ICICI Prudential has tailor made marketing collaterals, call centre support in five local languages, and created financial awareness through audio-visuals, simple application forms made available in eight regional languages for easier and better understanding of the local population. The Sarv Jana Suraksha Micro Insurance Policy which was first introduced by ICICI Prudential to provide protection and security to rural population at a very affordable cost.

Conclusion

It is very difficult to make a judgment on the costs and benefits of the regulation without actual primary research in the area. To begin with, the regulation has created a lot of curiosity and interest by regulated insurers to enter the micro insurance sector. Every insurance company has been given sales targets which are regulated by the IRDA and the quota rises each year, reaching a maximum of 16 per cent of the total number of policies sold for life insurance and five per cent of premium income for other types of insurance (after five years). Therefore, the regulated insurers are developing innovative new products and delivery channels and are bringing in their considerable resources to this task.

REFERENCES

1. Central Board for Workers Education (CBWE), Ministry of Labour and Employment, Government of India. Retrieved on 28th June 2014.
2. http://irdaeccdev.irdaonline.org:10000/
3. http://tataaiginsurance.in/
4. http://www.iciciprulife.com
5. http://www.policyholder.gov.in/Economically_Vulnerable.aspx

6. http://www.undp.org.in/report/IDF98/idfrural.htm).
7. Kulwant Rai Gupta (2009) Economics of Development and Planning. Atlantic Publishes & Distributors. ISBN 978-81-269-1011-3.
8. Microinsurance –Demand and Market prospects: India. Allianz AG, GTZ and UNDP, Public Private Partnership August 2006.
9. National Commission for Enterprises in the Unorganized Sector. Retrieved on 28th June 2014.
10. Report of the Committee on Unorganised Sector Statistics, National Statistical Commission, Government of India, February 2012.
11. Report on conditions of work and promotion of Livelihoods in the Unorganized Sector. Academic Foundation. January 2008. ISBN 978-81-7188-678-4.
12. Ruddar Datt (2008) Growth Poverty and Equity: Story of India's Economic Development. Deep and Deep Publications. ISBN 978-81-8450-088-2.
13. Social Security benefits for unorganized workers, Karnataka. Retrieved on 29th June 2014.
14. The Unorganised Workers' Social Security Act, 2008. The Gazette of India, Ministry of Law and Justice. Published by Authority, New Delhi. December 2008.
15. www.irda.gov.in

41

Economic Empowerment through Women Entrepreneurship—A Case Study of Mysore District

Divya, B.S., Dr Jagadish, V.V.

Abstract: *The emergence of the concept of the women entrepreneurship has taken foremost position in this modern world. Nowadays women are not confined to the four walls of their houses and they are not uneducated and do not fear for the age old and superstitious beliefs. Instead they are coming out of the atrocities and aspiring to touch the sky and becoming the brightest stars.*

Economic empowerment in this country is not only the most significant issue but also getting great relevance. To increase the confidence and to boost up woman's abilities many initiatives have been taken up. The notion of women entrepreneurship is considered to be an important focus point. It provides an opportunity to get dignified job for the women and gives her the opportunity to participate in decision-making process and to come out of the clutches of male-dominated society.

In this background the present study has made an attempt to understand the perception of women entrepreneurs of Mysore city and has analysed their opinion for opting their business activities and their experience. Simple random sampling method has been used to get information from the sample unit. Structured questionnaire method has been used to gather necessary information from the selected women entrepreneurs of the study area. Simple percentage method and tabular methods are applied to analyse the perception and demographic profile of respondents. The objectives of the present study are to study the factors responsible for the growth of women entrepreneurship, to analyse the demographic profile of woman entrepreneurship of study area and to understand the perceptions of woman entrepreneurs regarding their business activities.

Today woman has freedom to take part in decision making-process successfully. Now it has become her responsibility to get engaged in income generating activities to run chariot of her family. Therefore banks have also come forward to provide financial assistance with zeal and zest. When female group becomes economically stronger and get connected to the process of financial inclusion makes a positive impact on the growth process of an economy. Stronger woman builds stronger family and thereby a stronger nation.

Key words : Women Empowerment, Mysore City, Women Entrepreneurship, Banking Finance, Economic Empowerment.

Introduction

In this dynamic world women too have a significant role to play. They are the builder of any nation. They are psychologically stronger than men and they are the sources of inspiration and encouragement behind every successful man but unfortunately blind beliefs and negligence of this society have made them to cover up their talents, skills and capabilities. But today's expensive lifestyle has forced women folk to come out of the four walls of their sweet homes and new challenges have brought women force to job market. Women are gradually sinking in to the competitive and business world to enhance the financial status of their families.

The notion of Economic empowerment of women is gaining momentum nowadays. Women need to lead their life with dignity and have freedom to design their own life. Therefore empowering women is supreme goal of this era. When women get empowered it increases their economic opportunities.

What is women entrepreneurship?

Women entrepreneurship means, a woman by organising a group of female workers with set of goals run an enterprise to produce or provide goods and services. Economic conditions, educational background, socio-cultural factors and psychological attitude influence women to become an entrepreneur.

Today women entrepreneurship has become a 'buzzword'. Women are coming out of the traditional and gender biased environment to competitive business world and they are also playing a dynamic role with their extraordinary skills and potentialities.

Factors responsible for women entrepreneurship

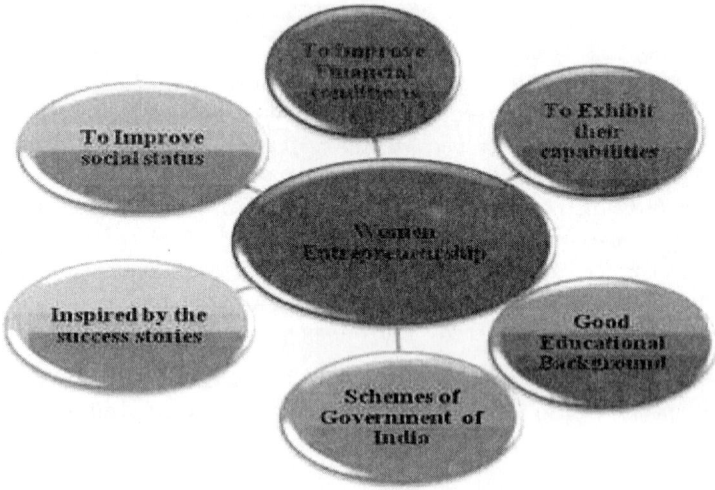

Women folk to get rid of their financial crisis are opening up their business shelter and utilising available resource to tap the maximum benefits. Entrepreneurship of women creates an opportunity for well-educated and well-trained youth to improve their carrier, enhance the capabilities and also to improve financial condition. It has helped them to meet various challenges and has brought them to the top of the social hierarchy. Government of India has also introduced various schemes such as Rural and Women Entrepreneurship Development Programme, Women's Development Cooperations, Marketing of Non Farm Products of Rural Women, Trade Related Entrepreneurship Assistance and Development, India Mahila Yojana etc. to promote a conducive business environment and to support the entrepreneurial initiatives among women.

Objectives

The present study is based on the following objectives. They are,

- To study the factors responsible for the growth of women entrepreneurship
- To analyse the demographic profile of woman entrepreneurship of study area

- To understand the perceptions of woman entrepreneurs regarding their business activities.

Methodology

Fifty women are selected on the basis of random sampling technique in Mysore city. The available data are collected through primary data. Secondary data are collected from books, journals, working papers, magazines etc. Structured questionnaire method is used to gather information from woman entrepreneurs. Tabulation and simple percentage method is used to analyse the available data.

Table 1: Reasons for opting entrepreneurship by women

Sl. No.	*Reasons*	*No. of respondents*	*Percentage*
1.	Poverty	35	70
2.	To exhibit their skills	04	8
3.	To improve social status	05	10
4.	Improved Qualification	03	6
5.	Schemes by Government	03	6
	Total	**50**	**100**

Source: Primary Data.

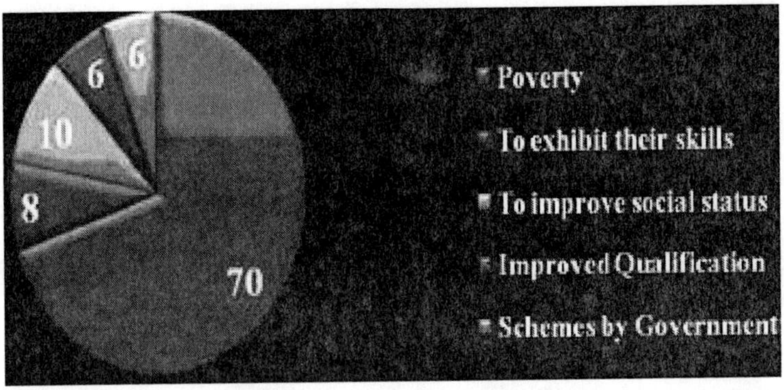

The above table and pie diagram shows that ten per cent of woman entrepreneurs are involved in business activities to improve their social status and to enhance their social prestige. eight per cent of respondents want to exhibit their skills in which they are well versed and well trained. Six per cent of respondents have prescribed educational qualification to use their skills. Remaining six per cent of respondents have got inspired by the various schemes launched by Government of India. It is noted that 70 per cent of women entrepreneurs are running their enterprises to come out of financial crisis and to overcome financial problems faced in their lives.

Table 2: Demographic Profile of Respondents

Sl. No.	*Age*	*No. of Respondents*	*Percentage*
1.	20 – 30	12	24
2.	30 – 40	20	40
3.	40 – 50	12	24
4.	50 & above	06	12
	Total	**50**	**100**

Source: Primary Data.

The above table shows that out of 50 respondents 40 per cent of respondents belong to 30 – 40 years of age group. Only 12 per cent of respondents come from the age group of 50 and above. It is observed that majority of respondents are young.

Table 3: Qualification-wise classification

Sl. No.	*Qualification*	*No. of Respondents*	*Percentage*
1.	Post Graduates	01	2
2.	Graduates	08	16
3.	SSLC Passed	41	82
	Total	**50**	**100**

Source: Primary Data.

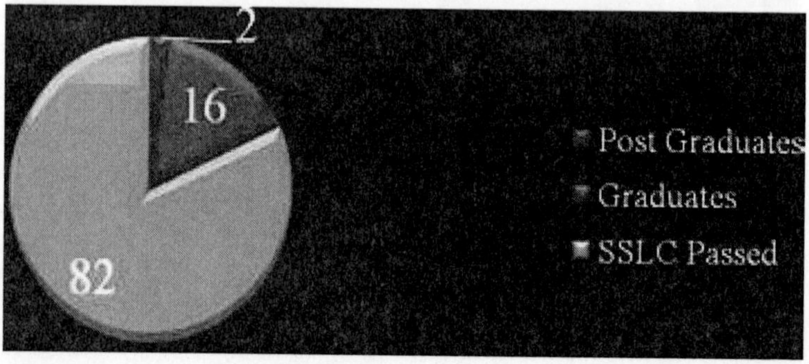

It is observed in the above figure that out of 50 respondents only one respondent has post graduation, eight respondents are graduates and 82 per cent of respondents are SSLC passed. Majority of selected women entrepreneurs are SSLC passed.

Table 4: Investments-wise classification

Sl. No.	*Investment in lakhs*	*No. of Respondents*	*Percentage*
1.	50,000 – 1,00,000	30	60
2.	1,00,000 – 1,50,000	15	30
3.	1,50,000 – 2,00,000	05	10

Source: Primary Data.

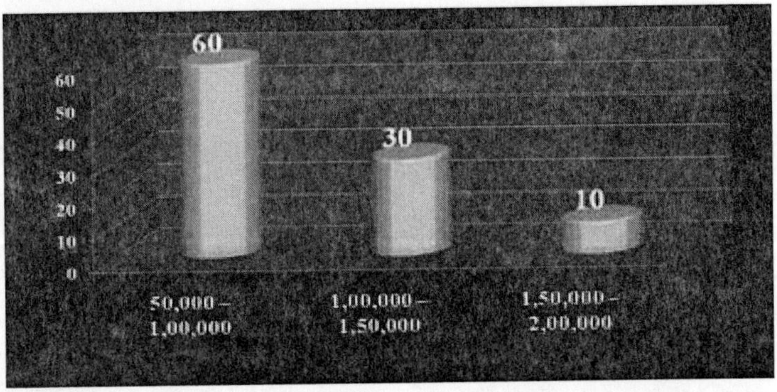

In the above table and diagram it is clear that 60 per cent of women entrepreneurs in the study area have invested their money between Rs 50,000 and Rs 1,00,000, 30 per cent of respondents have invested between Rs 1,00,000 and 1,50,000 and only ten per cent of respondents have invested more than Rs 1,50,000.

Table: Nature of business and respondents

Sl. No.	*Nature of Business*	*No. of Respondents*	*Percentage*
1.	Handicraft Business	10	20
2.	Condiments Business	22	44
3.	Tailoring and Boutique	18	36
4.	**Total**	**50**	**100**

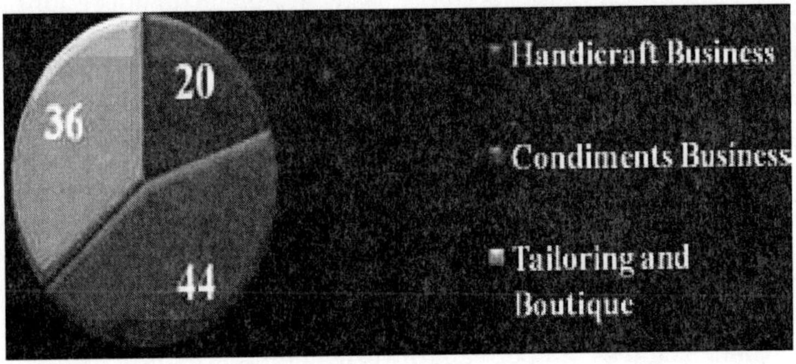

Out of 50 respondents 20 per cent of respondents are engaged in handicraft business, 44 per cent of respondents are doing condiments business and 36 per cent of respondents are running tailoring and boutique business.

Table: Perception of Women Entrepreneurs Regarding their Business Activities

Sl. No	*Level of Satisfaction*	*No. of respondents*	*Percentage*
1.	Highly Satisfied	15	30
2.	Satisfied	28	56
3.	Not Satisfied	07	14
	Total	**50**	**100**

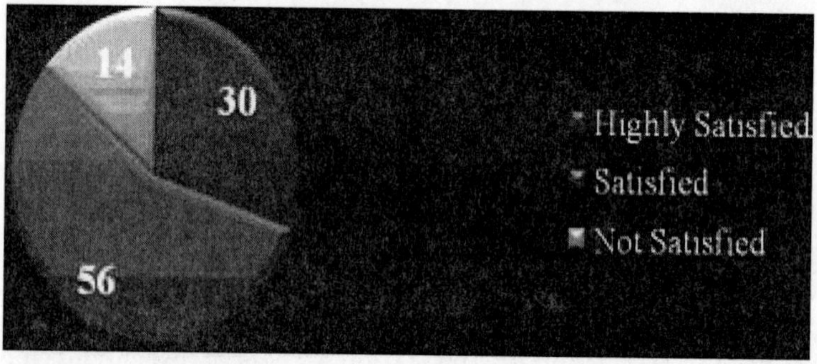

It is noted from the above table and diagram that 30 per cent of respondents are highly satisfied by being women entrepreneurs, 56 per cent of respondents are satisfied with their business activities and only 14 per cent of respondents are not satisfied with their business due to non availability of raw materials and downward trend of profit.

Findings and Conclusion

The traditional mindset of this society is changing. The transformation of Indian society has given wonderful opportunities to women folk to aspire for better living and economic independence. The following are the main findings of the study:

- Seventy per cent of women have stepped into entrepreneurship to get rid of their financial problems. Poverty has forced them to take this major step. Majority of them willingly have not taken up this business. Only eight per cent of respondents expressed that only to show their talents and utilise their skills have been engaged in business activities.
- Maximum numbers of women entrepreneurs are satisfied with their business. 30 per cent of respondents are highly satisfied and 56 per cent of respondents are satisfied but only 14 per cent

of respondents expressed their view that they are not satisfied with their business experience. They have to face some challenges such as marketing problems, non-availability of raw materials, non-cooperation from family members or over responsibilities of their families etc.

- 60 per cent of women entrepreneurs in this study area have invested their amount between Rs 50,000 and Rs 1,00,000, 30 per cent of respondents have invested Rs 1,00,000 – 1,50,000 only ten per cent have invested more than Rs 1,50,000. It indicates that with small amount investment they are successfully running their businesses.

Women entrepreneurship has given good opportunity to utilise their creativity in a positive way. They should also make use of suitable advanced technology to maximise their profit and enhance market. There is a need to stimulate and support women entrepreneurs' efforts to come forward in their lives to face personal challenges as well as to boost up their skills.

REFERENCES

1. Abadian, S. 1996 "Women's autonomy and its impact on fertility." World Development 24(12):1793-1809.
2. Acharya, Meena and Lynn Bennett 1981 "Rural Women of Nepal: An Aggregate Analysis and Summary of 8 Village Studies." The Status of Women in Nepal. Volume II, Part 9: Field Studies. Centre for Economic Development and Administration. Kathmandu: Tribhuvan University.
3. Attanapola, Chamila T., 2003 Multiple voices, multiple realities: female industrial workers' health in Sri Lanka. Norsk Geografisk Tidsskrift-Norwegian Journal of Geography, 57(3), pp.154-163.
4. Charlton S. E. (1984) Women in Third World Development, 240 pp. Boulder, Colorado: Westview Press. [One of the first studies to place women's political disadvantages on the agenda of development analysis.]
5. Charmes, Jacques; Wieringa, Saskia, 2003 Measuring women's empowerment: an
6. Dabindu Collective, 2001 Problems faced by women working in Sri Lanka's Export
7. Development index, Journal of Human Development, 1(2), pp. 191-195.
8. Dijkstra, A. Geske; Hanmer, Lucia C., 2000 Measuring Socio-Economic gender inequality: Toward an alternative to the UNDP Gender-Related Development Index,Feminist Economics, 6(2), pp.41-75.
9. Gomez, Shymala; Gomez, Mario 2004 Sri Lanka: the law's response to women
10. Goonesekere, Savatri. 2004 Overview: reflections on violence against women and the

11. Journal of Human Development, 7(2), 221-241. BOI, 2010. Industrial Relations Statistics of EPZs/IPs/EPPs in Sri Lanka, Board of Investment, Sri Lanka (As at 30/09/2010).
12. Social Indicators Research, 57(3), pp. 301-315. victim's of violence. In Savitri Goonesekere ed. Violence, Law & Women's Rights in South Asia. New Delhi: Sage. pp. 207-267.
13. Vidyarathne, D. B., 2009 Sri Lanka Labour Force Survey 2008 Final Report. Department of Census and Statistics, Ministry of Finance and Planning, Sri Lanka. Visvanathan, Nalini, 1997. Introduction. In Nalini Visvanathan et al. eds. The Women, Gender and Development Reader. London: Zed Books, pp.11-43.

42

Role of Microfinance in Rainwater Harvesting and Sanitation Programmes in India

R. Sambashivam and G. Harsha Dhar

Abstract: *Microfinance in India has been viewed as a progress tool which would alleviate poverty and enhance growth of the country through financial inclusion. Out of Six lakh villages in India, approximately 50,000 have access to finance. An India is a country which has the highest number of households which are excluded from banking. Our paper vitally assesses an attempt to create water related services, awareness and sanitation programs via microfinance loans with reference to the specific instance of rainwater harvesting. The micro financing of rainwater harvesting and sanitation is a private business model which requires households, agricultural lands and industrial sectors to privately recognize, internalize and capitalize the benefits from improved water and sanitation systems. But household water and sanitation, being closely linked to underlying common pool resources, and being merit goods, have strong public supplies characteristics and therefore depend on collective solutions. Despite their dissimilar settings and designs, evidence is found that both projects encountered similar and comparable problems at the collective level which individual microfinance loans could not address.*

The problems encountered warn against an emergent micro-privatisation of rainwater harvesting through microfinance.

Together with these things our study has made an endeavour by focusing a number of objectives those are; analyse the valuable position of microfinance for rainwater harvesting and sanitation programmes in India, evaluate the sustainable approaches of microfinance for water suppliers and Municipalities and lastly examine the global aspects of microfinance and rainwater harvesting system. A couple of hypotheses are as well set for our study; directly or indirectly microfinance contributes in the fever of water suppliers, municipals and rainwater harvesting adaptations and next sustainably, rainwater harvesting system offers an employment opportunity and circulates the capital to generate microfinance as strengthen. Finally, our paper revises the various attachment strategies related to rainwater harvesting, sanitation programmes and microfinance as for inclusive growth and emphasise which accordingly need of present economic situation.

Keywords: Sanitation, municipals, suppliers, private business, households, sustainably, MFIs.

Introduction

Microfinance is a moderately new source of funding in the rainwater harvesting and sanitation division and has potential to help increase access to water supply while improving the financial power of impoverished people. Assessing microfinance in the rainwater harvesting and sanitation segment provides a unique opportunity to analyse the implications such missions will have on women and gender empowerment. Microfinance institutions lend primarily to women. Because, women has also play a predominant position in water management and developing communities, as they are typically responsible for water related activities including water fetching, cooking, cleaning, washing and other similar activities. Using microfinance in the rainwater harvesting and sanitation sector provides a unique opportunity to increase access to water management services, create female ownership of such resources and promote gender equality.

However, microfinance is an extremely complicated source of funding and tasks must incorporate gender sensitivity and educational outreach in order to ensure that access to rainwater harvesting and sanitation sources occurs in a sustainable manner and to ensure that citizens are given a voice in the development of such services, and ultimately benefit from loans for water management services. Our paper sets out to give an extensive overview of the few components: microfinance, rainwater harvesting and sanitation.

Microfinance for Rainwater Harvesting and Sanitation Programmes

Water is conventionally seen as a public good, but with the introduction of new technologies as rainwater harvesting and sanitation programmes at household and community level, new business opportunities are emerging in the water management. It is typically noted in equivalent sectors that finance is often a constraint in creating access to such solutions especially for the low income segments. Drawing a parallel to the demand for water, a large number of Indian poor lack access to affordable financial services. Approximately in the last 20 years, microfinance has emerged as a tool that creates access to the unbanked segments of the population. The pioneers in microfinance have developed effective distribution models to reach the poor. It is in this context that a potential synergy can be explored with microfinance in creating access to rainwater harvesting and sanitation programmes.

The opportunities to integrate rainwater harvesting and sanitation programmes through microfinance have been identified in a many of successful pilot agendas around the world. However, only a few of these programmes have been able to move beyond the lead stage. Some of the constraints that these schedules have experienced include a supply driven technology focus and the lack of a sustainable saleable business model.

Microfinance, Water Supervision and Sanitation Services

Historically, microfinance has not been available for financing water supply and sanitation activities, because these are not usually perceived to be sufficiently attractive. A long-term is normally required for repayment and the direct link with income generation is not always obvious. Conversely, some microfinance institutions argue that the middle blockage to increased microfinance in the water management and sanitation sector is awareness of the business case for water supply and sanitation schemes.

Some time, in India microfinance has been used for append to the water projects; such as rainwater harvesting, watershed development, water sanitation, water management and additional programmes to revolving fund for various activities. Usually it is a first step to generate social awareness and for the productive uses for instance of backward gardening and livestock. But more recently, it has linked to cost recovery policies aiming to increase user's contributions and social attention. Microfinance is also being used to help pay for capital costs and to cover operation and maintenance expenses. Microfinance can also help households and communities to access water services when high lump sum costs have to be paid up front. This is especially the case in urban and agricultural areas, where utilities charge high connection costs.

Global Water Management and Sanitation Crisis

The global rainwater harvesting and sanitation crisis is one of the looming development issues of the 21st century. The World Health Organisation defines access to water as 50 to 100 liters of water might need each person as for every day. The source of water must meet the drinking-safety levels of national or local standards and should be within 1,000 meters of the home with collection time under more than 30 minutes.

The United Nations Development Programme claims that water should be affordable and recommends the price of water should not exceed three per cent of household income. The United Nations also acknowledges that "all water facilities and services must be culturally appropriate and sensitive to gender, lifecycle and privacy requirements". Access to sanitation is defined by the United Nations as access to facilities that separate human waste from human contact.

As of 2010, over 780 million people lacked access to clean water and 2.5 billion lacked access to improved sanitation, according to the 2012 Millennium Development Goal Progress Report by the WHO and UNE, Scientific, and Cultural Organisation's Joint Monitoring Programem. Joint Monitoring Programme's 2012 Progress Report announces that, as of 2010, the target for drinking water has been met, as over two billion people gained access to improved drinking water sources since 1990 (WHO/UNICEF JMP for Water Supply and Sanitation 2012). However, the JMP Report recognises that there still remains a great deal of work to be done to provide the remaining 780 million people with access to safe drinking water. It is important to note that even with access to water, as defined above, households still may not have access to piped water in their homes and women may still have to walk a mile to fetch water.

Microfinance through Water Suppliers and Municipalities

Small-scale water providers have been played a very significant role for water harvesting and water supply. Especially in poor urban areas are tending to lack access for credit, which would for example enable them to buy water storage facilities. Borehole operators need finance to drill boreholes and for build small water networks. Without such access, most operators rely on family and informal loans and limiting their potential for growth.

Besides small scale providers, municipalities often play a crucial character in providing water services. However, often municipalities are not allowed to access credit because of the legal framework also because they cannot obtain a credit rating as an independent assessment of the creditworthiness of a borrower. Either because they are insolvent and they do not have the resources to pay for the rating. This is a major constraint on their ability to provide water supply services. As a result there is increasing interest from International Finance Institutions and bilateral to support sub sovereign lending and guarantees for the water sector. These need to be adapted to the local realities of countries with weak also for non-existent financial markets.

Resourceful Position of Rainwater Harvesting for Microfinance

The Rainwater Harvesting and Sanitation scheme will raise incomes and improve the livelihoods of poor smallholder farmers in upland villages. It will support government efforts to limit further degradation of upland watersheds and improve the natural resource base. The mission will engage villagers in decisions and processes relating to the rehabilitation of natural resources. It will also build a strong sense of ownership among upland communities, thereby ensuring sustainability of the investments.

In national level some of our states have an ultimate irrigation potential of about 121.74 lakh hectare approximately. Proper assessment of ground water resources on yearly basis, promotion of rain water harvesting structures, financing of micro institution structures, drip and sprinkler irrigation would help in achieving this targeted scheme in other words it would be a good experimental action for coming generation.

Objectives

The broad objectives of the present study shall be:

- To analyse the valuable position of microfinance for rainwater harvesting and sanitation programmes in India.
- To evaluate the sustainable approaches of microfinance for water suppliers and Municipalities.
- To examine the global aspects of microfinance and rainwater harvesting system.

Hypotheses

The present study has set the following tentative hypotheses:

- Directly or indirectly microfinance contributes for the fever of water suppliers, municipals and rainwater harvesting adaptations.
- Sustainably, rainwater harvesting offers an employment opportunity and circulates the capital to generate microfinance as strengthen.

Methodology

The Methodology is very essential to construct any research work. Both qualitative and quantitative methods were used in the study. Our article has required Secondary data. Secondary data had gathered from published sources such as various journals, periodicals, articles, books, literatures and reports on the subject. For the purpose of gathering the latest, updated information on the topic E-sources will also consulted.

Micro Finance and Rainwater Harvesting from Global Perspective

In many countries, rainwater harvesting is still marginal and often goes unacknowledged as a means to improve the economic, social and environmental livelihoods of local urban and rural communities. However, the available resource of rainwater is a valuable component of integrated water resources management that contributes to the global efforts towards achieving the Millennium Development Goals and sustainable development.

Despite the potential of rainwater harvesting to empower local communities and enhance their development capacities, especially in developing countries, there are several perceived blockages. These include lack of awareness, lack of institutional framework in terms of non-existent or poor policies at national and local levels, information gaps, low investment in research and development and lack of private sector participation.

Another heavy burden on developing countries is poverty and water scarcity. Approximately, with over four billion people of the world's 6.5 billion at the bottom of the pyramid, delivering access to water and sanitation has never been more critical. In recent years, micro-finance has emerged as an important weapon against poverty and its potential to increase the accessibility to rainwater harvesting looks promising.

Rainwater harvesting and micro-finance share common structural characteristics, and as a result, the latter appears to be an efficient delivery mechanism to bring rainwater harvesting solutions to communities in developing countries. Microfinance can be defined as the provision of a wide range of financial services to low-income individuals and communities that could not otherwise have access to those services through formal financial institutions. Here are clear parallels between rainwater harvesting and microfinance from at least two stand points; firstly, microfinance institutions are in the process of expanding to rural and pre-urban areas where the need to deliver access to water and sanitation is most pressing. The rural microfinance sector means that such institutions are well positioned to understand specific needs to each community (locally based demand). Secondly, through practical assistance and capacity building, typically provided by microfinance institutions to their customers, microfinance contributes to empower and develop the entrepreneurial strength of rural communities.

Complementarities also arise in terms of how rainwater harvesting and microfinance are both community driven. The microfinance approach rests on group lending, where borrowers are jointly responsible for debt repayments, and peer pressure to provide finance without collateral as mainstream financial institutions usually require. Hence, provision of microcredit could enable poor communities to collectively access the financial resources needed to develop rainwater harvesting infrastructures that will yield benefits to all members of a community through positive spill-over effects related to improved quality of life.

Fundamentally, financing rainwater harvesting schemes and projects through microcredit offers the benefit of requiring less resource mobilisation in the long term, com-pared to donor-funded initiatives. As loans contracted to set up rainwater harvesting facilities are gradually paid back by individuals as benefiting from agricultural revenues, resources become available to channel into other schemes or to extend rainwater harvesting initiatives to reach more communities experiencing water scarcity. Micro-fiinance thus appears to be a sustainable delivery vehicle to enable communities address the challenges of access to water and sanitation through their own effort and ultimately brings a sense of ownership and responsibility.

Some thoughts on Microfinance in India

- There is a growing trend of expansion of urban microfinance: two urban MFIs in Bangalore, and one each in Ahmedabad, Kolkata and Mumbai, are negotiating with equity investors and lenders.

- One of the distinguishing features of Indian microfinance has been the lack of savings which have proven so successful in reaching and empowering mainly poor women elsewhere.
- Indian MFIs have one of the lowest interest rates in the world. For small start-up MFIs and for new products, unit transactions costs are particularly high. There is a need for MFIs to have mechanisms in place to recover realistic interest rates if they are to survive and grow. This does not mean that the costs have to be all charged to the clients, but overheads and other transaction costs need to be taken properly into account.
- The microfinance sector in India in its broadest sense is highly decentralised, with no single agency responsible for its development. Some useful information resources already exist but most information as bank lending to the MFI sector, investments by capital funds, information on new products, etc. is very disperse.

Findings

The major optimal findings are as follows:

- Under the microfinance some organisations are providing a loans and subsidies to adopt the rain water harvesting system.
- Environmental based microfinance organisations are strongly supports to implement the rainwater harvesting system.
- Microfinance is devoting their presence to increase our national income by contributing for rainwater harvesting and other water related sanitation business.
- Microfinance is preserving a good affiliation among the household, agricultural and industrial sectors by executing their water management facilities by implementing rain water harvesting system.

Suggestions

On the basis of above study, the following suggestions are recommended to overcome water scarcity/poverty. These are all vital perception of Rain Water Harvesting for effective and sustainable development of the nation with the valuable assist of Microfinance.

- The active awareness programs and workshops to be conducted/ organised to implement the rainwater harvesting system through Microfinance toward save the water energy.
- The government should take the correct action to observe the microfinance position as in rainwater harvesting system schemes, projects, acts, subsidies and loans.

- There is a need of conducting a survey to identify the beneficiaries and to examine the effects and affects of microfinance for rainwater harvesting system.
- It should be respond the microfinance demands to the accomplishment of rainwater harvesting system as successfully.
- It should recognise and support the microfinance organisations which are serving the society by executing the rainwater harvesting system to regenerate the water resource.

Conclusion

Accordingly our above study invisibly microfinance playing a friendly role to implement a rain water harvesting as successful for all household, industrial and agricultural sectors. But practically management/government have to respond the microfinance's activates by making effective projects, schemes, surveys and other related appreciable acts. Nowadays by following too much of advanced civilisation aspects knowingly or unknowingly we are losing our basic requirements and resources water foundations. Water scarcity, water poverty and water problem tasks are the tentative example for these things! The rain is a primary source for all kind of water resources. So it is only the way, if we want to save water energy? If we want to protect water for tomorrow's next generation, if we want to avoid water related dependency and if we want to survive in healthy society, we have to adopt rain water harvesting by following sanitation programmes instructions with the moral help of microfinance. So as for all these livelihoods microfinance have a superior responsibility in our eco-friendly society!

REFERENCES

1. Mehta M and Virjee K, "Financing Small Water Supply and Sanitation Service Providers: Exploring the Microfinance Option in Sub-Saharan", Water and Sanitation Program (Dec 2003); pp. 03–10.
2. Anil K. Khandelwal, "Microfinance Development Strategy for India", Economic and Political Weekly, (March – 31 – 2007); pp. 54.
3. NWP and IRC, "Microfinance for Water Sanitation and Hygiene", (October – 2007); pp. 03–19.
4. Reis N. and P. Mollinga, 'Microcredit for Rural Water Supply and Sanitation in the Mekong Delta: Policy Implementation between the Needs for Clean Water and "Beautiful Latrines", ZEF Working Paper 49. Bonn: Center for Development Research, ZEF, (2009).

5. Philip Mader, "Attempting the Production of Public Goods through Microfinance: The Case of Water and Sanitation", Journal of Infrastructure Development 13(1) 153–170, © 2011 India Development Foundation, SAGE Publications Los Angeles, London, New Delhi, Singapore, Washington DC, (March – 2011); pp. 06–08.
6. WHO/UNICEF and JMP, "Water Supply and Sanitation Progress on Drinking Water and Sanitation: 2012 Update", Progress Report, UNICEF and World Health Organisation, (2012); pp. 03–08.
7. Abby Waldorf, "Assessing the Role of Women in Microfinance for Water Supply and Sanitation Services", University of Pennsylvania Department of Earth and Environmental Studies, (July – 16 – 2012); pp. 19–24.
8. S. Sunitha., "A Comprehensive Study on Micro Finance Institutions in India", Galaxy International Interdisciplinary Research Journal: ISSN 2347-6915, GIIRJ, Vol. 2 (2), (Feb – 2014); pp. 06–10.
9. http://www.mfinindia.org
10. http://www.who.org
11. http://www.righttowater.info/code/General-Comment-15
12. http://www. mixmarket.org/mfi/country/India

43

Impact of Microfinance on Non-Agricultural Activities: an Empirical Investigation

Dinesha P.T. and Prasanna Kumar T.

Abstract: *Women's empowerment is critical to the process of development of the community and bringing women into the mainstream of development has been a major concern of the government since independence. Hence, after a series of efforts and strategies micro-finance through self help groups has been working as a powerful tool to fight poverty became the effective approach of financial inclusion. Several livelihood strategies have been adopted by the Self Help Group (SHG) member in general and the poor SHG member in particular to derive their bread and butter. Among these non-agricultural occupations like preparation of areca leaf plates, tailoring, petty shops, home industry etc are very popular. However, here also SHG women face several problems. Hence, the paper designed with the objective to discuss the investment and income of SHG members in non-agricultural activities across promoters, income and social groups and to suggest suitable policy prescriptions. The study found that the SHG members formed by NGO have made relatively more investment in non-agricultural occupations as compared to the SHG members formed by Cooperative and Government agencies. Across social groups, it was the SHG members* *belonging to other households who have invested more in non-agricultural activities as compared to the SHG members belonging to SCs and STs. Similarly, in the case of sample households with different levels of income groups, it was noticed that as the income level of the households tended to rise, the average micro credit invested in non-agricultural occupations increased up to certain level and then sharply declined. This shows that micro credit invested by the very high income group households tended to be lower as compared to that of low income group households.*

Introduction

Several livelihood strategies have been adopted by the Self Help Group (SHG) member in general and the poor SHG member in particular to derive their bread and butter. Their basic needs are not many, but they keep changing across space and time. The basic needs of them can be grouped into two categories, namely, physical needs- basic to survival, and livelihood needs, which can be regarded as essential for meeting basic family needs. The important physical needs are staple food, water, energy and shelter. The main livelihood needs are cash (needed for buying necessities, buying clothes, paying school, clinic fees, paying for small daily items such as soap, oil, tobacco, etc.), inputs to production, and cultural and community assets. A large chunk of the SHG members combine several strategies or diversify among the members to meet both physical and survival needs so that the decent standard of living can be ensured. Depending on the availability of their capital assets such as land, labour, savings, etc, the livelihood strategies are adopted by the SHG members to meet their physical and survival needs.The provision of micro credit not only generated employment for reasonable proportion of SHG members but it also created lots of employment for others, with varying degrees across different promoters and social groups. The provision of micro credit, therefore, has several economic effects; the generation of employment for both SHG member and non-SHG members is also one of them. Micro credit obtained to investment in agricultural and non-agricultural occupations to generate employment and income for their families. Most of the studies on microfinance and women empowerment speak about the positive side impact of microfinance on women's empowerment, but there are also some studies which question the ability of microfinance in empowering women and combating poverty. Studies like Carr *et al* (1996), Harper (1998), Dadhich (2001), Sudarshan Synghal (2002), Venkatarao (2009), Reddy Narasimhalu (2009), Vimala (2009) and Tankha *et al* (2005), Purohit (2003), Isabelle (2006) and Jayasheela and Palanna (2005) showed that participation of women in women organisations like SHGs has changed their lives economically, socially and politically. They argue that there is a positive correlation between women empowerment and SHG microfinance. A study by Hulme *et al*, (1996) Rajsekar (2004), Moyle *et al* (2006), Joanna (2000), Kamal Vatta (2003) and Gupta *et al* (2010) showed that just because women are clients of MFIs do not mean they will automatically become empowered and it is generally accepted that it is not a silver bullet to the problems of poverty reduction and women's empowerment.

Thus, a review of several studies conducted in regional, national and international level, brought-out divergent findings and conclusions on the ability of SHG microfinance in empowering women and poverty reduction. Moyle *et al* (2006) in his study found some negative appraisals of pressure, challenges and stress for most of the SHG members. Against this background, the present study is designed with the following objectives. 1. To know the investment and income of SHG members in non-agricultural activities across promoters, income and social groups; 2. To discuss the income of SHG members in Casual wage and self employment across promoters, income and social groups; 3.To suggest suitable policy prescriptions.

Research Design

The study is based on primary sources of data. The primary data were collected by canvassing the structured interview schedule for the sample households of 240 in Dakshina Kannada and Udupi districts of Karnataka State. The sample members of SHGs of three different promotes, i.e., NGO, Co-operative and Government were interviewed for collection of primary data. From each promoter, the members of SHGs belonging to the Scheduled Caste (SCs), the Scheduled Tribes (STs) and Others (Other castes including Other Backward Castes) were considered as the target group members. From each promoter 80 SHG members consisting 40 members from each district 20 members from each taluk ten SHG members from each village were selected for the interview. The data were analysed by using the simple percentage, average and indices, wherever appropriate.

Results and Discussion

Micro credit obtained to investment in agricultural and non-agricultural occupations to generate employment and income for their families. The important livelihood strategies adopted by most of the SHG members are related to the agricultural sector such as cultivation of paddy, dairy farming and sale of milk, milk made products, composite. In the case of non-agricultural occupations, the important activities are preparation of areca leaf plates, tailoring, petty shops, marketing of fish, dairy farming, home industry-candle making, pickle making, Incense Stick making, soap making, etc. They also undertake casual wage employment working in agricultural and non-agricultural occupations.

Investment and Income from Non-Agriculture through **Micro Credit**

An effort has been made to analyse the investment and income generated through the non-agricultural activities for which the micro credit was obtained. The data provided in Table 1 depicts that the average micro credit invested in non-agricultural occupations was worked out to be about Rs 2546, which is marginally higher as compared to that of in agricultural sector. The SHG members formed by NGO have made relatively more investment in non-agricultural occupations as compared to the SHG members formed by Cooperative and Government agencies. Across social groups, it was the SHG members belonging to other households who have invested more in non-agricultural activities as compared to the SHG members belonging to SCs and STs.

Table 1: Distribution of Average Investment and Income in Non-Agricultural Activities per SHG Member by Promoters, Social and Income Groups (Rs)

Particulars	*Average Investment through micro credit in non-agriculture*	*Average Income earned from non-agriculture*
	Promoters	
NGO	3959	5034
Co-operative	2370	2738
Government	1282	1052
Total	**2546**	**2968**
	Social Groups	
SCs	1776	2107
STs	2022	2148
Others	3092	3643
Total	**2546**	**2968**
	Income Groups	
LIGs	1826	1476
MIGs	2785	3339
HIGs	2797	2698
VHIGs	1000	2815
Total	**2546**	**2968**

Note: LIGs: Low income groups; MIGs Medium income groups; HIGs: High income groups; VHIGs: Very high income groups.

Source: Primary Survey.

Similarly, in the case of sample households with different levels of income groups[1], it was noticed that as the income level of the households tended to rise, the average micro credit invested in non-agricultural occupations increased up to certain level and then sharply declined. This shows that micro credit invested by the very high income group households tended to be lower as compared to that of low income group households.

As regards income earned from the non-agricultural activities, the average income was estimated to be at 2968, slightly lower than that earned from the agricultural occupations. The income earning patterns by the sample SHG members classified with different units were found to be the same as one observed in the case of agricultural occupations, except for income groups. It can be noted here that micro credit investment in agricultural activities was lower but the average earnings from them were found to be marginally higher as compared to that of non-agricultural occupations. The use of micro credit in agricultural activities seemed to have yielded better income to the sample SHG members. This is quite possible that most of the villages surveyed were irrigated and had fertile land suited to raise some market oriented cash crops.

Total Income Earned by SHG Members

An effort has also been made to estimate the average income earned by the SHG members from their wage labour without making any investment. The data provided in Table 2 indicate that the average income earned by way of wage labour was approximated with Rs 8885. This amount was found to be relatively more for the SHG members formed by Government followed by Co-operative as compared to that of NGO. This implies that NGO-led SHG members were motivated to take up more of self-employment in agricultural and non-agricultural sectors as compared to that of other promoting agencies.

The average income earned was found to be more in the case of SHG members belonging to SCs and STs as compared to other households. This implies that the dependency of SCs and STs on wage employment was more and less on self-employment due to limited savings, limited income and limited micro credit access and investment. Across different income groups, the average income earned by way of wage labour tended to decline as the income levels tended to rise. This show their reduced dependency on wage labour as their capability to invest more in self-employment either in agriculture and/or non-agricultural sectors tended rise.

As far as the average income earned by way of beedi rolling is concerned, it has been observed that the average income was found to be around Rs 4316, the second important source of income to the SHG members. No much variation was observed across different promoters, social and income groups. This is due to the fact that this activity was nothing to do with the formation of SHG; it was independent of the group concern.

Table 2: Source-wise Distribution of Average income earned by SHG Members

Particulars	*Casual wage employment*		*Self-employment*		*All Sources*
	Wage Labour	*Beedi Rolling*	*Agriculture*	*Non-Agriculture*	
Promoters					
NGO	6886	4764	3978	5034	20662
Co-operative	9016	3999	3506	2738	19259
Government	10797	4190	2442	1052	18481
Total	**8885**	**4316**	**3317**	**2968**	**19486**
Social Groups					
SCs	11828	3540	2330	2107	19804
STs	10932	4817	3465	2148	21362
Others	6790	4506	3721	3643	18660
Total	**8885**	**4316**	**3317**	**2968**	**19486**
Income Groups					
LIG	10313	3087	1750	1476	16626
MIG	9690	4526	2730	3339	20285
HIG	6464	4472	5329	2698	18963
VHIG	8835	3818	3150	2815	18618
Total	**8885**	**4316**	**3317**	**2968**	**19486**

Source: Primary Survey.

The average income earned by SHG members from all the sources was estimated to be around Rs 19486. This amount was found to be higher for the SHG members formed by NGO as compared to that of Cooperative and Government agencies. This shows that the NGO has taken proactive role in providing the micro credit and non-credit services and thereby contributing to an increased amount of income to the SHG members as compared to other agencies.

In the case of social groups, the average income of SHG members belonging to other households was estimated at Rs 18660, while the members of SCs with Rs 19804 and STs with Rs 21362. The average income of the members of STs was found to be higher mainly because of the wage earnings were found to be higher. Across the sample households with different levels of income groups, the figure was found to higher in the case of medium income groups followed by very low, high and very high income groups (Figure 1). It is evident that the members of SHG were involved in wage labour, beedi rolling, agricultural and non-agricultural self-employment. For these members, the income earned by way of wage labour was found to be higher and followed by beedi rolling as compared to the activities (agricultural and non-agricultural self-employment) for which micro credit was invested. This shows that for a large number of SHG members, the income from the micro-financed activities was found to be lower than those of other sources (wage labour and beedi rolling). This points out that there is a large space for NGOs and other promoting agencies to provide micro credit and encourage the members of SHG to take non-agricultural self-employment by providing appropriate training to them.

Figure 1: Source-wise Distributional Pattern of Average Income by sample households with different Income Groups

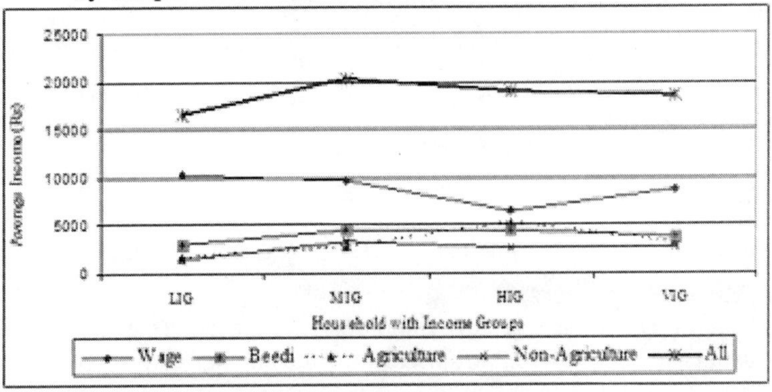

Proportion of income earned from Casual wage employment and Self-employment

The data provided in Table 3 indicates that the proportion of income earned from wage employment accounted for 45.6 per cent followed by beedi rolling (22.15 per cent), agriculture (17.02 per cent) and non-agricultural self-employment (15.23 per cent). This is not uniform across different promoters, social and income groups. The proportion of income from wage employment was much higher in the case of SHG members formed by Government (58.42 per cent) followed by Cooperative (46.82 per cent) and NGO (33.33 per cent). The data show that the income share earned by the micro-financed activities known as self-employment was found to be yet lower than those casual wage employment in all the promoters, leaving the huge space for access and usage of micro credit for their survival. This space was found to be quite significant in the case of SHG members formed by Government agencies and Co-operative agencies as compared to NGO (Figure 2). This means that the income uncertainty and degree of indecent work was found to be quite significant in the case of SHG members formed by Government and Co-operative agencies as compared to NGO.

Table 3: Source-wise Distribution of Income Share Earned by SHG Members

Particulars	*Casual wage employment*		*Self-employment*		*All Sources*
	Wage Labour	*Beedi Rolling*	*Agriculture*	*Non-Agriculture*	
Promoters					
NGO	33.33	23.06	19.25	24.36	100
Co-operative	46.82	20.76	18.21	14.21	100
Government	58.42	22.67	13.21	5.69	100
Total	**45.60**	**22.15**	**17.02**	**15.23**	**100**
Social Groups					
SCs	59.73	17.87	11.76	10.64	100
STs	51.17	22.55	16.22	10.05	100
Others	36.39	24.15	19.94	19.52	100
Total	**45.60**	**22.15**	**17.02**	**15.23**	**100**
Income Groups					
LIG	62.03	18.57	10.53	8.88	100
MIG	47.77	22.31	13.46	16.46	100
HIG	34.08	23.59	28.10	14.23	100
VHIG	47.46	20.50	16.92	15.12	100
Total	**45.60**	**22.15**	**17.02**	**15.23**	**100**

Source: Primary Survey.

In respect of social groups, the proportion of income earned by way of casual wage employment in agricultural and non-agricultural sectors was found to be quite higher for the SHG members belonging to SCs with 77.6 per cent and STs with 73.73 per cent as compared to those SHG members belonged to other households with 60.54 per cent. No SHG members belonging to any social groups tended to earn income from the micro financed activities more than 50 per cent. This points to the fact the SHG members belonging to SC and ST households may face greater uncertainty in income earnings and unsafe working conditions as compared to those SHG members belonging to other households (Figure 3).

Figure 2: Distribution of Income Share between Casual Wage Employment and Micro-financed Self-employment by Promoters

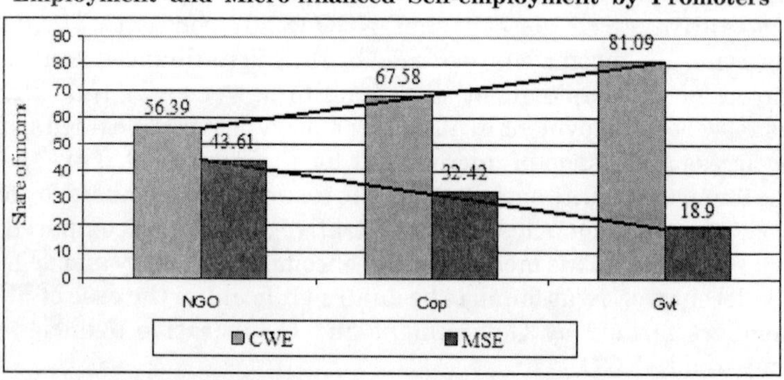

Note: CWE: Casual wage employment; MSE: Micro-financed self-employment.
Source: Table 3.

Figure 3: Distribution of Income Share between Casual Wage Employment and Micro-financed Self-employment by Social Groups

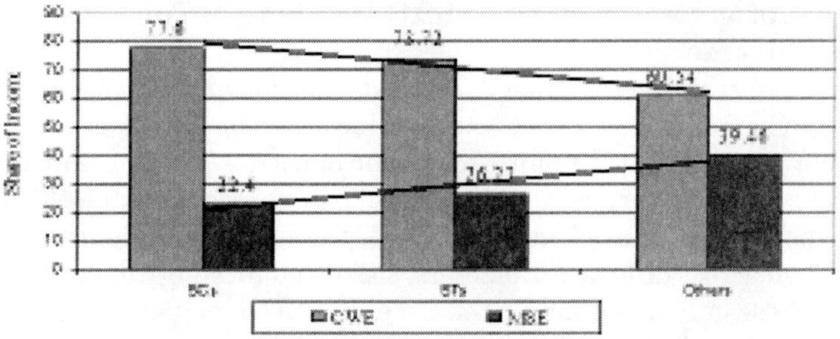

Note: CW: Casual wage employment; MSE: Micro-financed self-employment.
Source: Table 3.

It is very important for the promoters to note the point that in view of social inclusive and more broad-based growth, a greater importance may be accorded to those who are continued to be excluded from access of micro credit and other facilities.

In the case of the SHG members with different levels of household's income groups, the proportion of income earned through the casual wage employment was found to be expectedly higher for low income group households with 80.6 per cent followed by medium (70.08 per cent) and high income groups (57.6 per cent). Whereas in the case of very high income group households, the proportion of income from casual wage employment started to increase as compared to the low income group households. The proportion of income earned through the casual wage employment tended to decline sharply up to high income group households and then began to rise moderately for very high income group households (Figure 6.9). This may be attributed to the fact that in case of very high income group households, quite few members were high skilled causal workers in the study areas as also in nearby states and abroad.

Figure 4: Distribution of Income Share between Casual Wage Employment and Micro-financed Self-employment by Income Groups

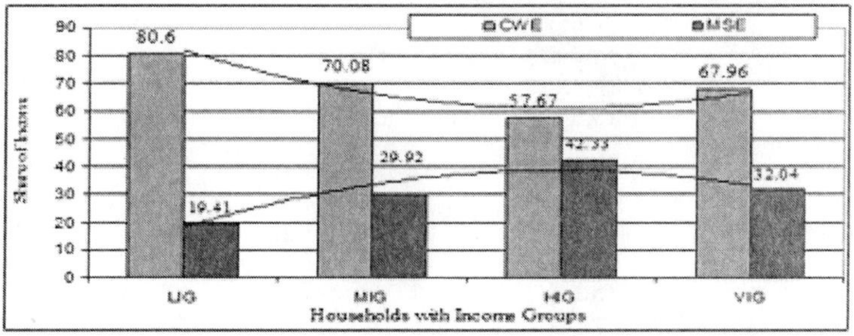

Note: CW: Casual wage employment; MSE: Micro-financed self-employment.
Source: Table 3.

Share of Income Earned by SHG Members in Total Household Income

An effort has been made to estimate the share of income earned by SHG members in total household income. The data presented in Table 4 shows that the share of income earned by SHG members in total household income was accounted a little less than one-third of the household annual income (27.40 per cent). This figure is not uniform across different promoters, social and income groups (Figure 5). It was much higher in the case of SHG members formed by Government followed by Cooperative and NGOs, belonged to SC and ST households as compared to others households and belonged to the low and medium income group households as compared to high and very high income group households (Figure 5).

Across different sources of income, the share of income earned by SHG members was found to be higher in the case of non-agricultural self-employment accounting for 78.5 per cent, followed by beedi rolling (70.69 per cent), agricultural self-employment (25 per cent) and wage labour (18.5 per cent). What is important is that the share of income from the activities for which micro credit was accessed and invested was found to be higher. This means that because of her joining to SHG the household annual income has gone up and women were expected to be respected and honoured at home.

Table 4: Share of Income Earned by SHG Members in Total Households Annul Income by Promoters, Social and Income Groups (per cent)

Particulars	*Casual wage employment*		*Self-employment*		*All Sources*
	Wage Labour	*Beedi Rolling*	*Agriculture*	*Non-Agriculture*	
Promoters					
NGO	12.97	71.78	22.89	94.64	25.07
Co-operative	18.54	70.84	30.78	73.12	28.16
Government	25.77	69.30	21.93	31.85	29.63
Total	**18.54**	**70.69**	**24.94**	**78.49**	**27.40**
Social Groups					
SCs	24.92	82.12	49.62	95.26	33.87
STs	25.46	69.52	40.13	90.83	35.16
Others	13.60	67.63	19.53	71.06	23.11
Total	**18.54**	**70.69**	**24.94**	**78.49**	**27.40**
Income Groups					
LIG	34.33	76.34	44.30	-	49.41
MIG	23.09	73.63	39.86	40.49	34.85
HIG	11.18	55.73	25.28	46.16	20.44
VHIG	10.57	39.44	6.09	52.72	12.90
Total	**18.54**	**70.69**	**24.94**	**78.49**	**27.40**

Source: Primary Survey.

Figure 5: Share of Income Earned by SHG Members in Total Household Annual Income by Promoters, Social and Income Groups

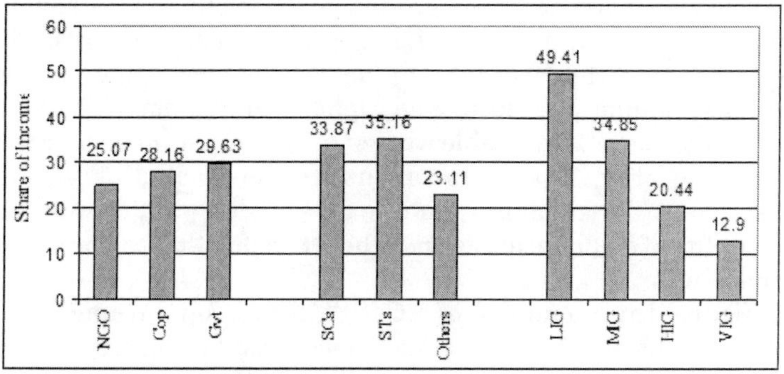

Source: Table 5.

The share of income from the non-agricultural self-employment (for which micro finance was provided) was higher for the SHG members formed by NGO (95 per cent) followed by Cooperative (73.1 per cent) as compared to that those formed by Government agencies, which accounted as low as 32 per cent. This can be noted that NGO formed SHG members have contributed a lot to the household annual income by way of joining SHG movement in the villages.

Across social groups, the share of income earned through agricultural and non-agricultural self-employment was found to be higher for the SHG members belonging to SCs and STs as compared to those belonged to other households. Similarly, in the case of households with different levels of income groups, the share of income earned through non-agricultural self-employment tended to increase and from agriculture tended to decline sharply as the income levels of the SHG households tended to rise. This shows that the household with lower income, the share of income earned by SHG members from agricultural was lower and that from non-agricultural self-employment was found to be higher as compared to the SHG households with high income groups. It is evident that SHG members played an important role in contributing to the annual household income by joining the SHG and also undertaking subsidiary occupations.

Suggestions and Conclusion

Based on the findings of the study, the following policy measures can be suggested for better functioning of SHGs and their sustainability to ensure women's empowerment and bring them on mainstream development: Firstly, government promoted group are availing much internal loans which is much less amount compared to external loans. They face the problem of lack of active support or guarantee agencies like NGOs. Hence, for such groups government should support through some policy measures. Loan amount should be increased to the extent that they can take up an income generating activity. Secondly, simple procedure and right encouragement from the financial agencies may enable women to form more and more SHGs in their locality. The financial institutions including various government departments should give wider publicity on the availability of credit facilities and others benefits that can be offered to the SHGs.

Thirdly, the members of SCs/ STs and low-income group households have not invested much micro credit on agriculture and related IGA's. The main problem of them is the lack of land. Even though these communities have some amount of land they are not suitable for cultivation. It is in mostly hilly regions and even irrigation facility is not good. Thus, for time being training should be given them to concentrate on much IGA's other than agriculture related like tailoring, soap, phenol making, agarbathi making since it does not need any land. Fourthly, Most of the SHG members especially streeshakti members avail micro credit for consumption purpose only. It is much more in low income groups and among SC and ST members. It is partly because many of the households have limited access to basic infrastructural facilities and also limited access to food grains obtained from PDS. Thus, government should think in this direction and should provide basic infrastructural facilities like electricity, water supply, house and adequate provision of food grains through PDS. The promoters should create awareness among the SC/ST and low income members to reduce consumption expenditure and concentrate on investment expenditure.

Fifthly, Groups formed by NGOs have motivated more members to undertake IGAs through micro credit. Hence, it is suggested that co-operatives and governments have to train their SHG members to undertake more and more IGAs. Special attention should be given to SC, ST and low income groups. Promotes have to motivate their and respective members to change their occupation in favour of better paid self employment. Sixthly, the main problem faced by the SHG members in adopting income generating activity is due to the lack of better marketing facilities. Even though the groups formed by NGOs has some ray of hope since their promoting agency created a Marketing agency called *'Siri'* to some extent they too face the problem of marketing for some goods. Hence, there is a need of aggressive policy by the state governments on the provision of marketing facilities. A place to market the products must be established in the gram panchayat area or village. So that the respondents can have access to market to sell their products and thereby grow in their business.

Sixthly, it can be suggested that training on innovative economic activities by using the resources in and around the taluk or district may be given to the SHGs members. The training should be given besides conventional or traditional business activities to all the members of the group. The training in the areas such as vermicelli making, beautician training, training on bakery unit may also be given. Because it provides a good income for them compared to other self employments. Since most of the SHG members are housewives, home-based production should be promoted so that the members can make optimum use of their time and get required assistance from her family members. Finally, simple procedure and right encouragement from the financial agencies may enable women to form more and more SHGs in their locality. The financial institutions including various government departments should give wider publicity on the availability of credit facilities and others benefits that can be offered to the SHGs.

It is evident that a larger proportion of SHG members have actively taken part in economic domains of their life. In the process of ensuring empowerment of women, there are several constraints such as illiteracy, rigid institutional and social factors which prevent women from going for work or taking part in any economic or social related functions, opposition from her husband or in-laws against what woman do and the like. Hence, to get better results through SHGs the capacity of women belonging to SCs and STs. It is required to be further improved and bring them into main stream development. In spite several intricacies in the process, NGO has been more successful in mobilising the women members and building their economic empowerment of them and thereby bringing them on to mainstream development of the rural economy. SHG- Microfinance has drawn attention to an entire sector of borrowers who had been previously poorly served by the formal financial sector. But the provision of micro credit is not a magic bullet to bring about far-reaching changes in the life of the women and there are no hundred per cent guarantees that microfinance always leads to empowerment of women and poverty eradication. The variations in performance of SHGs across the promoters, social and income groups need immediate attention. Government has to take proper initiative, so that the spread of SHGs movement can be streamlined across the country.

REFERENCES

1. Carr Marilyn, Martha Chen M. and Renana Jhabvala R. (1998), '*Speaking out Women's Economic Empowerment in South Asia*', Vistaar Publications, New Delhi.
2. Mayoux, Linda (2003), '*Women's Empowerment and Participation in Microfinance: Evidence, Issues and Ways Ahead*', in Linda Mayoux (Eds), Sustainable Learning for Women's Empowerment, SAMSKRITI, New Delhi.
3. Harper, Malcolm (1998), '*Profit for the Poor: Cases of Microfinance*', Oxford and IBH Publishing Company Private Limited, New Delhi.
4. Dadhich C.L (2001), 'Micro-finance –A Panacea for Poverty Alleviation: A Case Study of Oriental Grameen Project in India', *Indian Journal of Agricultural Economics*, Vol. 56, No. 3, pp. 419-421.
5. Sudarshan, Synghal (2002), 'Taking Micro-credit to Women', *Financing Agriculture*, Vol. 34, No. 2.
6. Venkatarao P (2009), 'Role of SHGs in the Empowerment of Women' *SEDME*, Vol. 35, No.1, pp. 29-45.
7. Reddy, Reddeppa A and K Narasimhalu (2009), 'SHG in India: A Tool for Urban Poverty', *Southern Economist*, Vol. 48, pp. 39-40.
8. Vimala P (2009), 'Kudumbashree, A Model for Women Empowerment', *Southern Economist*, Vol. 48, No. 14, pp. 37-38.
9. Tankha, Ajay Rewa Shankar Misra and Prabhat Labh (2005), 'Case for Microfinance in India', *Mainstream,* Vol. XLIII, No. 16, pp. 3-6.
10. Purohit, Sheela (2003), 'Microcredit and Women's Empowerment", *Swa Shakti Bulletin,* Matchup 15-20.
11. Isabelle Guerin, (2006), 'Women and Money: Lesson from Senegal', *Journal Development and Change,* Vol. 37, No. 3.
12. Jayasheela and Palanna V K (2005), 'Role of Self-Help Groups in Enhancing Sericulture Productivity: A case study in Karnataka'. *SEDME*, Vol. 32, No. 1.
13. Hulme, David, Montgomary, Richard, Debapriya Bhattacharya (1996), 'Credit for Poor in Bangladesh: The BRAC and TrDEP'. In David Hulme and Paul Mosely (Eds), 'Financing Against Poverty' Vol. 2, Routledge Publisher, London.
14. Rajasekhar D (2004), '*Microfinance, Poverty, and Empowerment of Women: A Case Study of two NGOs from Andhra Pradesh and Karnataka*', ISEC Publications, Bangalore.
15. Joanna Ledgerwood (2000), '*Sustainable Banking with the Poor-Microfinance Handbook: An Institutional and Financial Perspective,* 'The World Bank, Washington D C.
16. Kamal Vatta (2003), 'Microfinance and Poverty Alleviation', *Economic and Political Weekly,* Vol. 38, No. 05.
17. Gupta, Parameshwara A, Syed Rahmathulla and Shankar S.L. (2010): 'Impact of Microfinance: A Critical Analysis', *Southern Economist*, Vol. 48, No. 18, pp. 29-32.

44

NGOs, Microfinance Institutions and the Social Intermediation

Devaraja Nayaka and Nanjunda

Abstract: *NGOs as microfinance institutions have had some success in facilitation and social intermediation, there is small proof of the fact the NGOs as microfinance institutions have had some success in facilitation and social intermediate on, at they have had much achievement in poverty reduction. The expansion of a symbiotic association between NGOs and banks, with the former professionally utilising their strengths in social engineering and the latter focusing on pure financial intermediation. Such a planned company, the author feels, will help attain the or else indefinable targets of outreach to the poor and monetary sustainability. The position of NGOs needs reviewing from an operational perspective. It asserts that with a few notable exceptions, the record of NGOs in mainstreaming microfinance is a self-effacing one viewed from the context of NGOs as microfinance institutions (mFIs). The achievement of NGOs has though been creditable where facilitating and social intermediation criteria are practical. The planned company between banks and NGOs is balanced to alter the developmental intervention. While microfinance is never easy for other types of institutions trying to practice it (e.g. NGOs or credit unions), it is not, as will be explained, a field where a banker has natural compensation.*

Introduction

NGOs as microfinance institutions have had some success in facilitation and social intermediation, there is small proof of the fact that NGOs as microfinance institutions have had some success in facilitation and social intermediation, at they have had much achievement in poverty reduction. The expansion of a symbiotic association between NGOs and banks, with the former professionally utilising their strengths in social engineering and the latter focusing on pure financial intermediation. Such a planned company, the author feels, will help attain the or else indefinable targets of outreach to the poor and monetary sustainability. The position of NGOs needs reviewing from an operational perspective. It asserts that with a few notable exceptions, the record of NGOs in mainstreaming microfinance is a self-effacing one viewed from the context of NGOs as microfinance institutions (MFIs). The achievement of NGOs hast though been creditable where facilitating and social intermediation criteria are practical. The planned company between banks and NGOs is balanced to alter the developmental intervention. While microfinance is never easy for other types of institutions trying to practice it (e.g., NGOs or credit unions), it is not, as will be explained, a field where a banker has natural compensation. Social intermediation has been defined as a process in which investments are made in the development of both human resources and institutional capital, with the aim of increasing the self-reliance of marginalised groups, preparing them to engage in formal financial intermediation. A shorthand definition would be that social intermediation is financial intermediation with a capacity-building component, aimed at those sectors of society that lack access to credit and savings facilities (Edgcomb and Barton, 2012).

The best thing that has happened to microfinance globally is the metamorphosis of an NGO into a financial institution. Most of the MFIs which have emanated out of this transformation still maintain the social angle in every action of the MFI. Hundreds of such institutions globally are now talking about a double bottom-line in their balance sheets- one financial and the other social and have now started introducing a Social Performance Management system to keep a tag of the social development of their clientele. "Social intermediation is distinct from the provision of social welfare services in that social intermediation enables beneficiaries to become clients able to enter into a contract involving reciprocal obligations. The level, nature and time horizon of the investment required for social intermediation varies with the barriers facing a given target group. It is also likely to depend on the level of responsibility in financial intermediation that the client group is required or willing to acquire."- (Rhyne and Vogel, 1994).

Experts felt more than ten years from now there may not be a need for social intermediation as is being done now. The future MF customer armed with more literacy, empowerment and consumer awareness, should be in a position to choose financial services from a plethora of MFIs and banking institutions, through his/her own judgment and should not be under any societal/government/NGO pressure to seek services only through groups or use peer pressure to repay loans and pay insurance policies, in an open regulated market where private and government outlets will compete with each other to provide the best services at competitive rates for their services. Till that dream comes true, let us look at the economic empowerment of the poor, through professionally managed microfinance services, which involve both financial and social intermediation to create a total financial inclusion and the required social capital to face the competitive market and the socio-economic challenges to be faced in the future (Hwan, 1995).

Microfinance can contribute to social capital through social intermediation: peer group development that offsets the need for conventional collateral requirements among poor clients seeking MFI loans. Interaction within MFI groups can create cooperation and trust that not only facilitate microfinance activities, but also contribute benefits beyond loan access itself. Such benefit may include a greater sense of community, trust and reliance on the group in time of crisis, sharing of valuable social and market information, more positive social practices, etc. The networks and norms created by groups are thereby said to be a positive form of social capital, which in turn, can lay building blocks for other social capital development in a community.

Micrófinance sector has grown rapidly over the past few decades. Nobel Laureate Muhammad Yunus is credited with laying the foundation of the modern MFIs with establishment of Grameen Bank, Bangladesh in 1976. Today it has evolved into a vibrant industry exhibiting a variety of business models. Microfinance Institutions (MFIs) in India exist as NGOs (registered as societies or trusts), Section 25 companies and Non-Banking Financial Companies (NBFCs). Commercial Banks, Regional Rural Banks (RRBs), cooperative societies and other large lenders have played an important role in providing refinance facility to MFIs. Banks have also leveraged the Self-Help Group (SHGs) channel to provide direct credit to group borrowers. With financial inclusion emerging as a major policy objective in the country, Microfinance has occupied centre stage as a promising conduit for extending financial services to unbanked sections of population. At the same time, practices followed by certain lenders have subjected the sector to greater scrutiny and need for stricter regulation

Microfinance institutions that have embraced social capital and built strong ties with their clients, have been able to take advantage of low cost marketing, knowledge diffusion, low operational costs and the like. This has consequently enabled them to enjoy the economies of scale in the industry. In a related case, the created social capital normally creates an "information asset" for the active poor. The created "information asset" acts as the collective endorsement of character that each member of the group provides the other that will easily be accepted by the financial intermediary in lieu of other assets. Information asset, therefore, reduces information asymmetry; a barrier to financial intermediation. Besides, the increased level of awareness and transparency enable the communities to make viable financial decisions and selection of legitimate suppliers of financial services, which is key in hedging against commercial risk.

NGOs and Microfinance

Non-Governmental Organisations (NGOs) have played a substantial role in developing financial services for the poor (or microfinance). Their influence has been greatest in; • Pursuing a broader common vision and mission, particularly towards the poorest; • Offering clients a larger range of products and services; • Better engaging with industry regulators; • Advocating for microfinance generally and conducting research. Furthermore, even in cases where the role of these NGO Networks is no greater than other microfinance network support organisations, it appears the former are more willing to subsidise the costs of these benefits, such as with respect to innovation and creativity. Secondly, the financial performance of the NGO networks and the NGO microfinance institutions themselves do not suffer as a result. Based on the available evidence, there is no significant variation in the performance of NGO. MFIs around the world compared to the average for all MFIs. In India, the NGOs perform slightly worse than the average in three out of four indicators. Therefore, whilst the long-term trend is likely to see more formal and regulated financial institutions delivering microfinance, the NGO Networks themselves will retain a crucial role in the sector as a whole (Barclay O'Brien, 2008).

Non-governmental Organisations play a vital role in helping rural women to form Self-Help Groups and they motivated women to join Self-Help Groups. Non-governmental Organisations (NGOs) played a vital role in rural reconstruction, agricultural development and rural development even during pre-independent era in our country. In the post-independent period the NGOs became a supplementary agency for the developmental activities of the government and in some cases they become alternative to the government. After the introduction of microfinance through Self-Help Groups (SHG), they penetrated into each and every corner in India and actually the NGOs are responsible for converting the pilot project of microfinance into a major programme and the NGOs are responsible for making the microfinance through SHG as the largest programme in the world. Organisations helped them to form Self-Help Groups. Government departments and neighbouring Self-Help Groups play very negligible role in the formation of Self-Help Groups. It is revealed that NGOs and self motivation of women are the main motivational factors to join SHGs and Self-Help Group members also influence other women to join the groups in Kerala that NGOs played a major role and neighbours played a minimal role in group formation. People are well aware about the role of NGOs where NGOs are active in their quality of work rather than the no. of players and is reflected in the study. It is concluded that NGOs play an important role in SHG formation, linking the groups with the banks, arranging for loans and imparting training to start income generating activities.

Small businesses (and dynamic micro-enterprises) need to develop skills. NGOs can assist by creating institutions to train and teach, or work with existing institutions to make what they teach more relevant to the clients. Small businesses (and dynamic micro-enterprises) need to develop the capacity to become and remain competitive. NGOs with good community organising skills can work to get businesses to pool resources within a sub-sector to develop new products, new product designs, or new techniques for production that maximize local resources. Policy level constraints at the sub-sector level can be identified by NGOs who know the local market terrain, and NGOs can bring these issues to the policy-making table. Arguably, banking is more of a system than an art. Unarguably, working to facilitate the productivity of small businesses is really an art. And again, because of their grass roots orientation, because of their commitment, because they are less bureaucratic and encumbered than large development assistance organisations, NGOs are capable of overcoming a subtle but important barrier to successful facilitation – the 'packaging of knowledge and skills' (Kamukama and Natamba, 2013).

Once again, this is no case for discouraging NGOs from MF but to emphasise the role of emotional capital which will bring in an element of quality. The more NGOs, who are in microfinance, face the challenge of helping to bring about an increased articulation of the parts and the players in a local economy, the more they may need to get involved in such non-financial services. The effects of such services are difficult to measure in the short run. But NGOs can take on such tasks, many already do so.

Thus, NGOs will fill up an important void in quality at the grass roots level which will help the poor not only to borrow but also to become good investments for banks. This will help boost business at rural branch level and cover up inadequacies and constraints that might hamper a banker with the conflicting demands of his workload. Many banks and FIs have recognised the role of NGOs and have effected suitable policy initiatives. A larger recognition of this need is reflected in the statistical evidence on linkage patterns, which we have cited earlier (see the table), which establishes NGO-bank partnership over the Indian MF spectrum. A truer recognition at individual banker level might lead to business sense replacing customary skepticism for NGOs. This will be the strategic turning point in making India's relationship banking a showpiece and paradigm for the world's NGOs and bankers.

Recommendations

We must focus on ———

1. Proper Regulation
2. Field Supervision
3. Encourage rural penetration
4. Complete range of Products
5. Transparency of Interest rates
6. Technology to reduce Operating Cost
7. Alternative sources of Fund

Conclusion

Microfinance programmes can have tremendous impact on the empowerment process if their products and services take these structures into account. In the order for women to be empowered, she needs access to the material, human, and social resources necessary to make strategic choices in her life. Not only have women been historically disadvantaged in access to material resources like credit, property, and money, but they have also been excluded from social resources like education or knowledge of some businesses. Access to resources by the weaker sections alone does not automatically translate into empowerment or equality; however, women must also have the ability to use the resources to meet their goals. In order for resources to empower women, they must be too able to use them for a purpose that they choose. In this issue role of NGOs is also very crucial

REFERENCES

1. Christen, R, E Rhyne and R Vogel (1994), 'Maximising the Outreach of Microenterprise Finance: The Emerging Lessons of Successful Programmes', IMCC, September.
2. Elaine Edgcomb, Laura Barton(2012), Social Intermediation and Microfinance Programs (web article).
3. Elaine, Edgcomb and Barton, Laura (1998), "Social Intermediation and Microfinance Programmes: A Literature Review", USA: Micro-Enterprises Best Practices. The Network.
4. Kim Kyung-Hwan (1995) "Access to Credit, Term of Housing Finance and Affordability of Housing," Housing Finance International, 9(4), June 22-27.
5. Nixon Kamukama and Bazinzi Natamba (2013), Social intermediation and financial services access in Uganda's microfinance industry, African Journal of Economic and Management Studies, Vol. 4(3).
6. Nair, Tara S (2001), 'Institutionalising Microfinance in India: An Overview of Strategic Issues', *Economic and Political Weekly,* and January 27.

45

The Role of Micro-Finance in Rural Micro-Enterprise Development

Dhananjaya and Girish G.S.

Abstract: *The concept of microenterprise is recent and is still a developing one. Since independence our success in the development sector are only moderate. Unemployment and poverty still pose major challenge for us, especially in rural areas. It all happened irrespective of the high opportunities in employment generation lies in agriculture sector and rural non-farm sector. According to the criterion used by the Planning Commission of India 27.5 per cent of the population (or nearly 302 million people) were living below the poverty line in 2004-05, down from 51.3 per cent in 1977-78, and 36 per cent in 1993-94, marking a pace of reduction less than one per cent per year. About 221 million people (72 per cent of the poor) live in rural areas and most depend on subsistence farming for their livelihood. In this regard, microfinance and micro enterprise development play a crucial role in alleviating poverty and generation of self employment. In India, 92 per cent of the workforce is in the informal sector and micro enterprise is the main source of livelihood for many of them. Under SHG Bank Linkage programme promoted by NABARD, some of the SHG members have graduated to become micro entrepreneurs from the status of micro borrowers. It is important at this juncture to understand the impact of these micro enterprises on the livelihood of*

SHG members. Against to this background, this paper attempts an overview of varied dimensions, constraints and best practices related to rural microfinance and microenterprise.

Key Words: Micro-finance, Micro-enterprise, SHG, Livelihood, Poverty.

Introduction

Micro finance is a term used by many in different domains to fight poverty. Micro finance is not a new concept. It dates back in the 19th century when moneylenders were informally performing the role of now formal financial institutions. The informal financial institutions constitute; village banks, cooperative credit unions, state owned banks, and social venture capital funds to help the poor. These institutions are those that provide savings and credit services for small and medium size enterprises. They mobilise rural savings, have a simple and straightforward procedure that originates from local cultures, and are easily understood by the population. These funds are to finance the informal sector SMEs in developing countries and it known that these SMEs are more likely to fail. The creation of SMEs generates employment but these enterprises are short lived and consequently bound to die after a short while causing those who gained job positions to lose them and even go poorer than how they were. Banks do not lend to them because they do not have what is required to be granted a loan or to be provided with the bank services. The lack of financial power is a contributing factor to most of the societal problems. These problems emanate from poverty and it is known that with poverty one is bound to suffer so many consequences ranging from lack of good health care system, education, nutrition, micro finance have proved this bank concept to be wrong. They target the poor who are considered risky but the repayment rate turns to be positive as compared with the regular commercial banks.

This paper focuses on the role of microfinance in servicing the rural microenterprise sector. It explores changing issues in agriculture and rural enterprise and recommends measures for promoting sustainable access to microfinance in rural areas. The paper studies the specific needs and challenges of rural and women entrepreneurs with respect to financial services. It draws conclusions on factors essential for sustainable rural microfinance and identifies the roles of various stakeholders. The paper recommends measures for improving various aspects of rural enterprise and microfinance development. These include:

Factors Related to Demand-Supply of Micro-Finance

There is a vast unmet gap in the provisions of financial services to the poor. A very little segment of the poor people is being served by the formal financial system for micro-credit. Majority of the poor population depends on informal financial system for their credit needs. Let us look at some facts. According to the World Development Report (2000), 1.8 billion people live in extreme poverty, subsisting on less than $ 1 a day and almost half of the world population (2.8 billion) live on less than $ 2 a day. South Asia is the home to half of the world's poor families. In African countries, women account for more than 60 per cent of the agriculture labour force and contribute up to the 80 per cent of the total food production, yet receive less than ten per cent of the credit provided to small farmers. In India, various estimates put the requirements of micro credit at Rs 150 billion to Rs 500 billion per year. As against these estimates, bank advances to weaker section aggregated about Rs 100 billion per year and SHGs are estimated to provide about one billion per year. About 36 per cent of the rural households are outside the fold of institutional credit.

Micro-finance and Poverty Alleviation

Most poor people manage to mobilise resources to develop their enterprises and their dwellings slowly over time. Financial services could enable the poor to leverage their initiative, accelerating the process of building incomes, assets and economic security. However, conventional finance institutions seldom lend down-market to serve the needs of low-income families and women-headed households. They are very often denied access to credit for any purpose, making the discussion of the level of interest rate and other terms of finance irrelevant. Therefore the fundamental problem is not so much of unaffordable terms of loan as the lack of access to credit itself. The lack of access to credit for the poor is attributable to practical difficulties arising from the discrepancy between the mode of operation followed by financial institutions and the economic characteristics and financing needs of low-income households. For example, commercial lending institutions require that borrowers have a stable source of income out of which principal and interest can be paid back according to the agreed terms. However, the income of many-self employed households is not stable, regardless of its size. A large number of small loans are needed to serve the poor, but lenders prefer dealing with large loans in small numbers to minimise administration costs. They also look for collateral with a clear title - which many low-income households do not have. In addition bankers tend to consider low income households a bad risk imposing exceedingly high information monitoring costs on operation.

Rural India and Micro Finance

Micro financing has become important. To succeed in India, agribusiness must empower the farmer by making agriculture profitable, not by expropriating him for a particular purpose the farmer should be funded for their basic and small needs. Micro finance is expected to play a significant role in poverty alleviation and development. The need, therefore, is to share experiences and materials, which will help in not only understanding successes and failures but also provide knowledge and guidelines to strengthen and expand micro finance programmes. The ultimate aim is to attain social and economic empowerment. Successful intervention is therefore, dependent on how each of these stages has been carefully dealt with and the capabilities of the implementing organisations in achieving the final goal, e.g., if credit delivery takes place without consolidation of SHGs, it may have problems of self-sustainability and recovery. A number of schemes under banks, central and state governments offer direct credit to potential individuals without forcing them to join SHGs. Compilation and classification of the communication materials in the directory is done based on this development process.

Micro-Finance Institution Strategy

The approach of promoting MFIs is based on the premise that AFIs like SIDBI (Small Industries Development Bank of India), RMK and other donor agencies provide bulk lending, soft loan and some grant to such NGOs which can act as MFIs by on-lending the money to the poor people/ SHGs/ Federations/ smaller NGOs. These MFIs stimulate the credit demand of the poor people. They also provide technical support for the beneficiaries to ensure proper utilisation of loans and repayment. At the same time they meet their cost of funds, cost of credit management and cost of default through the spread of interest and generate surplus for the viable operation of micro-finance. The examples of such MFIs are Sewa Bank and FWWB in Gujarat, BASIX in Andhra Pradesh and RGVN (Rashtriya Grameen Vikas Nidhi) in north-eastern states, Orissa and Bihar.

A Critical Analysis of Institutional Initiatives of Poverty Alleviation in India

The institutional initiatives taken in extending micro-credit in India after independence can be understood in conjunction with the process of rural development and the role played by several developmental institutions for poverty alleviation and employment generation programmes. This process can be categorised under community development programme, RFIs (Rural Financial Institutions) programmes and development of co-operatives programmes. Apart from these, PDS (Public Distribution System) and agricultural / land reforms are also supposed to be major initiatives for providing the benefit to the poor section of the society and attacking poverty. There is a huge network of institutions of development in India to alleviate poverty and generate employment. However, several things went wrong. Anti-poverty programmes could not be implemented properly. Studies conducted by Ansari (1980), Jain (1984), Chaturvedi and Mitra (1987) and Ray (1992) show that the rural development programmes were centrally invented (lacking participation of local level institutions), politically motivated, having leakage and miss-appropriation and heavy administrative expenses. Consequently, poor quality assets were provided to the beneficiaries for productive purposes. Similar is the story of rural banking sector. Studies conducted by Basu (1979), Chippa (1987), Netherlands Development Co-operation (1992) and Rayudu (1992) show that rural credit schemes were politicised. Long-term credit institutions were more necessarily needed to finance for long period so as to enable the farmers to bring about lasting improvement. Nevertheless, this could not be done. There was lack of mobilising local savings. Regional distributions of agriculture credit were inequitable. Studies conducted by Choudhari (1972 *et al.*), Attwood (1984), Baviskar and Attwood (1984) and Attwood and Baviskar (1987) on the effectiveness of co-operatives in agriculture sector show that it is not only the process of production and distribution which leads to success or failure of cooperatives in different regions of India, but also more importantly, the social system has a bearing on the same. Participation of poorer members of co-operatives in decision-making was less. The rich members used loans and other financial facilities. Most of the co-operatives were formed with selfish motives of big landlords. In agriculture and land reforms, a strong lobby of agriculture landholders gradually started to dominate in the political systems, and made the political decisions in its favour.

Findings

1. Considerable gap between demand and supply for all financial services and majority of poor are excluded from financial services.

2. Savings of SHGs has increased by 46.5 per cent in the year 2008-2009. The increased deposits in banks indicate changing trends in rural savings, where the farmer intends to retain liquidity in his assets.
3. Regional Rural Banks are very popular among villagers as a place to save. It has attracted nearly 70.6 per cent savings of SHGs. The shift in investment to formal financial institutions has allowed rural consumers higher liquidity in recent years.
4. Commercial banks had lead in disbursement of loans to SHGs during 2008-2009 with 49.2 per cent followed by Co-operative banks with a share of 26 per cent and Regional Rural Banks with a share of 20.4 per cent.
5. Bankers feel that it is risky to finance poor people's because of their creditworthiness.
6. Commercial banks had the maximum share of outstanding bank loan to SHGs with a share of 40.7 per cent followed by cooperative banks with a share of 18.4 per cent and regional rural banks with a share of 18.2 per cent.
7. Outstanding bank loan to SHGs are due to high transaction costs.

Opportunities Call for Micro-Finance Sector in India

Rural population is a major population segment in India. According to the 2001 Census of India 2001, 72.22 per cent of the total population is rural and dependent on agriculture and allied activities for their livelihood. Due to the failure of agricultural reforms and not adopting a farmer-oriented agricultural policy, growth rate of employment in agriculture sector has declined from 2.32 per cent in 1972-73 to 1.2 per cent in 1983 to 0.65 per cent in 1985. Agriculture contributed only 31.7 per cent to GDP in 1993-94 down from 56.5 per cent in 1951. But this is not the complete picture of the rural economy. The rural economy has a strong base for employment generation. Rural economy still accounts nearly 40 per cent of India's GDP including 10 per cent of RNFS. Share of exports in GDP has increased from 6.2 per cent in 1991-92 to 9.2 per cent in 1994-95. Major contribution to exports comes from the agricultural and allied sectors such as handloom, power loom, gem and jewellery, handicrafts, carpets, leather and mineral products, all of which have at least one primary rural production base. The rural market share of both consumer durable and non-durable products exceeds 40-50 per cent for most items and is growing every year. Papola (1991) while analysing the trends in rural non-farm employment, based on the analysis of the data from the quinquennial rounds of the National Sample Survey during the 1970s and 1980s, reveals that the share of rural area in total employment has declined from around 82 per cent in 1977-78 to 78 per cent in 1987-88; that the share of the rural non-agricultural employment has increased from around 14 per cent to 17 per cent in total employment; and from 17 per cent to 22 per cent in rural employment. Employment in the rural non-agricultural activities has thus been growing much more rapidly than the overall employment, agricultural employment and also urban employment. In fact, the non-agricultural rural employment has grown at an average rate of about 5 per cent during the ten-year period 1977-78 to 1987-88. Consequently, there has been a shift from agriculture in which employment has grown at a rate of only 0.74 per cent, to the non-agricultural activities. It is because of decrease in self-employment and regular wages/ salaried employment in agriculture and increase in employment in non-agricultural sector. Micro-enterprises established in RNFS contribute about 40 per cent of the gross industrial turnover and 34 per cent of total exports. RNFS is the potential sector for employment generation through establishment of micro-enterprises. There is a need to match the decline in agriculture sector with the gain in non-farm activities, to absorb the surplus labour from agriculture.

Conclusion

Micro- finance interventions are well-recognised world over as an effective tool for poverty alleviation and improving socio-economic status of rural poor. In India too, micro- finance is making headway in its effort for reducing poverty and empowering rural poor and women. The need of micro finance arises because the rural India requires sources of finance for poverty alleviation, procurement of agricultural and farms inputs. Micro finance is a programme to support the poor rural people to pay its debt and maintain social and economic status in the villages. As we know that India is agriculture based economy, micro finance may be a tool to empower the farmers and rural peoples to make agriculture profitable.

REFERENCES

1. Ansari, A. Wahid (1980), The Changing Village India. Delhi: Chetna Publications.
2. Attwood, D.W. & Baviskar, B.S. (1987). "Study of Co-operatives in India: Approaches and Methods", Social Change, 17 (2), 8-15.
3. Attwood, Donald W. (1984), "Capital and the Transformation of Agrarian Class System: Sugar Production in India". in Meghnad Desai (et al.) Agrarian Power and

Agricultural Productivity in South Asia. Delhi: Oxford University Press. pp. 20-50.

4. Awasthi, Dinesh N. (1994), "Promoting Group Entrepreneurship" in Gautam Raj Jain and Debmuni Gupta (ed.) New Initiatives in Entrepreneurship Education and Training, Ahmedabad: Entrepreneurship Development Institute of India.
5. Awasthi, Dinesh N. (1996), "Rural Entrepreneurship Development: Relevance, Approach and Issues". Working Paper, Ahmedabad: Entrepreneurship Development Institute of India.
6. Basu, Subhas K. (1979), Commercial Banks and Agriculture Credit: A Study in Regional Disparity in India. New Delhi: Allied Publishers.
7. Baviskar, B.S. and Attwood, D.W. (1984), "Rural Co-operatives in India: A Comparative Analysis of their Economic Survival and Social Impact". Contribution to Indian Sociology (New Series), 18(1), 85-107.
8. Chakrabarti, Rajesh (2005), "The Indian Microfinance Experience - Accomplishments and Challenges", http://ssrn.com/abstract=649854
9. Gupta, M.S. 2008, "Micro Finance through Self Help Groups: An emerging Horizon for Rural Development", Indian Journal of Commerce, 61(3): 36-47.

46

The Study on "Extent of Rural Women's Participation in Agricultural and Household Activities in South Karnataka"

Padmegowda A.T.

Abstract: *In rural areas of India, women play a major role in agricultural production, livestock raising and cottage industries and remain busy from dawn to dusk to supply food to men in fields, fetch water, collect fuel wood, and manage livestock. They are equally efficient in seed bed preparation, tilling, sowing, fertiliser application, fodder cutting, weeding, intercultural operations, transplanting, husking, threshing, drying, storing cereals and fodder, selling agricultural commodities and harvesting of all the crops, fruits and vegetables (PARC, 1988; World Bank, 1989; Shah and Khan, 2004). Women often devote more time to carry out these tasks than men do and their participation is notably higher in food storage and processing. They carry out these tasks in addition to their normal household activities (Shaheed and Mumtaz, 1990; ESCAP, 1997).*

Women's contribution to agriculture is seldom recognised in spite of their active role in the agriculture as well as household activities in developed as well as developing world. In order to probe into the matter that to what, extent women participate in agricultural and household activities, the present study was designed. Both proportionate and simple random sampling technique was used for the selection of study respondents. Channagiri block of district Davanagere acted as central area for the present study. Out of the whole block four villages were randomly selected. From each of the selected village, 30 women were selected both from small and medium size families who were actively engage in farm as well as household activities. The data were collected with the help of validated interview schedule. The data, thus collected were analysed by using descriptive test statistics to formulate results and draw conclusions. It was concluded that women's participation is very much high in picking of cotton among farming activities. Among livestock activities, their participation was highest in cleaning of animal sheds. Looking after the family members was the main activity where women's participation was highest in household activities.

Introduction

Both men and women play an important role in feeding the world. According to an estimate, women produce more than 50 per cent of the total food (FAO, 1995). Women's contribution in agricultural labour force in developed countries is 36.7 per cent while, it is about 43.6 per cent in developing countries (FAO, 1999). In Asian countries, women account for approximately 50.0 per cent of food production overall in the region, with considerable variation from country to country. In the Philippines their participation in agricultural labour force is only 4.0 per cent, while 35.0 per cent in Malaysia, 54.0 per cent in Indonesia and over 60.0 per cent in Thailand. In Southwest Asia, women play a major role in rice production, particularly in sowing, transplanting, harvesting and processing (ESCAP, 1996). In addition to agricultural activities women often devote more time and resources under their control towards improving household concerns related to food security as compared to men and their involvement was significant in term of decision making authority (Saito and Weidman, 1990; Thomas, 1990 and Quisumbing et al., 1995). In rural areas of India, women play a major role in agricultural production, livestock rising and cottage industries and remain busy from dawn to dusk to supply food to men in fields, fetch water, collect fuel wood, and manage livestock. They are equally efficient in seed bed preparation, tilling, sowing, fertiliser application, fodder cutting, weeding, intercultural operations, transplanting, husking, threshing, drying, storing cereals and fodder, selling agricultural commodities and harvesting of all the crops, fruits and vegetables (PARC, 1988; World Bank, 1989; Shah and Khan, 2004). Women often devote more time to carry out these tasks than men do and their participation is notably higher in food storage and processing. They carry out these tasks in addition to their normal household activities (Shaheed and Mumtaz, 1990; ESCAP, 1997).

With respect to crops, women's participation is particularly high in cotton, rice, pulses and vegetables. Rice and cotton cultivation in Shivamogga and Davanagere jointly account for more than one-third of women's annual agricultural activities. It has been estimated that women account for 29.28 per cent of labour in rice production and 23.55 per cent in cotton areas. One study in rice and cotton producing villages in Karnataka showed that in agricultural activities women spent 39.34 and 50.42 per cent of their time in and cotton growing areas, respectively (Karanth and Jahan, 1982; UNDP, 1997 and Ramachandra, 2002). They are involved in various primary and secondary cotton operations, such as weeding and thinning (59.5 per cent), manuring (29.0 per cent), cotton cleaning (77.0 per cent) stick removing (72.5 per cent) and storage of seed cotton for domestic use (20.0 per cent) (Amith, 1994).

Women's participation in production of major field crops has been estimated to be approximately 30.0 per cent in rice, 25.0 per cent in cotton, 23.0 per cent in sugarcane, 18.0 per cent in arecanut and 26.0 per cent in vegetables (Kanthraj and Hussain, 2004). In Karnataka, caring for livestock takes up 35.0 per cent of a village women's time, and it is hard to walk around a village without seeing hens, goats, cows, and buffaloes etc. (Taranath, 1985). A rural woman in Karnataka works 12.50 hr a day, spending 5.50 hr in caring for livestock, but provides only 50 min for the care of her own children.

Women are responsible for 60.0 to 80.0 per cent of the feeding and milking of cattle (ESCAP, 1996). They also engaged in various activities related to livestock production like production of animals, sales of animal's products and by products (ghee, yoghurt), cleaning, watering and bathing the animals (Katuwal, 1991).

In addition to their participation in agricultural activities, they also involve in self-reliance decision-making in both economic and social spheres within the household as reported by Sathar and Kazi (1997) who examined various dimensions of women's autonomy by conducting a survey with the help of focus group interviews and separate focus group discussions both for men and women in the rural areas of Punjab. Women also perform various household tasks, such as, cooking, washing, house cleaning, fetching water, collecting fire woods and care of children and elderly members of the family (Khan and Bilquees, 1976; Ali and Ahmad, 1983; Sabir et al., 1989; Alderman and Chishti, 1991; Ahmad et al., 1993; FAO, 1997; AERC and PIDE, 1998). Many research studies observed that the average rural woman worked between 25 to 35 hr per week in household activities excluding child care (Chandrashekar and Ramesh, 1976; World Bank, 1990; Alderman and Chishti, 1991 and Ahmad et al., 1993).

Sathar and Desai (2006) conducted a research study in India and synthesised that women, living in nuclear families participate more intensively in household activities. In rural areas women fully involve during the whole day in domestic labour activities like looking after the children, cleaning the house, cooking, washing and the many other activities (Agha, 2005). Although their participation in agricultural and household activities are very high but the educational facilities and enrollment of female in primary education is hopeless because their enrollment has stayed roughly the same for the country as a whole, at about 30 per cent (Lloyed et al., 2002). Other than education women's full participation in economic and household activities impeded by cultural and legal constraints, which limits women's participation by women's relative lack of time and mobility due to their workloads and multiple roles (World Bank, 1995).

From above discussion it is crystal clear that women mostly participate in farming (agricultural) as well as household activities and they are the household activities and they are the household managers but their work is considered as non-productive, unorganised and un-documented throughout the world. They are deprived off not only in the field of agriculture, but also in all other fields like education, nutrition and health. For this purpose the present research study was designed to investigate that to what extent women participate in agricultural and household activities in rural Karnataka.

Materials and Methods

Four villages from Channagiri block of District Davanagere of Karnataka Province were selected through simple random sampling technique as the universe for the study. The district under study is equally important for crops, livestock and vegetable production with larger area under cultivation. A sample size of 30 women involved in agricultural and household activities was selected from both small and medium size families through proportionate random sampling technique and thus, making a total sample size of 120 respondents. The data were collected with the help of a pre-tested and validated interview schedule. The data thus collected were analysed by using Descriptive Test statistics to draw results, conclusions and present recommendations accordingly.

The extent of rural women participation in agricultural and household activities were assessed by using a three point continuum namely 'Mostly', 'Occasionally' and 'Not at all' which was assigned scores of 3, 2 and 1, respectively. For the purpose of ranking of different activities performed by rural women the frequency of responses from each of the three columns of a specific activity under major activity was tabulated and multiplied by concerned score. Then, they were added together to get the total score for each specific activity for the purpose of their ranking (Sailaja and Reddy, 2003).

Results and Discussions

Table I: Distribution of the respondents according to the extent of participation in faming activities (n=120)

Farming Activities	*Mostly(3)*		*Occasionally(2)*		*Not at all(1)*	
	F	*per cent*	*F*	*per cent*	*F*	*per cent*
Sed preparation	47	39.2	29	24.2	44	36.6
Sowing	46	38.3	29	24.2	45	37.5
Sealing	54	45.0	21	17.5	45	37.5
Spreading chemical	52	43.4	22	18.3	46	38.3
Taking off fodder	83	69.2	18	15.0	19	15.8
Weeding	82	68.3	20	16.7	18	15.0
Harvesting	90	75.0	14	11.7	16	13.3
Binding	91	75.8	12	10.0	17	14.2
Threshing	88	73.3	11	9.2	21	17.5
Drying	89	74.2	13	10.8	18	15.0
Storage of cereals and seed	99	82.5	10	8.3	11	9.2
Selling of Agricultural Commodities	40	33.3	6	5.0	74	61.7
Cotton picking	110	91.7	6	5.0	4	3.3

Table I reveals that 91.7, 82.5, 75.0, 74.2, 73.3, 69.2, 68.3, 45.0, 39.2, 38.3 and 33.3 per cent of the respondents were 'mostly' engaged and participated in cotton picking, storage of cereals and seed, binding, harvesting, drying, threshing, taking off fodder, weeding sealing, spreading chemical, seed preparation, sowing and selling of agricultural commodities, respectively. Whereas, on the other hand, 24.2, 24.2 and 18.3 per cent of the respondents participated 'occasionally' in seed preparation, sowing and spreading chemical, respectively., Selling of agricultural commodities was 'not at all' performed by 61.7 per cent of the respondents. These results were more or less similar to that of Ramesh (1998) and Nasir (2004).

Table II: Ranking of rural women's involvement in Farming Activities

Famming Activities	*Mean*	*SD*	*TS*	*R*
Sed preparation	2.03	0.874	243	11
Sowing	2.01	0.874	241	12
Sealing	2.08	0.909	249	9
Spreading Chemical	2.05	0.906	246	10
Taking off fodder	2.53	0.755	304	7.5
Weeding	2.53	0.744	304	7.5
Harvesting	2.62	0.712	314	3.5
Binding	2.62	0.724	314	3.5
Threshing	2.56	0.776	307	6
Drying	2.58	0.751	311	5
Storage of cereals and seed	2.73	0.618	328	2
Selling of agricultural commodities	1.70	0.940	206	13
Cotton picking	2.88	0.414	346	1

SD=Standard Deviation, TS=Total Score, R=Rank

The data presented in Table II reveals that women's participation in cotton piking is very much high having rank order '1' and mean '2.88' as compared to other farming activities because the major area in the selected block is under cotton cultivation and picking of cotton was totally the women's task throughout the cotton zone. It is followed by other farming activities like storage of cereals and seeds, harvesting, binding, drying, threshing, taking off fodder, weeding, sealing, spreading chemical, seed preparation and sowing with rank order 2, 3.5, 5, 6, 7.5, 9, 10, 11 and 12 and having mean value 2.73, 2.62, 2.62, 2.58, 2.56, 2.53, 2.53, 2.08, 2.05, 2.03 and 2.01, respectively. While on the other hand the activity in which women's participation was very much low with rank order '13' and mean value '1.70' was selling of agricultural commodities due to the cultural and social norms and values.

Rural Women's Participation in Agricultural and Household Activities

Table III: Distribution of the Respondents according to the extent of their participation in livestock activities (n=120)

Farming Activities	*Mostly(3)*		*Occasionally(2)*		*Not at all(1)*	
	F	*per cent*	*F*	*per cent*	*F*	*per cent*
Sed preparation	47	39.2	29	24.2	44	36.6
Cleaning of animal sheds	101	84.2	16	13.3	3	2.5
Watering of animals	94	78.5	50	16.7	6	5.0
Milking of animals	93	77.5	14	11.7	13	10.8
Preparing ghee	94	78.4	10	8.3	16	13.3
Egg collection of poultry birds	89	74.2	6	5.0	25	20.8
Grazing of animals	90	75.0	10	8.3	20	16.7
Feeding of animals	98	81.7	12	10.0	10	8.3

Table III reveals that an overwhelming majority (84.2 per cent) of the respondents participated 'mostly' in cleaning of animal sheds among livestock activities followed by feeding of animals (81.7 per cent), preparing ghee (78.4 per cent), watering of animals (78.3 per cent), milking of animals (77.5 per cent), grazing of animals (75.0 per cent) and egg collection of poultry birds (74.2 per cent). Women 'occasionally' participated in watering of animals and cleaning of animal sheds as responded by 16.7 per cent and 13.3 per cent of the respondents. But on the other side women 'not at all' participated in egg collection of poultry birds and grazing of animals as reported by 20.8 per cent and 16.7 per cent of the respondents, respectively. These findings are also confirmed by the research studies undertaken by Chandrasekhar and Ramesh (1997); Malathi and Mahjabeen (1998).

Table IV: Ranking of Rural Women's Participation in Livestock Activities

Livestock Activities	*Mean*	*SD*	*TS*	*R*
Sed preparation	2.03	0.874	243	11
Cleaning of animal sheds	2.82	0.449	338	1
Watering of animals	2.73	0.546	328	2.5
Milking of animals	2.67	0.665	320	4
Preparing Ghee	2.65	0.706	318	5
Egg collection of poultry birds	2.53	0.819	304	7
Grazing of animals	2.58	0.762	310	6
Feeding of animal	2.73	0.604	328	2.5

SD=Standard Deviation, TS=Total Score R=Rank

The data presented in Table IV depicts that 'cleaning of animal sheds' was the main activity with rank order '1' and mean '2.82', which was being performed by our rural women. The other livestock activities which was performed by women in rural areas were watering of animals, feeding of animals, milking of animals, preparation of ghee, grazing of animals and egg collection of poultry birds having rank order and means value 2.5, 2.5, 4, 5, 6 and 7 and 2.73, 2.73, 2.67, 2.65, 2.58 and 2.53, respectively.

Table V Distribution of the respondents according to the extent of their participation in household activities (n=120)

Household Activities	*Mostly(3)*		*Occasionally(2)*		*Not at all(1)*	
	F	*per cent*	*F*	*per cent*	*F*	*per cent*
Sed preparation	47	39.2	29	24.2	44	36.6
Food preparation	111	92.5	5	4.2	4	3.3
Fuel collection	97	80.8	16	13.4	7	5.8
Embroidery	48	40.0	14	11.7	58	48.3
Knitting	30	25.0	38	31.7	52	43.3
Other handicraft	36	30.0	5	4.2	79	65.8
Looking after all family members	117	97.5	0	–	3	2.5

Table V reveals that an overwhelming majority (97.5 per cent) of the respondents participated 'mostly' in looking after of all family members among household activities followed by preparation of food (92.5 per cent), fuel collection (80.8 per cent), embroidery (40.0 per cent), other handicrafts (30.0 per cent) and knitting (25.0 per cent). Women 'occasionally' participated in knitting and fuel collection as reported by 65.8 per cent, 48.3 per cent and 43.3 per cent of the respondents, respectively.

Table VI: Ranking of Rural Women's Participation in Household Activities

Livestock Activities	*Mean*	*SD*	*TS*	*R*
Sed preparation	2.03	0.874	243	11
Food preparation	2.89	0.406	347	2
Fuel collection	2.75	0.554	330	3
Embroidery	1.92	0.940	230	4
Knitting	1.82	0.809	218	5
Other handicraft	1.64	0.915	197	6
Looking after all family members	2.95	0.314	354	1

SD=Standard Deviation, TS=Total Score, R=Rank

The data presented in Table VI depicts that 'looking after of all family members' was the main activity among other household activities with rank order '1' and mean 2.95, where rural women's participation was maximum. The other household activities which were being performed by rural women were food preparation, fuel collection, embroidery, knitting and other handicraft with rank order and mean value 2, 3, 4, 5 and 6; and 2.89, 2.75, 1.92, 1.82 and 1.64, respectively.

Conclusions

It was concluded that in farming activities women 'mostly' participate in cotton picking as reported by 91.7 per cent of the respondents but 'occasionally' involve in seed preparation and 'not at all' involve in selling of agricultural commodities as responded by 24.2 per cent and 61.7 per cent of the respondents, respectively. Among livestock activities majority (84.2 per cent) of the respondents 'mostly' involve in cleaning of animal sheds but on the other hand 'occasionally' participate in watering of animals and 'not at all' participate in egg collection of poultry birds as resported by 16.7 per cent and 20.8 per cent of the respondents, respectively. It was also conclude that in addition to farming and livestock activities in household activities women 'mostly' participate in looking after of all family members (97.5 per cent) and 'occasionally' involve in knitting while 'not at all' participate in other handicraft as resported by 31.7 per cent and 65.8 per cent of the respondents, respectively.

Recommendations

On the basis of conclusions drawn from the research study, following recommendations have been formulated.

- For agriculture and livestock management, government should impart trainings to rural female through female extension agents with the collaboration of NGOs, and other rural development agencies.
- Educational level of rural females should be increased through adult and non-formal educational programmes.
- Indiscriminate laws related to land and credit should be eliminated.
- Various agricultural development programmes should be initiated by government for the betterment of rural women.

REFERENCES

1. Dreze, Jean, (1990), "Poverty in India and the IRDP delusion", Economic and Political Weekly, Vol. 25, No. 39.
2. Galab, S. (1990), "Some Micro-level Arrangements of Social Security in Andhra Pradesh', Indian Journal of Labour Economics, Vol. 42, No. 3.
3. Kanchanya, K. (1998), "Women and Development: A Case Study of DWCRA Programme in West Godavari District', Unpublished thesis submitted to Dr. B. R. A.O. University, Hyderabad.
4. Hanumantha Rao, C. H. (1987), "Poverty Alleviation Programmes and the Poor", Economic and Political Weekly, Vol. 22, No. 35.
5. Hanumantha Rao, C.H.(1994), "Agricultural Growth, Rural Poverty and Environmental Degradation in India", Oxford University Press, New Delhi.
6. Hanumantha Rao, C.H., and Linnermann, Hans (eds) (1996), "Economic Reforms and Poverty Alleviation in India", Sage Publications, New Delhi.
7. Mahendra Dev, et.al.,(1988), "Regional Disparities in Agricultural Labour Productivity and Rural Poverty in India", Indian Economic Review, Vol. 23, No. 2.
8. Mahendra Dev, S.,(1999), "An Overview of Social Security in Indian", India Journal of Labour Economics, Vol. 42, No. 3.
9. Parthasarathy, G.(1995), "Public Intervention and Rural Poverty: Case of Non Substainable Reduction in Andhra Pradesh", Economic and Political Weekly, Vol. XXX, No. 41 and 42, Oct., 14-21.
10. Lloyed, C.B., C.Mete and Z.A. Sathar, 2002, The effect of gender differences in primary school. Access, type and quality on the decision to enroll in rural India, Working Paper No. 164. Policy Research Division of Population Council, New Delhi.

11. Nazar, F., 2004, A sociological study of participation of rural women in agricultural activities in district Khanewal. M.Sc. Thesis, Rural sociology University of Agriculture, Delhi, PARC, 1988.
12. International Food Policy Research Institute (IFPRI) Washington, DC.
13. Saito, K.A. and C.J. Weidemann, 1990. Agricultural Extension for Women Farmers in Africa, World Bank discussion paper No. 103. The World Bank, Washington, D.C.

47

Women Entrepreneuership Development Programme

M.D. Umesha

Abstract: *Global economy in general and Indian economy in particular is poised for accelerated growth driven scope for entrepreneurship. In admits of environment of super mall culture we find plenty of scope for entrepreneurship in trading and manufacturing. We are at the crossroads of unemployment on one hand and talent crunch on the other hand. Skilled persons are scarcely available at all levels and in all fields. Besides the existing generation of entrepreneurship also is passing through the transition period. They experience financial resource limitation to promote or to develop venture and there is also need for research and innovation to meet with marketing challenges. Indian rural economy is also experiencing negative trends in respect of women employment opportunities.*

Introduction

Global economy in general and Indian economy in particular is poised for accelerated growth driven scope for entrepreneurship. In admits of environment of super mall culture we find plenty of scope for entrepreneurship in trading and manufacturing. We are at the crossroads of unemployment on one hand and talent crunch on the other hand. Skilled persons are scarcely available at all levels and in all fields. Besides the existing generation of entrepreneurship also is passing through the transition period. They experience financial resource limitation to promote or to develop venture and there is also need for research and innovation to meet with marketing challenges. Indian rural economy is also experiencing negative trends in respect of women employment opportunities.

That proper understanding between the banker and NGO's are inevitably essential for successful implementation of WEDP's, and Micro Credit Projects. "A growth and development of Network between the Bankers and NGO's will help to understand each other's role and brings mutual trust, co-operation and co-ordination with each other. at the same both can work on Micro Credit activities. There is need focus on experience sharing on WED and Micro Credit activities and lessons thereof strategy should be adopted for effectiveness of WEDP. It is also suggested that the Bankers and NGO's should pay a role to take care of the gaps identified and contribute to the effectiveness of WEDP's. It is also necessary gaps identified and contributes to the effectiveness of WEDP's. It is also necessary to find the strength and weakness of NGO's and Bankers to understand one another and to know each other's weaknesses. Both the bankers and NGO's are also requested to make some suggestions to each other to understand one another and develop positive attitude towards WEDP's. Both the Bankers and NGO's also requested to develop an action plan for strengthening to WEDP's. The present study which aims at are lying the effectiveness of entrepreneurship an development programmes is based upon the above said assumptions. To promote the women by self confidence and (i) To make them perfect and fulfilled women. It also aims at (ii) To creating self awareness and sustained effort to rise in life (iii) To encourage them to earn themselves by (iv) To motivating the women in promotion of handicraft products.

Methodology

The researchers have used the SWOT formula to assess the effectiveness of women entrepreneurship development programme. They have made three different working groups and discussed their problems and find out their possible solutions.

Working group-1

The strategy in terms of WEDP effectiveness and reliability.

WEDP approach is effective on the following fronts:

Selection of trainees and their group formation * Selection thrust activity Imparting training on marketing aspect ^Located the viable / honest/ sincere entrepreneur *Banker should provide loan in time (timely assistance) *Code of conducts between banker and NGO's

*Joint efforts to assist the entrepreneurs, Banker should and NGO's should understand each other's role "'Properly and work hand in hand for enlistment of rural mass : ^Bankers approach towards NGO's should be positive * NGO's should not interfere in political matters * There should not be any political pre sure on the banker * Assurance from bankers to Co-operate in pre promotion *Co-operate In pre Promotional plan, Bankers should be core faculty during training period, Bankers also act as a following committee members:

WEDP approach is replaceable to all the corners of the country should be chalked out and implemented as per natural resources available in the particular aea and economically viability of the activity.

P: Which components should the bankers should involved in and following components?

S: Selection of applicants group

- Evaluation of the activity economical employment generation *Infrastructure development

P: What are the inputs that should go into WEDP towards facilitating enterprise launching? -

S: Timely and adequate availability of Raw Material and machinery

- Smooth running of production cycle :Canvassing, publicity, marketing of services, products, publicity.

Marketing of services / products, pre tie up sale dealership network

- Fast, timely realisation of payments to be received and to meet payment of obligation.

P: What do you think are the facilitating factors for successful implementation of strategy?

S: Administrative skill

- Acceptability, social standing to the masses.
- NGO's should shoulder more responsibility towards all concerns goodwill.
- Pre and Post disbursement follow up *Changed banking scenario.
- Competition from private banks, co-op banks, co-op Society, mutual funds privatisation.
- Since most of the banks have gone to public issue, the public will be paid dividend.
- Liberalisation, globalisation, investment in information technology.
- Remove debt relief concept, each branch should be profitable counter.
- Bankers should develop positive attitude towards unit holders.

Working group-11:

Role of Bankers and NEGO's in WEDP and credit activities

P: The Bankers and the NGOs should play in the above to take care of the gaps identified and contribute to the effectiveness of WEDP's.

S: - The Bankers and NGOs should have a motto of Socio Economic Development.

- Joint survey for viable activities as per area and preparing list of existing activities in which no more expansion is viable (Negative list is to be prepared) Selection of entrepreneur with available tools both by NGOs and bank.
- Banks should be evolved to share their experience on various aspects and to share their experience.
  -Joint efforts are required between the banker and NGOs.
- Economically viable activities to the particular area for economic development of rural areas.
  -List of NGOs / list of the trainees will be given to the bank. Programme details should be given to the bank.
- Continuous interaction between banker and NGOs in each other activities and proper understanding in each other's roles and reconciliation of their roles.
  -Duties and responsibilities are to be fixed in both the organisations
  -Run the organisation systematically through understanding about do's and don'ts to sustain credibility in presence of the banker.
  P: The Banker / NGOs acquire capability to perform such roles?
  S: - Continuous interaction between NGOs and Banker.
- Fix the job roles and responsibility in both the organisations
- Readiness, platform to perform in time bound manner.
  P: What do you want to do as a Banker or NGOs to facilitate the Banker / NGO to play their identified role?
  S: As NGOs:
- Democratic / transparent / finest administrator of the unit
- Follow up till the smooth running of the project and 100 per cent repayment. As a Banker:
- Extend follow up Co-operation *Time bound and adequate disbursement.
  P: What do you think should be done to have role clarity by both Banker and NGOs?
  S:- To understand each others problem
- Evaluation of projects / procedures undergone
- Positive Approach *Avoid avoidable conflicts.

Working group-111:

Role of Bankers and NGOs in WEDP and credit activities

You are one aware of WEDP strategy, the role of credit in it and the different roles being played by bankers and NGOs in order to have better understanding between the NGOs and Bankers, it will be useful to undertake a strength and weaknesses analysis in a constructive manner, on other. Please deliberate on the following.

P: What are the strengths of NGOs Bankers which are consider as positive factors?

Si- Strength of NGO's

- Knowing culture and capability of the society
- Working for the people of the people and by the people - Always positive approach - Low cost establishment for the motto - Creating awareness for masses employment innovations and self development - A bridge between bankers and the enterer - They are well versed with rural development - Convincing ability and organisational structure is good - Liaison with the rural mass - Knowledge about the credit worthiness and potentiality of the rural mass.

Strength of Bankers

-Bankers have status, power - Clarity regarding business plan - Bankers are mathematical, logical skill, reasoning ability in decision making - To be point.

P:What are the weaknesses of NGOs? Bankers which consider as limiting factors?

S: Weaknesses of NGOs:

- Improper functioning - No transference, undemocratic way of functioning. - Accounting lapses, leading to political pressure - Target oriented and not quality consciousness.- Lack of knowledge, communication, and innovation- No long term Planning - No perdition of people - No self evaluation
- Poor follow up and monitoring -NGOs should not taking part in recovery of bank dues - They are impresses by the local leaders - They are target oriented - They act as if the proprietors of the organisation - Focus from the view point of publicity rather than more actual work.

Weakness of Bankers

- Favouritism, nepotism, partiality while sanctioning loans - Bankers do not want to take any risk - Suspicious mind towards new entrepreneurs -

Egoism, Interpretation of the power according to his wills - Cultural imbalance

P: What are the methods could use to get NGO's Bankers to supplement each other?

S:- Co-operation and understanding, regular interaction between NGO's and Bankers.

- Concurrent interaction, monthly meeting, got together between Banker and NGO's - Proper understanding, mutual trust on each other- Understand the banker and their limitations- Central Committee is found at district level. -Understand the banker and their limitations - NGO's and bankers interface at district level periodically.

P: What suggestions would to like take to the NGO's / Bankers to overcome the weaknesses?

S: - Should be quality consciousness

- Follow up till the task is competed - Proper and long-term planning - Evaluation and rectification - In-house infrastructure to meet the goal - Co-ordination and trust between each other - No's should have carry of ideas - NGO's should approach the banker for financial guidance - NGO's should maintain the liaison with the controlling authority.
- NGO's administrative set lip should be known to the bankers - Bankers should provide one window service - Bankers should be target oriented group - Creation of partnership, sharing of responsibility between NGO's and banker.

Recommendations for banking sector

- Every two years best Bankers-award should be given which has contributed a lot for rural enlistment of the society.
- Best motivates award - Banker should consider every aspect before financing to the unit - Basic managerial skill, on the job training. How to get finance, Marketing, Book Keeping, Good Economic background, proper Co-ordination between banker and Entrepreneurs. - Educating the banker about the financial discipline.
- Involvement in Fixation of area specific plan - NGO's list should be provided by NABARD to controlling office and circulated to branches - Branch managers should take interest for NGO's trainer motivate list. -Looking to the Indian economy banking sector should full. Fit social objectives.
- Bankers are to be involved only at the time of evaluation of the project -Bankers should assist the entrepreneurs in the field of

marketing potentialities of the areas, sources for obtaining machinery etc. - Bankers should involve, while selection of trains and group formation.

Suggestions to NGOs

NGOs should help the entrepreneurs in selection of the Industries. - NGOs should have administrative skill, communication skill, and positive attitude towards enlistment of rural mass for socio-economic development. - Bankers should be informed well in advance regarding the establishment of the unit. - NGO's should in form to the banker from time to time their activities that enable the banker for evaluation of their activities - NGOs should be committed, dedicated, self driving, proper remuneration should be given to NGOs - Proper control on field staff.

- NGOs should be independent, competent, knowledgeable, resourceful about marketing, finance - NGOs aware about the programmes of EDI - No's should motivate the trainees to be com-mitted, dedicated. - Entrepreneurs are to be trained properly.
- NGOs should assist the bankers in recovery of their dues. - Gross route level NGOs / workers / bankers should involve in framing EDP.
- NGOs should be knowledgeable and resourceful, fanatically sound. - A federation, platform is to be developed for NGOs suggestions can be sent to the Govt. Special allocations. - NGOs should be special / specified / field.
- Work should be qualitative - NGOs staff should be restricted to local -WEDP consider as National Programme -Duplication of scheme should be avoided - Concentrate only on one scheme - EDI should organise such programme at Block / District level.
- Work load should be diverted to co-operate banks too - One scheme should be implemented by one agency only. Suggestion to national financial institutions like NABARD / SIDBI - No. of Govt. scheme should be reduced EDI.
- Latest project profile should be provided to NGOs - Stamp duties should be exempted - NABARD should impress upon Government to expedite the recovery losses.

Suggestions to Government and EDII

- Advance cell with EDII - Public Money recovery act to be properly implemented - Advance Cell with EDII -Entrepreneur to NGOs to Standing Committee to Banks.

As a NGOs:

- Work with utmost Co-operation with bankers. - To promote saving capacity among the rural youth. - To educate rural youth regarding banking activities like approach, Project preparation and how to face the banker. - Try to maintain trust on each other. - To bring awareness among the rural masses about various schemes introduced by the bank from time to time - Proper control over diversification. - Helping in speedy recovery - Helping to the bank for accomplishment of rural development activities.

Conclusion

It is found that proper understanding between the banker and NGOs are necessary for effectiveness of women entrepreneurship development. The banker and NGOs play an important role to take care of the gaps identified and contribute to the effectiveness of W,E,D,P,'s. It is also found that Indian rural economy is also experiencing negative trends in respect of women employment opportunity.

NGOs in India have promoted micro finance through women's self- help groups. However different institutional forms are not value neutral and vested interest are involved.

Independence brought promise of equality of opportunity in all sphere to the Indian women and laws guaranteeing for their equal rights of participation in political process and equal opportunities and rights in education and employment where enacted. But, unfortunately, the government sponsored development activities have benefited only a small section of women. The large majority of them are still unaffected by change and it is revealed that development activities have benefited only a small section of women, i.e., the urban middle class women. The large majority of them are still unaffected by change and development.

REFERENCES

1. Arjun (2009), "Rural Development Women Self Help Group" Southern Economist, March 1.
2. Subbulakshmi A.V.V.S. (2008), "Micro Finance and Empowerment of Rural Women", The Economic Challenger, No. 11, Issue-41, October- December.
3. Gender Development Decision and Policies, Edited by Siddhartha Sarkar and Netten Narajana, Serials Publications, New Delhi, pp. 326.

4. Gurumurthy T.R. (2002), Economic empowerment through self reliance social welfare Delhi.
5. Rashmi R., Agnihotri, H.R and Dr. M.A. Konnur (2009), "Empowering Women Through SHGs", Third Concept, Vol. 23, No: 270, August.

48

Micro Finance and Women Entrepreneurs in India

R. Sambashivam and Shilpa M. Wodeyar

Abstract: *Micro-Finance is a type of banking service that is provided to unemployed or low-income individuals or groups who would otherwise have no other means of gaining financial services. Microfinance and also Self-help Group provides women with the financial banking they need to start business ventures and actively participate in economy. The emergence of women entrepreneurs and their contribution to the national economy is quite visible in India. It is discovered that women entrepreneurship could be an effective strategy for poverty reduction in a country; since women are the worst hit in such situation. However, it is discovered that women entrepreneurs, especially in developing countries, do not have easy access to microfinance factors for their entrepreneurial activity such as low business performance than their men counterparts. Whereas the rate of their participation in the informal sector of the economy is higher than males, and microfinance factors could have positive effect on enterprise performance.*

Considering the entrepreneurial environment, women's activities are very interesting as they offer a great source of knowledge and innovation. One important element, and perhaps the only characteristic that men will never have, is the possibility to transfer "motherhood skills" to job. These include fostering of other people's development through guiding, monitoring and sharing information.

Women are experienced in balancing claims, in organising and pacing, and in handling difficulties. For women and especially for poor women, micro-enterprise ownership has emerged as a strategy for economical survival. One of the most essential factors contributing to success in micro-entrepreneurship is access to capital and financial services. For various reasons; Women have had less access to these services than men. Some research has shown that investing in women offers the most effective means to improve health, nutrition, hygiene and educational standards for families and consequently for the whole of society. Thus, a special support for women in financial services is necessary.

Keywords: Microfinance, Women Entrepreneurs, Self-help Groups, Micro-Enterprises.

Introduction

Women Entrepreneurship plays a critical role in the economic development of societies in its smallest manifestation, it enhances livelihoods with the family while on larger and deeper levels, and national wealth accrues. However for long, Women Entrepreneurs have low business performance compared to their male counterparts. And this has been attributed to factors which normally affect entrepreneurial performance such as lack of credit, saving, education, or training, and social capital. Women entrepreneurs play a significant role in local economies and women developing countries are undertaking a good number of small-scale enterprises. In a developing country like India where economic status of women is very painful especially in rural pockets and opportunities of earning are very less, entrepreneurship in small enterprise is an option for women either individually or through SHGs. The growth rate of women's participation in economic activities is much lower than the expected rate. If we look at the developed countries we see that women are actively participative in the business and trade activities, including agriculture, without any social or other restrictions. But in India, there are still many social and cultural restrictions on women. Hence, women participation in entrepreneurial activities is less than the requirement of the fast growth of India. Microfinance serves as a means to empower the poor, and provides a valuable tool to assist the economic development process. While the main objective of the microfinance is to enable the poor to acquire productive assets, in practice the size of the loan being very small and the repayment period being very short, microfinance activity in India does not lead to the creation of sustainable micro enterprises. The nature of the target group and the absence of security for the loan generally tend to create an atmosphere of utmost caution, which is reflected in the size, and the duration of the loan. Further, microfinance is by its very nature a group activity and therefore may not promote individuals excelling to set up thriving micro-enterprises. The answer to this seems to be that the initial phase of microfinance activity should lead to a second phase of financing where individuals with proven record are picked up for commercial scale financing operations.

Micro Finance and Micro Enterprise

Microfinance means providing small loans to very poor families to help them engage in productive activities or grow their tiny business. Microfinance originally established to impel the moneylender out of business and to bridge the capital gap apparently unfilled by the rural co-operatives and commercial banks. Microfinance is a logical approach to development because it functions at the grass root level, can be sustainable, is capable of involving large segments of the population and builds both human and productive capacity. Microfinance is the provision of a broad range of financial services to low-income micro enterprise and households. Robinson (2001) defines microfinance as "small-scale finance services-primarily credit and savings-provided to people who farm, fish or herd" and adds that it " refers to all types of financing services provided to low-income households and enterprise". It is observed that the micro-finance activities are mainly offered by formal financial institutions with the help of SHGs. As a result, micro-finance programme is growing in those areas where there is incredible growth of formal financial institutions.

Micro Enterprise: Micro enterprise is a term used often in development programmes such as poverty alleviation and self-employment in particular. The micro and small sectors have been a major component of industrial growth in which these can be regarded as an absolute force of innovation and development. There was no definition of Micro enterprise earlier. In accordance with the provision of Micro, Small and Medium Enterprise Development (MSMED) Act, 2006 the Micro Enterprises are rather classified in two classes.

- **Manufacture Enterprises:** The micro manufacturing enterprise is defined in terms of investment in plant and machinery. The investment should not exceed twenty-five lakh rupees.

- **Service Enterprises:** The enterprises engaged in providing or rendering of services and are defined in terms of investment in equipment. The limit of investment in plant and machinery / equipment for micro service enterprises should not exceed ten lakh rupees.

Objectives of the Study

The basic objectives of this study are:

1. To discuss the significance of Women Development programmes in general.
2. To trace out the status of women in their ordinary business of life.
3. To analyse the levels of Attitude, Skill and Knowledge gained by women entrepreneurs through microfinance (SHGs).
4. To analyse the impact of empowerment of women entrepreneurs.
5. To suggest some remedial measures to improve upon the efficiency and effectiveness of Micro-finance in developing women entrepreneurship.

Statement of the Problem

In olden days women were restricted to take part in any social activities and not given roles in decision-making in her family. The situation was even more worsening in rural and remote areas. Now the situation has been changed. She is given freedom to do what she wishes. In today's scenario more women are engaged in income generating activities. This is because of NGO and other financial institution came forward to provide microfinance to poor women. They believe that a woman is the small credit risk and often benefits the whole family. The main aim of microfinance is to empower women. This induced the researcher to focus more on the empowerment of rural women who participates in the microfinance.

Woman Entrepreneur and her Qualities

She is a woman of commitment, independently employed, she has a close relationship with her father and after obtaining an undergraduate and subsequently a graduate degree in some area of liberal arts, marries, has children and starts her first significant entrepreneurial venture in the service area in her late 30s or early 40s. Her biggest problems at start-up later in the venture reflect a lack of business training and generally in the financial area.

Leadership Qualities

Some of the outstanding qualities of women entrepreneurs are:

Accept challenges	Ambitious
Drive	Enthusiastic
Hard work	Patience
Industrious	Motivator
Skilful	Potential Optimism
Adventurous	Conscious
Educated	Determination to excel
Keenness to learn and imbibe new ideas	Experienced
Intelligent	Perseverance
Studious	

In spite of the remarkable importance of women's participation, their jobs have been considered as an "extra income" to family survival or simply to improve its living conditions. Moreover, micro-enterprises owned by women have been considered as a way to meet primary needs instead of a profitable source of income. Women have had to lead fight against an adverse environment, which traditionally had been minimising and exploiting their capacities. As a consequence of this reality, in some cases, women are just satisfied with the non-financial benefits, such as the psychological satisfaction of social contact.

Benefits of a Women Entrepreneur:

First-born child of middle class parents
Father and /or mother in independent business
College-educated
Married
Early 30s for the first significant venture
Previous experience in new venture
Desires independence
Motivated by desire for independence and job satisfaction
Small and young business
Self-confident
Moderate risk-taker
High tolerance for ambiguity
High energy level Biggest problems in start-up
Lack of business training
Personnel management
Biggest problems in current operations:

- Lack of experience in financial planning
- Weak collateral position

- Cash flow management
- Taxation

With education and training, the women have gained confidence to do all work, which was the prerogative of man and do it excellently, rather better than men. Over the years, the educational women have become ambitious, acquired experience and basic skills of competency and self assurance.

Women's Micro-Enterprises - Main Characteristics

Considering the entrepreneurial environment, women's activities are very interesting as they offer a great source of knowledge and innovation. For example, there is no single type of female micro-entrepreneur; they differ in social background, educational level, experience and age. One important element, and perhaps the only characteristic that men will never have, is the possibility to transfer "motherhood skills" to job. These include fostering of other people's development through guiding, monitoring and sharing information. Women are experienced in balancing claims, in the organising and pacing, and in handling difficulties.

Businesswomen in developing countries share the following general characteristics:

- They are concentrated in market sectors that have low barriers to entry and low levels of outside communication (transfer to other markets) they focus on trade, services and light manufacturing activities.
- Their business is smaller than others, employing less than five employees.
- The owners have relatively little previous working experience.
- They use traditional technologies.
- Most employees are family related.
- They are often home based.
- Business growth strategies are affected by household responsibilities.
- Owners tend to have lower levels of education and literacy.
- Women start their enterprises with less professional work experience and knowledge of their sector than their male counterparts.

Women's Participation in Micro Finance Activities

Although men, as well as women, face difficulties in establishing an additional enterprise, women have barriers to overcome. Among them are negative socio-cultural attitudes, legal barriers, and practical external barriers, lack of education and personal difficulties.

In spite of this, for women and especially for poor women, micro-enterprise ownership has emerged as a strategy for economical survival. One of the most essential factors contributing to success in micro-entrepreneurship is access to capital and financial services. For various reasons, women have had less access to these services than men of collateral, frequent repayment schedules more appropriate to the cash flows of their enterprises, simpler application procedures and improved access to savings accounts. Surveys have shown that many elements contribute to make it more difficult for women in small business to make a profit.

SHGs Women Entrepreneurship Development

A Self Help Group is defined as a "self governed, peer controlled informal group of people with similar socio-economic background and having a desire to collectively perform common purpose."

The SHG is considered as a viable organisation of the rural poor particularly women for delivering micro credit in order to undertake entrepreneurial activities. Some of the SHGs managed by the rural poor women successfully demonstrated how to mobilise and manage thrift activities, appraise credit needs enforce financial disciplines, maintain credit linkages with banks and effectively undertake income generating activities. In the last decade, SHGs have gained increased attention among women entrepreneurs. They have become increasing important programme of the development process in the women in all of these main areas of work such as attitude, skill and knowledge. On the other hand, there is a current view that SHGs constitute a viable alternative to government as channels of development assistance, particularly in developing countries.

Microfinance is a critical tool in addressing the issues of financial exclusion is the inability of individuals, households or groups to access necessary financial services in an appropriate form. In India, microfinance scene is dominated by Self Help Groups (SHGs) - Banks linkage Programme, aimed at providing a cost effective mechanism for providing financial services to the 'unreached poor'.

In the last decade, SHGs have gained increased attention among women entrepreneurs. They have become increasing important programme of the development process in the women in all of these main areas of work such as attitude, skill and knowledge. On the other hand, there is a current view that SHGs constitute a viable alternative to government as channels of development assistance, particularly in developing countries.

Impact of Micro-Finance on Women

Microfinance in India is woman centric. Reports and evaluation studies indicate that these activities have led to creation of awareness among rural women, promotion of savings habit, better utilisation of money to generate income, and general improvement in the respect for women in the rural society.

At the same time, fear is expressed that in the social milieu where, the women can come under the family/male pressure, she might be forced to misdirect the loan. In other words, the women may be used as a front by the society. Such apprehension is quite realistic because of the still widely prevalent illiteracy among women. Therefore microfinance, as is envisaged, will succeed and will be sustainable in areas where female literacy is high and programme is accompanied by good amount of training and awareness building.

Progress of Micro- Finance Programme

Year	*SHGs financed by Banks during the Year*			*Bank Loan Outstanding*		
	No. (lakh)	*Amount (Rs.Crore)*	*Growth (per cent)*	*No. (lakh)*	*Amount (Crore)*	*Growth (per cent)*
2007-08	12.28	8849.26	-	36.26	16999.90	-
2008-09	16.09	12256.51	38.50	42.24	22679.85	33.41
2009-10	15.87	14453.30	17.90	48.52	28038.28	23.62
2010-11	11.96	14547.73	0.65	47.87	31221.17	11.35
2111-12	11.48	16534.77	13.66	43.54	36340.00	16.40

Source: NABARD.
Note; *Includes new as well as repeat loans to SHGs.

Under the SHG-Bank Linkage Programme, as on 31 March, 2012, 79.60 lakh SHG-held savings bank accounts with total savings of Rs 6,551 crore were in operation. By November 2012, another 2.14 lakh SHGs had come under the ambit of the programme, taking the cumulative number of savings-linked groups to 81.74. As on March 2012, 43.54 lakh SHGs had outstanding bank loans of Rs. 36 340 crore. During 2012-13 (up to November 2012) 3.67 lakh SHGs were financed with an amount Rs.6 664.15 crore.

This provides Sample evidence to the fact that micro finance through SHGs laid the seeds for social and economic empowerment of women. 'Banking the Unbankable' through micro finance is a valuable contribution to development planning as it presents an alternative way to development. Micro finance has ushered in a new life of liveliness, joy and jubilations for them. It has aided in making the passage from darkness to light for thousands of women struggling to breathe in the quagmire of poverty.

Reasons for Women choosing Entrepreneurship

Self-determination, expectation for recognition, self-esteem and career goal are the key drivers for taking up entrepreneurship by women. Sometimes, women chose such career path for discovering their inner potential, caliber in order to achieve self satisfaction. It can also provide a mean to make best use of their leisure hours. However, dismal economic conditions of the women arising out of unemployment in the family and divorce can compel women into entrepreneurial activities.

Obstacles for Women Entrepreneurship

The entrepreneurial process is same for men and women. Successful men and women entrepreneurs undergo similar motivations and thus achieve success in largely same way under similar challenges. They are also found to have access to fund from the same sources.

The same condition both men and women can be successful entrepreneurs. However, in practice most of the upcoming women entrepreneurs face problems that are of different dimensions and magnitudes than that faced by their male counterparts. These problems, generally, prevent these women entrepreneurs from realising their potential as entrepreneurs. The major hurdles that the women face during starting and running a company generally come from financing and balancing of life. The balancing of life is caused due to lack of family support for the women. The other hindering external factors include gender discrimination, inaccessibility to information, training opportunities, infrastructure etc. Some internal factors like risk aversion by women, lack of confidence, lack of vision of strategic leader etc. can also create obstacles for the women entrepreneurship development.

Problems of Women Entrepreneurship in India

Definitely, there are a number of problems regarding women entrepreneurship in India, researchers having identified issues relating to social aspects, economic life, skill problems, problems of family support, courage etc.

1. Absence of Definite Agenda of Life
2. Absence of Balance between Family and Career Obligations
3. Poor Degree of Financial Freedom
4. No Direct Ownership of the Property
5. Paradox of Entrepreneurial Skill and Finance

6. No Awareness about Capacities
7. Low Ability to Bear Risk
8. Problems of Work with Male Workers
9. Negligence by Financial Institutions
10. Lack of Self-Confidence
11. Lack of Professional Education
12. Mobility Constraints
13. Lack of Interaction with Successful Entrepreneurs
14. Measures to remove Obstacles

The elimination of obstacles for women entrepreneurship requires a major change in traditional attitudes and mindsets of people in society rather than being limited to only creation of opportunities for women. Hence, it is imperative to design programmes that will address to attitudinal changes, training, supportive services.

A. The basic requirement in development of women entrepreneurship is to make aware the women regarding her existence, her unique identity and her contribution towards the economic growth and development of country.

B. The basic instinct of entrepreneurship should be tried to be reaped into the minds of the women from their childhood. This could be achieved by carefully designing the curriculum that will impart the basic knowledge along with its practical implication regarding management (financial, legal etc.) of an enterprise.

C. Adopting a structured skill training package can pave the way for development of women entrepreneurship. Such programmes can train, motivate and assist the upcoming women entrepreneurship in achieving their ultimate goals. Various schemes like the World Bank sponsored programmes can be undertaken for such purposes. The course design should focus on imparting input on profitability, marketability and practical management lessons. Besides, there should be consideration in helping the women entrepreneurs in balancing their family life and work life.

D. As a special concern, computer illiterate women can be trained on Information Technology to take the advantage of new technology and automation. The established and successful women entrepreneurs can act as advisors for the upcoming women entrepreneurs.

E. The initiatives taken from these well established entrepreneurs for having interaction with such upcoming women entrepreneurs can be proved to be beneficial in terms of boosting their morale and confidence. It may result in more active involvement of women entrepreneurs in their enterprises.

F. Infrastructure set up plays a vital role for any enterprise. Government can set some priorities for women entrepreneurs for allocation of industrial plots, sheds and other amenities. However, precautionary measures should be undertaken to avoid the misuse of such facility by the men in the name of the women.

Even in today's era of modernisation the women entrepreneurs depend on males of their family for marketing activities. This is simply because they lack the skill and confidence for undertaking such activities. Women development corporations should come forward to help the women entrepreneurs in arranging frequent exhibitions and setting up marketing outlets to provide space for the display of products or advertisement about services made by women.

Measures to Increase and Support Women's Participation in Microfinance Activities

Governments should explore ways of developing innovative credit programmes using intermediary channels or institutions closer to the target groups such as co-operatives, women's group associations and other grassroots organisations. Savings and credit programmes should be designed in a way not to exclude women from participating. Additionally, there is a need to examine the impact of structural adjustment policies on men and women at the family level as well as within various sub-sectors of the labour market and within the small enterprise sector itself.

In general terms, in order to facilitate the participation of women in micro and small enterprise, donors should;

- Encourage micro-enterprise programmes to develop specific strategies for recruiting women as clients from within their existing target groups.
- Encourage micro-enterprise programmes to expand their target groups to include the sizes and types of enterprise activities in which women engage and/or experiment with, business and technical assistance according to the needs of these types of enterprises.
- Consider expanding support to a broader range of organisations, especially those organisations active in rural areas that aim at poverty eradication. Support for these organisations should include technical assistance and training in programme

planning, management and in developing teams of female staff to assist clients in business planning and management.

- Increase the availability of working capital;
- Experiment with lending programmes that do not require conventional forms of collateral;
- Replicate and expand existing successful methodologies for delivering small working –capital loans;
- Introduce savings mobilisation components in the context of credit or other enterprise assistance programmes;
- Promote credit policies that are open to both small-scale enterprise activities and enterprises operating in trade, commerce and other small enterprise sectors where women have higher participation rates.

Technical assistance for micro-enterprise development should focus more on basic training in product marketing and design concepts and on transmitting skills to increase and diversify production. Governments can also directly increase the market for micro-enterprise products by improving rural and urban infrastructures.

Findings and Suggestions

- Donor agencies should promote studies to support local women's groups in educational and promotional campaigns and launch special studies on specific policy problems related to the micro-enterprise sector and gender issues in microfinance activities.
- Short-term assistance programmes might aim at increasing the productivity of women's labour by providing credit, technology, and skill training.
- Long-term objectives could emphasise eliminating institutional constraints which limit women's access to productive resources, creating social, technological and economic mechanisms to reduce conflicts between women's productive and reproductive roles, as well as defining strategies to address traditional and legal barriers that hamper or preclude the active participation of women in the productive sectors of the economy.
- The key issue for successful microfinance programme focused on women should consider them in a broader context, as a family nucleus, that is vital for societal improvement and progress. Following this idea, microfinance programmes should provide women with specific adapted products through appropriate methodologies, which can offer competitiveness to their business but also well-being to them and their families.

Conclusion

Traditionally women have been marginalised. A high percentage of women are among the poorest of the poor. Microfinance activities can give them a means to climb out of poverty. Microfinance could be a solution to help them to extend their horizon and offer them social recognition and empowerment.

On the other hand, thanks to women's capabilities to combine productive and reproductive roles in microfinance activities and society has enabled them to produce a greater impact as they will increase at the same time the quality of life of the women micro entrepreneur and also of her family. The question is not whether we should focus on women or men. Both female and male play vital role in creating income and jobs. Their capacity for innovation stimulates general economic growth. Microfinance programmes should be accessible to both of them (male and female entrepreneurs) and offer adequate policies regarding to market interchange, access to financial services, and training and technical assistance.

Microfinance through SHGs laid the seeds for Social and Economic empowerment of women. 'Banking the Unbankable' through micro finance is valuable contribution to development planning as it presents an alternative way to development. Micro-finance has ushered in a new life of liveliness, joy and jubilations for them. It has aided in making the passage from darkness to light for thousands of women struggling to breathe in the quagmire of poverty.

REFERENCES

1. Sarumathi S. and K. Mohan, *Role of Micro Finance in Women's Empowerment* (An Empirical study in Pondicherry region rural SHG's), Journal of Management and Science Vol.1, No.1 (Sep. 2011) ISSN: 2249-1260.
2. Ruth Marjory AdhiamboOcholahSimeoOkeloCainanOjwang Fredrick Aila and Patrick B. Ojera, *Literature Review on the Relationship between Microfinance Provision and Women Enterprise Performance*, Greener Journal Social Sciences, GJSS ISSN: 2276-7800, Impact Factor 2012 (UJRI): 0.7863 ICV 2012: 5.99.
3. Dr. Jyotish Prakash Basu, Reader and Head, Department of Economics, Raja Peary Mohan College, Uttarpara, Hooghly, *Microfinance and Women Empowerment an Empirical Study with special reference to West Bengal.*
4. IsidoreEkpeNorsiahBinti Mat RazliCheRazak, *The Effect of Microfinance Factors on Women Entrepreneurs' Performance in Nigeria: A Conceptual Framework,* International Journal of Business and Social Science, Vol. 1 No. 2; November 2010.
5. Moin Qazi, *Microfinance and Women's Empowerment*, Himalaya Publishing House, Mumbai, 2007.

6. Vasant Desai, Director, Visvesvararaya Institute of Socio- Economic Research (VISER), Mumbai, *Small-scale Industries and Entrepreneurship,* Himalaya Publishing House, 2008.
7. Chanchal Charan, *Micro-Finance in India; Rural Development and Poverty Alleviation*, Southern Economist, Nov 15, 2013.
8. Sivakkolundu C. and Lognanthan, *Micro Finance and Self Help Groups*, Southern Economist, Nov 15, 2013.
9. Chakraborty K.C., *Financial Inclusion in India; Journey so far & way forward,* Southern Economist, Nov 15, 2013.
10. Angel Anila A., *Impact of EDP Curriculum on the SHG Women Entrepreneurship Development,* Southern Economist, July 1, 2013.

49

Micro Finance: an Instrument for Poverty Alleviation

Siddalingareddy

Abstract: *Micro finance is a tool for poverty alleviation and improving socio-economic conditions of the poor. Microfinance is a new method to meet the credit requirement in rural areas. Since bank borrowing requires collateral and the deprived class does not have any type of such collaterals, the success of Bangladesh Grameen Bank which was started by Prof. Mohamed Yunus, in 1976 attracted the attention of the India policy makers towards the micro finance and micro credit. Micro-finance institutions other than banks are engaged in the provision of financial services to low income clients, including consumers and the self-employed, who traditionally lack access to banking and related services.*

Those who promote micro finance generally believe that such access will help the poor people come out of poverty. Microfinance, therefore, is an emerging discipline in today's financial world. Indeed, it is a weapon in the hands of marginalized poor people to fight a war against poverty. The multi-facts of microfinance, thus, reflect acknowledging that saving services will help to improve well-being of the poor in general and of women in particular. Microfinance is emerging as a powerful instrument for poverty alleviation in the new economy. In India, micro-finance scene is dominated by Self Help Groups (SHGs) - Banks linkage Programme, aimed at providing a cost effective mechanism for providing financial services to the 'unreached poor'. The study aims at identifying the origin and concept of microfinance, role of microfinance in India, This paper attempts to identify effects of micro finance on poverty reduction.

Key words: Micro Finance, Poverty alleviation, SHGs.

Introduction

Micro-financing is a set of financial activities provided to the poor masses basically incorporating loans, savings and deposits, insurance, transfer services, etc. to enable them to utilise their resources and entrepreneurial skills including abilities to the fuller extent so as to improve the economic conditions and shield themselves against risks.Microfinance is the provision of thrift and other financial services and products of very small amount to the poor in rural, semi-urban areas for enabling them to raise their income levels and improve their living standards. Microfinance may be defined as: "Banking with service for the poor." Microfinance, therefore, is an emerging discipline in today's financial world. Indeed, it is a weapon in the hands of marginalised poor people to fight a war against poverty. The multi-facts of microfinance, thus, reflect acknowledging that saving services will help to improve well-being of the poor in general and of women in particular. microfinance is emerging as a powerful instrument for poverty alleviation in the new economy. In India, microfinance scene is dominated by Self Help Groups (SHGs) - Banks linkage Programme, aimed at providing a cost effective mechanism for providing financial services to the 'unreached poor'. Based on the philosophy of peer pressure and group savings as collateral substitute, the SHG. programme has been successful in not only designing financial products meeting peculiar needs of the rural poor, but also in strengthening collective self-help capacities of the poor at the local level, leading to their empowerment.

MFI can be classified into three categories as following:

1. Non-profit — public trusts, societies, companies registered under Sec. 25
2. Mutual Benefit—Self-Help Group and Federation and Co-operative societies
3. For Profit-Non Banking Financial Corporation.

In India the players in the microfinance sector can be classified in three main groups as following:

1. SHG—BL model accounting for about 58 per cent of the outstanding loan portfolio.
2. NBFC accounting 34 per cent of the outstanding loan portfolio.
3. Others including trusts, societies etc.accounting for the balance eight per cent of the outstanding loan portfolio.

In India, economic reforms with a human face have been accepted as the guiding principle of sustainable development. Keeping the poor at centre stage, the policies need to be re-oriented so as to develop and optimise the potential of such a large segment of the population and enable them to contribute in the growth process significantly in terms of output, income, employment and consumption.

Microfinance Terminology

1. **Micro credit:** This is a small amount of money loaned to a client by a bank or other institution. Micro credit can be offered, often without collateral, to an individual or through group lending.
2. **Microfinance:** This refers to loans, savings, insurance, transfer services and other financial products targeted at low-income clients.
3. **Micro insurance:** This is a system by which people, businesses and other organisations make payments to share risk. Access to insurance enables entrepreneurs to concentrate more on growing their businesses while mitigating other risks affecting property, health or the ability to work.
4. **Remittances:** These are transfer of funds from people in one place to people in another, usually across borders to family and friends. Compared with other sources of money that can fluctuate depending on the political or economic climate, remittances are a relatively steady source of funds.
5. **Micro savings:** These are deposit services that allow people to store small amounts of money for future use, often without minimum balance requirements. Savings accounts allow households to save small amounts of money to meet unexpected expenses and plan for future investments such as education and old age. Inclusive financial sectors: It allows poor and low-income people to access credit, insurance, remittances and savings products. In many countries, the financial sectors do

not provide these services to the lower income people. An inclusive financial sector will support the full participation of the lower income levels of the population.

6. **Micro entrepreneurs:** These are people who own small-scale businesses that are known as micro enterprises. These businesses usually employ less than five people and can be based out of the home. They can provide the sole source of family income or supplement other forms of income. Typical micro entrepreneur activities include retail kiosks sewing workshops, carpentry shops and market stalls.

Role of micro finance in poverty reduction

Microfinance is about providing financial services to the poor who are not served by the conventional formal financial institutions- it is about extending the frontiers of financial service provision. The provision of such financial services requires innovative delivery channels and methodologies. The need for financial services that allow people to both, take advantage of opportunities and better management of their resources. Micro finance can be one big effective tool amongst many for poverty alleviation. However, it should be used with caution-despite recent claims, the question between micro finance and poverty alleviation is not straightforword, because poverty is a complex phenomenon with many constraints that the poor in general have to cope with. We need to understand when and in what form micro finance is appropriate for the poorest; the delivery channel, methodology and products offered all are inter-linked and in turn affect the prospects and promise of poverty alleviation access to formal banking services is difficult for the poor. The main problem the poor have faced when trying to acquire from formal financial institutions is the demand for collateral asked by these institutions. In addition, the process of acquiring a loan entails many bureaucratic procedures, in general. Formal financial institutions show performance for urban over rural sectors, large scale over small scale transactions and non agricultural over agricultural loans.

Estimation of Poor House hold benefits through micro finance (Formal Banking)

Year	*No. of Beneficiaries(In Lakh)*	*Cumulative Beneficiaries (In Lakh)*	*Growth rate*
2002-03	167	167	-
2003-04	75.5	242.5	45.21 per cent
2004-05	87.3	329.8	36.00 per cent
2005-06	79.7	409.5	24 per cent
2006-07	170.5	580	41 per cent
2007-08	130	710	22.41 per cent

Source: Compiled from NABARD data base.

The above table shows that the SHG-Bank linkage programme helped 167 lakh (45.21 per cent) household members up to 2002-03, but during the 2007-08 financial year it was only 130 lakh (22.41 per cent) household members that benefited through SHG-Bank linkage programme. The linkage programme helps the poor people to get micro credit from formal financial institutions to improve their standard of living and economic conditions.

Salient Features of Micro Finance Programme of Government of India

1. **Arranging fixed deposits for MFIs/NGOs:** Under this scheme government of India arrange money to MFI/NGO like SIDBI for micro credit to poor.
2. **Training and studies on micro-finance programme:** Government of India would help SIDBI in meeting the training needs of NGOs, SHGs, intermediaries and entrepreneurs and also in enhancing awareness about the programme. Institution building for 'intermediaries' for identification of viable projects: The Government of India would help in institution building through identification and development of 'intermediary organisation', which would help the NGOs/SHGs in identification of product, preparation of project report, working out forward and backward linkages and in fixing marketing/ technology tie-ups. The SISIs would help in the identification of such intermediaries in different areas.
3. **Budgetary provision for the scheme during Tenth Plan:** There was a budgetary provision in Tenth five Year Plan and hoping more funds in next plan.
4. **Administrative arrangement:** A committee has been formed to control and monitor the administrative arrangement of MFI/ NGOs.

Schemes of Government of India

There are so many schemes for the upliftment of poor in India. One of them Micro-credit programmes is run primarily by NABARD in the field of agriculture and SIDBI in the field of Industry, Service and Business (ISB). The success of Micro-credit programme lies in diversification of services. Micro Finance Scheme of SIDBI is under operation since January, 1999 with a corpus of Rs 100 crore and a network of about 190 capacities assessed Rated MFIs/NGOs. Under the programme, total amount of Rs 191 crore have been sanctioned upto 31st December, 2003, benefiting over nine lakh beneficiaries.

Under the programme, NGOs/MFIs are supposed to provide equity support in order to avail SIDBI finance. But they find it difficult to manage the needed equity support because of their poor financial condition. The problem has got aggravate due to declining interest rate on deposits. The office of the development commissioner (Small Scale Industries) under Ministry of SSI is launching a new scheme of Micro Finance Programme to overcome the constraints in the existing scheme of SIDBI, whose reach is currently very low. It is felt that government's role can be critical in expanding reach of the scheme, ensuring long-term sustainability of NGOs / MFIs and development of Intermediaries for identification of viable projects.

Effect of micro-finance on poverty reduction

1. Micro credit and microfinance have received extensive recognition as a strategy for poverty reduction and for economic empowerment particularly in rural areas having poor population. Providing poor people the small amounts of credit at reasonable interest rates give them an opportunity to set up their own business at small scale.
2. Microfinance is an innovative step towards alleviating poverty. Microfinance facilities provided to the people help them to use and develop their skills and enable them to earn money through micro enterprises. Moreover provision of micro finance helps them to smooth their consumption level and manage unexpected risks. Micro finance helps the poor to built assets, educate their children and have a better quality of life.
3. Micro finance is the founding stone for poverty reduction. There is a fundamental linkage between microfinance and poverty eradication, in that the latter depends on the poor gaining access to, and control over, economically productive resources, which includes financial resources.
4. Micro finance directly improves quality of life and promotes poverty reduction. By getting loans the client become self-employed and protect himself for the external threats. By getting employment they become raised from the poverty line and the poverty decreased. Micro finance is in the initial stages and in these stages most of the peoples do not know about the reality of micro finance. Some peoples take that example of micro finance where the result of micro finance is negative. It is more important that the examples where the result of micro finance is more positive than negative should be highlighted so that

more and more peoples get benefit from micro finance and cross the poverty line.

5. Micro finance is that chemical through which the germ of poverty can be killed. Micro finance is equally profitable in the poor countries as in the rich countries.
6. Micro finance play an important role in poverty alleviation but the part of micro finance in poverty alleviation is like a drop of water in a sea. Micro finance helps in improving the standard of living of peoples
7. Micro finance increase the self confidence of the poor by meeting their emergency requirements, ensuring need-based timely credits and making the poor capable of savings. The credibility of microfinance in health related issues in a positive manner. It has been postulated that by making policy towards income generation and enhancement, ultimately to eradicate poverty alone can improve the health status through better, timely and easy access of healthcare.
8. Microfinance is the most important resource to provide loans and other basic financial services to increase the employment rate, productivity and earning capacity. It will impact the people's lives through removing poverty, improving living standards, such as health, education, food and other social impacts.

The microfinance sector is developed day by day in India. Most of the population of India is based on the rural area, where people live below the poverty line. The need for micro credit is higher in the rural area than urban area. The large numbers of microfinance borrowers show the market opportunity and need in India.

Conclusion

Creating self employment opportunities is one way of attacking poverty and solving the problems of unemployment. There are over 24 crore people below the poverty line in our country. The scheme of micro-finance has been found as an effective instrument for lifting the poor above the level of poverty by providing them increased self-employment opportunities and making them credit worthy with some effort substantial progress can be made in taking MFIs to the next orbit of significance and sustainability. There is a need of designing financially sustainable models and increase outreach and scale up operations for poor in India. People belong to villages are still unaware about banking policies and credit system. So NGO should communicate to them and share their view with villagers. Banks should convert and build up professional system into social banking system for poor. Government of India and state governments should also provide support for capacity building initiatives and ensure transparency and enhance credibility through disclosure.

REFERENCES

1. Sreedhar N and T.V. Seshaiah, *Role of Micro Finance in eradicating poverty in India, Women Empowerment during 21st Century in India"*, Himalaya Publishing House, Mumbai, 2013.
2. Muhammad K Durrani, Abid Usman, Muhammad Imran Malik, *Role of Micro Finance in Reducing Poverty: A Look at Social and Economic Factors,*International Journal of Business and Social Science Vol. 2, No. 21 [Special Issue – November 2011]
3. Rajesh Kumar Shastri, *Micro finance and poverty reduction in India (A comparative study with Asian Countries),* African Journal of Business Management Vol. 3 (4), pp. 136-140, April, 2009.
4. Sharada Kumari, Impact of Microfinance Institutions in the Eradication of Poverty in the Rural Areas of Bihar International Journal of Applied Research and Studies (IJARS) ISSN: 2278-9480 Volume 2, Issue 9, Sep – 2013.
5. Sibanjan Mishra, Manmohan Mall, P K Mishra, *"Microfinance a Tool for Poverty Alleviation",* American International Journal of Research in Humanities, Arts and Social Sciences, Jun-Aug., 2013.

www.laghuudyog.com/schemes/microfinance.htm.

50

Micro Finance—A Tool for Poverty Alleviation in India

B. Jayarama Bhat

Abstract:- *Today there is a dire need to ensure decent and comfortable living for the hitherto neglected sections in our society. In India's development paradigm, micro-finance has evolved as a need-based programme for poverty alleviation and empowerment of the deprived groups. Poverty, which is a bane to humanity in any place can be eradicated by enhancing the capacity building of the vulnerable section, which in turn, can be enhanced only by making the easy credit accessibility to the poor. Micro-finance has become one of the most effective interventions for poverty alleviation. Micro finance, thus, is an emerged efficacious strategy to reach the rural and urban poor and is emerging as a movement. The micro credit system has been strengthened by institution of Self-Help Group (SHGs).*

Self-Help Groups (SHGs) are the thrift and credit groups formed in formal way whose members pool savings and relend within the group on rotational or needs basis. These groups operate on co-operative principles and act collectively. Besides providing banking services to their members' doorsteps, they make regular savings and use the pooled savings for the benefit of their members. Poverty may be alleviated and a decent living may be ensured when a free flow of credit is assured to the poor. Under the circumstances, an attempt is made here, to peep into the different dimension of Self-Help Groups and Micro Finance as a tool for poverty alleviation in India. The paper depends on secondary data.[1]

1. Introduction

Nobody never denies that poverty eradication is one of the greatest challenges of our times. Both the market and the State are said to have failed in safeguarding the interest of the poor. Poverty is a great curse on humanity and is no disgrace. In recent years, many civil societies such as Non-Governmental Organisations (NGOs), Self-Help Groups (SHGs), and Voluntary Organisations (VOs) have emerged as important links between the poor people and the formal system. Empowering the poor is sure to alleviate poverty and thereby ensures comfortable and decent living for them. The inability to get the basic needs- food, clothing and shelter- as a consequence of low income, lack of productive assets partial use of human resource owing to inadequate access to education and health and no access to break out poverty due to weak economic and social status are the important aspects of poverty.[1]

The seriousness of the problem can be understood from the following information:

- More than eight million people die every year in India.
- One out of six people live in extreme poverty defined as living on less than $ 1 a day.
- More than 800 people go hungry each day.
- Every year, over six million children die from malnutrition before their fifth birthday.
- Over 11 million children die from preventable diseases like malaria, diarrhea, and pneumonia.
- Every 36 seconds another person dies of starvation and large majority are children under the age of five.
- Over 100 million primary school age children cannot go to school.

Such is the malady of poverty! This certainly necessitates every need for innovative measure to ensure a strategic approach both to empower the poor people to eke out their livelihood and improve their social status. Providing financial services to the poor and underprivileged section of the society has been given top priority on the agenda of many anti-poverty programme initiated by the Government of India ever since independence. This involves formal financial institutions. In spite of the best efforts of these financial institutions, in reaching the deprived sections of the society living in rural areas, still, a large chunk rural under privileged poor failed to get their due share from the institutional finance.

Even by early 1990s, the share of informal financial institutions (informal sector) was quite high at 39.6 per cent of the total credit as per the data provided by the RBI. It was in this backdrop, the need for alternative financial innovation that should penetrate into rural hinterland and provide formal financial services without any hurdles was strongly felt. It was in such an environment micro finance emerged as a strong and suitable innovation that fills the existing gap. Pandit Jawaharlal Nehru rightly said that "over 80 per cent of our people live in our villages. India is poor because the villages of our country are poor. India will be rich if villages can be made rich. Therefore, the basic problem of years ago the Zamindari and Jagirdari systems in various parts of India were abolished because the villages could not progress under a semi-feudal system of landownership".

Despite the efforts of the Government of India to initiate various poverty alleviation programme no much difference is seen in the magnitude of poverty. Poverty in any place can be eradicated by enhancing the capacity building of the vulnerable section and capacity building can be enhanced only by making easy accessibility of credit to the poor. Over the last two decades, micro finance has acquired a greater dimension and recognition as an instrument for meeting the credit needs of the poor for starting income generating activities of micro enterprises.[5] The institution of Self-Help Group (SHGs) has provided strength to micro credit system.

Paper Scheme

The paper depends on secondary data for its analysis. The data gathered are presented in the form of a table and are analysed using simple percentage.

2. Objectives

The specific objectives of the study are:

- To present the brief history of the origin of micro finance,
- To describe the concept of SHGs and its role,
- To highlight the need for micro finance and SHGs, and
- To focus as how SHG-Bank linkage helps in the poverty eradication.

3. Origin and History of Bank Linkages

Muhammed Yunus, of Bangladesh, was an initiator of an action research project 'Grameen Bank'. The project was started in 1976 and later this was recognised as a formal bank by the Government of Bangladesh. It got the status of Scheduled Bank (SB) in 1986 and started lending to landless poor particularly women to promote them for self employment.

The Bangladesh Rural Advancement Committee (BRAC), the Association for Social Advancement (ASA) and PROSHIKA are the other micro finance giants operating for over two decades. The BRAC is the largest Non-Governmental Organisation (NGO) addressed the issues of poverty alleviation and empowerment of poor especially women in the rural areas of the country. It has spread its functions in the fields of literacy, legal education and human rights, health, nutrition and other supportive services.

In India, banks are considered to be the predominant agency for delivery of micro credit. In 1970s, Ilaben Bhat, Founder Member of Self Employed Women's Association (SEWA), Ahmadabad had developed a concept of Women and Micro Finance. The Annapurna Mahila Mandal in Maharashtra and Working Women's Forum in Tamil Nadu and many NABARD sponsored groups have followed the path of SEWA. Since 1987, Mysore Resettlement and Development Agency (MYRADA) promoted Credit Management Groups (CMGs) which are similar to SHGs with an aim to bestow social empowerment of women. In 1991-92, the NABARD started promoting SHGs in a large scale and it was the real take-off point for the SHG movement in India. With an addition to this, in 1993, the Reserve Bank of India (RBI) allowed SHGs to open saving accounts in banks and avail the banking services and it was the major boost to the movement.

4. The Concept of Micro Finance

Micro finance programmes extend small loans to poor people for self employment projects that generate income, allowing them to care for themselves and their families. In most cases, they offer a combination of services and resources to their clients in addition to credit for self employment. These include savings, training, networking, and peer support.

5. Need for Micro Finance

In rural areas, the poor people have been dependent on money lenders for meeting their financial needs. Money lenders exploit the situation mercilessly. The formal credit system of banks by and large is beyond their reach. The prime need of the hour is to ensure that the poor people live with dignity sufficiency and responsibility. In this context, the activities of the SHGs have emerged as a sustainable approach to make credit facilities available to the poor.

6. Concept of SHGs

In recent years Self-Help Groups have been emerging as a major strategy for the promotion of informal credit to the rural poor. In 1992 RBI-NABARD have launched a 'pilot project' and issued necessary guidelines to the banking system for lending to the SHGs. After careful thought and study both by the RBI and NABARD, assisting the SHGs became 'normal lending programme' under priority sector and service area approach in 1996.

The SHG is a small economically homogeneous and affinity group of rural people generally not exceeding 20 members voluntarily coming together to save small amounts regularly to mutually agree to contribute to a common fund, to have collective decision-making to solve conflicts through collective leadership and mutual discussions and to provide collateral free loans at terms decided by the group at market driven rates.[6] The members of SHGs are the ultimate beneficiaries. And SHGs may be registered or unregistered.[7]

The SHGs play a vital role in the upliftment of the rural poor by providing loans at a reasonable interest rate. This helps the rural poor to improve employment and economic support. SHGs in most of the villages have been successful in breaking the clutches of money lenders. SHGs bank linkage programme has been advantageous not only to the members of SHGs but also to the banks[8]. The advantages to the banks are the lower transaction cost by providing loan to the groups for internal lending. There is no recovery problem for banks in loans given to SHGs, i.e., near zero non-performing assets. The SHGs will help economic independence of the rural people and economic development of our country.

7. Necessity of SHG

In recent years, there has been a phenomenal expansion of formal credit system in the country but dependence of the poor on the informal finance still persists.[9] Formal sector financing institutions are characterised by absence of linkages between infrastructure, skills and market, heavy transaction costs both for lenders and borrowers while financing micro enterprises and their credit programme and failure to promote savings habits among poor are impediments in repayment ethics.

8. SHG-Bank Linkage Programme

The initiative of 1992 to make the traditional and formal banks to extend financial services to deprived sections through informal Self-Help Groups (SHGs), has now blossomed into a "monolith" micro finance initiative. It has been recognised as a decentralised, cost effective and the fastest growing micro finance initiative. The linkage with banks has provided the members of the groups both the facility of pooling their thrift /savings and access to credit from the banking system and created a platform through which they could launch a number of livelihood initiatives and also facilitate the empowerment process.[10] The SHG –Bank linkage is presented in Table-1.

Table-1: SHG - Bank Linkage

Year	*No. of SHGs*	*Bank Loan (Rs.Crores)*	*No. of Families Assisted (In lakhs)*	*Average Loan per SHG (Rs)*	*Average Loan per Families*
01	02	03	04	05	06
2000-01	1,49,050	28,789	25.33	19,315	1,136
2001-02	197,653	54,554	33.60	27,601	1,624
2002-03	2,55,882	1,02,231	37.54	26.985	1,799
2003-04	3,61,731	1,85,550	45.86	36,180	2,412
2004-05	5,18,173	2,96,180	77.74	42,971	2,864
2005-06	4,82,598	3,09,613	72.38	64,155	4,277
2006-07	11,05,749	6,57,039	154.80	59,420	3,961
2007-08	12,27,770	8,84,926	171.88	72,076	5,148
2008-09	16,09,586	12,25,351	225.64	76,108	5,436
2009-10	15,87,000	14,45,330	222.18	91,073	6,505
2010-11	11,96,000	14,54,773	167.44	1,21,636	8,688
2011-12	17,60,346	16,63,477	191.53	94,497	9,685
per cent Change over 2000	1081	5678	656	389	753

Note: The percentage change is computed.
Source: NABARD-Micro Finance Status in India 2011-12.

The data presented in the Table1 reveal that the number of SHGs registered an increase of 1081 per cent in 2011-12 over 2000-01. Similarly the bank loan witnessed an increase of 5678 per cent during the same period. It is obvious that over a period of time the average loan per family did increase from Rs 19,315 lakhs in 2000-01 to Rs 1,21,639 lakhs up to 2010-11 but during 2011-12 it showed a decline. It is easy to comprehend that the average loan per families also registered an increase with a percentage share of 753. The savings, fresh loans and the loans outstanding of SHGs are reflected in the Figure below.

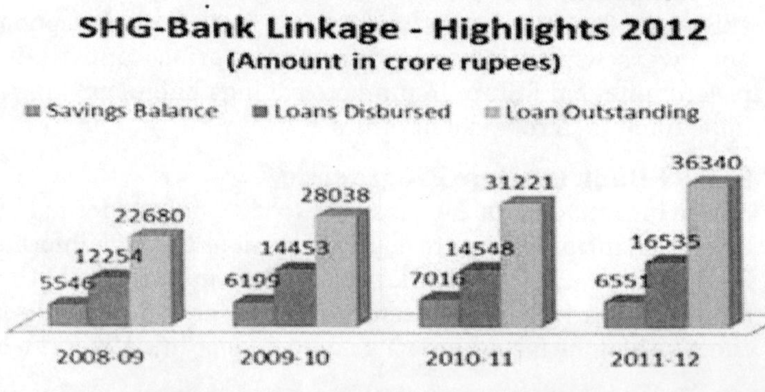

The above Figure gives a picture of the savings, fresh loans and the loan outstanding of SHGs with banks for the last four years which is self explanatory. It is found that the total bank loans outstanding against the SHGs have registered to be over Rs 36340 crore in 2011-2012 indicating an increase in absolute number over 2008-09. Further, it can also be showcased that the fresh loans extended to the SHGs were to the extent of Rs 16535 crore during 2011-12 by all banks. The fresh lending to SHGs during the year registered an increase constituting 13.7 per cent over the previous year.

9. Conclusion

To sum up, Micro Finance has proved to be an efficacious and alternative approach for the existing system of credit disbursement by banks. It is indisputable that the Micro Finance by promoting thriftiness amongst the rural poor, enabling them to generate income and enhancing their capacity building goes a long way in alleviating poverty in India. The significance of micro finance can be cognised by the fact that the formal credit institutions and the existing informal lending has either failed to deliver or has not stood the expectation. The results are certainly promising. However, more meticulous and expeditious endeavour is warranted to make the new approach more fruit bearing in the days to come. Let us hope for the best.

Notes

1. See, Ramesh Babu et.al. Micro Finance : An Approach for Poverty Alleviation; Southern Economist, Vol. 49 (10) Bangalore p. 23.
2. See Dinesh.B.Raghuwanshi,' Micro Fincance : Present Scenario and Emerging Challenges' Southern Economist Vol. 49 (1) p.15.
3. *Ibid*. p. 15.
4. Gopal Jain, Management of Rural Development and Resources, Mangaldeep Publication, Jaipur, 2002, p. 11.
5. "Micro Finance and Self Help Groups", Unoose Begum in Micro Finance and Women Empowerment (Ed.) Rais Ahmed, Mittal Publication, New Delhi p. 259.
6. SHGs and Micro Finance-A Instrument for Poverty Alleviation, pp. 672-676.
7. Somanath, MF- Redefining Future, Excel Books, New Delhi, 2009 p.107.

8. Ganismurthy and K.S. Vasan Poverty Alleviation through Micro Finance, M. Rais Ahmed (Ed), Micro Finance and Empowerment, pp. 641-64.
9. SHGs and Micro Finance-A Instrument for Poverty Alleviation, pp. 672-676.
10. NABARD, Status of Micro Finance in India, 2011-12, p. 3.

REFERENCES

1. NABARD, Status of Micro Finance in India, 2010-11, 2011-12.
2. Rais Ahmed (2009) (Ed.), Micro Finance and Women Empowerment, Mittal Publication, New Delhi.
3. Somanath,V.S., (2009) Micro Finance -Redefining the Future, Excel Books, New Delhi.

Index

E

G

J

K

L

M

S

V

W